C++ Programming: An Object-Oriented Approach

Behrouz A. Forouzan
Richard F. Gilberg

Mc Graw Hill Education

C++ PROGRAMMING: AN OBJECT-ORIENTED APPROACH

This book is printed on acid-free paper.

1 2 3 4 5 6 7 8 9 LWI 21 20 19

ISBN 978-0-07-352338-5 (bound edition)
MHID 0-07-352338-0 (bound edition)
ISBN 978-1-259-57145-9 (loose-leaf edition)
MHID 1-259-57145-9 (loose-leaf edition)

Executive Portfolio Manager: *Suzy Bainbridge*
Product Developer: *Heather Ervolino*
Marketing Manager: *Shannon O'Donnell*
Content Project Managers: *Jane Mohr and Sandra Schnee*
Buyer: *Laura Fuller*
Designer: *Egzon Shaqiri*
Content Licensing Specialist: *Shawntel Schmitt*
Cover Image: ©*McGraw-Hill Education*
Compositor: *MPS Limited*

All credits appearing on page or at the end of the book are considered to be an extension of the copyright page.

Library of Congress Cataloging-in-Publication Data

Forouzan, Behrouz A., author. | Gilberg, Richard F., author.
C++ programming : an object-oriented approach / Behrouz A. Forouzan, Richard F. Gilberg.
First edition. | New York, NY : McGraw-Hill Education, [2020] |
Includes index.
LCCN 2018030975| ISBN 9780073523385 (bound edition : acid-free paper) |
ISBN 0073523380 (bound edition : acid-free paper) | ISBN 9781259571459 (loose-leaf edition) |
ISBN 1259571459 (loose-leaf edition)
LCSH: Object-oriented programming (Computer science) | C++ (Computer program language)
LCC QA76.64 .F684 2019 | DDC 005.1/17—dc23
LC record available at https://lccn.loc.gov/2018030975

mheducation.com/highered

To my wife, Faezeh
Behrouz A. Forouzan

To my wife, Evelyn
Richard F. Gilberg

Online Appendices

This book complements a course designed to teach object-oriented programming using the syntax of the C++ language. It will also prepare students for advanced concepts such as data structure and design patterns. Students who have completed this course will be ready to take on any other object-oriented language course, a data-structure course, or a course about design patterns.

What Is the C++ Language?

C++ is a progressive programming language derived from its predecessors, the C language and the B language. The C++ language expands the idea of a *struct* to a *class* in which different objects can be created from one single definition of a class with different values for each data element.

Furthermore, the C++ language explores the idea of object-oriented languages that simulate real life. In real life, we define a type and then we have objects of that type. In the C++ language, we define a class and then we create objects from that class. C++ also includes the idea of *inheritance*. In inheritance, we can create a class and then extend the definition to create other classes, just as in real life where the idea of an animal can be extended to create the idea of a horse, a cow, a dog, and so on.

Perhaps the most interesting addition to C++ is the idea of *polymorphism*. Polymorphism gives us the ability to write several versions of an action with the same name to be used by different objects. This practice is found in real life when we use the verb *open*. We can say that we open a business, open a can, open a door, and so on. Although the word *open* is used in all cases, it elicits different actions on different objects.

The most recent additions to C++ include the Standard Template Library (STL), a collection of predefined complex objects and actions that can be applied to those objects, as well as design patterns to make problem solving more efficient and coherent.

Why This Book?

The book has five distinctive goals as discussed below.

Teach Computer Programming

The book can be used as the first course in computer programming using the C++ language as the vehicle. Chapters 1 to 6 are designed for this purpose. They discuss computer systems and languages. They also discuss the basics of the C++ syntax and program controls, such as decisions and repetitions. Chapters 1 to 6 are essential to learning programming using the C++ language.

Teach the Syntax of the C++ Language

Chapters 7 to 12 are essential in the study of object-oriented programming. Although Chapters 8 and 9 are not directly related to the object-oriented features of C++, we believe that these two chapters can be taught after students understand the basics of object-oriented programming, which are discussed in Chapter 7.

Present New Features of C++

Chapters 13 to 17 discuss other topics normally taught in a first or second course in programming. They can be taught in any order.

Discuss Data Structure and Introduce the STL Library

Chapters 18 and 19 are an introduction to data structures. They prepare students for a course in data structures.

Introduce Design Patterns

Chapter 20 (which can be found online) gives simple and alternative solutions to some typical problems in object-oriented programming that would be more difficult to solve if patterns were not used. Chapter 20 gives students an insight to object-oriented programming through a set of standard solutions to specific problems. Although design patterns are normally taught in computer graphics courses, we have applied them to nongraphic problems for students who have no graphical programming experience.

Course Outline

The twenty chapters of the book are outlined in the following figure.

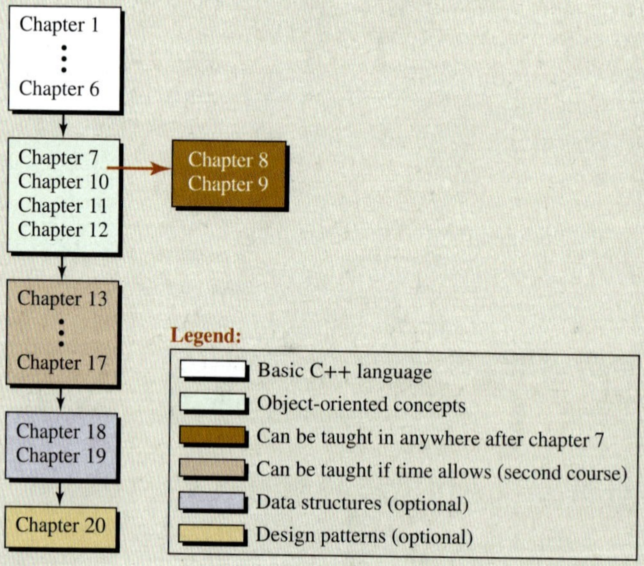

Appendices

Appendices can be found online and are divided into six categories.

References

Appendices A to E are designed to be used as references for students. Students may need to consult these appendices when studying chapters in the book.

Language Knowledge

Appendices F and G give students information about how C++ prepares a source code for compilation and how it handles names in different sections.

Advanced Topics

Appendixes H to O discuss some advanced topics that were added to C++. They can be taught in the class, or students can use them as a source of additional information.

Brief Review of C++ 11

Appendix P gives a brief review of C++ 11 topics that were not discussed in the appendices that discussed advanced topics.

Brief Review of UML

We have used UML diagrams in the text. Appendix Q provides general insight into UML as a tool for designing object-oriented projects.

Bitset

The concept of bitset becomes more popular when C++ is used in network programming. We have included this topic in Appendix R.

Instructor Resources

Accompanying this text are several additional resources which can be found online at www.mhhe.com/forouzan1e. These include CheckPoint questions that help instructors gauge student understanding after reading each section of a chapter. True/false and review questions are also available to further test student's knowledge. Complete solutions to the CheckPoint features, true/false questions, review questions, and problems are provided as well. Lastly, Lecture PPTs, text image files, and sample programs are provided as well.

Acknowledgments

We would like to express our gratitude to the reviewers of this text. Their insight and suggestions over the last few years greatly influenced this first edition. In alphabetical order, the reviewers are as follows:

Vicki H. Allan, *Utah State University*
Kanad Biswas, *Institute of Technology, Delhi*
Gary Dickerson, *Union College*
Max I. Formitchev, *Maximus Energy*
Cynthia C. Fry, *Baylor University*
Barbara Guillott, *Q&A Analyst, CGI, Lafayette, LA*
Jon Hanrath, *Illinois Institute of Technology*
David Keathly, *University of North Texas*
Robert Kramer, *Youngstown State University*
Kami Makki, *Lamar University*
Christopher J. Mallery, *Principal Software Engineering Lead for Microsoft*
Michael L. Mick, *Purdue University, Calumet*
Amar Raheja, *California State Polytechnic University, Pomona*
Brendan Sheehan, *University of Nevada–Reno*

At McGraw-Hill, we would like to thank the following editorial and production staff: Thomas Scaife, Senior Portfolio Manager; Suzy Bainbridge, Executive Portfolio Manager; Heather Ervolino, Product Developer; Shannon O'Donnell, Marketing Manager; Patrick Diller, Business Project Manager; and Jane Mohr, Content Project Manager.

In this chapter, we describe the components of a computer system and discuss the general ideas behind computer languages. The overview provided in this chapter will help prepare you for future chapters. You can skip the chapter in the first reading and return to it when you have a better understanding of programming.

Objectives

After you have read and studied this chapter, you should be able to:

- Discuss the two major components of a computer: hardware and software.
- Describe the six parts of hardware: CPU, primary memory, secondary storage, input system, output system, and communication system.
- Describe the two major categories of software: system software and application software.
- Describe the evolution of computer languages from machine languages, to assembly languages, and to high-level languages.
- Discuss four different paradigms of computer languages: procedural, object-oriented, functional, and logic.
- Describe the two steps of program design: understand the problem and develop a solution.
- Describe the multistep procedure that transforms a program written in the C++ language to an executable program.

1.1 COMPUTER SYSTEM

A **computer system** is made of two major components: hardware and software. The **computer hardware** is the physical equipment. The **software** is the collection of programs (instructions) that allow the hardware to do its job.

1.1.1 Computer Hardware

The **hardware** of a computer system consists of six parts: a central processing unit (CPU), main memory, secondary storage, the input system, the output system, and the communication system. These components are connected together by what is called a bus. Figure 1.1 shows these six components and their connection.

Central Processing Unit (CPU)

The **central processing unit (CPU)** consists of the **arithmetic-logical unit (ALU),** the control unit, and a set of registers to hold data temporarily while being processed. The control unit is the traffic cop of the system; it coordinates all the operations of the system. The ALU

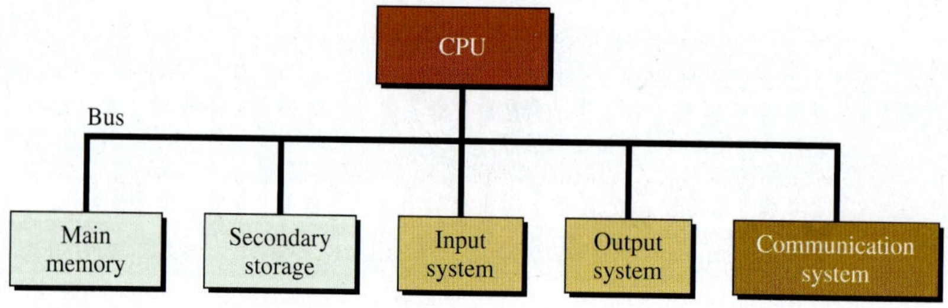

Figure 1.1 Basic hardware components

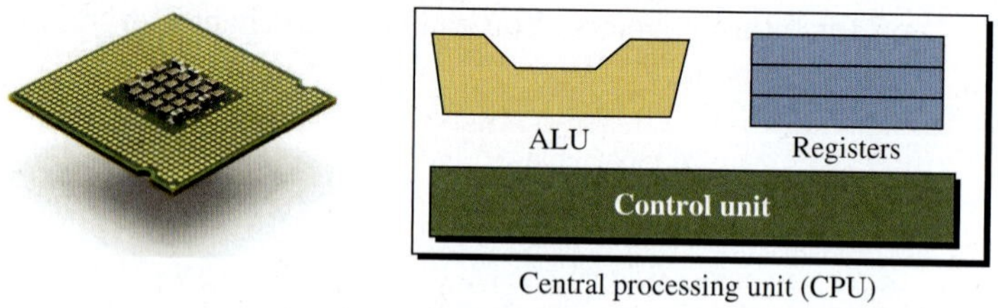

Figure 1.2 Central processing unit
(photo) ©leungchopan/Getty Images

executes instructions such as arithmetic calculations and comparisons among data. Figure 1.2 shows the general idea behind a central processing unit.

Primary Memory

Primary memory is where programs and data are stored temporarily during processing. The contents of primary memory are lost when we turn off the computer. Figure 1.3 shows primary memory in more detail. Each storage location in memory has an address, much like a street address, that is used to reference the memory's contents. The addresses in Figure 1.3(a) are shown on the left as numbers ranging from zero to $(n - 1)$, where n is the size of memory. In Figure 1.3(b) the address is shown symbolically as x.

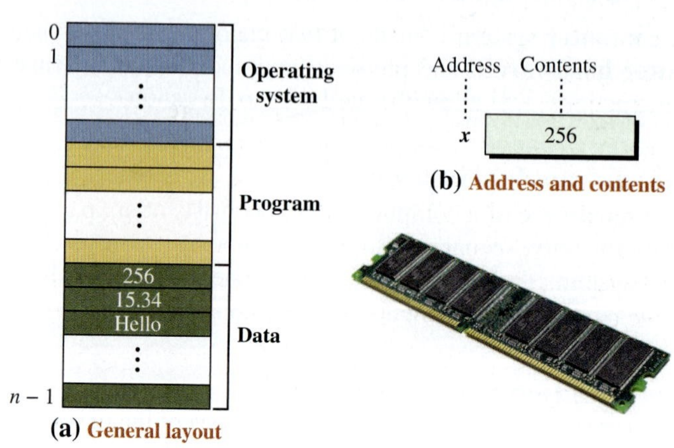

Figure 1.3 Primary memory
(photo) ©Simon Belcher/Alamy

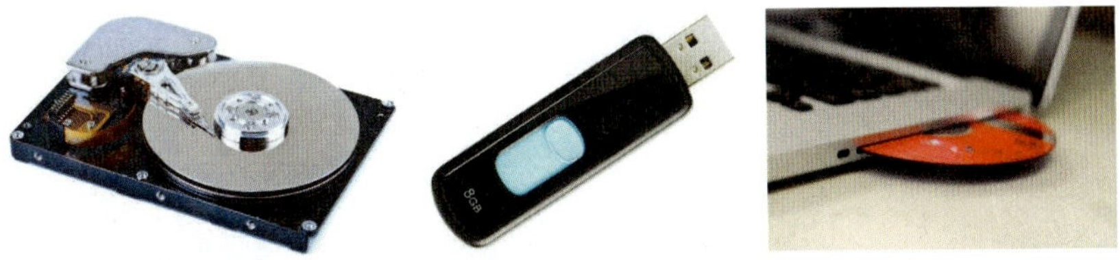

Figure 1.4 Some secondary storage devices
©Shutterstock/PaulPaladin; ©David Arky/Getty Images; ©McGraw-Hill Education

Figure 1.5 Some input systems
©JG Photography/Alamy; ©Keith Eng 2007

Generally, each address refers to a fixed amount of memory. In personal computers, the amount of storage accessed is usually one, two, or four bytes. In large computers, it can be many bytes. When more than one byte is accessed at a time, *word* rather than *byte* is usually used for the memory size.

In general, primary memory is used for three purposes: to store the operating system, to store the program, and to store data. The type of data stored is dependent on the application. In Figure 1.3, we demonstrate three different types of data: an integer (256), a real number (15.34), and a string (Hello).

Secondary Storage

Programs and data are stored permanently in **secondary storage.** When we turn off the computer, our programs and data remain in the secondary storage ready for the next time we need them. Examples of secondary storage include hard disks, CDs and DVDs, and flash drives (Figure 1.4).

Input System

The **input system** is usually a keyboard where programs and data are entered into the computer. Examples of other input devices include a mouse, a pen or stylus, a touch screen, or an audio input unit (Figure 1.5).

Output System

The **output system** is usually a monitor or a printer where the output is displayed or printed. If the output is displayed on the monitor, we say we have a soft copy. If it is printed on the printer, we say we have a hard copy (Figure 1.6).

Communication System

We can create a network of computers by connecting several computers. Communication devices are installed on a computer system for this purpose. Figure 1.7 shows some of these devices.

Figure 1.6 Some output systems
©Roy Wylam/Alamy; ©Stephen VanHorn/Alamy

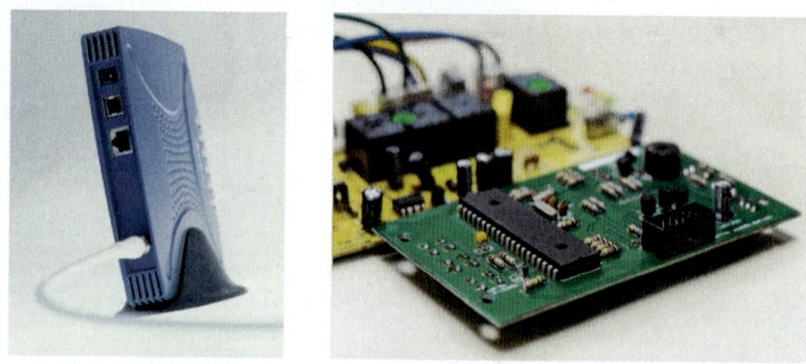

Figure 1.7 Some communication devices
©Ingram Publishing; ©somnuek saelim/123RF

1.1.2 Computer Software

Computer software is divided into two broad categories: **system software** and **application software.** This is true regardless of the hardware system architecture. System software manages the computer resources. Application software, on the other hand, is directly responsible for helping users solve their problems.

System Software

System software consists of programs that manage the hardware resources of a computer and perform required information processing. These programs are divided into three groups: the **operating system, system support,** and **system development.**

Operating System The operating system provides services such as a user interface, file and database access, and interfaces to communication systems. The primary purpose of this software is to operate the system in an efficient manner while allowing users access to the system.

System Support System support provides system utilities and other operating services. Examples of system utilities are sort programs and disk format programs. Operating services consist of programs that provide performance statistics for the operational staff and security monitors to protect the system and data.

System Development System development software includes the language translators that convert programs into machine language for execution, debugging tools to assure that the programs are error-free, and computer-assisted software engineering (CASE) systems that are beyond the scope of this book.

Application Software

Application software is broken into two categories: **general-purpose software** and **application-specific software.**

General-Purpose Software General-purpose software is purchased from a software developer and can be used for more than one application. Examples of general-purpose software include word processors, database management systems, and computer-aided design systems. These programs are called general purpose because they can solve a variety of user computing problems.

Application-Specific Software Application-specific software can be used only for its intended purpose. A general ledger system used by accountants and a material requirements planning system used by engineers are examples of application-specific software. They can be used only for the task they were designed for; they cannot be used for other generalized tasks.

1.2 COMPUTER LANGUAGES

To write a program for a computer, we must use a **computer language.** Over the years, computer languages have evolved from machine to symbolic to high-level languages and beyond. A time line for computer languages is seen in Figure 1.8.

1.2.1 Machine Languages

In the earliest days of computers, the only programming languages available were **machine languages.** While each computer still has its own machine language, which is made of streams of 0s and 1s, we no longer program in machine language.

The only language understood by a computer is its machine language.

1.2.2 Symbolic Languages

It became obvious that not many programs would be written if programmers continued to work in machine language. In the early 1950s, Grace Hopper, a mathematician and a member of the United States Navy, developed the concept of a special computer program for converting programs into machine language (see Figure 1.9).

Her work led to the use of programming languages, which simply mirrored the machine languages using symbols, or mnemonics, to represent the various machine language instructions. Because they used symbols, these languages were known as **symbolic languages.** A special program called an **assembler** is used to translate symbolic code into machine language. Because symbolic languages have to be assembled into machine language, they soon became known as **assembly languages.** This name is still used today for symbolic languages that closely represent the machine language of their computer.

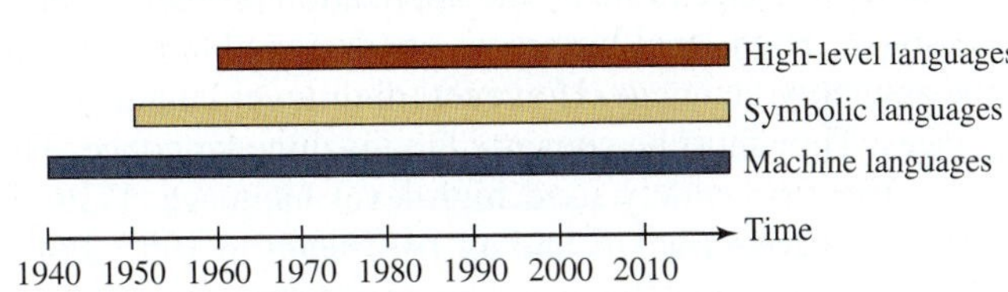

Figure 1.8 Computer language evolution

Figure 1.9 Grace Hopper
©Cynthia Johnson/Getty Images

Symbolic language uses mnemonic symbols to represent machine language instructions.

1.2.3 High-Level Languages

Although symbolic languages greatly improved programming efficiency, they still required programmers to concentrate on the hardware they were using. Working with symbolic languages was also very tedious because each machine instruction had to be individually coded. The desire to improve programmer efficiency and to change the focus from the computer to the problem being solved led to the development of **high-level languages.**

High-level languages are portable to many different computers, which allows the programmer to concentrate on the application problem at hand rather than the intricacies of the computer. High-level languages are designed to relieve the programmer from the details of the assembly language. However, high-level languages share one thing with symbolic languages: They must be converted to machine language. This process is called *compilation.*

The first widely used high-level language, FORTRAN (Formula Translation), was created by John Backus and an IBM team in 1957. Following soon after FORTRAN was COBOL (Common Business-Oriented Language). Admiral Grace Hopper was again a key figure, this time in the development of the COBOL business language.

Over the years, several other languages—most notably BASIC, Pascal, Ada, C, C++, and Java—were developed. Today, one of the popular high-level languages for system software and new application code is C++, which we discuss in this book.

1.3 LANGUAGE PARADIGMS

Computer languages can be categorized according to the approach they use in solving a problem. A paradigm is a model or a framework for describing how a program handles data. Although there are several taxonomies for dividing current languages into a set of paradigms, we discuss only four: procedural, object-oriented, functional, and logic, as shown in Figure 1.10. The figure also shows which language belongs to which paradigm according to our taxonomy.

Note that the C++ language can be used both as a procedural and an object-oriented paradigm, as we will see in future chapters.

1.3.1 Procedural Paradigm

In a **procedural** (also called **imperative**) paradigm, a program is a set of commands. The execution of each command changes the state of the memory related to that problem. For example, assume we want to find the sum of any two values. We reserve three memory locations and call them `a`, `b`, and `sum`. The combination of these three memory locations comprises a state in this case. Figure 1.11 shows how a procedural paradigm uses four commands to change the state of memory four times. Note that the memory locations in gray show the original state, wherein the locations are reserved for the program.

To get the value of the first number, `a`, into memory, we use an input command (input *a*). After execution of this command, the computer waits for us to enter a number on the keyboard. We entered 6. When we press the enter key on the keyboard, the number 6 is stored in the first memory location and the state of memory is changed. After the second command, again the state of the memory is changed and now both 6 and 8 are stored in memory. The third command changes the memory state by adding the values of `a` and `b` and storing the result in `sum`. Although the last command (output `sum`) does not look like it is changing the memory state, it is considered a change because the value of `sum` is output.

The way we have written the code in Figure 1.11 is very inefficient for two reasons. First, it contains some commands that can be repeated in the same program or other programs. Second, if the set of data to be handled is large, we need to handle them one by one. To remove these two inefficiencies, the procedural paradigm allows packaging commands and **data items.**

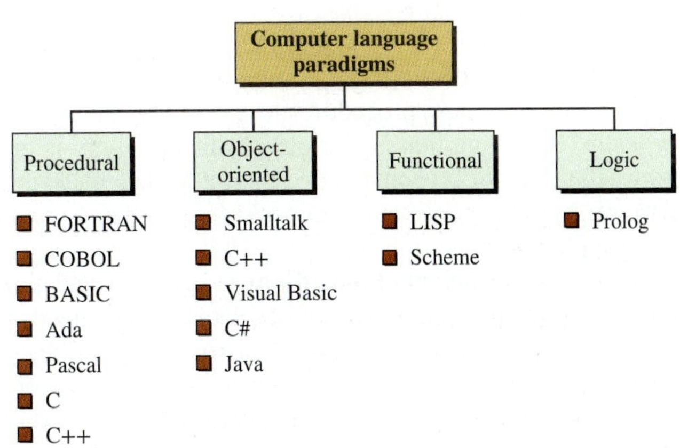

Figure 1.10 Language paradigms

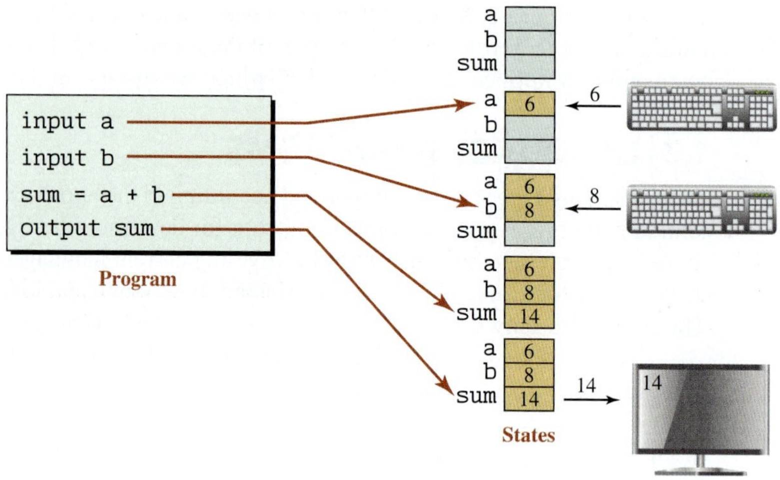

Figure 1.11 An example of a procedural paradigm

a. If we are writing code for different programs, we can package the code and create what is called a **procedure** (or **function**). A procedure can be written once and then copied in different programs. The standard procedures can be stored in the language library and be used instead of rewritten.

b. If we are handling a large set of data items (for example, hundred or thousands of numbers), we need to store them in a package (called different names such as array or record) and input them all together, process them all together, and output them all at the same time. The operation at the background is still done one data item at a time, but the program can see the data items as packages.

The following shows how a procedural paradigm uses three lines of code to sort a list of numbers of any size. Of course, we must have already written the procedures and already packaged data items into a `list`.

```
input (list);
sort (list);
output (list);
```

1.3.2 Object-Oriented Paradigm

In the procedural paradigm, the often-used procedures can be created and saved. We then apply a subset of these procedures to the corresponding data packages to solve our particular problem. One thing that is obvious in this paradigm is that there is no explicit relationship between the set of procedures and the set of data packages. When we want to solve a problem, we need to choose our data package and then go and find the appropriate procedure(s) to be applied to it.

The **object-oriented paradigm** goes further and defines that the set of procedures that can be applied to a particular type of data package needs to be packaged with the data. The whole is referred to as an *object*. In other words, an object is a package containing all possible operations that can be applied to a particular type of data structure.

This is the same concept we find in some physical objects in our daily life. For example, let us think about a dish-washing machine as an object. The minimum operations we expect from a dishwasher are washing, rinsing, and drying. All of these operations are included

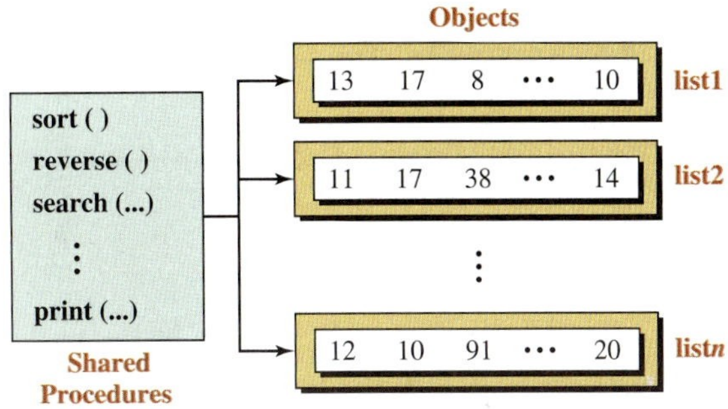

Figure 1.12 An example of an object-oriented paradigm

in any typical dish-washing machine. However, each time we load the machine with a different set of dishes (same as a different set of data). We need to be careful, however, not to load the machine with a load it is not designed for (not to wash clothes, for example, in the dish-washing machine).

In the real world, all the hardware necessary for an operation is included in an object; in the object-oriented programming world, each object holds only data, but the code that defines the procedures is shared. Figure 1.12 shows the relationship between the procedures and data in the object-oriented paradigm.

1.3.3 Functional Paradigm

In the **functional paradigm,** a program is a mathematical function. In this context, a function is a black box that maps a list of inputs to a list of outputs. For example, adding numbers can be considered as a function in which the input is a list of numbers to be added and the output is a list with only one item, the sum. In other words, the functional paradigm is concerned with the result of a mathematical function. In this paradigm, we are not using commands and we are not following the memory state. The idea is that we have some primitive functions, such as add, subtract, multiply, divide. We also have some primitive functions that create a list or extract the first element or the rest of the elements from a list. We can write a program or a new function by combining these primitive functions. Figure 1.13 shows how we add two numbers using the functional paradigm. The code is symbolic, but each language in this paradigm has its own definition for a function. Note also that in our code, we distinguish between a number and a list. We have a number as 8, but a list with one

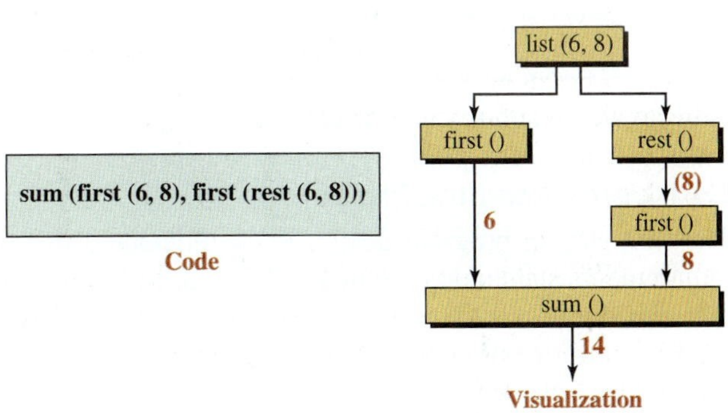

Figure 1.13 An example of a functional paradigm

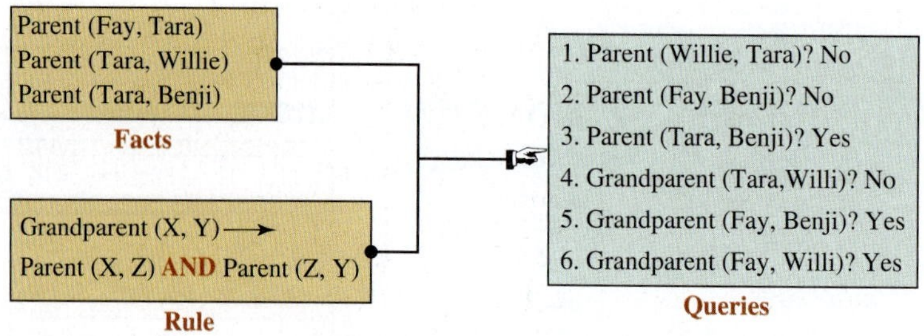

Figure 1.14 An example of a logic paradigm

element is (8). The function `first` gets a number, but the function `rest` gets a list. To get the second number in the list, we first use the function `rest` to get the list (8) and then use the function `first` to get 8.

1.3.4 Logic Paradigm

The **logic paradigm** uses a set of facts and a set of rules to answer queries. It is based on formal logic as defined by Greek mathematicians. We first give the program the facts and rules before asking queries. Figure 1.14 shows a simplified and symbolic version of a logic paradigm. A fact such as Parent (Fay, Tara) is read as "Fay is the parent of Tara."

1.3.5 Paradigms in C++ Language

Our discussion of four paradigms might lead you to wonder where the C++ language stands. C++ is an extension to the C language and is based on the procedural paradigm. However, the existence of classes and objects allows the language to be used as an object-oriented language. In this book we use C++ mostly as a procedural paradigm in early chapters (except for input/output that are done using objects). However, we use the language as an object-oriented paradigm after the introductory chapters.

1.4 PROGRAM DESIGN

Program design is a two-step process that requires understanding the problem and then developing a solution. When we are given the assignment to develop a program, we are given a program requirements statement and the design of any program interfaces. In other words, we are told what the program needs to do. Our job is to determine how to take the inputs we are given and convert them to the outputs that have been specified. To understand how this process works, let's look at a simple problem.

Find the largest number in a list of numbers.

How do we go about doing this?

1.4.1 Understand the Problem

The first step in program design is to understand the problem. We begin by reading the requirements statement carefully. When we fully understand it, we review our understanding with the user. Often this involves asking questions to confirm our understanding. For example, after reading our simple requirements statement, we should ask several clarifying questions.

What type of numbers are we dealing with (with fractions or without fractions)?

Are the numbers arranged in any special sequence, such as lowest to highest?

How many numbers can we expect?

If we don't clarify the problem—that is, if we make assumptions about the input or the output—we may supply the wrong answer. To answer our questions, we need to process integers arranged in any sequence. There is no limit as to the number of integers.

As this example shows, even the simplest problem statements may require clarification. Imagine how many questions must be asked for a program that contains hundreds or thousands of detailed statements.

1.4.2 Develop the Solution

Once we fully understand the problem and have clarified any questions we may have, we develop a solution in the form of an algorithm. An **algorithm** is a set of logical steps necessary to solve a problem. Algorithms have two important characteristics: first, they are independent of the computer system. This means that they can be used to implement a manual system in an office as well as a program in a computer. Second, an algorithm accepts data as input and processes the data into an output.

To write the algorithm for our problem, we use an intuitive approach, calling not only on the problem statement but also our knowledge and experience. We start with a small set of five numbers: Once we have developed a solution for five numbers, we extend it to any number of integers.

```
13    7    19    29    23
```

We begin with a simple assumption: The algorithm processes the numbers one at a time. We name the algorithm `FindLargest`. Every algorithm has a name to identify it. `FindLargest` looks at each number in turn without knowing the values of the others. As it processes each number, it compares it to the largest number known to that point and determines if the new number is larger. It then looks at the next number to see if it is larger, and then the next number and the next number until all of the numbers have been processed. Figure 1.15 shows the steps in determining the largest among five integers.

The algorithm requires that we keep track of two values, the current number and the largest number found. We determine the largest number using the following steps.

- **Step 1:** We input the first number, 13. Since `largest` has no value, we set it to the value of the first number.
- **Step 2:** We input the second number, 7. Since 7 is less than 13, the value of *largest* does not need to be changed.
- **Step 3:** We input the third number 19. When we compare 19 to the value of *largest*, 13, we see that 19 is larger. We therefore set *largest* to 19.
- **Step 4:** We input the fourth number, 29. When we compare 29 to the value of *largest,* 19, we see that 29 is larger. We set *largest* to 29.
- **Step 5:** We input the fifth number, 23. Because it is smaller than 29, *largest* does not need to be changed. Because there is no more input, we are done and we have determined that the largest value is 29.
- **Step 6:** We output the value of *largest*, which is 29.

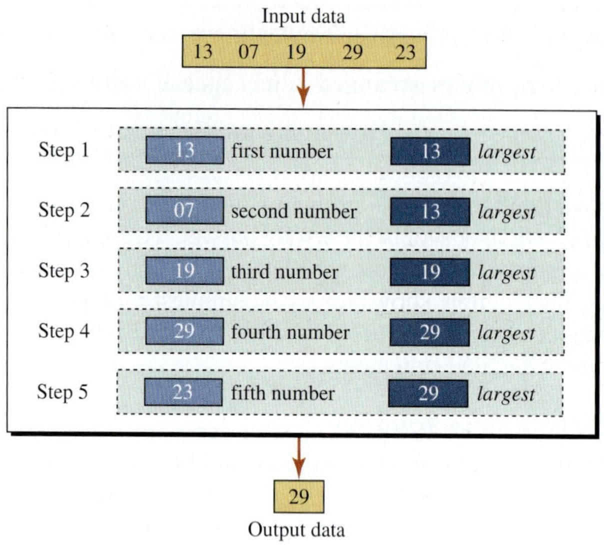

Figure 1.15 Find the largest among five integers

Algorithm Generalization

The algorithm shown in Figure 1.15 does not quite solve our original problem definition because it only handles five numbers. To make it work for all number series, we need to replace steps 2 through 5 to process an undetermined number of values. This requires that we generalize the statements so that they are the same. We can do this with a minor rephrasing of the statements as shown below.

If the current number is greater than *largest*, set *largest* to the current number.

We then include the rephrased statement in a repeat statement that executes the steps until all numbers are processed. The resulting algorithm is shown in Figure 1.16.

It is important to realize that the design is done *before* we write the program. In this respect, it is like the architect's blueprint. No one would start to build a house without a detailed set of plans, yet one of the most common errors of both experienced and new

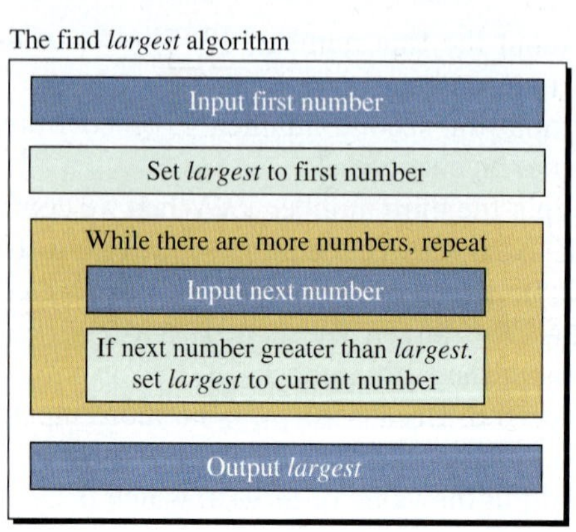

Figure 1.16 Algorithm to find `largest` among *n* numbers

programmers alike is to start coding a program before the design is complete and fully documented.

This rush to start is partially because programmers think they fully understand the problem and partially because they are excited about getting on with a new problem to solve. In the first case, they find that they did not fully understand the problem. By taking the time to design the program, they raise more questions that must be answered and therefore gain a better understanding of the problem.

The second reason programmers code before completing the design is just human nature. Programming is a tremendously exciting task. To see your design begin to take shape, to see your program creation working for the first time, brings a form of personal satisfaction that is a natural high.

Unified Modeling Language (UML)

The **Unified Modeling Language** (UML) is a standard tool for designing, specifying, and documenting many aspects of a computing system. For example, it can be used to design large complex systems, programs, and objects within a program. It can also be used to show the relationship between objects in an object-oriented language such as C++. We discuss UML in future chapters when we learn to design programs.

1.5 PROGRAM DEVELOPMENT

Figure 1.17 shows the general procedure for turning a program written in any language into machine language. The procedure for a C++ program is a little bit more involved. The process is presented in a straightforward, linear fashion, but we need to recognize that these steps are repeated many times during the development process to correct errors and make improvements to the code.

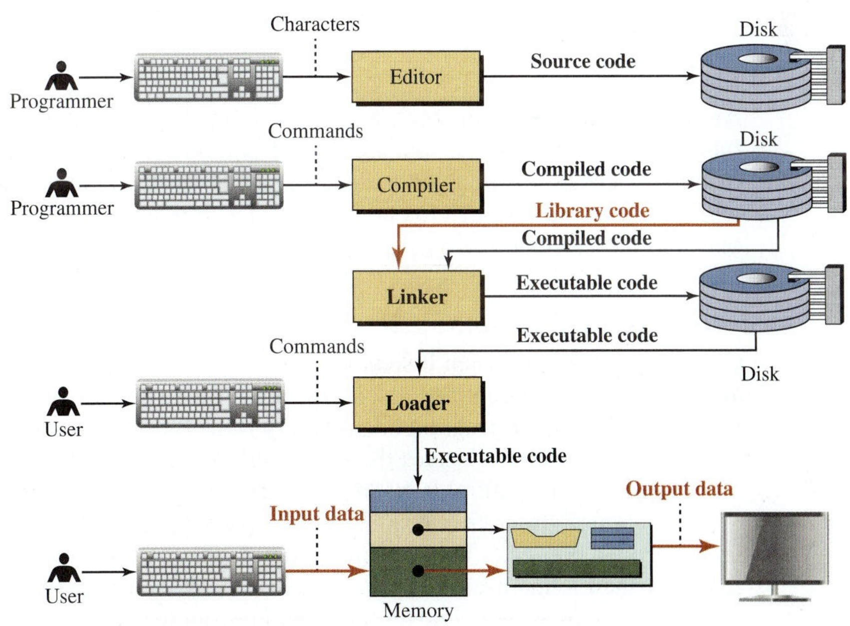

Figure 1.17 Writing, editing, and executing a program

It is the job of the programmer to write the program and then to turn it into an **executable file.** There are four steps in this process:

a. Write and edit the program.
b. Compile the program.
c. Link the program with the required library modules (normally done automatically).
d. Execute the program. From our point of view, executing the program is one step. From the computer point of view, however, it is two substeps: load the program and run the program.

1.5.1 Write and Edit Programs

The software used to write programs is known as a **text editor.** A text editor helps us enter, change, and store character data. Depending on the editor on our system, we could use it for writing letters, creating reports, or writing programs. The big difference between the other forms of text processing and writing programs is that programs are oriented around lines of code, while most text processing is oriented around characters and paragraphs.

The text editor could be a generalized word processor, but it is more often a special editor provided by the company that supplies the compiler. Some of the features we look for in an editor are search commands that are used to locate and replace statements, copy-and-paste commands that can be used to copy or move statements from one part of a program to another, formatting commands that use colors to display key parts of the program, and automatic formatting that aligns and indents parts of the program.

After we complete a program, we save our file to disk. This file then becomes the input to the compiler; it is known as a **source file.**

1.5.2 Compile Programs

The information in a source file stored on disk must be translated into machine language so the computer can understand it. This is the job of the **compiler.**

1.5.3 Link Programs

As we will see later in the text, a program is made up of many functions. Some of these functions are written by us and are part of our source program. However, there are other functions, such as input/output processes and mathematical library functions, that exist elsewhere and must be attached to our program. The **linker** assembles the system functions and ours into the executable file.

1.5.4 Execute Program

Once the program has been linked, it is ready for execution. To execute a program we use an operating system command, such as `run`, to load the program into main memory and execute it. Getting the program into memory is the function of an operating system program known as the **loader.** It locates the **executable program** and reads it into memory. When everything is ready, control is given to the program and it begins execution.

In a typical program execution, the program reads data for processing, either from the user or from a file. After the program processes the data, it prepares the output. Data output can be written to the user's monitor or to a file. When the program is finished, it tells the operating system, which removes the program from memory.

1.6 TESTING

After we write the program, we must test it. **Program testing** can be a very tedious and time-consuming part of program development. As the programmer, we are responsible for completely testing it. We must make sure that every instruction and every possible situation have been tested.

1.6.1 Designing Test Data

Test data should be developed throughout the design and development of a program. As we design the program, we create test cases to verify the design. These test cases then become part of the test data after we write the program.

In addition, as we design the program, we ask ourself what situations, especially unusual situations, we need to test, and then we make a note of them. For example, in `FindLargest`, what if only one number is input? Similarly, what if the data were in sequence or all the same? When we design the program, we review it with an eye toward test cases and make additional notes of the cases needed. Finally, while we code the program, we make more notes of test cases.

When it comes time to construct the test cases, we review our notes and organize them into logical sets. Except for very simple student programs, one set of test data never completely validates a program. For large-scale development projects, 20, 30, or even more test cases may need to be run to validate a program. All of these test cases become what is known as a test plan.

One set of test data *never* completely validates a program.

Finally, as we test the program, we discover more test cases. Again, we write them down and incorporate them into the test plan. When the program is finished and in production, we still need the test plan for modifications to the program. Testing of modifications is known as **regression testing** and should start with the test plan developed when we wrote the program.

How do we know when our program is completely tested? In reality, there is no way to know for sure, but there are a few things we can do to help the odds. While some of these concepts will not be clear until we get to later chapters, we include them here for completeness.

a. Verify that every line of code has been executed at least once. Fortunately, there are programming tools on the market today that help us do this.

b. Verify that every conditional statement in the program has executed both the true and false branches, even if one of them is null.

c. For every condition that has a range, make sure the tests include the first and last items in the range, as well as items before the first and after the last. The most common mistakes in range tests occur at the extremes of the range.

d. If error conditions are being checked, make sure all error logic is tested. This may require a temporary modification to the program to force the errors; for instance, an input/output error usually cannot be created—it must be simulated.

1.6.2 Program Errors

There are three general classifications of errors: **specification errors, code errors,** and **logic errors.**

Specification Errors

Specification errors occur when the problem definition is either incorrectly stated or misinterpreted. Specification errors should be caught when we review our design with analysts and users.

Code Errors

Code errors usually generate a compiler error message. These errors are the easiest to correct. Some code errors generate what is known as a warning message, which usually means that the compiler has made an assumption about the code and needs to have it verified. It may be right, or it may be wrong. Even though the program may run with a warning message, the code should be changed so that all warning messages are eliminated.

Logic Errors

The most difficult errors to find and correct are logic errors. Examples of logic errors are division by zero or forgetting to store the first number in `largest` in `FindLargest`. They can be corrected only by thorough testing. And remember, before we run a test case, we should know what the correct answer is. Don't assume that the computer's answer is correct; if there's a logic error, the answer will be wrong.

Key Terms

algorithm
application software
application-specific software
arithmetic-logical unit (ALU)
assembler
assembly language
central processing unit (CPU)
code errors
compiler
computer hardware
computer language
computer software
computer system
data item
executable file
executable program
function
functional paradigm
general-purpose software
hardware
high-level language
imperative paradigm
linker
input system
loader
logic errors
logic paradigm
machine language
object-oriented paradigm
operating system
output system
primary memory
procedural paradigm
procedure
program design
program errors
program testing
regression testing
secondary storage
software
source file
specification errors
symbolic language
system development software
system software
system support software
text editor
Unified Modeling Language (UML)

Summary

Computer systems are made up of two major components: hardware (CPU, memory, secondary storage, output system, and communication system) and software (system software and application software).

Computer languages are used to develop software. The computers themselves run in machine language. Over the years programming languages have progressed through symbolic languages to the many high-level languages used today.

Language paradigms (procedural, object-oriented, functional, logic) describe the approach used to solve problems on the computer. C++ is based on the procedural and object-oriented paradigms.

Program design is a two-step process that requires understanding the problem and then developing a solution.

Algorithms have two important characteristics; they are independent of the computer system and they accept data as input and process data into an output.

Program development turns the program design into a computer system in four steps: write the program, compile it, link it, and execute it.

Testing a program requires that every instruction and every possible situation is validated.

Problems

PR-1. Show the state of the memory for the following example of a procedural paradigm (see Figure 1.11).

```
input a
input b
input c
sum = a + b + c
output sum
```

PR-2. Show the state of the memory for the following example of a procedural paradigm (see Figure 1.11). Assume that values of *length* and *width* are 12 and 8, respectively, and represent the sides of a rectangle.

```
input length
input width
area = length × width
parameter = 2 × (length + width)
```

PR-3. Imagine we need to create a bank account object using an object-oriented paradigm. Show the data and list of procedures you think need to be encapsulated with the data (see Figure 1.12).

PR-4. In a functional paradigm, show the result of the following function (see Figure 1.13).

```
first (rest (rest (a, b, c)))
```

PR-5. In a functional paradigm, show the result of the following function, assuming that the list (...) makes a list of given elements (see Figure 1.13).

```
list (first (rest (a, b)), first (a, b))
```

PR-6. Based on Figure 1.14, what is the result of the following queries?

```
Parent (Benji, Tara)?
GrandParent (Fay, Willi)?
```

PR-7. Based on Figure 1.14, what is the result of the following queries?

```
Parent (Fay, Tara)?
GrandParent (Tara, Willi)?
```

PR-8. Show the value of *sum* after the following algorithm is executed.

```
sum = 0
sum = sum + 10
sum = sum × 10
sum = sum − 10
```

PR-9. Show the value of *x* after the following algorithm is executed.

```
x = 5
x = x + 1
x = x - 10
```

PR-10. Show the value of *x*, *y*, and *z* after the following algorithm is executed.

```
x = 2
y = 5
x = x + 1
y = y - 10
z = 8
z = x + y
x = y + z
y = x + y + z
```

PR-11. Design an algorithm that converts a value in centimeters to a value in inches using the following formula:

1 inch = 2.54 centimeters

PR-12. Design an algorithm that converts a value in inches to a value in centimeters using the following formula:

1 centimeter = 0.3937 inch

PR-13. Design an algorithm that converts a temperature value in Fahrenheit (F) to a value in Celsius (C) using the following formula:

$$C = (F - 32) \times (100/180)$$

PR-14. Design an algorithm to find the sales tax and the total sale value of a transaction made of two soft drinks (1 dollar each), three bottles of milk (2 dollars each), and one can of coffee (3 dollars). The tax is 9 percent.

PR-15. Design an algorithm that finds the smallest among a list of numbers.

PR-16. Design an algorithm that finds the sum of a list of numbers.

PR-17. Design an algorithm that finds the product of a list of numbers.

PR-18. Design an algorithm that adds numbers from 1 to 100.

This chapter sets the foundation of computer programming in C++. Each C++ program involves input, output, and assignment. First, we discuss how these activities can be achieved using two objects and an operator. Next, we introduce the fundamental data types in C++. **Fundamental data types** are primitive built-in data types that can be used without being declared. We then discuss variables, values, and constants and how they can be used in a program. Finally, we discuss two components of a program, namely, **tokens** and **comments.**

Objectives

After you have read and studied this chapter, you should be able to:

- Discuss variables, values, and constants and how they are used in C++ programs.
- Discuss the general components of a C++ program that is made of tokens and comments.
- Discuss the fundamental data types in C++ and their size.
- Show how we can use integer data types in programs.
- Show how we can use character data types in programs.
- Show how we can use Boolean data types in programs.
- Show how we can use floating-point data types in programs.
- Discuss the void data type and discuss its use.
- Introduce C++ strings and briefly discuss their use.
- Introduce and discuss some simple programs in C++.

2.1 C++ PROGRAMS

Every C++ program is made of several sections, and each section is made of several parts. Each section or part must follow the rules defined in the C++ language, just as documents written in one of the natural languages follow the rules of that language.

Before we formally delve into the structure of a C++ program and explore some of the pertinent rules, we study some sample programs.

2.1.1 First Program

Program 2.1 shows a simple example of a C++ program and will help us gain a basic understanding of C++ programs.

Program 2.1 The first simple program

```
1  #include <iostream>
2
3  int main ()
4  {
5     std :: cout << "This is a simple program in C++ ";
6     std :: cout << "to show the main structure." << std :: endl;
7     std :: cout << "We learn more about the language ";
8     std :: cout << "in this chapter and the rest of the book.";
9     return 0;
10 }
```

Run:

```
This is a simple program in C++ to show the main structure.
We learn more about the language in this chapter and in the rest of the book.
```

Box and Background Coloring

We have shown the program in a table made of two columns and several rows with some boxes and some colored or shaded backgrounds. These decorations are just for demonstration in this book. They are not part of the C++ language. Other books may use other decorations to make the components of a program more visible.

> **Box and background coloring are not part of a C++ program; they are used in this book to show different sections of a program.**

Separation of Code and Result

We have divided the program into two sections vertically. The top section, in two columns, shows the code that we have written. The bottom section shows the result of the program when it runs. Note that the first line of the second section (`Run:`) is not part of the program or its results after running. It is added by us to show that this section is the result of running the program. If we run the program more than once, you will see multiple sections each starting with (`Run:`). The results of the program are normally shown on the screen of the computer on which we compile and run the program, but we show them at the bottom of each program inside a shaded area for quick reference.

> **We separate the code from the results of the program for demonstration; the results of the program are normally shown on the screen.**

Case Sensitivity

Every C++ program is case-sensitive. We must use the terms exactly as defined in the language. If we change the case of a letter in a term that is part of the language, we get a compilation error. In other words, we cannot use the word `Include` or `IOSTREAM` instead of `include` or `iostream` in line 1 of the program. We cannot use the word `Main` instead of `main` in line 3. This is also true with terms like `std`, `cout`, `endl`, and `return`.

> **C++ language is case-sensitive. The term that names an entity must be used as it is defined without changing the case of its letters.**

Program Lines

Although it is not necessary to do so, we divide our programs into lines to show the different sections and to increase readability. When we discuss the program, we use line numbers for ease of reference. Line numbers are not part of the program and should not be included in the program when we create the source code. Note that we also add blank lines to separate different sections of the program (for example, line 2 in Program 2.1).

Line numbers are not part of the program and should not be included in the source code. They are used in this book for reference to each line.

Indention

In Program 2.1, we have indented lines in the function body. Although it is not necessary to do so we believe it improves the readability of the program. We always indent lines that belong to an enclosing entity. Lines 5 to 9 belong to the function body, and we have indented them to show that they are inside the two braces.

Line indention improves the readability of a program and we strongly recommend it.

Program Analysis

We briefly analyze the program line by line (except for line 2, which is blank to increase readability to indicate the separation of the two sections).

Line 1: Preprocessor Directive A **preprocessor** directive is a command to the compiler to take some action before it compiles the program. Line 1 of the program (without the line number) is a preprocessor directive as shown below:

```
#include <iostream>
```

A C++ program needs some predefined lines of code that are not written by us. These lines of code are very complex and sometimes access the hardware of the computer, which means they depend on the type of computer we are using. The C++ designers created these lines of code and included them in files referred to as **header files.** We do not have to write these lines; we can simply copy the contents of these files into our code. To copy them, we need to know the name of the file, `iostream`, which stands for *input/output stream* in this case. To tell the complier that we need to include the contents of this file, we need to have an `include` line as shown above. The `include` line starts with the `#` symbol. When a line in a program starts with this symbol, it is an indication to the compiler that something needs to be done before the program can be compiled. Before the compiler starts compiling our code, it runs another program, called *preprocessor,* that checks all preprocessor commands (the **include** directive is one of them). The compiler does what is needed in the command (such as including the contents of the header file) and then removes the preprocessor directive. After all preprocessor directives have been taken care of and are removed, the program is ready for compilation. Note that each preprocessing command needs to be in a single line by itself with the first nonblank, character, the symbol `#` (pound sign). In the include directive, the name of the file must be enclosed in two pointed brackets such as `<filename>` after the term `include`. We discuss preprocessing in more details in Appendix F.

Note that no semicolon should be put after any include directive. The compiler may generate an error if it finds one.

Line 3: Function Header Line 3 of the program (without the line number) is shown below:

```
int main ()
```

A C++ program is normally made of a number of *functions*. A function, as we will see in future chapters, is a section that groups a number of lines of code. A C++ program consists of one or more functions, but it must contain one function named `main`. The execution of a C++ program starts with the `main` function and terminates when the `main` function is terminated.

Execution of each C++ program starts with the main function, which means that each program must have one function named main.

Each function has a *header* and a *body*. The header defines the name of the function and what goes into the function (inside the parentheses) and what type of information comes out of the function, mentioned before the name **int** in this case. Line 3 is the header of the `main` function. It shows that the name of the function is `main`; nothing will be passed to the function (parentheses are empty); an integer value will be returned from the function (**int** is C++ for an integer) and given to the operating system.

Lines 4 and 10: Opening and Closing Braces Lines 4 and 10 are a combination of an opening and a closing brace (curly brackets) that need to go together to enclose the whole body of the function. It is a compilation error to have one without the other. The following shows these lines.

```
{
    ...
}
```

Every function definition in C++ needs a body enclosed between an opening and a closing brace.

It is a major error to have an opening brace without a closing one or a closing brace without an opening one.

Line 5: The First Line of Body Let us now discuss the contents of the body, line by line, starting with line 5 that is shown below:

```
std :: cout << "This is a simple program in C++ ";
```

Most of the lines in the body of a function are commands that tell the computer what to do. As we see in a natural language, a command (an imperative sentence) is made of a verb, a direct object, an indirect object (target or recipient), and a terminator (normally a period). This is what we see in a command line in a function although in a different order. In

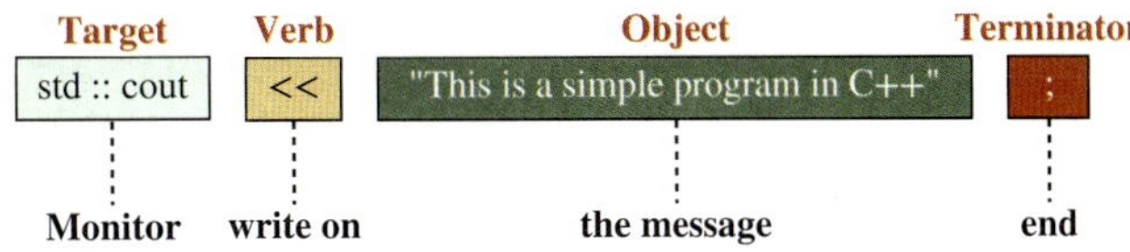

Figure 2.1 Analysis of line 5

this case. the target object (`cout`, which is the monitor) comes first, the verb (write) comes next, and what to write (direct object, a string) comes last. The command is terminated with a semicolon (instead of a period). With this explanation, line 5 of Program 2.1 says that the computer should write the object string (`This is a simple program in C++`) on the monitor and move to the next command. Note that the two quotation marks are part of the language syntax; they are not written on the screen. Figure 2.1 shows a graphical analysis of line 5.

We will see that each object in C++ (as an object-oriented language) has a name. The monitor connected to our computer also has a name in C++. It is called **std :: cout**. Note that the name in this case is made of two parts, `std` and `cout`, separated by a colon. Just like people in real life are recognized by two identifiers, last name and first name, an object in C++ also has a last name and a first name. The monitor's last name is `std` (abbreviation for standard); its first name is `cout` (abbreviation for console out). The last name defines the group (family) to which the object belongs; the first name defines the actual name of the object in the group. In summary, line 5 tells the computer to write the given message on the screen.

Line 6: The Second Line of Body Line 6 of the program is as shown below:

```
std :: cout << "to show the main structure. " << std :: endl;
```

This line is very similar to line 5 with some exceptions. First, the message is different, "to show the main structure." Second, after the message is written, the verb (`<<`) is repeated. Third, no new message is defined, but the program writes a predefined object called `std :: endl`. This is a different object, an object that when sent to the monitor adds a **new line** at the end of the previous message, which causes the output to move to the next line. This object, `endl`, is an abbreviation of (end line). The next output will be printed on the next line. Figure 2.2 shows that the destination is the same (mentioned only once) but the verb and the object are repeated. In the first section, the object is a string object; in the second it is **endl** (note that the last character is a lowercase L, not a one).

Lines 7 and 8 Lines 7 and 8 are similar to lines 5 and 6, but there is no `endl` object because line 8 is the last line of text and there is no need for the `endl` object.

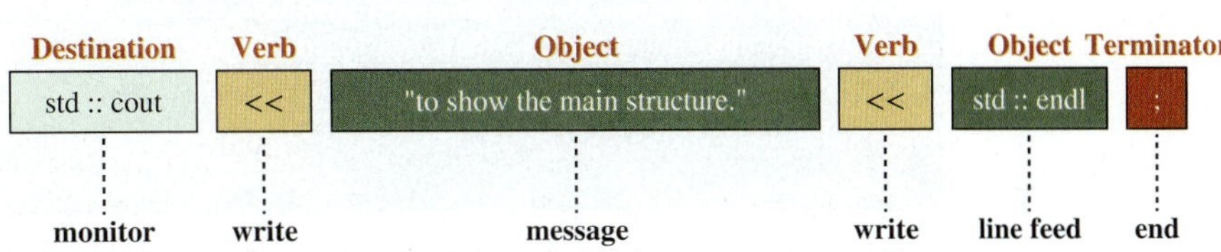

Figure 2.2 Analysis of line 6

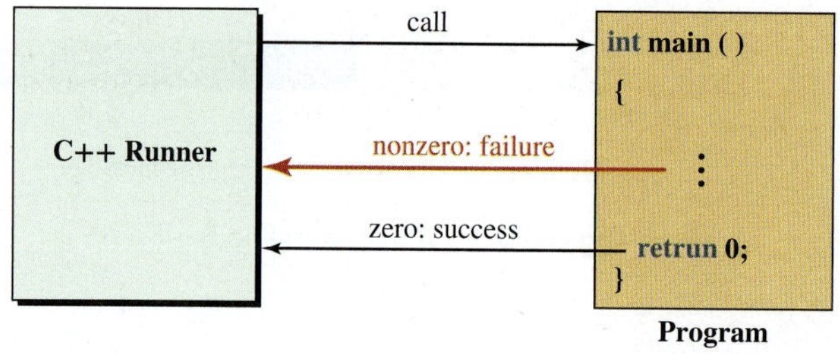

Figure 2.3 Relationship between the runner and our program

Line 9 The last line in the body of the function is different from other lines:

```
return 0;
```

This line is still a command, but there is no explicit target object. The target object is implicit here. It is an entity in the C++ system that is called the *runner*. Figure 2.3 shows the situation.

The runner starts the `main` function running from the first command in the body; the runner expects the function to return a value that shows if the program has been successful or not. The returned value defines the success or failure. If the program reaches the last line in the function and returns 0, it means success. Figure 2.3 shows a simple version of the program as started and stopped by the runner.

Program Output

The result of the execution of the commands whose target object is `cout` is shown on the monitor connected to the computer on which we are running the program. In this case, we have two lines of text to be shown on the monitor. Figure 2.4 shows the monitor (console) window where our program output is displayed (the details are platform dependent).

2.1.2 Second Program

In this section we write another program in C++ similar to the first one, but with some modification and addition. Although many puritans believe that every object in the program should be coded with both a last name and a first name, such as `std :: cout` or `std :: endl`, most programmers believe that we do not need to mention the last name of each object individually. They believe we should give the group (last) name at the top of the program and then use only the first name. We discuss this issue in more detail in Appendix G, namespaces. Program 2.2 shows our second program.

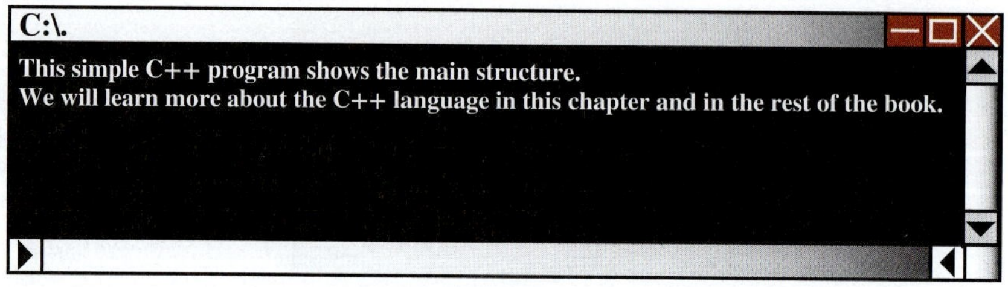

Figure 2.4 The console (cout object) where the output is shown.

Program 2.2 The second simple program

```
1  /**************************************************************
2   * This program shows how we can print a square of asterisks.  *
3   **************************************************************/
4  #include <iostream>
5  using namespace std;
6  int main ()
7
8  {
9     // Printing a square of asterisks
10    cout << "******" << endl;
11    cout << "******" << endl;
12    cout << "******" << endl;
13    cout << "******" << endl;
14    cout << "******" << endl;
15    cout << "******";
16    return 0;
17 }
```

```
Run:
******
******
******
******
******
******
```

Analysis

We briefly analyze the lines in Program 2.2 that are different from the corresponding lines in the first program.

Lines 1 to 3: Block Comment Lines 1 to 3 in the second program are different from the first program. They are what we call a **block comment.** A block comment is one or more lines that are considered comments for the user or reviewer of the code and are totally ignored by the compiler (block comments are erased before the program is compiled). The format is shown below:

```
/* Text to be ignored
Text to be ignored
Text to be ignored */
```

The comment has a starting section and ending section. The starting section is made of two characters (`/*`), and the ending section is made of the same two characters but in the reverse order (`*/`). Everything in between is considered a comment and is ignored. Note that we can have any character between the starting section and the ending section (including `*` and `/`) but not in combination to create a starting section or an ending section. Inside the program we use colored text for the whole comment. Note that in lines 1 to 3, we have used some asterisks as text to create a frame for our comment, but this is a personal choice.

Line 5 This line is also new in this program, as shown below:

```
using namespace std;
```

Line 5 tells the compiler that when it cannot see the last name of an object, insert `std::` in front of it to make the name complete. In other words, it tells the compiler that some names that we use in the program belong to the `namespace std`. With this single line, we can use the `cout` and `endl` objects without qualifying them with the `std` namespace.

Line 9 This line is also a comment, but a **line comment** (instead of a block comment). This type of comment starts with two slashes and continues with text as a comment (up to the end of the line). The whole line is ignored by the compiler.

```
// Printing a square of asterisks
```

This type of comment can span only a single line. If we need two lines of comments, we must start another line comment or use a block comment.

Lines 10 to 15 These lines do the same thing as similar ones in the first program, but we can use `cout` and `endl` without (`std ::`). Each line prints a line of six asterisks on the monitor to create a square of asterisks. In Program 2.2 we have used a yellow background to highlight the body of the function here. This is not needed; it is only used for readability.

2.2 VARIABLE, VALUE, AND CONSTANT

Before we can write more programs, we need to understand three concepts: *variables, values, and constants.*

2.2.1 Variables

Programs written in the C++ language receive input data, manipulate them, and create output data. Since the input and output data may change, we must be able to store the input data, store the intermediate data, and store the output data in memory. For this reason, C++, like most programming languages, uses the concept of variables. A **variable** in computer language parlance is a memory chunk that needs to have a *name* and a *type*. It is called a variable because its contents may change during the execution of the program. It's purpose is to store and retrieve data. It must have a *type* because we use different data types for different purposes.

A variable is a memory location, with a name and a type, that stores different values in each moment of a program's execution.

Before we use a variable, we must define it. We must tell the compiler that we want to use a memory location with the given name and the given type. The name is used to refer to the variable; the type is used to tell what type of data is stored in the variable.

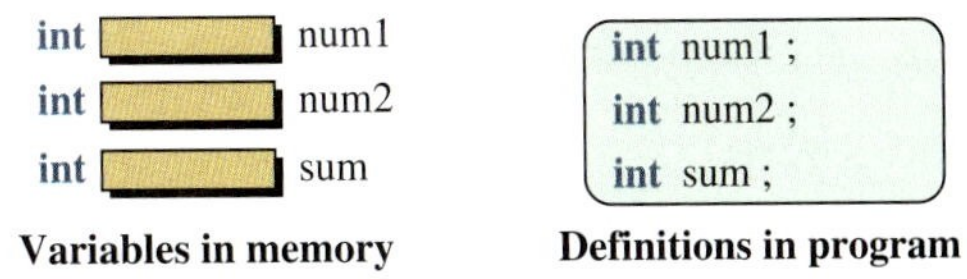

Figure 2.5 Variables in memory and their definition in a program

EXAMPLE 2.1

Figure 2.5 shows three variables with their types and names. The figure also shows how we define them to ensure that the compiler will know the variable to which we are referring.

We have not discussed data types yet, but we specify that all three data types are integer types (**int**) that represent a whole number (without fractions), such as 17, 35, 100, and so on, but not 23.67.

2.2.2 Values

The contents of a variable are referred to as its **value.** For example, if `num1` at this moment holds the integer 17, its value is 17. When we use the name of a variable in a program, sometimes we mean the variable itself, sometimes the value it holds. The next example shows the difference.

EXAMPLE 2.2

Assume we want to write a program that accepts any two whole numbers, adds them together, and displays the result. While we not have studied data types yet, we understand that the two numbers and the result are integer types (**int** in C++). To store the two numbers and the result of the addition, we need to give them names. We call them **num1**, **num2**, and **sum**, respectively. We then write a program that, each time it runs, finds the sum of two numbers entered at the keyboard and prints them (Program 2.3).

Program 2.3 A program that adds two values

```
/*********************************************************************
 * This program gets the values for two numbers from the keyboard,   *
 * adds them together and prints the result on the monitor.          *
 *********************************************************************/
#include <iostream>
using namespace std;

int main ()
{
   // Definition
   int num1;
   int num2;
   int sum;
   // Getting inputs
   cout << "Enter the first number: ";
```

(continued)

Program 2.3 A program that adds two values (Continued)

```
16     cin >> num1;
17     cout << "Enter the second number: ";
18     cin >> num2;
19     // Calculation and storing result
20     sum = num1 + num2;
21     // Display output
22     cout << "The sum is: " << sum;
23     return 0;
24 }
```

```
Run:
Enter the first number: 23
Enter the second number: 35
The sum is: 58
```

```
Run:
Enter the first number: 7
Enter the second number: 110
The sum is: 117
```

We examine the contents of lines 11 to 13 as shown below:

```
int num1;
int num2;
int sum;
```

These three lines declare variables. Declaration of a variable means reservation of memory with a corresponding name. In the case of the above three declarations, we have the situation shown previously in Figure 2.5. Note that no values are stored in the program at this moment.

Now we examine lines 15 to 18 as shown below:

```
cout << "Enter the first number: ";
cin >> num1;
cout << "Enter the second number: ";
cin >> num2;
```

We are familiar with the first line. The first line prints a message, which is referred to as *prompt,* on the screen. It tells the user what to do next. The second line is new for us. It uses a target object, `cin` (for console in) and a command (`>>`), which means *read*. This command waits for the user of the program to enter a value (an integer in this case) on the keyboard and hit the enter key. The program then stores the value entered in variable `num1`. The third line is the same as the first one. The fourth line is the same as the second line, but it stores the value entered by the user in variable `num2`. After these four lines, two values are stored

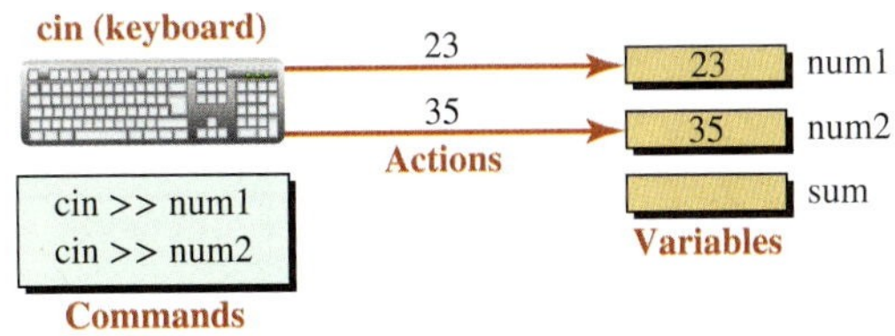

Figure 2.6 Variable contents before and after two input commands

in two variables. If we assume that we entered 23 and 35, the memory location now looks like Figure 2.6.

Now we analyze line 20 as shown below:

```
sum = num1 + num2;
```

In this line, we use two *operators*: assignment (=) and addition (+). We discuss operators in the next chapter in more detail. For the moment, let us describe their roles in this line. The assignment operator (=) means store. It stores the value on the right-hand side and the variable on the left-hand side. In other words, it is of the form

```
variable = value;
```

In this case, the variable on the left-hand side is `sum`, and the value on the right-hand side is a copy of the value stored in `num1` added to a copy of the value stored in **num2**, as shown in Figure 2.7.

Line 22 is similar to what we have seen before. It is

```
cout << "The sum is: " << sum;
```

In this case two entities are shown on the screen. The first is the message; the second is the value of variable `sum` as shown in Figure 2.8.

The cin and the cout Objects

The concept of variable and value are closely tied to the concept of the `cin` and `cout` objects in the previous program. The `cin` object is the source of data; the `cout` object is the desti-

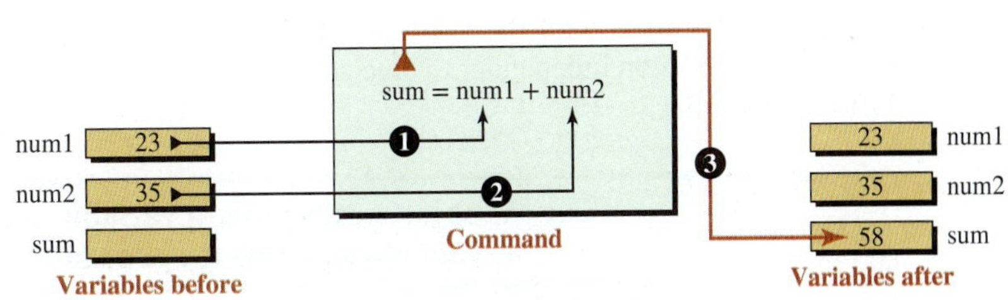

Figure 2.7 Variable contents before and after assignment

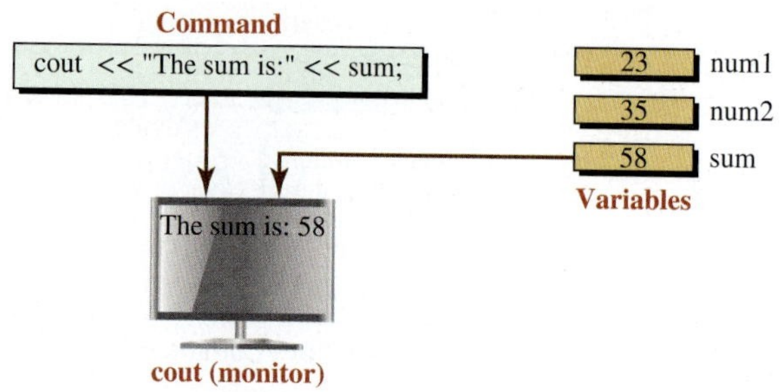

Figure 2.8 Situation of variables and monitor after line 22

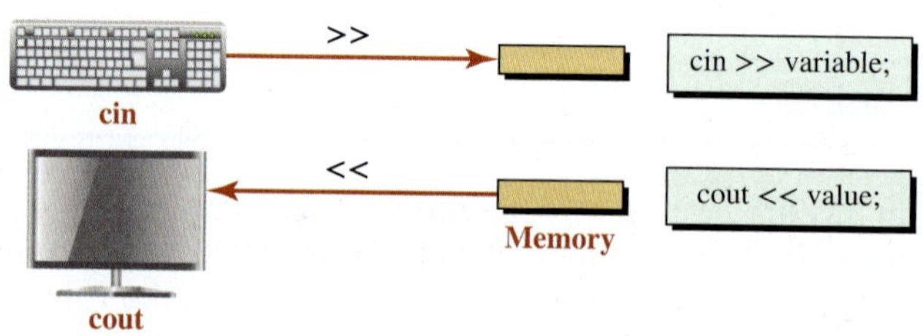

Figure 2.9 Keyboard and monitor as the source and destination of date

nation of data. The `cin` object uses an input device (such as the keyboard) as the source of data. The `cout` object uses an output device (such as the monitor) as the destination of data. The `cin` object uses the operators (`>>`) to get the data; the `cout` object uses the operator (`<<`) to deliver the data. We can better understand the role of these objects if we see them together with their memory as shown in Figure 2.9.

To remember which operators we need to use, we can think of (`>>`) and (`<<`) as double arrows in the direction of data movement. In the case of input, data moves to the right; in the case of output, data moves to the left.

The most important point that we need to remember about the `cin` object is that we need a variable name (as the destination of data). On the other hand, we need a value as the source of data for the `cout` object. However, we have seen that we use a command such as `cout << sum`, where the `sum` is the name of a variable. We should be aware that in this case, we mean the value of `sum`, not the name of `sum`. This is an important issue that we need to remember. The name of the variable sometimes means the physical variable as the destination; sometimes, it means a copy of the value stored in it.

The value used with the `cout` object does not necessarily have to be the value of a variable; it can be an independent value such as (`cout << 12`), which means send the value 12 to the monitor.

The *cin* object needs to see a variable name;
the *cout* object needs to see a value.

The following examples clarify these important concepts.

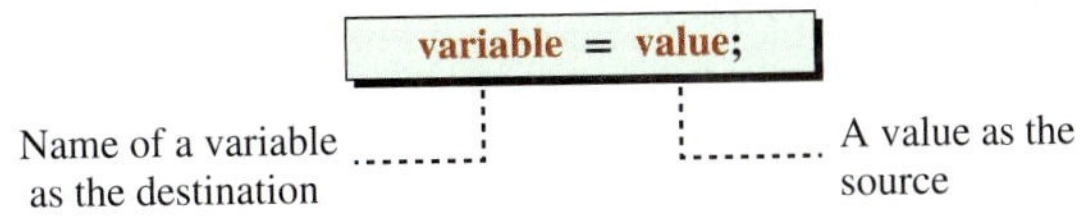

Figure 2.10 Source and destination in an assignment

```
cin >> x;         // Get a value from keyboard and store it in variable x.
cout << x;        // Get the value of variable x and display it; value of x will not change.
cout << 4;        // Display the value 4 on the screen.
cin >> 4          // Error. The cin object needs a variable, not a value.
```

Assignment Operator

Another entity related to the concept of value and variable is the assignment operator. The assignment operator (=) needs a variable on the left-hand side and a value on the right-hand side as shown in Figure 2.10.

When we talk about a value related to the assignment operator, we mean the value of a variable whose name is given, an independent value, or a combination of values to make a single value. Examples are as follows:

```
x = y;            // Store the value of variable y into variable x.
x = 5;            // Store 5 into variable x.
x = y + 6;        // Take value of y, add 6 to it, and store the result in variable x.
x = x + 3;        // Take value of x, add 3 to it, and store the result back in variable x.
x = x + y;        // Take value of x, add value of y to it, and store the result back in x.
```

Note that the terms x and y on the left- and right-hand sides of the assignment operator mean different things.

A variable on the right-hand side of an assignment operator means copy the value of the variable (as a source); a variable on the left-hand side of the assignment operator means store the value in that variable (as a destination).

2.2.3 Constants

The last entity that we discuss in this section is a **constant.** A constant is a storage entity whose value cannot be changed. Its value is fixed. We declare the memory location that holds it, we qualify the name with the **const** modifier, and we use the assignment operator to store the value we want to be held by it no matter how many times we reference it. The format is shown for the value of π in mathematics. Note that the term **double** represents a number with fraction such as 3.14159 or 7.2.

```
const double PI = 3.14159;        // Definition of a constant
```

The above definition tells us that we want to store the value of π in a memory location named PI, but we want its value to be fixed and not changed during the program run. In other words, we can access the value, but we cannot change the value. This means that we cannot use the name PI on the left-hand side of an assignment operator (except when we define it) and we cannot use it with the `cin` object as shown below:

```
PI = x;                 // Error the value of PI cannot be changed
cin >> PI;              // Error PI cannot receive a value
cout << PI;             // The value of PI can be shown on the monitor
x = PI;                 // The value of PI be stored in a variable
```

Another way we can use a constant value in a program is to use it as a **literal.** We use a literal value in our program without storing it in a memory location. The experts, however, forbid the use of literals in a program unless their use is completely clear to everyone who looks at the program. The following shows how we can use both a stored constant and a literal constant to find the perimeter of a circle when its radius is given (the asterisk in this case means multiplication).

```
perimeter = 2 * PI * radius;         // 2 is a literal, PI is an stored constant
```

2.3 COMPONENTS OF A C++ PROGRAM

Now that we have discussed some programs in C++ and have analyzed them, we introduce the components of a C++ program. To write in a new natural language like French or Spanish, we must know the components of the language. We must know the meaning of the set of words we use and how to combine them to make sentences. We must also be familiar with the punctuation symbols used in the language. Learning to create a program in a new computer language, such as C++, is much simpler because it has a limited number of words and symbols to master.

What we see in a C++ program (referred to as source code) is usually made of two things interleaved with each other. The first is the code that is used by the compiler to create the runnable program (in machine language). The second is comments added by the programmer to explain the purpose of the whole or a part of the program. The first uses the *tokens* of the C++ language; the second uses words in the English language and a few predefined symbols.

2.3.1 Tokens

A C++ program without comments is a sequence of *tokens*. A token can be an *identifier*, a *literal*, or a *symbol*. We discuss each next.

Identifiers

An **identifier** is the name of an entity in the C++ language. To be a valid identifier, a name must start with a letter or an underscore, and it can have zero or more digits, letters, or underscores. There is no limit to the number of characters in an identifier.

An identifier must start with a letter or an underscore, and it can have zero or more letters, digits, or underscores.

As we mentioned before, the C++ language is case-sensitive. Many programmers use identifiers made of lowercase letters, but it is becoming more and more common to use two-word or three-word identifiers with the first word all in lowercase and subsequent words starting with an uppercase letter, such as *lowerValue*, *upperValue*, *firstTest*, *secondTest*, *timeOfWithdraw*, and so on. The library of the C++ language also uses identifiers with several words separated by an underscore, but we need to avoid them in our programs.

EXAMPLE 2.3

The list of identifiers in Program 2.1 is shown below:

```
include, iostream, int, main, std, cout, endl, return
```

They can be categoried as *keywords*, *predefined identifiers*, and *user-defined identifiers*. We discuss each category next.

Keywords A **keyword** (sometimes called reserved word) is an identifier that is reserved by the C++ language and cannot be redefined by the programmer or the library of the language. We show in color the keywords in the text and in programs to distinguish them from other identifiers. Table 2.1 shows the list of 84 keywords in C++. These keywords are made according to the rules of identifiers we discussed before.

Table 2.1 Keywords

alignas	alignof	and	and_eq	asm
auto	bitand	bitor	bool	break
case	catch	char	char16_t	char32_t
class	compl	const	const_cast	constexpr
continue	decltype	default	delete	do
double	dynamic_cast	else	enum	explicit
export	extern	false	float	for
friend	goto	if	inline	int
long	mutable	namespace	new	noexcept
not	not_eq	nullptr	operator	or
or_eq	private	protected	public	register
reinterpret_cast	return	short	signed	sizeof
static	static_assert	static_cast	struct	switch
template	this	thread_local	throw	true
try	typedef	typeid	typename	union
unsigned	using	virtual	void	volatile
wchar_t	while	xor	xor_eq	

EXAMPLE 2.4

Find how many of the identifiers in Program 2.1 are keywords. We see that only two of them are keywords that are shown in color. We use blue in this text to distinguish keywords from other identifiers.

```
int, return
```

Predefined Identifiers We encounter some identifiers in the C++ language that are not keywords but are predefined in the language. Although we can redefine them and use them in our programs, it is better not to do so to avoid confusion.

EXAMPLE 2.5

Find how many of the predefined identifiers we have used in Program 2.1. There are six of them as shown below:

```
include, iostream, main, std, cout, endl
```

User-Defined Identifiers Users of the language (programmers) can define a set of identifiers to be used in their programs as long as they follow the rules of identifiers we discussed before. The following are some valid programmer identifiers:

```
z          z12          _3          sum          average          result2          counter
```

However, we do not recommend the first three identifiers. The first two are not descriptive (the name does not say anything about the entity); the third starts with an underscore, which is usually used only for predefined identifiers.

The following are all invalid (illegal) identifiers and create a compilation error. The first three start with a digit. The third, fourth, and fifth have some symbols other than digits or letters. The last two are keywords and cannot be redefined by a programmer.

```
3z          13          3?2          sum@          count-2          delete          double
```

EXAMPLE 2.6

We did not define any identifiers in Program 2.1 or Program 2.2. However, we have created three identifiers in Program 2.3 as shown below:

```
num1, num2, sum
```

Literals

Another set of tokens we encounter in a program are literals. Literals are constant values of different types. We will discuss some literals in this chapter after we discuss the data types in the C++ language.

Table 2.2 Symbols in C++

<table>
<tr><td>{</td><td>}</td><td>[</td><td>]</td><td>#</td><td>##</td><td>(</td><td>)</td><td><:</td><td>:></td></tr>
<tr><td><%</td><td>%></td><td>%:</td><td>%:%:</td><td>;</td><td>:</td><td>...</td><td>,</td><td>.</td><td>+</td></tr>
<tr><td>–</td><td>*</td><td>/</td><td>%</td><td>^</td><td>&</td><td>|</td><td>?</td><td>::</td><td>.*</td></tr>
<tr><td>–></td><td>–>*</td><td>~</td><td>!</td><td>=</td><td>==</td><td><</td><td>></td><td><=</td><td>>=</td></tr>
<tr><td>|=</td><td><<</td><td>>></td><td><<=</td><td>>>=</td><td>-=</td><td>+=</td><td>*=</td><td>/=</td><td>%=</td></tr>
<tr><td>&=</td><td>!=</td><td>^=</td><td>++</td><td>– –</td><td></td><td></td><td></td><td></td><td></td></tr>
</table>

EXAMPLE 2.7

We have used five literals in Program 2.1: one integer literal and four string literals.

```
0                                                  // numeric literal
"This is a simple program in C++ "                 // string literal
"to show the main structure."                      // string literal
"We learn more about the language ";               // string literal
"in this chapter and the rest of the book.";       // string literal
```

Symbols

C++ uses nonalphabetic symbols as operators and punctuation. We discuss some of the operators later in the chapter. Here we discuss some of the punctuation symbols in sample programs. Table 2.2 shows the symbols used in the C++ language.

EXAMPLE 2.8

Find the symbols used in Program 2.1. They are shown below:

```
# (  ) {  ::  <<  ;  }
```

2.3.2 Comments

We briefly discussed comments when we introduced our second program. Comments are explanations added to the program to make it understandable for people who read the source code. They are text that is removed by the preprocessor, which is a program that prepares the source code for compilation.

Single-Line Comments

If we need a short comment, we can use a single-line comment. A single-line comment starts with // and terminates at the end of the line. It can start at any point in a line, but it consumes the rest of the line. The rest of the line after // is ignored by the compiler. In this book we show comments in red.

```
cout << "Hello World";                  // This prints the first line.
```

Multiple-Line Comments

A multiple-line comment can span several lines. It has two markers, one to define the beginning and another to define the end of the comment. The opening marker is /* while the closing marker is */. When the opening marker (/*) is encountered by the preprocessor, the rest of the text is ignored until the preprocessor encounters the closing marker (*/). The following shows a multiple-line command:

```
/* This is a program to show how we can print a message of two lines
using the output object cout defined in the iostream file. */
```

Nesting Comments

C++ does not support nested comments, although new programmers often try to nest them. A little thought about how comments are processed by the compiler will clarify the issue.

1. A line comment cannot be nested inside a line comment because when the compiler sees the line comment token (//) it ignores everything else on the line. The line is simply printed.
2. Nesting either a line comment or another multiple-line comment inside a multiple-line comment also doesn't work because again the compiler ignores everything from the opening token to the end token (/* ... */).
3. The one situation that can create an error is nesting a multiple-line comment in a single line comment. Let's look at this situation more closely.

```
// Single line comment. /* Start of multiple-line comment.
Line two of comments
*/ End of multiple-line comments
```

There are several problems with this error:

a. The compiler does not see the start of the multiple-line comment because it ignores everything on the line after the opening token (//).
b. The comments that follow on the second and successive lines are most likely English or mathematical descriptions. They will generate one or more error messages.
c. The compiler generates an error message when the end token (*/) is found because it doesn't have a start token. Remember, the start token was ignored.

2.4 DATA TYPES

A program written in the C++ language, in a procedural or an object-oriented paradigm, needs to manipulate data. In other words, a program in C++ is like a machine that accepts some input data, manipulates them, and produces the output data. To make manipulating data efficient, C++ recognizes different **data types.** The number of data types defined in the C++ language is very large, but we can divide these types into two broad categories: built-in and user-defined, with each category divided into two groups as shown in Figure 2.11.

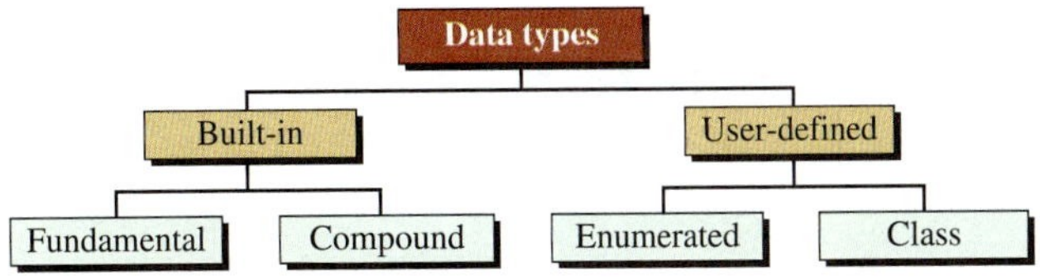

Figure 2.11 Data types in C++

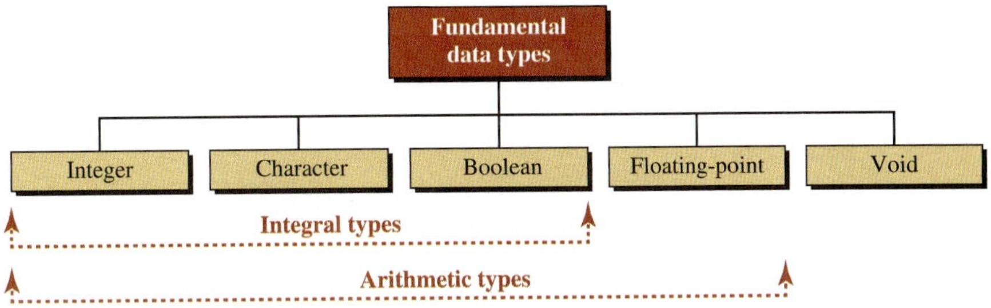

Figure 2.12 Fundamental data types

The **built-in data types** are those defined by the language. The language distinguishes two groups in this category: *fundamental* (or *primitive*) and *compound*. The fundamental types are very basic; we can use them immediately; the compound types are derived from the fundamental types (discussed in future chapters). The language also divides the user-defined type into two categories: **enumerated** and **class.**

The fundamental data types themselves are divided into five categories based on the nature of what they define as shown in Figure 2.12.

In this section, we only discuss fundamental types and one of the class types (string class). We discuss compound types in future chapters.

2.4.1 Integer Type

A number without a fraction is called an **integer.** For example, the number 1376 is an integer, but the number 1376.25 is not. C++ allows three different sizes of integers: **short int**, **int**, **long int** (in appendix M, we discuss a new integer data type defined in C++11). However, the term **int** can be omitted if there is no ambiguity. The size of these types is platform dependent, which means that **long int** can be 4 bytes in one machine and 8 bytes in another. Each of these three different types can be either signed or unsigned (the default is signed). We use a prefix to show that. In other words, C++ actually defines six different **integer data types.**

Table 2.3 shows the range of numbers used in a typical machine. Note that we have assumed 4 bytes (32 bits) for the size of **long int**, but some platforms use 8 bytes for this purpose.

Although the language does not define the exact size and ranges of the different integer data types, it emphasizes their relative sizes. It defines the following relationship, in which the symbol ≤ means "less than or equal."

```
short int  ≤  int  ≤  long int
```

To better visualize these different integer types and their sizes, we can look at Figure 2.13.

Table 2.3 Ranges of integers in a typical machine

Type	Sign	Range	
short int	signed	−32,768	+32,767
	unsigned	0	65,536
int	signed	−2,147,483,648	+2,147,483,647
	unsigned	0	4,294,967,295
long int	signed	−2,147,483,648	+2,147,483,647
	unsigned	0	4,294,967,295

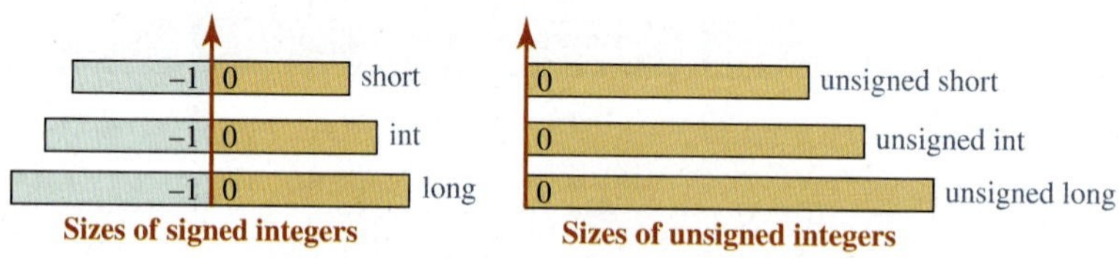

Figure 2.13 The relative sizes of integer data types

The signed types can be positive or negative; the unsigned types are only positive. Note that the total range of a type is the same in the signed and unsigned version, but the range is divided into two equally divided sections in the signed version (0 is considered as part of the signed section).

If we do not explicitly define the sign of an integer, it is signed.

Integer Variables

We can use integer variables in our program if we explicitly define a variable of type integer: **short int**, **int**, and **long int** (**short int** and **long int** can be abbreviated to **short** or **long**). At the same time, we can define the sign of the integer: **signed** or **unsigned** (the default is **signed**).

EXAMPLE 2.9

The following shows the definition of six variables, each a different integer type.

```
// Long format
unsigned short int first;
signed short int second;
unsigned int third;
signed int fourth;
unsigned long int fifth;
signed long int six;
```

```
// Short format
unsigned short first;
short second;
unsigned int third;
int fourth;
unsigned long fifth;
long int six;
```

EXAMPLE 2.10

Assume we need to find the value of any set of coins (dollars, quarters, dimes, nickels, pennies) in pennies. Since the value of each coin is predefined and always positive, we can use unsigned integer constants as shown in Program 2.4.

Program 2.4 Using unsigned integers

```
/*******************************************************************
 * Finding the total value of a set of coins                       *
 *******************************************************************/
#include <iostream>
using namespace std;

int main ()
{
  // Defining constants
   const unsigned int pennyValue = 1;
   const unsigned int nickelValue = 5;
   const unsigned int dimeValue = 10;
   const unsigned int quarterValue = 25;
   const unsigned int dollarValue = 100;
  // Defining variables (number of each coin)
   unsigned int pennies;
   unsigned int nickels;
   unsigned int dimes;
   unsigned int quarters;
   unsigned int dollars;
  // Defining total value
   unsigned long totalValue;
  // Inputting number of different coins
   cout << "Enter the number of pennies: ";
   cin >> pennies;
   cout << "Enter the number of nickels: ";
   cin >> nickels;
   cout << "Enter the number of dimes: ";
   cin >> dimes;
   cout << "Enter the number of quarters: ";
   cin >> quarters;
   cout << "Enter the number of dollars: ";
   cin >> dollars;
  // Calculating total value
   totalValue = pennies * pennyValue + nickels * nickelValue +
      dimes * dimeValue + quarters * quarterValue + dollars * dollarValue;
  // Outputting result
   cout << "The total value is: " << totalValue << " pennies." ;
   return 0;
}
```

Run:

```
Enter the number of pennies: 20
Enter the number of nickels: 5
Enter the number of dimes: 10
Enter the number of quarters: 4
Enter the number of dollars: 6
The total value is: 845 pennies.
```

Program 2.5 Using signed integers in a program

```
/*****************************************************************
 * Finding the balance of an account after three transactions   *
 *****************************************************************/
#include <iostream>
using namespace std;

int main ()
{
  // Definition of variables
  int balance = 0;
  int transaction;
  // Inputting first transaction and adjusting the balance
  cout << "Enter the value of the first transaction: ";
  cin >> transaction;
  balance = balance + transaction;
  // Inputting second transaction and adjusting the balance
  cout << "Enter the value of the second transaction: ";
  cin >> transaction;
  balance = balance + transaction;
  // Inputting third transaction and adjusting the balance
  cout << "Enter the value of the third transaction: ";
  cin >> transaction;
  balance = balance + transaction;
  // Outputting the final balance
  cout << "The total balance is: " << balance << " dollars. ";
  return 0;
}
```

```
Run:
Enter the value of the first transaction: 70
Enter the value of the second transaction: -50
Enter the value of the third transaction: 35
The total balance in your account is: 55 dollars.
```

EXAMPLE 2.11

We need to consider signed integers when dealing with bank transactions. A deposit is a positive-value transaction; a withdrawal is a negative-value transaction. Program 2.5 shows the balance of an account after three transactions when we open the account with a balance of zero dollars. Note that because we use both positive and negative integers, we let each customer withdraw money even if the balance is negative.

EXAMPLE 2.12

Later in the book, we discuss more about the size and maximum and minimum values of each type. At this time, we write a small program (Program 2.6) and use the **sizeof** operator

Program 2.6 Finding size of integer types

```
/***************************************************************
 * A program to find the size of all three integer types        *
 ***************************************************************/
#include <iostream>
using namespace std;

int main ()
{
   cout << "Size of short int is " << sizeof (short int) << " bytes." << endl;
   cout << "Size of int is " << sizeof (int) << " bytes." << endl;
   cout << "Size of long int is " << sizeof (long int) << " bytes." << endl;
   return 0;
}
```

```
Run:
Size of short int: 2 bytes.
Size of int: 4 bytes.
Size of long int: 4 bytes.
```

to find the size of the integer data types in the platform we are working on. This may help us to avoid using data values out of the range for the type.

Note that the size of an **int** and a **long int** are the same in the computer we used to run the program.

Integer Literals

When we explicitly use a value of any type in our program, it is referred to as a literal. An **integer literal,** when used in a program, has a constant value; its value does not change when the program executes. If the programmer does not define the size and the sign of an integer literal, the system uses the smallest size (`int` or `long`) that can fit the value. If the integer is positive, the literal would be *unsigned*; if it is negative, the literal would be *signed*. The programmer can explicitly define the size and the sign of the literal using suffixes as defined in Table 2.4.

Note that `short int` is not used for literals. The default value is `int` (no suffix). To tell the compiler that we want `long`, we can use the suffix l or L (lowercase or uppercase). Numeric literals are signed by default: to explicitly say that we want them unsigned, we need to us the suffix u or U (lowercase or uppercase). Note, however, that we do not

Table 2.4 Suffixes for explicit size and sign of an integer literal

Size	*Suffixes*	*Sign*	*Suffixes*
int	None	signed int or signed long	None
long	l or L	unsigned int or unsigned long	u or U

recommend using the lowercase formats (l or u). The first is too easily confused with the digit 1.

To explicitly define the size or sign of an integer literal, we use suffixes.

EXAMPLE 2.13

The following shows the only four cases we can have when we use an integer as a literal:

```
1234        // The system uses signed integer
1234U       // The system uses unsigned integer
1234L       // The system uses signed long int
1234UL      // The system uses unsigned long int
```

Integer literals can be used for two purposes. They can be used as a stand-alone value in a calculation or they can be used to initialize a variable.

Integer Literals Used for Initialization When we declare a variable, we can initialize it to a value. This does not mean that we cannot later change the value of the variable. It just means that if a new value is not assigned to the variable, the variable holds the initial value. Later in the book, we discuss default initialization values for variables, but until then we should remember to initialize a variable with an appropriate value.

To show why we need to be careful when we use integer literals to initialize variables, let us run Program 2.7.

Program 2.7 Initialization with integer literals

```
/***************************************************************
 * Using some literal values as variable initializers          *
 ***************************************************************/
#include <iostream>
using namespace std;

int main ()
{
  // Declaration and initialization
  int x = -1245;
  unsigned int y = 1245;
  unsigned int z = -2367;
  unsigned int t = 14.56;
  // Outputting initialized values
  cout << x << endl;
  cout << y << endl;
  cout << z << endl;
  cout << t;
```

(continued)

Program 2.7 Initialization with integer literals (Continued)

```
19      return 0;
20  }
```

```
Run:
Value of x: -1245          // OK.
Value of y: 1245           // OK.
Value of z: 4294964929     // Logical error. A negative value is changed to positive.
Value of t: 14             // The value is truncated.
```

The result shows that there is a logic error in line 12. We defined the variable z to be an unsigned integer and we stored the value -2367 in it. This number is interpreted as 4294964929 and stored in z. We will discuss this logical error in the next chapter, but this is not what we intended it to be. The result in line 18 is another surprise. Since we defined the variable t to be of type unsigned integer and we stored a noninteger value in it, the system changed the literal to an integer value by dropping the fraction part after the decimal point. Most puritans consider this case a logical error.

Integer Literals Used as Stand-Alone Values We can also use an integer literal as a stand-alone value in a program. In this case, the value seen by the program depends on both the literal value and its contents.

EXAMPLE 2.14

Program 2.8 shows a few cases that test the aforementioned situations.

Program 2.8 Use of some literals

```
/***************************************************************
 * Using some stand alone literal values                       *
 ***************************************************************/
#include <iostream>
using namespace std;

int main ()
{
   // Variable definition
   int x;
   unsigned long int y;
   // Assignments
   x = 1456;
   y = -14567;
   // Outputs
   cout << x << endl;
   cout << y << endl;
```

(continued)

Program 2.8 Use of some literals (Continued)

```
18      cout << 1234 << endl;
19      cout << 143267L << endl;
20      return 0;
21  }
```

```
Run:
1456            // OK.
4294952729      // Wrong value. The variable is unsigned; the value is signed.
1234            // OK.
143267          // OK.
```

Note that in line 14 an unsigned literal must be stored in variable y, but we assigned a negative value to it. In the next chapter, we will see the reason for this behavior.

2.4.2 Character Type

The second integral type we discuss is the **character type.** It is called **char**. We can think of **char** as an integer smaller than an **unsigned short int**. The size of a char as originally defined in C++ is 1 byte and it was implicitly unsigned. Today, however, we sometimes see characters of 1 byte, 2 bytes, or even 4 bytes in size. We even hear about signed and unsigned characters. These new types are designed to support the internationalization of the C++ language. We discuss some of these types in Appendix A. In this chapter, we assume that a **char** data type is a 1 byte integral type that defines a character in the **ASCII** encoding system (see Appendix A). The ASCII encoding system defines 128 characters using integral values from 0 to 127.

Character Variables

We can use character variables in our program just as we can use integer variables. However, we avoid signed and unsigned qualifiers in this chapter. The following shows some examples of declaring two variables of type **char**.

```
char first;
char second;
```

Character Literals

We can use two types of **character literals.** We can use alphabet characters as defined in the ASCII table (Appendix A) inside two **single quotes.** We can also use the integer value of the characters as defined in the ASCII table. As long as it is unambiguous that we mean character literals, the compiler stores the corresponding character in memory. Program 2.9 gives a very simple example using four character variables and character literals to initialize them.

Note the values printed for the first and second variables are the same. We have used a literal character for the first and a literal integer for the second. This is the case for the third and fourth variables.

Program 2.9 Character variables and literals

```
/*******************************************************************
 * Using some char variables and initialize them                   *
 *******************************************************************/
#include <iostream>
using namespace std;

int main ()
{
  // Defining and initializing some variables of char type
   char first = 'A';
   char second = 65;
   char third = 'B';
   char fourth = 66;
  // Printing values
   cout << "Value of first: " << first << endl;
   cout << "Value of second: " << second << endl;
   cout << "Value of third: " << third << endl;
   cout << "Value of fourth: " << fourth;
   return 0;
}
```

```
Run:
Value of first: A
Value of second: A
Value of third: B
Value of fourth: B
```

A character literal is always enclosed in a pair of single quotes.

We can use an escape sequence (**backslash** followed by a symbol) to define some special characters as shown in Table 2.5.

We use a backslash in front of the first five characters because they are not printable characters. The single quote is used to delimit a character, so we must use the backslash to mean we want the single quote itself, not the delimiter. This is the same with the

Table 2.5 Some special characters

Sequence	*Description*	*Sequence*	*Description*
\n	New line (line feed)	\f	Form feed
\t	Tab	\'	Single quote
\b	Backspace	\"	Double quote
\r	Carriage return	\\	Backslash

double quote, but it is used to delimit the string. Therefore, we need to use the a backslash to tell the program that we literally need this character, not the delimiter. If we want to literally use a backslash, we must escape it with another backslash.

EXAMPLE 2.15

Although we can define variables and assign any of these escape sequences, the better way is to show their effect when they are used in strings. Program 2.10 shows how we use seven of them in seven strings. The form feed cannot be used with the monitor; it is designed to feed a new page to the printer.

2.4.3 Boolean Type

The C++ language defines a type called **Boolean** (named after the French mathematician/philosopher George Bool) to represent a value that can be either **true** or **false**. The type is referred to as Boolean, but the type name used in a program is actually **bool**, which is a keyword.

This type is mostly used to represent the result of comparing two values. For example, if we compare the integers 23 and 24 for equality, we get **false**. However, if we compare them for inequality, we get **true**.

Program 2.10 Effect of some special characters

```
/***************************************************************
 * Using some special characters in strings                   *
 ***************************************************************/
#include <iostream>
using namespace std;

int main ()
{
  cout << "Hello\n";
  cout << "Hi\t friends." << endl;
  cout << "Buenos dias  \bamigos." << endl; // two space after dias
  cout << "Hello\rBonjour mes amis." << endl;
  cout << "This is a single quote\'." << endl;
  cout << "This is a double quote\"." <<endl;
  cout << "This is how to print a backslash \\.";
  return 0;
}
```

```
Run:
Hello    // \n has the same effect as endl
Hi friends.    // effect of tab
Buenos dias amigos.  // \b deletes the previous character (one of the spaces)
Bonjour mes amis.     //\r moves control to beginning of line (Hello will be gone)
This is a single quote'.  // A single quote is displayed
This is a double quote".  // A double quote is displayed
This is how to a print backslash \. // A backslash is displayed
```

Boolean Variables

In almost all implementations, a value of type **bool** is stored in a 1 byte chunk of memory. In other words, the size is 1 byte or 8 bits. If we compare a variable of type **char** with a variable of type **bool**, we see that both use 1 byte of memory and we can store integers in both of them. The difference is that the integer stored in type **char** is interpreted as a character; the integer stored in type **bool** is interpreted as a logical value (0 or 1) or (`false` or `true`).

> **The size of a bool data type is 1 byte.**

Boolean data types are used in decision-making processes that we discuss in future chapters.

Boolean Literals

Since a Boolean type is in fact a 1 byte integer, we could use a small integer to represent a **Boolean literal.** Traditionally, any zero value is interpreted as *false*; any nonzero value is interpreted as *true*. When the value of a Boolean type is output, it is either 0 or 1. In a future chapter, we show how to print the literals **false** or **true** instead.

EXAMPLE 2.16

Program 2.11 is a simple program to test Boolean values.

Program 2.11 Boolean type

```
/***************************************************************
 * The use of Boolean variables and values                     *
 ***************************************************************/
#include <iostream>
using namespace std;

int main ()
{
  // Variable definitions
   bool x = 123;
   bool y = -8;
   bool z = 0;
   bool t = -0;
   bool u = true;
   bool v = false;
  // Outputting values
   cout << "Value of x: " << x << endl;
   cout << "Value of y: " << y << endl;
   cout << "Value of z: " << z << endl;
```

(continued)

Program 2.11 Boolean type (Continued)

```
    cout << "Value of t: " << t << endl;
    cout << "Value of u: " << u << endl;
    cout << "Value of v: " << v << endl;
    return 0;
}
```

```
Run:
Value of x: 1        // 123 is interpreted as 1 (true)
Value of y: 1        // -8 is interpreted as 1 (true)
Value of z: 0        // 0 is interpreted as 0 (false)
Value of t: 0        // -0 is interpreted as 0 (false)
Value of u: 1        // true is output as 1
Value of v: 0        // false is output as 0
```

Note that any nonzero value (positive or negative) is interpreted as `true`; any zero value is interpreted as `false`. The Boolean values are displayed as 1 or 0 unless we explicitly change them to `true` or `false`, as we will discuss in a future chapter.

2.4.4 Floating-Point Type

A number with a fraction is called a **floating-point** type in C++. To make computation efficient, C++ defines three different floating-point sizes: **float**, **double**, and **long double**. All floating-point numbers are signed.

All floating-point numbers are signed.

Floating-point numbers are stored in the computer using the IEEE standard (see Appendix S for the range). Although the language does not define the exact size and ranges of the different floating-point data types, it emphasizes their relative sizes. It defines the following relationship in which the symbol <= "means less than or equal."

```
float  ≤  double  ≤  long double
```

Figure 2.14 shows this relationship graphically. Note that all floating-point data types are signed so the relationship is simpler than in the case of integer data types.

Floating-Point Variables

We can define floating-point variables in the same way that we have defined integers. We can initialize them when we declare them or we can assign values to them later.

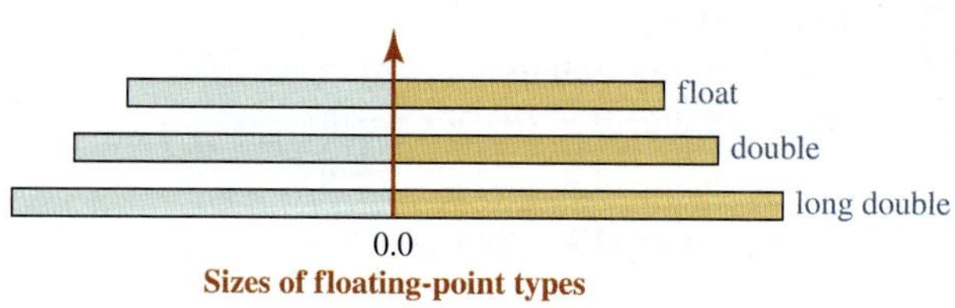

Figure 2.14 Relative sizes of floating-point types

Table 2.6 Suffixes to define the size of a literal

Floating-point type	*Suffixes*	*Example*
float	f or F	12.23F, 12345.45F, –1436F
double	**None**	1425.36, 1234.34, 123454
long double	l or L	2456.23L, 143679.00004 L, –0.02345L

Floating-Point Literals

Floating-point literals are numeric values with fractions such as 32.78, 141.123, 123456.0, and -2472.657. The programmer can explicitly define the size by using suffixes as shown in Table 2.6

The default size of a floating-point literal is double.

EXAMPLE 2.17

We discussed previously how to calculate the area and perimeter of a circle. Program 2.12 calculates the area and perimeter of any circle given its radius.

Program 2.12 Calculating area and perimeter of a circle

```
/*****************************************************************
 * This program calculates the area and perimeter of a circle.    *
 *****************************************************************/
#include <iostream>
using namespace std;

int main ().
{
  // Defining a stored constant
   const double PI = 3.14159;
  // Defining three variables
   double radius;
   double perimeter;
   double area;
  // Inputting value for radius
   cout << "Enter the radius of the circle: ";
   cin >> radius;
  // Calculating perimeter and area and storing them in variables
   perimeter = 2 *  PI * radius;    // 2 is used as a constant literal
   area = PI * PI * radius;
```

(*continued*)

Program 2.12 Calculating area and perimeter of a circle (Continued)

```
    // Outputing the value of radius, perimeter, and area
    cout << "The radius is: " << radius << endl;
    cout << "The perimeter is: " << perimeter << endl;
    cout << "The area is: " << area;
    return 0;
}
```

```
Run:
Enter the radius of the circle: 10.5
The radius is: 10.5
The perimeter is: 65.9734
The area is: 103.631
```

2.4.5 Void Type

The **void type** is a special type that has no value. However, it is useful because it can show the lack of any value. For example, we can use **void** to show that a function returns no value. The lack of value is the same concept we use in real life when we say a *void check*, which is a check that is used for other purposes but has no value. The **void** type can be used, for example, to show that a function returns nothing.

2.4.6 String Class

The string that we have used so far in this chapter is inherited from the C language. It is a collection of characters ending in a null character. For example, the string `"John"` can be thought of as a collection of five characters 'J','o', 'h', 'n', and '\0', the latter of which defines a null character (terminator). We see this type of string in more details when we discuss arrays (collection of elements) in a future chapter.

C++ defines a new string class that is a user-defined type (see Figure 2.11). The **string class** is defined in the C++ library and is more sophisticated and easier to use because many operations are defined for it. We use the **C++ strings** instead of **C strings** gradually until we discuss this class in full in a future chapter.

To use the C++ string, we must include the header file `<string>` in our program as shown below:

```
# include <string>
```

We declare a variable of type `string` using the following definition:

```
string name;
```

in which `name` is the name of the variable. An object of class string can also be created using double quotes such as `"John"`. One of the differences between the literal of the C string and the object of the C++ string is that the first is made of five characters; the second only of four characters (no null character is needed in a C++ string). The main difference and the advantage of the C++ string will reveal itself as we gradually learn to use operations on the objects of this class.

One of the interesting things that we can do with C++ string is concatenation. We can simply use the addition operator (+) to concatenate two or more strings together, as we see in the next example.

EXAMPLE 2.18

In this example we write a simple program (Program 2.13) that uses C++ strings. We declare the first name, last name, and initial of a person and, using concatenation, we print the whole name. This is just a simple example of a string class; the most powerful examples are discussed in future chapters.

Program 2.13 Using string class

```
/*****************************************************************
 * This program prints the full name of a person given the first,   *
 * the middle, and the last name.                                    *
 *****************************************************************/
#include <iostream>
#include <string>              // Need to use the string class
using namespace std;

int main ()
{
  // Defining variables
   string first;
   string initial;
   string last;
   string space = " ";
   string dot = ".";
   string fullName;
  // Input data for first name, initial, and last name
   cout << "Enter the first name: ";
   cin >> first;
   cout << "Enter the initial: ";
   cin >> middle;
   cout << "Enter the last name: ";
   cin >> last;
  // Formation of full name using concatenation operator
   fullName = first + space + initial + dot + space + last;
  // Outputting full name
   cout << "The full name is: " << fullName;
   return 0;
}
```

```
Run:
Enter the first name: John
Enter the initial: A
Enter the last name: Brown
The full name is: John A. Brown
```

Key Terms

ASCII
backslash
block comment
Boolean
Boolean literal
built-in data type
C string
C++ string
character type
character literal
class
comment
constant
data type
double
double quote
enumerated
floating-point
floating-point literal
fundamental data type
identifier
include
include directive
integer
integer data type
integer literal
keyword
line comment
literal
new line
preprocessor
single quotes
string class
token
value
variable

Summary

The C++ language is case-sensitive. We normally divide our programs into lines to improve readability. The header file in a program includes predefined code at the top of the program. Every C++ program needs at least one function named `main`.

A program in C++ uses variables, which have a `name` and a `type`.

The `cin` and `cout` objects we use in a program are closely related to the ideas of variable and value. The *cin* object gets data from a keyboard and stores it in a variable; the *cout* object sends a value to the monitor.

The source code in a C++ program is usually made of two things interleaved with each other: code and comments. The code uses the *tokens* of the C++ language; the comments are words in English. A *token* can be an *identifier*, a *literal*, or a *symbol*.

A program written in the C++ language manipulates data. C++ recognizes different types of data: *built-in* (*fundamental and compound*) and *user-defined* (*enumerated and class*). The fundamental data types are divided into three categories: integer, character, and floating-point type. An *integer* is a number without a fraction. A character data type defines a letter. The Boolean data type represents a `true` or `false` value. The floating-point type represents a number with a fraction.

The C++ language uses two string types: the first is called C-string; the second is called C++ string.

Problems

PR-1. Locate the errors (if any) in the following program.

```
#include <iostream>
using namespace std

```

```
int main ()
{
	cout << 25;
	cout << first;
	return 0;
}
```

PR-2. Locate the errors (if any) in the following program.

```
#include <iostream>

int main ()
{
	cout << 35;
	cout << 45;
	return 0;
}
```

PR-3. Locate the errors (if any) in the following program.

```
#include <iostream>
using namespace std

int main ();
{
	std :: cout << 35 << endl;
	std :: cout << 45;
}
```

PR-4. Locate the errors (if any) in the following program.

```
#include <iostream>
using namespace std

int main ()
{
	int a = 25;
	a + 30 = a ;
	cout << a;
	return 0;
}
```

PR-5. Locate the errors (if any) in the following program.

```
#include <iostream>
using namespace std;

int main ()
{
	string name;
	cout << name;
	return 1;
}
```

PR-6. Locate the errors (if any) in the following program.

```
using namespace std;

int main ()
{
    double = 24;
    cout << double ;
    return 0
}
```

PR-7. Locate the errors (if any) in the following program.

```
#include <iostream>
using namespace std;

int main ()
{
    int y = 32.34;
    cout << y ;
    return 0;
}
```

PR-8. Locate the errors (if any) in the following program.

```
#include <iostream>
using namespace std;

int main ()
{
    float y = 32.34;
    cout << y ;
    return 0;
}
```

PR-9. Locate the errors (if any) in the following program.

```
#include <iostream>
using namespace std;

int main ()
{
    double y = 32.34;
    cout << ;
    return 0;
}
```

PR-10. Locate the errors (if any) in the following program.

```
#include <iostream>
using namespace std;

int main ()
```

```
{
    char y = 32;
    char t = 78;
    char z = y + t;
    cout << z;
    return 0;
}
```

PR-11. What is printed from the following program?

```
#include <iostream>
using namespace std;

int main ()
{
    int x = 12;
    int y = 14;
    int z = x + y;
    cout << z;
    return 0;
}
```

PR-12. What is printed from the following program?

```
#include <iostream>
using namespace std;

int main ()
{
    double x = 12.24;
    double y = 14.32;
    cout << x  << " + " << y;
    return 0;
}
```

PR-13. What is printed from the following program?

```
#include <iostream>
using namespace std;

int main ()
{
    char x = 'A';
    char y = 'B';
    cout << x  << y;
    return 0;
}
```

PR-14. What is printed from the following program?

```
#include <iostream>
using namespace std;

```

```
int main ()
{
    bool truth = true;
    bool lie = false;
    bool result = truth + lie;
    cout << result;
    return 0;
}
```

PR-15. List all keywords in the following program.

```
#include <iostream>
using namespace std;

int main ()
{
    int x = 0;
    int y = 1;
    cout << x << y;
    return 0;
}
```

PR-16. Find all non-keyword identifiers in the following program.

```
#include <iostream>
using namespace std;

int main ()
{
    int x = 4;
    int y = 22;
    cout << x << y;
    return 0;
}
```

PR-17. Find all variables in the following program.

```
#include <iostream>
using namespace std;

int main ()
{
    int x = 4;
    int y = 22;
    cout << x << y;
    return 0;
}
```

PR-18. Give the line numbers containing line comments in the following program.

```
1 #include <iostream>
2 using namespace std;
3
```

```
int main ()
{
    // Declaration and initialization of two variables
    int x = 4;
    int y = 22;
    // Print the value of x and y
    cout << x << " " << y;
    return 0;
}
```

PR-19. Give the line numbers containing block comments in the following program.

```
1  /*********************************************************
2   * A small program to print two values.                  *
3   *********************************************************/
4  #include <iostream>
5  using namespace std;
6
7  int main ()
8  {
9      int x = 4;
10     int y = 22;
11     cout << x << " " << y;
12     return 0;
13 }
```

Programming Projects

PRG-1. Write a program that prints the following triangle of asterisks.

```
*
**
***
```

PRG-2. Write a program that prints the following figure using asterisks.

```
*
**
***
**
*
```

PRG-3. Write a program that prints a big letter `H` as shown below.

```
H  H
H  H
HHHH
H  H
H  H
```

PRG-4. Write a program that, given the time duration of a task in the number of hours, minutes, and seconds, calculates the duration in seconds.

PRG-5. Write a program that inputs four integer values and calculates and prints the sum of them.

PRG-6. Write a program that calculates and prints the area and the perimeter of a square when the size of one side is given.

PRG-7. Write a program that, using a C++ string, prints your name in the format shown below after being prompted to input your first and the last name. Note that the last name should come before the first name as shown.

```
Your full name is: last, first
```

PRG-8. Write a program that prompts the user to enter two integers. It then prints their sum. Run your program several times, each with different values for variables.

PRG-9. Write a program that calculates the sales tax of a transaction given the sale amount. Assume that the tax is 9 percent. Use a constant to define the tax rate. Run your program several times, each with different values for sale amount. Use the following format for output.

```
Sale amount: ...
Tax amount: ...
Total amount due: ...
```

PRG-10. Write a program that, given street number, street name, city name, state name, and zip code, prints the address in the following format.

```
street-number, street city, state zip-code
```

In this chapter, we introduce two main components of a program: expressions and statements. An expression in a C++ program looks like a phrase in a natural language like English; a statement in a C++ program looks like a sentence in English. If we want to use a natural language correctly, we need to understand phrases and sentences and how they are formed. To understand the C++ language and how to create a program in this language, we need to understand expressions and statements.

In C++ we have several types of expressions and several types of statements. We cannot discuss all of them in this chapter, but we discuss enough to be able to write simple programs. The discussion of expressions and statements will be continued in the next few chapters until we master all of them.

Objectives

After you have read and studied this chapter, you should be able to:

- Discuss expressions, how they are formed, and how they are evaluated and discuss primary expressions, unary expressions, multiplicative expressions, additive expressions, and assignment expressions.
- Discuss type conversion in an expression, including implicit and explicit conversion.
- Discuss the order of evaluation of simple expressions in a complex expression using precedence and associativity of subexpressions.
- Discuss overflow and underflow in both integer and floating-point data types.
- Show how to format input and output data using manipulators with no argument and with one argument.
- Discuss statements and show some simple types of statements, including declaration statements, expression statements, null statements, compound statements, and return statements.
- Discuss three steps in program design: understanding the problem, developing an algorithm, and writing the code.

3.1 EXPRESSIONS

We have seen that a program is a value manipulator. It takes values, manipulates them, and creates new values. To do so, a program defines several small entities called expressions. An **expression** is an entity with a value that can change the state of memory (*side effect*).

An expression is an entity that has a value and may have a side effect.

Table 3.1 Partial list of C++ expressions

Group	Name	Operator	Expression	Pred	Assoc
Primary	literal name parenthetic expr		literal name (expr)	19	→
Unary	plus minus sizeof	+ – sizeof	+ expr – expr size expr	17	←
Multiplicative	multiplication division remainder	* / %	expr * expr expr / expr expr % expr	14	→
Additive	addition subtraction	+ –	expr + expr expr – expr	13	→
Assignment	simple assignment comp. assignment	= op=	variable = expr variable op = expr	3	←

An expression can be a simple value. An expression can also use *operators* to combine values to create a new value. In C++, we can have an expression with no operator, with one operator, with two operators, or with three operators. We can also combine expressions to create another expression.

To handle expressions, we need a list of expressions with the corresponding operators they use to create expressions. This list is given in Appendix C, but for the purpose of this chapter we need only a part of the list as shown in Table 3.1. Note that we have used some abbreviations in this list such as Pred (for precedence), Assoc (for associativity), *expr* (for expression), and *op* (for operator).

Before we discuss the expressions in each group, let us give some information about Table 3.1.

1. The table lists only five groups of expressions, but C++ today has nineteen groups of expressions as depicted in Appendix C.
2. The first column defines the group of the expressions. The second column defines the name normally used for each subgroup. The third column defines the symbol or term used as the operator. The fourth column shows how the operator combines expressions to create a new expression.
3. The fifth column defines the *precedence* (Pred) of the operator. We discuss precedence later in the chapter; it tells us the order of evaluation when we have a collection of expressions with different precedences; the one with the highest precedence is evaluated first. Note that we have nineteen levels of precedence, but we have shown only five of them in Table 3.1.
4. The sixth column defines the *associativity* (Assoc) of the operator. We also discuss associativity later in the chapter; it tells us the order of evaluation when we have expressions with the same precedence. The associativity can be either left-to-right (→) or right-to-left (←).

We now discuss the five groups of expressions we defined in Table 3.1.

3.1.1 Primary Expressions

A **primary expression** is a simple expression with no operator. It is the basic building block for making more complex expressions. A primary expression has precedence 19, which means it has the highest precedence among all expressions. We have several primary expressions, as shown in Appendix C, but we describe only those shown in Table 3.1.

Literal

We have discussed **literals** (values that are used in a program). A *literal* in a program is a primary expression; it has a value, but no side-effect. The following shows some literals as primary expressions. Note that there are no short literals:

Literal	Description	Literal	Description
false	// Boolean literal	12897234L	// long integer literal
'A'	// character literal	245.78F	// float literal
"Hello"	// string literal	114.7892	// double literal
234	// integer literal	245.784321L	// long double literal

EXAMPLE 3.1

As we have seen, a literal can be used for the sake of its value, as shown in Program 3.1.

Name

When we use a **name** in our program we are using a primary expression. An *identifier* as a name can be a variable, an object name, a function name, and so on. The simplest name we can use in our program is the name of a variable. It is a primary expression with a value, the

Program 3.1 Literal expressions

```
/*****************************************************************
 * The program shows some literal expressions.                   *
 *****************************************************************/
#include <iostream>
using namespace std;

int main ()
{
    cout << false << " " << 'A' << " " << "Hello" << endl;
    cout << 23412 << " " << 12897234L << endl;
    cout << 245.78F << "  " << 114.782 << "  " << 2.051L;
    return 0;
}
```

```
Run:
0 A Hello                // A Boolean , a character, a string
23412 12897234           // An integer, a long integer (there is no short literal)
24.78  114.782  2.051    // A float, a double, a long double
```

value stored in the corresponding variable. As we saw in the previous chapter, we can also use a qualified name (a name with the group name and the individual name separated by double colon).

Expression	Description
x	// Can be a name of a variable
cout	// The name of an object
std :: cout	// A name qualified with its namespace

Parenthetical Expression

When we have an expression of a lower level of precedence that we want to change to a primary expression, we enclose it in parentheses. This is done to use the complex expression in a place where we need a primary expression. Sometimes we also need to evaluate part of an expression before evaluating the rest of it. A primary expression has the highest level of precedence, so we add parentheses to force the expression inside the parentheses to be evaluated first. We will see some parenthetical expressions later in the chapter, but the following shows two examples.

Expression	Description
(x + 3) * 5	// After adding the value of x with 3, multiply the result by 5
12 / (x + 2)	// After adding x with 2, then divide 12 by the result

In both cases, if we remove the parentheses, the value of the expressions will be changed and will not be what we intended, as the next program shows.

EXAMPLE 3.2

Program 3.2 shows how it makes a big difference when we use parentheses. We use the two expressions described above with and without parentheses to see the differences.

Program 3.2 Parenthetical expression

```
/***************************************************************
 * The program shows the use of parenthetical expressions.     *
 ***************************************************************/
#include <iostream>
using namespace std;

int main ()
{
  // Variable declaration
  int x = 4;
  // Printing the first expression with and without parentheses
  cout << "Value with parentheses: " << (x + 3) * 5 << endl;
  cout << "Value without parentheses: " << x + 3 * 5 << endl << endl;
```

(*continued*)

Program 3.2 Parenthetical expression (Continued)

```
    // Printing the second expression with and without parentheses
    cout << "Value with parentheses: " << 12 / ( x + 2) << endl;
    cout << "Value without parentheses: " << 12 / x + 2;
    return 0;
}
```

```
Run:
Value with parentheses: 35
Value without parentheses: 19

Value with parentheses: 2
Value without parentheses: 5
```

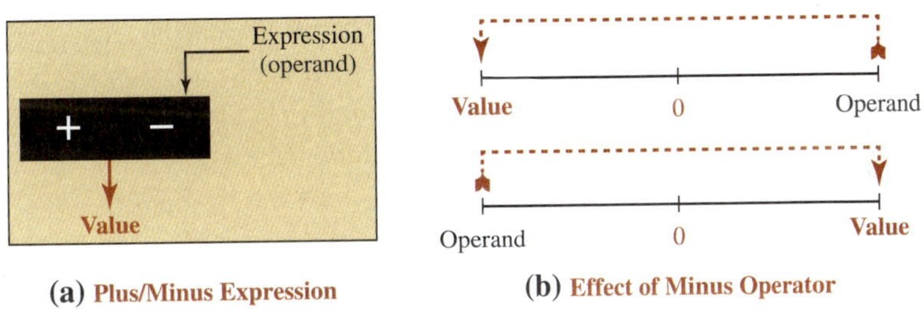

Figure 3.1 Plus and minus expression

3.1.2 Unary Expressions

A **unary expression** is an expression made of an operator applied to a single value (called an operand), which must be a primary expression, (if not, it must be first converted to a primary expression, as discussed later in the chapter). The result is a primary expression. In a unary expression the operator comes before the operand.

Plus and Minus Expressions

We have two expression named **plus expression** and **minus expression,** but we discuss them together. In both expression types, the operator comes before the operand, as shown in Figure 3.1.

The plus operator does not change the value of its operand (it is only for emphasis); the minus operator does change the value of its operand (it flips the value). If the value is originally positive, the operator changes it to negative and vice versa.

EXAMPLE 3.3

Program 3.3 shows how we can apply the plus/minus operator on primary expressions.

The sizeof Expression

Another unary expression is when we use the **sizeof** operator as shown in Figure 3.2. There are two versions of this operator: one that finds the size of an expression and one that finds the size of a type. The first version evaluates the expression (finds its value) and then finds

Program 3.3 Testing plus/minus expressions

```
/*************************************************************
 * The program shows the use of plus/minus expressions        *
 *************************************************************/
#include <iostream>
using namespace std;

int main ()
{
  // Declaration and initialization
  int x = 4;
  int y = –10;
  // Applying plus and minus operator on variable x
  cout << "Using plus operator on x: " << +x  << endl;
  cout << "Using minus operator on x: " << -x << endl;
  // Applying plus and minus operator on variable y
  cout << "Using plus operator on y: " << +y  << endl;
  cout << "Using minus operator on y: " << -y;
  return 0;
}
```

Run:

```
Using plus operator on x: 4
Using minus operator on x: -4
Using plus operator on y:-10
Using minus operator on y: 10
```

the size of the value. The second finds the size of the type as defined by the C++ implementation. The following shows examples of these two versions:

```
sizeof expression      // Finds the size of an expression.
sizeof (type)          // Finds the size of a type.
```

However, note that the *expression* in the first version needs to be a primary expression. So if we have an expression that contains an operator, we need to enclose it in parentheses. The result of the second expression is, of course, system dependent because the size of the data

The *size of* Expression

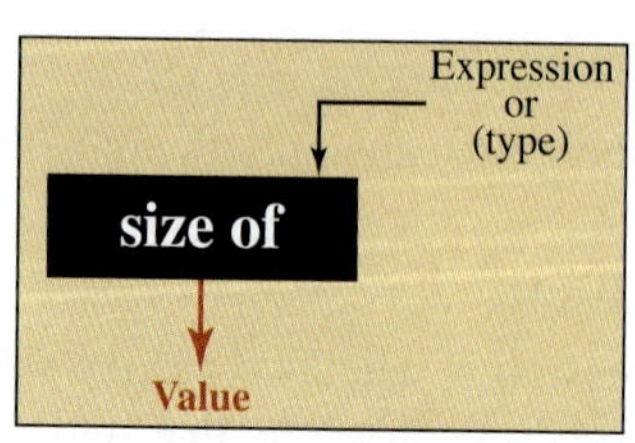

Note:
The operator can find the size of an expression or the size of a type.

Figure 3.2 The size of expression

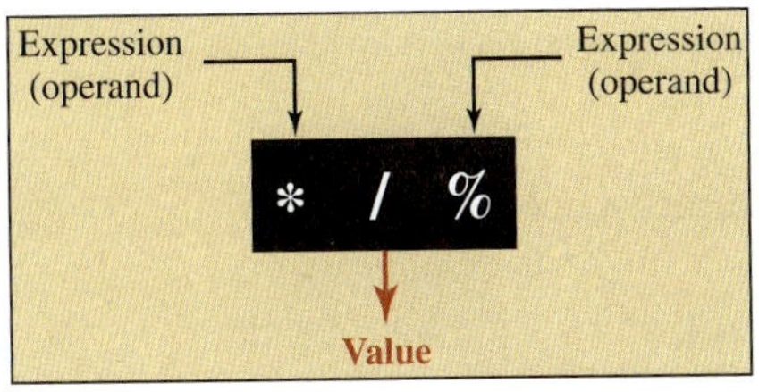

Note: For multiplication and division operators, if the the operands are of the same sign, the result is a positive value; otherwise the result is a negative value. For the remainder operator, the sign of the result is system dependent.

Figure 3.3 Multiplicative expression

type is system dependent. We discuss other unary expressions in future chapters when we use them.

3.1.3 Multiplicative Expressions

A **multiplicative expression** is a binary expression in which there are two operands: left and right. There are three operators that create multiplicative expressions, as shown in Figure 3.3 (*multiplication*, *division*, and *remainder*).

Multiplication

To multiply two values, we use a multiplication operator whose symbol is * (asterisk). Some type change may occur if the two operands are not the same type, as discussed later.

Division

To divide one value by another, we use a division operator whose symbol is / (forward slash). The result is an integer value if the two operands are both integers. The result can be a floating-point value if one of the operands is floating-point.

Remainder

To find the remainder of one integer value when divided by another integer value, we use a remainder operator whose symbol is the percent sign (%). The two operands need to be positive integral types. If either of the operand is a negative integral type, the result is system dependent.

EXAMPLE 3.4

Program 3.4 tests some multiplicative expressions.

Program 3.4 Multiplicative expressions

```
/***************************************************************
 * Shows effects of multiplicative expressions                 *
 ***************************************************************/
#include <iostream>
using namespace std;

int main ()
{
```

(continued)

Program 3.4 Multiplicative expressions (Continued)

```
    // Multiplication
    cout << "Testing multiplication operator" << endl;
    cout << "Value of 3 * 4 = " << 3 * 4 << endl;
    cout << "Value of 2.4 * 4.1 = " << 2.4 * 4.1 << endl;
    cout << "Value of -3 * 4 = " << -3 * 4  << endl;
    // Division
    cout << "Testing division operator" << endl;
    cout << "Value of 30 / 5 = " << 30 / 5  << endl;
    cout << "Value of 4 / 7 =  " << 4 / 7 << endl;
    // Remainder
    cout << "Testing remainder operator" << endl;
    cout << "Value of 30 % 5 = " << 30 % 5 << endl;
    cout << "Value of 30 % 4 = " << 30 % 4 << endl;
    cout << "Value of 3 % 7 = " << 3 % 7 << endl;
    return 0;
}
```

Run:

```
Testing multiplication operator
Value of 3 * 4 = 12
Value of 2.4 * 4.1 = 9.84
Value of -3 * 4 = -12
Testing division operator
Value of 30 / 5 = 6
Value of 4 / 7 = 0
Testing remainder operator
Value of 30 % 5 = 0
Value of 30 % 4 = 2
Value of 3 % 7 = 3
```

3.1.4 Additive Expressions

An additive expression is a binary expression in which there are two operands: the left and right operands. We have two additive expressions: **addition** and **subtraction** (both are referred to as additive expressions) as shown in Figure 3.4.

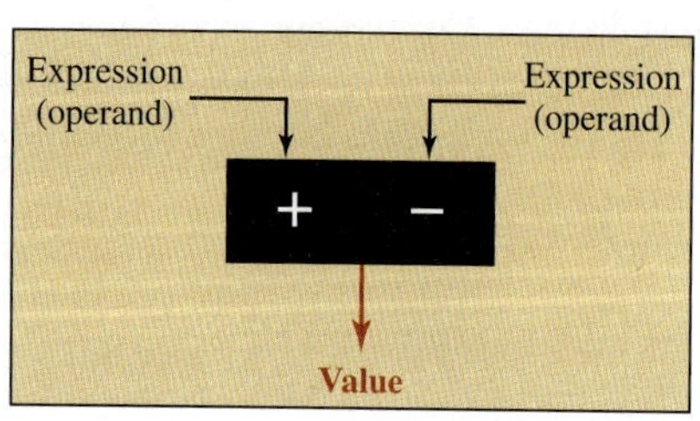

Note: When we subtract one operand from another, the sign of the result is the sign of the larger operand.

Figure 3.4 Additive expressions

Program 3.5 Addition and subtraction

```
/***********************************************************************
 * Shows effects of addition and subtraction operators                 *
 ***********************************************************************/
#include <iostream>
using namespace std;

int main ()
{
  // Testing some add operations
   cout << "Some addition operations" << endl;
   cout << "Value of 30 + 5 = " << 30 + 5 << endl;
   cout << "Value of 20.5 + 6.2 = " << 20.5 + 6.2 << endl;
  // Testing some subtract operations
   cout << "Some subtraction operations" << endl;
   cout << "Value of 5 - 30 = " << 5 - 30 << endl;
   cout << "Value of 51.2 - 30.4 = " << 51.2 - 30.4 << endl;
   return 0;
}
```

```
Run:
Some addition operations
Value of 30 + 5 = 35
Value of 20.5 + 6.2 = 26.7
Some subtraction operations
Value of 5 - 30 = -25
Value of 51.2 - 30.4 = 20.8
```

EXAMPLE 3.5

Program 3.5 shows how we can test some additive expressions.

3.1.5 Assignment Expressions

An assignment expression creates a value and has a side effect. It changes the memory state of the computer. There are two assignment expressions: simple and compound. We discuss the simple assignments and some compound assignments here, and we leave the discussion of the rest of the compound assignments for future chapters.

Simple Assignment

The **simple assignment** operator uses the = symbol. Although the symbol looks like equality in mathematics, it is called *assigned to* in C++. It is a binary operator with two operands. The left operand is a variable name. The right operand is an expression to be evaluated by the operator. Figure 3.5 shows the idea.

We can summarize the action of a simple assignment in two steps:

1. The operator stores the value of the expression in the variable. This is called the side effect because the previous value of the variable is lost and a new value is stored in it.
2. The operator returns the value obtained in step 1 to be used in more complex expressions.

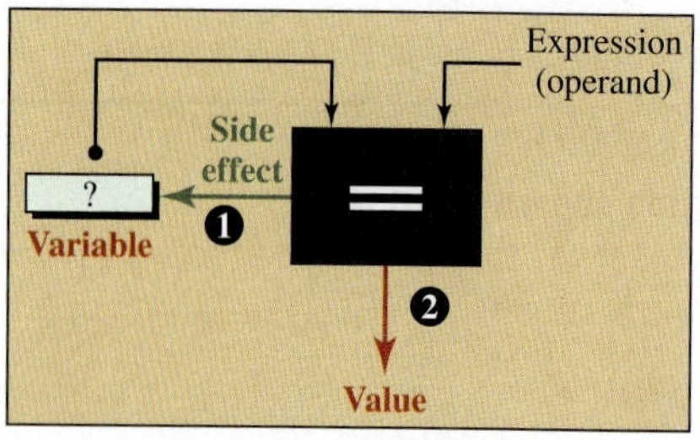

Note:

The left operand needs to be a variable.

The original value of the variable is lost, and the value of the right expression is stored in the variable as a side effect.

The side effect is done first; the value is returned next.

Figure 3.5 Simple assignment

In an assignment, the value of right expression is stored in the variable (side effect) before the expression value is returned.

EXAMPLE 3.6

Program 3.6 shows how we can test the return value and the side effect. We first do the assignment that returns the value to be printed (we need to use the parentheses to make the assignment expression be done first). We then print the value of the variable to check the side effect.

Program 3.6 Simple assignment operator

```
/***************************************************************
 * Testing some simple assignment expressions                  *
 ***************************************************************/
#include <iostream>
using namespace std;

int main ()
{
  // Variable Declaration
   int x;
   int y;
  // First assignment
   cout << "Return value of assignment expression: " << (x = 14) << endl;
   cout << "Value of variable x: " << x << endl;
  // Second assignment
   cout << "Return value of assignment expression: " << (y = 87) << endl;
   cout << "Value of variable y: " << y;
   return 0;
}
```

```
Run:
Return value of assignment expression: 14
Value of variable x: 14
Return value of assignment expression: 87
Value of variable y: 87
```

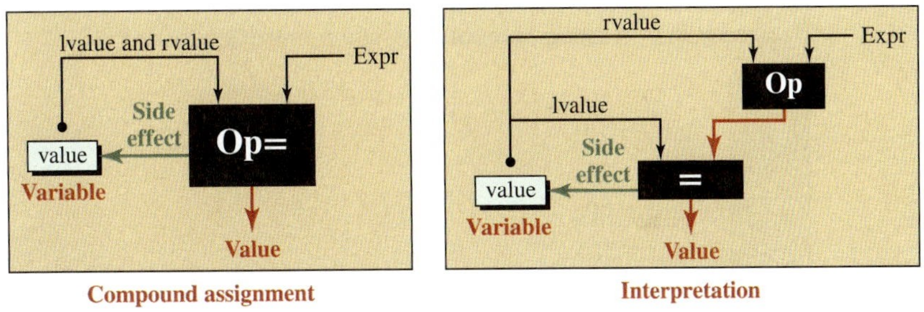

Figure 3.6 Compound assignment and its interpretation

Compound Assignments

Figure 3.6 shows the **compound assignment** and its interpretation. In programming, we often need to *change* the contents of a variable and store the result back into the variable, such as `x = x + 5`. The name of the variable is used two times in each expression: once in the left expression and once in the right expression. We need to understand that the same identifier here means two different things. At the right side of the assignment operator, the identifier *x* means a copy of the original value; at the left side, it means calculate the value of the right expression and store the result in variable *x*. Since expressions like the above are very common in programming, C++ provides a shortcut for this type of expression. It combines the assignment operator and the operator at the right side into one single operator called a compound assignment and uses the variable identifier only once. The expression becomes `x += 5`.

The following shows some compound assignment expressions and their interpretation by the compiler.

```
x += 5      // It is interpreted by the compiler as     x = x + 5
y -= 3      // It is interpreted by the compiler as     y = y - 3
z *= 10     // It is interpreted by the compiler as     z = z * 10
t /= 8      // It is interpreted by the compiler as     t = t / 8
u %= 7      // It is interpreted by the compiler as     u = u % 7
```

Note that each compound assignment operator is made of two operators; we cannot separate them from each other. In other words, we get an error if we use `z * = 10` instead of `z *= 10`.

EXAMPLE 3.7

Program 3.7 tests the side effect of some compound assignments.

Program 3.7 Testing compound assignments

```
/***************************************************************
 * Testing some compound-assignment expressions                *
 ***************************************************************/
#include <iostream>
using namespace std;

int main ()
{
```

(*continued*)

Program 3.7 Testing compound assignments (Continued)

```
   // Declaration of five variables
   int x = 20;
   int y = 30;
   int z = 40;
   int t = 50;
   int u = 60;
   // Use compound assignments
   x += 5;
   y -= 3;
   z *= 10;
   t /= 8;
   u %= 7;
   // Output results
   cout << "Value of x: " << x << endl;
   cout << "Value of y: " << y << endl;
   cout << "Value of z: " << z << endl;
   cout << "Value of t: " << t << endl;
   cout << "Value of u: " << u;
   return 0;
}
```

```
Run:
Value of x: 25
Value of y: 27
Value of z: 400
Value of t: 6
Value of u: 4
```

The first result can be thought of as `x = x + 5` or `x = 20 + 5`, which is actually `x = 25`. The last result can be thought of as `u = u % 7` or `u = 60 % 7`, which is actually `u = 4`.

3.1.6 The concepts of *lvalue* and *rvalue*

In C++ any entity that can be put at the left-hand side of the assignment operator is called an **lvalue** (left value). On the other hand, any entity that can be put at the right-hand side of an assignment is called an **rvalue** (right value). The name is sometimes misleading. It is clearer to say that an entity that can be a destination of a value is called an `lvalue`; an entity that can be the source of a value is an `rvalue`. A variable is an `lvalue` when it is at the left-hand side of an assignment and acts as a destination. The same variable is an `rvalue` when it is located at the right-hand side of an assignment and acts as a source. In a compound assignment, the variable acts both as an `lvalue` and an `rvalue`. This can be seen when we expand an expression like `x += 3` to `x = x + 3`.

An *lvalue* can be thought as the destination of a value;
an *rvalue* can be thought as the source of a value.

3.2 TYPE CONVERSION

We have discussed some arithmetic data types, some operators, and some expressions, but we need to remember that operators operate on data. We now need to answer two questions before we can find the return value and side effect (if any) of an arithmetic operation.

1. What happens when we apply an arithmetic operator to nonarithmetic data types such as Boolean or character? For example, what happens if we add two Boolean data items or multiply two characters?
2. When using binary operators, what happens if the operands are of different types? What is the type of the return value?

To answer these questions, we need to discuss two different processes: *implicit type conversion* and *explicit type conversion*. In the first process, the data types are implicitly changed to answer the above questions; in the second process, we force **type conversion**.

The C++ language provides a tool to test the type of any expression as shown below:

```
typeid (expression).name()
```

The expression is the one for which we need to know its type. The tool returns an abbreviation of the type (`i` for **int**, `d` for **double**, and so on). To use this tool, we need to include the `<typeinfo>` header file.

3.2.1 Implicit Conversion

Every time we use an operation on a data type for which that operation is not defined, the C++ compiler performs **implicit type conversion** before giving us the result. Implicit type conversion means changing the type of the operand(s) to another type on which the operation can be applied. This is done in two steps: *implicit type promotion* (promoting the type of the operand to a larger size) and *implicit type change* (changing the type of one operand to the other's type in a binary operation to make them of the same type). We discuss each step separately.

Implicit type conversion is done automatically by the compiler.

Implicit Type Promotion

Implicit type promotion is automatically applied to any operand to make it suitable for an arithmetic operation. This is done for two reasons. First, the type of the operand is not suitable for an arithmetic operation (Boolean and character). Second, there is no arithmetic operator defined for the type (**short** and **float**) because if we apply an arithmetic operator on a **short** or **float** value, the result may not fit in a **short** or **float** (think about multiplying two data items). To avoid these problems, the compiler applies five rules for implicit type promotion, as shown in Table 3.2.

Table 3.2 Implicit type promotion

Rule	Original Type	Promoted Type
1	bool	int
2	char	int
3	short	int
3	unsigned short	unsigned int
4	float	double

EXAMPLE 3.8

Program 3.8 shows how implicit type promotion occurs to change the type of a **bool**, a **char**, and a **short** data type to an **int** data type. It also shows how the type of **float** data is changed to a **double** data type. Note that no arithmetic data types are defined for these data types. So if we can use an arithmetic operation (addition in this case), this means that an implicit promotion has occurred.

Program 3.8 Implicit promotion of data types

```
/***************************************************************
 * Testing implicit type conversion for types with no arithmetic      *
 * operations: bool, char, short, and float                           *
 ***************************************************************/
#include <iostream>
#include <typeinfo>
using namespace std;

int main ( )
{
  // Declarations
   bool x = true;
   char y = 'A';
   short z = 14;
   float t = 24.5;
  // Type conversion from bool to int
   cout << "Type of x + 100: " << typeid (x + 100).name() << endl;
   cout << "Value of x + 100: " << x + 100 << endl;
  // Type conversion from char to int
   cout << "Type of y + 1000: " << typeid (y + 1000).name() << endl;
   cout << "Value of y + 1000: " << y + 1000 << endl;
  // Type conversion from short to int
   cout << "Type of z * 100: " << typeid (z * 10).name() << endl;
   cout << "Value of z * 100: " << z * 100 << endl;
  // Type conversion from float to double
   cout << "Type of t + 15000.2: " << typeid (t + 15000.2).name() << endl;
   cout << "Value of t + 15000.2: " << t + 15000.2;
   return 0;
}
```

```
Run:
Type of x + 100: i                // Type is integer
Value of x + 100: 101
Type of y + 1000: i               // Type is integer
Value of y + 1000: 1065
Type of z * 100: i                // Type is integer
Value of z * 100: 1400
Type of t + 15000.2: d            // Type is double
Value of t + 15000.2: 15024.7
```

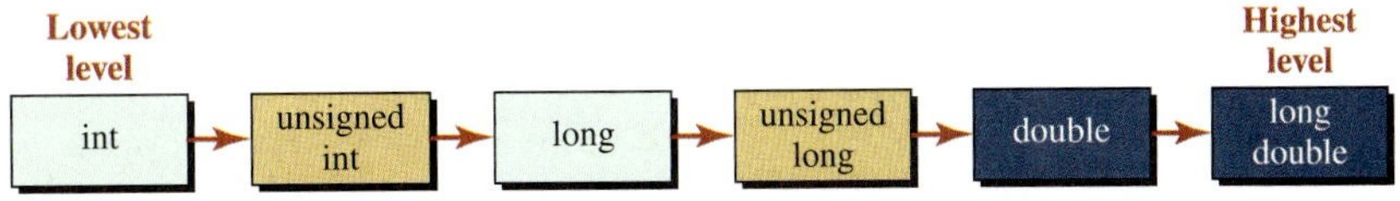

Figure 3.7 Hierarchy of types for implicit conversion

Implicit Type Change

After implicit promotion of each operand according to the rules we discussed above, the compiler may or may not perform implicit type change. **Implicit type change** occurs when the two operands are of different types; after the change, both operands are of the same type. If the operation is unary, there is no need for implicit conversion; if the operation is binary, the implicit type change may be needed to make the types of both operands the same. We discuss two cases.

Expressions with No Side Effect In this case, the operand in the lower level of hierarchy (smaller size) needs to be converted to the type of the higher level of hierarchy according to the hierarchy of types defined in Figure 3.7. Note that the types that are already promoted in the previous section are not included in this list. For example, data items of type **bool**, **char**, **short**, **unsigned short**, and **float** are not in this list because they are already implicitly promoted as described in the previous section.

The recipe followed by the compiler finds the operand with the higher level and converts the other one to that level.

EXAMPLE 3.9

Program 3.9 shows an example. We have three variables.

Program 3.9 Implicit type conversion (no side effect)

```
/***************************************************************
 * Implicit type conversion in an expression of mixed types when  *
 * there is no side effect.                                       *
 ***************************************************************/
#include <iostream>
#include <typeinfo>
using namespace std;

int main ( )
{
  // Declarations
  int x = 123;
  long y = 140;
  double z = 114.56;
  // Check the type and value of expression x + y
  cout << "Type of x + y: " << typeid (x + y).name ()<<endl;
  cout << "Value of x + y: " << x + y << endl << endl;
```

(continued)

Program 3.9 Implicit type conversion (no side effect) (Continued)

```
    // Check the type and value of expression x + y + z
    cout << "Type of x + y + z: " << typeid (x + y + z).name ()<< endl;
    cout << "Value of x + y + z: " << x + y + z << endl;
    return 0;
}
```

```
Run:
Type of x + y: l                    // Type is long
Value of x + y: 263

Type of x + y + z: d                // Type is double
Value of x + y + z: 377.56
```

Expression with Side Effects In some operations or activities, in which a value is supposed to go to a destination of a predefined type, we cannot change the type of the destination because it is already defined. For example, this happens when we assign a value to a variable of a different type. In these cases, the compiler performs implicit type change. The compiler changes the source type to fit in the destination type. For example, if we assign a floating-point value to an integer, the compiler truncates the source value and assigns the integral part to the destination variable. On the other hand, if we try to assign an integer value to a variable of a floating-point type, then the compiler adds a fraction part (of zero value) to the integer to make it a floating-point value.

EXAMPLE 3.10

Program 3.10 shows how a floating-point value is truncated to an integer to be stored in a variable of **int** type and how an integer value is changed to a floating-point type to be stored in a variable of type **double**.

Program 3.10 Implicit type conversion (with side effect)

```
/***************************************************************
 * Checking type conversion in an expression of mixed types   *
 ***************************************************************/
#include <iostream>
#include <typeinfo>
using namespace std;

int main ( )
{
    // Declaration
    int x;
    double y;
    // Assignment
    x = 23.67;
    y = 130;
```

(continued)

Program 3.10 Implicit type conversion (with side effect) (Continued)

```
    // Checking type and value of x
    cout << "Type of x = 23.67: " << typeid (x = 23.67).name ()<<endl;
    cout << "Value of x after assignment: " << x << endl << endl;
    // Checking type and value of x
    cout << "Type of y = 130: " << typeid (y = 130).name ()<<endl;
    cout << "Value of y after assignment: " << y << endl;
    return 0;
}
```

```
Run:
Type of x = 23.67: i                    // Type is int
Value of x after assignment: 23

Type of y = 130: d                      // Type is double
Value of y after assignment: 130
```

Note that the value of y is printed as 130, but it is actually 130.0; we need a manipulator to show the fraction part (discussed later in the chapter).

3.2.2 Explicit Type Conversion (Casting)

Sometimes we need or we want to change the type of an operand explicitly. This can be done using **explicit type conversion**, a process called **casting.** Casting is done in C++ in several ways, but we show only one of them, `static_cast`, which was described in a previous section.

```
static_cast <type> (expression)
```

EXAMPLE 3.11

Program 3.11 shows the difference between implicit and explicit type conversion. We have two variables of different types. We can add the values of these two variables and thereby allow implicit type conversion, or we can use explicit type conversion. In the first case, the complier changes the value of y to a **double**; in the second case, we force the value of x to change to an **int**. Note that in implicit conversion, the value of y is changed to 30.0 and added to 23.56, resulting in 53.56. In explicit conversion, the value of 23.56 is changed to 23 and added with 30, resulting in 53.

Program 3.11 Explicit conversion

```
/***************************************************************
 * Comparing implicit and explicit conversion in an expression   *
 ***************************************************************/
#include <iostream>
using namespace std;

int main ( )
{
```

(continued)

Program 3.11 Explicit conversion (Continued)

```
    // Declaration
    double x = 23.56;
    int y = 30;
    // Allowing implicit conversion
    cout << "Without casting: " << x + y <<endl;
    // Forcing explicit conversion
    cout << "With casting: " << static_cast <int> (x) + y;
    return 0;
}
```

```
Run:
Without casting: 53.56
With casting: 53
```

3.3 ORDER OF EVALUATION

We discussed a few expression types in the last two sections. The reader may ask what happens if we have a complex expression with more than one operator. How does the computer evaluate the expression? For example, what is the value of the following expression made of four operators?

```
3 + 4 * 7 / 22 - 8
```

To answer this question, we need to think of two properties of operators: **precedence** and **associativity.** Appendix C gives the list of all operators and expressions used in C++, but for the purpose of this chapter, we need only a partial list as shown previously in Table 3.1.

3.3.1 Precedence

When we have a complex expression with several simple expressions of different precedence levels, we need to use the following steps to find the value of the complex expression:

1. We evaluate the simple expression with the highest level of precedence and replace it with its value. Now we have a new expression.
2. We repeat step 1 until the whole expression is evaluated.

EXAMPLE 3.12

Program 3.12 shows how we can find the result of the expression `5 + 7 * 4` when evaluated by C++. The program shows both the result and the evaluation steps. Note that the multiplication has precedence 14, but addition has precedence 13.

Program 3.12 Evaluating a simple expression

```
/***************************************************************
 * Evaluating a simple expression with two levels of precedence  *
 ***************************************************************/
```

(continued)

Program 3.12 Evaluating a simple expression (Continued)

```
#include <iostream>
using namespace std;

int main ( )
{
   cout << "Result of expression: " << 5 + 7 * 4 << endl;
   return 0;
}
```

Run:

```
Result of expression: 33
```

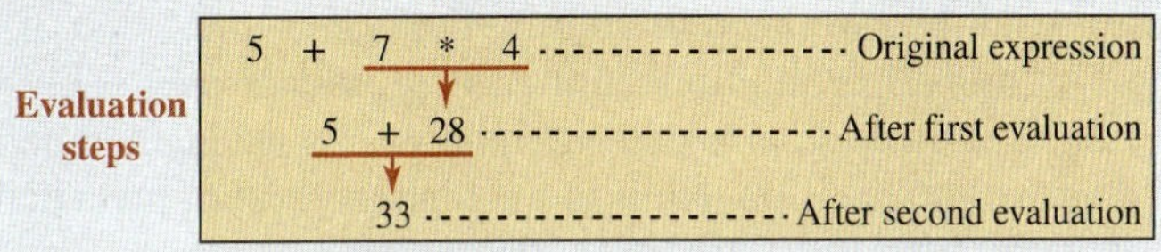

EXAMPLE 3.13

Program 3.13 shows how we evaluate the complex expression `result = 5 - 15 % 4`, which is made of three operators—assignment, subtraction, and remainder—each with a different level of precedence.

Program 3.13 Evaluating a complex expression

```
/***************************************************************
 * Evaluating an expression with three levels of precedence    *
 ***************************************************************/
#include <iostream>
using namespace std;

int main ( )
{
   // Declare one variable
   int result;
   // Evaluate the expression and store the result in the variable
   result = 5 - 15 % 4;
   // Output the result stored in the variable
   cout << "The value stored in result: " << result;
   return 0;
}
```

Run:

```
The value stored in result: 2
```

(continued)

Program 3.13 Evaluating a complex expression (Continued)

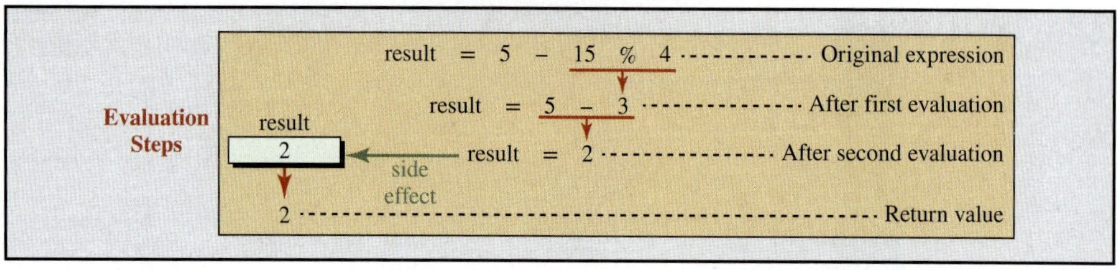

EXAMPLE 3.14

Now assume that we need to purposely change the precedence level of a simple expression. For example, we need to add the literal 6 to the value of variable x and then multiply the result by 7. Here multiplication has precedence over addition, but we need to do the addition first. The solution is to use parentheses. As we learned before, a pair of parentheses creates a primary expression that is at the highest level of precedence. Program 3.14 shows how we write and evaluate the expression.

EXAMPLE 3.15

As another example, assume the original values of x and y are 8 and 10, respectively. Program 3.15 shows how we can find the value of y after evaluation of the following expression:

Program 3.14 Simple expression with parentheses

```
/***************************************************************
 * Evaluating simple expression including parentheses          *
 ***************************************************************/
#include <iostream>
using namespace std;

int main ( )
{
  // Declaration
  int x = 5;
  // Outputting value of expression
  cout << "Value of (x + 6) * 7: " << (x + 6) * 7 ;
  return 0;
}
```

Run:

```
Value of (x + 6) * 7: 77
```

Program 3.15 Expression with side effects

```
/*****************************************************************
 * Evaluating a simple expression with side effect              *
 *****************************************************************/
#include <iostream>
using namespace std;

int main ( )
{
  // Declaration and initialization
  int x = 8;
  int y = 10;
  // Assignment
  y *= x + 5;
  // Outputting value of variable y
  cout << "Value of y: " << y ;
  return 0;
}
```

```
Run:
Value of y: 130
```

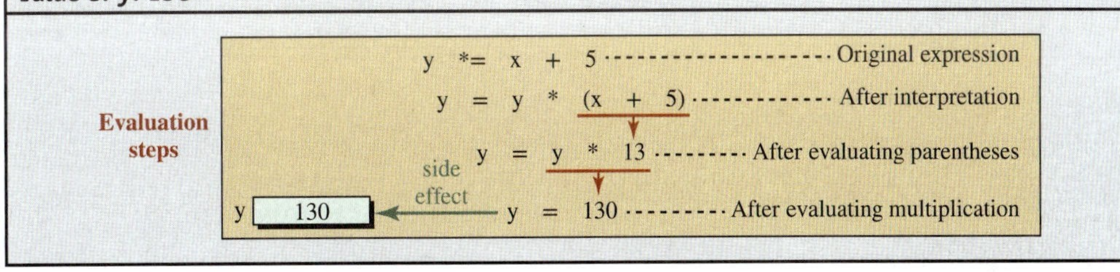

y *= x + 5. Note that the expression at the right-hand side of the compound assignment operator is considered a primary expression when we expand the compound assignment to a simple assignment. In other words, the compound assignment is actually **y *= (x + 5)**, which is expanded to **y = y * (x + 5)**.

3.3.2 Associativity

In each previous example, the complex expression we used had only one single instance of an expression type (multiplicative, additive, or assignment). What happens if a complex expression has more than one expression at the same level of precedence (for example, two multiplicative expressions). In this case, we need to use the associativity of the simple expressions. Associativity of an operator is either left-to-right or right-to-left (see Table 3.1). When we need to evaluate a particular expression with more than one instance of an expression type, we need to evaluate the expressions according to their associativity.

EXAMPLE 3.16

Let us find the value of an expression with two multiplicative operators and two additive operators: **5 - 30 / 4 * 8 + 10**. Program 3.16 shows how C++ evaluates this expression.

Program 3.16 Precedence and associativity

```
/***************************************************************
 * Evaluation involving both precedence and associativity      *
 ***************************************************************/
#include <iostream>
using namespace std;

int main ( )
{
  cout << "Value of expression: " << 5 - 30 / 4 * 8 + 10 ;
  return 0;
}
```

Run:

```
Value of expression: −41
```

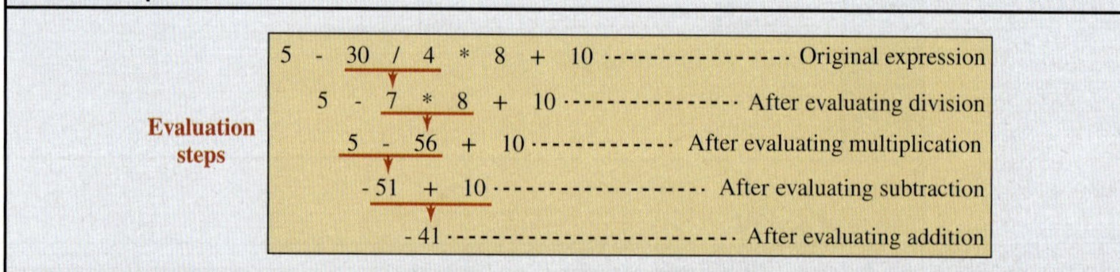

In this complex expression, the multiplicative expressions are evaluated first because of their precedence. Furthermore, they are evaluated from the left because of their associativity (left to right).

EXAMPLE 3.17

Program 3.17 shows how the system evaluates two expression involving operators (compound assignment) with the same precedence, but with associativity from right to left.

Program 3.17 Expressions with the same precedence

```
/***************************************************************
 * Evaluating expression with right-to-left associativity      *
 ***************************************************************/
#include <iostream>
using namespace std;

int main ( )
{
```

(*continued*)

Program 3.17 Expressions with the same precedence (Continued)

```
    // Declaration and initialization
    int x = 10;
    int y = 20;
    // Assignment
    y += x *= 40;
    // Printing values of x and y
    cout << "Value of x: " << x << endl;
    cout << "Value of y: " << y;
    return 0;
}
```

Run:

```
Value of x: 400
Value of y: 420
```

Evaluation steps

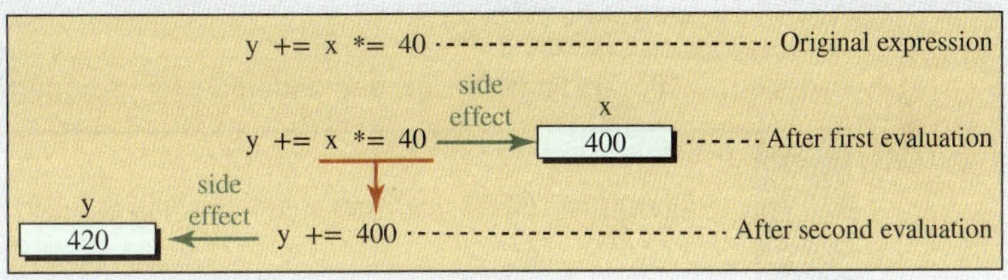

3.4 OVERFLOW AND UNDERFLOW

Before we write more programs, we discuss an issue all programmers need to understand: *overflow* and *underflow*. In real life, it is possible to write a very large number on paper. However, the memory allocation for data types in each computer system is limited. What happens if we try to store a number larger than the maximum value or smaller than the minimum value for a type? The result is **overflow** or **underflow.** C++ does not create an error message during the compilation, although it may give us a warning. What happens is that the result is not what we expected. The overflow and underflow behavior is different for integers and floating-point values (other types are promoted to either integer to floating-point, as we discussed before).

3.4.1 Overflow and Underflow In Integers

As we know, integer data types can be unsigned or signed. The overflow and underflow error is different for unsigned and signed integers. We discuss each case separately.

Overflow and Underflow in Unsigned Integers

The range of an unsigned integer is from zero to the positive maximum value. We want to see what happens when we try to use a value larger than the maximum value or a value less than zero. In the first case, we have an overflow situation; in the second case, we have an underflow situation. Both are shown in Figure 3.8. In either case, the values are wrapped back

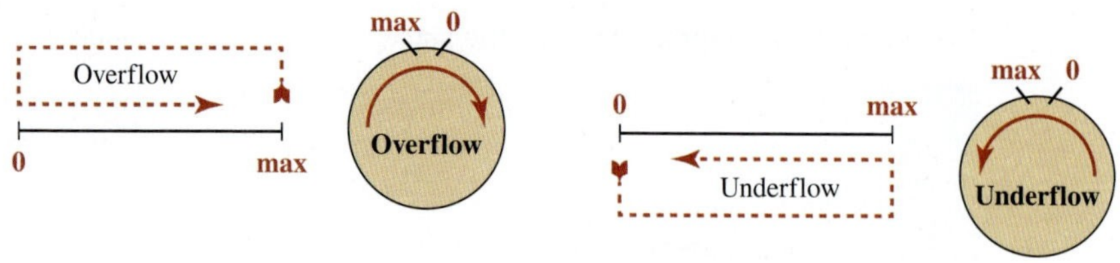

Figure 3.8 Overflow and underflow in unsigned integers

into the valid range. The circular notation better shows the effect of overflow and underflow. Adding is clockwise; subtracting is counterclockwise.

Program 3.18 shows the effect of overflow and underflow in an **unsigned int** type. We initialize a variable (`num1`) to the maximum value and then try to add one to it. We initialize another variable (`num2`) to zero and then try to subtract one from it. The output result shows that wrapping has occurred. Since maximum and minimum values are system dependent, we use a library function in lines 11 and 12 to set the values.

Program 3.18 Testing overflow and underflow for unsigned integers

```
1  /***************************************************************
2   * A program to test overflow and underflow in unsigned integers       *
3   ***************************************************************/
4  #include <iostream>
5  #include <limits>
6  using namespace std;
7  
8  int main ( )
9  {
10   // Create two unsigned integer of maximum and minimum values
11   unsigned int num1 = numeric_limits <unsigned int> :: max();
12   unsigned int num2 = numeric_limits <unsigned int> :: min();
13   // Print the maximum and minimum values
14   cout << "The value of maximum unsigned int: " << num1 << endl;
15   cout << "The value of minimum unsigned int: " << num2 << endl;
16   // Force the integers to overflow
17   num1 += 1;
18   num2 -= 1;
19   // Print the overflowed values
20   cout << "The value of num1 + 1 after overflow: " << num1 << endl;
21   cout << "The value of num2 – 1 after underflow: " << num2 << endl;
22   return 0;
23 }
```

Run:

```
The value of maximum unsigned int: 4294967295
The value of minimum unsigned int: 0
The value of num1 + 1 after overflow: 0
The value of num2 – 1 after underflow: 4294967295
```

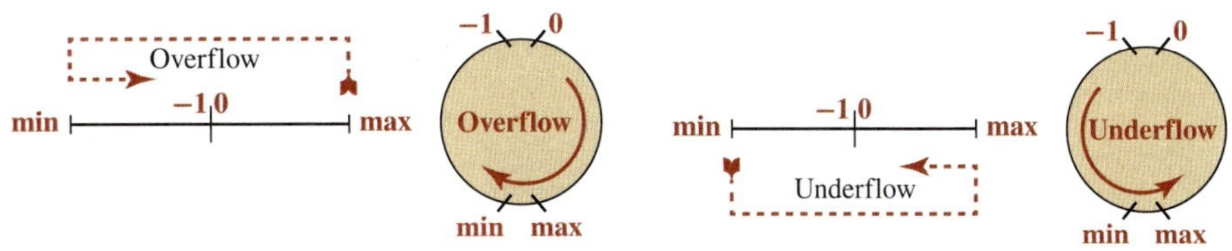

Figure 3.9 Overflow and underflow in signed integers

Overflow and Underflow in Signed Integers

The range of a signed integer is from a negative minimum to a positive maximum value. We want to see what happens when we try to use a value larger than the maximum value or a value less than the minimum value. We have an overflow situation in the first case; we have underflow situation in the second case. Both are shown in Figure 3.9. In other words, the values are wrapped back into the valid range. A positive value larger than the positive maximum becomes a negative value; a negative value smaller than the negative minimum becomes a positive value.

Program 3.19 shows the effect of overflow and underflow in a **signed int** type. We initialize a variable (`num1`) to the maximum value and then try to add one to it. We initialize another variable (`num2`) to the minimum value and then try to subtract one from it. The output result shows that wrapping has occurred. Since maximum and minimum values are system dependent, we use a library function in lines 11 and 12 to set the values.

Program 3.19 Testing overflow and underflow in signed integers

```
1  /**************************************************************
2   * A program to test overflow and underflow in signed integers  *
3   **************************************************************/
4  #include <iostream>
5  #include <limits>
6  using namespace std;
7
8  int main ( )
9  {
10   // Find the maximum and minimum of an integer
11   int num1 = numeric_limits <int> :: max();
12   int num2 = numeric_limits <int> :: min();
13   // Print the maximum and minimum values
14   cout << "Value of maximum signed int: " << num1 << endl;
15   cout << "Value of minimum signed int: " << num2 << endl;
16   // Cause num1 and num2 to overflow
17   num1 += 1;
18   num2 -= 1;
19   // Print the overflowed values
20   cout << "The value of num1 + 1 after overflow: " << num1 << endl;
21   cout << "The value of num2 - 1 after underflow: " << num2 << endl;
```

(continued)

Program 3.19 Testing overflow and underflow in signed integers (Continued)

```
    return 0;
}
```

```
Run:
The value of maximum signed int: 2147483647
The value of minimum signed int: -2147483648
The value of num1 + 1 after overflow: -2147483648
The value of num2 - 1 after underflow: 2147483647
```

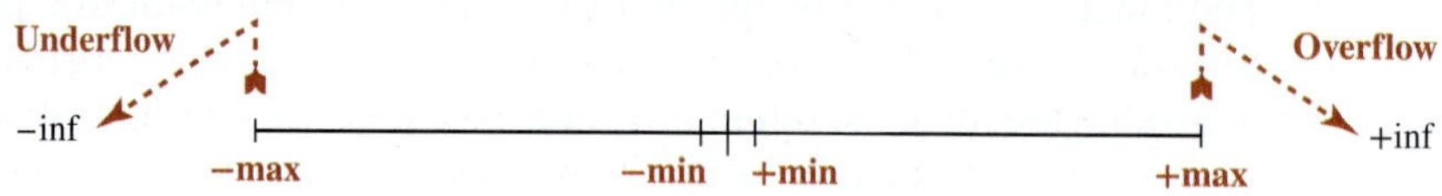

Figure 3.10 Overflow and underflow in floating-point values

3.4.2 Overflow and Underflow in Floating-Point Values

We also have overflow and underflow in floating-point values; however, there are two differences here. First, all floating-point values are signed. Second, there is no wrapping when overflow and underflow occurs; instead we have *sinking*. Overflow results in sinking to +infinity; underflow results in sinking to −infinity. Figure 3.10 shows the concept.

Note that we have two `max` values and two `min` values. The `min` values define the small numbers nearest zero. The positive `max` and negative `max` values may create positive or negative infinity when increased or decreased, respectively. Program 3.20 initializes `num1` and `num2` to positive `max` and negative `max` values and then multiplies each number by 1000.00 to make the values overflow to `+inf` and `-inf`. Since positive maximum and negative maximum values are system dependent, we use a library function in lines 11 and 12 to instigate them.

Program 3.20 Overflow and underflow in doubles

```
1  /***************************************************************
2   * A program to test overflow and underflow in doubles          *
3   ***************************************************************/
4  #include <iostream>
5  #include <limits>
6  using namespace std;
7  
8  int main ( )
9  {
10   // Find the positive and negative maximum double
11   double num1 = +numeric_limits <double> :: max ();
12   double num2 = -numeric_limits <double> :: max ();
```

(continued)

Program 3.20 Overflow and underflow in doubles (Continued)

```
    // Print the positive and negative maximum double
    cout << "The value of maximum double: " << num1 << endl;
    cout << "The value of minimum double: " << num2 << endl;
    // Multiply the values by 1000.00
    num1 *= 1000.00;
    num2 *= 1000.00;
    // Print the overflowed values
    cout << "The value of num1 * 1000 after overflow: " << num1 << endl;
    cout << "The value of num2 * 1000 after underflow: " << num2 << endl;
    return 0;
}
```

```
Run:
The value of maximum double: 1.79769e+308
The value of minimum double: -1.79769e+308
The value of num1 * 1000 after overflow: INF
The value of num2 * 1000 after underflow: -INF
```

3.5 FORMATTING DATA

The programs we have used in the previous section input or output data in a standard (default) format. For example, Boolean data are input and output as 0 or 1. The integer values are input and output in decimal format (see Appendix B). The floating-point values are input in a standard format (integral part followed by a decimal point and the fraction part) and output as required by the application. Sometimes we need to change this behavior. We need to format data as we like. This is done with the help of predefined objects called **manipulators**. We have manipulators for outputting data and manipulators for inputting data. We first discuss the manipulators for outputting data, which are more common and extensive; we then discuss manipulators for inputting data.

3.5.1 Manipulators for Output

As we mentioned before, output operations are done using output objects. We use the predefined output object (`cout`). So far, we have only passed data items to the insertion operator (`<<`); we have not defined how the data should be formatted when displayed or printed. An output manipulator is an object that can be passed to the insertion operator to change the behavior of the output. We have two different kinds of output manipulators: with no argument and with one argument. We discuss each next.

No-Argument Manipulators

There are several output manipulators that need no argument. The no-argument manipulators are part of `<iostream>`, which means no extra header file is needed. We show the common no-argument manipulators in Table 3.3.

The manipulators for each category (except `endl`) come in groups of two or three. One of the manipulators in each group is the default. If we do not use a manipulator in that group, it is set to the default value. In Table 3.3 we show the default values in red. Note that the term (**none**) means that there is no default: The system uses the fixed or scientific based on

Table 3.3 No-argument manipulators for output stream

Manipulator	*Boolean*	*Character*	*Integer*	*Floating point*
endl	√	√	√	√
noboolalpha, boolalpha	√			
dec, oct, hex			√	
noshowbase, showbase			√	
(none), fixed, scientific				√
noshowpoint, showpoint				√
noshowpos, showpos			√	√
nouppercase, uppercase			√	√
left, right, internal	√	√	√	√

the value of the floating-point data unless we explicitly define one of the other two choices. All manipulators except `endl` change the state of the output stream. When we choose one of the manipulators in the group, the output stream uses that manipulator until we change the state using a different one. This means that we can apply one of the manipulators for all output data until we need to change it.

All no-argument manipulators except endl change the state of the output stream.

The endl Manipulator We have used this manipulator from the beginning of the book. It is designed to add a `'\n'` character at the end of the data to force the next output to move to the next line. It is the only no-argument manipulator that does not change the state of the stream. We must repeat it every time we need it.

Manipulators for Boolean Literals (noboolalpha, boolalpha) The first category of manipulators in Table 3.3 can be used only with Boolean data types. The `noboolalpha` manipulator outputs a Boolean value as an integer (0 or 1); the `boolalpha` outputs the bool value as a literal (**false** or **true**). Program 3.21 shows a test. Note that we do not need the manipulator in line 17; the state of the output has already been changed in line 16.

Program 3.21 Testing `boolalpha` manipulator

```
1 /***************************************************************
2  * A program to test boolalpha manipulator for logical values  *
3  ***************************************************************/
4 #include <iostream>
5 using namespace std;
6
7 int main ( )
8 {
```

(continued)

Program 3.21 Testing `boolalpha` Manipulator (Continued)

```
    // Declaration
    bool x = true;
    bool y = false;
    // Testing values without manipulators
    cout << "Value of x using default: " << x << endl;
    cout << "Value of y using default: " << y << endl;
    // Testing values using manipulators
    cout << "Value of x using manipulator: " << boolalpha << x << endl;
    cout << "Value of y: " << y;
    return 0;
}
```

```
Run:
Value of x using default: 1
Value of y using default: 0
Value of x using manipulator: true
Value of y: false
```

Manipulator for Different Bases (dec, oct, hex) Although all integers are stored in the computer in binary base 2 (see Appendix B), we may need to output them in our program in one of the three different formats: `dec` (base 10), `oct` (base 8), or `hex` (base 16). The default is `dec`. Presentation does not affect the size, sign, or value in the computer; it is only for the programmer's convenience. It allows the programmer to use the format that is most convenient. For example, we can print the integer 1237 as 1237 (decimal), 2325 (octal), or 4D5 (hexadecimal).

Manipulators for Base Prefix (noshowbase, showbase) When we output an integer in different bases, we have the choice not to show the base of the number (default) or show the base of the number. The base is shown as a prefix (nothing for decimal, 0 for octal, and 0x for hexadecimal).

EXAMPLE 3.18

Program 3.22 shows how we can use manipulators to convert an integer in different bases and show or not show the prefix of the base.

Program 3.22 Testing manipulator for the base of integers

```
/***************************************************************
 * A program to print data in different bases (decimal,octal,   *
 * and hexadecimal)                                             *
 ***************************************************************/
#include <iostream>
using namespace std;

```

(continued)

Program 3.22 Testing manipulator for the base of integers (Continued)

```
int main ( )
{
  // Declaration of variable x
  int x = 1237;
  // Outputting x in three bases without showbase
  cout << "x in decimal: " << x << endl;
  cout << "x in octal: " << oct << x << endl;
  cout << "x in hexadecimal: " << hex << x << endl << endl;
  // Outputting x in three bases with showbase
  cout << "x in decimal: " << x << endl;
  cout << "x in octal: " << showbase << oct << x << endl;
  cout << "x in hexadecimal: " << showbase << hex << x;
  return 0;
}
```

```
Run:
x in decimal: 1237
x in octal: 2325
x in hexadecimal: 4d5

x in decimal: 1237
x in octal: 02325           // 0 shows that the number is in octal
x in hexadecimal: 0x4d5     // 0x shows that the number is in hexadecimal
```

Manipulators for Fixed or Scientific Notation We have two ways to show a floating-point type value: *fixed* or *scientific*. Both are shown in Figure 3.11.

In the **fixed format,** a floating-point value is shown as an integer part and the fraction part separated by a decimal point such as (dddd.ddd) in which each d is a digit. The number is preceded by a minus sign if it is negative. In the **scientific format,** the number is shown as a number in fixed format multiplied by an exponent (10^n) if the number is very large or (10^{-n}) if the number is very small.

Manipulators for Showing the Decimal Point If the fraction part of a floating-point value is zero, C++ does not print the decimal point. We can force the output to show the decimal point with a zero fraction using the **showpoint** manipulator.

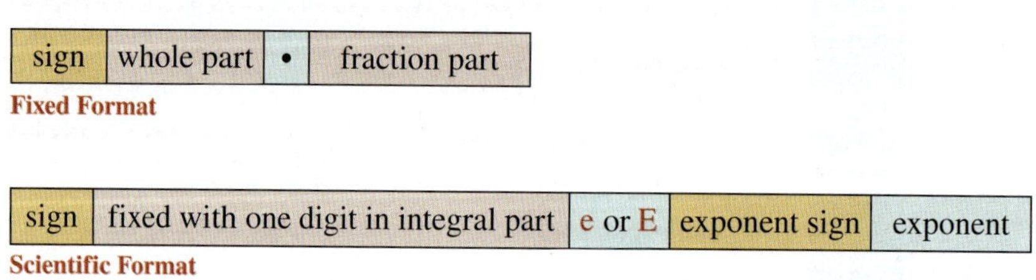

Figure 3.11 Fixed and scientific format for manipulators

Program 3.23 Testing floating-point manipulators

```
/****************************************************************
 * A program to test some manipulators for floating-point types *
 ****************************************************************/
#include <iostream>
using namespace std;

int main ( )
{
  // Declarations
   double x = 1237;
   double y = 12376745.5623;
  //Using fixed (default) and showpoint manipulator
   cout << "x in fixed_point format: " << x << endl;
   cout << "x in fixed_point format: " << showpoint << x << endl;
  //Using scientific manipulator
   cout << "y in scientific format: " << y << scientific;
   return 0;
}
```

```
Run:
x in fixed_point format: 1237          // We have not used showpoint
x in fixed_point format: 1237.00       // We have used showpoint
y in scientific format: 1.23767e+007
```

EXAMPLE 3.19

Program 3.23 shows how we use manipulators for the floating-point types.

Manipulators for Showing the Positive Sign C++ does not show a positive sign (+) if the number is positive (the negative sign is always shown). To force a positive number to be printed with the positive sign, we can use the **showpos** manipulator.

Manipulators for Showing Letters in Uppercase We have seen that the integer and floating-point values sometimes include alphabetic characters (a, b, c, d, e, f) for values in hexadecimal notation, x for hexadecimal notation, and e for scientific notation. These characters are printed in lowercase by default. If we want them to be printed in uppercase, we use the manipulator **uppercase.**

Manipulator for Adjusting Numbers in a Field Later we see how we can define the size of a field (number of characters occupied) to print a value using manipulators with arguments. After the size is determined, we need to decide how we want to adjust the value and the sign (if any) in the field. C++ uses three formats for this as shown in Figure 3.12.

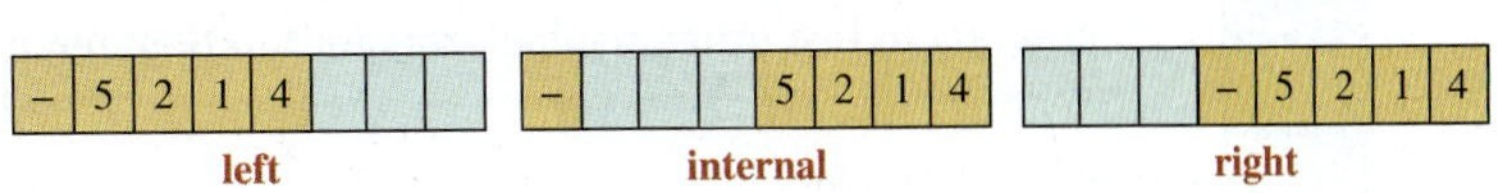

Figure 3.12 Adjusting a value in a field

Table 3.4 One-argument manipulators for output stream

Manipulator	Boolean	Character	Integer	Floating point
setprecision (n)				√
setw (n)	√	√	√	√
setfill (ch)	√	√	√	√

In the left format (default), the number and sign are located at the left of the field and the rest of field is filled with padding (as we explain shortly). In the internal format, the sign occupies the leftmost part of the field, the number occupies the rightmost parts, and the remaining part is filled with padding. In the right format, the sign and the number occupy the rightmost part and the left part is filled with padding. Note that this manipulator does not change the state of the stream.

Manipulators with Arguments

We discuss only three manipulators that take one argument (an integer or a character) as shown in Table 3.4. To use these manipulators, we need to include the `<iomanip>` header in our program. They are not defined in `<iostream>`.

Manipulator setprecision (n) This manipulator is used only for fixed (not scientific) floating-point values. The integer inside the parentheses (*n*) defines the number of digits after the decimal point.

Manipulator setw (n) This manipulator is used to define the size of the field that we want our value to occupy. Note that in the case of the floating-point data type, we need to consider space for the whole part, decimal point, and the fraction part. Note that this manipulator does not change the state of the stream. It needs to be set for each value individually.

Manipulator setfill (ch) This manipulator shows how we can fill the field with padding if the actual size of our value is less than the size defined by `setw` (*n*). The argument inside parentheses is a literal character used as padding. The manipulators left, internal, and right that we discussed before can then determine where the padding is located.

> **All manipulators with arguments except setw change the state of the output stream. We must repeat setw where we need it.**

EXAMPLE 3.20

Program 3.24 shows how we can test manipulators with arguments.

Program 3.24 Using manipulators with arguments

```
/***************************************************************
 * A program to test other manipulators for floating-point types     *
 ***************************************************************/
#include <iostream>
```

(continued)

Program 3.24 Using manipulators with arguments (Continued)

```
#include <iomanip>
using namespace std;

int main ( )
{
  // Declaration
  double x = 1237234.1235;
  // Applying common formats
  cout << fixed << setprecision(2) << showpos << setfill('*');
  // Printing x in three formats
  cout << setw(15) << left << x << endl;
  cout << setw(15) << internal << x << endl;
  cout << setw(15) << right << x;
  return 0;
}
```

```
Run:
+1237234.12****
+****1237234.12
****+1237234.12
```

Table 3.5 Manipulator for input stream

Manipulator	*Boolean*	*Character*	*Integer*	*Floating-point*
noboolalpha, boolalpha	√			
dec, oct, hex			√	

3.5.2 Manipulators for Input

There are manipulators that can be used with input. We mention only two of them here and discuss the rest in Chapter 16. They are shown in Table 3.5. Note that they are the same as the first two for output streams but they are used for input streams. In the first case, we can enter a Boolean value as true or false instead of 0 or 1. In the second case, we can enter the integer values in octal or hexadecimal.

EXAMPLE 3.21

Program 3.25 shows how we can enter a false or true value for a Boolean and then print it as 0 or 1.

Program 3.25 Testing input for Boolean values

```
/***************************************************************
 * A program to input Boolean values as false or true          *
 ***************************************************************/
```

(continued)

Program 3.25 Testing input for Boolean values (Continued)

```
#include <iostream>
using namespace std;

int main ( )
{
  // Declaration
  bool flag;
  // Input value using manipulator
  cout << "Enter true or false for flag: ";
  cin >> boolalpha >> flag;
  // Output value
  cout << flag ;
  return 0;
}
```

```
Run:
Enter true or false for flag: false
0
```

```
Run:
Enter true or false for flag: true
1
```

EXAMPLE 3.22

Program 3.26 shows how we input the value of three variables in decimal, octal, and hexadecimal format.We then print the three values in decimal.

Program 3.26 Inputting integers in different bases

```
/***************************************************************
 * A program to input integer value in any base               *
 ***************************************************************/
#include <iostream>
using namespace std;

int main ( )
{
  // Declaration
  int num1, num2, num3;
  // Input first number in decimal (no manipulator)
  cout << "Enter the first number in decimal: ";
  cin >> num1;
  // Input second number in octal
  cout << "Enter the second number in octal: ";
  cin >> oct >> num2;
```

(continued)

Program 3.26 Inputting integers in different bases (Continued)

```
    // Input second number in hexadecimal
    cout << "Enter the third number in hexadecimal: ";
    cin >> hex >> num3;
    // Output values
    cout << num1 << endl;
    cout << num2 << endl;
    cout << num3;
    return 0;
}
```

```
Run:
Enter the first number in decimal: 124
Enter the second number in octal: 76
Enter the third number in hexadecimal: 2ab
124
62
683
```

3.6 STATEMENTS

We have studied expressions, but we also need statements to create a program in the C++ language. A C++ program is made of a sequence of **statements.** Each statement is executed by the computer, in the order dictated by the program, to achieve the goal of the program.

If we compare the C++ language with a natural language such as English, we find that a statement in C++ plays the role of a sentence in a natural language. When reading text in English, for example, a sentence is a unit of information we must interpret and understand before moving to the next sentence. A statement in a C++ program is a command that the C++ running environment must execute before going to the next statement. However, a programming language, like C++, has some statements that change the order of execution to move from one point in the program to another.

C++ provides many different types of statements, each with a predefined task. We discuss only some of them here. We discuss the rest gradually in future chapters.

Some statements need a semicolon to terminate the statement. On the other hand, some statements do not need a semicolon because they have another token at the end that is used as a terminator.

Some statements need a semicolon at the end as the terminator, but some already have a built-in terminator.

3.6.1 Declaration Statement

There are two terms in C++ that must be explained: *declaration* and *definition*. **Declaration** introduces an entity by mentioning its type and giving it a name (an identifier). **Definition,** on the other hand, means to allocate memory for the entity. There are many entities that need to be declared and defined for a complex program, but for now we limit ourselves only to variable and constant declaration.

Variable Declaration

We discussed the concept of variables in a previous section. To use a variable in our program, we must declare it. **Variable declaration** is in fact both declaration and definition unless we add an extra modifier (called **extern**) to postpone the definition to some other part of the program. Variable declaration statements require a semicolon to indicate statement termination.

A variable declaration statement requires a semicolon to terminate the statement.

Single Declaration A **single declaration** gives a name to a variable and defines its type. It also reserves a physical location in memory, suitable to hold a data item of the declared type. We declare and define three variables below: `test`, `sum`, and `average`. Note that each declaration needs a semicolon to terminate the statement.

```
short test;
int sum;
double average;
```

Multiple Declaration If we need to declare several variables of the same type, we can combine them and use only one declaration statement. For example, the following shows how we declare three variables of type **int**, two variables of type **double**, and one variable of type **char**. Note that we need to separate the variable names by a comma, but we need only one semicolon to terminate the statement. Note also that there is no need to add a space after the comma, but we strongly recommend at least one space after each comma to make the program readable.

```
int first, second, third;
double average, mean;
char ch;
```

Initialization When we declare a variable, we give the variable a name and we ask the computer to allocate a memory location of the corresponding type. The declaration, however, does not say what should be stored in the memory location initially, but we can initialize the variables when we declare them as shown in the following declarations.

```
int first = 0;
double average = 0.0, mean = 0.0;
char ch = 'a';
```

We may ask what happens if the variables are not initialized. We encounter two cases.

Global Variables If a variable is global (declared outside any function), it is initialized to default values (integers are initialized to 0, floating points to 0.0). Note that characters and Boolean data types are special (small) integers and are initialized to 0.

Local Variables If a variable is local (declared inside a function), it is not initialized, but the variable holds some garbage left over from the previous use. Before using a local variable, we need to either initialize it or change the garbage stored in it by other means.

Before using a local variable, we need to store a value in it.

Constant Declaration

In a previous section we discussed that a *constant* is a memory location in which its value is initialized and cannot be changed. To use a constant, we need to declare it (declaration in this case also means definition). A **constant declaration** is similar to variable declaration but with four differences. First, we need to use the keyword **const** in front of the type. Second, we must initialize a constant when it is declared. Third, it is customary to use uppercase letters to name a constant to distinguish it from the variables in the program (if the name involves more than one word, the words are separated by underscores). Fourth, constants are normally declared in the global area of the program (before any function, including `main`), which makes them visible in all functions. The following are examples of using constants.

```
const int FOOT_TO_INCH = 12;
const double TAX_RATE = 8.5;
const double PI = 3.1415926536;
```

Constants must be initialized when they are declared.

3.6.2 Expression Statement

An **expression statement** is an expression ended by a semicolon (as the terminator). We learned in the previous section that an *expression* has a value and possibly a side effect. When an *expression statement* is found in a program, the computer determines its value and performs its side effect. The value is thrown away, but the side effect changes the memory state of the computer. This means that expression statements in which the expression has no side effect are useless as statements; we need to avoid them although the compiler does not create an error.

The computer evaluates the value of the expression and performs its side effect. The value is thrown away.

EXAMPLE 3.23

The following are expression statements. Some are useful and some pointless. Only the last one creates a compilation error.

```
num = 24;              // Expression statement
num *= 10;             // Expression statement
num = data + 6;        // Expression statement
num1 + num2;           // Useless. There is no side effect
num1 * 6;              // Useless. There is no side effect.
num;                   // Useless. There is no side effect.
6;                     // Useless. There is no side effect.
cout << "Hello!";      // Input.
cin >> data            // Output
```

In some of the literature, an expression statement is called an assignment statement. There is no assignment statement in the syntax of the C++ language, only an expression statement. We follow the formal language specification.

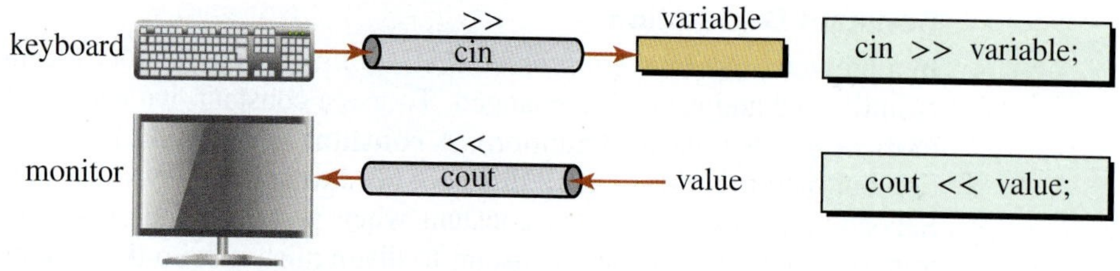

Figure 3.13 Input/output objects and operations

Although we need to input data into our program and send the results out of our programs, there are no input/output statements in C++. In C++, input and output operations are done using stream objects (`cin` and `cout`), as shown in Figure 3.13.

A stream object can be thought of as a conduit connecting the program to the physical input device (such as a keyboard) or a physical output device (such as a monitor). The stream connected to the keyboard is called `cin`; the stream connected to the monitor is called `cout`. The symbol `>>` (called extraction operator) is in fact an operator defined for the `cin` object; the symbol `<<` (called insertion operator) is in fact an operator defined for the `cout` object.

On the surface, when we use an input/output command, it looks like it is a new type of statement, but it is not. An input/output command is in fact an expression statement, and it needs a semicolon at the end.

Input/output commands that we have used in our programs are in fact expression statements and need a semicolon as a terminator.

3.6.3 Null Statement

A **null statement** is a statement that does nothing. We will see in the next two chapters that there are occasions in which the C++ syntax needs a statement but does not need a side effect. We will discuss some of the applications of the null statements in future chapters, but for the moment assume that by mistake we added two semicolons at the end of an expression. The compiler does not complain because it thinks we are using two statements: one expression statement and one a null statement. The following shows the case.

```
num = 24; ;                // We have an expression statement and a null statement.
```

3.6.4 Compound Statement

Sometimes we need to treat several statements as a single statement. In this case, we enclose the statements in a pair of braces. We can combine any number of statements (zero or more) inside a pair of braces. The process creates a single statement called a **compound statement,** which is also referred to as a *block*. We must use a compound statement whenever C++ syntax needs a single statement, but we need more than one statement. As we will see in future chapters, sometimes we even enclose a single statement in a pair of braces to improve readability and avoid confusion. Note that we do not need a semicolon at the end of a compound statement; the closing brace serves as the terminator. The following shows a compound statement with two statements.

```
{
   int num = 8;
   cout << num << endl;
}
```

What happens if we add a semicolon at end of the compound statement? Nothing. The compiler thinks that we have a compound followed by a null statement.

EXAMPLE 3.24

The body of a function needs a compound statement after the header as shown below:

```
int main ()
{
  ...
  return 0;
}
```

3.6.5 Return Statement

Another statement we have used in our programs is the **return statement,** which may return a value to the entity that called the function, such as `main` that returns 0 to the system. This statement belongs to the category of control statements that we discuss in chapter 4 in more detail.

EXAMPLE 3.25

In this example we write a program in C++; the program will input three integers, calculate the sum, and print the sum (Program 3.27). Various statements are used in the program.

Program 3.27 Input three integers and print the sum of them

```
/***************************************************************
 * A program to add three integers and print the result        *
 ***************************************************************/
#include <iostream>
#include <iomanip>
using namespace std;

int main ( )
{
  // Variables declaration
   int first, second, third, sum;
  // Prompts and inputs
   cout << "Enter the first integer: ";
   cin >> first;
   cout << "Enter the second integer: ";
   cin >> second;
   cout << "Enter the third integer: ";
   cin >> third;
  // Calculation
   sum = first + second + third;
  // Output
   cout << "The sum of the three integers is: " << sum;
```

(continued)

Program 3.27 Input three integers and print the sum of them (Continued)

```
23     return 0;
24 }
```

```
Run:
Enter the first integer: 20
Enter the second integer: 30
Enter the third integer: 10
The sum of the three integers is: 60
```

```
Run:
Enter the first integer: 10
Enter the second integer: 8
Enter the third integer: 3
The sum of the three integers is: 21
```

Let us analyze the statements we have used in this program. The program starts with the definition of the `main` function. The body of the `main` function (lines 10 through 23) is a compound statement. Line 11 is a declaration statement. Lines 13 through 18 are expression statements (input/output commands). Line 20 is an expression statement (addition). Line 22 is an expression statement (output command). Line 23 is a return statement. The compound statement in lines 10 through 23 is a combination of several statements (excluding the comments) that are enclosed between two delimiters: the opening and closing braces.

3.7 PROGRAM DESIGN

In this section, we design and implement five programs. We use a *software development process* that consists of three steps.

- **Understand the Problem.** In the first step, we see if we understand the problem to be solved.
- **Develop the Algorithm.** In the second step, we develop an algorithm for the problem. We have several tools to do so, but we use only the informal description in this chapter because the programs we write are very simple.
- **Write the Code.** In the third step, we use the developed algorithm to write the C++ code.

3.7.1 Extracting Parts of a Floating-Point Number

Let us design and implement a program that, given a floating-point value, extracts and prints the integral and the fraction parts.

Understand the Problem

A floating-point number is given; we want to separate the fractional part and the integral part. For example, given 123.78, we want to output 123 and 0.78.

Develop the Algorithm

The algorithm in this case is simple. We input a number, extract its integral and fraction parts, and output the original number, the integral part, and the fraction part. The step-by-step algorithm is shown below:

1. **Input**
   a. **Input a number.**
2. **Process**
   a. **Extract the integral part.**
   b. **Extract the fraction part.**
3. **Output**
   a. **Output the original number.**
   b. **Output the integral part.**
   c. **Output the fraction part.**

Write the Code

Now that we have formalized all of the elements of the program—input section, processing section, and output section—we can write the code (see Program 3.28).

Program 3.28 Extracting integral and fractional parts of a floating-point number

```
/***************************************************************
 * This program shows how to extract the integral part and the    *
 * fractional part of a floating-point number                     *
 ***************************************************************/
#include <iostream>
#include <iomanip>
using namespace std;

int main ( )
{
  // Variable Declaration
   double number;
   int intPart;
   double fractPart;
  // Input
   cout << "Enter a floating-point number: ";
   cin >> number;
  // Processing
   intPart = static_cast <int> (number);
   fractPart = number - intPart;
  // Output
   cout << fixed << showpoint << setprecision (2);
   cout << "The original number: " << number << endl;
   cout << "The integral part: " << intPart << endl;
   cout << "The fractional part: " << fractPart;
   return 0;
} // End of main
```

(continued)

Program 3.28 Extracting integral and fractional parts of a floating-point number (Continued)

```
Run:
Enter the floating-point number: 145.72
The original number: 145.72
The integral part: 145
The fractional part: 0.72
```

```
Run:
Enter the floating-point number: -546
The original number: -546.00
The integral part: -546
The fractional part: 0.00
```

```
Run:
Enter the floating-point number: -0.14
The original number: -0.14
The integral part: 0
The fractional part: -0.14
```

We have used the `fixed`, `showpoint`, and `setprecision` manipulators to format our output. Note that in each run we enter only one floating-point value. One way to test if our program does its job is to add the integral and fraction part in each run and see if we can get the original number. In the first run, we have $145 + 0.72 = 145.72$.

3.7.2 Extracting the First Digit of an Integer

Let us design and implement a program that, given an integer, extracts and prints the first (rightmost) digit of an integer.

Understand the Problem

An integer is given; we want to extract the first digit of the number. For example, given 6759, we want to output 9.

Develop the Algorithm

The algorithm in this case is simple. We input an integer and extract its first digit. We then print the original integer and the first digit. The algorithm is shown below:

1. Input
- **a. Input an integer.**

2. Process
- **a. Extract the first (rightmost) digit.**

3. Output
- **a. Output the original number.**
- **b. Output the first digit.**

Write the Code

We write the program by using the input, processing, and output sections we defined (Program 3.29).

Program 3.29 Extracting the first digit of a given integer

```
/***********************************************************************
 * This program extracts the first digit of an input integer.          *
 ***********************************************************************/
#include <iostream>
using namespace std;

int main ( )
{
  // Variables Declaration
   unsigned int givenInt, firstDigit;
  // Prompt and Input
   cout << "Enter a positive integer: ";
   cin >> givenInt;
  // Processing
   firstDigit = givenInt % 10 ;
  // Output
   cout << "Entered integer: " << givenInt << endl;
   cout << "Extracted first digit: " << firstDigit << endl;
   return 0;
}
```

```
Run:
Enter a positive integer: 253
Entered integer: 253
Extracted first digit: 3
```

```
Run:
Enter a positive integer: 45672
Entered integer: 45672
Extracted first digit: 2
```

3.7.3 Changing a Duration of Time to Its Components

Let us design and implement another problem. Find how many hours, minutes, and second are in a time duration given in seconds.

Understand the Problem

We are given a large integer such as 234,572 as the number of seconds to perform a task. We need to find how many hours, minutes, and seconds it took to perform the task.

Develop the Algorithm

The algorithm in this case is simple. We input a number representing seconds and extract the hours, minutes, and seconds in it. We then print the number of hours, minutes, and seconds. The algorithm is shown below:

1. Input
   a. Input an integer representing the duration in seconds.
2. Process
   a. Extract the number of hours that can fit in the seconds.
   b. Extract the number of minutes that can fit in the rest of the seconds.
   c. Find the left-over seconds.
3. Output
   a. Output the duration value given in seconds.
   b. Output the number of extracted hours.
   c. Output the number of extracted minutes.
   d. Output the number of left-over seconds.

Write the Code

Now we can create the program code based on the preceding algorithm (Program 3.30).

Program 3.30 Change a time duration to its components

```
/****************************************************************
 * This program changes a duration of time in seconds to hours        *
 * minutes, and seconds.                                              *
 ****************************************************************/
#include <iostream>
using namespace std;

int main ( )
{
  // Variables Declaration
   unsigned long duration, hours, minutes, seconds;
  // Prompt and Input
   cout << "Enter a positive integer for the number of seconds: ";
   cin >> duration;
  // Processing
   hours = duration / 3600L;
   minutes = (duration - (hours * 3600L)) / 60L;
   seconds = duration - (hours * 3600L) - (minutes * 60);
  // Output
   cout << "Given Duration in seconds: " << duration << endl;
   cout << "Result: ";
   cout << hours << " hours, ";
   cout << minutes <<  " minutes, and ";
   cout << seconds << " seconds.";
   return 0;
} // End main
```

(continued)

Program 3.30 Change a time duration to its components (Continued)

```
Run:
Enter a positive integer for the number of seconds: 4000
Given duration in seconds: 4000
Result: 1 hours, 6 minutes, and 40 seconds.
```

```
Run:
Enter a positive integer for the number of seconds: 39250
Given duration in seconds: 39250
Result: 10 hours, 54 minutes, and 10 seconds.
```

We cannot say that the answer is right by just looking at the result. We should test some of the results to be certain that our program is correctly designed. For example, we can go backward and find the input from the output in both runs as shown below:

```
Run 1: (1 * 3600) + (6 * 60) + 40 = 3600 + 360 + 40 = 4000 seconds
Run 2: (10 * 3600) + (54 * 60) + 10 = 36000 + 3240 + 10 = 39250 seconds
```

Since we get the same value we gave for the duration, the program is working properly.

3.7.4 Calculating Average and Deviation

In this problem, we want to read three integers, calculate their average, and determine the deviation of each integer from the average.

Understand the Problem

The average of a list of numbers can be found by adding them together and dividing the result by the size of the list. The deviation of each number means how far that number is from the average, positive or negative. For example, we have three numbers: 10, 14, and 15. The sum of the numbers is 39. The average is 39/3 or 13. The deviation of the first number is $10 - 13 = -3$, the deviation of the second number is $14 - 13 = 1$, and the deviation of the fourth number is $15 - 13 = 2$.

Develop the Algorithm

The algorithm in this case is somewhat involved. We input three integers. We calculate the sum and the average. We calculate the deviation of each number from the average. We then output the sum, the average, and the deviation for each number. The algorithm is shown below:

1. **Input**
   a. **Input three numbers.**
2. **Process**
   a. **Add three numbers to find the sum.**
   b. **Divide the sum by 3 to find the average.**
   c. **Find the deviation of each number from the average.**
3. **Output**
   a. **Output the value of sum.**
   b. **Output the value of average.**
   c. **Output the deviation of each number.**

Write the Code

We now write the code (Program 3.31).

Program 3.31 Finding the sum, the average, and deviations

```
/**************************************************************
 * This program takes three integers, adds them, finds their     *
 * average and the deviation of each from the average.            *
 **************************************************************/
#include <iostream>
#include <iomanip>
using namespace std;

int main ( )
{
  // Variable declaration
   int num1, num2, num3;
   int sum;
   double average;
   double dev1, dev2, dev3;
  // Prompt and Input
   cout << "Enter the first integer: ";
   cin >> num1;
   cout << "Enter the second integer: ";
   cin >> num2;
   cout << "Enter the third integer: ";
   cin >> num3;
  // Processing
   sum = num1 + num2 + num3;
   average = static_cast <double> (sum) / 3;
   dev1 = num1 - average;
   dev2 = num2 - average;
   dev3 = num3 - average;
  // Output
   cout << fixed << setprecision (2) << showpos;
   cout << "Sum of three numbers: " << sum << endl;
   cout << "Average: " << setw(9) << average << endl;
   cout << "Deviation of number 1: " << setw(9) << dev1 << endl;
   cout << "Deviation of number 2: " << setw(9) << dev2 << endl;
   cout << "Deviation of number 3: " << setw(9) << dev3 << endl;
   return 0;
}
```

```
Run:
Enter the first integer: 100
Enter the second integer: 101
Enter the third integer: 103
```

(*continued*)

Program 3.31 Finding the sum, the average, and deviations (Continued)

```
Sum of three numbers: 304
Average:  101.33
Deviation of number 1:   -1.33
Deviation of number 2:   -0.33
Deviation of number 3:   +1.67
```

We need to be sure the results are correct. If we add each deviation to the average, we should get the original number. However, this calculation may result in an approximation. We have

a. $101.33 + (-1.33) = 100$ (first number).
b. $101.33 + (-0.33) = 101$ (second number).
c. $101.33 + (+1.67) = 103$ (third number).

Key Terms

addition
associativity
casting
compound assignment
compound statement
constant declaration
declaration
definition
explicit type conversion
expression
expression statement
fixed format
implicit type change
implicit type conversion
implicit type promotion
literal
lvalue
manipulator
minus expression
multiple declaration
multiplicative *expression*
name
null *statement*
overflow
plus expression
precedence
primary expression
return statement
rvalue
scientific format
showpoint
simple assignment
single declaraton
sizeof
statement
subtraction
type conversion
unary expression
underflow
uppercase
variable declaration

Summary

An expression is an entity with a value and possibly a side effect. An expression can be made of a simple value or multiple values combined with operators. A primary expression contains one value and no operator. A unary expression contains one value and one operator. A binary expression contains one operator and two values. A ternary expression is made of two operators and three values. Expression evaluation may involve type conversion, which can be implicit or explicit.

To find the order of evaluation of simple expression in a complex expression, we need to think of two properties of operators: precedence and associativity. Precedence is used when we have an expression of different levels of precedence; associativity is used when we have expressions of the same precedence.

Overflow and underflow define the rules for determining what happens when a number is either too large or too small for a variable.

Sometimes we need to format data. This is done with the help of predefined objects called manipulators. We have manipulators for outputting data and manipulators for inputting data.

To write a program in C++, we need statements. C++ provides many different types of statements, each with a pre-defined task. We discusses five types of statements in this chapter: declaration statement, expression statement, null statement, compound statement, and return statement.

Program design is a process that needs to be carefully followed using at least three steps: understanding the program, developing algorithms, and writing the code.

Problems

PR-1. Evaluate the following integer expressions in decimal. Find any errors.

a. `0723` b. `0491`
c. `-0241` d. `-0412`

PR-2. Evaluate the following integer expressions in decimal. Find any errors.

a. `-0x1A12` b. `-0xH21B`
c. `0xA2EF` d. `0x4`

PR-3. Evaluate the following floating-point expressions. Find any errors.

a. `0.0712F` b. `6.0712`
c. `1.234E2` d. `1123E-2`

PR-4. Evaluate the following expressions.

`3 + 7 * 2` `4 * 2 + 7` `7 / 4 + 3 * 4`

PR-5. Evaluate the following expressions.

`4 / 3 * 6 / 2 + 8 % 3` `24 % 5 + 16 % 5 * 4 / 2`

PR-6. Assume x = 3, y = 5, and z = 6. Evaluate the following expressions (assume each expression is independent).

`x - 3 + y * 2 - z / 2` `(x + 2) % (y * y)`

PR-7. Assume x = 3, y = 5, and z = 6. Evaluate the following expressions (assume each expression is independent).

`(y / 3 + x) * z % x` `y - 2 - x * y`

PR-8. Assume x = 4 and y = 2. Find the value of x after evaluating each of the following expressions.

`x -= y - 2;` `x += y + 2;`

PR-9. Assume x = 4, y = 2, and z = 5. Find the value of z after evaluating each of the following expressions.

`z /= x + y + 4;` `z %= y * 2 + 3;`

PR-10. What is the value of each expression?

```
2 + 4          3 % 5;          3.2 * 2;          5 + 3.2;
```

PR-11. What is the value of each expression?

```
'A' - 2          'B' + 3.2;          4.5 + 'D';          'C' * 2;
```

PR-12. If `x` is `integer`, `y` is `float`, and `z` is `double`, what are the values of `x`, `y`, and `z`?

```
x = 'A'          y = 3          z = 2          z = 2.5 + 2
```

PR-13. Change the following simple assignments to compound assignments.

```
x = x + 4;          y = y - 2;          z = z + 2 - t          t = t / 5;
```

PR-14. Change the following compound assignments to simple assignments.

```
x += 8          y -= 8 + x          z *= t + 2          t %= x + 5
```

PR-15. Given that `x` is `character`, `y` is `short integer`, `z` is `integer`, and `t` is `long integer`, find any errors in the following statements.

```
x = 105.2;          y = 4.6;          z = 27;          t = 'A';
```

PR-16. Which of the following variables are correctly declared?

```
a. char letter = 'A';
b. int first, second;
c. double average, tax = 8.5;
d. long double 3x;
```

PR-17. Which of the following variables are correctly declared?

```
a. char letter, grade;
b. int sum = 5;
c. double average * 3;
d. long double 34.123;
```

PR-18. Assume the following statements occur one after another in a program. Show the values of `x`, `y`, and `z` after all statements have been executed.

```
int x = 2, y = 4, z = 5;
x = y - 2;
y += x;
z /= x + y + 4;
z %= y * 2 + 3;
```

PR-19. Assume the following statements occur one after another in a program. Show the values of `x`, `y`, and `z` after all statements have been executed.

```
double x = 2.5, y = 3.2, z = 5.1;
x = y + 2 ;
y += x - 1.5;
z += x + y * 4;
```

PR-20. Declare two variables of type **int**, two of type **float**, three of type **double**, and one of type **char**.

PR-21. Declare `x`, `y`, `z`, and `t` to be constants of type **char**, **short**, **int**, and **float**, respectively. Use appropriate values for each constant.

PR-22. Which of the following statements gives a compile-time error? Explain your answer.

a. `2 + x = 4;`
b. `z = z + 2 = 6;`
c. `y = x + 2 % 5;`
d. `t = z = 4 + 5;`

PR-23. Assume the following statements occur one after another in a program. Show the values of x, y, and z after all statements have been executed.

```
int x = 2, y, z;
x = y = x + 2 ;
y += y - 6;
z = y + 5;
```

PR-24. Assume the following statements occur one after another in a program. Show the values of x and y after all statements have been executed. Are the values of x and y swapped? Explain.

```
int x = 2, y = 10;
y = x ;
x = y;
```

PR-25. Assume the following statements occur one after another in a program. Show the values of x and y after all statements have been executed. Are the values of x and y are swapped? Explain.

```
int x = 2, y = 10;
int temp;
temp = x ;
x = y;
y = temp ;
```

PR-26. What would be printed from the following lines of code?

```
cout << fixed << setprecision (2) << 124.78560 << endl;
cout << fixed << setprecision (2) << 0.14 << endl;
cout << fixed << setprecision (2) << 20 << endl;
cout << fixed << setprecision (2) << 14767.0 << endl;
```

PR-27. What would be printed from the following lines of code?

```
cout << fixed << setprecision (4) << 124.79 << endl;
cout << fixed << setprecision (4) << 0.14 << endl;
cout << fixed << setprecision (4) << 20.0 << endl;
cout << fixed << setprecision (4) << 14767.00 << endl;
```

PR-28. Write the following expression statements in C++. Each statement is independent.

```
increment the value of x
decrement the value of y
set the value of t to 5.14
copy the current value of variable first to the variable second.
```

PR-29. Write the following expression statements in C++. Each statement is independent.

```
add 2 to the contents of variable x
multiply the value of variable y by 7
```

```
add value of x with y and store the result in z
set the value of flag (of type bool) to false
```

PR-30. Find any error in each of the following statements (x, y, z, and t are numeric types).

```
x += 7;
y *= y;
z + 6 = z;
3t = 12;
```

PR-31. Find any error in each of the following statements (assuming that all variables are numeric types).

```
x = 7 = 4;
y *= y = 6;
z = z + 5 = 8;
hello = 12;
```

PR-32. Assume x is of type bool, y is of type char, z is of type short, and t is of type float. What implicit promotion takes place in each of the following expressions, and what is the value of each expression?

```
x + 4
y * 2
z - 24;
t + 23.4;
```

PR-33. Assume x is of type int, y is of type long, z is of type long long, and t is of type long double. What implicit promotion takes place in each of the following expressions?

```
x + y
y * z
z - t;
```

PR-34. What will be output from the following program segment?

```
double x = -909.245;
cout << fixed << setprecision (2) << x << endl;
cout << fixed << setw (15) << setprecision (3) << setfill ('*') << x;
```

PR-35. What will be output from the following program segment?

```
int x = 50;
cout << setw(10) << setfill ('*') << x;
```

PR-36. What will be output from the following program segment?

```
int n1 = 10, n2 = 20;
char ch = '$';
cout << setw(n1) << setfill (ch) << 241 << endl;
cout << setw(n2) << setfill (ch) << 14672;
```

PR-37. What will be output from the following program segment?

```
int n1 = 8, n2 = 12;
char ch = '#';
```

```
cout << setw(n1) << setprecision (3) << setfill (ch) << 475.12 << endl;
cout << setw(n2) << setprecision (4) << setfill (ch) << 0.151;
```

PR-38. What will be output when the following code is executed and we enter the Boolean value `false`?

```
bool x;
cin >> boolalpha >> x;
cout << x ;
```

PR-39. What will be output when the following code is run and we input `72`?

```
int x;
cin >> oct >> x;
cout << x;
```

PR-40. What will be output when the following code is run and we input `72`?

```
int x;
cin >> hex >> x;
cout << x;
```

Programs

PRG-1. Write a program that finds the maximum and minimum values for a **short** and **unsigned int** in your computer.

PRG-2. Write a program that finds the minimum and maximum values for a **long**, and a **long long** in your computer.

PRG-3. Write a program that finds the minimum and maximum values for a **float** and a **double** in your computer.

PRG-4. Write a program that extracts and prints the second digit of an input data of type **int**.

PRG-5. Write a program that individually extracts the rightmost three digits of an input data of type **int**.

PRG-6. Write a program that, given a three-digit integer, constructs and prints another integer whose digits are in the reverse order of the given one. For example, given 372, the program prints 273.

PRG-7. Write a program that, given a number of hours, calculates the number of weeks, days, and hours included in that number.

PRG-8. Write a program that, given the time duration of a task in the number of hours, minutes, and seconds, calculates duration in seconds.

PRG-9. Write a program that inputs the number of seconds (a long value) and changes it to days, hours, minutes, and seconds.

PRG-10. Write a program that inputs four scores (`int` values) and finds and prints the average of the scores (a double value).

PRG-11. Write a program that helps a cashier at a store find the amount of change given, the amount of a purchase in dollars and cents, and the amount of dollars and cents given by the customer. The answer should be in dollars, quarters, dimes, nickels, and pennies.

PRG-12. Write a program that, given a temperature in Celsius, calculates and prints the temperature in Fahrenheit using the formula F = (9/5) C + 32.

PRG-13. Write a program that, given a temperature in Fahrenheit, calculates and prints the temperature in Centigrade using the formula C = (F – 32) * 5/9.

PRG-14. Assume a party of three couples dines in a restaurant. The first family has two children. Each of the other families has one child. Write a program that divides the bill among each family if a child is charged 3/4 of an adult share. The total charge (before tax) is given as an input. The tax is 9.5 percent, and 20 percent must be added for service.

PRG-15. An hourly employee is paid regular pay per hour for 40 hours a week. She will be paid 60 percent more for every hour she works over 40 hours. Write a program that asks an employee to enter the number of extra hours worked last week and the weekly rate and then calculates and prints total payment.

PRG-16. Write a program to create a customer's bill for a company. The company sells only three products: TV sets, DVD players, and remote controllers. The unit prices are $1400.00, $220.00, and $35.20, respectively. The program must read from the keyboard the quantity of each piece of equipment purchased. It then calculates the cost of each item, the subtotal, and the total cost after an 8.25 percent sales tax.

The programs we wrote in previous chapters were based on a sequential execution of statements. The programs were mostly made of input statements, calculation statements, and output statements. Every time we ran the program, all statements in the program were executed one after another. The sequential execution of statements may solve simple problems, but we also need to have control statements. In this chapter, we discuss the first group of control statements: selection statements. A selection statement allows the programmer to choose between different actions based on one or more conditions.

Objectives

After you have read and studied this chapter, you should be able to:

- Discuss the need for relational and equality expressions in achieving simple selections.
- Understand how we can make a one-way selection using the *if* statement.
- Understand how we can make a two-way selection using the *if-else* statement.
- Understand how we can make a multiway selection using the nested *if-else* statement.
- Show how complex decisions can be made by combining relational/equality expressions with logical expressions.
- Understand how we can make a multiway selection in which the decision is based on discrete values using a *switch* statement.
- Show how we can use a *conditional expression* instead of a simple *if-else* statement.

4.1 SIMPLE SELECTION

To solve some problems, we must make decisions based on the test of a *true-false* condition. If the condition is true, we need to execute a set of statements; if the condition is false, we need to execute another set of statements (or no statements). This process is referred to as selection. The question is, How do we create the condition that should be tested? The answer is that we use expressions whose values are either *true* or *false*.

4.1.1 Relational and Equality Expressions

To make simple decisions, we need either relational or equality expressions. These expressions are shown in Appendix C, but we show them in Table 4.1 for quick reference. We distinguish between the two groups because they occupy different levels of precedence (11 and 10).

Table 4.1 Relational and equality expressions

Group	Name	Operator	Expression	Pred	Assoc
Relational	less less or equal greater greater or equal	< <= > >=	expr < expr expr <= expr expr > expr expr >= expr	11	→
Equality	equal not equal	== !=	expr == expr expr != expr	10	→

Relational Expressions

As Table 4.1 shows, **relational expressions** use four relational operators to compare two values. Note that the result of `(a <= b)` is *true* if *a* is equal to or if *a* is less than *b*; it is *false* if *a* is greater than *b*. Similarly, the result of `(a >= b)` is *true* if *a* is greater than or equal to *b*; the result is *false* if *a* is less than *b*. The type of the left and the right expression must be the same when the comparison is evaluated. If the two expressions are not the same type, the conversion we discussed in Chapter 3 is applied. The following shows some examples of relational operators.

```
3 < 4            // The result is true because 3 is less than 4.
12.78 < 7.36     // The result is false because 12.78 is not less than 7.36.
5 <= 3.24        // The left operand is first promoted to 5.0. The result is false.
5.0 <= 5         // The  right operand is first promoted to 5.0. The result is true.
3 > false        // The right operand is promoted to 0. The result is true.
5 >= 2.2         // The left operand is promoted to 5.0. The result is true.
```

Equality Expressions

Table 4.1 also shows two **equality expressions** that determine if two entities are equal or not. Note that the result of ($a == b$) is *true* if *a* is equal to b; it is *false* if *a* is not equal to *b*. Similarly, the result of (a != b) is *true* if the value of *a* is different from the value of *b*; the result is false if they are equal. The type of the left and the right expressions must be the same when the comparison is evaluated. If the two expressions are not the same type, the conversion we discussed in Chapter 3 is applied. The following shows some equality expressions and their results.

```
3 == 4           // The result is false.
true == false    // The exprssion is converted to (1 == 0). The result is false.
true != false    // The expression is converted to (1 != 0). The result is true.
3 != false       // The right operand is changed to 0. The result is true.
65 != 'A'        // The result is false because 'A' is converted to 65.
```

Precedence and Associativity

When we try to evaluate a complex expression involving relational and equality expressions, we need to pay attention to the precedence and associativity of these two groups. In a complex expression, parentheses help to indicate the order of evaluation. The following shows some examples:

```
3 < 4 == 1        // Using precedence we have (3 < 4) == 1. The result is true.
2 < 3 < 0         // Using associativity we have (2 < 3) < 0. The result is false.
3 <= 6 < 5        // Using associativity we have (3 <= 6) < 5. The result is true.
4 == 4 < 2        // Using precedence we have 4 == (4 < 2) or 4 == 0. The result is false.
```

Pitfall

We should avoid using either of the equality operators with floating-point values because we do not know with what precision these values are stored in memory. In other words, the result is system dependent.

```
x == 2.78123      //The result may be false even if the value of x is 2.78123.
x != 14.67823     // Even if the value of x is close to 14.67823, the result may be true.
```

4.1.2 One-Way Selection: The *if* Statement

The most common structure for making decisions is one-way selection, which is accomplished in C++ by the ***if* statement.** Figure 4.1 shows the logic of one-way selection and the syntax of the if statement in C++.

In this type of statement, we use an expression to test a condition. The program executes the statement (or the set of statements) if the result of the test is true; it skips the statement (or the set of statements) if the result is false. Note that if we have more than one statement to be executed, we need to use a compound statement.

This type of selection is often referred to as **one-way selection:** to do a task or not to do a task. Note that the selection expression makes sense only if each time we run the program, the result is unpredictable (based on the tested condition). In other words, the result of the relational or equality expression should be based on the input to the program; otherwise, the decision making does not make sense.

Note that the statement to be executed when the result of the testing is true is one single statement, but this single statement can be a compound statement (a set of statements inside two braces). Some programmers discard the braces when there is only one statement to be executed. We strongly discourage this practice. The braces clearly show the flow of the program even when there is only one statement to be executed.

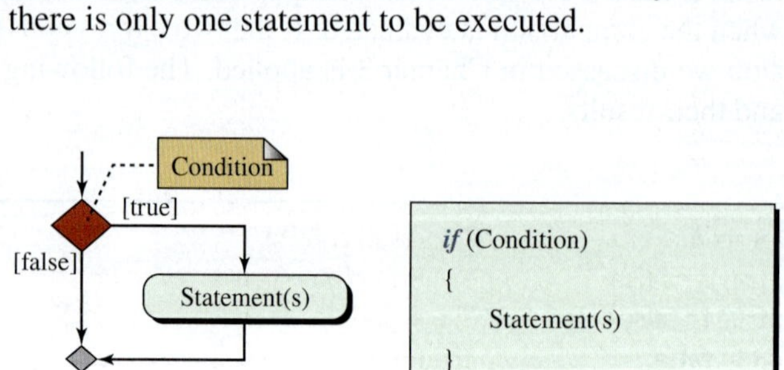

(a) Flow diagram (b) C++ syntax

Figure 4.1 One-way selection

Program 4.1 Printing absolute value

```
1  /*****************************************************************
2   * Using if-statement to print the absolute value of a number     *
3   *****************************************************************/
4  #include <iostream>
5  using namespace std;
6
7  int main ()
8  {
9    // Declaration
10   int number;
11   // Getting input
12   cout << "Enter an integer: ";
13   cin >> number;
14   // Finding the absolute value
15   if (number < 0)
16   {
17       number = -number;
18   }
19   // Printing the absolute value
20   cout << "Absolute value of the number you entered is: " << number;
21   return 0;
22 }
```

```
Run:
Enter an integer: 25
Absolute value of the number you entered is: 25
```

```
Run:
Enter an integer: -17
Absolute value of the number you entered is: 17
```

EXAMPLE 4.1

Program 4.1 shows a very simple use of an *if* statement to find the absolute value of an integer entered by the user of the program. If the user enters a negative integer, the programs changes it to a positive integer of the same magnitude; otherwise, the program does nothing. After the program exits the decision-making section (lines 15 to 18), it prints the absolute value of the integer entered.

Note that we do not need the braces (lines 16 and 18) in this simple example, but it is a good practice to use them.

EXAMPLE 4.2

Program 4.2 also demonstrates the use of an *if* statement. It calculates the weekly gross earnings for an employee. If the employee works more than 40 hours during the week, the overtime pay rate for the extra hours is 130 percent of the base pay rate.

Program 4.2 Gross payment of an employee

```
/*****************************************************************
 * Use of if-statement to find gross payment of an employee      *
 *****************************************************************/
#include <iostream>
#include <iomanip>;
using namespace std;

int main ()
{
  // Declaration;
   double hours;
   double rate;
   double regularPay;
   double overPay;
   double totalPay;
  // Input
   cout << "Enter hours worked: ";
   cin >> hours;
   cout << "Enter pay rate: ";
   cin >> rate;
  // Calculation that does not depend on decision
   regularPay = hours * rate;
   overPay = 0.0;
  // Calculation that is skipped if hours worked is not more than 40
   if (hours > 40.0)
   {
        overPay = (hours - 40.0) * rate * 0.30;
   } // End if
  // Rest of the calculation
   totalPay = regularPay + overPay;
  // Printing output
   cout << fixed << showpoint;
   cout << "Regular pay  = " << setprecision (2) << regularPay << endl;
   cout << "Over time pay = " << setprecision (2) <<  overPay << endl;
   cout << "Total pay = " << setprecision (2) << totalPay << endl;
   return 0;
}
```

```
Run:
Enter hours worked: 30
Enter pay rate: 22.00
Regular pay = 660.00
Over time pay = 0.00
Total pay = 660.00
```

(continued)

Program 4.2 Gross payment of an employee (Continued)

```
Run:
Enter hours worked: 45
Enter pay rate: 25.00
Regular pay = 1125.00
Over time pay = 37.50
Total pay = 1162.50
```

In the first run, since the employee worked less than 40 hours, the program ignores the statement in line 27. The overtime pay remains 0.0 as initialized. In the second run, since the employee worked more than 40 hours, statement 27 is executed, the overtime pay is calculated as $37.50, and it is added to *regularPay*, which makes *totalPay* $1162.50.

Some Pitfalls

When we use an *if* statement for one-way selection, we must look carefully for pitfalls. These errors normally are not caught by the compiler because they are logic errors, not syntactical ones. We compile and run the program, but we find that the result is not correct.

Using the Assignment Operator Instead of the Equality Operator A common mistake is to use the assignment operator (=) instead of the equality operator (==). The following shows an example:

```
if (x = 0)              // This statement is always false.
{
   statement;           // The statement is never executed.
}
```

Note that in this case the condition is always *false* no matter what the value of x is. The expression changes the value of x to 0 (which we did not intend). The result of the expression is the value of x, which is 0. We have seen that the value of 0 is interpreted as *false* in an expression that needs a Boolean value. This means the statement is never executed.

Similarly, if we have `(x = 5)` instead of `(x == 5)`, the result is always *true* and the statement is always executed as shown below:

```
if (x = 5)              // This condition is always true.
{
   statement;           // The statement is always executed.
}
```

Forgetting Braces Another common mistake is to forget the braces when we have more than one statement to be executed:

```
if (x == 0)
   statement1;          // Statement1 is executed if x is equal to 0.
   statement2;          // Statement2 is always executed.
```

In the above example, the compiler interprets the body of the *if* statement as only one statement (statment1) and then always executes statement2. Our recommendation is to always use the braces to avoid this confusion.

Extra Semicolon The *if* statement is one statement that is made of the header and a compound statement as the body. If we put an extra semicolon at the end of the header, the compiler thinks that the body is empty. In the following example, `statement1` and `statement2` are executed no matter what the value of `x` is. In other words, statement1 and statement2 are considered a compound statement separate from the *if* statement.

```
if (x == 0);          // Semicolon makes the body of if statement empty.
{
  statement1;         // Statement1 is always executed.
  statement2;         // Statement2 is always executed.
}
```

4.1.3 Two-Way Selection: *if-else* Statement

The second statement we discuss for selection is **two-way selection** using the *if-else* statement as shown in Figure 4.2. When the program reaches the ***if-else* statement** during execution, it first evaluates the Boolean expression. If the value of this expression is *true*, the program executes statement1 and ignores statement2; otherwise, the program executes statement2 and ignores statement1. Note that in each run, only one of the two statements, `statement1` or `statement2`, is executed but never both. Also note that `statement1` and `statement2` can be either a single statement or a compound statement. However, we always recommend using braces (a compound statement) even if we have only one statement for either branch. The *if-else* statement is used whenever we have to do something, no matter what the result of the decision is.

EXAMPLE 4.3

Program 4.3 prints a pass/no-pass grade for a student based on a test score. After entering the score, we use an *if-else* statement to check if the score is equal to or above 70. In this case, the *if* branch and the *else* branch each have only one statement. The program executes either line 17 or 21 but never both.

Note that in this case, we print the result of the test as a pass/no-pass grade, no matter what the value of the grade is. However, it is also possible to use only the *if* statement when we use a variable to hold the result, as we will see in future chapters.

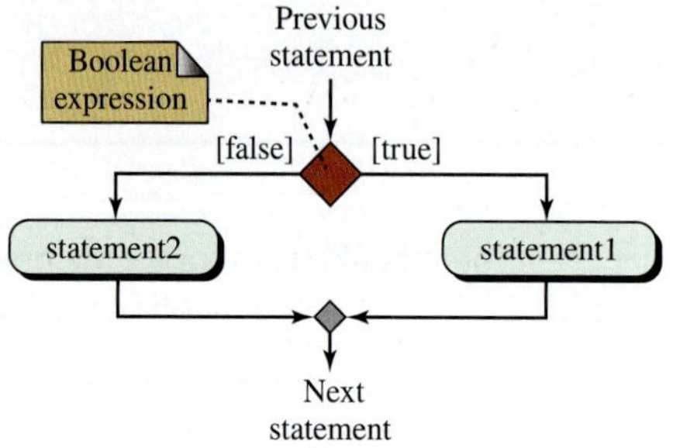

(a) Flow diagram

```
if (boolean-expression)
{
    statement1;
}
else
{
    statement2;
}
```

(b) C++ syntax

Figure 4.2 *if-else* statement

Program 4.3 Find pass/no-pass grade

```
/*****************************************************************
 * Use of an if-else statement to find a pass/no-pass grade      *
 *****************************************************************/
#include <iostream>
using namespace std;

int main ()
{
  // Local Declaration
  int score;
  // Input
  cout << "Enter a score between 0 and 100: ";
  cin >> score;
  // Decision
  if (score  >= 70)
  {
      cout << "Grade is pass" << endl;
  } // End if
  else
  {
      cout << "Grade is nopass" << endl;
  } // End else
  return 0;
}
```

```
Run:
Enter a score between 0 and 100: 65
Grade is nopass.
```

```
Run:
Enter a score between 0 and 100: 92
Grade is pass.
```

EXAMPLE 4.4

Program 4.4 asks the user to enter two integers and prints the larger one.

Program 4.4 Finding larger of two numbers

```
/*****************************************************************
 * Use of if-else statement to print larger between two numbers  *
 * or print the first if numbers are equal                       *
 *****************************************************************/
#include <iostream>
```

(continued)

Program 4.4 Finding larger of two numbers (Continued)

```
using namespace std;

int main ()
{
  // Declaration
   int num1, num2;
   int larger;
  // Input Statements
   cout << "Enter the first number: ";
   cin >> num1;
   cout << "Enter the second number: ";
   cin >> num2;
  // Decision
   if (num1 >= num2)
   {
        larger = num1;
   } // End if
   else
   {
        larger = num2;
   } // End else
  // Printing result
   cout << "The larger number is: " << larger;
   return 0;
}
```

```
Run:
Enter the first number: 40
Enter the second number: 25
The larger number is: 40
```

```
Run:
Enter the first number: 22
Enter the second number: 67
The larger number is: 67
```

Note that in the above program, we separate the output from the decision-making process. We do not print the larger value in the decision section. We store the larger value in a variable (called `larger`), and then we print it after the decision process is complete. This is a better strategy than the one used in the previous program because we separate the tasks.

Another Pitfall: Extra Semicolon An extra semicolon in the header creates the same problem we saw for one-way selection. However, the error here is different; it is a compilation error. The program does not compile because the compiler thinks that we are using an *else* clause without an *if* clause. This is a less dangerous error because it forces us to make the correction and recompile. Compile-time errors are better than run-time errors.

// Coded	// Interpreted by the compiler
`if (b);  // Extra semicolon`	`if (b) ; // Empty statement`
`{`	`{`
`statement1;`	`statement1`
`}`	`}`
`else`	`else // Error here (else without if)`
`{`	`{`
`statement2;`	`statement2`
`}`	`}`

Nested *if-else* Statement

As we discussed in the previous section, each branch in an *if-else* statement can be any type of statement. This means that each branch can be another *if-else* statement. This situation is referred to as a *nested if-else* statement. Although we can have as many levels of nesting as we desire, the program becomes very complicated after a few levels. Figure 4.3 shows a nested *if-else* statement with two levels. Note that nesting can occur in the *if* branch or the *else* branch or both. The figure shows the nesting in both branches.

EXAMPLE 4.5

Let's write a program that determines if one number is greater than, equal to, or less than a second number. The flow diagram is shown in Figure 4.4. Note that the *else* branch in this case has only one task.

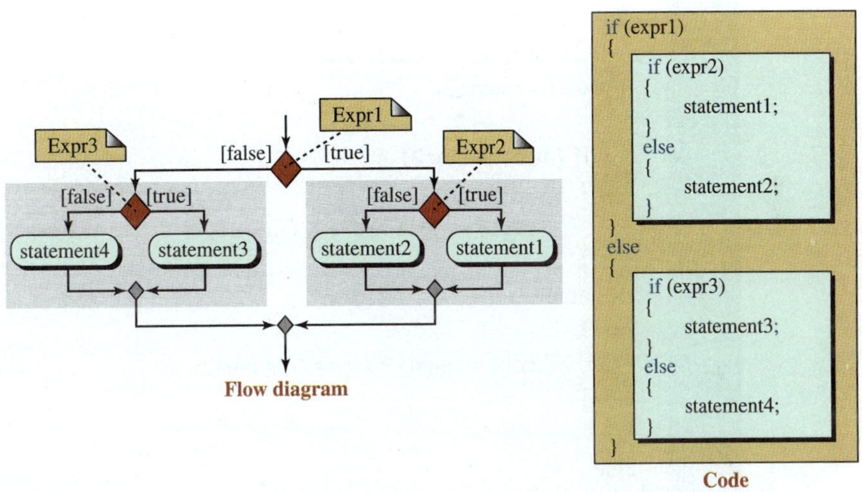

Figure 4.3 Nested *if-else* statement

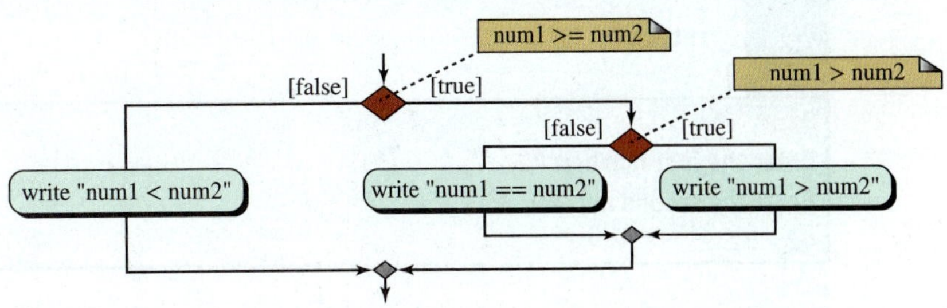

Figure 4.4 The diagram for finding the relationship between two numbers

The solution first determines if the first number is greater than or equal to the second number. If this condition is false, the program has established that `num1` is less than `num2`. If `num1` is greater than or equal to `num2`, the program tests further to find the exact relationship. This is an example of a nested *if-else* statement in which the left branch is just a simple statement. The code is shown in Program 4.5.

Program 4.5 Finding the relationship between two numbers

```
/***************************************************************
 * Find if a number is greater than, equal, or less than another   *
 ***************************************************************/
#include <iostream>
using namespace std;

int main ()
{
  // Declaration
  int num1, num2;
  // Get input values
  cout << "Enter the first number: ";
  cin >> num1;
  cout << "Enter the second number: ";
  cin >> num2;
  // Decision using nested if-else statement
  if (num1 >= num2)
  {
       if (num1 > num2)
       {
            cout << num1 << " > " << num2;
       }
       else
       {
            cout << num1 << " == " << num2;
       }
  }
  else
  {
       cout << num1 << " < " << num2;
  }
  return 0;
}
```

```
Run:
Enter the first number: 42
Enter the second number: 32
42 > 32
```

(continued)

Program 4.5 Find the relationship between two numbers (Continued)

```
Run
Enter the first number: 12
Enter the second number: 12
12 == 12
```

```
Run
Enter the first number: 12
Enter the second number: 28
12 < 28
```

A Serious Pitfall: Dangling Else Problem Nested *if-else* statements may create a classic problem known as the **dangling else.** If in a nested *if-else* statement we can have more *if* branches than *else* branches, we need to know which *if* branch should be paired with which *else* branch. The answer is that the complier matches an *else* with the most recent unpaired *if*. This is done regardless of how we have intended our code.

An *else* is always paired with the most recent unpaired *if*.

Figure 4.5 shows one flow diagram and two coded solutions.

The first code does not correspond with the diagram because the *if* and the *else* sections are wrongly paired. In cases like this, we must use a compound statement as shown in the second code to be sure that the *else* statement is paired with the first *if* statement, not the second. We will see later that there is another solution to this problem: using logical expressions.

Always use compound statements to avoid a dangling else problem.

4.1.4 Multiway Selection

Sometimes we need to solve a problem with several conditions, as shown below. Note that each statement could be a compound statement:

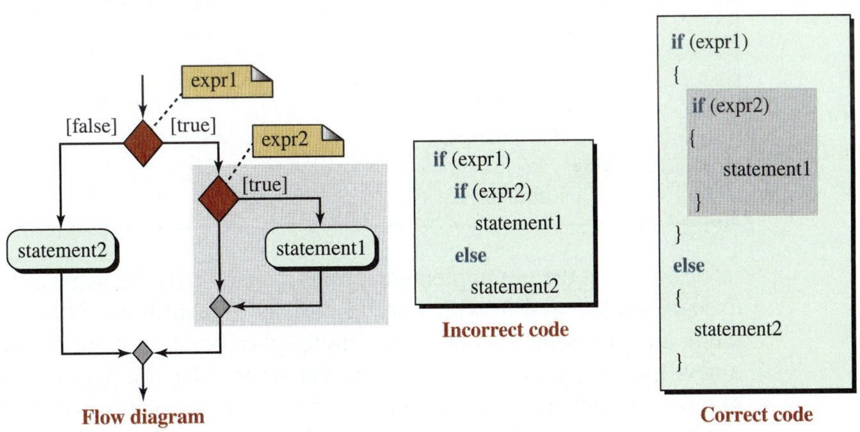

Figure 4.5 Dangling else problem

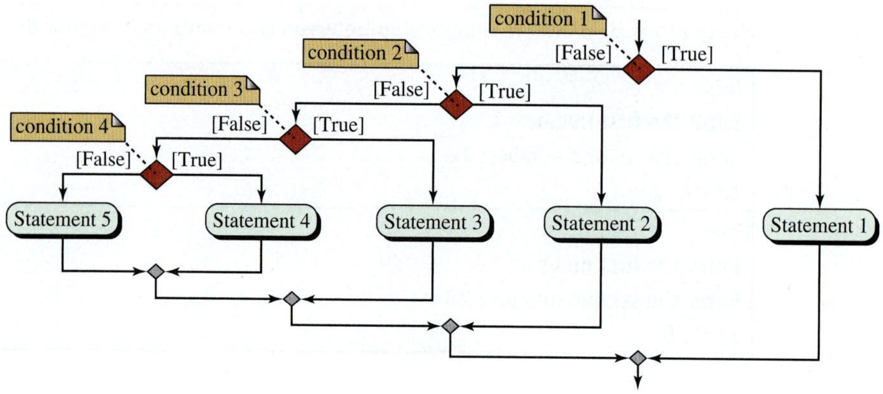

Figure 4.6 Multiway *if-else* selection

```
If condition 1 is true, do statement 1
If condition 2 is true, do statement 2
...
If none of the above conditions is true, do statement n
```

This is known as a **multiway selection.** We can use a nested *if-else* statement to achieve multiway selection. Figure 4.6 shows the flow diagram for multiway conditions with five different statements.

We can format the multiway selection in Figure 4.6 in two different ways, as shown below:

Non-Compact

```
if (condition 1)
  statement 1;
else
  if (condition 2)
      statement 2;
  else
      if (condition 3)
          statement 3;
      else
          if (condition 4)
              statement 4;
          else
              statement 5;
```

Compact

```
if (condition 1)
  statement 1;
else if (condition 2)
  statement 2;
else if (condition 3)
  statement 3;
else if (condition 4)
  statement 4;
else
  statement 5;
```

Note that the left implementation is syntactically the same as the right implementation except that *else* and *if*, which are in two subsequent lines without any statement between them, are combined with only one single space between them. As far as C++ is concerned, a new line character and a space are the same. The compact format is both shorter in the number of lines and requires less indentions. It is much easier to read. To keep the code short, we have not used braces. Braces should always be used in a program, as shown in the next example.

EXAMPLE 4.6

Assume a professor wants to write a program to determine the letter grade (A, B, C, D, and F) for a test score between 0 and 100. The code, using multiway selection, is shown in Program 4.6.

Program 4.6 Finding a grade related to a score

```
/********************************************************************
 * Find a grade given a score using the multi-way selection         *
 ********************************************************************/
#include <iostream>
using namespace std;

int main ()
{
  // Declaration
  int score;
  char grade;
  // Get Input
  cout << "Enter a score between 0 and 100: ";
  cin >> score;
  // Multi-way decision using if-else
  if (score >= 90)
  {
       grade = 'A';
  }
  else if (score >= 80)
  {
       grade = 'B';
  }
  else if (score >= 70)
  {
       grade = 'C';
  }
  else if (score >= 60)
  {
       grade = 'D';
  }
  else
  {
       grade = 'F';
  }
  // Output
  cout << "The grade is: " << grade;
  return 0;
} // End main
```

(continued)

Program 4.6 Finding a grade related to a score (Continued)

```
Run:
Enter a score between 0 and 100: 83
The grade is B
```

```
Run:
Enter a score between 0 and 100: 65
The grade is D
```

```
Run:
Enter a score between 0 and 100: 95
The grade is A
```

4.2 COMPLEX DECISIONS

In the previous section, we solved some decision-making problems using the relational and equality expressions. Sometimes the decision to be made is more complex and we need more expression types to define it. For example, we cannot make a decision based on a value in a specific range, such as *x* should be between 5 and 10. We need to deploy more expressions. In this section, we introduce three logical expressions that facilitate more complex decisions. These logical expressions can be used in other areas of computer programming, such as repetition, that we discuss in future chapters.

4.2.1 Logical Expressions

Logical expressions use logical operators that take one or two operands of Boolean type and create a Boolean type. We have three logical operators: NOT (!), AND (&&), and OR (||). Appendix C shows all C++ expressions; we include only those expressions we need in this section in Table 4.2. We also include the relational and equality expressions in Table 4.2 so we can see the relationship among all expressions that are necessary in creating selection statements. Note that the ***logical-not*** **expression** has a very high precedence (even more than relational and equality expressions), but ***logical-and*** and ***logical-or*** **expressions** have a very low precedence. We must also pay attention to the associativity of the *logical-not* (which is right to left).

Table 4.2 Precedence and associativity of some expressions

Group	Name	Operator	Expression	Pred	Assoc
Unary	logical not	!	! expr	17	←
Relational	less less or equal greater greater or equal	< <= > >=	expr < expr expr <= expr expr > expr expr >= expr	11	→
Equality	equal not equal	== !=	expr == expr expr != expr	10	→
Logical AND	logical and	&&	expr && expr	6	→
Logical OR	logical or	||	expr || expr	5	→

NOT

Operand	Result
false	true
true	false

AND

Left	Right	Result
false	false	false
false	true	false
true	false	false
true	true	true

OR

Left	Right	Result
false	false	false
false	true	true
true	false	true
true	true	true

Figure 4.7 Logical expression and their truth tables

The best way to show the result of a logical expression is to use a truth table. Figure 4.7 shows the three logical operators and their interpretations.

In the case of the *not* expression, we have only one input. Note that conversion occurs if we use operands other than true or false for this operator. The following shows some examples of using the *logical-not* expression.

```
!true        // The result is false.
!false       // The result is true.
!5           // First, 5 is converted to Boolean true. The result is false.
!0           // First, 0 is converted to Boolean false. The result is true.
```

The *and* expression needs to see two Boolean values as its operands. The result is the Boolean value *true* if and only if both operands are *true*; the result is *false* if either of the operands is *false*. Again note that conversion occurs if we use operands other than true or false for these operators. The following shows some examples of using the logical *and* expression.

```
true && true          // The result is true.
false && true         // The result is false.
(3 < 5) && (4 > 2)    // It is true && true. The result is true.
(4 < 6) && (2 == 3)   // It is true && false. The result is false.
6 && false            // First, 6 is converted to true. The result is false.
4 && 0                // First 4 is converted to true and 0 to false. The result is false.
```

The *or* expression also needs to see two Boolean values as its operands. The result is the Boolean value *false* if and only if both operands are *false*; the result is *true* if either of the operands is *true*. Again note that conversion occurs if we use operands other than true or false for these operators.The following shows some logical *or* expressions and their results.

```
true || true          // The result is true.
false || false        // The result is false.
(1 < 4) || (2 ==3)    // It is (true || false). The result is true.
(4 < 3) || (4 <= 3)   // It is (false || false). The result is false.
3 || false            // First, 3 is converted to true. The result is true.
0 || false            // First 0 is converted to false. The result is false.
```

The following shows how precedence and associativity affect calculation of the complex expressions. Adding parentheses in our calculation helps us find the result.

```
!false && true              // This is (!false) && true. The result is true.
false || true && false      // This is false || (true && false). The result is false.
2 == 2 || 5 < 6 && false    // This is true || (false && false). The result is true.
```

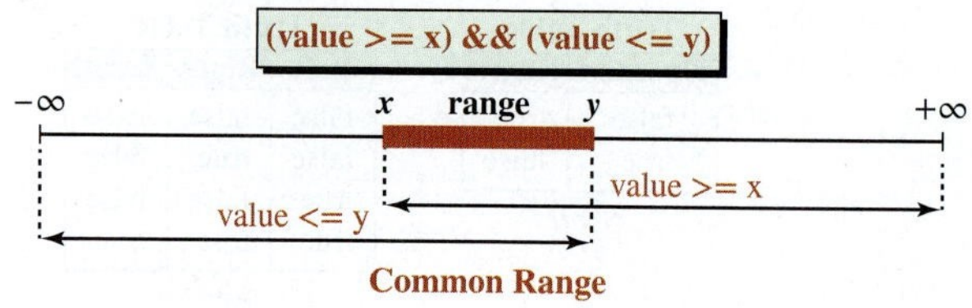

Figure 4.8 A common range as the combination of two relations

4.2.2 Use of Logical Expressions

We can code complex selection criteria using the combination of relational/equality expressions and logical expressions. Let's take a look at some cases.

Use Of AND Expression

Since the result of an *and* expression is *true* when both operands are true, we can use an *and* expression when we need the two conditions to be true to do something. In other words, the expression

```
condition1 && condition2
```

is true when both condition1 and condition2 are true. For example, to test if a number is inside a range, we need two conditions, as shown in Figure 4.8.

EXAMPLE 4.7

Assume a car rental company defines the minimum and maximum age to rent a car to be 25 and 100, respectively. Program 4.7 shows how a person's age can be tested using a simple decision-making code.

Program 4.7 Finding age eligibility

```
/*******************************************************************
 * Find age eligibility to rent a car                              *
 *******************************************************************/
#include <iostream>
using namespace std;

int main ()
{
  // Declaration of variables
  int age;
  bool eligible;
  // Getting input
  cout << "Enter your age: ";
  cin >> age;
```

(*continued*)

Program 4.7 Finding age eligibility (Continued)

```
    // Setting the condition
    eligible = (age >=25) && (age <= 100);
    // Testing the condition and output
    if (eligible)
    {
        cout << "You are eligible to rent a car.";
    }
    else
    {
        cout << "Sorry! You are not eligible to rent a car.";
    }
    return 0;
}
```

```
Run:
Enter your age: 27
You are eligible to rent a car.
```

```
Run:
Enter your age: 54
You are eligible to rent a car.
```

```
Run:
Enter your age: 103
Sorry! You are not eligible to rent a car.
```

```
Run:
Enter your age: 21
Sorry! You are not eligible to rent a car.
```

Use of OR Expression

Since the result of an *or* expression is *true* when either of the operands is true, we must think of an *or* operator when we need to test if at least one of the two conditions is true in a decision. In other words, the expression

```
condition1 || condition2
```

is true when either condition1 or condition2 (or both) is *true*. For example, to test if a number is outside a range, we need to test two conditions, as shown in Figure 4.9.

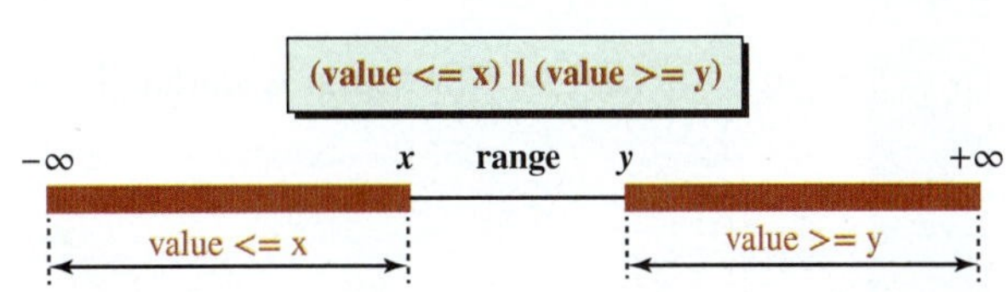

Figure 4.9 A disjoint range as the combination of two relations

Note that for the test to work, x and y must be distinct and y must be larger than x. Otherwise, there is an overlap and the range is not distinct.

EXAMPLE 4.8

Assume we want the air-conditioning system in a house to be on when the inside temperature is above 75 degrees or below 60 degrees Fahrenheit. We can simulate this by inputting the temperature and turning on the air-conditioning system as shown in Program 4.8. After the system is on, the program can decide to turn on the heater or the cooler. Note that for either the heater or the cooler to be on, the air-conditioning system must be turned on first.

Program 4.8 Turning the air-conditioning system on and off

```
/*************************************************************
 * Turn the air conditioning system on if the temperature is  *
 * below or above a certain temperature.                      *
 *************************************************************/
#include <iostream>
using namespace std;

int main ()
{
  // Variable declaration
   int temperature;
   bool hot;
   bool cold;
  // Input the temperature
   cout << "Enter the temperature: ";
   cin >> temperature;
  // Set two conditions
   hot = temperature >= 75;
   cold = temperature <= 65;
  // Make the decision
   if (hot || cold)
   {
        cout << "The air condition system is turned on!" << endl;
        if (hot)
        {
             cout << "The cooler is working!" << endl;
        }
        else
        {
             cout << "The heater is working!" << endl;
        }
   }
   else
   {
```

(continued)

Program 4.8 Turning the air-conditioning system on and off (Continued)

```
            cout << "The air condition system is turned off!" << endl;
        }
        return 0;
    }
```

```
Run:
Enter the temperature: 73
The air condition system is turned off!
```

```
Run:
Enter the temperature: 63
The air condition system is turned on!
The heater is working!
```

```
Run:
Enter the temperature: 82
The air condition system is turned on!
The cooler is working!
```

Use of NOT Expression

The *not* operator flips the value of a logical expression. If the logical expression is originally *true*, the result is *false*; if the logical expression is originally *false*, the result is *true*. In other words, the result of the following expression is the inverse of the given condition.

```
!condition
```

EXAMPLE 4.9

In our current calendar, the month of February has 28 days instead of 29. To check for a leap year, we need to check three conditions. If a year is divisible by 400, it is definitely a leap year. Otherwise, if the year is divisible by 4, but not by 100, it is also a leap year. The condition can be written using the logical expression shown below:

```
leapYear = (divisibleBy400) || (divisibleBy4 && !(divisibleBy100))
```

Program 4.9 shows how we can use the above condition to test if a given year is a leap year.

Program 4.9 Finding if a given year is a leap year

```
/***************************************************************
  * Find if a given year is a leap year testing three conditions     *
  ***************************************************************/
#include <iostream>
using namespace std;

int main ()
{
```

(*continued*)

Program 4.9 Finding if a given year is a leap year (Continued)

```
    // Variable declaration
    int year;
    bool divBy400, divBy4, divBy100;
    bool leapYear;
    // Input year
    cout << "Enter the year: ";
    cin >> year;
    // Set conditions
    divBy400 = ((year % 400) == 0);
    divBy4 = ((year % 4) == 0);
    divBy100 = ((year % 100) == 0);
    leapYear = (divBy400) || (divBy4 && !(divBy100));
    // Decision and output
    if (leapYear)
    {
        cout << "Year " << year << " is a leap year." << endl;
    }
    else
    {
        cout << "Year " << year << " is not a leap year." << endl;
    }
    return 0;
}
```

```
Run:
Enter the year: 2000
Year 2000 is a leap year.
```

```
Run:
Enter the year: 1900
Year 1900 is not a leap year.
```

```
Run:
Enter the year: 2012
Year 2012 is a leap year.
```

```
Run:
Enter the year: 2014
Year 2014 is not a leap year.
```

Removal of Not Operator

There are occasions when we write a condition and we end up with a *not* operator in front of the expression, which sometimes can be difficult to comprehend or interpret.

Expressions Involving Relational or Equality Operators If the expression after the *not* operator is relational or an inequality, it is simple to remove the *not* operator and change the expression because we can easily find another expression that is the opposite of the one we have. The following shows how to remove a *not* operator in front of a relational or equality expression.

!(x < 7)	⟶	(x >= 7)	!(x >= 7)	⟶	(x < 7)
!(x > 7)	⟶	(x <= 7)	!(x <= 7)	⟶	(x > 7)
!(x == 7)	⟶	(x != 7)	!(x != 7)	⟶	(x == 7)

Expressions Involving Logical-And or Logical-Or Operators When an expression involves a *logical-and* or a *logical-or* operator, the case is not simple. We need to use one of the two forms of what is called **De Morgan's law,** named after logician August De Morgan (1806–1871). The two forms are shown below:

!(x && y)	⟶	(!x || !y)	!(x || y)	⟶	(!x && !y)

In other words, we can remove the *not* operator in front of the *logical-and* expression if we change the *logical-and* operator to the *logical-or* operator and insert the *not* operator in front of each expression. Conversely, we can remove the *not* operator in front of the *logical-or* expression if we change the *logical-or* operator to the *logical-and* operator and insert the *not* operator in front of each expression.

At first glance, it looks like we are elongating the expression by removing one *not* operator and adding two *not* operators, but we are simplifying the expression and making it easier to understand.

EXAMPLE 4.10

Assume we want to stop jogging when the temperature is below 35 degrees Fahrenheit (too cold) or above 90 degrees Fahrenheit (too hot). We can write the stop condition as

```
Stop Condition ⟶ (temp < 35) || (temp > 90)
```

If we want to find the continue jogging conditions, we can easily negate the above expression as

```
Continue Condition ⟶ !((temp < 35) || (temp > 90))
```

The second form of De Morgan's law allows us to write the expression as

```
Continue Condition ⟶ (!(temp < 35) && !(temp > 90))
```

Although we have two *logical-not* operators here, we can simplify the expression (using the rules we learn in this section) to get a better picture.

```
Continue Condition ⟶ (temp >= 35) && (temp <= 90)
```

The last version says that we can continue to jog as long as the temperature is between 35 and 90.

Swapping *if* and *else* Blocks

Sometimes we want to swap the *if* and *else* blocks in an *if-else* statement. We can do this by flipping the condition in the *if* clause. This is helpful when the *if* block is empty as shown below. By swapping the *if* and *else* blocks, we can make the *else* block empty, and the empty block can be removed to a simple decision. Note that we cannot eliminate the empty *if* block, but we can eliminate the empty *else* block. Let us see how this can help to simplify the code as shown below:

// Original code	// After swapping	//After simplifying

if (x)
{
 	
}
else
{
  statement;
}
	if (!x)
	{
	  statement;
	}
	else
	{
	
	}
		if (!x)
		{
		  statement;
		}

Short-Circuit Behavior: A Problem to Be Aware Of

C++ tries to be efficient and uses what is called **short-circuit behavior.** This behavior can happen in both logical *and* and logical *or* expressions.

Short-Circuit Behavior with Logical AND Operator In an *and* expression, C++ evaluates the left operand. If it is *false*, it does not evaluate the right operand because the result is *false* regardless of the value of the right operand. If the left operand is *true*, then the right operand is evaluated. Although this behavior does not affect our program in many cases, it may affect our program when the right operand has a side effect. This means that we should avoid using expressions with side effects as the right operand. The following shows two examples.

```
(3 < 2) && (x = 2)        // The second operand is ignored. x is not changed.
(2 < 6) && (x = 2)        // The second operand is evaluated. The integer 2 is stored in x.
```

Short-Circuit Behavior with Logical OR Operator In an *or* expression, C++ evaluates the left operand. If it is *true*, it does not evaluate the right operand because the result is *true* regardless of the value of the right operand. If the left operand is *false*, then the right operand is evaluated. Although this behavior does not affect our program in many cases, it may affect our program when the right operand has a side effect. This means that we should avoid using expressions with side effects as the right operand with the logical-or operator. The following shows two examples.

```
(2 < 5) || (x = 3)        // The second operand is ignored. x is not changed.
(7 < 6) || (x = 5)        // The second operand is evaluated. The integer 5 is stored in x.
```

We recommend avoiding side effects in a logical expression.

4.3 DECISIONS ON SPECIFIC VALUES

In the previous two sections we discussed decision-making processes that depend on Boolean conditions. We tested a single condition and multiple conditions. In each case, if the condition was *true*, we did something; otherwise, we did something else or nothing. Sometimes we need to make multiple decisions, but the decision to be made in each case is not based on Boolean conditions; the decision is based on some specific integral values. For example, we may have to do a different task on each day of the week. This is a decision-making process

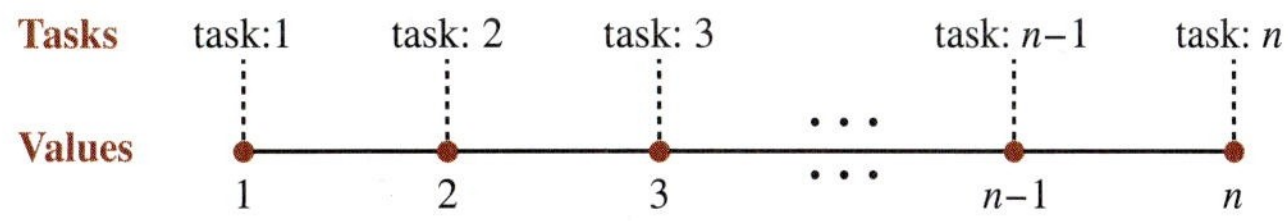

Figure 4.10 Decision based on integral values

based on one of the seven values for the day: 1, 2, 3, 4, 5, 6, or 7. Although we can still use seven conditions (day == 1), (day == 2) , … , (day == 7) and use a multiple *if-else* statement, C++ has a better solution for us: the *switch* statement, which we discuss next.

4.3.1 Switch Statement

Another multiway decision construct in C++ is the ***switch* statement**, in which the decision is based on specific values. Figure 4.10 shows the case in which we must test specific values (1 to *n*) and, based on the result, we must do one of the *n* tasks.

Structure of Switch Statement

Before we discuss how the *switch* statement can be used for multivalue decisions, let us look at the structure of this statement. The basic *switch* statement is designed for what is called a *fall through* flow. Figure 4.11 shows the flow diagram and the syntax of a switch statement with four cases (we can have as many cases as we need).

The *switch* statement makes a decision to enter the *fall through* flow when the value of the expression matches a value defined in one of the cases. In other words, entering the *fall through* is based on a value, but when the flow enters the *fall through*, it goes all the way to the end and executes all remaining fall through statements.

In the figure, the value of the expression is first compared to the value1. If there is a match, `statement1` through `statement4` are all executed. If the value of the expression does not match `value1`, but matches `value2`, `statement2` through `statement4` are executed (`statement1` is skipped). If none of the values are matched, no statement is executed. The value in the *case* clauses should be unique.

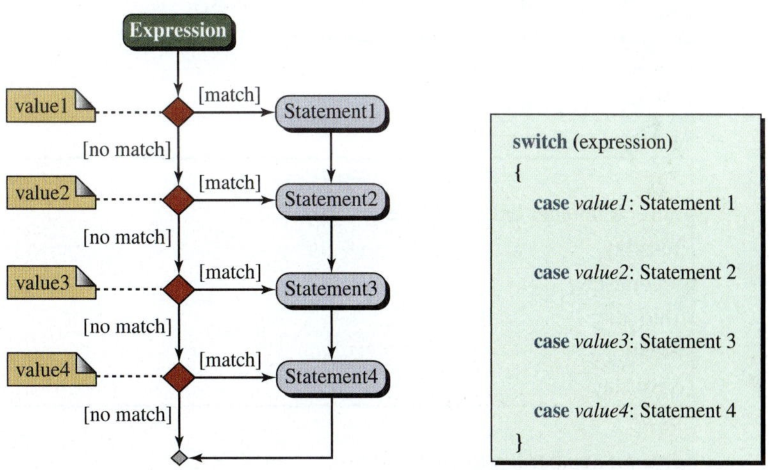

(a) Flow diagram **(b) Switch statement**

Figure 4.11 Water fall flow of a switch statement

EXAMPLE 4.11

To show how a switch statement works, we use Program 4.10. In this program, we assign integer values, 0 to 6, to the days of the week (Sunday through Saturday) and see how a switch statement enters the week at a specific day (defined by the input value) and prints the name of the day and the names of the rest of the days in the week.

Program 4.10 Printing the days of the week

```
/*****************************************************************
 * Use a switch statement to print the days of the weeks from a    *
 * specific day to the end of the week.                            *
 *****************************************************************/
#include <iostream>
using namespace std;

int main ()
{
  // Declaration
  int day;
  // Input
  cout << "Enter a number between 0 and 6: ";
  cin >> day;
  // Switch statement (decision and output)
  switch (day)
  {
      case 0: cout << "Sunday" << endl;
      case 1: cout << "Monday" << endl;
      case 2: cout << "Tuesday" << endl;
      case 3: cout << "Wednesday" << endl;
      case 4:  cout << "Thursday" << endl;
      case 5: cout << "Friday" << endl;
      case 6: cout <<"Saturday" << endl;
  } // End switch
  return 0;
}// End main
```

```
Run:
Enter a number between 0 and 6: 2
Tuesday
Wednesday
Thursday
Friday
Saturday
```

```
Run:
Enter a number between 1 and 6: 4
Thursday
```

(continued)

Program 4.10 Printing the days of the week (Continued)

```
Friday
Saturday
Run:
Enter a number between 1 and 6: 6
Saturday
Run:
Enter a number between 1 and 6: 8
```

We run the program four times. The first time we enter 2 for the integer day; the switch enters at the case 2 and prints the rest of the week (Tuesday through Saturday). In the second run, we enter 4 for the integer day; the *switch* statement enters at the case 4 and prints the rest of the week (Thursday through Saturday). In the third run, we enter 6; the program only prints the last day of the week (Saturday). In the fourth run, we enter 8, which is not in the list of integral values; nothing is printed.

Switch Statement with Breaks

To use the switch statement for multivalue selection, we must add *break* statements. A *break* statement breaks the flow of the program at the time the statement is encountered and jumps to the end of the *switch* statement. Figure 4.12 shows the *switch* statement with the break statement added at each branch. We can see that each time we enter the *switch* statement, only one path is followed, the one that matches the expression. Compare the flow diagrams of Figure 4.11 and Figure 4.12 to see the differences. Figure 4.11 uses fall through; Figure 4.12 uses selection.

EXAMPLE 4.12

Let us change Program 4.10 to a *switch* statement with breaks. Program 4.11 shows the result. In each run of the program only one day is printed. Like before, we enter 3 for the

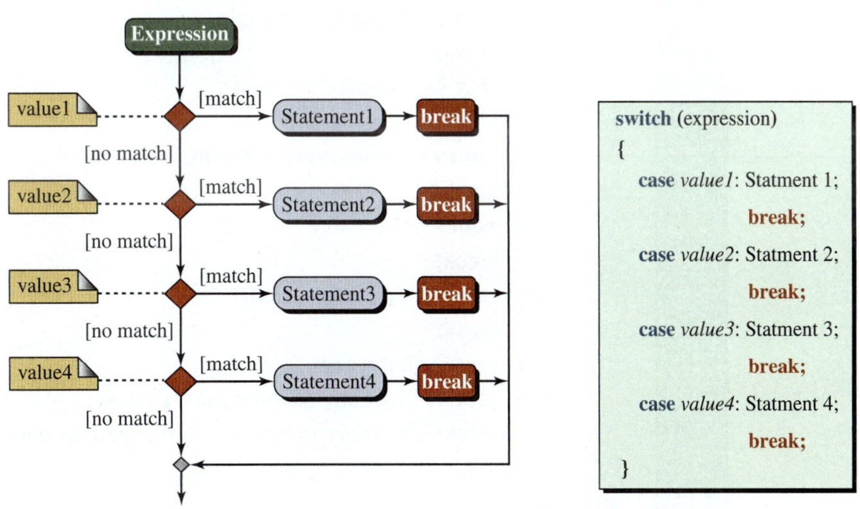

(a) Flow diagram (b) Switch statement

Figure 4.12 Switch statement with breaks

integer day in the first run; the result is Tuesday. In the second run, we enter 5 for the integer day; the result is Thursday. When we enter 8 for the integer day, none of the cases match and nothing is printed. Note that the last break is not really needed, but good programmers add it to make the symmetry complete. Note also that we have added a second output in the first and last cases to demonstrate that multiple statements can also be executed in any case branch.

Program 4.11 Printing the day of the week from a given day

```
/****************************************************************
 * Use a swith statement with break to print the name of the     *
 * week day.                                                     *
 ****************************************************************/
#include <iostream>
using namespace std;

int main ()
{
  // Declaration
  int day;
  // Input
  cout << "Enter a number between 0 and 6: ";
  cin >> day;
  // Switch statement (Decision and output)
  switch (day)
  {
      case 0: cout << "Sunday" << endl;
              cout << "First day of the week " << endl;
              break;
      case 1: cout << "Monday" << endl;
              break;
      case 2: cout << "Tuesday" << endl;
              break;
      case 3:  cout << "Wednesday" << endl;
              break;
      case 4:  cout << "Thursday" << endl;
              break;
      case 5: cout << "Friday" << endl;
              break;
      case 6: cout <<"Saturday" << endl;
              cout << "Last day of the week " << endl;
              break; // This is not needed, but added for parallelism
  } // End switch
  return 0;
}// End main
```

(continued)

Program 4.11 Printing the day of the week from a given day (Continued)

```
Run:
Enter a number between 0 and 6: 0
Sunday
First day of the week
```

```
Run:
Enter a number between 0 and 6: 4
Thursday
```

```
Run:
Enter a number between 0 and 6: 6
Saturday
Last day of the week
```

```
Run:
Enter a number between 0 and 6: 8
```

Adding Default

Sometimes we have several cases that need to take the same action. In this case, if all of the cases are at the end of the switch statement, we can make the statement shorter by adding a **default case.** A *default* case is entered when none of the cases match.

The *default* case can also be used for error detection. It can be used to detect the error when none of the cases match the given value. However, we need to know that the *default* case can be used only once, as the last case.

The *default* case must be the last case in a *switch* statement.

This means if we use the *default* to catch several case values, it cannot be used for error detection. We need to use other tools. The next example shows the use of a *default* case.

EXAMPLE 4.13

Let us show how we can use the *switch* statement to change a test score to a letter grade. We have a problem that needs to be solved; the grade is based on a range of scores, not a single value. For example, if a score is in the range 90 to 100, the grade should be assigned the letter 'A'. However, we can solve the problem using a *switch* statement if we change the ranges to single values using the division operator. If we divide a score between 0 and 100 by 10, we get a value between 0 and 10. Program 4.12 shows how to solve the problem using this technique.

Program 4.12 Printing a grade from a score

```
/***************************************************************
 * Use a swith statement to print a grade from a given score.  *
 ***************************************************************/
#include <iostream>
using namespace std;

```

(continued)

Program 4.12 Printing a grade from a score (Continued)

```
int main ()
{
  // Declaration
  int score;
  char grade;
  // Input
  cout << "Enter a score between 0 and 100: ";
  cin >> score;
  // Decision making using switch statement
  switch (score / 10)
  {
       case 10: grade = 'A';
                break;
       case 9 : grade = 'A';
                break;
       case 8 : grade = 'B';
                break;
       case 7 : grade = 'C';
                break;
       case 6 : grade = 'D';
                break;
       default: grade = 'F';
       } // End switch
  // Output
  cout << "Score: " << score << endl;
  cout << "Grade: " << grade << endl;
  return 0;
}
```

```
Run:
Enter a score between 0 and 100: 71
Score: 71
Grade: C
```

```
Run:
Enter a score between 0 and 100: 93
Score: 93
Grade: A
```

```
Run:
Enter a score between 0 and 100: 24
Score: 24
Grade: F
```

As you can see, we have used a *default* case to handle several cases (5, 4, 3, 2, 1, 0), which means all grades less than 60. However, we still have a problem. What if the user enters a score less than 0 or greater than 100? The program will give the grade F. To handle this problem, we need to test the validity of the input first. One way to do this is as follows.

```
cout << "Enter a score between 0 and 100: ";
cin >> score;
if (score > 100)
{
  score = 100;
}
if (score < 0)
{
  score = 0;
}
```

We will see a better input validation strategy when we discuss repetition in the next chapter.

Combining Cases

If the task performed by several cases is the same, we can combine the cases. This is possible because the *fall through* nature of the *switch* statement allows the program to go through the cases until a *break* statement is encountered. We show the idea in the next example.

EXAMPLE 4.14

In Program 4.13 we read a letter grade and print a pass/no-pass grade. The default statement serves as the error detector.

Program 4.13 Finding a pass/no-pass grade

```
/***************************************************************
 * Use a switch statement to find a pass/nopass grade.        *
 ***************************************************************/
#include <iostream>
using namespace std;

int main ()
{
  // Declaration
   char grade;
  // Input
   cout << "Enter a grade (A, B, C, D, F): ";
   cin >> grade;
  // Decision section using switch statement
   switch (grade)
   {
       case 'A':
```

(*continued*)

Program 4.13 Finding a pass/no-pass grade (Continued)

```
        case 'B':
        case 'C': cout << "Grade is pass";
                break;
        case 'D':
        case 'F': cout << "Grade is nopass";
                break;
        default: cout <<"Error in the input. Try again.";
    } // End switch
    return 0;
}// End main
```

```
Run:
Enter a grade (A, B, C, D, F): A
Grade is pass
```

```
Run:
Enter a grade (A, B, C, D, F): D
Grade is nopass
```

```
Run:
Enter a grade (A, B, C, D, F): F
Grade is nopass
```

```
Run:
Enter a grade (A, B, C, D, F): G
Error in the input. Try again.
```

```
Run:
Enter a grade (A, B, C, D, F): B
Grade is pass
```

```
Run:
Enter a grade (A, B, C, D, F): C
Grade is pass
```

4.4 CONDITIONAL EXPRESSIONS

Another construct that can be used for decision making is the **conditional expression.** It is the only *ternary* expression in C++. It uses two operators and three operands, as discussed next.

4.4.1 Structure of a Conditional Expression

The following shows the syntax of a conditional expression.

```
condition ? expression1 : expression2
```

Table 4.3 shows the location of conditional expressions in the list of expressions in Appendix C.

Table 4.3 Conditional expression

Group	Name	Operator	Expression	Pred	Assoc
Conditional	conditional	? :	expr1 ? expr2 : expr3	4	←

The type *expr1* must be a Boolean expression with a *true* or *false* value. The type *expr2* and *expr3* must be the same, but the common type can be any type discussed in previous chapters. The whole construct is also an expression with a value. The value of the whole expression is the value of *expr2* if *expr1* is *true*; otherwise, it is the value of *expr3*.

The conditional expression can be used anywhere an expression can be used.

4.4.2 Comparison

Let us compare the conditional expression with the two-way *if-else* statement as shown in Figure 4.13.

- The two-way *if-else* statement is made of a Boolean expression with a true branch and a false branch. The logical expression is made of a Boolean expression and two expressions, one for *true* and one for *false*.
- A two-way *if-else* statement is a statement; it can be used anywhere we can use a statement. The *conditional expression* is an expression, it can also be used anywhere we can use an expression. We can use it in one of the following ways:
  a. We can use as an expression in a statement.
  b. We can add a semicolon at the end to change it to a stand-alone statement. This method is useful when both the second and third statements have a side effect.

EXAMPLE 4.15

In Program 4.14 we print the larger of two integers using a *conditional* expression.

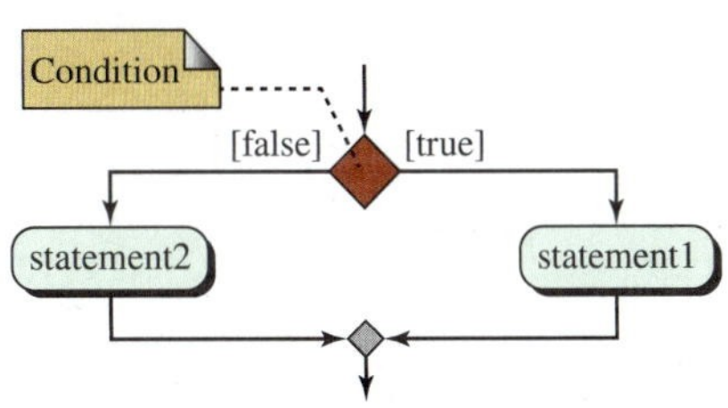

(a) Flow diagram

```
if (condition)
        statement1;
else
        statement2;
```

(b) Using if-else statement

```
x = condition ? statement1 : stateemnt2;      // As part of another statement
condition ?  statement1 : statement2;         // As an expression statement
```

(c) Using a condtional expression

Figure 4.13 Comparing *if-else* statement and conditional expression

Program 4.14 Conditional expression

```
/**************************************************************
 * Uses a conditional expression to print the larger of two    *
 * numbers or the first if the numbers are equal               *
 **************************************************************/
#include <iostream>
using namespace std;

int main ()
{
  // Declaration
   int num1, num2;
   int larger;
  // Input
   cout << "Enter the first number: ";
   cin >> num1;
   cout << "Enter the second number: ";
   cin >> num2;
  // Decision making
   larger = num1 >= num2 ? num1 : num2;
  // Output
   cout << "The larger is: " << larger;
   return 0;
}// End main
```

```
Run:
Enter the first number: 40
Enter the second number: 25
The larger is: 40
```

```
Run:
Enter the first number: 22
Enter the second number: 67
The larger is: 67
```

4.5 PROGRAM DESIGN

In this section, we design and implement four programs. We use the software development process we discussed in Chapter 3: *understand the problem*, *develop an algorithm*, and *write the code*.

4.5.1 Student's Score

Let us create a program that helps a professor find the score of a student in a class based on the result of three tests. The professor believes that the student's score should be the average of the maximum and minimum of the three scores.

Understand the Problem

We need input, processing, and output. We need to input the three scores. Next we must find the maximum and the minimum scores of the three input scores. Finally, we must find the average of the two and set the student's score to the average. Although there are more efficient methods discussed in future chapters, we first find the maximum score and then the minimum score using nested if-else structure. The student score is the average of the minimum and the maximum scores.

Develop the Algorithm

Based on our understanding, we can create the following algorithm.

```
1. Input
   a. input score1
   b. input score2
   c. input score3
2. Process
   a. find the maxScore
      1. if score1 is greater than the other two, maxScore is score1
      2. else if score2 is greater than the other two, maxScore is score2
      3. else maxScore is score3
   b. find the minScore
      1. if score1 is smaller than the other two, minScore is score1
      2. else if score2 is smaller than the other two, minScore is score2
      3. else minScore is score3
   c. find the student's score
      1. add maxScore and minScore
      2. divide the result by two to get the student's score
3. Output
   a. Output three scores
   b. Output minScore and maxScoe
   c. Output the student's score
```

Write the Code

Now we can write the code based on the developed algorithm (Program 4.15). The only section of the program that needs some explanation is lines 47 to 52. The maximum and minimum scores are of type integer, and we want the student score to be of type integer. If the sum of the maximum and minimum scores is odd, we add 1 to it to make the sum even. Adding 1 effectively rounds the result of the division up to the higher score; otherwise, the score would be truncated to the lower score.

Program 4.15 Finding the student score based on three tests

```
1  /**************************************************************
2   * Finding the student score based on the given three scores        *
3   * The program sets the student score to the average of maximum     *
4   * and minimum of the three scores                                  *
5   **************************************************************/
```

(continued)

Program 4.15 Finding the student score based on three tests (Continued)

```
#include <iostream>
using namespace std;

int main ( )
{
  // Declarations
  int score1, score2, score3, maxScore, minScore, score;
  // Input
  cout << "Enter the first score: ";
  cin >> score1;
  cout << "Enter the second score: ";
  cin >> score2;
  cout << "Enter the third score: ";
  cin >> score3;
  // Find maximum score
  if (score1 > score2 && score1 > score3)
  {
       maxScore = score1;
  }
  else if (score2 > score1 && score2 > score3)
  {
       maxScore = score2;
  }
  else
  {
       maxScore = score3;
  }
  // Find minimum score
  if (score1 < score2 && score1 < score3)
  {
       minScore = score1;
  }
  else if (score2 < score1 && score2 <= score3)
  {
       minScore = score2;
  }
  else
  {
       minScore = score3;
  }
  // Find and round the student score
  int temp = maxScore + minScore;
  if (temp % 2 == 1)
```

(*continued*)

Program 4.15 Finding the student score based on three tests (Continued)

```
    {
        temp += 1;
    }
    score = temp / 2;
    // Print results
    cout << "Scores: " << score1 << " " << score2 << " " << score3 << endl;
    cout << "minimum and maximum scores: ";
    cout << minScore << " " << maxScore << endl;
    cout << "Student score: " << score;
    return 0;
}
```

```
Run:
Enter the first score: 78
Enter the second score: 92
Enter the third score: 79
Scores: 78 92 79
minimum and maximum scores: 78 92
Student score: 85
```

```
Run:
Enter the first score: 65
Enter the second score: 93
Enter the third score: 60
Scores: 65 93 60
minimum and maximum scores: 60 93
Student score: 77
```

4.5.2 Finding the Tax for a Given Income

Let us design a program that calculates and prints the tax for a given income.

Understand the Problem

Income tax in many countries is bracketed, which means there are different tax rates for each bracket as shown in Figure 4.14.

The total tax is the sum of the taxes in each bracket (Table 4.4). A person in bracket1 pays tax1. A person in bracket2 pays the sum of tax1 and tax2. A person in bracket3 pays tax1, tax2, and tax3. A person in bracket4 pays tax1, tax2, tax3, and tax4. The *diff* in the table means the difference between the income and the previous limit.

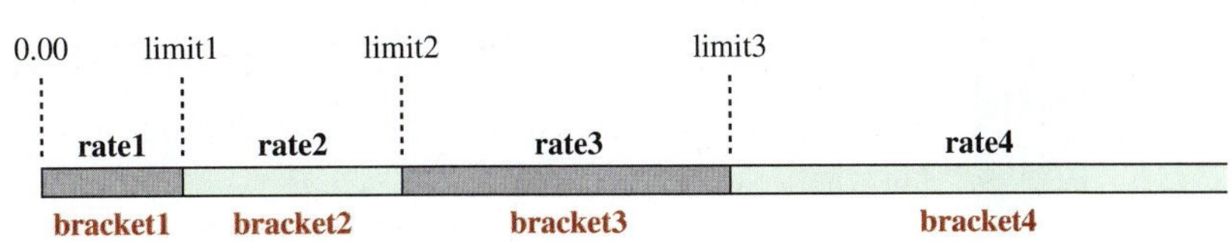

Figure 4.14 Concept of bracketed tax

Table 4.4 Tax brackets

Bracket	Tax1	Tax2	Tax3	Tax4
bracket 1	diff × rate1			
bracket 2	limit1 × rate1	diff × rate2		
bracket 3	limit1 × rate1	limit2 × rate2	diff × rate3	
bracket 4	limit1 × rate1	limit2 × rate2	limit3 × rate3	diff × rate4

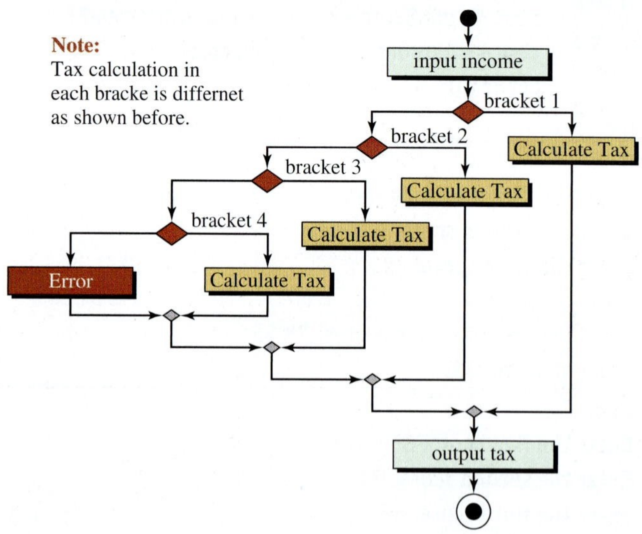

Figure 4.15 Flow diagram for design of calculating income tax

Develop the Algorithm

The algorithm in this case is simple. We input the income, calculate the tax using nested if-else constructs, and then print the tax amounts as shown in Figure 4.15.

Write the Code

We create a program based on the two previous sections, we make the program reusable when the rate and the bracket ranges change in the future, and we declare the rate and limit instead of literally coding them in the program. We also create four Boolean variables that define in which bracket the income belongs (bracket1 to bracket4). If bracket1 is true, the income is in the first bracket and so on. To prevent errors (like a negative input for income), we create another branch in the *if-else* statement to handle error conditions. If the user enters a negative income, the program prints a message and immediately returns lines 44 and 45. The return statement in line 45 is needed to print the result in lines 48 and 49. See Program 4.16.

Program 4.16 An individual's tax burden

```
1  /***************************************************************
2   * Finding the tax of an individual using four different tax     *
3   * brackets                                                      *
4   ***************************************************************/
```

(continued)

Program 4.16 An individual's tax burden (Continued)

```
#include <iostream>
using namespace std;

int main ( )
{
  // Declaration and initialization
   double income, tax ;
   bool bracket1, bracket2, bracket3, bracket4;
   double limit1 = 10000.00, limit2 = 50000.00, limit3 = 100000.00;
   double rate1 = 0.05, rate2 = 0.10, rate3 = 0.15, rate4 = 0.20;
  // Input
   cout << "Enter income in dollars: " ;
   cin >> income;
  // Defining brackets
   bracket1 = (income <= limit1) && (income >=0) ;
   bracket2 = (income > limit1) && (income <= limit2);
   bracket3 = (income > limit2) && (income <= limit3);
   bracket4 = (income > limit3);
  // Calculating tax
   if (bracket1)
   {
       tax = income * rate1;
   }
   else if (bracket2)
   {
       tax = limit1 * rate1 + (income - limit1) * rate2 ;
   }
   else if (bracket3)
   {
       tax = limit1 * rate1 + (limit2 - limit1) * rate2 +
                                  (income - limit2) * rate3 ;
   }
   else if (bracket4)
   {
       tax = limit1 * rate1 + (limit2 - limit1) * rate2 +
                   (limit3 - limit2) * rate3 + (income - limit3) * rate4 ;
   }
   else
   {
       cout << "Error! Invalid income!";
       return 0;
   }
   // Printing income and tax
```

(continued)

Program 4.16 An individual's tax burden (Continued)

```
    cout << "Income: " << income << endl;
    cout << "Tax due: " << tax;
    return 0;
}
```

```
Run:
Enter income in dollars: 8500
Income: 8500
Tax due: 425
```

```
Run:
Enter income in dollars: 14500
Income: 14500
Tax due: 950
```

```
Run:
Enter income in dollars: -5
Error! Invalid income!
```

```
Run:
Enter income in dollars: 123000
Income: 123000
Tax due: 16600
```

The income in the third run (−5) is invalid; otherwise, the income in each run is in one of the brackets. In the first run, the tax payer is in bracket1 and pays 5 percent of her income to taxes (425). In the second run, the tax payer is in bracket2. She pays 500 for bracket1 (the first 10000 dollars) and 450 for the bracket 2 (the remaining 4500 dollars), and so on. Verify that each result is correct.

4.5.3 Day Number

Assume we give all days in the year a day number. For example, January 1 is day1 and December 31 is day365. We want to find the day number in a year given the month and the day of the month.

Understand the Problem

To solve the problem, we need the month and the day of that month. We need the month because we must calculate the number of days passed in all previous months.

Develop the Algorithm

We need two tasks in this algorithm: adding the number of days in all past months and adding the day number in the current month. The first is done in a *switch* statement, one case for each month. The second is done after the *switch* statement. The *switch* statement using the fall through approach (without *break* statements) is very suitable for this problem because we need to accumulate the number of days passed in the previous months. To make the *switch* statement work, we start from the last month of the year and go to the first month. If we are in month 7, for example, we enter the case 7, but we add the number of days from month 6 to month 1. When we come out of the *switch* statement, we add the number of days in the current month.

Write the Code

Program 4.17 follows the algorithm. Note that we have ignored the case of a leap year, in which February contains 29 days. We leave the case of a leap year for an exercise. We have also ignored input errors, which we discuss in a future chapter.

Program 4.17 Day number

```
/***************************************************************
  * Finding the number of days passed from the beginning of the     *
  * the year including the current day                               *
  ***************************************************************/
#include <iostream>
using namespace std;

int main ( )
{
  // Declaration
   int month;
   int day;
   int totalDays = 0;
  // Input current month and current day of the month
   cout << "Enter month: ";
   cin >> month;
   cout << "Enter day of month: ";
   cin >> day;
  // Number of days in months
   int m01 = 31;
   int m02 = 28;
   int m03 = 31;
   int m04 = 30;
   int m05 = 31;
   int m06 = 30;
   int m07 = 31;
   int m08 = 31;
   int m09 = 30;
   int m10 = 31;
   int m11 = 30;
  // Switch statement find the total days using fall through
   switch (month)
   {
       case 12 : totalDays += m11;
       case 11 : totalDays += m10;
       case 10 : totalDays += m09;
       case 9  : totalDays += m08;
       case 8  : totalDays += m07;
```

(continued)

Program 4.17 Day number (Continued)

```
            case 7 : totalDays += m06;
            case 6 : totalDays += m05;
            case 5 : totalDays += m04;
            case 4 : totalDays += m03;
            case 3 : totalDays += m02;
            case 2 : totalDays += m01;
            case 1 : totalDays += 0;
    }
    // Adding the day of the month to the previous total days
    totalDays +=  day;
    // Printing the result
    cout << "Day number: " << totalDays;
    return 0;
}
```

```
Run:
Enter month: 1
Enter day of month: 23
Day number: 23
```

```
Run:
Enter month: 4
Enter day of month: 12
Day number: 102
```

```
Run:
Enter month: 11
Enter day of month: 24
Day number: 328
```

```
Run:
Enter month: 12
Enter day of month: 31
Day number: 365
```

Key Terms

conditional expression
dangling else
De Morgan's law
default case
equality expression
if statement
if-else statement
logical-and expression
logical expression
logical-not expression
logical-or expression
multiway selection
one-way selection
relational expression
short-circuit behavior
switch statement
two-way selection

Summary

To solve some problems, we need to make a decision based on the test of a true-false condition. This is referred to as *selection*. The most common structure for making a decision is the one way selection, accomplished in C++ by the *if statement*. The second statement we discussed for selection is the two-way selection using the *if-else statement*.

Sometimes decision-making problems are too complex to be solved by using the relational and equality expressions. We can combine relational and equality expressions with logical expressions to achieve a selection. We discussed three logical operators: NOT, AND, and OR.

Another multiway decision construct in C++ is the *switch statement* in which the decision is based on specific values.

Another construct that can be used for decision making is called the *conditional expression*. It is the only *ternary* expression in C++. It uses two operators and three operands.

Problems

PR-1. If originally x = 4 and y = 0, what are the values of x and y after executing the following code?

```
if (x != 0)
{
     y = 3;
}
```

PR-2. If originally x = 4, y = 0, and z = 2, what are the values of x, y, and z after executing the following code?

```
if ( z == 2 )
{
     y = 1;
}
else
{
     x = 3;
}
```

PR-3. If originally x = 4, y = 0, and z = 2, what are the values of x, y, and z after executing the following code?

```
if ( x > y || y < z )
{
     x = 10;
}
```

PR-4. If originally x = *true*, y = *false*, and z = *true*, what are the values of x, y, and z after executing the following code?

```
if ( x )
{
     if ( y )
     {
          z = false;
```

```
        }
        else
        {
            y = true;
        }
}
```

PR-5. If originally x = 4, y = 0, and z = 2, what are the values of x, y, and z after executing the following code?

```
if ( z == 0 || y != 0 )
{
    if ( z <= 2 )
    {
        z = 4;
    }
}
else
{
    y = 5;
    z = y + x;
}
```

PR-6. If originally x = 0, y = 0, and z = 1, what are the values of x, y, and z after executing the following code?

```
switch ( x )
{
    case 0 :  x = 2;
              y = 3;
    case 1 :  x = 4;
    default : y = 5;
              x = 1;
}
```

PR-7. If originally x = 2, y = 1, and z = 1, what are the values of x, y, and z after executing the following code?

```
switch ( x )
{
    case 0 :  x = 3;
              y = 2;
    case 1 :  x = 2;
    default : y = 3;
              x = 4;
}
```

PR-8. Rewrite the following multiway selection using a *switch* statement.

```
if ( x == 2 )
{
    x++;
```

```
}
else if (x == 3)
{
    x--;
}
else
{
    cout << "End!";
}
```

PR-9. Rewrite the following switch statement using a multiway *if-else* statement.

```
switch (x)
{
    case 1: cout << "One" << endl;
        break;
    case 2: cout << "Two" << endl;
        break;
    default: cout << "Any" << endl;
        break;
}
```

PR-10. Rewrite the following code fragment using one *switch* statement.

```
if (ch == 'A' || ch == 'a')
    countA++;
else if (ch == 'E' || ch == 'e')
    countE++;
else if (ch == 'I' || ch == 'i')
    countI++;
else
    cout << "Error--Not A, E, or I " << endl;
```

PR-11. Write a code fragment that will assign the value 1 to the variable *best* if the integer variable score is 90 or greater.

PR-12. Write a code fragment to add 4 to an integer variable *num* if a float variable *amount* is greater than 5.4.

PR-13. Write a code fragment to print the value of the integer *num* if the variable *flag* is *true*.

PR-14. Write a code fragment to do the following: If the variable *divisor* is not zero, divide the variable *dividend* by *divisor* and store the result in *quotient*. If *divisor* is zero, assign it to *quotient*. Then print all three variables. Assume that the variables *dividend* and *divisor* are integers and *quotient* is a double.

PR-15. Write a code fragment to check if the variable flag is *true*; if *true*, read values of integer variables *num1* and *num2*. Then calculate and print the values of the sum and average of both inputs. If the variable flag is *false*, do nothing.

PR-16. Write a code fragment that tests the value of an integer *num*1. If the value is 10, square *num*1. If it is 9, read a new value into *num*1. If it is 2 or 3, multiply *num*1 by 99 and print out the result. Implement your code using nested *if* statements, not a *switch* statement.

Programs

PRG-1. Write a program that accept only two-digit unsigned integers from the user and then reverses the digits and prints them. Use an *if* statement to terminate the program if the input number has more than two digits.

PRG-2. Write a program that, given three integers, prints the smallest one.

PRG-3. Write a program that, given an integer between 1 and 12 (inclusive), prints the corresponding month of the year.

PRG-4. Write a program that, given the type of vehicle ('c' for car, 'b' for bus, 't' for truck) and the hours a vehicle spent in the parking lot, returns the parking charge based on the rates shown below.

```
car: $2 per hour          bus:$3 per hour          truck: $4 per hour
```

PRG-5. Write a program that determines a student's grade. It reads three test scores (between 0 and 100) and calculates the grade based on the following rules:

a. If the average score is 90 or more, the grade is 'A'.
b. If the average score is between 80 and 90, the program checks the third score. If the third score is more than 90, the grade is 'A'; otherwise, the grade is 'B'.
c. If the average score is between 70 and 80, the program checks the third score. If the third score is more than 80, the grade is 'B'; otherwise, the grade is 'C'.
d. If the average score is between 60 and 70, the program checks the third score. If the third score is more than 70, the grade is 'C'; otherwise, the grade is 'D'.
e. If the average score is less than 60, the program checks the third score. If the third score is more than 60, the grade is 'D'; otherwise, the grade is 'F'.

PRG-6. Write a program that calculates and prints a student's total tuition at a college. The students pay a fee of \$10 per unit for up to 12 units; once they have paid for 12 units, they have no additional per-unit fee. The registration fee is \$10 per student.

PRG-7. A wholesale store gives a discount on the number of items purchased, as shown below.

Quantity	Discount	Quantity	Discount
1 to 9	0%	50 to 99	5%
10 to 49	3%	100 or more	10%

Write a program that, given the quantity and unit price of an item, calculates the total price after the discount.

PRG-8. Write a program that prints the quarter (1, 2, 3, and 4) of a point in the Cartesian (rectangular) system given the values of x and y for the point. For example, if both x and y are positive, the point is located in the first quadrant. If both x and y are negative, the point is located in the third quadrant, and so on.

PRG-9. Change Program 4.17 to consider the extra day in a leap year (February is 29 days instead of 28 days). The program must get the year from the user and use the following formula to find if the year is a leap year.

```
leapYear = (year % 400) || (year % 4 && ! (year % 100))
```

PRG-10. Write a program that finds the day of the week for any given date using Zeller's congruence. Zeller found the following formula to calculate the day of the week using the day of the month, the month, and the year.

```
weekday = (day + 26 * (month + 1) / 10 +
                     year + year / 4 – year /100 + year /400 ) % 7
```

The formula is based on the following:

a. There are seven days in the week so the calculation must be done modulo 7.
b. The first term, *day*, shows that each day of the month moves the weekday forward by 1.
c. The second term, 26 * (*month* + 1) / 10, is the Zeller congruence. Instead of worrying about the number of days in each month, Zeller devised this solution. Zeller's formula works for a solar system when the year starts from March, not January. Therefore, we must consider the months January and February as months 13 and 14 of the previous year. In other words, January of 2017 must be considered as month 13 of *year* 2016.
d. The next term, *year,* moves the week day one day for each year because **a non-leap year** is 365 **and** when divided by 7 the result is 1.
e. The next term, *year* / 4, is the contribution of the leap year. We know that each year divided by 4 **could** be a leap year **that adds** one day to the week day.
f. The next term, *year / 100,* is the term that excludes the year divided by 100 from the previous year.
g. The next term, *year / 400,* is the term that defines if a year divided by 400 is a leap year and needs to add 1 to the calculation.

PRG-11. Change the menu-driven calculator program (Program 4.18) to do calculations on floating-point numbers.

PRG-12. Write a program that, given a dollar value, prints the minimum number of bill denominations in 100s, 50s, 20s, 10s, 5s, and 1s. Use the conditional expression (: ?) to print only nonzero numbers of bills.

The programs we have written in the previous chapters were based on sequential statements or selection statements. In most programs, we need to repeat lines of code. Repetition allows the program to iterate a section of code multiple times. C++ provides three constructs for repeating a set of statements without physically repeating them in the code: *while statements, for statements*, and *do-while statements.* To use any of these constructs, we need more expression types.

Objectives

After you have read and studied this chapter, you should be able to:

- Review the expressions that can be used as counters in repetition statements.
- Understand the syntax of a *while* statement and its use in creating a counter-controlled or event-controlled repetition.
- Understand how to initialize and update a counter in a counter-controlled repetition statement.
- Understand how to use a sentinel, an end of file (EOF) marker, or a flag in an event-controlled repetition statement.
- Understand the syntax of a *for* statement as a replacement for a counter-controlled *while* statement.
- Understand how initialization, testing, and counter updating are all done in the header of a *for* statement.
- Understand the syntax of a *do-while* statement and how it can be used for data validation.
- Analyze and compare the three repetition constructs.
- Discuss other statements related to repetition and how we can avoid them by changing the structure of the repetition statements.

5.1 INTRODUCTION

Although we can solve many problems in computer science using only the sequence and selection constructs, this approach will not solve all problems. Assume we want to change 100 test scores to their corresponding letter grades. We have three choices:

a. We can write a program with only one selection statement and run it 100 times. This approach is very time consuming.

Table 5.1 Prefix and postfix expressions

Group	Name	Operator	Expression	Pred	Assoc
postfix	postfix increment postfix decrement	++ --	lvalue++ lvalue--	18	→
unary	prefix increment prefix decrement	++ --	++lvalue --lvalue	17	←

b. We can write one program with 100 selection statements. This approach is long and must be changed if the number of students changes.

c. We can use *repetition statements* (also called *loops*) that allow us to repeat one activity or a set of activities as many times as we desire.

5.1.1 Prefix and Postfix Expressions

When we use repetition statements, we often need to use a *counter* to check how many times something is repeated and to terminate the repetition when we have done enough. Two groups of expressions are designed to simulate a counter: *postfix increment/decrement* and *prefix increment/decrement*. These two types of expressions are part of the C++ expressions discussed in Appendix C. For quick reference, we have copied them in Table 5.1. Note that postfix increment/decrement expressions belong to the group *postfix* and prefix increment/decrement expressions belong to the group *unary*.

Postfix Increment and Postfix Decrement Expressions

Postfix increment and **postfix decrement expressions** are made of a single operand and one operator (++ or −−) that are placed after the operand, as shown in Figure 5.1.

In each expression the operand is the name of a variable (an *lvalue* as we discussed before). The previous value of the variable is the return value, but the value of the variable is incremented or decremented (side effect). In other words, if the value of variable `x` is 3, the `x++` expression returns 3 and increments the contents of `x` to be 4. Similarly, if the value of `y--` is 8, the expression returns 8 and decrements `y` to be 7, as shown in Figure 5.2.

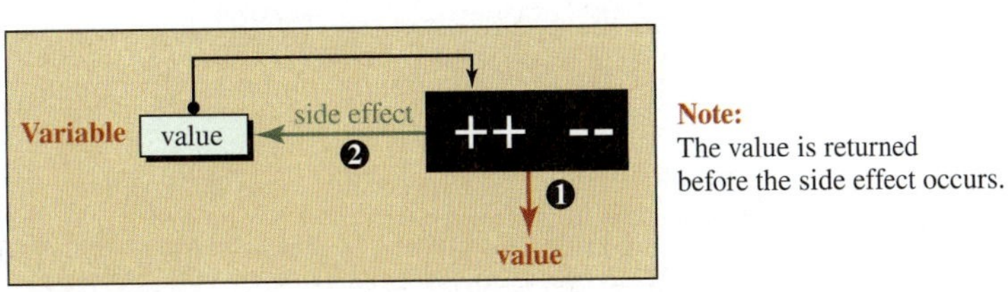

Figure 5.1 Postfix increment and postfix decrement expressions

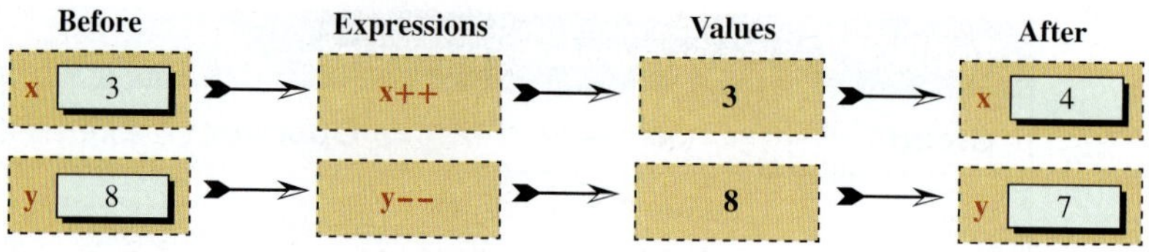

Figure 5.2 Values and side effects of postfix expressions

EXAMPLE 5.1

Figure 5.2 tells us that we can use the side effect of expression *x++* as a count-up counter and the side effect of expression *y--* as a count-down counter if we continuously increment variable *x* and decrement variable *y*.

// Using x as count-up counter	// Using y as count-down counter
int x = 3;	int y = 8;
x++;	y--;
x++;	y--;
x++;	y--;
cout << x; // 6 is printed	cout << y; // 5 is printed

Prefix Increment and Prefix Decrement Expressions

Prefix increment and **prefix decrement expressions** are made of a single operand and one operator (++ or −−) that are placed before the operand, as shown in Figure 5.3.

In each expression the side effect occurs (the variable is incremented or decremented) before the value is returned. Figure 5.4 shows the result of incrementing or decrementing a variable using these expressions.

EXAMPLE 5.2

Figure 5.4 tells us that we can use the side effect of the expression *++x* as a count-up counter and the side effect of the expression *--y* as a count-down counter if we continuously increment variable x and decrement variable y.

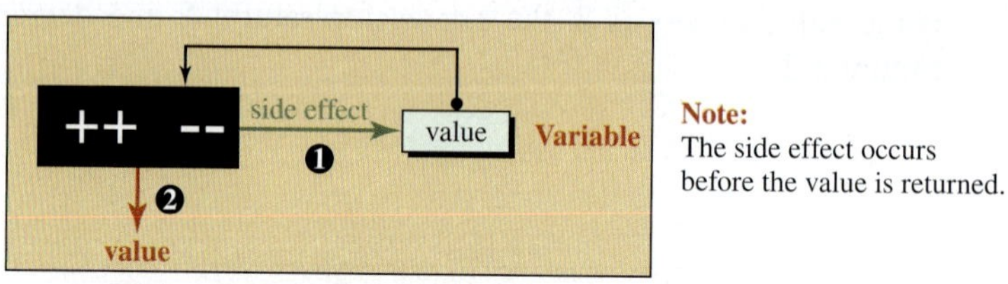

Figure 5.3 Prefix increment and prefix decrement expressions

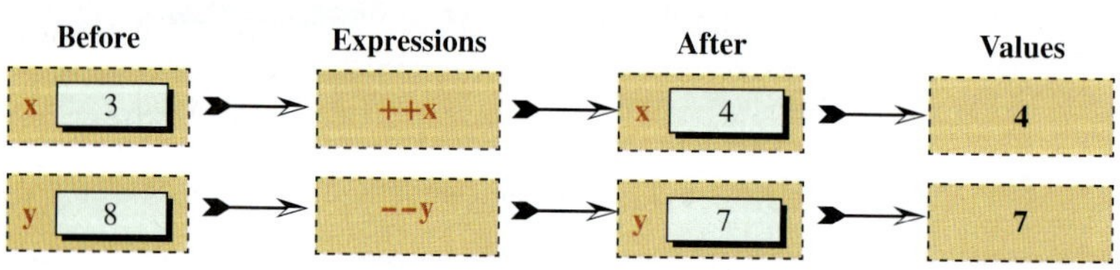

Figure 5.4 Values and side effects of prefix expressions

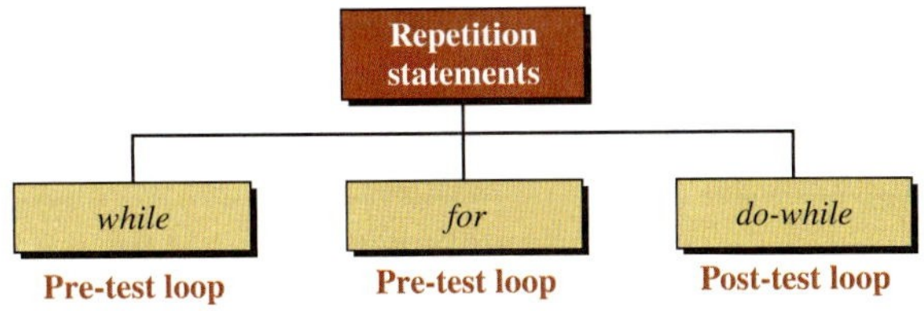

Figure 5.5 Three repetition statements in C++

// Using x as count-up counter	// Using y as count-down counter
int x = 3;	int y = 8;
++x;	y--;
++x;	y--;
++x;	y--;
cout << x; // 6 is printed	cout << y; // 5 is printed

Comparison between Postfix and Prefix Expressions

When we compare the postfix and prefix expressions, we see that they behave the same if we are only interested in their side effects (contents of the variable). The difference is in the return values. The return value of the postfix expression is the original value of the variable; the return value of the prefix expression is the value of the variable after the side effect. In other words, if we are using any of these expressions as a counter, there is no difference. Traditionally programmers use the postfix expressions.

5.1.2 Repetition Statements

Three repetition statements are used in C++: the *while* statement, the *for* statement, and the *do-while* statement, as shown in Figure 5.5. We discuss all three in this chapter.

5.2 THE *while* STATEMENT

The first repetition statement we discuss is the **while statement** (or *while* loop). Figure 5.6 shows the flow diagram and the syntax of this statement. The *while* statement is made of the reserved word *while*, followed by a Boolean expression (called the condition) in parentheses, followed by a single statement, which is the body of the *while* statement.

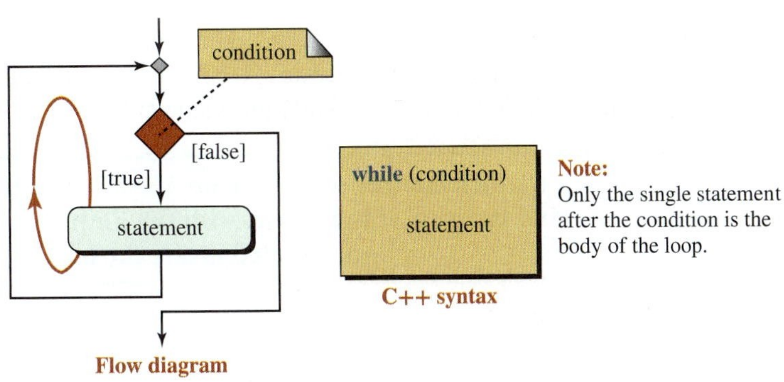

Figure 5.6 Flow diagram and syntax of the *while* statement

The structure repeatedly evaluates the condition and executes the statement as long as the condition is *true*. When the condition becomes *false*, the repetition stops. In that moment, the control passes to the next statement after the *while* statement.

The *while* statement does not need a semicolon at the end.

The body of the loop must be a single statement. If we need to execute more than one statement in the body of the loop, we enclose the statements in a compound statement to make them a single statement to the *while* loop. However, it is good practice to always use a compound statement as the body no matter how many statements we need to execute the body. The following shows the code that we normally see as a *while* statement.

```
while (condition)
{
  statement-1;
  ...
  statement-n;
}
```

The body of the *while* statement must be a single statement.

The construct in Figure 5.6 is the general idea behind the *while* statement. It does not define what the condition checks and how we can design the condition to be *true* when we want to repeat the statement or to be *false* when we need to stop repeating the statement. C++ provides two types of *while* statements: *counter-controlled* and *event-controlled*. Each type answers these questions differently.

5.2.1 Counter-Controlled *while* Statement

Often, we know how many times the body of the loop must be repeated. In these cases, we can use a counter. We can set the counter to an initial value before the loop, increment or decrement the counter in each iteration, and stop the loop when we are done. For example, if we have decided to do 20 push-ups every morning, we are using a **counter-controlled loop.** We know how many times we want to repeat it. We count the number of push-ups and we stop when we are done.

To change the general *while* loop structure we showed in Figure 5.6 to a counter-controlled loop, we must add one statement before the loop to initialize the counter and augment the body of the loop to update the counter. Now the body of the loop must be a compound statement that includes the actions to be taken and the counter update. Figure 5.7 shows the flow diagram and the C++ code. Besides a counter, we also need a limit value against which to check the value of the counter. The limit value can be either specific or implicit.

In a counter-controlled *while* loop, the counter is initialized before entering the loop, it is checked with the limit in each iteration, and it is updated inside the loop.

EXAMPLE 5.3

Assume we need to print the message "Hello world!" 10 times. We can use a *while* loop instead of repeating the message 10 times. Here the limit (10) can be literally given in the condition of the loop, as shown in Program 5.1.

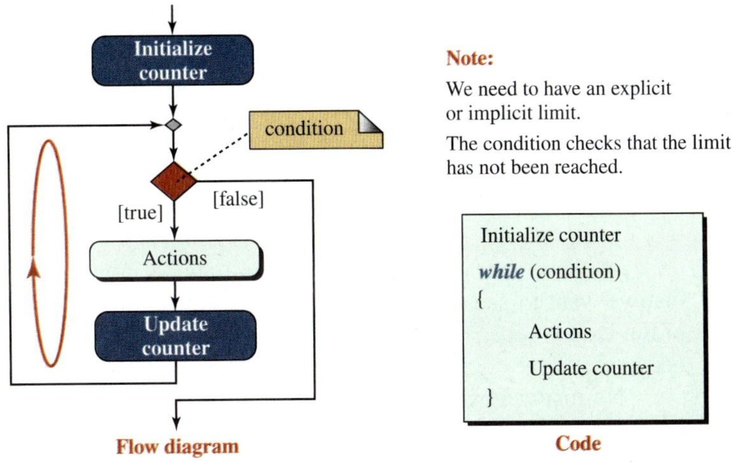

Figure 5.7 Flow diagram and the code for a counter-controlled *while* statement

Program 5.1 A counter-controlled *while* statement

```
/********************************************************************
 * Use of a while statement to print a message 10 times            *
 ********************************************************************/
#include <iostream>
using namespace std;

int main ( )
{
  // Declaration and initialization of counter
   int counter = 0;
  // While statement
   while (counter < 10)  // The number of repetition is fixed to 10
   {
        cout << "Hello world!" << endl;
        counter++;
   }
   return 0;
}
```

```
Run:
Hello world!
Hello world!
Hello world!
Hello world!
Hello world!
Hello world!
Hello world!
Hello world!
Hello world!
Hello world!
```

Table 5.2 Values of counter and Boolean expression in each iteration

Counter	**0**	**1**	**2**	**3**	**4**	**5**	**6**	**7**	**8**	**9**	**10**
Condition	true	true	true	true	true	true	true	true	true	true	**false**
Body executed?	yes	yes	yes	yes	yes	yes	yes	yes	yes	yes	**no**

We have used a counter, which is initialized at line 10 and updated at line 15. The limit that we want to use (10) is literally coded as the condition of the loop in line 12. The body of the loop is repeated when the counter is 0, 1, 2, 3, 4, 5, 6, 7, 8, and 9. When the counter becomes 10, we come out of the loop as shown in Table 5.2.

No matter how many times we run the program, the message is printed 10 times because the number of the repetitions is fixed.

EXAMPLE 5.4

Now let us assume that a professor needs to write a program to determine the average score for each student during the term. The professor gives four exams in each term to each student. This is also a case in which the iteration limit is fixed, but the professor can run the program several times with the scores for different students. Program 5.2 shows the case.

Program 5.2 Finding the average of a set of scores

```
/***************************************************************
 * Use of the counter-controlled while loop to find the average    *
 * of scores for each student.                                     *
 ***************************************************************/
#include <iostream>
#include <iomanip>
using namespace std;

int main ()
{
  // Declaration
  int score;
  int sum = 0;
  double average;
  // Loop
  int counter = 0; // initialize the counter
  while (counter < 4)  // Test the counter
  {
      // Process (Read and add score to the sum)
      cout << "Enter the next score (between 0 and 100): ";
      cin >> score;
      sum = sum + score;
      counter++; // Increment the counter
  }
```

(continued)

Program 5.2 Finding the average of a set of scores (Continued)

```
    // Result
    average = static_cast <double> (sum) / 4;
    cout << fixed << setprecision (2) << showpoint;
    cout << "The average of scores is: " << average;
    return 0;
}
```

```
Run:
Enter the next score (between 0 and 100): 78
Enter the next score (between 0 and 100): 68
Enter the next score (between 0 and 100): 92
Enter the next score (between 0 and 100): 88
The average of scores is: 81.50
```

```
Run:
Enter the next score (between 0 and 100): 80
Enter the next score (between 0 and 100): 90
Enter the next score (between 0 and 100): 76
Enter the next score (between 0 and 100): 74
The average of scores is: 80.00
```

EXAMPLE 5.5

In the previous program, the limit that controls the loop iteration was set to a fixed value. We can also have a counter-controlled loop in which the limit can be changed for each run. For example, Program 5.3 shows how we can print the integers from 1 to a limit in which the limit is given by the user in each run. Note that in this program, we actually print the value of the count variable.

Program 5.3 Printing *n* integers

```
/*****************************************************************
 * Use of a while statement loop to print integers from 0 to n         *
 *****************************************************************/
#include <iostream>
using namespace std;

int main ()
{
  // Declaration of the limit and counter
  int n, count;
  // Input the value of n (limit)
  cout << "Enter the number of integers to print: ";
  cin >> n;
  // Printing integers
  count = 0;
```

(*continued*)

Program 5.3 Printing *n* integers (Continued)

```
16     while (count < n)
17     {
18         cout << count << endl;
19         count++;
20     }
21     return 0;
22 }
```

```
Run:
Enter the number of integers to print: 5
0
1
2
3
4
```

```
Run:
Enter the number of integers to print: 0
```

```
Run:
Enter the number of integers to print: -3
```

Note that in the last two runs the condition `(count < n)` is false in line 16 and the program never enters the body of the loop.

EXAMPLE 5.6

We know from mathematics that the sum of the following series is as shown below:

$$1 + 2 + 3 + 4 + \ldots \; + n = n\,(n+1) \,/\, 2$$
$$1 + 4 + 9 + 16 + \ldots + n^2 = n\,(n+1)\,(2n + 1) \,/\, 6$$
$$1 + 8 + 27 + 64 + \ldots \; + n^3 = n^2\,(n+1)^2 \,/\, 4$$

We can check the result of this series using a simple counter-controlled *while* statement as shown in Program 5.4. Note that the counter in each case is the value of n in the above formulas. Also note that the counter in this case needs to start from 1 (not zero) and the condition should be `(counter <= n)`.

Program 5.4 Using the *while* loop to calculate a series

```
/***************************************************************
 * Use of a while statement to calculate the sum of three series   *
 ***************************************************************/
#include <iostream>
using namespace std;

int main ()
```

(continued)

Program 5.4 Using the *while* loop to calculate a series (Continued)

```
{
  // Declaration and initialization
   int sum1 = 0, sum2 = 0, sum3 = 0;
   int n;
   // Input value of n (limit)
   cout << "Enter the value of n: ";
   cin >> n;
  // The while statement
   int counter = 1;   // Initialize counter
   while (counter <= n)
   {
        sum1 += counter;
        sum2 += counter * counter;
        sum3 += counter * counter * counter;
        counter++; // Update counter
   }
  // Printing results
   cout << "Value of n: " << n << endl;
   cout << "Value of sum1: " << sum1 << endl;
   cout << "Value of sum2: " << sum2 << endl;
   cout << "Value of sum3: " << sum3 << endl;
   return 0;
}
```

```
Run:
Enter the value of n: 5
Value of n: 5
Value of sum1: 15
Value of sum2: 55
Value of sum3: 225
```

```
Run:
Enter the value of n: 15
Value of n: 15
Value of sum1: 120
Value of sum2: 1240
Value of sum3: 14400
```

5.2.2 Event-Controlled *while* Loop

Sometimes we want to repeat an activity, but we do not know how many times we need to do it. We know that we should stop when an *event* occurs. This may also happen in real life. For example, we want to do push-ups in the morning, but we do not know how far we can go. We think we should stop when we get tired. In other words, *tiredness* is the event we are looking for to stop the repetition. Figure 5.8 shows an **event-controlled loop.**

The events that occur in computer programming can be several things, but the most encountered events are the appearance of a *sentinel*, the appearance of the *end-of-file* marker, and the occurrence of a *condition*.

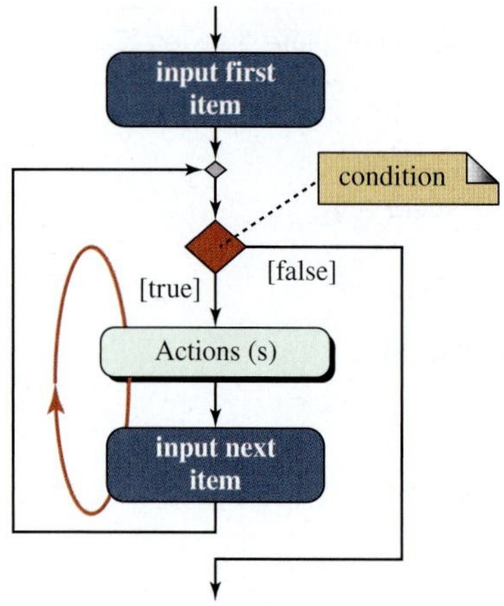

Flow diagram

Note:
An event should occur to stop the loop.

```
input first item
while (event did not occur)
{
      Actions (s)
      input next item
}
```

Code

Figure 5.8 Event-controlled *while* loop

Sentinel-Controlled while Loop

A **sentinel** is a guard who prevents unauthorized persons from passing a point. In data processing, a sentinel is a value that is added to the list of data to show when we need to stop processing. The type of the sentinel is the same as the rest of the data, but its value must be different from all of the data items before it. Note that when we use the *while* loop as the **sentinel-controlled loop,** the sentinel is not to be processed (the *while* loop is a pre-test loop).

> **In an sentinel-controlled *while* loop, the sentinel is not to be processed.**

EXAMPLE 5.7

Assume we have a long list of positive numbers to add. We do not want to count the numbers before entering them into the computer. Since we know that there are no negative numbers in the list, we can add a negative number at the end of the list to serve as the sentinel, as shown below:

> 14 23 71 87 … 66 12 −1

The sentinel in this case is the integer −1. With it the numbers can be added as shown in Program 5.5. Note that we have used a prompt statement before the loop and in the loop to let the user know what to do. Program 5.5 shows how we use the sentinel to control the iteration.

Program 5.5 The sentinel-controlled loop

```
/*****************************************************************
 * Use of the sentinel-controlled while loop to find the sum     *
 * of some numbers                                               *
 *****************************************************************/
#include <iostream>
using namespace std;

int main ()
```

(*continued*)

Program 5.5 The sentinel-controlled loop (Continued)

```
{
    // Declaration
    int sum = 0;
    int num;
    // Loop including the first input
    cout << "Enter an integer (-1 to stop): ";
    cin >> num;
    while (num != -1)
    {
        sum = sum + num;
        cout << "Enter an integer (-1 to stop): ";
        cin >> num ; // Sentinel update
    }
    // Outputting result
    cout << "The sum is: " << sum;
    return 0;
}
```

```
Run:
Enter an integer (-1 to stop): 25
Enter an integer (-1 to stop): 22
Enter an integer (-1 to stop): 12
Enter an integer (-1 to stop): 67
Enter an integer (-1 to stop): -1
The sum is: 126
```

EOF-Controlled *while* Loop

We can read data from the keyboard or from a file. In both cases, we can use the EOF marker that serves as a sentinel sentinel in an ***eof-controlled loop.*** It can be added to the keyboard and is always present in a file. It is a marker that defines that no more data will be entered through the keyboard or that we have reached the end of the file. The EOF marker allows us to read the data items and control the repetition of the loop. If we are using the keyboard as the source of data, the EOF is (`ctrl + d`) in the Unix environment and (`ctrl + z`) in the Windows environment (the first means "hold the control key and press d"; the second means "hold the control key and press z"). On the other hand, if we are using a file as the source of data, the EOF marker is added when the file is created. Figure 5.9 shows both cases.

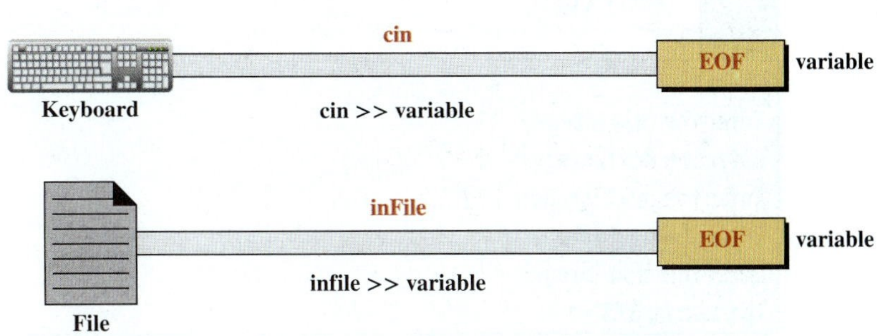

Figure 5.9 EOF marker for keyboard object and file object

How can we use EOF? Fortunately, the >> operator has a side effect and a return value. It reads the next item in the stream. If the next item is EOF, it discards it and returns **false** (the loop is terminated). If the next item is not EOF, it stores the next item in the variable defined after the operator >> and returns **true** (the loop continues).

```
// Reading from keyboard
while (cin >> num)
{
  process;
}
```

```
// Reading from a file
while (infile >> num)
{
  process;
}
```

EXAMPLE 5.8

Program 5.6 is the repetition of the previous example but using EOF to control the loop.

Program 5.6 Using EOF

```
/*****************************************************************
 * Use of the EOF-controlled while loop to find the sum          *
 * of some numbers entered on the keyboard                       *
 *****************************************************************/
#include <iostream>
using namespace std;

int main ()
{
  // Declaration
  int sum = 0;
  int num;
  // Loop including initialization
  cout << "Enter the first integer (EOF to stop): ";
  while (cin >> num)
  {
      sum = sum + num;
      cout << "Enter the next integer: ";  // update
  }
  // Output
  cout << "The sum is: " << sum;
  return 0;
}
```

```
Run:
Enter the first integer: 24
Enter the next integer: 12
Enter the next integer: 123
Enter the next integer: 14
Enter the next integer: ^Z
The sum is: 173
```

EXAMPLE 5.9

We can do the same with a file named numbers.dat that has five numbers in it: 100, 200, 300, 400, and 500 as shown in Program 5.7.

Flag-Controlled *while* Loop

Sometimes the event we are looking for does not necessarily happen at the end of a list of items like we saw with a sentinel or an EOF. The event can be a condition that may occur anywhere in a list of items. For example, assume that we are searching for the first integer greater than or equal to 100 in a list of integers. We cannot use a sentinel because we are not looking for a particular value such as 100 to stop the loop. The number that will stop the loop can be 100, 132, 150, and so on. We cannot use EOF because we do not want to process all integers. We are looking for a condition that can be defined as (number >=100). The solution is a **flag-controlled loop**. We create a Boolean variable referred to as a flag. We set the flag to false before entering the loop; we set it to true when the condition occurs. However, we need to combine the flag with other tools to avoid an infinitive loop if the condition never occurs. In other words, we combine the flag-controlled condition with a sentinel-controlled or EOF-controlled condition.

Program 5.7 Using EOF on a file

```
/***************************************************************
 * Use of the EOF-controlled while loop to find the sum        *
 * of some numbers stored in a file                            *
 ***************************************************************/
#include <iostream>
#include <fstream>
using namespace std;

int main ()
{
  // Declarations
  int sum = 0;
  int num;
  ifstream infile;
  // Openning file
  infile.open ("numbers.dat");
  // While loop
  while (infile >> num)
  {
       sum = sum + num;
  }
  // Output result
  cout << "The sum is: " << sum;
  infile.close ();
  return 0;
}
```

```
Run:
The sum is: 1500
```

The flag-controlled mechanism is normally combined with another mechanism to prevent an infinite loop.

EXAMPLE 5.10

Assume we want to print the first integer that is greater than or equal to 150 in a list of integers. We can use a Boolean flag that is set to *false* before entering the loop. If the number is found, we set the flag to *true* and come out of the loop. Otherwise, we let the EOF marker terminate the loop. Program 5.8 uses this design.

Program 5.8 Use of a flag

```
/*****************************************************************
 * Use of both EOF and a flag to terminate a loop                *
 *****************************************************************/
#include <iostream>
#include <fstream>
using namespace std;

int main ()
{
  // Declarations
   ifstream infile;
   int num;
   bool flag;
  // Open file
   infile.open ("numbers.dat");
  // Loop to find a number greater than 150
   flag = false;
   while (infile >> num && !flag )
   {
        if (num >= 150)
        {
                cout << "The number is: " << num;
                flag = true;
        }
   }
  // Check flag
   if (!flag)
   {
        cout << "The number was not found!";
   }
   infile.close ();
   return 0;
}
```

(continued)

Program 5.8 Use of a flag (Continued)

```
Run:
The number is: 170
```

```
Run:
The number was not found!
```

Note that we test the program with the same file and two different contents. In the first run, the contents of the file is

90 110 120 135 170 200 230 EOF

We come out of the loop when 170 is read because it matches the condition we are looking (it is greater than 150). The flag is set to *true,* which means !flag is *false* and the loop is terminated although the other condition (infile >> num) is *true.* In the second run the contents of the file is

90 110 120 135 137 140 EOF

The flag never becomes *true,* but when we reach the EOF, the other condition *(infile >> num)* becomes *false* and the loop is terminated.

If the number is found inside the loop, we print it. If the loop is terminated, the flag is still *false* and we know that we have reached the end of file.

Pitfalls

Although there are many pitfalls to be avoided with the *while* statement, we mention only four here.

Zero-Iteration Loop We must avoid a loop that never iterates. This happens when the Boolean expression is *false* when it is tested for the first time. In this case, the body of the loop never executes no matter how many times we run the program. Unfortunately, this problem is not caught during compilation-time or run-time. We must be very careful to avoid this situation. The following are two cases of zero iteration.

```
while (false)                              while (2 == 3)
{                                          {
  ...                                        ...
}                                          }
```

Infinite-Iteration Loop Another example of a *while* statement pitfall is a loop that repeats its body forever. This happens when the Boolean expression is *true* each time it is tested. In this case, the loop never stops. This type of a loop should normally be avoided, but, as we will discuss in the next section, we create such a loop to let a server program run forever.

```
while (true)                        while (2 != 3)
{                                   {
   ...                                 ...
}                                   }
```

Empty-Body Loop Sometimes we accidentally create a loop whose body is empty. This happens, for example, if we add a semicolon after the header of the *while* statement. The compiler thinks that we do not want to use braces and that there is a null statement before the semicolon. The actual body is interpreted as a stand-alone statement that is executed once after the loop. The compiler does not give an error, but the program does not do what we expected (logical error).

```
while (expression); // Empty expression (compound expression ignored)
{
   ...
}
```

Use of Floating-Point Values in Boolean Expressions As we discuss in a previous chapter, floating-point values depend on the precision of the numbers in any system. For example, 3.141516 and 3.1415 are not equal but may appear to be equal if the precision is only four places after the decimal point. For this reason, we must be very careful when testing floating-point numbers for equality.

Creating a Delay

C++ provides several tools (discussed in future chapters) to create a delay in a program. We can also create a delay using a *while* statement. We can use a counter-controlled *while* statement whose body has only the updating statement. The loop does not do anything but go through iterations, which creates a delay. The following is an example. The code creates a 10-second delay if the computer performs 10,000 iterations in a second, which means this type of delay depends on the speed of the computer.

```
int counter = 0;
while (counter < 100000)
{
   counter++;
}
```

5.2.3 Analysis of a *while* Statement

We can better understand the behavior of the *while* statement if we think of it as a combination of decision-making statements as shown in Figure 5.10. In each loop execution, there is a *true path* and a *false path*. Figure 5.10 shows that the number of tests is always one more than the number of repetitions. If the body of the loop is repeated n times, $n + 1$ tests are made. In the first n tests, the result is *true*; in the last test, the result is *false*. This means that even if the body is not executed at all, we need to make one test and the result should be false. The above analysis shows that the *while* statement is a **pre-test loop.** A test must be done in each iteration before the body is executed.

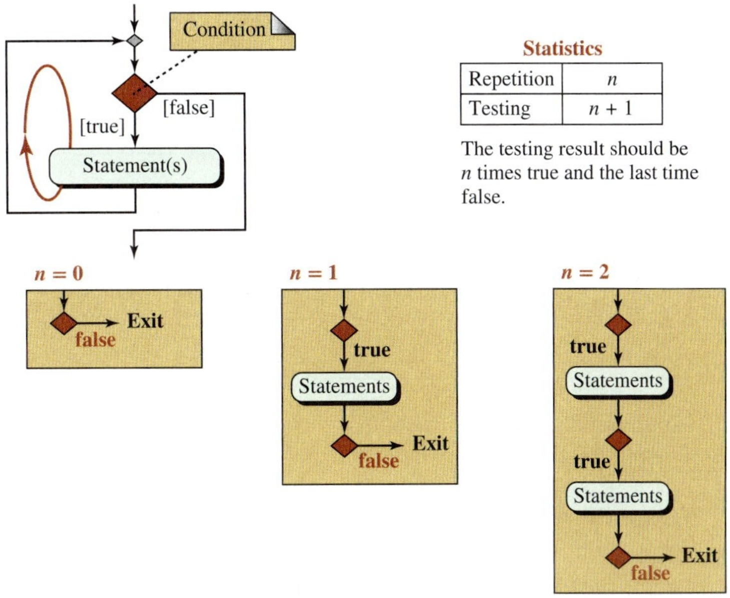

Statistics

Repetition	n
Testing	$n + 1$

The testing result should be n times true and the last time false.

Figure 5.10 Analysis of a *while* statement

> **A *while* statement is a pre-test loop.**
> **If the body is executed n times,**
> **the condition has been tested $(n + 1)$ times.**

5.3 THE *for* STATEMENT

As we discussed in the previous section, we can always use the *while* statement as a counter-controlled loop. C++ provides another loop construct, however, called the ***for* statement,** that is particularly useful when we need counter-controlled iteration. It combines the three elements of a loop—initialization, conditional test, and update—into the loop construct itself. A quick comparison between the two loops shows that the *for* statement is much more compact than using a *while* statement for counter-controlled looping, as shown in Figure 5.11.

5.3.1 Header

We now discuss in detail each of the three sections in the header of a *for* statement.

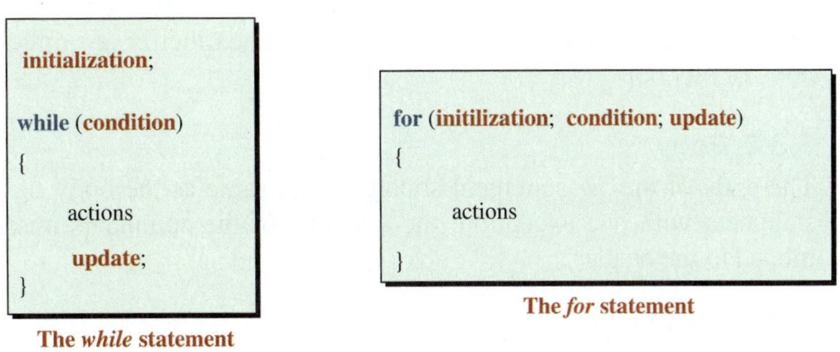

Figure 5.11 Comparison between a *while* loop and a *for* loop

Initialization

The initialization section is an expression that initializes the counter. It is customary to use lowercase variables such *i*, *j*, *k*, for the counter. We can declare the counter before the header of the loop or declare the counter at the same time that we initialize it.

// Counter declaration before the header	// Counter declaration inside the header

int i;
for (i = 0 ; ... ; ...)
{
  actions
}
	
	for (int i = 0 ; ... ; ...)
	{
	  actions
	}

In the first method, the scope of the counter extends beyond the boundary of the loop; in the second method, the scope of the counter is only inside the loop.

Condition

The condition section is the second part in the header. As in the *while* statement, the condition in the *for* statement is a Boolean expression. If the condition is true, the body of the loop is executed; otherwise, the loop exits, which indicates that the *for* statement is a pre-test loop. If the condition section is empty (between the first and the second semicolons), it is defaulted to true.

If the condition second is empty, it is defaulted to true.

EXAMPLE 5.11

The following *for* loop does not compile because the condition section in the header is missing.

```
for (int i = 0 ; i++) {...}
```

EXAMPLE 5.12

The following *for* loop compiles and creates an infinite loop because the condition section is missing and is defaulted to true section is empty.

```
for (int i = 0 ; ; i++) {...}
```

Updating

The updating section is executed after the body of the loop is executed. After updating, the condition is tested again to see if the body should be executed once more. The updating section can be missing, which means updating, explicitly or implicitly, must be done in the body of the loop.

5.3.2 Body

The body of the *for* statement should be the same as the body of the corresponding *while* statement with one exception: the updating of the counter is missing because it has been moved to the header.

EXAMPLE 5.13

We can change Program 5.3, which used a *while* statement, to Program 5.9, which uses a *for* statement. We can see that the result is the same, but the *for* statement makes the program shorter and easier to understand.

Program 5.9 Printing *n* integers using a *for* statement

```
/*****************************************************************
 * Use of a for loop to print n integers                         *
 *****************************************************************/
#include <iostream>
using namespace std;

int main ()
{
  // Declaration
   int n;
  // Get the value of n
   cout << "Enter the number of integers to print: ";
   cin >> n;
  // Loop
   for (int counter = 0; counter < n; counter++)
   {
        cout << counter << " ";
   }
   return 0;
}
```

```
Run:
Enter the number of integers to print: 5
0 1 2 3 4
```

```
Run:
Enter the number of integers to print: 3
0 1 2
```

EXAMPLE 5.14

Assume we want to print integers from 1 to 300 that are divisible by 7. The output, however, is to be printed in a table made of 10 columns. Program 5.10 shows the solution.

We know that the last number must be less than or equal to 300, but we do not know the number of rows and columns in the output. We print data in a row until the number of columns becomes 10. At this point, we move to the next row.

Program 5.10 Printing the integers divisible by 7

```
/*****************************************************************
 * Prints numbers divisible by 7 in the range 1 to 300 in a      *
 * table made of 10 columns.                                     *
 *****************************************************************/
#include <iostream>
#include <iomanip>
```

(continued)

Program 5.10 Printing the integers divisible by 7 (Continued)

```
using namespace std;

int main ()
{
  // Declaration including initialization
  int lower = 1;
  int higher = 300;
  int divisor = 7;
  int col = 1;
  // Processing loop
  for (int i = lower; i < higher ; i++)
  {
      if (i % divisor == 0)
      {
            cout << setw(4) << i;
            col++;
            if (col > 10 )
            {
                cout << endl;
                col = 1;
            }
      }
  }
  return 0;
}
```

Run:

```
   7  14  21  28  35  42  49  56  63  70
  77  84  91  98 105 112 119 126 133 140
 147 154 161 168 175 182 189 196 203 210
 217 224 231 238 245 252 259 266 273 280
 287 294
```

EXAMPLE 5.15

Assume we want to print a month when the number of days in the month and the first week day in the month (0 to 6 for Sunday through Saturday) is given. Program 5.11 shows a solution.

Program 5.11 Printing a calendar for a month

```
/*******************************************************************
 * Prints a month's calendar when we are given the number of days   *
 * and the first day of the month.                                  *
 *******************************************************************/
#include <iostream>
```

(continued)

Program 5.11 Printing a calendar for a month (Continued)

```
#include <iomanip>
using namespace std;

int main ()
{
  // Declaration including initialization
   int startDay;
   int daysInMonth;
   int col = 1;
  // Validation of days In a Month
   do
   {
        cout << "Enter the number of days in the month (28, 29, 30, or 31): ";
        cin >> daysInMonth;
   } while (daysInMonth < 28 || daysInMonth > 31);
  // Validation of start day
   do
   {
        cout << "Enter start day (0 to 6): ";
        cin >> startDay;
   } while (startDay < 0 || startDay > 6);
  // Print titles
   cout << endl;
   cout << "Sun Mon Tue Wed Thr Fri Sat" << endl;
   cout << "--- --- --- --- --- --- ---" << endl;
  // Print spaces before the startday
   for (int space = 0; space < startDay; space++)
   {
        cout << "    ";
        col++;
   }
  // Print the calendar
   for (int day = 1; day <= daysInMonth; day++)
   {
        cout << setw(3) << day << " ";
        col++;
        if (col > 7)
        {
              cout << endl;
              col = 1;
        }
   }
   return 0;
} // End main
```

(continued)

Program 5.11 Printing a calendar for a month (Continued)

```
Run:
Enter the number of days in the month (28, 29, 30, or 31): 31
Enter start day (0 to 6): 3

Sun Mon Tue Wed Thr  Fri  Sat
--- --- --- --- --- --- ---
                1   2    3    4
  5   6   7     8   9   10   11
 12  13  14    15  16   17   18
 19  20  21    22  23   24   25
 26  27  28    29  30   31
```

5.4 THE *do-while* STATEMENT

The last repetition statement we discuss is the ***do-while*** **statement,** in which the logical expression is tested at the end of each iteration instead of at the beginning. For this reason, the *do-while* loop is a **post-test loop.** Since the logical expression in each iteration is tested after the body of the loop is executed, the body of the loop in a *do-while* statement is always executed at least once (Figure 5.12).

The *do-while* statement consists of five parts: the reserved word *do*, the statement that is the body of the loop (usually a compound statement enclosed in braces), the reserved word *while*, a logical expression in parentheses, and a semicolon. Note that the semicolon is required at the end of the *do-while* statement.

A semicolon is required at the end of the *do-while* statement.

5.4.1 Event-Controlled Loop

The *do-while* statement is designed to be used as an event-controlled loop. However, the post-test feature of the *do-while* loop requires a different provision to control the loop.

At Least One Iteration

The *do-while* loop is the recommended solution when a problem requires that the body of the loop be executed at least once.

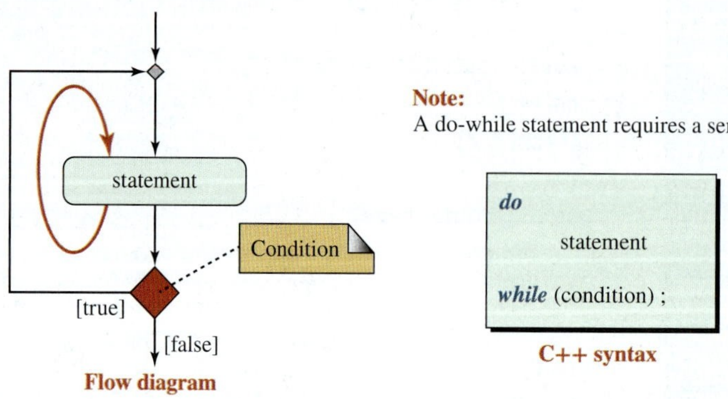

Figure 5.12 Flow diagram and syntax for a do-while statement

We use a *do-while* loop when the problem requires that the body of the loop be executed at least once.

EXAMPLE 5.16

We want to write a program that extracts and prints the left-most digit of any nonnegative integer. In other words, if the input integer is 247, the digit 2 should be printed, and if the integer is 7562, the digit 7 should be printed. Program 5.12 contains the solution for this problem.

In the first run, the number has only one digit. The first iteration of the loop extracts the only digit, and the value of *num* becomes 0, which means that the loop is terminated.

Program 5.12 Extracting the left most digit of an integer

```
/***************************************************************
 * Demonstrate the use of the do-while loop to extract the      *
 * left-most digit of an integer.                               *
 ***************************************************************/
#include <iostream>
using namespace std;

int main ( )
{
  // Declaration
  int num;
  short leftDigit;
  // Input
  cout << "Enter a non-negative integer: ";
  cin >> num;
  // Loop
  do
  {
      leftDigit = num % 10;
      num = num / 10;
  } while (num > 0);
  // Output
  cout << "The leftmost digit is: " << leftDigit << endl;
  return 0;
}
```

```
Run:
Enter a non-negative integer: 5
The leftmost digit is: 5
```

```
Run:
Enter a non-negative integer: 4567
The leftmost digit is: 4
```

In the second run, the number has three digits. Here the first iteration extracts the right most digit (1), but the second iteration discards this digit and replaces it with the new right most digit (3) because when we enter the second iteration, the value of *num* is 23. A number with three digits goes through three iterations. The problem shows that we definitely need at least one iteration because the number entered has at least one digit (even if the number is 0).

Data Validation

Another common example that requires at least one iteration is **data validation.** Data validation should be included in a program whenever a user enters data that must match a set of criteria. For example, when we enter flight information in an airline reservation system, some of the data are required and some are optional. Data validation ensures that we have entered all of the required data in the proper format.

EXAMPLE 5.17

Data entry often requires the data be in a predefined range. For example, when we change a numeric score to a grade, test scores are usually in the range of 0 and 100. If the user enters a number out of the range, the program needs to repeat the request until the user enters a number that is in the correct range. Program 5.13 demonstrates this data

Program 5.13 Using a *do-while* loop for validation

```
/***************************************************************
 * Demonstrate the use of the do-while loop to validate data   *
 ***************************************************************/
#include <iostream>
using namespace std;

int main ( )
{
  // Declaration
   int score;
   char grade;
   // Input validation loop
   do
   {
       cout << "Enter a score between 0 and 100: ";
       cin >> score;
   } while (score < 0 || score > 100);
  // Decision
   switch (score / 10)
   {
       case 10: grade = 'A';
```

(continued)

Program 5.13 Using a *do-while* loop for validation (Continued)

```
            break;
            case 9: grade = 'A';
            break;
            case 8: grade = 'B';
            break;
            case 7: grade = 'C';
            break;
            case 6: grade = 'D';
            break;
            default: grade = 'F';
        }
        // Output
        cout << "The grade is " << grade << endl;
        return 0;
}
```

```
Run:
Enter a score between 0 and 100: 83
The grade is B
```

```
Run:
Enter a score between 0 and 100: 111
Enter a score between 0 and 100: 97
The grade is A
```

validation. Note the use of *logical-or* and *inequality* expressions to define the unacceptable range.

In the first run, the user enters a score in the valid range. The body of the loop is executed only once, and the score is accepted. In the second run, the user enters an out-of-range score two times. The body of the loop is repeated three times; the score entered in the first two iterations is discarded and the score entered in the third iteration is accepted. The program shows that a *do-while* loop is an appropriate design for data validation.

5.4.2 Analysis of a *do-while* Loop

We analyzed the *while* loop in a previous section to find out that the *while* loop is a pre-test loop in which the number of tests is one more than the number of iterations. We said that a *for* loop is a variant of the *while* loop, which means it follows the specification of the *while* loop. It is useful to analyze the *do-while* loop and compare it with the *while* loop. To do so, we unfold a *do-while* loop as we did with the *while* loop (Figure 5.13).

> **In a *do-while* loop, if a body is executed *n* times, the condition is tested *n* times.**

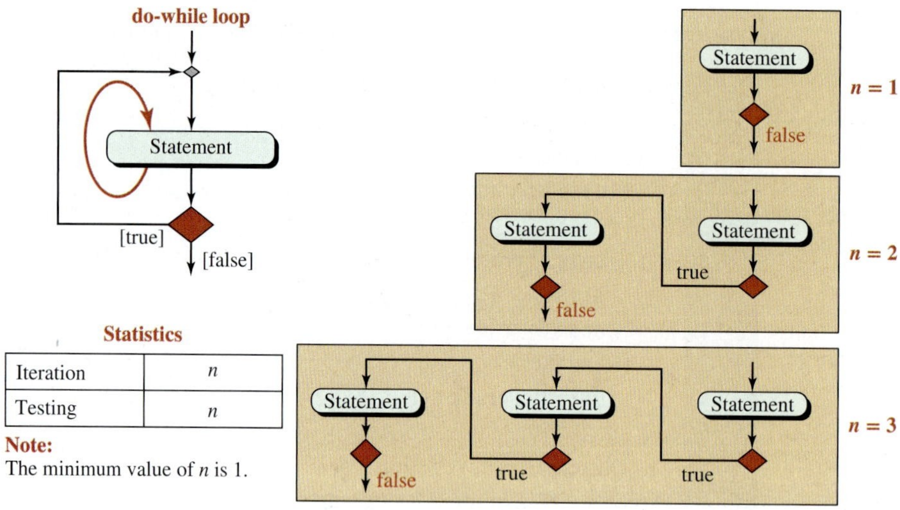

Figure 5.13 Analysis of a *do-while* loop

5.5 MORE ABOUT LOOPS

In this section, we first compare the three loop constructs: *while* loop, *for* loop, and *do-while* loop. We then see how we can combine them to create nested loops, which are helpful in solving problems.

5.5.1 Comparison of Three Loops

The three loop statements discussed in the previous sections have some common and some different features. Table 5.3 shows the comparison summary for n iterations.

- The *while* loop and the *for* loop are pre-test loops. The *do-while* loop is a post-test loop.
- The *while* and the *do-while* loops are primarily designed as event-controlled loops; the *for* loop is primarily designed as a counter-controlled loop.
- The *while* loop and the *for* loop can iterate zero times; the *do-while* loop iterates at least once.
- If we want n iterations in a loop, then we need $n + 1$ tests in the *while* loop and the *for* loop, but only n tests in the *do-while* loop.

5.5.2 Nested Loops

We can have a **nested loop,** a loop inside another loop. The inside loop does not have to be of the same type as the outside loop.

Table 5.3 Comparison of *while, for,* and *do-while* Loops

Feature	*while* Loop	*for* Loop	*do-while* Loop
Test type	pre-test	pre-test	post-test
Primary design	event-controlled	counter-controlled	event-controlled
Minimum iterations	0	0	1
Number of tests	$n + 1$	$n + 1$	n

EXAMPLE 5.18

We can use nested *for* loops to print a set of asterisks horizontally and vertically; that is, to print a rectangle of asterisks. The outside loop controls the rows; the inside loop controls the columns. For each iteration of the outside loop, the inside loop is repeated once for each column. To print a rectangle of four lines (rows) with eight asterisks (columns) in each line, the outside loop uses 4 iterations; the inside loop uses 32 (4 × 8) iterations. Program 5.14 shows the code and two sample runs.

Program 5.14 A *for* statement inside another *for* statement

```
/***************************************************************
 * Use a for loop inside another loop to print a patterns of    *
 * asterisks horizontally and vertically                        *
 ***************************************************************/
#include <iostream>
using namespace std;

int main ( )
{
  // Declaration
  int rows;    // Number of rows
  int cols;    // Number of columns
  // Inputs
  cout << "Enter the number of rows: ";
  cin >> rows;
  cout << "Enter the number of columns: ";
  cin >> cols;
  // Output
  for (int count1 = 1; count1 <= rows; count1++)
  {
      for (int count2 = 1; count2 <= cols; count2++)
      {
              cout << "*";
      }
      cout << endl;
  }
  return 0;
}
```

```
Run:
Enter the number of rows: 3
Enter the number of columns: 8
********
********
********
```

```
Run:
Enter the number of rows: 2
Enter the number of columns: 6
******
******
```

EXAMPLE 5.19

Let's look at another example. This time the value of the outside loop counter controls the starting value of the inside loop counter (Program 5.15).

Program 5.15 Printing a pattern of digits

```
/*********************************************************************
 * Use a for loop inside another loop to print a patterns of          *
 * digits horizontally and vertically                                 *
 *********************************************************************/
#include <iostream>
using namespace std;

int main ( )
{
  // Delcaration
   int rows;    // Number of rows
   int cols;    // Number of columns
  // Inputs
   cout << "Enter the number of rows: ";
   cin >> rows;
   cout << "Enter the number of columns: ";
   cin >> cols;
  // Nested loops
   for (int i = 1; i <= rows; i++)
   {
        for (int j = i; j <= i + cols -1; j++)
        {
               cout << j << " ";
        } // End inner loop
        cout << endl;
   }
   return 0;
}
```

```
Run:
Enter the number of rows: 3
Enter the number of columns: 6
1 2 3 4 5 6
2 3 4 5 6 7
3 4 5 6 7 8
```

```
Run:
Enter the number of rows: 2
Enter the number of columns: 8
1 2 3 4 5 6 7 8
2 3 4 5 6 7 8 9
```

EXAMPLE 5.20

Program 5.16 shows how to create the multiplication table for size 2 to 10. The size is input by the user. Note that the value in row *i* and column *j* is in fact the value of (i * j).

Program 5.16 Creating a multiplication table

```
/***************************************************************
 * Use a for loop inside another loop to print a multiplication    *
 * table of size 2 to 10.                                          *
 ***************************************************************/
#include <iostream>
#include <iomanip>
using namespace std;

int main ()
{
    // Declaration of size
    int size;
    // Input and validation
    do
    {
        cout << "Enter table size (2 to 10): " ;
        cin >> size;
    } while (size < 2 || size > 10);
    // Printing the table (nested loops)
    for (int i = 1 ; i <= size; i++)
    {
        for (int j = 1 ; j <= size ; j++)
        {
            cout << setw (4) << i * j;
        }
        cout << endl;
    }
    return 0;
}
```

```
Run:
Enter table size (2 to 10): 4
   1   2   3   4
   2   4   6   8
   3   6   9  12
   4   8  12  16
```

(continued)

Program 5.16 Creating a multiplication table (Continued)

```
Run:
Enter table size (2 to 10): 11
Enter table size (2 to 10): 9
 1   2   3   4   5   6   7   8   9
 2   4   6   8  10  12  14  16  18
 3   6   9  12  15  18  21  24  27
 4   8  12  16  20  24  28  32  36
 5  10  15  20  25  30  35  40  45
 6  12  18  24  30  36  42  48  54
 7  14  21  28  35  42  49  56  63
 8  16  24  32  40  48  56  64  72
 9  18  27  36  45  54  63  72  81
```

5.6 OTHER RELATED STATEMENTS

In addition to three repetition statements, C++ defines another group of statements that are normally used with repetition statements: *return, break, continue,* and *goto.* Figure 5.14 shows the taxonomy of these statements.

5.6.1 The *return* Statement

The **return statement** terminates the current function immediately and returns control to the function caller. The use of a *return* statement in a loop causes the loop to terminate and, at the same time, the function in which the loop is iterating (such as *main*) to be terminated.

EXAMPLE 5.21

In mathematics, we can divide the positive integers into three groups: 1, *prime*, and *composite*. A prime number is divisible only by itself and 1. A composite number is not a prime. Prime numbers play a very important role in computer science and security. To determine if a number is prime, we can use the following steps (although there are more efficient, but more complex ways).

a. If the number is 1, we know the number is not a prime.
b. If the number is divisible by any number less than itself, it is not prime; it is composite.

Note that we do not have to test all numbers from 2 to the number itself; as soon as we find any integer 2 or greater that divides the number, we can announce that the number is not prime and terminate the loop. Program 5.17 shows one solution.

Note that we have inserted a *return* statement at line23, a *return* statement at line 32, and a *return* statement at line 37. All three can terminate the program.

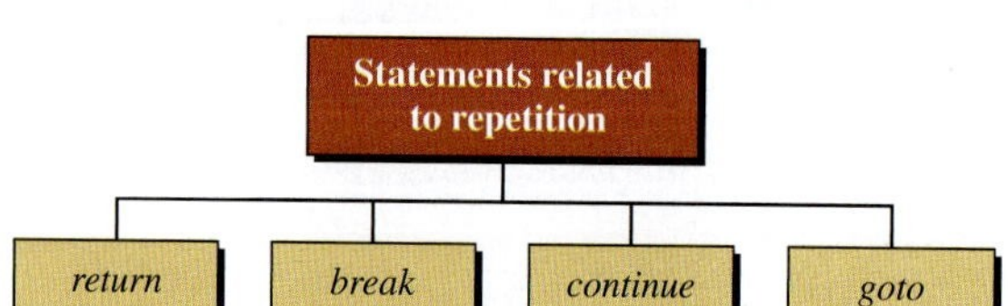

Figure 5.14 Statements related to repetition

Program 5.17 Finding if a number is a prime

```
/*****************************************************************
 * Use a return statement to find if a number is a prime or not.    *
 * The program returns from the main function as soon if finds      *
 * if a number is 1 or composite.                                   *
 *****************************************************************/
#include <iostream>
using namespace std;

int main ()
{
  // Declaration
  int num;
  // Input validation loop
  do
  {
        cout << "Enter a positive integer: " ;
        cin >> num;
  } while (num <= 0);
  // Testing if the input is 1
  if (num == 1)
  {
        cout << "1 is not a composite nor a prime.";
        return 0;
  }
  // Testing for composite
  for (int i = 2; i < num ; i++)
  {
        if (num % i == 0)
        {
              cout << num << "is composite." << endl;
              cout << "The first divisor is " << i << endl;
              return 0;
        }
  }
  // Output Result
  cout << num << " is a prime." << endl;
  return 0;
}
```

```
Run:
Enter a positive integer: 1
1 is not a composite nor a prime.
```

```
Run:
Enter a positive integer: 12
12 is composite.
The first divisor is 2
```

(continued)

Program 5.17 Finding if a number is a prime (Continued)

```
Run:
Enter a positive integer: 23
23 is a prime.
```

```
Run:
Enter a positive integer: 97
97 is a prime.
```

5.6.2 The *break* Statement

The **break statement** in C++ can be used in the body of a loop or a *switch* statement. We saw the use of the *break* statement in a *switch* statement in Chapter 4. We can also use a *break* statement to come out of a loop prematurely when we need to. All three loop statements can be terminated by the *break* statement. The *break* statement transfers control to the end of the loop. Most computer science professionals consider the use of the *break* in a loop non structural. They believe the Boolean expression in the loop should be redesigned to avoid using a *break* statement. The following code shows two different loops, with and without a *break* statement; both code segments do the same thing. (Statement1 and Statement2 are symbolic and can be any statement, including a compound statement.)

```
while (expression)                    while (expression && !condition)
{                                     {
   Statement1                            Statement1
   if (condition)                        if (!condition)
       break;                                Statement2
   Statement2                         }
}
```

5.6.3 The *continue* Statement

The next statement related to looping is the ***continue*** **statement.** As we saw before, a *break* statement terminates a loop if a condition occurs. But sometimes we do not want to terminate the loop; we just want to terminate one iteration and continue with the remaining iterations. In this case, we can use a *continue* statement, but we need to be careful because in the *while* and *do-while* loops, control is transferred to the Boolean expression. Therefore, any required updating must be included in the statements before the continue statement. In a *for* loop, however, the control is transferred to the updating statement in the header of the loop because the updating is explicitly there. Figure 5.15 shows the transfer point in each loop.

5.6.4 The *goto* Statement

Another statement in C++ that can be used with a loop statement is the ***goto*** **statement.** The following shows the format of this statement.

```
goto label
```

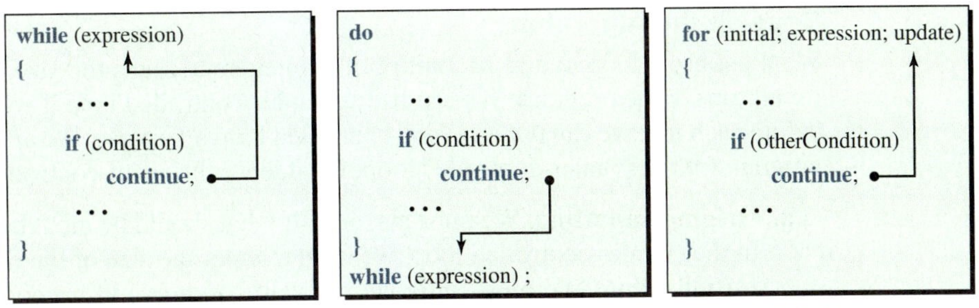

(a) A *while* loop (b) A *do-while* loop (c) A *for* loop

Figure 5.15 The *continue* statement

in which *label* is an identifier referring to a *labeled* statement in the same function. Although the *goto* statement is still part of the C++ language, puritan programmers consider the use of the *goto* statement unstructured. Its use may create *spaghetti* code that is hard and time consuming to debug. For this reason, we do not discuss this statement in depth here, and we do not need to discuss label statements.

5.7 PROGRAM DESIGN

In this section, we show how to use selection and repetition statements to solve some classic problems in computer science. We give some basic solutions to these problems, but in future chapters we will provide more structured and efficient solutions.

5.7.1 Summation and Products

Although in previous sections we have written some programs that add numbers, in this section we give a formal solution to problems involving summation and products. Summation means to add a list of numbers; multiplication means to multiply a list of numbers. The following shows the idea of adding or multiplying a set of reals.

sum	=	**17.0**	+	**14.4**	+	**...**	+	**71.2**
product	=	**17.0**	×	**14.4**	×	**...**	×	**71.2**

Understand the Problem

We have a list of floating-point numbers to add (or multiply). We can initialize a variable *sum* (or *product*) to hold the result of the summation (or multiplication) and use a loop to add each integer to *sum* (or multiply each integer with *product*) as shown below:

Initialization	sum = 0.0	product = 1.0
Iteration 1	sum += 17.0	product *= 17.0
Iteration 2	sum += 14.4	product *= 14.4
...	...	...
Iteration *n*	sum += 71.2	product *= 71.2
Printing result	sum	product

Note that the initialization is different for sum and product. For the sum, the initialization is sum = 0.0; for the product, the initialization is product = 1.0.

Develop the Algorithm

We must use a loop to add or multiply the integers because the size of the list is not fixed for all runs of the program. We can use a counter-controlled loop if we are given the list size before each run; we can use an event-controlled loop otherwise. We'll give the algorithm and program for the counter-controlled loop; we'll leave the event-controlled loop as an exercise.

a. **Original inputting.** We must ask ourself what should be input before starting the loop. In the counter-controlled loop, we need to enter the size of the list.
b. **Initialization.** We must initialize the value of *sum* and *product*. In other words, we must set (sum = 0.0) and (product = 1.0). We also must initialize the counter when we use the counter-controlled loop.
c. **Processing in each iteration.** In each iteration, we must read the next number, add it to *sum*, and multiply it by *product*. We also must increment the counter. The number of iterations is controlled by the counter.
d. **Creating the result.** The results (*sum* and *product*) can be printed after the loop is terminated.

Using the following steps, we can give the informal algorithm:

1. Input
 a. input size
2. Initialize
 a. initialize sum to 0.0
 b. initialize product to 1.0
 c. initialize counter to 0
3. Repeat as long as the counter is less than the size
 a. read the next number
 b. set new sum to previous sum plus number
 c. set new product to previous product times number
 d. update counter
4. Output
 a. output the sum
 b. output the product

Write the Program

Program 5.18 shows the code based on the algorithm. The types of the sum and product are long double, so it is rare that we get overflow or underflow. However, if you want, you can add code to test for them.

Program 5.18 Finding the product of a list of numbers

```
/***************************************************************
 * It shows how to add and multiply a list of integers when the   *
 * size of the list is predefined                                 *
 ***************************************************************/
```

(continued)

Program 5.18 Finding the product of a list of numbers (Continued)

```
#include <iostream>
#include <iomanip>
using namespace std;

int main ( )
{
  // Variable declaration
  int size;
  long double number;
  long double sum, product;
  // input validation for the size
  do
  {
       cout << "Enter a non-negative integer value for size: " ;
       cin >> size;
  } while (size < 0);
  // Initialization
  sum = 0;
  product = 1;
  // Processing
  for (int i = 1; i <= size; i++)
  {
       cout << "Enter the next integer: ";
       cin >> number;
       sum += number;
       product *= number;
  }
  // Output
  cout << fixed << setprecision (2);
  cout << "sum =  " << sum << endl;
  cout << "product =  " << product;
  return 0;
}
```

```
Run:
Enter a non-negative integer value for size: 6
Enter the next number: 12
Enter the next number: 13.45
Enter the next number: 15
Enter the next number: 22.10
Enter the next number: 11.34
Enter the next number: 14
sum = 87.89
product = 8494310.92
```

(*continued*)

Program 5.18 Finding the product of a list of numbers (Continued)

```
Run:
Enter a non-negative integer value for n: 0
sum = 0.00
product = 1.00
```

The first run multiplies seven numbers. The second run shows that if the list is empty (*size* = 0), the result is the initial value for the variables *sum* and *product*. It is good practice to show that the list is empty.

5.7.2 Factorial

Another calculation that we encounter in programming is to find the **factorial** of a number.

Understand the Problem

Factorial is a special kind of multiplication in which the numbers to be multiplied are positive integers (from 1 to the factorial number). In other words, we are looking for the result of $(1 \times 2 \times 3 \times \cdots \times n)$, where n is the size of the list. This is referred to as factorial n (called $n!$ in mathematics). The only information we need from the user is the last number in the series (n).

Develop the Algorithm

The algorithm to find the factorial is the same as the one we discussed for multiplication in the previous problem. However, since in each iteration we must multiply the counter by the factorial, we must start the counter from 1 (not zero); otherwise the value of the factorial becomes zero in the first iteration and remains zero for the rest of the algorithm. Since we start the counter from 1, we need to come out of the loop when the counter is $n + 1$ instead of n.

1. Input
   a. input *n*
2. Initialize
   a. initialize factorial to 1
   b. initialize counter to 1
3. Repeat as long as the counter is less than *n + 1*
   a. set new factorial to previous factorial times counter
   b. update counter
4. Output
   a. output factorial

Write the Program

Based on the program components, it is very simple to write the code for this problem. However, we must be concerned about one potential problem: overflow in the result value. Depending on the size of the *unsigned long* type in the system, the result could overflow with a large value for n (Program 5.19).

Program 5.19 Factorial

```
/*****************************************************************
 * It uses the idea of list multiplication to find the value    *
 * of n! (factorial n)                                          *
 *****************************************************************/
#include <iostream>
using namespace std;

int main ( )
{
  // Variable declaration
   int n;
   unsigned long long factorial;
  // Input
   do
   {
       cout << "Enter the factorial size: ";
       cin >> n;
   } while (n < 0);
  // initialization
   factorial = 1;
  // Processing
   for (int i = 1; i < n + 1; i++)
   {
       factorial *= i;
   }
  // Output
   cout << n << "! = " << factorial;
   return 0;
}
```

```
Run:
Enter the factorial size: 0
0! = 1
```

```
Run:
Enter the factorial size: 4
4! = 24
```

```
Run:
Enter the factorial size: 12
12! = 479001600
```

```
Run:
Enter the factorial size: 22
22! = 17196083355034583040
```

```
Run:
Enter the factorial size: 30
30! = 9682165104862298112
```

Let us analyze the outputs: The first output defines $0! = 1$, which is according to the definition. The second output is obvious; when n is 4, we have $4! = 1 \times 2 \times 3 \times 4 = 24$. The third output shows that the factorial calculation really becomes large when n is 12. The results of the fourth and fifth outputs are strange. The result of 30! is less than the result of 22!. This means overflow has occurred, but we do not know where. It could have occurred for values less than $n = 22$.

5.7.3 Power

Another interesting example of multiplication is calculating the power of a number (b^n) in which b is called the base and n is called the exponent.

Understand the Problem

This is an example of multiplication in which the list is the repetition of the same value, the base. In other words, we multiply the base n times by itself.

$$power = b^n = b \times b \times b \times \ldots \times b \times b \quad n \text{ times}$$

The library of C++ provides a function that calculates the power of any base to any exponent. The numbers used in this function are all floating-point values. Sometimes we need to use unsigned integers, which is what we do in this section.

Develop the Algorithm

The following is the informal description of the algorithm.

1. **Input**
   - a. **input *base***
   - b. **input *exponent***
2. **Initialize**
   - a. **power to 1**
   - b. **set counter to 0**
3. **Repeat as long as the counter is less than *exponent***
   - a. **set new power to previous power times base**
   - b. **update counter**
4. **Output**
   - a. **output power**

Write the Program

Since we know how to handle overflow, we give the final version of the program in Program 5.20.

Program 5.20 Calcuating a base to a power (b ^ n)

```
/*************************************************************
 * It uses the idea of multiplication to find the value of a  *
 * base to the power of an exponent (b^n).                    *
 *************************************************************/
```

(continued)

Program 5.20 Calcuating a base to a power (b ^ n) (Continued)

```
#include <iostream>
using namespace std;

int main ( )
{
  // Variable declaration
  int base, exponent;
  unsigned long int power, temp;
  bool overflow;
  // input validation for base
  do
  {
      cout << "Enter a non-negative integer value for b: " ;
      cin >> base;
  } while (base < 0);
  // input validation for exponent
  do
  {
      cout << "Enter a non-negative integer value for n: " ;
      cin >> exponent;
  } while (exponent < 0);
  // initialization
  power = 1;
  temp = power;
  overflow = false;
  // Processing
  for (int i = 1; (i <= exponent) && (!overflow); i++)
  {
      power * = base;
      if (power / base != temp)
      {
          overflow = true; // terminate the loop
      }
      temp = power;
  }
  // Output
  if (overflow)
  {
      cout << "Overflow occurred! Try again with smaller b or n." ;
  }
  else
  {
      cout << base << "^" << exponent << " = " << power;
  }
```

(continued)

Program 5.20 Calcuating a base to a power (b ^ n) (Continued)

```
    return 0;
}
```

```
Run:
Enter a non-negative integer value for b: 22
Enter a non-negative integer value for n: 5
22^5 = 5153632
```

```
Run:
Enter a non-negative integer value for b: 5
Enter a non-negative integer value for n: 25
5^25 = 298023223876953125
```

```
Run:
Enter a non-negative integer value for b: 5
Enter a non-negative integer value for n: 28
Overflow occurred! Try again with smaller b or n.
```

The first point about Program 5.20 is that we may be tempted to allow negative values for the b (*base*). If we do so, the result would be negative when the value of *n* (*exponent*) is odd. Therefore, we use an unsigned value for *power* and *temp* to keep the overflow checking simple.

The second point is that the variable *power* overflows in the last test, which means our system cannot accept 5^{28}. The difference between this problem and the pervious one is that the overflow depends on the value of *b* and *n* together. So it is more difficult to determine what caused overflow.

5.7.4 The Smallest and the Largest

Two other common activities in computer science are to find the smallest and the largest values among a list of numbers.

Understand the Problem

Assume that we have the following list of numbers: 17, 14, 12, 18, and 71. We initialize the variable *smallest* to +infinity before entering the loop. In each step, we determine the smaller between the result of the last iteration and the next number. We do this by using an *if* statement. The following demonstrates the process for the smallest. The process for the largest is similar. We set the variable *largest* to −infinity before entering the loop. In each iteration, we determine the larger between the previous largest and the next number.

Numbers	smallest = + infinity
17	smallest = smaller of 17 and previous smallest (+infinity) = 17
14	smallest = smaller of 14 and previous smallest (17) = 14
12	smallest = smaller of 12 and previous smallest (14) = 12
71	smallest = smaller of 71 and previous smallest (12) = 12
Result	12

Some literature initializes *smallest* (or *largest*) to the first number. Although this practice works for almost all cases, it does not work if the list is empty. In other words, it is not a general solution. You may wonder why we set *smallest* to +infinity. The reason is that we want *smallest* to be the value of the first number in the list after the first iteration. The procedure is similar for *largest*.

Develop the Algorithm

The following is the informal description of the algorithm.

1. Input
- **a. input *size***

2. Initialize
- **a. initialize smallest to (+infinity)**
- **a. initialize largest to (−infinity)**
- **b. initialize counter to 0**

3. Repeat as long as the counter is less than *size*
- **a. read next number**
- **b. set smallest to the smaller of previous smallest and the number**
- **b. set largest to the larger of previous largest and the number**
- **b. update counter**

4. Output
- **b. output smallest**
- **a. output largest**

Write the Program

Program 5.21 shows how we can combine the components we discussed to find the smallest and the largest among a list of integers.

Program 5.21 Finding the smallest and the largest in a list

```
/***************************************************************
 * The program finds the smallest and the largest among a list        *
 * of integers when the size of the list is known.                    *
 ***************************************************************/
#include <iostream>
#include <limits>                 // Header file for numeric limits
using namespace std;

int main ( )
{
  // Variable declaration
  int size;
  int number, smallest, largest;
  // Initialization
  smallest = numeric_limits <int> :: max();
```

(continued)

Program 5.21 Finding the smallest and the largest in a list (Continued)

```
    largest = numeric_limits <int> :: min() ;
    // Size Input
    do
    {
        cout << "Enter the size of the list (non-negative): ";
        cin >> size;
    } while (size <= 0);
    // Processing
    for (int i = 1; i <= size; i++)
    {
        cout << "Enter the next item: ";
        cin >> number;
        if (number < smallest)
        {
                smallest = number;
        }
        if (number > largest)
        {
                largest = number;
        }
    } // End for
    // Result output
    cout << "The smallest item is: " << smallest << endl;
    cout << "The largest item is: " << largest << endl;
    return 0;
}
```

Run:

```
Enter the size of the list (non-negative): 6
Enter the next item: 12
Enter the next item: -3
Enter the next item: 14
Enter the next item: 15
Enter the next item: 27
Enter the next item: -7
The smallest item is: -7
The largest item is: 27
```

Run:

```
Enter the size of the list (non-negative): 3
Enter the next item: 1
Enter the next item: 87
Enter the next item: 45
The smallest item is: 1
The largest item is: 87
```

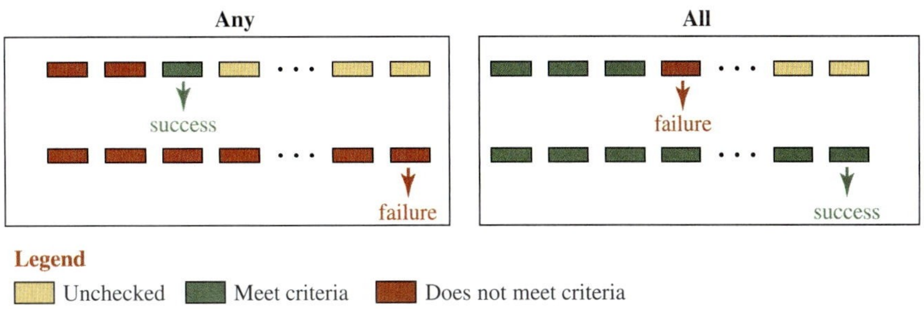

Figure 5.16 The search looking for *any* or *all*

5.7.5 Any or All Queries

Another common activity in computer science is to search a list of items using specified criteria. In particular, we often need to see if any item meets the criteria or if all items meet the criteria.

Understand the Problem

If we are looking for any item that meets the criteria, we stop the search as soon as we find the first item that does. If we want to check if all items meet the criteria, we stop the search as soon as we find the first item that does not. Figure 5.16 shows the search process.

Develop the Algorithm

Since we need to stop the search when we find an item meeting the criteria (in *any*) or when we find the item not meeting the criteria (in *all*), we need to use a combination of a counter-controlled (or sentinel or EOF) and a flag-controlled loop. We call this flag *success.* We initialize *success* to *false* for *any* and to *true* for *all*. In the case of *any,* we are successful if success turns to *true* during the loop. In the case of *all*, we are successful if *success* remains *true* for the entire duration. The best way to find the condition of either loop is to think about the condition for exiting the loop and use De Morgan's law to change it to the condition for staying in the loop.

Problem	Terminating condition	Staying condition
any:	(no more item) or (success)	(more item) and (not success)
all:	(no more item) or (not success)	(more item) and (success)

The following is the separate informal description of the algorithm for *any* and *all* queries. Note that we have written separate descriptions for each problem because the condition for terminating the loop and the output result is different for each problem.

Description for any	Description for all
1. input	**1. input**
a. input size	**a. input size**
2. Initialize	**2. Initialize**
a. success = *false*	**a. success = *true***
b. counter = *0*	**b. counter = *0***

3. Repeat (counter < size or !success)	**3. Repeat (counter < size or success)**
a. read next item	**a. read next item**
b. success = criteria	**b. success = criteria**
c. counter++	**c. counter++**
4. if success	**4. if success**
a. write success message	**a. write success message**
5. else	**5. else**
a. write failure message	**a. write failure message**

Write the Program

Since the two programs are very similar, we give the code for the case of *any* and leave the case of *all* as an exercise. Program 5.22 shows the code. We have a validation loop, a search loop, and a post-loop decision to check if the item meeting the given criterion was found or not.

Program 5.22 Finding if *any* item in a list meets a given criterion

```
/***************************************************************
 * The program search a list of item to find if any item is     *
 * divisible by 7.                                              *
 ***************************************************************/
#include <iostream>
using namespace std;

int main ( )
{
  // Declaration
   bool success;
   int size;
   int item;
  // Input Validation
   do
   {
        cout << "Enter the number of items in the list: ";
        cin >> size;
   } while (size < 0);
  // Processing
   for (int i = 0; (i < size ) && (!success); i++)
   {
        cout << "Enter the next item: ";
        cin >> item;
         success = (item %7 == 0);
   }
  // Checking success or failure
```

(*continued*)

Program 5.22 Finding if *any* item in a list meets a given criterion (Continued)

```
    if (success)
    {
        cout << "The number " << item << " is divisible by 7." << endl;
    }
    else
    {
        cout << "None of the numbers is divisible by 7." << endl;
    }
    return 0;
}
```

```
Run:
Enter the number of items in the list: 5
Enter the next item: 12
Enter the next item: 32
Enter the next item: 28
The number 28 is divisible by 7.
```

```
Run:
Enter the number of items in the list: 5
Enter the next item: 6
Enter the next item: 12
Enter the next item: 15
Enter the next item: 17
Enter the next item: 22
None of the numbers is divisible by 7.
```

Key Terms

break statement
continue statement
counter-controlled loop
data validation
do-while statement
EOF-controlled loop
event-controlled loop
flag-controlled loop
for statement
goto statement
nested loop
post-test loop
postfix increment expression
postfix decrement expression
pre-test loop
prefix increment expression
prefix decrement expression
return statement
sentinel
sentinel-controlled loop
while statement

Summary

Repetition allows the program to iterate a section of code multiple times. When we are using repetition statements, we need to use a *counter* to check how many times something is repeated. Two groups of expressions are designed to simulate a counter: *postfix increment/decrement* and *prefix increment/decrement*. There are three repetition statements: the *while* loop, the *for* loop, and the *do-while* loop.

The *while* loop contains a condition, a Boolean expression, followed by a single statement known as the body of the loop. The *for* statement combines the three elements: loop-initialization, conditional test, and update. The *do-while* loop is similar to the *while* loop except that the logical expression is tested at the end of each iteration.

There are four other statements that may be used with the loop construct: *return, break, continue,* and *goto*. The return statement terminates a function. The break statement jumps to the end of a loop prematurely and discontinues repetition. The continue statement in a loop is used to immediately terminate one iteration, but the next iteration will be executed. The *goto* statement transfers control to a labeled statement. It is considered non-structured and should not be used.

Problems

PR-1. How many times is the body of the following loop executed? What is the value of *x* after the loop termination?

```
int x = 5;
while ( x < 9 )
{
    x++;
}
```

PR-2. How many times is the body of the following loop executed? What is the value of *x* after the loop termination?

```
int x = 5;
while ( x < 11 )
{
    x += 2;
}
```

PR-3. How many times is the body of the following loop executed? What is the value of *x* after the loop termination?

```
int x = 7;
while ( x < 3 )
{
    x++;
}
```

PR-4. How many times is the body of the following loop executed? What are the values of *x* and *y* after the loop termination?

```
int x = 7;
int y = 5;
while ( x < 11 && y > 3 )
{
    x++;
    y--;
}
```

PR-5. How many times is the body of the following loop executed? What is the value of x after the loop termination?

```
int x = 7;
while ( false )
{
      x++;
}
```

PR-6. How many times is the body of the following loop executed? What is the value of x after the loop termination?

```
int x = 10;
while ( true )
{
      x--;
}
```

PR-7. How many times is the body of the following loop executed? What is the value of x after the loop termination?

```
int x = 5;
do
{
      x -= 2;
} while (x != 4);
```

PR-8. How many times is the body of the following loop executed? What is the value of x after the loop termination?

```
int x = 15;
do
{
      x -= 2;
      if (x < 9)
      break;
} while (true);
```

PR-9. What is printed from the following program segment?

```
int x = 13;
while (x > 7)
{
      cout << x << " ";
      x--;
}
```

PR-10. What is printed from the following program segment?

```
for (int x = 13; x > 7; x--)
{
      cout << x << "  ";
}
```

PR-11. What is printed from the following program segment?

```
int x = 13;
do
{
    cout << x << "  ";
    x--;
} while (x > 7);
```

PR-12. Change the following *do-while* loop to a *while* loop.

```
int x = 10;
do
{
    cout << x << end;
    x++;
} while (true);
```

Both *do-while* and *while* are infinite loops.

PR-13. Change the following *while* loop to a *for* loop.

```
int x = 10;
while (x < 20)
{
    cout << x << endl;
    x++;
}
```

PR-14. Change the following *for* loop to a *while* loop.

```
for (int x = 20; x < 10; x--)
{
    cout << x << endl;
}
```

Programs

PRG-1. Write a program to print any of the following four patterns. The pattern type (1 to 4) and the size of the pattern (1 to 9) are given by the user.

```
type 1          type 2          type 3          type 4
*               *****           *****               *
**              ****             ****              **
***             ***               ***             ***
****            **                 **            ****
*****           *                   *           *****
```

PRG-2. Write a program to print one of the following patterns. The pattern type and size (number of rows) are given by the user (between 1 and 6).

```
  type 1        type 2
 ********          *
  *******         ***
   *****         *****
    ***         *******
     *         *********
```

PRG-3. Write a program that reads a list of positive integers less than 1000 from a keyboard. The program prints the sum and the average of the numbers. The program will stop when the user types 1000 as a sentinel.

PRG-4. Write a program that asks the user to enter a list of positive or negative integers using the integer 0 as the sentinel. The program then counts the number of positive and negative integers entered.

PRG-5. Write a program that asks the user to enter two positive integers. The program then prints a list of even and a list of odd numbers between the given integers.

PRG-6. Write a program that prints all numbers between 1 and 100 that are divisible by 7.

PRG-7. Write a program that prints all numbers between 1 and 100 that are divisible by both 5 and 7.

PRG-8. Write a program that reads a positive integer between 1 and 100 and prints its factors (divisors). A factor is a number that divides another number. For example, the factors of 10 are 1, 2, 5, and 10. The factors of 12 are 1, 2, 3, 4, 6, and 12.

PRG-9. Write a program that reads two integers between 1 and 100 and prints their common factors (divisors).

PRG-10. Write a program that finds the greatest common divisor of two integers m and n using the following algorithm:

a. Let $m = m - n$ and swap m and n if $m < n$ after subtraction.
b. Repeat step (a) until n is 0. The greatest common divisor is m. Test your programs with the following pairs of data: 9 and 12; 7 and 11; and 12 and 140.

PRG-11. Write a program that reads a list of scores between 0 and 100 and finds and prints the smallest and the largest scores. The program needs to ask for the number of the scores from the user; this number must be less than or equal to 10.

PRG-12. Write a program to display the leap years in the years 2000 to 2099. A leap year is a year that is divisible by 4, but if it is divisible by 100, it should also be divisible by 400.

PRG-13. Write a program that asks the user to enter a positive integer. The program then prints the sum of the digits.

PRG-14. Write a program that asks the user to enter a positive integer. The program then prints the integer in reverse order. For example, if the user enters 359, the program prints 953.

PRG-15. Write a program that asks the user to enter a positive integer. The program then checks to see if the number is a palindrome. A palindrome integer is an integer that is the same when the order of digits is reversed. For example, 353 and 376673 are palindromes. Hint: Use the result of the program in PRG-14.

PRG-16. Write a program that creates a table of Celsius/Fahrenheit conversions between 0 and 99 degree Celsius. The conversion formula is as follows:

```
Fahrenheit = Celcius * 180.0 / 100.0 + 32
```

The programs we have presented thus far have been very simple. They solve problems that can be understood without too much effort. As we consider increasingly larger and more complex programs, however, we will discover that it is not possible to understand all aspects of most programs without somehow first reducing them to more elementary parts.

Breaking a complex problem into smaller parts is a common practice. We divide programs into modules that are tractable. In this chapter, we discuss functions, an abstraction in computer programming that helps to divide a large program into smaller parts.

Objectives

After you have read and studied this chapter, you should be able to:

- Introduce functions and discuss the benefits of dividing the task of a program into smaller tasks, each assigned to a function.
- Give the elements of a function: definition, declaration, and call.
- Group the functions in C++ into library functions and user-defined functions.
- Discuss library functions that we can use without defining them, such as mathematical functions, character functions, time functions, and random-number generators.
- Introduce the idea of user-defined functions by dividing them into four groups: void functions with no parameters, void functions with parameters, data-returning functions with no parameters, and data-returning functions with parameters.
- Discuss the mechanism of data exchange between the calling function and the called function: data pass and data return.
- Discuss default parameters and function overloading in which two or more functions can be defined with different signatures.
- Discuss the scope of entities in a program: local and global.
- Discuss the lifetime of entities in a program, including automatic and static variables.
- Design and write programs using functions.

6.1 INTRODUCTION

A **function** is an entity designed to do a task; it has a header and a set of statements enclosed in opening and closing braces. In previous chapters, we used one single function, *main*, to do the whole task of the program. In other words, we put the whole responsibility of solving a problem on the *main* function. This approach works for small programs in which the task is very simple and the program is short.

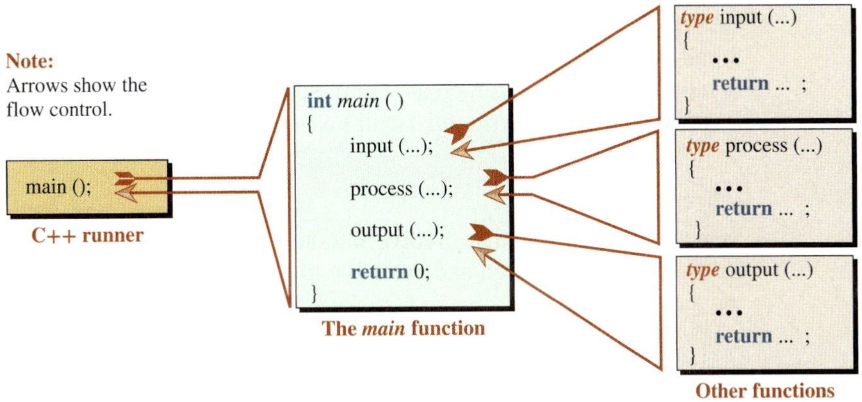

Figure 6.1 A program made of several functions

When a task is more complicated, we divide the task into smaller tasks, in which each task is responsible for a part of the job. We see this approach in many other situations. For example, manufacturing a car is divided into several tasks. The body is made at one location, the engine is made somewhere else, another entity is responsible for making tires, and so on. When all of the parts are made and ready, the car is assembled.

The same approach can be applied to programming. We can divide a program into different sections, in which each section is responsible for a part of the task. Each section in this case is called a function in C++, although other terms with the same meaning, such as *method* or *procedure,* are also used. Figure 6.1 shows this approach.

In the figure, the responsibility of the program is still on the shoulder of the *main* function, but *main* calls other functions to do part of the job. The statements *input* (…), *process* (…), and *output* (…) are function calls that invoke the corresponding functions and let them do part of the job. When each function terminates, the control returns to the *main* function. The figure also shows that the *main* function is called by the C++ runner. When we run the program, the *main* function is invoked and does its task. In other words, we have used the concept of a function from the first program we wrote in the first chapter of this book. In this chapter, we develop the idea and learn how we can write more functions.

6.1.1 Benefits

You may wonder about the benefit of dividing a task into several small tasks when doing so involves writing more code because of the overhead involved in each function. Despite the extra work, there are benefits to task division, including the following.

Easier to Write Simpler Task

Everyone knows that doing simple tasks is easier than doing difficult tasks. It is easier to concentrate on manufacturing tires for cars than manufacturing the whole car.

Error Checking (Debugging)

One of the big headaches of programming is finding errors (called bugs). Error checking (or debugging) is much more simple when a program is divided into small functions. Each function can be debugged and then put together as one program.

Reusability

Small tasks can be reused in many large tasks. If we isolate these small tasks and write a function for each, we can create many large programs by assembling these small functions. We do not need to rewrite the small task over and over again.

Library of Functions

Some common tasks that involve interaction with the operating system and the computer hardware are pre-written and available to the user. We can use these functions without writing the code for them.

6.1.2 Definition, Declaration, and Call

To work with a function, we must consider three entities: function definition, function declaration, and function call. We briefly discuss these here.

Function Definition

The **function definition** creates the function. Like any other entity in C++, the definition of a function must follow syntax rules. Figure 6.2 shows the basic syntax of a function definition.

As the figure shows, the definition is made of two sections: the **function header** and the **function body.** The header defines the name of the function, the type of data that will be returned from the function, and the **parameter list,** which consists of the data items (with their types) that are passed to the function. The body defines what is done by the function.

EXAMPLE 6.1

The following shows the definition of a function that finds and returns the larger of two given integers.

```
int larger (int first, int second)    // header
{
   int temp;
   if (first > second)
   {
      temp = first;
   }
   else
   {
      temp = second;
   }
   return temp;
}
```

```
return-type function-name (parameter list)
{
        Body
}
```

Figure 6.2 Syntax of function definition

Table 6.1 Function call

Group	Name	Operator	Expression	Pred	Assoc
postfix	function call	(...)	name (expr, ...)	18	→

The return type is integer. There are two parameters each of type integer. The body is a compound statement, as we have seen in the *main* function in previous chapters.

Function Declaration

The **function declaration** (also called **function prototype**) is only the header of the function followed by a semicolon. The parameter names are optional; the types are required. The function declaration is used to show how the function should be called. It tells us what goes into the function and what comes out of it without defining the action performed by the function.

EXAMPLE 6.2

The following shows the declaration of the function defined in Example 6.1. We have given two versions, with and without the names of the parameters.

```
int larger (int first, int second);     // With the names of the parameters
int larger (int, int );                 // Without the names of the parameters
```

Function Call

A **function call** is a postfix expression that invokes a function to do its job. As with the expressions we learned in previous chapters, we need to know the syntax of this expression to call it. It belongs to the postfix group (like the postfix-increment and postfix-decrement expressions). Table 6.1 shows the position of the function call expression with relation to other expressions as discussed in Appendix C.

Figure 6.3 shows more information about a function call expression.

If we compare the syntax of the function call with other postfix expressions, such as postfix-increment or postfix-decrement, we see that the operand in this case is a name (the name of the function). The operator is a pair of parentheses with a list of zero or more values. A function call can have a side effect, a return value, or both. If it has only a side effect, it needs to be used as an expression statement. If it returns a value (with or without a side effect), it can be used in any situation where a value is needed. Our larger function is called as *larger* (*value1*, *value2*), as shown in the next example.

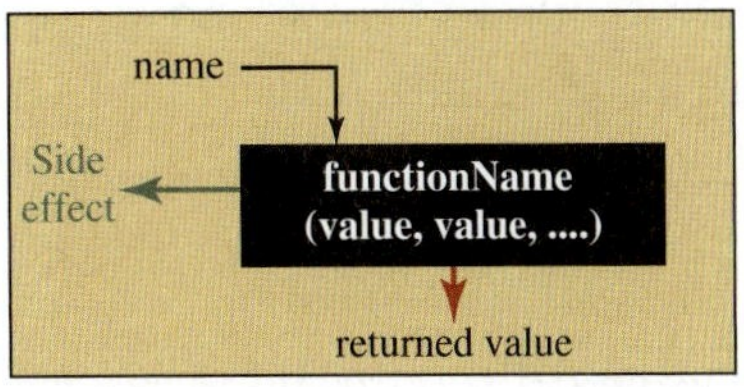

Note:
A function call can have a side effect, a return value, or both.

Figure 6.3 Function call operator

EXAMPLE 6.3

The following shows how we can call our larger function in *main* as many times as we want.

```
int main ()
{
    cout << larger (3, 13);
    cout << larger (10, 12);
    cout << larger (2, 12);
    return 0;
}
```

You may have noticed that the *main* function we used in previous chapters is itself the definition of a function. The function is called by the C++ run-time environment. Its header tells us that it returns an integer, but its parameter list is empty (Appendix N shows the *main* function with a parameter list).

Arguments and Parameters

Before we close this section, we discuss two terms used in functions: arguments and parameters. A *parameter* is a variable declared in the header of the function definition; an *argument* is a value that initializes the parameter when the function is called. In other words, a parameter is like a variable on the left-hand side of an assignment statement; the corresponding argument is like the value used on the right-hand side of the assignment statement. The initialization of the parameter is done explicitly by the system when a function is called.

The following shows the function call with the assignment statement. The parameter *x* is initialized with argument 5.

```
int main ()
{
    ...
    fun (5);                // Function call; 5 is an argument
    ...
}
void fun (int x)            // Function definition; x is a parameter
{
    ...
}
```

As we will see, the argument can be a variable or even an object, but only its value takes part in the function call.

6.1.3 Library and User-Defined Functions

To use functions in a program, we must have a function definition and a function call. However, we must choose between two types: library functions and user-defined functions.

Library Functions

The C++ library contains predefined functions. We need only the declaration of the functions to call them. We study some of these functions later in this chapter.

User-Defined Functions

There are a lot of functions that we need, but there are no predefined functions for them. We must define these functions first and then call them. We learn how to do so later in the chapter.

6.2 LIBRARY FUNCTIONS

As we said before, if a there is a predefined function in library, we do not need to worry about the function definition. We only add the corresponding header file in which the function is defined. However, we must call the function, which means that we must know the declaration of the function.

6.2.1 Mathematical Functions

C++ defines a set of mathematical functions that can be called in our program. These functions are predefined and collected under the <cmath> header. The prefix "c" in the name of the header emphasizes that it is inherited (with some changes) from the C language.

We need the <cmath> header to use the mathematical functions.

Numeric Functions

Numeric functions are used in numeric calculations. The parameters are normally one or more numeric values and the result is also a numeric value. Table 6.2 shows some of the common functions in this category as well as function declarations.

The type is *float, double,* or *long double.* In the case of the *pow* function, the second argument can also be an integer. All of these functions can accept different types of arguments and can return a value of a different type. This means these functions are *overloaded* (we discuss overloading later in the chapter).

EXAMPLE 6.4

Program 6.1 shows the return values of the functions given in Table 6.2.

Table 6.2 Some numeric functions defined in <cmath>

Function declaration	Explanation
type abs (type *x*);	Returns absolute value of *x*
type ceil (type *x*);	Returns largest integral value less than or equal to *x*
type floor (type *x*);	Returns smallest integral value less than or equal to *x*
type log (type *x*);	Returns the natural (base e) logarithm of *x*
type log10 (type *x*);	Returns the common (base 10) logarithm of *x*
type exp (type *x*);	Returns e^x
type pow (type *x*, type *y*);	Returns x^y; note that y can also be of type int in this case
type sqrt (type *x*);	Returns the square root of *x* ($x^{1/2}$)

Program 6.1 Testing some numeric functions

```
/***************************************************************
 * This program shows how to use some of the numeric functions   *
 * defined in the <cmath> header file.                           *
 ***************************************************************/
#include <iostream>
#include <cmath>
using namespace std;

int main ( )
{
  // abs function with two different arguments
  cout << "abs (8) = " << abs (8) << endl;
  cout << "abs (-8) = " << abs (-8) << endl;
  // floor and ceil functions with the same argument
  cout << "floor (12.78) = " << floor (12.78) << endl;
  cout << "ceil (12.78) = " << ceil (12.78) << endl;
  // log and log10 functions
  cout << "log (100) =  " << log (100) << endl;
  cout << "log10 (100) =  " << log10 (100) << endl;
  // exp and pow functions
  cout << "exp (5) =  " << exp (5) << endl;
  cout << "pow (2, 3) = " << pow (2,3) << endl;
  // sqrt function
  cout << "sqrt (100)    " << sqrt (100);
  return 0;
}
```

Run:

```
abs(8) = 8
abs(-8) = 8
floor(12.78) = 12
ceil(12.78) = 13
log(100) = 4.60517
log10 (100) = 2
exp(5) = 148.413
pow(2, 3) = 8
sqrt(100) = 10
```

Note that since none of the functions has a side effect, the return value will be thrown away when we use any of the functions as an expression statement. We must use each function where a value is needed, such as an argument to the insertion operator (<<).

EXAMPLE 6.5

For an application of one of these functions, *pow*, let us find the roots of the quadratic equation $ax^2 + bx + c = 0$ as we have seen in mathematics. We know that three situations can happen depending on the value of $(b^2 - 4ac)$, which we call the *term*:

a. If the value of the *term* is negative, there are no real roots (they are complex).

b. If the value of the *term* is zero, the two roots are the same and the common value is $-b/2a$.

c. If the value of the *term* is positive, the two roots are distinct and their values are $-b + (b^2 - 4ac)^{1/2}$ and $-b - (b^2 - 4ac)^{1/2}$.

We can use these three facts to find the roots of any quadratic expression, as shown in Program 6.2.

Program 6.2 Calculating the root of a quadratic equation

```
/***************************************************************
 * This program finds the roots of the quadratic equations      *
 ***************************************************************/
#include <iostream>
#include <cmath>
using namespace std;

int main ( )
{
   // Declaration of variables
   int a, b, c;
   double term;
   // Inputting the value of three coefficients
   cout << "Enter the value of coefficient a: ";
   cin >> a;
   cout << "Enter the value of coefficient b: ";
   cin >> b;
   cout << "Enter the value of coefficient c: ";
   cin >> c;
   // Calculating the value of term (b² – 4ac)
   term = pow (b, 2) – 4 * a * c;
   if (term < 0 )
   {
        cout << "There is no root!" << endl;
   }
   else if (term == 0)
   {
        cout << "The two roots are equal." << endl;
        cout << "x1 = x2 = " << –b / (2 * a) << endl;
   }
   else
   {
        cout << "There are two distinct roots: " << endl;
        cout << "x1 = " << (–b + sqrt (term)) / (2 * a) << endl;
        cout << "x2 = " << (–b – sqrt (term )) / (2 * a) << endl;
```

(continued)

Program 6.2 Calculating the root of a quadratic equation (Continued)

```
    }
    return 0;
}
```

```
Run:
Enter the value of coefficient a: 3
Enter the value of coefficient b: 5
Enter the value of coefficient c: 4
There is no root!
```

```
Run:
Enter the value of coefficient a: 1
Enter the value of coefficient b: 2
Enter the value of coefficient c: 1
The two roots are equal.
x1 = x2 = -1
```

```
Run:
Enter the value of coefficient a: 4
Enter the value of coefficient b: -9
Enter the value of coefficient c: 2
There are two distinct roots:
x1 = 2
x2 = 0.25
```

Trigonometric Functions

Table 6.3 gives the list of common trigonometric functions. Note that all of these functions are also overloaded. The type entries (colored red) represent one of the floating-point types (*float, double,* and *long double*).

Note that the argument of the first three functions needs to be in radians, in which 180 degrees = π radians and ($\pi = 3.14159265358979323846 2$) approximately.

EXAMPLE 6.6

Program 6.3 shows the use of some trigonometric functions.

Table 6.3 Trigonometric functions

Function declaration	Function explanation	Argument units	Returned range
type cos (type *x*);	Returns the cosine	radians	[−1, +1]
type sin (type *x*);	Returns the sine	radians	[−1, +1]
type tan (type *x*);	Returns the tangent	radians	any
type acos (type *x*);	Returns the inverse cosine	[−1, +1]	[0, π]
type asin (type *x*);	Returns the inverse sine	[−1, +1]	[0, π]
type atan (type *x*);	Returns the inverse tangent	any	[−π/2, +π/2]

Program 6.3 Trigonometric functions

```
/***************************************************************
 * A program to test some trigonometric functions              *
 ***************************************************************/
#include <iostream>
#include <cmath>
using namespace std;

int main ( )
{
  // Defining constant PI and an angle of 45 degrees
  const double PI = 3.141592653589793238462;
  double degree = PI / 4;
  // Finding the sin, cos, and tan of an angle of 45 degrees
  cout << "sin (45): " << sin (degree) << endl;
  cout << "cos (45): " << cos (degree) << endl;
  cout << "tan (45): " << tan (degree);
  return 0;
}
```

```
Run:
sin (45): 0.707107
cos (45): 0.707107
tan (45): 1
```

EXAMPLE 6.7

Trigonometry tells us that we can find the perimeter and area of a polygon with four or more sides given the number of sides and the length of each side, as shown in Figure 6.4.

Program 6.4 shows how we can find the perimeter and the area of any polygon.

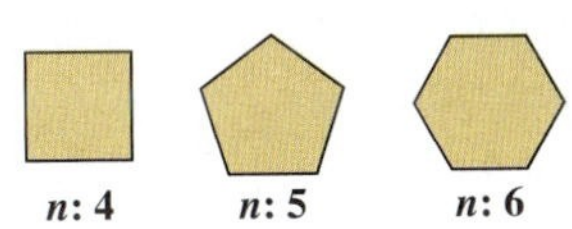

$$\textbf{perimeter} = n \times s$$

$$\textbf{area} = \frac{n \times s^2}{4 \times \tan(\pi/n)}$$

Figure 6.4 Perimeter and area of polygons

Program 6.4 Calculating the perimeter and area of a polygon

```
/***************************************************************
 * This program finds the perimeter and the area of a polygon  *
 * given the number of sides and the length of a side          *
 ***************************************************************/
#include <iostream>
#include <cmath>
using namespace std;

```

(continued)

Program 6.4 Calculating the perimeter and area of a polygon (Continued)

```
int main ( )
{
   // Declarations
   const double PI = 3.14159265358979323846;
   int n;
   double s, peri, area;
   // Inputting number of sides
   do
   {
        cout << "Enter the number of sides (4 or more): ";
        cin >> n;
   } while (n < 4);
   // Inputting the length of each side
   do
   {
        cout << "Enter length of each side: ";
        cin >> s;
   } while (s <= 0.0);
   // Calculating perimeter and area
   peri = n * s;
   area = (n * pow (s, 2)) / (n * tan (PI / n));
   // Printing results
   cout << "Perimeter: " << peri << endl;
   cout << "Area: " << area;
   return 0;
}
```

```
Run:
Enter the number of sides (4 or more): 2
Enter the number of sides (4 or more): 3
Enter the number of sides (4 or more): 4
Enter length of each side: 5
Perimeter: 20
Area: 25
```

```
Run:
Enter the number of sides (4 or more): 5
Enter length of each side: 5
Perimeter: 25
Area: 34.4095
```

6.2.2 Character Functions

We discussed characters as a fundamental type in Chapter 2. We can apply most of the operations we discussed for fundamental types to character types. We can also use input/output operations on characters.

Table 6.4 Character classification functions

Function declaration	Explanation
int isalnum (int x);	Is the parameter an alphanumeric character?
int isalpha (int x);	Is the parameter an alphabetic character?
int iscntrl (int x);	Is the parameter a control character?
int isdigit (int x);	Is the parameter a decimal digit (0 to 9)?
int isgraph (int x);	Is the parameter a printable character other than space?
int islower (int x);	Is the parameter a lowercase letter (a to z)?
int isprint (int x);	Is the parameter a printable character (including space)?
int ispunct (int x);	Is the parameter a punctuation character?
int isspace (int x);	Is the parameter a whitespace character (space, return, or tab)?
int isupper (int x);	Is the parameter an uppercase character (A to Z)?
int isxdigit (int x);	Is the parameter a hexadecimal character (0–9, a–f, or A–F)?

In addition, there are several library functions that handle characters in C++. All character handling functions are found in the <cctype> library (abbreviation of C Character Type). They are inherited from the C language.

We need the <cctype> header to use the character functions.

Character Classification Functions

All of the classification function names start with the prefix *is,* such as *iscontrol*, *isupper*, an so on. If the argument belongs to the category defined by the function name, the function returns 1 (which can be interpreted as *true*); otherwise, the function returns 0 (which can be interpreted as *false*). Table 6.4 shows the list of these functions. Note that the parameter in each function is of type *int,* but we always pass a character as the parameter (a character is an integer smaller than short integer).

Character Conversion Functions

Two functions in C++ are used to convert a character from one class to another. These functions start with the prefix *to* and return an integer that is the value of the converted character. Table 6.5 shows these two functions.

Note that the return value of these functions is defined as an integer, but we can always convert the return value (implicitly or explicitly) to a character as shown in Program 6.5.

Program 6.5 shows an example of using the predefined functions *isalpha* and *toupper* to change the characters in the text to uppercase and to count the alphabetic characters.

Table 6.5 Character conversion functions

Declaration	Explanation
int tolower (int x)	Returns the lowercase version of its parameter.
int toupper (int x)	Returns the uppercase version of its parameter.

Program 6.5 Using character functions

```
/**************************************************************
 * A program that changes every lowercase letter to an uppercase   *
 * letter and counts the alphabetic characters.                     *
 **************************************************************/
#include <iostream>
#include <cctype>
using namespace std;

int main ( )
{
   // Declaration
   char ch;
   int count = 0;
   // Inputting characters and processing
   while (cin >> noskipws >> ch)
   {
        if (isalpha (ch))
        {
              count++;
        }
        ch = toupper (ch);
        cout << ch ;
   }
   // Printing the count of characters
   cout << "The count of alphabetic characters is: " << count;
   return 0;
}
```

```
Run:
This is a line made of more than 10 characters.
THIS IS A LINE MADE OF MORE THAN 10 CHARACTERS.
^Z
The count of alphabetic characters is: 35
```

6.2.3 Handling Time

One of the library functions we often encounter in C++ programming is the *time* function defined in the <ctime> header file. We discuss this function in more detail in Appendix I, but for the moment, it is enough to say that this function returns the number of seconds elapsed from the Unix epoch (midnight of January 1, 1970) when the argument passed to the function is 0. In other words, *time*(0) gives the count of seconds from the epoch until the time that the function is called, as shown in Figure 6.5.

To find the day, month, and year of the current time, we need more sophisticated functions, which we discuss in a future chapter (leap years must be considered). However, it is easy to find the hours, minutes, and seconds of the current time, as shown in the next example.

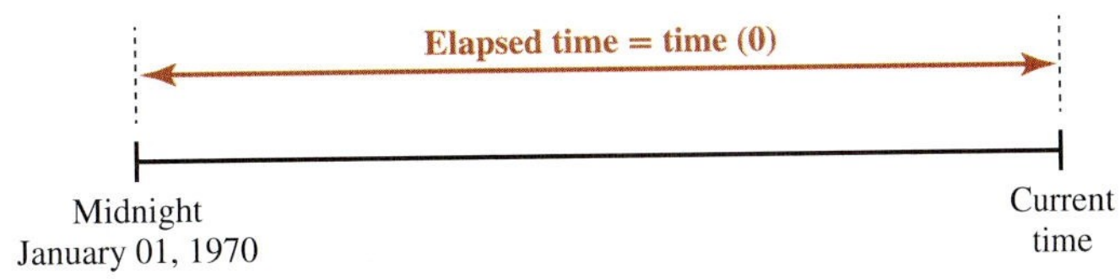

Figure 6.5 Number of seconds defined by *time*(0) function

EXAMPLE 6.8

Program 6.6 shows how we can use the *time*(0) function to print the current time. We need to know that the time calculated is Greenwich mean time (GMT), not the local time.

Note the use of / and % operators in Program 6.6. The first finds the elapsed unit; the second finds the current unit. Note also that if you want to find the current time in your location, you must add or subtract the difference between your local time and the GMT time.

6.2.4 Random Number Generation

The C++ 11 standard defined classes to create random numbers in any distribution as defined in probability theory. We discuss these classes later in the book. In this chapter, we

Program 6.6 Finding current time

```
/*****************************************************************
 * A program finding the current time using time (0) function     *
 *****************************************************************/
#include <iostream>
#include <ctime>
using namespace std;

int main ( )
{
   // Finding elapsed seconds and current second
   long elapsedSeconds = time (0);
   int currentSecond = elapsedSeconds % 60;
   // Finding elapsed minutes and current minute
   long elpasedMinutes = elapsedSeconds / 60;
   int currentMinute = elpasedMinutes % 60;
   // Finding elapsed hours and current hour
   long elapsedHours = elpasedMinutes / 60;
   int currentHour = elapsedHours % 24;
   // Printing current time
   cout << "Current time: ";
   cout << currentHour << " : " << currentMinute << " : " << currentSecond;
   return 0;
}
```

```
Run:
Current time: 20 : 57 : 59
```

```
Run:
Current time: 20 : 58 : 22
```

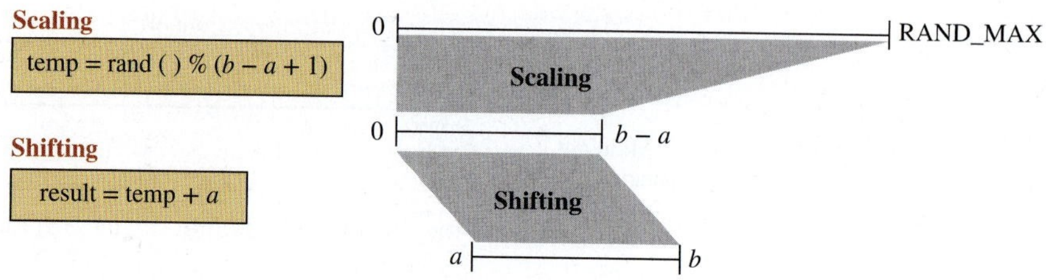

Figure 6.6 Scaling and shifting a random number

introduce the random number generator inherited from the C language and defined in the <cstdlib> header file. The function is called *rand*. It generates a random integer between 0 and RAND_MAX, a value that is system dependent but is normally set to 32,767 ($2^{15} - 1$), which means one of the 32,768 different values if we include 0.

This function is pseudorandom: It generates the same set of random numbers in each run of the program because it uses the same *seed* to start the random series. The seed is set to 1, which means that the same series is always generated. To get a different series in each run, we must give a different seed to the *rand* function each time we run the program. The best choice is to use the function *time*(0), which is the number of seconds passed from the epoch, as we discussed before. Each time we run the program, the value of *time*(0) is different, which means we get a different set of random numbers. To do so, we simply pass the return value of *time*(0) to another function named *srand* (seed for random) and then call the *rand* function.

We often need to create a random number in the range *a* to *b* (inclusive). To do so, we must create a random number using the *rand* function. We then must scale it to the range `0` to `(b - a)`. We finally shift it as shown in Figure 6.6.

EXAMPLE 6.9

As an application of generating a random number, we have created a number-guessing game (see Program 6.7). We generate a random number between two limits (*low* and *high*) and let the user guess a limited number of times to find it. In each try, if the guess is not correct, we give a clue to the user.

Program 6.7 A guessing game

```
/***************************************************************
 * A program simulating a guessing game using a random number  *
 ***************************************************************/
#include <iostream>
#include <cstdlib>
#include <ctime>
using namespace std;

int main ( )
{
  // Declaration and initialization
  int low = 5;
```

(continued)

Program 6.7 A guessing game (Continued)

```
int high = 15;
int tryLimit = 5;
int guess;
// Generation of random number
srand (time (0));
int temp = rand();
int num = temp % (high - low + 1) + low;
// Guessing loop
int counter = 1;
bool found = false;
while (counter <= tryLimit  && !found)
{
      do
      {
            cout << "Enter your guess between 5 to 15 (inclusive): ";
            cin >> guess;
      } while (guess < 5 || guess > 15);

      if (guess == num)
      {
            found = true;
      }
      else if (guess > num)
      {
            cout << "Your guess was too high!" << endl;
      }
      else
      {
            cout << "Your guess was too low!" << endl;
      }
      counter++;
}
// Success response
if (found)
{
      cout << "Congratulation: You found it. ";
      cout << "The number was: " << num;
}
// Failure response
else
{
      cout << "Sorry, you did not find it! ";
      cout << "The number was: " << num;
```

(continued)

Program 6.7 A guessing game (Continued)

```
    }
    return 0;
}
```

```
Run:
Enter your guess between 5 to 15 (inclusive): 7
Your guess was too low!
Enter your guess between 5 to 15 (inclusive): 8
Congratulation: You found it. The number was: 8
```

```
Run:
Enter your guess between 5 to 15 (inclusive): 15
Your guess was too high!
Enter your guess between 5 to 15 (inclusive): 14
Your guess was too high!
Enter your guess between 5 to 15 (inclusive): 13
Your guess was too high!
Enter your guess between 5 to 15 (inclusive): 12
Your guess was too high!
Enter your guess between 5 to 15 (inclusive): 11
Your guess was too high!
Sorry, you did not find it! The number was: 10
```

6.3 USER-DEFINED FUNCTIONS

Not all functions we need are defined in the C++ library. To call a function that is not defined in the library, we must first define it in our program.

6.3.1 Four Categories of Functions

We showed the general syntax of a function definition in Figure 6.2 and the syntax of the function call operator in Figure 6.3. In this section, we develop the function concept further by giving the syntax details for the four types of functions that we encounter in C++: *void* functions with no parameters, *void* functions with parameters, value-returning functions with no parameters, and value-returning functions with parameters as shown in Figure 6.7. We also discuss the applications of each type so that when we want to design a function, we know which type we need.

```
void name ( )
{
    ...
    return;
}
```

Void with no parameters

```
void name (type parameter, ...)
{
    ...
    return;
}
```

Void with parameters

```
type name ( )
{
    ...
    return value;
}
```

Value-returning with no parameters

```
type name (type parameter, ...)
{
    ...
    return value;
}
```

Value-returning with parameters

Figure 6.7 Four categories of functions in C++

Void Function with No Parameters

Probably the simplest case is a **void function** with no parameters. The function takes no parameters and returns nothing. This type of function is only defined for its side effect, which occurs inside the function; otherwise, the function is useless. Since the function does not return a value, we cannot use it where a value is needed. We can only use this function as a postfix expression in which its side effect is used.

EXAMPLE 6.10

Let us create a *void* function with no parameters that prints a message, such as a greeting, on the screen (side effect) as shown in Program 6.8. Note that we have used a different background color for the function definition. Note also that the function definition (lines 13 to 19) comes before the function call (line 23) in the *main* function. In fact, we have two function definitions, one for the *greeting* function and one for the *main* function. The *greeting* function is called from inside of the *main* function; the *main* function is called by the C++ runner.

Program 6.8 Using a void function with no argument

```
1  /****************************************************************
2   * A program that prints a boxed greeting using a void function      *
3   ****************************************************************/
4  #include <iostream>
5  using namespace std;
6
7  /****************************************************************
8   * Function definition for the greeting function. This is a void      *
9   * function with no parameters that creates a three-line message.     *
10  * The function returns nothing to its caller. It has only a side     *
11  * effect (displaying three lines)                                    *
12  ****************************************************************/
13 void greeting ( )
14 {
15   cout <<"********************" << endl;
16   cout <<"* Hello Friends          *" << endl;
17   cout <<"********************" ;
18   return;
19 }
20
21 int main ( )
22 {
23   greeting(); // Calling the greeting function (expression statement)
24   return 0;
25 }
```

```
Run:
*****************
* Hello Friends     *
*****************
```

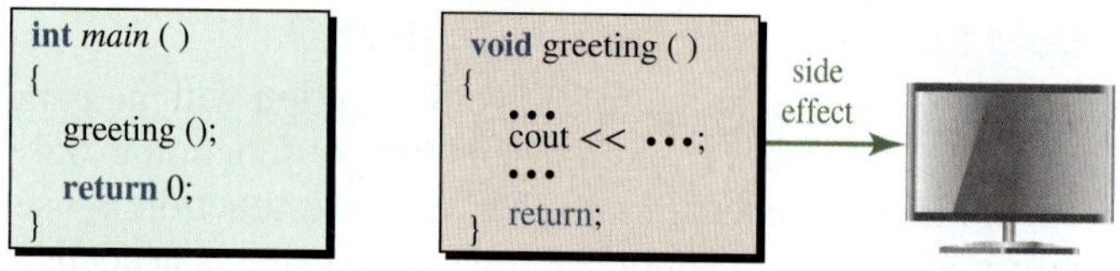

Figure 6.8 Communication between the main function and the greeting function

Figure 6.8 shows the communication between the *main* function and the *greeting* function. Although no data is exchanged between the *main* and *greeting* functions, there is a side effect. The *main* function first calls the *greeting* function. The *greeting* function prints the greeting on the screen (side effect). The control then returns to the *main* function (void return).

Void Function with Parameters

The next choice is to create a function with parameters. The function is passed values (arguments) that sit in the place of parameters. The function has a side effect but does not return data to its caller. This type of function is used when we need only the side effect of the function but we also need to pass some information, such as what is to be output each time we call the function. As we will see later, the void function with parameters is a good choice for the output module in the input-process-output design.

EXAMPLE 6.11

Program 6.9 shows an example in which the parameter tells the function how to format the pattern in each execution. Lines 14 to 25 are the function definition; line 38 is the function call.

Program 6.9 A void function with a parameter

```
1  /*****************************************************************
2   * This program shows how we can create different patterns using     *
3   * a void function with a parameter.                                  *
4   *****************************************************************/
5  #include <iostream>
6  using namespace std;
7
8  /*****************************************************************
9   * Function definition for the pattern function. This is a void       *
10  * function with one parameter that accepts its size from the         *
11  * user each time the program is called. The parameter is used        *
12  * to create a different size for the pattern.                        *
13  *****************************************************************/
14 void pattern (int size)
15 {
16   for (int i = 0; i < size; i++)
17   {
18       for (int j = 0; j < size; j++)
```

(*continued*)

Program 6.9 A void function with a parameter (Continued)

```
        {
            cout << "*" ;
        }
        cout << endl;
    }
    return;
}

int main()
{
    // Declaration
    int patternSize;   // Argument to be pass to the square function
    // Input validation
    do
    {
        cout << "Enter the size of the pattern: ";
        cin >> patternSize;
    } while (patternSize <=0);
    // Function call
    pattern (patternSize); // patternSize is the argument
    return 0;
}
```

```
Run
Enter the size of the pattern: 3
***
***
***
```

```
Run
Enter the size of the pattern: 4
****
****
****
****
```

Figure 6.9 shows the communication between *main* and the *pattern* function. Each time we run the program, we get a value for *patternSize* and pass that value to the function call to control the size of the printed pattern. In other words, the *patternSize* value is stored in the *size* parameter each time we call the function.

Value-Returning Function with No Parameters

This type of function is designed only for its return value. The function normally has an input side effect and returns the input value to the calling function. As we will see later, it is a good choice for the input module in the input-process-output design. Program 6.10 demonstrates the design concept. It calls an input function, *getData*, that reads an integer from the keyboard and returns it to the *main* function for processing.

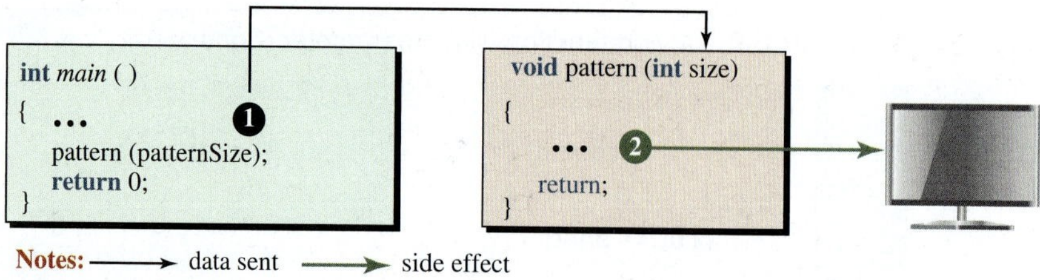

Figure 6.9 Communication between the main function and the pattern function

Program 6.10 A value-returning function without parameters

```
/***************************************************************
 * This program shows how to define a function to get a positive    *
 * integer from the keyboard and print its right-most digit.        *
 ***************************************************************/
#include <iostream>
using namespace std;

/***************************************************************
 * The getdata function is a returning-value function with          *
 * no parameters. It takes the user input (side effect) from        *
 * the keyboard and returns the value to the main function          *
 * after validating that the number is positive.                    *
 ***************************************************************/
int getData()
{
  int data;
  do
  {
      cout << "Enter a positive integer: ";
      cin >> data;
  } while (data <= 0);
  return data;
}

int main()
{
  int number = getData(); // Function call with no argument
  cout << "Right-most digit: " << number % 10;
  return 0;
}
```

Run

```
Enter a positive integer: 56
Right-most digit: 6
```

(continued)

Program 6.10 A value-returning function without parameters (Continued)

```
Run
Enter a positive integer: -72
Enter a positive integer: 72
Right-most digit: 2
```

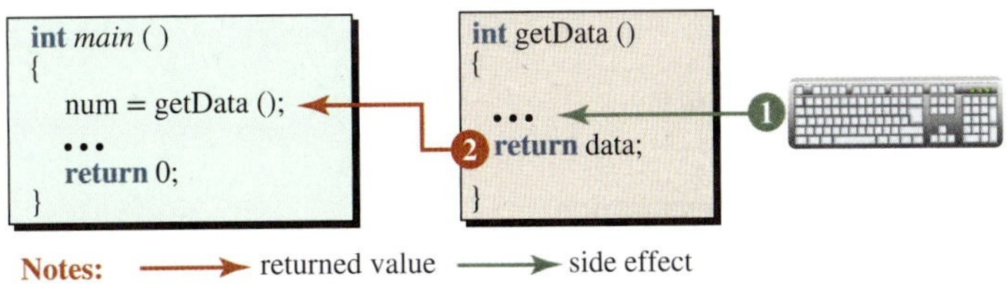

Figure 6.10 Communication between the main function and the pattern function

Figure 6.10 shows the communication between the *main* function and the *getData* function. Each time we run the program, we get an integer from the keyboard, validate that it is positive, and return it to the *main* function.

Value-Returning Function with Parameters

Program 6.11 shows how we can have a function with parameters that returns a value. The *larger* function accepts two values from the *main* function, finds the larger of the two, and returns the result.

Program 6.11 A value-returning function with parameters

```
/***************************************************************
 * This program shows how to define a function to find the      *
 * larger of any two positive integers given by the user.       *
 ***************************************************************/
#include <iostream>
using namespace std;

/***************************************************************
 * The larger function is a value-returning function with two   *
 * parameters that gets two values from the calling function    *
 * and returns the larger one. The function has no side effect. *
 ***************************************************************/
int larger (int fst, int snd)
{
   int max;
   if (fst > snd)
   {
        max = fst;
   }
```

(*continued*)

Program 6.11 A value-returning function with parameters (Continued)

```
   else
   {
       max = snd;
   }
   return (max);
} // End larger

int main()
{
   // Declaration
   int first, second;
   // Get inputs
   cout << "Enter the first number: ";
   cin >> first;
   cout << "Enter the second number: ";
   cin >> second;
   // Function call
   cout << "Larger: " << larger (first, second); // Function call
   return 0;
}
```

```
Run
Enter the first number: 56
Enter the second number: 71
Larger: 71
```

```
Run
Enter the first number: -10
Enter the second number: 8
Larger: 8
```

Figure 6.11 shows the communication between the *main* function and the *larger* function. The *main* function sends two values (arguments) to *larger*. The *larger* function finds the larger of the two and returns it.

6.3.2 Using Declarations

In all of the previous examples, we have put the function definition before the function call. Another approach is to put a declaration (prototype) of the function before the function call

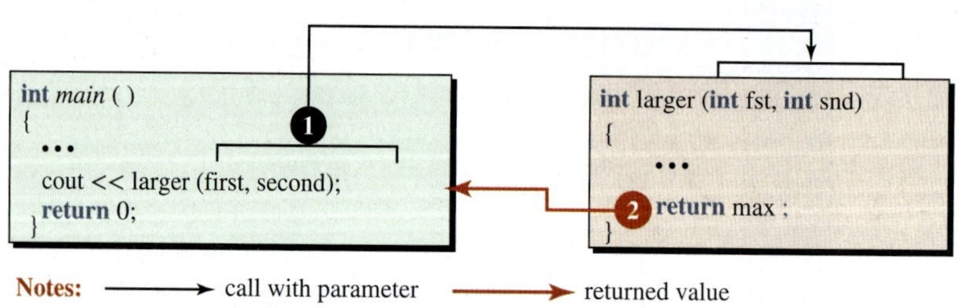

Figure 6.11 Function call, returns, and side effect

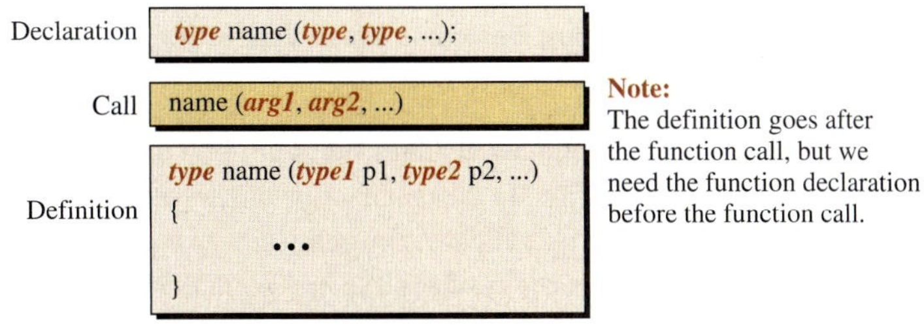

Figure 6.12 Setting function definition after function call

and put the function definition after the function call, as shown in Figure 6.12. Note that the declaration must have a semicolon at the end.

A semicolon is needed at the end of a function declaration.

EXAMPLE 6.12

Program 6.12 follows the principle of modular programming: input-process-output. The *main* function is responsible for only three calls: input call, processing call, and output call. The rest is done by three functions: *input*, *process*, *output*. Program 6.12 is designed to get the value of a year from the user (input), find if the year is a leap year (processing), and print the result (output). We previously discussed that a year needs to satisfy two criteria to be a leap year. First, it must be divisible by 4. Second, if it is divisible by 100, it must also be divisible by 400.

Program 6.12 Finding if a year is a leap year

```
/***************************************************************
 * This program shows how to use three functions: input an     *
 * integer representing a year, check if it is a leap year,    *
 * and print the result.                                        *
 ***************************************************************/
#include <iostream>
using namespace std;

// Declarations (prototypes)
int input ();
bool process (int year);
void output (int year, bool result);

int main ()
{
   // Input, processing, output
   int year = input();
   bool result = process (year);
   output (year, result);
}
```

(continued)

Program 6.12 Finding if a year is a leap year (Continued)

```
/***************************************************************
 * The definition of the input function. It is called in the   *
 * main function. It takes the value of the year from the user  *
 * (side effect), validates the year to be greater than 1582,   *
 * and returns the result to the main function. The function is *
 * value-returning, with no parameters, but with a side effect. *
 ***************************************************************/
int input ()
{
  int year;
  do
  {
       cout << "Enter a year after 1582: " ;
       cin >> year;
  } while (year <= 1582);
  return year;
}
/***************************************************************
 * The definition of the process function. It takes the value of *
 * the year from the main function as a parameter. It checks to *
 * to see if it is a leap year and returns a boolean value back *
 * to main. It is a value-returning function with a parameter   *
 * and no side effect.                                          *
 ***************************************************************/
bool process (int year)
{
  bool criteria1 = (year % 4 == 0);
  bool criteria2 = (year % 100 != 0) || (year % 400 == 0);
  return (criteria1) && (criteria2);
}
/***************************************************************
 * The output function takes the year value and the Boolean value *
 * returned from the process function. It prints the results on *
 * the monitor. It is a void function with two parameters.      *
 ***************************************************************/
void output (int year, bool result)
{
  if (result)
  {
       cout << "Year " << year << " is a leap year.";
  }
  else
  {
```

(continued)

Program 6.12 Finding if a year is a leap year (Continued)

```
        cout << "Year " << year << " is not a leap year.";
    }
    return;
}
```

```
Run
Enter a year after 1582: 1900
Year 1900 is not a leap year.
```

```
Run
Enter a year after 1582: 1500
Enter a year after 1582: 1600
Year 1600 is a leap year.
```

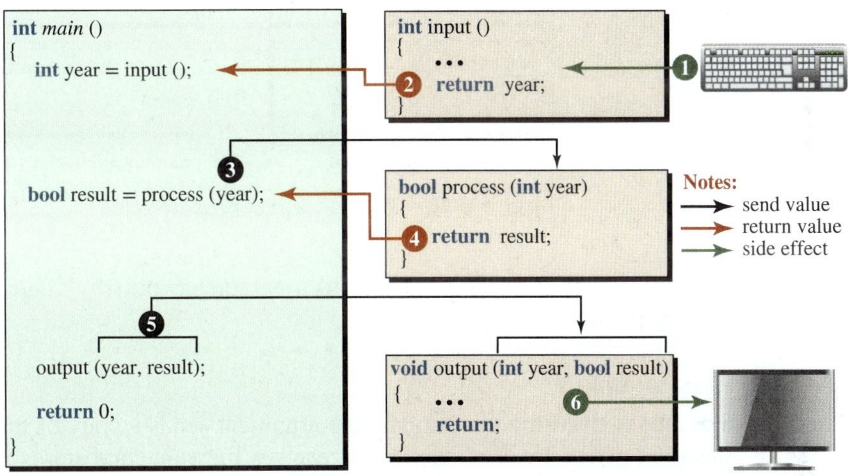

Figure 6.13 Relation between the *main* function and three called functions

Figure 6.13 shows the communication between the *main* function and the other three functions. The numbers define the order of communication. The *main* function first calls the *input* function, which gets input from the keyboard and returns a value (after validation) to the *main* function. The *main* function then calls the *process* function and passes the value of the year to it to determine if the year is a leap year and to return the result. The *main* function then calls the output function to print the value of the year and indicate if it is a leap year or not.

6.4 DATA EXCHANGE

In the previous section, we showed that a calling function can communicate with the called function. During communication, the two functions can exchange data in two directions: forward and backward, as shown in Figure 6.14. We discuss each case separately.

6.4.1 Passing Data

If the parameter list of the called function is not empty, data is passed from each argument to the corresponding parameter. Depending on the application, we can use three mechanisms

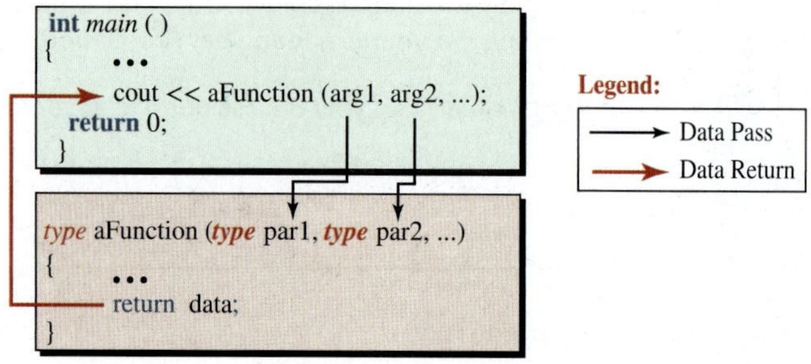

Figure 6.14 Data exchange between a caller and a called function

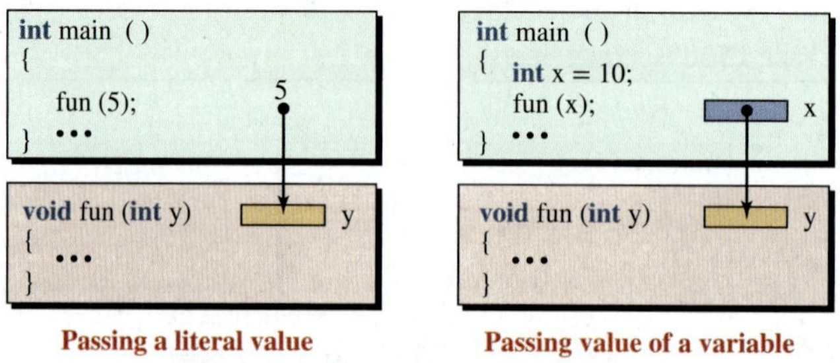

Figure 6.15 The concept of pass-by-value

for passing data from an argument to a parameter: pass-by-value, pass-by-reference, and pass-by-pointer.

Pass-by-Value

In the **pass-by-value** mechanism, the argument sends a copy of the data item to the corresponding parameter. The parameter receives the value and stores it. Since the exchange is made through a value, the argument can be a literal value or the value of a variable, as shown in Figure 6.15.

We use pass-by-value when we do not want a called function changing the value of the arguments passed to it. In other words, the called function can only read the value of the arguments; it cannot modify them. In computer parlance, this is referred to as read-only access.

The pass-by-value method initializes a parameter with a copy of the corresponding argument.

EXAMPLE 6.13

Program 6.13 shows a simple example to demonstrate the idea behind pass-by-value. We increment the value of parameter *y* in the called function (*fun*), but the value of the corresponding argument *x* is not incremented.

We see examples of pass-by-value in real life. When a friend wants to borrow a valuable document from you, you can give her a copy of the document. Your friend can do whatever she likes with the document, but your original document remains untouched.

Pass-by-Reference

In the **pass-by-reference** mechanism, a memory location is shared between the argument and the corresponding parameter. The calling and the called functions can refer to that memory

Program 6.13 Testing pass-by-value

```
/*************************************************************
 * This program shows how a change in the parameter cannot    *
 * affect the corresponding argument in pass-by-value.        *
 *************************************************************/
#include <iostream>
using namespace std;

// Function declaration
void fun (int y);

int main ()
{
   // Declaration and initialization of an argument
   int x = 10;
   // Calling function fun and passing x as an argument
   fun (x);
   // Printing the value of x to see no change
   cout << "Value of x in main: " << x << endl;
   return 0;
}
/*************************************************************
 * Fun is a function that receives the value of x by value and *
 * stores it in parameter y. The locations x and y are two     *
 * independent memory locations. The value of y is incremented *
 * in fun, but the value of x in main remains unchanged.       *
 *************************************************************/
void fun (int y)
{
   y++;
   cout << "Value of y in fun: " << y << endl;
   return;
}
```

```
Run
Value of y in fun: 11    // y in the called function is incremented.
Value of x in main: 10   // x in the main is not affected.
```

location by the same name or different names (different names are preferred). The parameter name is an *alias* for the argument name. Figure 6.16 shows the concept.

In the figure, the two names, *x* and *y*, are actually referring to the same variable location, which is created by the calling function and used by the called function. However, to tell the compiler that *y* is not a new memory location, C++ requires that we declare *y* as an alias to an integer location (*int*& y), not a new integer location (*int* y).

EXAMPLE 6.14

Program 6.14 repeats the previous example, but we have used pass-by-reference instead of pass-by-value.

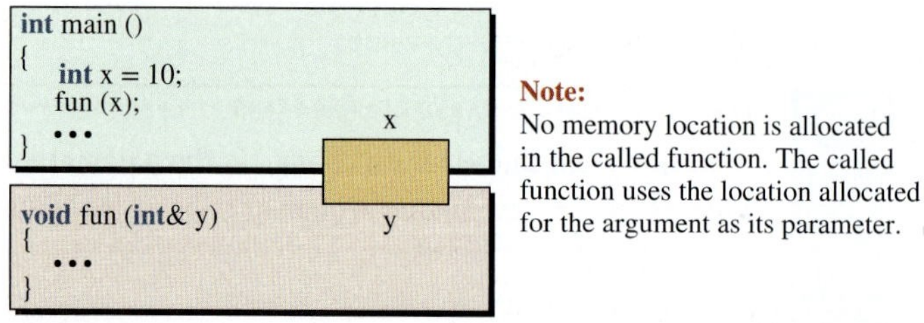

Figure 6.16 The concept of pass-by-reference

Program 6.14 Testing pass-by-reference

```
/***************************************************************
 * This program shows how a change in the parameter can change the      *
 * corresponding argument when data is passed by reference.             *
 ***************************************************************/
#include <iostream>
using namespace std;

// Function declaration;
void fun (int&  y);  // The ampersand tell us that y is an alliance

int main ()
{
   // Declaration and initialization of an argument
   int x = 10;
   // Calling function fun and passing x as an argument
   fun (x);
   // Printing the value of x to see change
   cout << "Value of x in main: " << x << endl;
   return 0;
}
/***************************************************************
 * Fun is a function that receives the value of y by reference,         *
 * which means the parameter y is an alias for the argument x in        *
 * the function call. This function increments its parameters, which   *
 * results in incrementing the argument in main.                        *
 ***************************************************************/
void fun (int&  y)
{
   y++;
   cout << "Value of y in fun: " << y << endl;
   return;
}
```

```
Run
Value of y in fun: 11
Value of x in main: 11       // Change of y in fun, has changed x in main
```

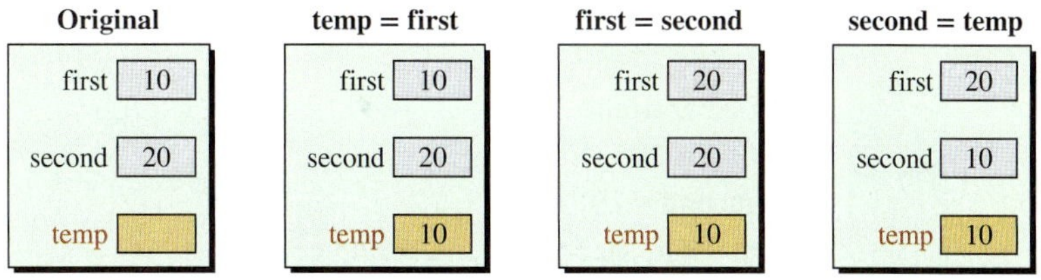

Figure 6.17 Using a temporary variable to swap two values

Note that we call the function *fun* with argument *x* of value 10. The *fun* function increments the value of *y* and prints it as 11. Since the *main* function and the *fun* function are sharing the same memory location, the value of *x* in the *main* function was also incremented as shown.

We see examples of pass-by-reference in real life. When we pass a document to a friend for editing, we are sharing the original document with her. Any change to the document by our friend changes it for us when the document is returned.

In computer parlance, we sometimes refer to pass-by-reference as *read-write* communication, which means the called function can read the value of the arguments in the calling function, and it can also change them.

EXAMPLE 6.15

As a classical example, we show the process of *swapping* the values of two variables, *first* and *second*. After swapping, the variable *first* holds what was originally stored in *second*; the variable *second* holds what was originally stored in *first*. For example, if the value of the variables *first* and *second* was 10 and 20, respectively, the variables should hold 20 and 10 after swapping. We should convince ourselves that using the simple assignment *first* = *second* and *second* = *first* sets both variables to 10 or 20. We must use a temporary variable and three assignments as shown in Figure 6.17. Note that the name of each variable must appear once at the left-hand side and once at the right-hand side of the assignment operator.

Swapping is used in sorting and other algorithms and is repeated so many times in each algorithm that it is worth having a function and calling the function whenever we need it. However, the called function cannot swap the variables in the calling function if we use pass-by-value because the data are exchanged in the called function but not in the calling function. This is a case where we need to use pass-by-reference, as shown in Program 6.15.

Program 6.15 Using a swap function

```
/***************************************************************
 * This program shows how pass-by-reference can swap two values  *
 * in the calling function.                                      *
 ***************************************************************/
#include <iostream>
using namespace std;

void swap (int& first, int& second); // Function declaration

int main ( )
{
```

(continued)

Program 6.15 Using a swap function (Continued)

```
   // Declaration
   int first = 10;
   int second = 20;
   swap (first, second); // Function call
   // Printing to test swapping
   cout << "Value of first in main: " << first << endl;
   cout << "Value of second in main: " << second;
   return 0;
}
/***************************************************************
 * The swap function takes two parameters as pass-by-reference.   *
 * It then swaps the values of fst and snd using a temporary      *
 * variable named temp. Since the data are passed by reference,   *
 * changing the parameters in the swap means changing values in   *
 * the arguments (first and second in main).                      *
 ***************************************************************/
void swap (int& fst, int& snd)
{
   int temp = fst;
   fst = snd;
   snd = temp;
   return;
}
```

```
Run:
Value of first in main: 20
Value of second in main: 10
```

Pass-by-Pointer

In the **pass-by-pointer** mechanism, the argument sends a memory address to the corresponding parameter. The parameter stores the address and can access the value stored in the argument through that address. The pass-by-pointer mechanism is used in the C language because pass-by-reference does not exist in C. It is still used to some extent in C++. We discuss pass-by-pointer after we discuss pointers in Chapter 9.

Advantages and Disadvantages

Before closing this section, we briefly review the advantages and disadvantages of each method.

a. Pass-by-value is very simple and protects arguments from being changed by the called function. However, it has one disadvantage: The argument object needs to be copied and passed from the calling function to the called function. If the object is small, like the built-in data types we have used so far, copying is not expensive and we should use this method. We will see in Chapter 9, however, that we do not use pass-by-value in object-oriented programming when the object size is large. We use the other methods (pass-by-reference and pass-by-pointer).

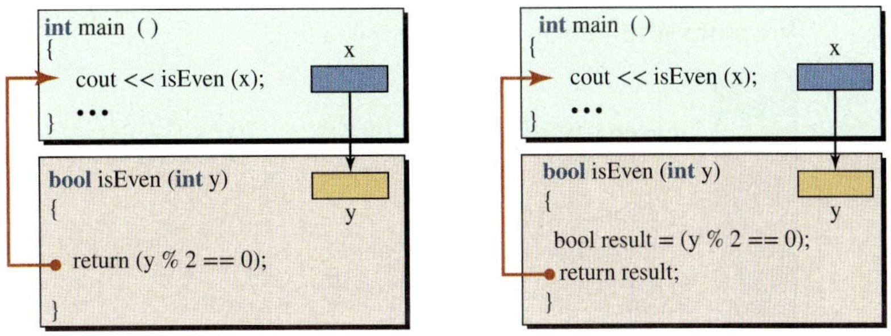

Returning a literal value **Returning value of a variable**

Figure 6.18 Return-by-value

b. Pass-by-reference changes the arguments in the calling function when the parameters are changed by the called function. If this is the purpose of the function, such as the case in swapping, pass-by-reference is the best choice. This method has the advantage that copying is not needed; the objects in the calling function and the called function are the same with different names. This means that for large objects, when copying can be expensive, we should use this method.

c. Pass-by-pointer has the same advantage as pass-by-reference. It is normally avoided in C++, but it can be used if the nature of the data to be passed involves pointers (such as C-type strings and arrays, both of which are discussed in future chapters).

6.4.2 Returning Data

We have seen that a *void* function is designed for its side effect; it does not return anything to the calling function. On the other hand, a non-void function needs to return a value to its caller. This can be done in three ways: return-by-value, return-by-reference, and return-by-pointer.

Return-by-Value

The most common return method is *return-by-value*. The called function creates an expression in its body and returns it to the calling function. In this case, the function-call expression must be called in a situation that needs a value. Figure 6.18 shows two examples of the value of an expression being returned to the called function.

EXAMPLE 6.16

Program 6.16 demonstrates return-by-value.

Program 6.16 Returning a literal value from a function

```
/*********************************************************************
 * This program shows how we can return a value from a function.     *
 *********************************************************************/
#include <iostream>
using namespace std;

// Function declaration
bool isEven (int y);
```

(continued)

Program 6.16 Returning a literal value from a function (Continued)

```

int main ( )
{
  // Function call
  cout << boolalpha << isEven (5) << endl;
  cout << boolalpha << isEven (10);
  return 0;
}
/*****************************************************************
 * The isEven function takes one parameter y. It then checks to   *
 * see if the value of y is even by getting the remainder of y.   *
 * The function then returns the result by value (literal value). *
 *****************************************************************/
bool isEven (int y)
{
  return ((y % 2) == 0);
}
```

```
Run:
false
true
```

Return-by-Reference

Most of the functions we encounter in C++ (when used as a procedural programming language) return data by value. It is easy and straightforward to use return-by-value. However, return-by-value has a drawback. The compiler must make a copy of the object to be returned by the called function and then return it to the calling function. In the case of the built-in data types, this is normally no problem. However, in object-oriented programming we encounter large objects that must be returned. For efficiency we should return them by reference. A problem occurs, however, when the called function creates the object because after the function terminates, the object does not exist anymore; it cannot be returned by reference. We discuss return-by-reference in Chapater 9.

Return-by-Pointer

Return-by-pointer can yield the same effect as return-by-reference, but this practice is seldom used.

6.4.3 A Comprehensive Example

In this section we consider a program that uses the principles of modular programming. We must create a program that gets a score, calculates the corresponding grade, and prints the result. The relationship among the modules is shown in Figure 6.19.

EXAMPLE 6.17

Program 6.17 shows how we can create functions for each task. The first two are value-returning functions; the third is a *void* function.

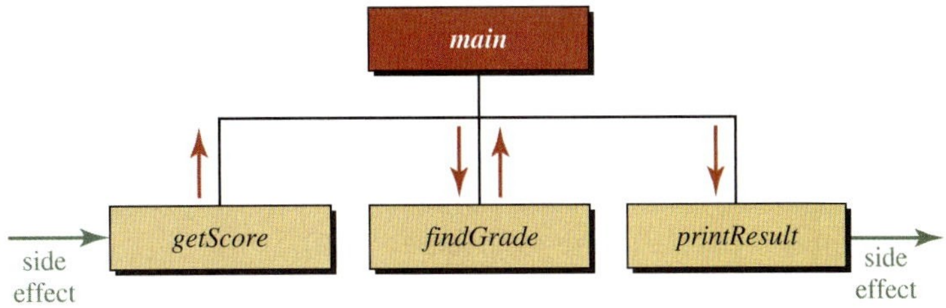

Figure 6.19 A structure chart for calculating and printing grades and scores

Program 6.17 Calculating a grade based on a score value

```
/***************************************************************
 * This program shows how to use three functions to input,     *
 * calculate, and print the score and grade of a student.      *
 ***************************************************************/
#include <iostream>
using namespace std;

// Function declarations
int getScore ();
char findGrade (int score);
void printResult (int score, char grade);

int main ()
{
   // Declaration
   int score;
   char grade;
   // Function calls
   score = getScore ();
   grade = findGrade (score);
   printResult (score, grade);
   return 0;
}
/***************************************************************
  * The getScore function is an input function with a side effect  *
  * that gets the input from the user and returns the score by     *
  * value to the main function. It uses a local variable (score)   *
  * whose value is returned to the main function. The function     *
  * also validates the score to be between 0 and 100.              *
  ***************************************************************/
int getScore ()
{
   int score;  // Local declaration
   do
```

(continued)

Program 6.17 Calculating a grade based on a score value (Continued)

```
    {
        cout << "Enter a score between 0 and 100: ";
        cin >> score;
    } while (score < 0 || score > 100);
    return score;
}
/***********************************************************************
 * The findGrade function calculates and returns a character          *
 * grade (A, B, C, D, F) related to the scored passed to it.          *
 * It uses pass-by-value to get the value of the score. It            *
 * use return-by-value to return the grade to the main function.      *
 * We have used a nested if-else construct, but it can also be        *
 * be done using a switch statement.                                  *
 ***********************************************************************/
char findGrade (int score)
{
    char grade; // Local declaration
    if (score >= 90)
    {
        grade = 'A';
    }
    else if (score >= 80)
    {
        grade = 'B';
    }
    else if (score >= 70)
    {
        grade = 'C';
    }
    else if (score >= 60)
    {
        grade = 'D';
    }
    else
    {
        grade = 'F';
    }
    return grade;
}
/***********************************************************************
 * The last function prints the score and corresponding grade.        *
 ***********************************************************************/
void printResult (int score, char grade)
```

(continued)

Program 6.17 Calculating a grade based on a score value (Continued)

```
{
   cout << endl << "Result of the test." << endl;
   cout << "Score: " << score << " out of 100"<< endl;
   cout << "Grade: ";
}
```

```
Run:
Enter a score between 0 and 100: 87
Result of the test.
Score: 87 out of 100
Grade: B
```

```
Run:
Enter a score between 0 and 100: 93
Result of the test.
Score: 93 out of 100
Grade: A
```

Figure 6.20 shows the communication between the *main* function and the three called functions.

When we analyze the small program in Figure 6.20, we find that the *main* function is responsible for coordinating the job of each of the other three functions. The first function, *getScore*, gets the data (*score*) from outside and gives it back to *main*. The second function, *findGrade*, receives the data (*score)* from *main*, processes it, and return the result (*grade*) back to *main*. The third function, *printResult*, receives two data items (*score* and *grade*) from *main* and sends them to the monitor.

Note that we have used the same name for the parameters and local variables that handle the score. We call all of them *score* without any confusion in the program. The reason is that they are in different territories (or scope, as we explain later). We have four storage locations called *score*, one in each entity. The ones in *getScore* and *main* are local variables; the ones in *findGrade* and *printResult* are parameters. We have also three storage locations named *grade*, two local variables and one parameter.

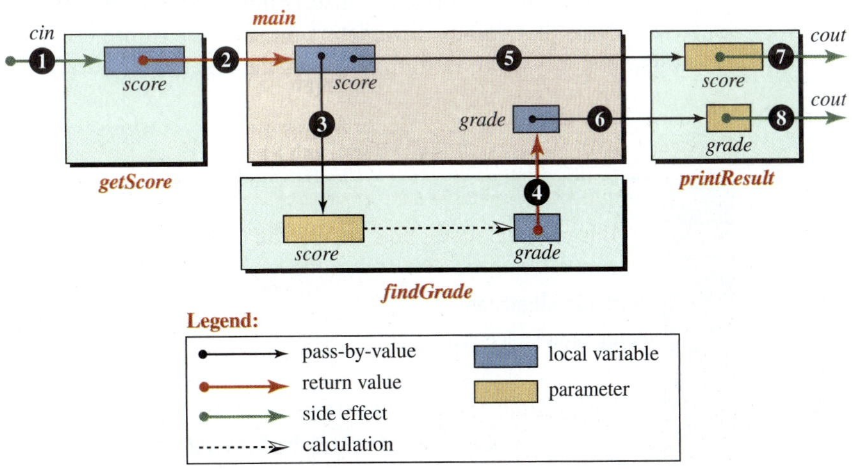

Figure 6.20 Passing data between *main* and called functions

6.5 MORE ABOUT PARAMETERS

There are two other issues related to parameters that we must discuss: default parameters and overloaded functions.

6.5.1 Default Parameters

A program may call a function several times. If the function is designed with pass-by-value parameters, it may happen that the value of a parameter is the same most of the time. In this case, we can use a **default parameter** value for one or more of the parameter values (including all parameters). If only some parameters have default parameters, they must be the rightmost parameters.

EXAMPLE 6.18

Assume that we have designed a function named *calcEarnings* that calculates the weekly gross earnings for a group of employees. The function uses two parameters, *rate* and *hours*. Most of the employees work 40 hours; some, however, work less. We assume that no employee can work more than 40 hours (company regulation). We can use the default value 40 for the parameter hours in this function by simply assigning the default value to the parameter in the parameter list. The following declaration statement shows the declaration for a function named *calcEarnings* with a default of 40 hours.

```
double calcEarnings (double rate, double hours = 40.0);
```

Note that if there is no function declaration (when the function definition comes before the function call), then the function definition, as we discussed before, serves as function declaration. This means the default parameters must be defined in the header of the function definition.

When an employee works 40 hours, we can call *calcEarnings* by passing just the argument for the *rate* parameter. When the employee works less than 40 hours, we pass both the *rate* and the *hours*. The following examples demonstrate the default parameter concept.

```
calcEarnings (payRate);
calcEarnings (payRate, hourWorked);
```

In the first call, the program inserts the default value 40 for the hours worked by the employee. Note that default parameters must be the rightmost (last) parameters in the function's parameter list. Program 6.18 shows the idea.

Program 6.18 Using a default value

```
/*****************************************************************
 * This program shows how we use the default parameter value.   *
 *****************************************************************/
#include <iostream>
using namespace std;

// Declaration: the second parameter uses a default value of 40
double calcEarnings (double rate, double hours = 40);
```

(*continued*)

Program 6.18 Using a default value (Continued)

```

int main ( )
{
  // The first function call uses the default value
  cout << "Emplyee 1 pay: " << calcEarnings (22.0) << endl;
  cout << "Emplyee 2 pay: " << calcEarnings (12.50, 18);
  return 0;
}
/****************************************************************
 * The function definition has two parameters, but we do not     *
 * have to show the default parameter in the defintion because   *
 * it is the declaration that contains the default value.        *
 ****************************************************************/
double calcEarnings (double rate, double hours)
{
  double pay;
  pay = hours * rate;
  return pay;
} // End of calcEarnings
```

```
Run:
Emplyee 1 pay: 880
Emplyee 2 pay: 225
```

6.5.2 Function Overloading

Can we have two functions with the same name? The answer is positive if their parameter lists are different (in type, in number, or in order). In C++, the practice is called **function overloading.** The criteria the compiler uses to allow two functions with the same name in a program is referred to as the **function signature.** The signature of a function is the combination of the name and the types in the parameter list. If two function definitions have different signatures, the compiler can distinguish between them. Note that the return type of a function is not included in the signature because C++ must select between overloaded functions when the function is called; the return type is not included in the syntax of the function call.

The return value of a function is not included in its signature.

EXAMPLE 6.19

The following shows how to define different functions to find the maximum between two integers and two floating-point values.

```
int max (int a, int b)
{
  ...
}
```

```
double max (double a, double b)
{
  ...
}
```

The above two functions are considered two different (overloaded) functions because their signatures are different. The first function (the one on the left) has the signature *max* (*int, int*); the second function has the signature *max* (*double, double*).

EXAMPLE 6.20

The following two functions are not recognized as two overloaded functions because their signatures are the same.

```
int get ()                                double get ()
{                                         {
  ...                                       ...
}                                         }
```

The first function has the signature *get* ( ); the second function has also the signature *get* ( ). If we write a program with the above two definitions, it does not compile.

The compiler does not compile a program that contains two function definitions with the same signature.

EXAMPLE 6.21

Overloading can help us call one function from inside another. For example, we can write three overloaded functions to find the maximum of two integers, the maximum of three integers, and the maximum of four integers. The second function calls the first function in its definition; the third function calls the second. Program 6.19 demonstrates the concept.

Program 6.19 Creating three overloaded functions

```
/***************************************************************
  * This program shows how we can use different signatures to     *
  * create three overloaded functions.                            *
  ***************************************************************/
#include <iostream>
using namespace std;

// Function Declaration
int max (int num1, int num2);
int max (int num1, int num2, int num3);
int max (int num1, int num2, int num3, int num4);

int main ()
{
   // Three calls to overloaded max functions
   cout << "maximum (5, 7): " << max (5, 7) << endl;
   cout << "maximum (7, 9, 8): " << max (7, 9, 8) << endl;
   cout << "maximum (14, 3, 12, 11): " << max (14, 3, 12, 11);
```

(continued)

Program 6.19 Creating three overloaded functions (Continued)

```
    return 0;
}// End main
/*****************************************************************
 * The following is the definition for the max function with       *
 * two arguments num1 and num2. It returns the maximum of the       *
 * parameters.                                                      *
 *****************************************************************/
int max (int num1, int num2)
{
    int larger; // Local variable
    if (num1 >= num2)
    {
        larger = num1;
    }
    else
    {
        larger = num2;
    }
    return larger;
}
/*****************************************************************
 * The following is the definition for the max function with       *
 * three arguments num1, num2, and num3. It uses a call to          *
 * the function with two arguments to first find the maximum        *
 * of the first two. It then makes another call to the first        *
 * function to find the maximum of the result and the num3.         *
 *****************************************************************/
int max (int num1, int num2, int num3)
{
    return max(max(num1, num2), num3);
}
/*****************************************************************
 * The following is the definition for the max function with       *
 * four arguments num1, num2, and num3, and num4. It uses a         *
 * a call to the function with three arguments first to find        *
 * the maximum of the first three, and then calls the function      *
 * with two arguments to find the max of the previous result        *
 * and the fourth number.                                           *
 *****************************************************************/
int max (int num1, int num2, int num3, int num4)
{
    return max(max(num1, num2, num3), num4);
} // End max function with four parameters
```

(continued)

Program 6.19 Creating three overloaded functions (Continued)

```
Run:
maximum (5, 7): 7
maximum (7, 9, 8): 9
maximum (14, 3, 12, 11): 14
```

6.6 SCOPE AND LIFETIME

In this section we discuss two concepts that affect the design and use of functions: *scope* and *lifetime*.

6.6.1 Scope

Scope defines where in the source code a named entity (constant, variable, object, function, and so on) is visible. To define the scope of an entity, we must first define scope. Scope is a region in the source code that has one or more declarations. In other words, when we declare an entity, we create a scope for that entity.

Scope is a region with a declaration.

Local Scope

An entity that has **local scope** is visible from the point it is declared until the end of the block (defined by the closing brace). Local scope can start in the header that comes before the block (such as function header or loop header) or immediately after the beginning of the block (after opening brace) or sometimes in the middle of the block. However, the end of a local scope is always where the closing brace is seen.

Figure 6.21 shows three cases of a local scope. The first case shows the scope of a parameter declared in the header of a function. The second case shows the scope of a counter declared in a *for*-loop. The third case shows the scope of a local variable declared in the body of the *main* function.

Overlapped Scopes We cannot have two entities with the same name in a block; doing so creates a compilation error. Figure 6.22 shows situation in which we have declared two variables with the same name: one in the function header and one in the function body. The scope of the two variables is the function body, although one scope is declared before the other. The two scopes overlapp and we get an error during compilation.

Nested Blocks When we write a program, we often see **nested blocks:** a block inside another block. What is the scope of the entities declared in the outer block and in the inner block? The entity in the outer block has a larger scope that includes the inner block; the entity that is declared inside the inner block has a smaller scope that includes only the inner block. Figure 6.23 shows the difference.

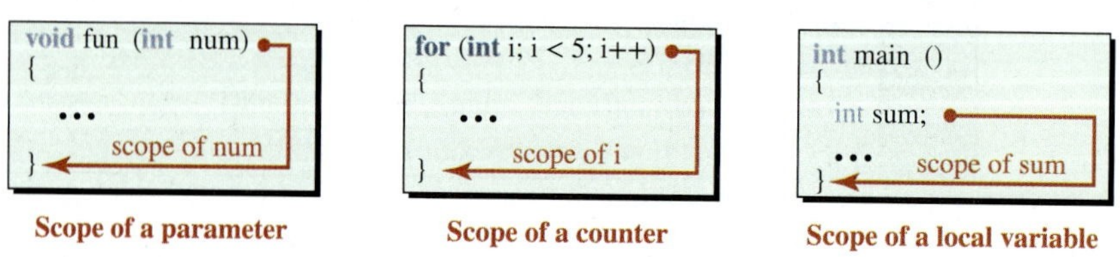

Figure 6.21 Three cases of a local scope

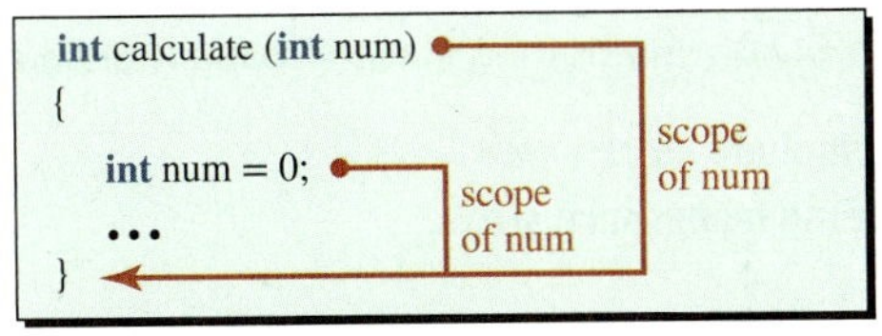

Error: Overlapping scopes in a single block

Figure 6.22 Overlapping scopes (error in this case)

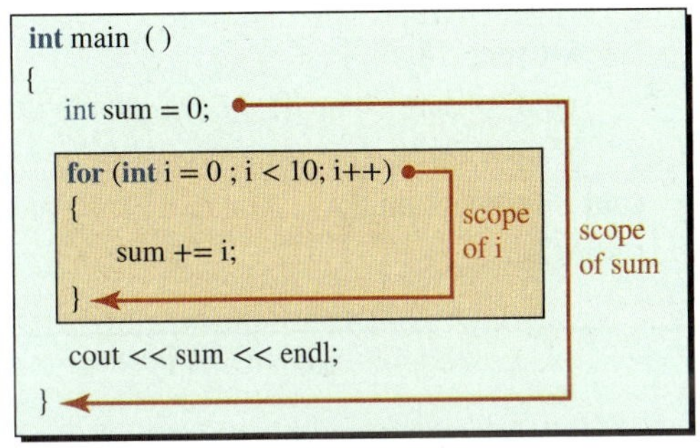

A nested block

Figure 6.23 Scope in a nested block

The variable *sum* is declared inside the outer block; it is visible in the outer and the inner blocks. The variable *i* (the counter of the loop) is declared in the header of the inner block; it is visible only in the inner block. If we try to use the variable *i* outside of the inner block, we get a compilation error.

Shadowing in Local Scopes In the previous case of nested blocks, the names were different. What happens if we declare two entities with the same name, one in the outer block and one in the inner block? What are the visibilities? Although this looks like overlapping scope, the situation is different because of the two distinct scopes (inner and outer). In this case, known as **function shadowing,** the visibility of the entity in the inner block shadows the visibility of the entity in the outer block. In other words, once the duplicate name is declared in the inner block, the corresponding entity is the only one that can be seen until it goes out of scope at the end of the block. The outer block entity is visible until the inner block's entity is defined and after the inner block terminates.

Program 6.20 shows a simple example of visibility. We have two variables named *sum*. The one in the outer block is initialized to 5 and the one in the inner block is initialized to 3. When we print the *sum* in the inner block, the one declared in the outer block is shadowed. The system sees only the one initialized to 3 and prints its contents (3). When we leave the inner block, the *sum* in the outer block becomes visible again and its contents (5) are printed.

Program 6.20 Shadowing in local scope

```
/***************************************************************
 * A variable declared inside a block shadows another variable  *
 * with the same name declared outside the block                *
 ***************************************************************/
```

(continued)

Program 6.20 Shadowing in local scope (Continued)

```
#include <iostream>
using namespace std;

int main ( )
{
   int sum = 5;
   cout << sum << endl;
   {
        int sum = 3;
        cout << sum << endl; // The sum in the inner block is visible
   }
   cout << sum << endl; // The sum in the outer block is visible
   return 0;
}
```

```
Run
5
3
5
```

Global Scope

An entity has a **global scope** if it is declared outside all functions. A global entity is visible from the location it is declared to the end of the program. Figure 6.24 shows the scope of a variable named *sum* declared outside *main* and *print*. It is visible in both functions.

Shadowing in Global Scope We discussed shadowing for local scope. If we consider global scope as the largest block in a program that extends from the beginning of the program to the end of the program, we can see that shadowing also applies to the global scope. In other words, a local scope shadows a global scope. Program 6.21 shows the point. We have two variables named *num*: a global and a local. The local variable shadows the global variable.

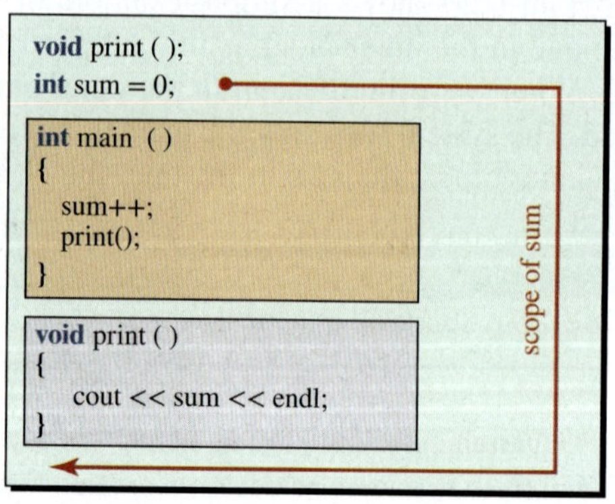

Figure 6.24 Scope of a global entity

Program 6.21 Shadowing in global scope

```
/***************************************************************
  * A program to test shadowing of global scope                *
  ***************************************************************/
#include <iostream>
using namespace std;

int num = 5;  // Global variable

int main ( )
{
   cout << num << endl;  // global num
   int num = 25;  // Local variable
   cout << num;  // local num shadows global num
   return 0;
} // End of main
```

```
Run
5
25
```

Version with one operand   Version with two operands

Figure 6.25 Two versions of scope resolution operator

Scope Resolution Operator Sometimes we may need to override the shadowing and access a global entity inside a local block. C++ provides an operator (::) that can explicitly or implicitly define the scope of the entity. Figure 6.25 shows the two versions of this operator. The first version takes one right operand; the second version takes two operands.

In the first version, the name of the scope is implicit (it means the global scope of the program). In the second version, we must give the name of the scope. Program 6.22 shows the use of the first version of the scope operator.

Program 6.22 Using the scope resolution operator

```
/***************************************************************
  * A program to test the use of scope operator                *
  ***************************************************************/
#include <iostream>
using namespace std;
```

(continued)

Program 6.22 Using the scope resolution operator (Continued)

```

int num = 5; // A global variable

int main ( )
{
   int num = 25; // A local variable
   cout <<" Value of Global num: " << ::num << endl;
   cout <<" Value of Local num: " << num << endl;
   return 0;
} // End of main
```

Run

```
Value of Global num: 5
Value of Local num: 25
```

Scopes Related to Functions

It can be challenging to understand the scope of functions. A function has a name, and the parameters of the function also have names. We must distinguish between the two.

Scope of Function Names A function is an entity with a name; it has a scope. The **function scope** is from the point that it is declared until the end of the program. We have discussed that we can eliminate the function declaration (prototype) by inserting the function definition before the *main* function. In this case, the function definition serves both as declaration and definition. Figure 6.26 shows the scope of a function name in both cases.

In the first case, the scope of the function name (*print*) starts at the point where the function is declared and extends until the end of the program. In the second case, the definition serves both as the declaration and definition, which means the scope of the function name (*print*) starts at the function header and extends to the end of the program.

Scope of Function Parameters In addition to the function name, function parameters are other entities with names, which means they also have scope. Their scope starts from the point they are declared up to the point when the function block is terminated. However,

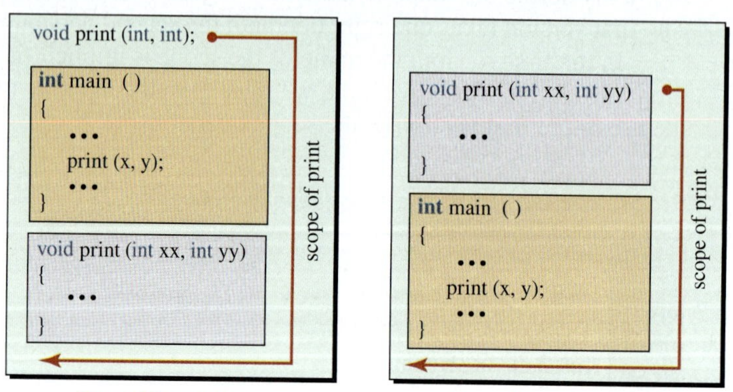

Case with prototype **Case without prototype**

Figure 6.26 Scope of function name

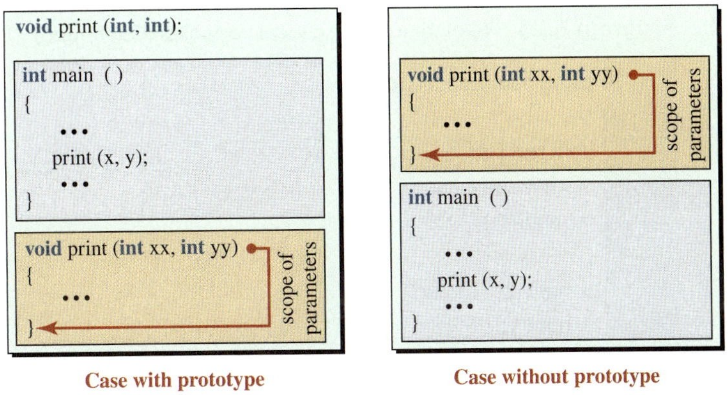

Figure 6.27 Scope of function parameter

we must caution that the parameters are not declared in the function declaration (prototype); they are declared in the header of the function definition. Function declaration just declares the name of the function and gives its structures (types of parameters). This is why we can have a function declaration without mentioning the parameter names. Figure 6.27 shows the scope of the parameters in the *print* function shown in Figure 6.26. We have omitted the names of the parameter in the declaration to emphasize that the compiler does not need them and the scope does not start from that point. However, we strongly recommend that they be included in the declaration for documentation.

Note that in both cases, the parameter scope is local to the function definition. That is the reason we need pass-by-value, pass-by-reference, and pass-by-pointer even if we use the same names for a parameter and its corresponding argument. The scope of a parameter is local to the definition of the called function; the scope of an argument is local to the calling function.

6.6.2 Lifetime

Every entity in a program has a **lifetime:** It is born and it dies. However, in this section we discuss only the lifetime of local variables in a function. The lifetime of a variable in a function is important because we may call a function several times. We have two types of local variables in a function: automatic and static.

Automatic Local Variable

An **automatic local variable** is born when the function is called and dies when the function terminates. By default all local variables in a function have automatic lifetime, but we can explicitly use the modifier *auto* in front of the variable declaration to emphasize that local variables are reborn each time the function is called. Program 6.23 shows the idea.

Program 6.23 Testing automatic local variables

```
/***************************************************************
 * A program to test the use of an automatic local variable    *
 ***************************************************************/
#include <iostream>
```

(continued)

Program 6.23 Testing automatic local variables (Continued)

```
using namespace std;

void fun ( );

int main ( )
{
   fun ( );
   fun ( );
   fun ( );
   return 0;
}
/**************************************************************
 * The function has two automatic local variables, num and count.    *
 * In each function call, these variables are initialized.           *
 **************************************************************/
void fun ( )
{
   int num = 3;                     // implicit auto variable
   auto int count = 0;              // explicit auto variable
   num++;
   count++;
   cout << "num = " << num << " and " << "count = " << count << endl;
}
```

Run

```
num = 4 and count = 1
num = 4 and count = 1
num = 4 and count = 1
```

The program calls the function *fun* three times. In each call, the two variables are born, initialized to 3 and 0, and incremented. Each time the function *fun* terminates, these variables die. In other words, the system does not keep track of these variables. In each call, two new variables are created.

Static Local Variable

The modifier *static* has three applications in C++, but we discuss only the one related to local variables. A **static local variable** is created by using the *static* modifier. The lifetime of a *static* variable is the lifetime of the program in which it is defined. A *static* variable is initialized only once, but the system keeps track of its contents as long as the program is running. This means it is initialized in the first call to the function, but it can be changed during subsequent function calls. We can change the variable *count* in the previous program to a *static* variable and see how the system keeps the value of *count* from call to call. Program 6.24 shows how we can use a static variable to tell how many times the function *fun* was called.

Program 6.24 Testing static variables

```
/****************************************************************
 * A program to test the use of static variables                *
 ****************************************************************/
#include <iostream>
using namespace std;

void fun ( );

int main ( )
{
    fun ( );
    fun ( );
    fun ( );
    return 0;
}
/****************************************************************
 * The function has one static variable named count. It is     *
 * initialized in the first call, but it holds its value for   *
 * the next time. This means value is incremented in each call. *
 ****************************************************************/
void fun ( )
{
    static int count = 0;  // explicit static variable
    count++;
    cout << "count = " << count << endl;
}
```

```
Run
count = 1
count = 2
count = 3
```

Note that the program ignores the initialization in the second and third calls, but it keeps the value of *count* after each call. After termination of the first call, the count value is 1; after termination of the second call, the value is 2; and after the termination of the third call, the value is 3.

We used the *static* variable in the previous program to count how many times the function *fun* was called. The static variable can be used in other ways. For example, we can use a static variable to find the maximum or minimum value of an argument when the function is called several times.

Initialization

It is worthwhile to compare the initialization of a global variable, an automatic local variable, and a static local variable. If an automatic local variable is not explicitly initialized, it

Program 6.25 Initializing different variable types

```
/***************************************************************
 * A program to test the initialization of variables           *
 ***************************************************************/
#include <iostream>
using namespace std;

int global; // A global variable

int main ( )
{
  static int sLocal; // A static local variable
  auto int aLocal;   // An automatic local variable
  // Printing values
  cout << "Global = " << global << endl;
  cout << "Static Local = " << sLocal << endl;
  cout << "Automatic Local = " << aLocal << endl;
  return 0;
}
```

```
Run
Global = 0
Static Local = 0
Automatic Local = 4202830 // Garbage value
```

holds the garbage left over from the previous use. Global and static local variables, on the other hand, are initialized to default values (0 for integral types, 0.0 for floating-point types, and false for Boolean types) if they are not initialized explicitly. In other words, global and static local variables behave the same with respect to initialization.

> **If not initialized explicitly, global and static local variables are initialized to default values, but local variables contain garbage left over from previous use.**

Program 6.25 shows how the three variables (one global, one static local, and one automatic local) are initialized implicitly. The global and the static local variables are initialized to default values; the automatic local variable keeps the garbage value left over from previous use.

6.7 PROGRAM DESIGN

In this section we show how to use functions in three programs. The three programs are all related to finance. They are classical programs and are discussed in computer-science literature.

6.7.1 Future Value of a Fixed Investment

We want to write a program that uses functions and introduces the concepts of a *factor* and a *multiplier*. These concepts are used in the next two programs to calculate the future value of a periodic investment and to find the monthly payment of a loan.

Understand the Problem

The future value of a fixed investment can be calculated as:

$$\textbf{future value} = \textbf{investment} \times (\textbf{1} + \textbf{rate})^{\textbf{term}}$$

in which *rate* is the periodic interest rate and *term* is the number of periods (years or months). We can think of (1 + rate) as a *factor* that shows the value of a one-dollar investment at the end of the next period. We can also think about (factor ^{term}) as a multiplier that shows the value of a one-dollar investment at the end of the term. With these assumptions, we have

$$\textbf{factor} = (\textbf{1} + \textbf{rate})$$
$$\textbf{multiplier} = \textbf{factor}^{\textbf{term}}$$
$$\textbf{future value} = \textbf{investment} \times \textbf{multiplier}$$

In other words, to find the future value of an investment, we must find the future value of one dollar (using multiplier) and then multiply it by the amount of the investment.

Develop the Algorithm

Structure Chart In the structure chart shown in Figure 6.28, we divide the task among three functions: *input*, *process*, and *output*. Each of these functions calls other functions. The *input* function calls the *getInput* function three times to get the investment, rate, and term (number of periods). The *process* function calls another function named *findMultiplier* to get the multiplier and multiply it by the investment to find the future value of the investment. The output function first calls the *printData* function to print the given data. It then calls *printResult* to print the result (multiplier and future value). We divide the output into two categories to show what was given (collected by the *input* function) and what was calculated (found in the *process* function).

The *main* function The *main* function calls three functions: *input*, *process*, and *output*.

The *input* function The *input* function is a *void* function that gets three values from the user and passes them to the *main* function using pass-by-reference. To get the input, it calls another function, *getInput,* that displays a different message each time it is called. It gets the amount of investment, the interest rate, and the term (number of years).

The *process* function The *process* function calculates the future value. We use pass-by-value for the first three parameters and pass-by-reference for the last two because they need to change the value of *multiplier* and *futureValue* in *main*. The *process* function calls another

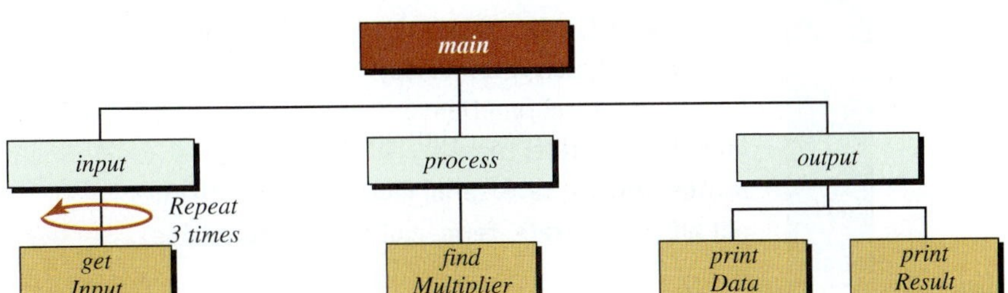

Figure 6.28 Structure chart for investment problem

function, *findMultiplier*, to calculate the *multiplier*. The *multiplier* is a number that must be multiplied by the original investment to give the future value at the end of the period. It can be defined as (multiplier = $\text{factor}^{\text{term}}$), in which the factor is (1 + rate /100).

The *output* function The *output* function calls two functions, *printData* and *printResult,* to show what was input by the user and what was calculated.

Write the Program

Program 6.26 shows the *main* function and the three functions called by *main*: *input*, *process*, and *output*. It also gives the definition of the *getInput* (called by *input*), *findMultliplier* (called by *process*), and *printData* and *printResult* (called by *output*).

Program 6.26 Finding the future value of a fixed investment

```
/***************************************************************
  * The program shows how to use functions to calculate the future     *
  * value of an investment that earns compound interest.               *
  ***************************************************************/
#include <iostream>
#include <iomanip>
#include <cmath>
using namespace std;

// Declaration of top-level functions
void input (double& invest, double& rate, double& term);
void process (double invest, double rate, double term,
                              double& multiplier, double& futureValue);
void output (double invest, double rate, double term,
                              double multiplier, double futureValue);
// Declaration of low-level functions
double getInput (string message);
double findMultiplier (double rate, double period);
void printData (double invest, double rate, double term);
void printResult (double multiplier, double value);

int main ( )
{
  // Variable Declaration
  double invest, rate, term;              // For input
  double multiplier, futureValue;         // For Result
  // Call first level functions
  input (invest, rate, term);
  process (invest, rate, term, multiplier, futureValue);
  output (invest, rate, term, multiplier, futureValue);
  return 0;
}
```

(continued)

Program 6.26 Finding the future value of a fixed investment (Continued)

```
/***************************************************************
 * The input function gets three inputs by calling the getInput  *
 * function three times. It uses pass-by-reference to send back  *
 * the values to main. After the function termination, the       *
 * data values are stored in invest, rate, and term.             *
 ***************************************************************/
void input (double& invest, double& rate, double& term)
{
  invest = getInput ("Enter the value of investment: ");
  rate = getInput ("Enter the interest rate per year: ");
  term = getInput("Enter the term (number of years): ");
}
/***************************************************************
 * The process function calls findMultiplier to calculate the    *
 * the multiplier. It then multiplies the return value by the value *
 * invested to find the future value.                            *
 ***************************************************************/
void process (double invest, double rate, double term,
                            double& multiplier, double& futureValue)
{
  multiplier = findMultiplier (rate, term);
  futureValue  = multiplier * invest;
}
/***************************************************************
 * The output function calls printData to print three given values. *
 * It then calls printResult to print the two calculated values.  *
 ***************************************************************/
void output (double invest, double rate, double term,
                             double multiplier, double futureValue)
{
  printData (invest, rate, term);
  printResult (multiplier, futureValue);
}
/***************************************************************
 * The getInput function gets the input from the user. Its only  *
 * parameter is an object of type string that contains a         *
 * different message in each call to ask the user to input       *
 * the appropriate data. It validates the data and sends it      *
 * back to the calling expression in the input function.         *
 ***************************************************************/
double getInput (string message )
{
  double input;
  do
```

(*continued*)

Program 6.26 Finding the future value of a fixed investment (Continued)

```
    {
        cout << message;
        cin >> input;
    } while (input < 0.0);
    return input;
}
/*****************************************************************
 * The findMultiplier is very simple. The two values, rate and term,   *
 * are passed to it by value. It first calculates the factor. It        *
 * then returns the multiplier using the pow function.                  *
 *****************************************************************/
double findMultiplier (double rate, double term)
{
    double factor = 1 + rate/100;
    return pow (factor , term);
}
/*****************************************************************
 * The printData function prints the three data items input by          *
 * the user with appropriate explanations. It is a void function         *
 * with only side effects.                                               *
 *****************************************************************/
void printData (double invest, double rate, double term)
{
    cout << endl << "Information about investment" << endl;
    cout << "Investment: " << fixed << setprecision (2) << invest << endl;
    cout << "Interest rate: " << rate << fixed << setprecision (2);
    cout << " percent per year" << endl;
    cout << "Term: " << term << " years" << endl << endl;
}
/*****************************************************************
 * The printResult function prints the two results of the program.      *
 * It prints the multiplier and the futureValue of the investment.      *
 * It is also a void function with only side effects.                    *
 *****************************************************************/
void printResult (double multiplier, double futureValue)
{
    cout << "Investment is multiplied by: " << fixed << setprecision (8);
    cout << multiplier << endl;
    cout << "Future value: " << fixed << setprecision(2);
    cout << futureValue << endl;
}
```

Run:

```
Enter the value of investment: 360000
Enter the interest rate per year: 5
Enter the term (number of years): 30
```

(continued)

Program 6.26 Finding the future value of a fixed investment (Continued)

```
Information about investment
Investment: 360000.00
Interest rate: 5.00 percent per year
Term: 30.00 years

Investment is multiplied by: 4.32194238
Future value: 1555899.26
```

The result shows that the multiplier is 4.32194238. Any dollar invested with 5 percent interest per year for 30 years results in 4.32194238 dollars. We can test the program with different investment values but the same *rate* and *term* to see that the multiplier is the same; only the future value will be changed.

6.7.2 Future Value of a Periodic Investment

Instead of a one-time investment, we can periodically invest in a bank account that pays compound interest. For example, we may invest the same amount each month.

Understand the Problem

1. We assume that the periodic investment is the same in each period.
2. We assume that the investment interval and the interval to pay the interest are the same. In other words, if we invest monthly, the interest is also calculated and added to the previous value monthly.

Develop the Algorithm

Based on the previous two assumptions, we need only change the calculation of the multiplier in the previous program to make it work for a periodic investment. In this case, we actually have n multipliers, one for each period, in which $n = term \times period$. The multiplier for the second investment should be calculated for $(n - 1)$ periods. The multiplier for the third investment should be calculated for $(n - 2)$ periods. Finally, the multiplier for the last investment should be calculated for only one period. In other words, the total multiplier is

$$\textbf{multiplier} = (1 + \textbf{factor})^n + (1 + \textbf{factor})^{n-1} + \ldots + (1 + \textbf{factor})^1$$

This is a power series that has a solution in mathematics, but we can easily use a loop to simulate it. So the *findMultiplier* function in the previous program can be changed to simulate the series in a *for* loop.

```
double findMultiplier (double rate, double term)
{
   double multiplier = 0;
   double factor = 1 + rate/100;
   for (int i = term; i >=0; i--)
   {
       multiplier += pow (factor , i);
   }
   return multiplier;
}
```

Write the Program

Based on the preceding explanation, we can repeat the program for the fixed investment to find the future value of a periodic investment (Program 6.27).

Program 6.27 Finding the future value of periodic investments

```
/******************************************************************
 * This program shows the use of functions to calculate the future   *
 * value of periodic investments each of the same amount.            *
 *****************************************************************/
#include <iostream>
#include <iomanip>
#include <cmath>
#include <string>
using namespace std;

// Declaration of top-level functions
void input(double& invest, double& rate, double& term);
void process (double invest, double rate, double term,
                  double& multiplier, double& futureValue);
void output (double invest, double rate, double term,
                  double multiplier, double futureValue);
// Declaration  of low-level functions
double getInput (string message);
double findMultiplier (double rate, double period);
void printData (double invest, double rate, double term);
void printResult (double multiplier, double value);

int main ( )
{
  // Variable Declaration
  double invest, rate, term;           // For input
  double multiplier, futureValue;      // For Result
  // Call first level functions
  input (invest, rate, term);
  process (invest, rate, term, multiplier, futureValue);
  output (invest, rate, term, multiplier, futureValue);
  return 0;
}
/******************************************************************
 * The input function gets three inputs by calling the getInput      *
 * function three times. It uses pass-by-reference to send back      *
 * the values to main. After the function termination, the           *
 * data values are stored in invest, rate, and term.                  *
 *****************************************************************/
```

(continued)

Program 6.27 Finding the future value of periodic investments (Continued)

```
void input (double& invest, double& rate, double& term)
{
  invest = getInput ("Enter the value of periodic investment: ");
  rate = getInput ("Enter the interest rate per year: ");
  term = getInput("Enter the term (number of years): ");
}
/*****************************************************************
 * The process function calls findMultiplier to calculate the        *
 * the multiplier. It then multiplies the return value by the value  *
 * invested to find the future value.                                *
 *****************************************************************/
void process (double invest, double rate, double term,
              double& multiplier, double& futureValue)
{
  multiplier = findMultiplier (rate, term);
  futureValue  = multiplier * invest;
}
/*****************************************************************
 * The output function calls printData to print three given values.  *
 * It then calls printResult to print the two calculated values.     *
 *****************************************************************/
void output (double invest, double rate, double term,
             double multiplier, double futureValue)
{
  printData (invest, rate, term);
  printResult (multiplier, futureValue);
}
/*****************************************************************
 * The getInput function gets the input from the user. Its           *
 * only parameter is an object of type string that contains          *
 * a different message in each call to force the user to input       *
 * the appropriate data. It then validates data and sends it back    *
 * to the calling expression in the input function.                  *
 *****************************************************************/
double getInput(string message )
{
  double input;
  do
  {
      cout << message;
      cin >> input;
  } while (input < 0.0);
  return input;
```

(continued)

Program 6.27 Finding the future value of periodic investments (Continued)

```
}
/*****************************************************************
 * This findMultiplier in this case needs to add all multipliers   *
 * calculated for each year together, each with a different exponent. *
 * The function then returns the result to the process function.   *
 *****************************************************************/
double findMultiplier (double rate, double term)
{
  double multiplier = 0;
  double factor = 1 + rate/100;
  for (int i = term; i > 0 ; i– –)
  {
       multiplier += pow (factor , i);
  }
  return multiplier;
}
/*****************************************************************
 * The printData function prints the three data items input by     *
 * the user with appropriate explanations.                          *
 *****************************************************************/
void printData (double invest, double rate, double term)
{
  cout << endl << "Information about period invesment" << endl;
  cout << "Periodic Investment: " << fixed << setprecision (2)
                                             << invest << endl;
  cout << "Interest rate: " << rate << fixed << setprecision (2);
  cout << " percent per year" << endl;
  cout << "Term: " << term << " years" << endl << endl;
}
/*****************************************************************
 * The printResult function prints the two results of the program. *
 * It prints the multiplier and the futureValue of the investment. *
 *****************************************************************/
void printResult (double multiplier, double futureValue)
{
  cout << "Result of investment" << endl;
  cout << "Investment is multiplied by :" << fixed << setprecision (8);
  cout << multiplier << endl;
  cout << "Future value: " << fixed << setprecision(2);
  cout << futureValue << endl;
}
```

Run:

```
Enter the value of periodic investment: 12000
Enter the interest rate per year: 5
```

(*continued*)

Program 6.27 Find the future value of periodic investments (Continued)

```
Enter the term (number of years): 30

Information about period invesment
Periodic Investment: 12000.00
Interest rate: 5.00 percent per year
Term: 30.00 years

Result of investment
Investment is multiplied by: 69.76078988
Future value: 837129.48
```

Note that the total investment in Program 6.26 and Program 6.27 is $360,000, but the future value of the second program is less. This is natural because when we invest periodically, the dollars are not totally invested for the full term.

Key Terms

automatic local variable
default parameter
function
function body
function call
function declaration
function definition
function header
function overloading
function prototype
function scope
function shadowing
function signature
global scope
lifetime
local scope
nested block
parameter list
pass-by-pointer
pass-by-reference
pass-by-value
scope
static local variable
void function

Summary

A function is an entity with a header and a set of statements that are designed to do a task. As programs become more complex, we divide the task into smaller tasks, each of which is responsible for a part of the job. There are four benefits to dividing a task into several small tasks: easier to write, easier to debug. reusable, and can be saved for future use. Three entities are associated with a function: function definition, function declaration, and function call.

In a library function, the definition is already created in the C++ library; we only need to include the corresponding header file in our program and then call the function. In a user-defined function, we declare, define, and call the function.

Functions in a program may need to exchange data. We refer to this activity as *data pass* and *data return*. Each can be done using one of the three methods: by value, by reference, or by pointer.

We can have one or more default parameters with predefined values in a function declaration.

Function overloading provides several definitions for a function with the same name but with different *signatures*, which means a different number of parameters, or different types of parameters, or both. The return value of a function is not part of its signature.

Scope and lifetime are two concepts that affect the design and use of functions. Scope defines where in the source code a named entity is visible. An entity in a program has a lifetime: It is born and it dies.

Problems

PR-1. Find the signature associated with each of the following function declarations:

```
int firstFunction (int x, float y, int z);
void secondFunction (int x, boolean y);
void thirdFunction (double x, double y);
void fourthFunction ();
```

PR-2. Given the declaration of the following two functions, determine if they are overloaded versions of each other.

```
int fun (int x, int y);
void fun (int a, int b);
```

PR-3. Given the declaration of the following two functions, determine if they are overloaded versions of each other.

```
int fun (int x, int y);
void fun (float a, float b);
```

PR-4. Given the declaration of the following two functions, determine if they are overloaded versions of each other.

```
int fun (int x, int y, int z);
float fun (int a, int b);
```

PR-5. Given the declaration of the following two functions, determine if they are overloaded versions of each other.

```
int functionOne (int x, int y);
int functionTwo (int a, int b);
```

PR-6. Given the declaration of the following two functions, determine if they are overloaded versions of each other.

```
int fun ();
float fun ();
```

PR-7. Find the valid function declarations among the following:

```
a. float one (int a, int b);
b. boolean two (int a, b);
c. float (int a, int b);
d. void three (void);
e. int ();
```

PR-8. Find any errors in the following function definition:

```
void one (int a)
{
    return a;
}
```

PR-9. Find any errors in the following function definition:

```
int two (int a)
{
    int b = a * a;
}
```

PR-10. Find any errors in the following function definition:

```
int three (int a, int b)
{
    c = a * b;
    return c;
}
```

PR-11. Find any errors in the following function definition:

```
void one ()
{
    cout << "In One" << endl;
    void two ()
    {
        cout << "In Two" << endl;
        return;
    }
    return;
}
```

PR-12. Find any errors in the following function definition:

```
int wrong (int x)
{
    double x = 2.7;
    return x;
}
```

PR-13. What would be returned when the following function is called?

```
int test ()
{
    return 3.25;
}
```

PR-14. What would be returned when the following function is called?

```
char test ()
{
    return 67;
}
```

PR-15. What would be returned when the following function is called?

```
double test ()
{
    return 9;
}
```

PR-16. What would be printed from the following program?

```
include <iostream>
using namespace std;

int main ()
{

       int x;
       cout << x;
       return 0;
}
```

PR-17. What would be printed from the following program?

```
# include <iostream>
using namespace std;

int x;

int main ()
{
     cout << x;
     return 0;
}
```

PR-18. What would be printed from the following program?

```
# include <iostream>
using namespace std;

int x;

int main ()
{

     int x;
     cout << x;
}
```

PR-19. What would be printed from the following program?

```
#include <iostream>
#include <cmath>
using namespace std;

int main ()
```

```
{
    double x = 23.671;
    cout << floor (x * 10 + 0.5) / 10 << endl;
    return 0;
}
```

PR-20. What would be printed from the following program?

```
#include <iostream>
#include <cmath>
using namespace std;

int main ()
{
    double x = −23.671;
    cout << floor (x * 10 − 0.5) / 10  << endl;
    return 0;
}
```

Programs

PRG-1. Write a short program to find the result of the following function calls.

```
a. abs (25) and abs (−23)
b. floor (44.56) and floor (−23.78)
c. ceil (25.23) and ceil (−2.89)
```

PRG-2. Write a short program to find the result of the following function calls.

```
a. pow (5.0, 3) and  pow (5, −3)
b. sqrt (44.56)
c. exp (−6.2) and exp (44.26)
d. log (16.2) and log10 (14.24)
```

PRG-3. Write a short program to find the result of the following function calls. The value of PI is defined in the text.

```
a. sin (0) and sin (PI)
b. cos (0) and cos (PI)
c. tan (0) and tan (1)
d. asin (0) and asin (1)
e. acos (0) and acos (1)
f. atan (0) and atan (1)
```

PRG-4. Show how we can use the *round* function to round a value. For example, the number 23.2 should be changed to 23, number 23.8 should be changed to 24, the number −23.2 should be changed to −23, and the number −23.8 should be changed to −24.

PRG-5. To show the behavior of the random number generator, generate 5 sets of random numbers in which each set contains 10 random numbers between 10 and 99 (two-digit values). Then find the sum of the numbers in each set to see the variations.

PRG-6. Show how to call the *rand* function to create a random number that can only be 0 or 1 and simulates the tossing of a coin.

PRG-7. Show how to call the *rand* function to create a random number between 0.1 and 0.9 with only one digit after the decimal point. Hint: Find random numbers between 1 and 9 and then divide the result by 10 to get a double value. Write a program to test your answer with 10 numbers.

PRG-8. Show how to call the *rand* function to create a random number belonging to the following set: 2, 4, 6, 8, 10.

PRG-9. Write a program that prints the square root of the first 10 integers using the corresponding function in the <cmath> header. Tabulate your result with appropriate headers.

PRG-10. Write a program that prints the cubic root of the first 10 integers using the *pow* function in the <cmath> header. Tabulate your result with appropriate headers.

PRG-11. Write a function that finds $\log_2 x$ using the log functions in the <cmath> header file. Note that we have $\log_a x = \log_b x / \log_b a$. Test your function in a program with values of x from 1 to 10. Tabulate your result with appropriate headers.

PRG-12. Write a function that, given a temperature in Celsius, returns the temperature in Fahrenheit. Use your function in a program and test it with Celsius values 0, 37, 40, and 100. The conversion from Celsius to Fahrenheit is given below:

Fahrenheit = Celcius ∗ 180.0 / 100.0 + 32

PRG-13. Write a function that, given a temperature in Fahrenheit, returns the temperature in Celsius. Use your function in a program and test it with Fahrenheit values 32, 98.6, 104, and 212. The conversion from Fahrenheit to Celsius is given below:

Celcius = (Fahrenheit − 32) ∗ (100.0 / 180.0)

PRG-14. Write a function to find the factorial of a positive number as shown below. Then use the function in a program to get the value of n from the user and print the factorial value. Test your program with values of n between 1 and 20 to avoid overflow.

$$\textbf{factorial}\ (n) = n * (n-1) * (n-2) * \ldots * 3 * 2 * 1$$

PRG-15. The permutation of n objects k at a time can be defined as shown below. The equation tells us how many permutations of n objects can be formed k elements at a time.

$$P(n, k) = \textbf{factorial}\ (n) / \textbf{factorial}\ (n-k)$$

PRG-16. The combination of n objects k at a time can be defined as shown below. The equation tells us how many combination of n objects can be formed k elements at a time.

$$P(n, k) = \textbf{factorial}\ (n) / (\textbf{factorial}\ (n-k) * \textbf{factorial}\ (k))$$

PRG-17. The Pascal triangle defines the coefficient of the terms (C_n) in the expansion of the binomial

$$(x+y)^n = C_0 x^0 y^n + C_1 x^1 y^{n-1} + \ldots + C_{n-1} x^{n-1} y^1 + C_n x^n y^0$$

The following shows the coefficient related to each n from 0 to 5. Note that both rows and columns start from 0.

```
n = 0        1
n = 1        1  1
n = 2        1  2  1
n = 3        1  3  3  1
n = 4        1  4  6  4  1
n = 5        1  5  10  10  5  1
```

Note that the value of each coefficient in a row and column is the sum of the coefficients in the previous row and previous column added with the coefficient in the previous row and the same column as shown below.

Pascal (row, col) = pascal (row – 1, col – 1) + pascal (row – 1 , col)

Write a function to find the value's coefficients for any n. Test your function to print the coefficient for n from 1 to 10 in rows and columns.

PRG-18. The value of PI (π) in trigonometry can be calculated as shown below:

$$\pi = 4 \times [\, 1 - 1/3 + 1/5 + \ldots + (-1)^{i+1} / (2i - 1) \,]$$

in which i varies from 1 to n. As n becomes increasingly larger, we get the value of π increasingly closer to the actual value. Write a function to return the value of π for the given value of n. Then write a program to tabulate the values of i and π for i from 1 to 2001 in increments of 200.

PRG-19. Write a function to create four-digit random integers in the range 1111 to 9999. Eliminate any number that has a zero in it. Then create 100 numbers and print them in a table with 10 numbers to a line.

PRG-20. Write two functions. The first finds the average of any set of three integers. The second finds the median of any set of three integers. A median is the number in the middle when the set is sorted (for example, the median of 4, 9, 6 is 6 because if the numbers are sorted the set is (4, 6, 9)). Then call each function in the program to find the average and median of any three integers. Test your program for at least five different sets and tabulate the result.

PRG-21. Write a function that finds the count of the digits in any positive integer (greater than 0). The integer is to be read from the keyboard. For example, the number of digits in 367 is 3. Hint: Divide the given integer by 10 continuously and increment the count until the integer is 0. Test the function in a program and tabulate the number of digits for at least 10 integers.

PRG-22. Write a function that finds the sum of the digits in any given integer. For example, the sum of the digits in 367 is 16. Write a program to tabulate at least five integers and print the sum of their digits.

PRG-23. Write a function that reverses the digits in its argument. For example, given the integer 378, the function returns 873. Test your program with a few integers with different numbers of digits.

PRG-24. An integer is a palindrome if it can be read backward and forward. For example 5, 121, 12321, 1347431 are all palindromes. Write a function to determine if a number is a palindrome. Use the function developed in PRG-23 to reverse the given integer before testing if it is a palindrome.

PRG-25. An integer is a prime if it is divisible only by itself and 1. Note that the integer 1 is not a prime. Write a function to test if a given number is prime. Then use a program to print the prime numbers less than 100 in a table of 10 columns.

PRG-26. Another way to find if a number is a prime is to find if it is divisible only by itself and not any other number in the range 1 to its square root. Write a function to test if a given number is a prime using this method. Then use a program to print the prime numbers less than 500 in a table of 10 columns.

PRG-27. An integer is *emirp* (prime spelled backward) if, when we inverse the digits, it is also a prime number. Write a function to print the *emirp* integers from 1 to 1000 ten numbers in a line.

PRG-28. Write a program that finds all the factors of a given number. A factor is a number less than the given number that divides the number. The program should use a function to test if a number is divisible by another number. Test your function with numbers between 1 and 100.

PRG-29. Write a function that finds all of the prime factors of a given number. A prime factor is a prime and also a factor. Use the idea of finding a prime in PRG-23. Test your function with numbers between 1 and 100.

PRG-30. Write a program that, given the desired future value, the number of years, and the interest rate, finds the value of the fixed amount to be invested. Hint: First find the multiplier.

PRG-31. Write a program that, given the monthly payment, the number of years, and the interest rate, finds the value of the loan one can borrow. Hint: First find the multipliers.

This is the first chapter in which we use C++ as an object-oriented language. In previous chapters we discussed the basics, and we will need what we learned in those chapters to understand the materials we use in this chapter and the rest of the book. In this chapter, we show how to create new types and how to use them. The mechanism for creating new types uses a *class* or an enumerated type. We will discuss classes in this chapter but we will ignore discussion on enumerated types because they are not common.

Objectives

After you have read and studied this chapter, you should be able to:

- Introduce object-oriented concepts, including types and instances, attributes and behaviors, and data members and member functions.
- Discuss the class definition that declares data members and member functions.
- Discuss three types of constructors: parameter constructors, default constructors, and copy constructors.
- Discuss destructors that are used to clean up the objects before they are recycled.
- Discuss instance data members and instance member functions.
- Discuss static data members and static member functions.
- Discuss how we divide the three sections of a program into three separate files—interface file, implementation file, and application file—and achieve one of the goals of object-oriented programming: encapsulation.

7.1 INTRODUCTION

In Chapter 1, we mentioned that C++ is a combination of a procedural and an object-oriented language. In previous chapters, we have used the language mostly as a procedural language; in this chapter we start using it as an object-oriented language.

7.1.1 Types and Instances in Real Life

A *type* is a concept from which an *instance* is created. In other words, a type is an abstraction; an **instance** of that type is a concrete entity. The word *clock* is a type; it defines a general concept that we are familiar with. The clock in John's office, the clock in Sue's office, or the clock in a train station are instances of this type. The word *circle* is a type. We can draw circles with different radii as instances of that type. We can even go further and say that the word *person* is a type, and that John, Sue, and Michelle are instances of the type person.

The relationship between a type and its instances is a one-to-many relation. We can have many instances from one single type. Figure 7.1 shows the type *Circle* and four instances that we call *circle1*, *circle2*, *circle3*, and *circle4*.

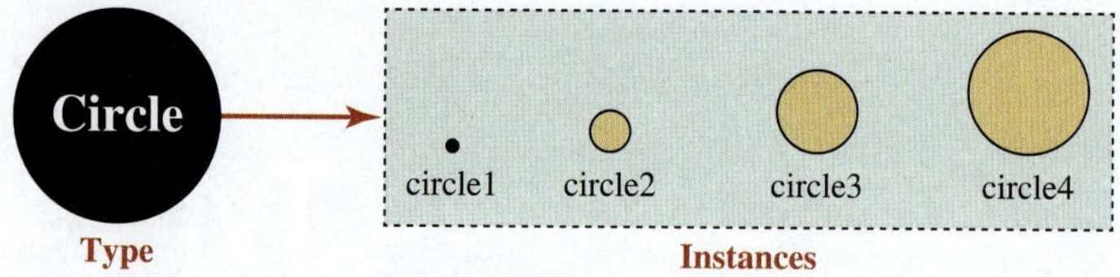

Figure 7.1 A type and its instances

Any instance we encounter in this world has a set of attributes and a set of behaviors.

Attributes

In real life an attribute is a characteristic ascribed to an instance. In computer science, an **attribute** is any characteristic that interests us in an instance. For example, if the instance is an employee, we may be interested only in the employee's *name*, *address*, *position*, and *salary*. On the other hand, if the instance is a student in a university, we may be interested only in the student's *name*, *year*, *courses taken*, and *grades*. If the instance is a circle, we may be interested only in its *radius*, *perimeter*, and *area*.

An attribute is a characteristic of an instance that we are interested in.

Behaviors

When we think about instances, we also think about their behaviors. In this sense, a **behavior** is an operation that an instance can perform on itself. For example, if an instance is an employee, we assume that she can give her *name*, her *address*, and her *salary*. On the other hand, if an instance is a circle, we assume that it can give its *radius*, its *perimeter*, and its *area*. Note that in object-oriented programming, we assume that an instance is capable of performing an operation on itself.

A behavior is an operation that we assume an instance can perform on itself.

7.1.2 Classes and Objects in Programs

In object-oriented programming, we still use the terms *type* and *instance*. In C++, a user-defined type can be created using a construct named **class.** An instance of a class is referred to as an **object.** This means that we use *type* and *class*. We also use *instances* and *objects*. In object-oriented programming, attributes and behaviors of an object are represented as *data members* and *member functions*.

Data Members

A **data member** of an object is a variable whose value represents an attribute. For example, the radius of a circle object can be represented by the value of a variable of type *double*. In other words, the attribute of an object of type *circle* can be effectively represented as a variable of type *double* that holds the value of the radius for that instance. However, some attributes of an instance are not independent; they may depend on values of other attributes. For example, the perimeter and the area of a circle may be two attributes for a mathematician, but we do not represent them as data members because both depend on the value of the radius.

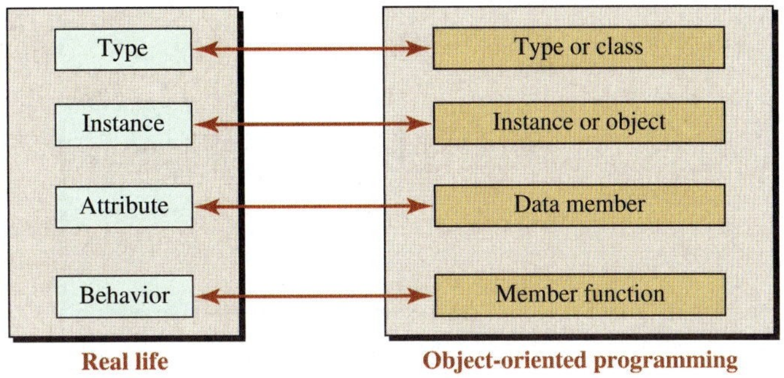

Figure 7.2 Comparison of terms in real life and in object-oriented programming

> **Attributes of an object in object-oriented programming are simulated using data members.**

Member Function

In programming, a function is an entity that can do something. A **member function** in object-oriented programming is a function that simulates one of the behaviors of an object. For example, we can write a function that allows a circle to give its radius, its area, and its perimeter. We can also write a function that a circle can use to set its radius, but we should be aware of dependent attributes when we do so.

> **Behaviors of an object in object-oriented programming are simulated using member functions.**

7.1.3 Comparison

Figure 7.2 shows the terms we use in real life and in object-oriented programming. The figure can be used throughout the chapter to better understand the concepts we discuss.

7.2 CLASSES

Although C++ has many predefined (built-in) types such as *int, double, char,* and *bool,* it also allows programmers to create new types. In C++, new types are mostly created using a **class.** To write object-oriented programs, we need to create a class, as a type, and then instantiate objects as instances of that type. In procedural programming, we need only write an *application* program (the *main* function and some other functions) to use objects of built-in types. In object-oriented programming we need three sections: the *class definition*, the *member function definition*, and the *application* (which uses the objects created from the class). In other words, if we want to write object-oriented programs versus writing procedural programs, we should always think about these three sections. We will see that sometimes each section is designed and saved by different entities. We have seen that in some cases, the first two sections (class definition and member function definitions) are created and stored in the C++ library (like the string and file classes), but the principle is the same: We need all three sections, as shown in Figure 7.3.

In the *class definition* section, we declare the data members and member functions. In the *member function definition* section, we define all member functions. In the *application* section, we instantiate objects and apply the member function to those objects.

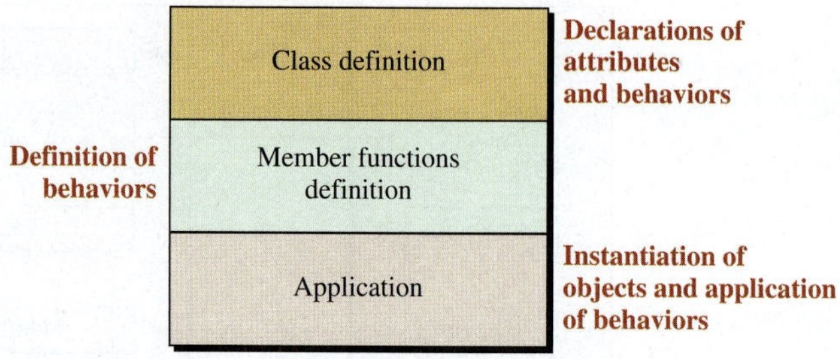

Figure 7.3 Three sections of a C++ program in object-oriented paradigm

7.2.1 An Example

Before we formally discuss these three sections, we use them in Program 7.1. We know that there are many issues that we have not discussed yet, but the program will be used to discuss them gradually.

Program 7.1 Creating and handling two circle objects

```
/***************************************************************
 * A program to use a class in object-oriented programming    *
 ***************************************************************/
#include <iostream>
using namespace std;

/***************************************************************
 * Class definition: the declaration of data members and member *
 * functions of the class                                       *
 ***************************************************************/
class Circle
{
  private:
       double radius;
  public:
       double getRadius () const;
       double getArea () const;
       double getPerimeter () const;
       void setRadius (double value);
};
/***************************************************************
 * Members function definition. Each function declared in the  *
 * class definition section is defined in this section.        *
 ***************************************************************/
// Definition of getRadius member function
double Circle :: getRadius () const
{
  return radius;
}
```

(continued)

Program 7.1 Creating and handling two circle objects (Continued)

```
// Definition of getArea member function
double Circle :: getArea () const
{
   const double PI = 3.14;
   return (PI * radius * radius);
}
// Definition of getPerimeter member function
double Circle :: getPerimeter () const
{
   const double PI = 3.14;
   return (2 * PI * radius);
}
// Definition of setRadius member function
void Circle :: setRadius (double value)
{
   radius = value;
}
/***************************************************************
 * Application section: Objects are instantiated in this section.       *
 * Objects use member functions to get or set their attributes.        *
 ***************************************************************/
int main ( )
{
   // Creating first circle and applying member functions
   cout << "Circle 1: " << endl;
   Circle circle1;
   circle1.setRadius (10.0);
   cout << "Radius: " << circle1.getRadius() << endl;
   cout << "Area: " << circle1.getArea() << endl;
   cout << "Perimeter: " << circle1.getPerimeter() << endl << endl;
   // Creating second circle and applying member functions
   cout << "Circle 2: " << endl;
   Circle circle2;
   circle2.setRadius (20.0);
   cout << "Radius: " << circle2.getRadius() << endl;
   cout << "Area: " << circle2.getArea() << endl;
   cout << "Perimeter: " << circle2.getPerimeter();
   return 0;
}
```

Run:

```
Circle 1:
Radius: 10
Area: 314
Perimeter: 62.8
```

(continued)

Program 7.1 Creating and handling two circle objects (Continued)

```
Circle 2:
Radius: 20
Area: 1256
Perimeter: 125.6
```

Lines 11 to 20 are the *class definition*. Lines 25 to 46 are *member functions definitions*, and lines 51 to 68 are the *application*. We will discuss each section in detail by referring to this program.

7.2.2 Class Definition

To create a new type, we must first write a **class definition.** A class definition is made of three parts: a *header*, a *body*, and a *semicolon*. A **class header** is made of the reserved word *class* followed by the name given by the designer. Although we are free to use lowercase or uppercase letters when we define user-defined types, we follow a convention that recommends that class names start with an uppercase letter to distinguish them from library classes, which start with lowercase letters. The **class body** is a block (starting with an opening brace and ending with a closing brace) that holds the declaration of *data members* and *member functions* in the block. The third element of a class declaration is a semicolon that terminates the definition. We repeat the class definition for our class:

```
class Circle  // Header
{
    private:
        double radius;                      // Data member declaration
    public:
        double getRadius () const;          // Member function declaration
        double getArea () const;            // Member function declaration
        double getPerimeter () const;       // Member function declaration
        void setRadius (double value);      // Member function declaration
}; // A semicolon is needed at the end of class definition
```

Declaring Data Members

One part of the class definition declares data members of the class, variables or constants of built-in types or other previously defined class types. The data members of a class simulate the attributes of the objects that are instantiated from the class. However, in any object we may have several attributes, some of which are dependent on the others and can be calculated given the other attributes. Among the dependent attributes, we need to select the simplest and the most basic ones. For example, in our circle class, we have three attributes: *radius*, *area*, and *perimeter*. Each of them can be calculated given one of the other two, but the radius is the most primitive and most basic. We have chosen the radius to be a data member. Selecting more than one attribute among the dependent attributes can cause an error in the program; we may change one of them and forget to change the others. For example, if we have chosen both *radius* and *area* as data members, changing the *radius* using a member function and not changing the *area* at the same time creates a circle whose area is calculated erroneously and vice versa.

Figure 7.4 Access modifier

Data members in a class must not depend on each other.

Declaring Member Functions

The second part of the class definition declares the member functions of the class; that is, it declares all functions that are used to simulate the behavior of the class. This section is similar to the prototype declaration we used when we were working with global functions in previous chapters. There is, however, one difference: Some functions have the *const* qualifier at the end and some do not. Those that change something in the object cannot use this qualifier; those that are not allowed to change anything need this qualifier. We will return to this issue later in the chapter.

Access Modifiers

The **access modifier** determines how a class can be accessed. The declaration of data members and member functions in a class is by default private. These members and member functions cannot be accessed for retrieving or changing.

When there is no access modifier for a member, it is private by default.

To circumvent this limitation, C++ defines three access modifiers. The designer of a class can apply an access modifier to the declaration of a member to control access to that member. C++ uses three modifiers for this purpose: *private, protected,* and *public* as shown in Figure 7.4. Table 7.1 gives the general idea behind each modifier.

When a member is *private*, it can only be accessed inside the class (through member functions). When a member is *public*, it can be accessed from anywhere (inside the same class, inside the subclasses, and in the application). We discuss *protected* members when we discuss subclasses in Chapter 11.

Access Modifiers for Data Members The modifiers for data members are normally set to *private* for emphasis (although no modifier means private). This means that the data members are not accessible directly. They must be accessed through the member functions.

Table 7.1 Member Access for each modifier

Modifier	Access from same class	Access from subclass	Access from anywhere
private	Yes	No	No
protected	Yes	Yes	No
public	Yes	Yes	Yes

However, privacy does not mean privacy in visibility; it means privacy in access. A private data member is visible, but it cannot be accessed except through a member function.

The data members of a class are normally set to private.

Access Modifiers for Member Functions To operate on the data members, the application must use member functions, which means that the declaration of member functions usually must be set to *public*.

The instance member functions of a class are normally set to public.

However, sometimes the modifier of a member function must be set to private, such as when a member function must help other member functions but is not allowed to be called by functions outside the class. We will discuss this issue later in this chapter.

Group Modifier Access You may have noticed that we have used only one keyword, *private,* and one keyword, *public,* in the whole class definition. This is referred to as group modification. We have collected all data members under one group and have used the *private* keyword followed by a colon to say that all of the keywords are private. We have also grouped all member functions and used one *public* keyword followed by a colon to say that all of them are public. In other words, a modifier is valid until we encounter a new one. We could have defined the modifier followed by a colon for each data member or member function, but it is not necessary. Indention after the modifier is for clarity.

7.2.3 Member Functions Definition

The declaration of a member function gives its prototype; each member function also needs a definition. The definition of a function must be done separately except in some situations, which we discuss later in this chapter. In Program 7.1 we created a definition for each member function based on the declaration defined in the class definition.

```
double Circle :: getRadius () const
{
   return radius;
}
double Circle :: getArea () const
{
   const double PI = 3.14;
   return (PI * radius * radius);
}
double Circle :: getPerimeter () const
{
   const double PI = 3.14;
   return (2 * PI * radius);
}
void Circle :: setRadius (double value)
{
   radius = value;
}
```

Table 7.2 Class scope

Group	Name	Operator	Expression	Pred	Assoc
Primary	class scope	::	class :: name	19	→

The definition of each member function is similar to the definition that we have used in previous chapters, but with two differences. The first is the qualifier (*const*) that is applied to some member function. The second is the name of the function that must be qualified with the name of the class. This is similar to when we know two people with the name Sue, one coming from the Brown family and the other from the White family. In C++, we need to mention the class name (family name) first followed by a *class scope* (::) symbol to achieve this goal. The class scope is a primary expression as shown in Appendix C, but it is repeated in Table 7.2 for convenience.

You may ask why we did not include the last name of a data member or a member function in the class declaration. The reason is that these members are enclosed in the class definition; they belong to that class. This is similar to the case in which we do not mention the last name of an individual when she is in the family; the last name is used when we are out of the family circle. Figure 7.5 shows the difference.

Note that the return type of the function always comes before the whole name. In the class declaration, there is no explicit last name, so it comes before the first name. In the function definition, it must come before the whole name.

7.2.4 Inline Functions

When the body of a function is short, the execution time involved in the function call (storing the arguments, transferring control, retrieving the argument, and storing the return value) may be greater than executing the code inside the function. To improve program performance, we can declare a function as an **inline function** to indicate that the compiler can replace the function call with the actual code in the function. However, the compiler may ignore this request. We have not used inline functions in our previous programs and will not do so, but you are free to use this option.

Implicit Inline Function

A function is defined as an **implicit inline function** when we replace its declaration (in the class definition) with its definition. This is not recommended for two reasons. First, it makes the definition more difficult to read. Second, it violates the principle of encapsulation, which we discuss shortly. The following shows a partial definition of the *Circle* class with an implicit inline function.

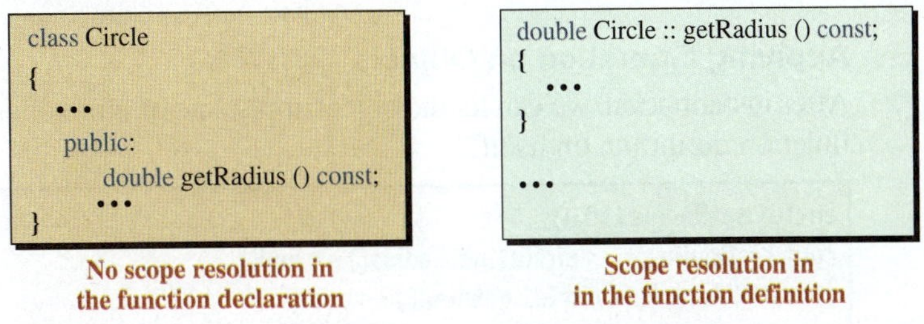

Figure 7.5 Using names in the class definition and member functions

```
class Circle
{
    // Data Members
    private:
        double radius;
    // Member functions
    public:
        double getRadius () const { return radius }
        ...
};
```

We have included the definition of the *getRadius* function in the class definition, which means that there is no need to include the definition of this function separately.

Explicit Inline Function

A function is defined as an **explicit inline function** by adding the keyword *inline* in front of the function definition. In this case, the definition remained unchanged with the exception of adding the *inline* keyword.

```
inline double Circle :: getRadius()      const
{
   return radius;
}
```

7.2.5 Application

The class definition and member function definition must be used. We need an application section—the *main* function, for example—to instantiate objects of the class and apply the member functions on the those objects as shown in Program 7.1. We first instantiated one object named *circle1* using the following format (we discuss this format and similar ones later in the chapter).

Object Instantiation

Before using any member function, we must instantiate an object of the class as shown below:

```
Circle circle1;
```

After this line we have an object named *circle1* that encapsulates one single data member (variable) of type *double* named *radius,* which contains the garbage left over from the previous operation. We must change the value of this variable before using it.

Applying Operation on Objects

After instantiation, we can let the object apply one or more operations defined in the member function definition on itself.

```
circle1.setRadius (10.0);
cout << "Radius: " << circle1.getRadius() << endl;
cout << "Area: " << circle1.getArea() << endl;
cout << "Perimeter: " << circle1.getPerimeter() << endl << endl;
```

The first line sets the radius of *circle1*. The second line gets the value of the circle's radius. The next two lines calculate and print the area and perimeter of the object named *circle1*.

Member Selection

You may wonder why we are using a *dot* between the object name and the member function that is supposed to operate on the object. This is called the *member select* operator, and we discuss it later in the chapter. In other words, we can apply the same function on different objects using this operator as shown below:

```
circle1.getRadius();          // circle1 is supposed to get its radius
circle2.getRadius();          // circle2 is supposed to get its radius
```

7.2.6 Structs

We sometimes encounter a construct in C++ that is in fact a legacy from the C language: *struct.* A **struct** in the C++ language is actually a *class* with one difference: In a *struct*, all members are public by default; in a *class*, all members are private by default. We can always create a *class* to simulate a *struct* as shown below:

```
struct                        class
{                             {
   string first;                 public:
   char middle;                      string first;
   string last;                      char middle;
};                                   string last;
                              };
```

Some programmers still use a *struct* instead of a *class* because doing so allows them to access the elements in a *struct* directly (they are public) without using a member function. This can be seen in some programs that aggregate data items into one item, such as a *node* in a *linked-list* structure; we will discuss these in Chapter 13. Our recommendation is to use a *class* instead of a *struct*.

7.3 CONSTRUCTORS AND DESTRUCTORS

In object-oriented programming, an instance is an object that encapsulates the data members defined in the class definition. If we want an object to perform some operations on itself, we should first create the object and initialize its data members. Creation is done when a special member function named a **constructor** is called in the application; initialization is when the body of a constructor is executed.

On the other hand, when we do not need an object anymore, the object should be cleaned up and the memory occupied by the object should be recycled. Cleanup is automatically done when another special member function named a **destructor** is called, the object goes out of scope, and the body of the destructor is executed; recycling is done when the program is terminated.

A constructor is a special member function that creates and initializes an object.
A destructor is a special member function that cleans and destroys an object.

In other words, as shown in Figure 7.6, an object goes through five steps. It is created and initialized by a special member function called a *constructor*. It applies some operations

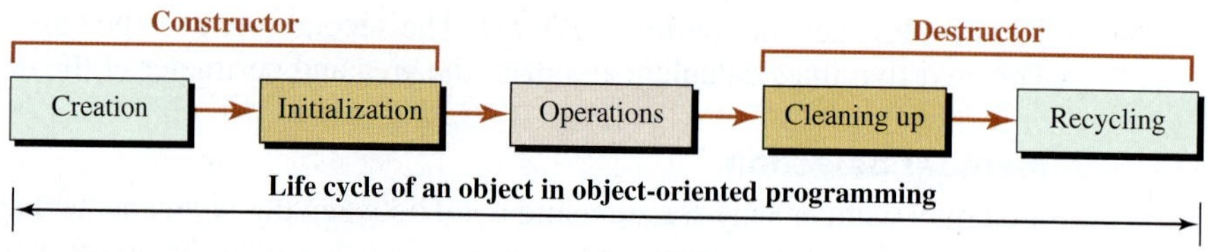

Figure 7.6 Life cycle of an object

requested by the application on itself. It is cleaned up and recycled by another special member function called a *destructor*.

7.3.1 Constructors

A constructor is a member function that creates an object when it is called and initializes the data members of an object when it is executed. The declaration of the data members in the class definition does not initialize the data members; the declaration just gives the names and the types of the data members.

A constructor has two characteristics: It does not have a return value, and its name is the same as the name of the class. A constructor cannot have a return value (not even *void*) because it is not designed to return anything; its purpose is different. It creates an object and initializes the data members. Although we will see that a constructor may also do some other tasks, such as validation of values, these tasks are also considered part of the initialization.

We can have three types of constructors in a class: *parameter constructors, default constructors,* and *copy constructors.*

Constructor Declaration

A constructor is a member function of the class, which means it must be declared in the class definition. A constructor has no return value, its name is the same as the name of the class, and it cannot have the *const* qualifier because the constructor initializes the value of the data members (more about this later). The following shows how we add the declaration of three constructors to our *Circle* class.

```
class Circle
{
  ...
  public:
      Circle (double radius);              // Parameter Constructor
      Circle ();                           // Default Constructor
      Circle (const Circle& circle);       // Copy Constructor
      ...
}
```

Note that all constructors of the class are normally public, so the application can call any of the constructors to initialize an object of the class.

Parameter Constructor Normally we have a **parameter constructor** that initializes the data members of each instance with specified values. The parameter constructor can be overloaded, which means that we can have several parameter constructors each with a different signature. The advantage of the parameter constructor is that we can initialize the data members of each object with a specific value. In other words, if we use a parameter constructor, the radius of one circle can be initialized to 3.1, another one to 4.6, and so on.

The parameter constructor can be overloaded for a class.

Default Constructor The default constructor is a constructor with no parameters. It is used to create objects with each data member for all objects set to some literal values or default values. Note that we cannot overload the default constructor because it has no parameter list and therefore is not eligible for overloading.

The default constructor cannot be overloaded for a class.

Copy Constructor Sometimes we want to initialize each data member of an object to the same value as a corresponding data member of a previously created object. We can use a copy constructor in this case. A copy constructor copies the data member values of the given object to the new object just created. After calling the copy constructor, the source and the destination objects have exactly the same value for each data member, although they are different objects. The copy constructor has only one parameter that receives the source object by reference. The *const* modifier in front of the parameter type guarantees that the pass-by-reference cannot change the source object. Remember that pass-by-reference has two characteristics. First, there is no need to physically copy the object. Second, a change in the destination means the same change in the source. Using the *const* modifier, we keep the first characteristic, but we forbid the second. Also note that we cannot overload the copy constructor because the parameter list is fixed and we cannot have an alternative form.

The copy constructor cannot be overloaded for a class.

Constructor Definition

As we said, a constructor is a member function, but a special one. It cannot have a return value, and its name is the same as the name of the class. The following shows the definition of the three constructors for our *Circle* class.

```
// Definition of a parameter constructor
Circle :: Circle (double rds)
: radius (rds)          // Initialization list
{
    // Any other statements
}
// Definition of a default constructor
Circle :: Circle ()
: radius (1.0) // Initialization list. If it is missing, radius is set to garbage values
{
    // Any other statements
}
// Definition of a copy constructor
Circle :: Circle (const Circle& cr)
: radius (cr.radius)     // Initialization list
{
    // Any other statements
}
```

The main difference between the definition of a constructor and definition of other member functions is that a constructor can have an initialization list after the header to initialize the data members. The initialization list is put after the header and before the body of the constructor and it starts with a colon. In our *Circle* class, we have only one data member to initialize. If we need to initialize more than one data member, the initialization of each data member must be separated by a comma from other data members. In general, the initialization list has the following format:

```
: dataMemember (parameter), ... , dataMember (parameter)
```

We can think of each initialization as an assignment statement that assigns the parameter to the data member, such as *dataMember* = parameter. There is no terminator for the initialization list. The next line is the body of the constructor. The *dataMember* name must be the same as the one defined in the declaration of the data member, but the name of each parameter is determined by the programmer.

Another important point is that a constant data member of an object must be initialized when the object is created. As we have seen in previous chapters, we cannot change a constant entity after it has been declared, but C++ allows us to initialize it in the initialization section of a constructor.

Sometimes, however, we must use the body of the constructor to initialize complex data members (through assignments) that cannot be simply initialized in the initialization list. The body of a constructor can also be used for additional processing, such as validating a parameter, opening files if needed, or even printing a message to verify that the constructor was called.

7.3.2 Destructors

Like a constructor, a destructor has two special characteristics. First, the name of the destructor is the name of the class preceded by a tilde symbol (~), but the tilde is added to the first name, not the last name (the last name is the same for all member functions). Second, like a constructor, a destructor cannot have a return value (not even *void*) because it returns nothing. A destructor is guaranteed to be automatically called and executed by the system when the object instantiated from the class goes out of scope. In other words, if we have instantiated five objects from the class, the destructor is automatically called five times to guarantee that all objects are cleaned up. Cleanup is most important if the constructed has called resources such as files. After the program is terminated, the allocated memory is recycled. A destructor can take no arguments, which means it cannot be overloaded.

A destructor is a special-purpose member function with no parameter and is designed to clean up and recycle an object.

Destructor Declaration

The following shows the declaration of the destructor in the class definition.

```
class Circle
{
    ...
  public:
    ...
    ~Circle ();                          // Destructor
}
```

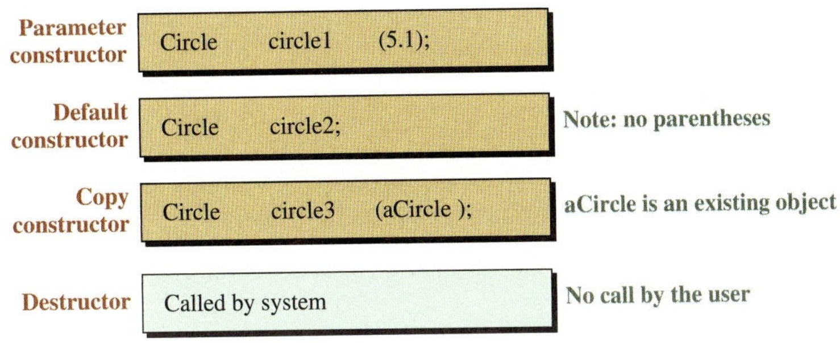

Figure 7.7 Object construction and destruction for a class type

Destructor Definition

The definition of a destructor is similar to the definition of the other three member functions, but it must have a tilde (~) in front of the first name. A destructor should be public like all constructors.

```
// Definition of a destructor
Circle :: ~Circle ()
{
    // Any statements as needed
}
```

7.3.3 Creating and Destroying Objects

We are now ready to show how we can instantiate objects when they are needed and how we can destroy them when they are not needed. Note that calling a constructor creates an object. When the constructor is executed, it initializes the data members. Similarly, when a destructor is executed, the data members are cleaned up. When the program is terminated, the memory locations are released.

Figure 7.7 shows the syntax for calling a parameter constructor, a default constructor, and a copy constructor. There is no syntax to call a destructor because it is called by the system. We must pay attention to the call of a default constructor. In C++ the default constructor does not need empty parentheses. If we use empty parentheses when we call the default constructor, the system thinks we want to call an overloaded parameter constructor with no parameters; if such a constructor is not defined, we get an error.

Note that the literature sometimes includes the *assignment operator* as part of the group, but the assignment operator just copies the data member of one object to another. The two objects must exist already. We will discuss the assignment operator in Chapter 13 and will explain its relation to the above four member functions when we do.

Table 7.3 compares the creation of variables when dealing with built-in types to the creation of objects when dealing with objects of class types.

Table 7.3 Comparison between creation of variables and objects of classes

Member	Class type	Built-in type
Parameter constructor	Circle circle1 (10.0);	`double x1 = 10.0;`
Default constructor	Circle circle2;	`double x2;`
Copy constructor	Circle circle3 (circle1);	None
Destructor	No call	No call

Note:
We need at least one member from each group. If we do not define at least one member from each group, the system provides one.

Figure 7.8 Grouping constructors and destructor

7.3.4 Required Member Functions

We may ask, which of these four member functions are required for a class? What happens if we ignore declaring and defining one or more of them as we did in the case of our *Circle* class? We can best answer this question if we put these member functions into three groups as shown in Figure 7.8. Each group is independent when it comes to its requirements.

Group 1

Group 1 consists of the parameter constructor and the default constructor. We must have at least one of these constructors; we may sometimes need both. If we provide either of them, the system does not provide any for us. If we provide neither of them, the system provides a default constructor, referred to as a *synthetic default constructor*, that initializes each member to what is left over as garbage in the system. That is what happened in our first definition of the *Circle*. We needed one of the two constructors in the first group, but we did not provide one. The system provided one for us with garbage stored in the *radius* data member. We did not use the object created before we re-initialized the constructors with the *setRadius* member function. To be safe, we can always provide both of the constructors in Group 1.

We normally declare and define both parameter and default constructors in our class.

Group 2

The second group is the copy constructor. A class must have one and only one copy constructor, but if we do not provide one, the system provides one for us, which is referred to as the *synthetic copy constructor*. Most of the time it is better to create our own copy constructor.

Group 3

The third group is the destructor. A class must have one and only one destructor, but if we do not provide one, the system provides one for us, which is referred to as the *synthetic destructor*. Most of the time, the synthesized destructor is not what we want. It is better to create our own destructor.

EXAMPLE 7.1

Program 7.2 repeats our *Circle* class with the constructors and the destructor provided. We include a message in the body of each constructor and the destructor to show when they are called.

Program 7.2 A complete *Circle* class

```
/****************************************************************
 * A program to use a class in object-oriented programming       *
 ****************************************************************/
#include <iostream>
using namespace std;

/****************************************************************
 * Class Definition:                                              *
 * declaration of parameter constructor, default constructor,     *
 * copy constructor, destructor, and other member functions       *
 ****************************************************************/
class Circle
{
  private:
      double radius;
  public:
      Circle (double radius);        // Parameter Constructor
      Circle ();                     // Default Constructor
      ~Circle ();                    // Destructor
      Circle (const Circle& circle);      // Copy Constructor
      void setRadius (double radius);     // Mutator
      double getRadius () const;          // Accessor
      double getArea () const;            // Accessor
      double getPerimeter () const;       // Accessor
};
/****************************************************************
 * Member Function Definition:                                    *
 * Definition of parameter constructor, default constructor,      *
 * copy constructor, destructor, and other member functions       *
 ****************************************************************/
// Definition of parameter constructor
Circle :: Circle (double rds)
: radius (rds)
{
  cout << "The parameter constructor was called. " << endl;
}
// Definition of default constructor
Circle :: Circle ()
: radius (0.0)
{
  cout << "The default constructor was called. " << endl;
}
// Definition of copy constructor
Circle :: Circle (const Circle& circle)
```

(continued)

Program 7.2 A complete *Circle* class (Continued)

```
: radius (circle.radius)
{
  cout << "The copy constructor was called. " << endl;
}
// Definition of destructor
Circle :: ~Circle ()
{
  cout << "The destructor was called for circle with radius " ;
  cout << endl;
}
// Definition of setRadius member function
void Circle :: setRadius (double value)
{
  radius = value;
}
// Definition of getRadius member function
double Circle :: getRadius () const
{
  return radius;
}
// Definition of getArea member function
double Circle :: getArea () const
{
  const double PI = 3.14;
  return (PI * radius * radius);
}
// Definition of getPerimeter member function
double Circle :: getPerimeter () const
{
  const double PI = 3.14;
  return (2 * PI * radius);
}
/*****************************************************************
 * Application :                                                 *
 * Creating three objects of class Circle (circle1, circle2,     *
 * and circle3) and applying some operation on each object       *
 *****************************************************************/
int main ( )
{
  // Instantiation of circle1 and applying operations on it
  Circle circle1 (5.2);
  cout << "Radius: " << circle1.getRadius() << endl;
  cout << "Area: " << circle1.getArea() << endl;
  cout << "Perimeter: " << circle1.getPerimeter() << endl << endl;
```

(continued)

Program 7.2 A complete *Circle* class (Continued)

```
    // Instantiation of circle2 and applying operations on it
    Circle circle2 (circle1);
    cout << "Radius: " << circle2.getRadius() << endl;
    cout << "Area: " << circle2.getArea() << endl;
    cout << "Perimeter: " << circle2.getPerimeter() << endl << endl;
    // Instantiation of circle3 and applying operations on it
    Circle circle3;
    cout << "Radius: " << circle3.getRadius() << endl;
    cout << "Area: " << circle3.getArea() << endl;
    cout << "Perimeter: " << circle3.getPerimeter() << endl << endl;
    // Calls to destructors occur here
    return 0;
}
```

```
Run:
The parameter constructor was called.
Radius: 5.2
Area: 84.9056
Perimeter: 32.656

The copy constructor was called.
Radius: 5.2
Area: 84.9056
Perimeter: 32.656

The default constructor was called.
Radius: 0
Area: 0
Perimeter: 0

The destructor was called for circle with radius: 0
The destructor was called for circle with radius: 5.2
The destructor was called for circle with radius: 5.2
```

Note that the application creates three objects, *circle1, circle2,* and *circle3,* using a parameter constructor, a copy constructor, and a default constructor. Note that the application does not call the destructor but the system calls it when the object goes out of scope. The interesting point is that the objects are destroyed in the reverse order in which they are constructed. The last created object is destroyed first; the first created object is destroyed last. We will discuss the reason in Chapter 14 when we show that the objects are created in *stack memory.* In a stack, the last item inserted is the first item that can be removed (like a stack of dishes).

EXAMPLE 7.2

Sometimes we need only the parameter constructor because the default and copy constructors do not make sense. We discussed the use of random number generation in Chapter 6.

We know that for each random number, we need to call the *seed* function with an appropriate argument (such as *time*(0)). We then call the *random* function. Finally we need to scale and shift the generated random number to get a random number in the desired range. All of this work can be done in a class. We instantiate an object of the class to create a random number, as shown in Program 7.3.

Program 7.3 Defining and creating three random numbers

```
/***************************************************************
 * A program to declare, define, and use a class that generates      *
 * a random-number integer between any given range defined in        *
 * the constructor of the class.                                     *
 ***************************************************************/
#include <iostream>
#include <cstdlib>
#include <ctime>
using namespace std;

/***************************************************************
 * Class Definition (Declaration of data members and member          *
 * functions) for a Random-number generator.                         *
 ***************************************************************/
class RandomInteger
{
  private:
     int low;    // Data member
     int high;   // Data member
     int value;  // Data member
  public:
     RandomInteger (int low, int high); // Constructor
     ~RandomInteger (); // Destructor
     // Preventing a synthesized copy constructor
     RandomInteger (const RandomInteger& random) = delete;
     void print () const;  // Accessor member function
};
/***************************************************************
 * Definitions of constructor, destructor, and accessor member       *
 * functions for the random number generator class                   *
 ***************************************************************/
// Constructor
RandomInteger :: RandomInteger (int lw, int hh)
:low (lw), high (hh)
{
  srand (time (0));
  int temp = rand ();
```

(continued)

Program 7.3 Defining and creating three random numbers (Continued)

```
    value = temp % (high - low + 1) + low;
}
// Destructor
RandomInteger :: ~RandomInteger ()
{
}
// Accessor member function
void RandomInteger :: print () const
{
    cout << value << endl;
}
/***************************************************************
 * Application to instantiate random number objects and print   *
 * the value of the random number                                *
 ***************************************************************/
int main ( )
{
    // Generating a random integer between 100 and 200
    RandomInteger r1 (100, 200);
    cout << "Random number between 100 and 200: ";
    r1.print ();
    // Generating a random integer between 400 and 600
    RandomInteger r2 (400, 600);
    cout << "Random number between 400 and 600: ";
    r2.print ();
    // Generating a random integer between 400 and 600          ;
    RandomInteger r3 (1500, 2000);
    cout << "Random number between 1500 and 2000: ";
    r3.print ();
    return 0;
}
```

Run:

```
Random number between 100 and 200: 130
Random number between 400 and 600: 570
Random number between 1500 and 2000: 1720
```

There are four points we must mention about this program.

- This is an example in which we do not need a default constructor because creation of a random number with literal values does not make sense. Since we have defined a parameter constructor, the system does not create a default constructor in this case, which is what we want.
- We do not need a copy constructor for this class (it does not make sense to create the same random number), but we cannot stop the system from defining a synthesized one. In this case, the new C++11 standard comes to the rescue. It allows us to declare

a copy constructor and set it to the keyword *delete,* which prevents the system from providing a synthesized copy constructor (see the class definition, line 25).

- Although we have three data members, only two of them (*low* and *high*) are initialized in the initialization list of the constructor. The third data member (*value*) is calculated in the body of the constructor. The calculation is too complex to be done in the initializer list. The only accessor member function is the *print* function, which prints the value of the created random number.
- Finally, we have no mutator member functions because we do not want to change the created random number.

7.4 INSTANCE MEMBERS

In the previous three sections, we learned how to define classes, how to instantiate objects from classes, and how to apply member functions on the data members of objects. In this section and the next, we learn more about these members and the interaction among members in the background; doing so will help us design better classes. When we design a class, we can have two groups of members: *instance members* and *class members.*

7.4.1 Instance Data Members

An **instance data member** defines the attributes of an instance, which means that each object must *encapsulate* the set of data members defined in the class. These data members belong exclusively to the corresponding instance and cannot be accessed by other instances. The term *encapsulation* here means that separate regions of memory are assigned for each object and each region stores possibly different values for each data member. Figure 7.9 shows the concept of encapsulation.

Access Modifier for Instance Data Member

Although an instance data member can have a private or a public access modifier, it makes more sense for instance data members to be private. If we make the data members of an instance member public, they can be directly accessed by the application without calling an instance member function. That is not the goal of object-oriented programming. In object-oriented programming we want the objects to apply their behaviors on their attributes. In other words, we must make the instance data members private so that they can be accessed only through instance member functions.

The instance data members of a class are normally private and can be accessed only through instance member functions.

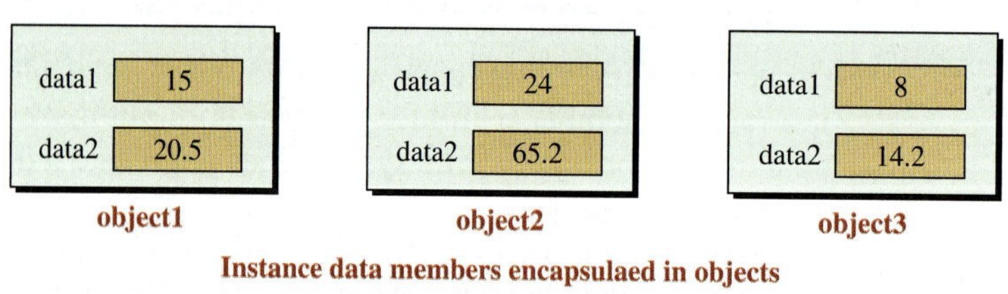

Figure 7.9 Encapsulation of data members in objects

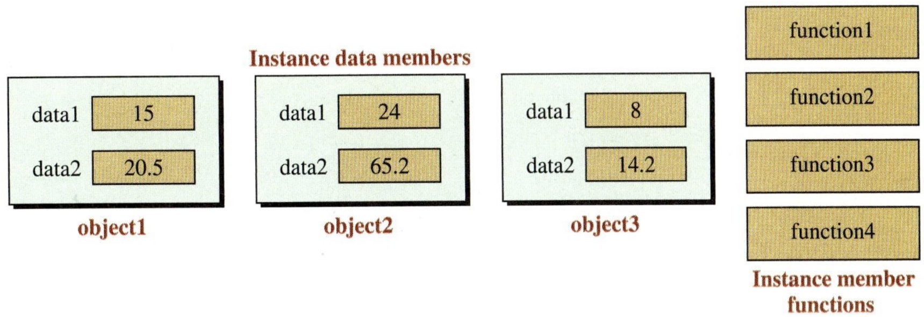

Figure 7.10 A class with two data members and four member functions

7.4.2 Instance Member Functions

An **instance member function** defines one of the behaviors that can be applied on the instance data members of an object. Although each object has its own instance data members, there is only one copy of each instance member function in memory and it must be shared by all instances. Figure 7.10 shows the case of a class with two instance data members and four instance member functions.

Since we have created three objects from this class, we have three pairs of instance data members and four instance member functions; each member function is shared among the objects (one object at a time).

Access Modifier for Instance Member Functions

Unlike instance data members, the access modifier for an instance member function is normally public and allows access from outside the class (the application) unless the instance member function is supposed to be used only by other instance member functions within the class.

> **The instance member function of a class must be public so it can be accessed from outside the class.**

Instance Member Function Selectors

An application (for example, the *main* function) can call an instance member function to operate on an instance. In object-oriented programming, this call must be done through the instance. The application must first construct an instance and then let the instance call the instance member function. In other words, it looks like the instance is operating on itself. The C++ language defines two operators, called **member selector operators,** for this purpose. They are defined in Appendix C as part of the postfix expression and repeated in Table 7.4 for quick reference.

Table 7.4 Member selector operators

Group	Name	Operator	Expression	Pred	Assoc
Postfix	member selector	.	object.member	18	→
	member selector	->	pointer -> member	18	→

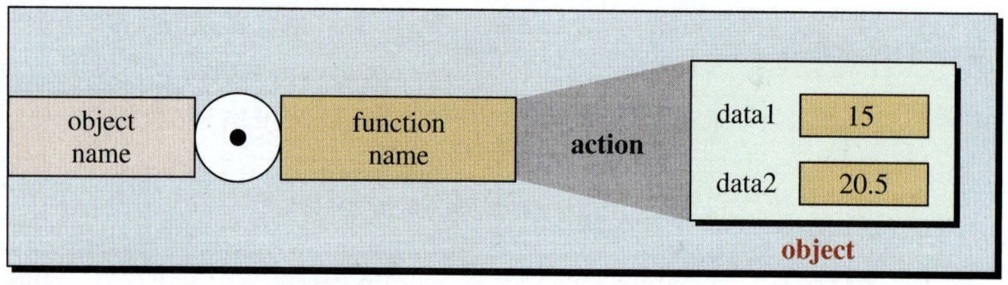

Figure 7.11 Use of member select operator to apply an operation on an instance

Figure 7.11 shows how the first *member select operator* can be used to select a member function given the name of the object. We discuss the use of the second one shortly when we discuss locking and unlocking an instance.

We used the dot member select operator in Program 7.2 and Program 7.3 to let the objects call their member functions.

Locking and Unlocking

If there is only one copy of a member function, how can that function be used by one object at one time and by another object at another time? The more important question is, When a function is being used by one object, how can we prevent other objects from using it? In other words, how we can *lock* a function when it is being used and *unlock* it when the function is terminated (returned) so that it can be used by another object later?

The answer is that locking and unlocking are done in the background. C++ adds a pointer (a variable that holds the address of an object) to each member function. So while we use the dot member selector depicted in Figure 7.11, the compiler changes it to a pointer member selector depicted in Figure 7.12, in which each member function has a hidden pointer named the **this pointer.** The function is employed by the object to which the *this pointer* is pointing at the time. In other words, the function code is applied to the data members of the object pointed to by the *this* pointer.

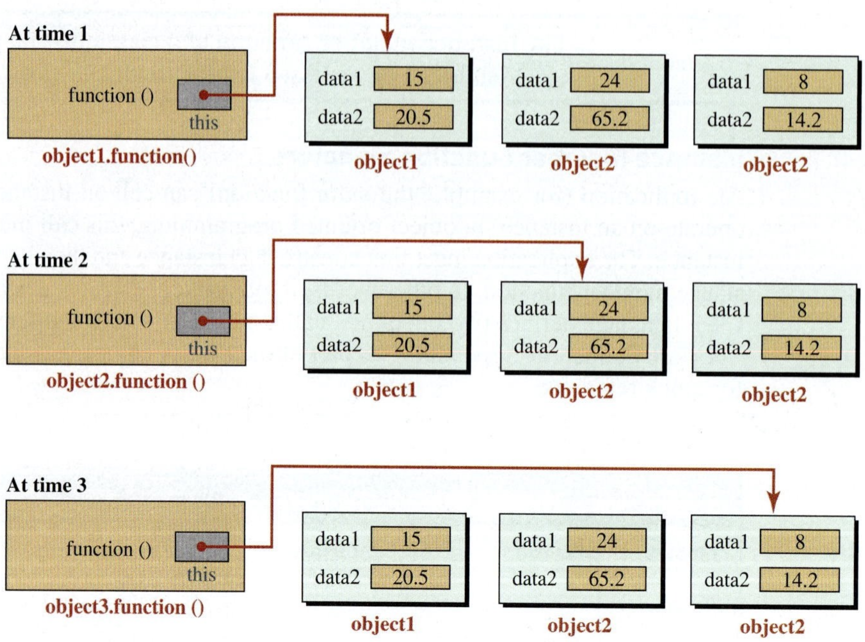

Figure 7.12 Locking and unlocking a function to a particular object

Figure 7.12 shows one member function that is used by different objects at different times. The function is the same, but the object being operated on is different at different times. Since each function has only one *this* pointer and we can call only one function at a time, we should be convinced that locking and unlocking are done properly.

Hidden Parameter How does an instance member function get a *this* pointer? It is added as a parameter to the instance member function by the compiler as shown below:

```
// Written by the user              // Changed by the compiler
double getRadius () const           double getRadius (Circle* this) const
{                                   {
   return radius;                      return (this -> radius);
}                                   }
```

The operator (−>) is a special operator that is the combination of the indirection operator and the member operation. In other words, we have the following relation:

```
this -> radius              is the same as              (*this).radius
```

When we use the member operator to call an instance member function, the compiler changes the call statement into two statements, as shown below:

```
// Written by the user              // Changed by the system
circle1.getRadius();                this = &circle1;
                                    getRadius (this);
```

Explicit Use of this Pointer

We can use the *this* pointer in our program to refer to a data member instead of using the data member itself, and we can use the name of the data member as a parameter. In this way, we do not have to use abbreviated names as we did in the past. The following shows coding *setRadius* for the *Circle* class without and with the use of the *this* pointer.

```
// Without using the this pointer        // Using the this pointer
void Circle :: setRadius (double rds)    void Circle :: setRadius (double radius)
{                                        {
   radius = rds;                            this -> radius = radius;
}                                        }
```

We must remember that the *this* pointer cannot be used in the initialization list of a constructor because at that point, the host object has not been constructed; however, it can be used in the body of the constructor if needed.

Host Object

When an instance member function is being executed, there is always a **host object.** The host object is the object that the instance member function is operating on at a given moment. In other words, the host object is the object that is pointed to by the *this* pointer. There is only one host object during the execution of an instance member function. Figure 7.12 depicts the situations we discuss next.

The host object of an instance member function is the object pointed to by the *this* pointer.

Accessor Member Function

An **accessor member function** (sometimes called a *getter*) gets information from the host object but does not change the state of the object. In other words, it makes the host object a read-only object. It gets the value of one or more data members but does not change their values in the host object. For example, an instance member function that returns the value of the *radius* in a *Circle* object is an accessor instance member function. To guarantee that an accessor instance member function does not change the state of the object, we must add the *const* qualifier at the end of the function header (both in the declaration and the definition) as shown below:

```
double getRadius () const;       // const qualifier makes the host object read-only
double getPerimeter () const;    // const qualifier makes the host object read-only
double getArea() const;          // const qualifier makes the host object read-only
```

The parameter list of an accessor member function is normally empty. The *const* modifier at the end of the header defines the host object as a constant object that cannot be changed.

An accessor instance function must not change the state of the host object; it needs the const modifier.

An accessor member function does not have to return the value of a data member; it can be used to create a side effect (through outputting a value, for example) as long as there is no change in the state of the object. For example, we can have an *output* function that prints the value of the radius, the perimeter, and the area of an object of the *Circle* class with no return value as shown below.

```
void Circle :: print () const
{
   cout << "Radius: " << radius << endl;
   cout << "Perimeter: " << 2 * radius * 3.14 << endl;
   cout << "Area: " << radius * radius * 3.14 << endl;
}
```

In Chapter 16 we will see that the extraction operator (<<) is in fact an accessor function applied to the *cout* object.

Mutator Member Function

The objects of a class type in a program are normally initialized by the parameter constructor. This means that the state of the object is set when it is constructed. However, sometimes we must change the original state. For example, if we create a class representing a bank account, the data member that represents the balance changes over time (with each deposit and withdrawal). This means we may need instance member functions that can change the state of their host objects. Such a function is called a **mutator member function** (sometimes called a *setter*). This function must not have the constant qualifier because it is supposed to change the state of the host object. In our *Circle* class, we have only one instance mutator member functions as shown below:

```
void setRadius (double rds);        // No const qualifier for a mutator
```

A mutator instance member function does not need to have a parameter to change the value of a data member; it can be a function with no parameters and a side effect (through inputting a value, for example).

A mutator instance function changes the state of the host object; it cannot have the const modifier.

For example, we can have an *input* function that inputs the value of the radius of an object of the *Circle* class with no return value as shown below.

```
void Circle :: input()
{
   cout << "Enter the radius of the circle object: ";
   cin << radius;
}
```

In Chapter 16 we will see that the insertion operator (>>) is in fact a mutator function applied to the *cin* object.

Note that constructors and destructors can be thought as mutator member functions because they initialize or clean up objects (thereby changing the state).

7.4.3 Class Invariants

One of the important issues in a class's design is class invariants. A **class invariant** is one or more conditions that we must impose on some or all of the instance data members of a class and that we should enforce through instance member functions. In other words, it is an issue related to both instance data members and instance member functions. When we look in our *Circle* class, we see that the radius of a circle must be a positive value; a circle with a negative value does not make sense. The compiler does not catch this problem because we have defined the radius as type *double,* and a *double* value can be negative.

An invariant is one or more conditions that must be imposed on some or all class data members.

We enforce the invariant of a class through instance data member functions that create objects (parameter constructors) or mutator member functions that change the value of a data member. For example, we can change the parameter constructor of our *Circle* class to guarantee the invariant of the class. The following shows how to change the constructor.

```
Circle :: Circle (double rds)
: radius (rds)
{
   if (radius <= 0.0))
   {
        cout << "No circle can be made!" << endl;
        cout << "The program is aborted" << endl;
        assert (false);
   }
}
```

In this case we must abort the program because the corresponding object cannot be created, and the lack of the object may affect the rest of the program. The *assert* function is a library function that has no effect when its argument is set to *true;* it aborts the program when its argument is set to *false.* We have used it with the *false* argument to abort the program in case the invariant is not satisfied. To use the *assert* function, we must include the <cassert> header file in our program.

EXAMPLE 7.3

In this example we create a new class, *Rectangle,* that represents a rectangle type with two data members: *length* and *height* as shown in Program 7.4. Note that we have not used any mutator member functions because we do not want to resize a rectangle after it has been created, but they could be added easily. Also note that instead of using two accessor functions to get *length* and *height* separately, we have used one accessor function, *print*, that prints both of them.

Program 7.4 Using the class Rectangle

```
/***************************************************************
 * A program to declare, define, and use a Rectangle class      *
 ***************************************************************/
#include <iostream>
#include <cassert>
using namespace std;
/***************************************************************
 * Class Definition (Declaration of data members and member     *
 * functions) for a Rectangle class.                            *
 ***************************************************************/
class Rectangle
{
  private:
      double length;                              // Data member
      double height;                              // Data member
  public:
      Rectangle (double length, double height);   // Constructor
      Rectangle (const Rectangle& rect);          // Copy constructor
      ~Rectangle ();                              // Destructor
      void print () const;                        // Accessor member
      double getArea () const;                    // Accessor member
      double getPerimeter () const;               // Accessor member
};
/***************************************************************
 * Definitions of constructors, destructor, and the accessor    *
 * instance member functions                                    *
 ***************************************************************/
// Parameter constructor
Rectangle :: Rectangle (double len, double hgt)
: length (len), height (hgt)
```

(continued)

Program 7.4 Using the class Rectangle (Continued)

```
{
    if ((length <= 0.0) || (height <= 0.0 ))
    {
        cout << "No rectangle can be made!" << endl;
        assert (false);
    }
}
// Copy constructor
Rectangle :: Rectangle (const Rectangle& rect)
: length (rect.length), height (rect.height)
{
}
// Destructor
Rectangle :: ~Rectangle ()
{
}
// Accessor member function: Print length and height
void Rectangle :: print() const
{
    cout << "A rectangle of " << length << " by " << height << endl;
}
// Accessor member function: Get area
double Rectangle :: getArea () const
{
    return (length * height);
}
// Accessor member function: Get perimeter
double Rectangle :: getPerimeter () const
{
    return (2 * (length + height));
}
/*****************************************************************
 * Application to instantiate three objects and use them         *
 *****************************************************************/
int main ( )
{
    // Instantiation of three objects
    Rectangle rect1 (3.0, 4.2);          // Using parameter constructor
    Rectangle rect2 (5.1, 10.2);         // Using parameter constructor
    Rectangle rect3 (rect2);             // Using copy constructor
    // Operations on first rectangle
    cout << "Rectangle 1: ";
    rect1.print();
```

(continued)

Program 7.4 Using the class Rectangle (Continued)

```
    cout << "Area: " << rect1.getArea() << endl;
    cout << "Perimeter: " << rect1.getPerimeter() << endl << endl;
    // Operations on second rectangle
    cout << "Rectangle 2: ";
    rect2.print();
    cout << "Area: " << rect2.getArea() << endl;
    cout << "Perimeter: " << rect2.getPerimeter() << endl << endl;
    // Operations on third rectangle
    cout << "Rectangle 3: ";
    rect3.print();
    cout << "Area: " << rect3.getArea() << endl;
    cout << "Perimeter: " << rect3.getPerimeter() << endl << endl;
    return 0;
}
```

Run

```
Rectangle 1: A rectangle of 3 by 4.2
Area: 12.6
Perimeter: 14.4

Rectangle 2: A rectangle of 5.1 by 10.2
Area: 52.02
Perimeter: 30.6

Rectangle 3: A rectangle of 5.1 by 10.2
Area: 52.02
Perimeter: 30.6
```

7.5 STATIC MEMBERS

As we mentioned, a class type can have two types of members: *instance members* and *static members*. We discussed instance members in the previous section; we discuss static members in this section. As with instance members, we can have *static data members* and *static member functions*. We discuss them separately.

7.5.1 Static Data Members

A **static data member** is a data member that belongs to all instances; it also belongs to the class itself. As an example of a *static* data member, assume that we want to keep track of the number of current instances in our program. We can create a *static* data member, called *count*, which is initialized to 0. We can change the definition of all constructors to increment this *static* member every time an instance is created. We can change the definition of the destructor to decrement it when an object is destroyed (goes out of scope). A *static* data member has other applications that we will see later in this chapter and in other chapters.

Declaring Static Data Members

Data members belong to the class, and their declarations must be included in the class definition; static members must be qualified with the keyword *static*. The following shows how we declare a *static* data member named *count* inside the class definition.

```
class Rectangle
{
   private:
      ...
      static int count;                         // Static data member
   public:
      ...
}
```

Initializing Static Data Members

We know that an instance data member is normally initialized in a constructor, but a *static* data member belongs to no instance, which means it cannot be initialized in a constructor. A static data member must be initialized after the class definition. This means it must be initialized in a global area of the program. We code it after the class definition. We must show that it belongs to the class by adding the class name and the class scope operator (::) to the definition, but the *static* qualifier should not be added. It is already qualified as a *static* data member in the definition section of the class. The following shows how we initialize the *static* member *count*, which is already declared inside the class.

```
int Rectangle :: count = 0;            // initialization of static data member
```

7.5.2 Static Member Functions

After declaring and initialing a *static* data member, we must find a way to access it (for example, to print its value). Since a *static* data member is normally *private*, we need a *public* member function to do so. Although this can be done by an instance member function, normally we use a **static member function** for this purpose. A static member function can access the static data member through an object and also through the name of the class when no object exists. In other words, the use of a static member function enables us to access the corresponding static data member when an instance wants to access it or when the application needs to access it. Note that a static member function has no host object because it is not associated with any instance.

A static member function has no host object.

Declaring Static Member Functions

A static member function, like a static data member, belongs to the class. It should be declared inside the class but must be qualified with the keyword *static*. The following shows how we can add a static member function *getCount* to retrieve the value of the static data member *count* in our *Rectangle* class.

```
class Rectangle
{
  private:
      ...
      static int count;            // Static data member
  public:
      static int getCount();       // Static member function
      ...
}
```

Defining Static Member Functions

A static member function must be defined outside of the class, like an instance member function. There is no difference between the definition of a static member function and an instance member function. If we want to see if a function definition is an instance or a static one, we need to refer to the declaration.

```
int Rectangle :: getCount()
{
  return count;
}
```

Note that we cannot use the *const* qualifier because there is no host object.

Calling Static Member Functions

A static member function can be called either through an instance or through the class (for example, *Rectangle*). To call a static member function through an instance, we use the same syntax we use to call an instance member function; to call a static member function through the class, we use the name of the class and the class resolution operator (::). The following shows both methods.

```
rect.getCount ();             // Through an instance
Rectangle :: getCount();      // Through the class
```

Warning: We cannot use a static member function to access an instance data member because a static member function does not have the hidden *this* pointer, which defines the instance that needs to be referenced.

A static member function cannot be used to access instance data members because it has no *this* pointer parameter.

On the other hand, an instance member function can be used to access static data members (the *this* pointer is not used), but we usually avoid this. A good practice is to use instance member functions to access instance data members and static member functions to access static data members. We recommend that the territory of instance members in the program be separated from static members symbolically, as shown in Figure 7.13.

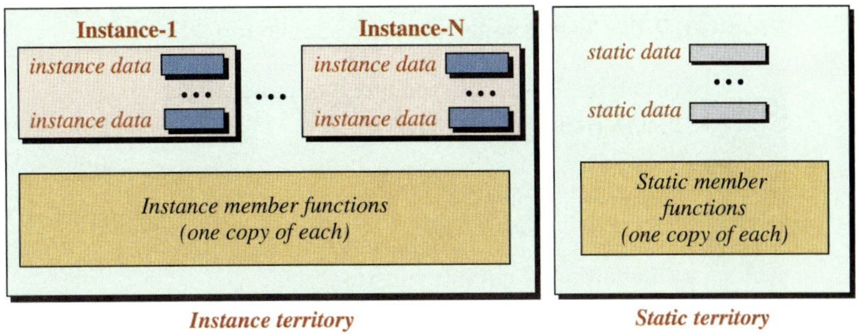

Figure 7.13 Separation of instance and static territory

EXAMPLE 7.4

In this example we write a program that tests a static data member and the corresponding static member function using the *Rectangle* class. Program 7.5 also shows how we can count the instances.

Program 7.5 Testing static members

```
/***************************************************************
 * A program to create objects and count them.               *
 ***************************************************************/
#include <iostream>
using namespace std;
/***************************************************************
 * Definitions of the class Rectangle                         *
 ***************************************************************/
class Rectangle
{
  private:
      double length;
      double height;
      static int count;    //Static data member
  public:
      Rectangle (double length, double height);
      Rectangle ();
      ~Rectangle ();
      Rectangle (const Rectangle& rect);
      static int getCount ();  // Static member function
};
// Initialization of static data member
int Rectangle :: count = 0;
/***************************************************************
 * Definitions of instance member functions                   *
 ***************************************************************/
// Definition of parameter constructor
```

(continued)

Program 7.5 Testing static members (Continued)

```
Rectangle :: Rectangle (double len, double hgt)
: length (len), height (hgt)
{
  count++;
}
// Definition of default constructor
Rectangle :: Rectangle ()
: length (0.0), height (0.0)
{
  count++;
}
// Definition of copy constructor
Rectangle :: Rectangle (const Rectangle& rect)
:length (rect.length), height (rect.height)
{
  count++;
}
// Definition of destructor
Rectangle :: ~Rectangle ()
{
  count--;
}
/*************************************************************
 * Definitions of the static member function                 *
 *************************************************************/
int Rectangle :: getCount ()
{
  return count;
}

/*************************************************************
 * Application to create and count Rectangle objects         *
 *************************************************************/
int main ( )
{
  {
      Rectangle rect1 (3.2, 1.2);
      Rectangle rect2 (1.5, 2.1);
      Rectangle rect3;
      Rectangle rect4 (rect1);
      Rectangle rect5 (rect2);
      cout << "Count of objects: " << rect5.getCount() << endl;
  }
```

(continued)

Program 7.5 Testing static members (Continued)

```
71      cout << "Count of objects: " << Rectangle :: getCount();
72      return 0;
73  }
```

Run:

```
Count of objects: 5
Count of objects: 0
```

Declaration of the static member is done in line 14 using the keyword *static*. Initialization of this member is done in line 23 outside the class. The definition of the function is done in lines 53–56. We have added a nested block (lines 63–70) in the *main* function to create a scope in which the objects are created. This means that outside this block, there is no instance, but we can check the value of the static data member using the class name. We create five instances before we go out of the block; we check the value of the static data member through the last object and find it to be 5. After we go out of the block, all the instances are destroyed and we can check the value of the static data member through the class name to see that it is 0.

EXAMPLE 7.5

In this example we design a class that represents a checking account. The only two instance data members we designed for this class are the *account number* and *balance*. Although the balance can be initialized by the user of the class during creation of an instance, the account number cannot be entered by the user because it must be unique. To prevent duplication of the account number, we have used a static data member, called *base*, that is initialized to 0 and incremented with the opening of each new account. We add 100000 to this static data member to make it a large number as is customary. We do not need a static member function because we are not checking the value of the static data member. Program 7.6 shows this class and its application.

Program 7.6 An example of a bank account

```
/***************************************************************
 * A program to declare, define, and use a bank account class   *
 ***************************************************************/
#include <iostream>
#include <cassert>
using namespace std;

/***************************************************************
 * Class Definition (Declaration of all members)                *
 ***************************************************************/
class Account
{
  private:
      long accNumber;
      double balance;
```

(continued)

Program 7.6 An example of a bank account (Continued)

```
        static int base; // Static data member
    public:
        Account (double bal); // Constructor
        ~Account (); // Destructor
        void checkBalance () const;                 // Accessor
        void deposit (double amount);               // Mutator
        void withdraw (double amount);              // Mutator
};
// Initialization of static data member
int Account :: base = 0;
/*************************************************************
 * Definition of all member functions                        *
 *************************************************************/
// Parameter Constructor
Account :: Account (double bal)
:balance (bal)
{
    if (bal < 0.0)
    {
        cout << "Balance is negative; program terminates";
        assert (false);
    }
    base++;
    accNumber = 100000 + base;

    cout << "Account " << accNumber << " is opened. " << endl;
    cout << "Balance $" << balance << endl << endl;
}
// Destructor
Account :: ~Account ()
{
    cout << "Account #: " << accNumber << " is closed." << endl;
    cout << "$" << balance << " was sent to the customer." << endl <<endl;
}
// Accessor member function
void Account :: checkBalance () const
{
    cout << "Account #: " << accNumber << endl;
    cout << "Transaction: balance check" << endl;
    cout << "Balance: $" << balance << endl<< endl;
}
// Mutator Member function
void Account :: deposit (double amount)
```

(continued)

Program 7.6 An example of a bank account (Continued)

```
{
  if (amount > 0.0)
  {
      balance += amount;
      cout << "Account #: " << accNumber << endl;
      cout << "Transaction: deposit of $" << amount << endl;
      cout << "New balance: $" << balance << endl << endl;
  }
  else
  {
      cout << "Transaction aborted." << endl;
  }
}
// Mutator member function
void Account :: withdraw (double amount)
{
  if (amount > balance)
  {
      amount = balance;
  }
  balance -= amount;
  cout << "Account #: " << accNumber << endl;
  cout << "Transaction: withdraw of $" << amount << endl;
  cout << "New balance: $" << balance << endl << endl;
}
/*****************************************************************
 * Application (the main function) to use the account class      *
 *****************************************************************/
int main ( )
{
  // Creation of three accounts
  Account acc1 (2000);
  Account acc2 (5000);
  Account acc3 (1000);
  // Transaction
  acc1.deposit (150);
  acc2.checkBalance ();
  acc1.checkBalance ();
  acc3.withdraw (800);
  acc1.withdraw (1000);
  acc2.deposit (120);
  return 0;
}
```

(continued)

Program 7.6 An example of a bank account (Continued)

```
Run:
Account 100001 is opened.
Balance $2000

Account 100002 is opened.
Balance $5000

Account 100003 is opened.
Balance $1000

Account #: 100001
Transaction: deposit of $150
New balance: $2150

Account #: 100002
Transaction: balance check
Balance: $5000

Account #: 100001
Transaction: balance check
Balance: $2150

Account #: 100003
Transaction: withdraw of $800
New balance: $200

Account #: 100001
Transaction: withdraw of $1000
New balance: $1150

Account #: 100002
Transaction: deposit of $120
New balance: $5120

Account #: 100003 is closed.
$200 was sent to the customer.

Account #: 100002 is closed.
$5120 was sent to the customer.

Account #: 100001 is closed.
$1150 was sent to the customer.
```

There are several points that we must explain about this program.

- Although we could have used a member function to let the user close each account, we let the account be closed when the program terminates. In our design, when the destructor is called, the account is closed and the remaining balance is sent to the bank customer.
- We have defined a parameter constructor, which means that the system will not create a synthesized constructor (which is not desirable in this class because of the initialization of the account number).
- Since we have not defined a copy constructor, the system has created a synthesized copy constructor that the application can call in this situation. We must avoid this situation because we cannot have two accounts with the same account number. The best way to prevent this situation is to declare a copy constructor and set to it the keyword *delete,* which automatically prevents the system from creating a synthesized copy constructor, as shown below:

```
Account (const Account& acc) = delete;
```

However, this feature was introduced in the C++11 standard, which means the program must be compiled with a C++11 compiler.

- We have used the *assert* library function (discussed previously) in the constructor to ensure that no account is opened with a negative balance.

7.6 OBJECT-ORIENTED PROGRAMMING

We now move from procedural programming to object-oriented programming. Doing so requires that we change some procedures we were using in previous chapters. We need to implement some changes in the way we compile and run programs. We will use the approaches we introduce in this section in future chapters.

7.6.1 Separate Files

As we have learned, when C++ is used as an object-oriented programming language, there are normally three code sections: *class definition*, *member function definition*, and *application*. So far we have used only one file that includes these sections. For the reason that we will discuss shortly, C++ allows us to create three separate files, one for each section as shown in Figure 7.14.

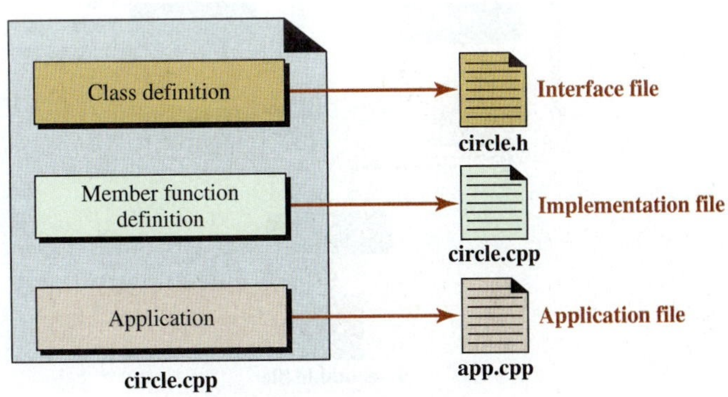

Figure 7.14 Three files created in C++ for a class

Interface File

The **interface file** is a file that contains the class definition (data member declarations and member function declarations). It gives the general picture of the class to be used by the other files; that is, it defines the *type* that is used by the other two files. The name of this file is normally the name of the class with an *h* extension, such as *circle.h*. The letter *h* designates it as a header file.

Implementation File

This **implementation file** contains the definition of member functions. It is the code for all member function declarations given in the interface file. The name of this file is normally the name of the class with a *cpp* extension, such as *circle.cpp*, although the extension may vary in different C++ environments.

Application File

The **application file** includes the *main* function that is used to instantiate objects and let each object perform operations on themselves. The application file must also have the extension cpp, but the name of the file is usually chosen by the user. The name we use is *app.cpp,* although the extension may vary in different C++ environments.

7.6.2 Separate Compilation

After creating three separate files, we must compile them to create an executable file. In C++, the process is referred to as **separate compilation** (Figure 7.15).

Note that although the process is the same for each operating system, the name of the compilation commands and the name of the created files may be different in different environments.

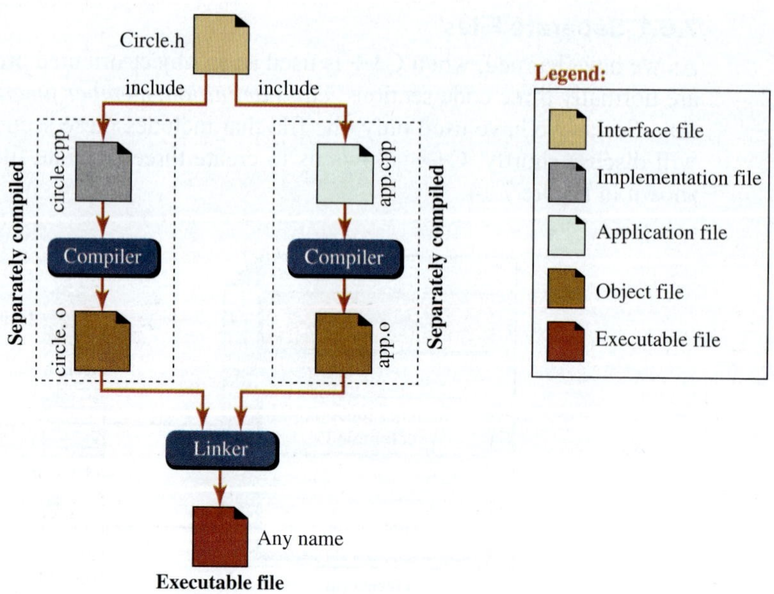

Figure 7.15 Process of separate compilation

Step-by-Step Process

The following is the step-by-step process:

a. The *interface file* is created containing only the class definition (declaration of data members and member functions). This file must be included in the *implementation file* and the *application file*, as we show shortly. In our *Circle* class, we can call this file *circle.h*.

b. The *implementation file* (member function definitions) is created with the interface file by including an *include directive*. The option *−c* indicates that we want only compilation.

```
c++ –c circle.cpp
```

If the compilation is successful, we have an object file with the extension *o*. In our example, the name of the file would be *circle.o*.

c. The *application file* (the *main* function) is created in which the interface file is also added to the beginning of the file using the *include directive*. This file is compiled using the following command. The option *−c* indicates that we want only compilation.

```
c++ –c app.cpp
```

If the compilation is successful, we have an object file with the extension o. In our example, the name of the file would be *app.o*.

d. We then link the two object files together with the −o option to create an executable file as shown below:

```
c++ –o application circle.o app.o
```

e. The result is an executable file that can be run to as shown below:

```
c++ application
```

Example

Here we apply the process of separate compilation on our *Circle* class. We will do the same for all classes that we design from now on.

Creating the Interface File We create the interface file that includes the class definition (declaration of data members and member functions) as shown in Program 7.7. The only three lines that are new in this file are lines 7, 8, and 25. These three lines prevent the duplication of this file by other files in the compilation that also include it. We discuss this issue shortly.

Program 7.7 The interface file

```
1  /***********************************************************************
2   * This is the interface file that defines the class Circle.          *
3   * It gives declaration of data members and member functions.         *
4   * This file will be included at the top of the implementation        *
5   * and application files.                                             *
6   ***********************************************************************/
```

(continued)

Program 7.7 The interface file (Continued)

```
#ifndef CIRCLE_H
#define CIRCLE_H
#include <iostream>
#include <cassert>
#include "circle.h"
using namespace std;
// Class Definition
class Circle
{
    private:
        double radius;
    public:
        Circle (double radius);              // Parameter constructor
        Circle ();                           // Default constructor
        Circle (const Circle& circle);       // Copy constructor
        ~Circle ();                          // Destructor
        void setRadius (double radius);      // Mutator function
        double getRadius () const;           // Accessor function
        double getArea () const;             // Accessor function
        double getPerimeter () const;        // Accessor function
};
#endif
```

Creating the Implementation File Program 7.8 shows the implementation containing the definitions of all member functions. To compile this file separately, the compiler must see the declaration of the data member and member functions. We include a copy of the interface file at line 8. Note that the include statement actually copies, line by line, all declarations and inserts them after line 8.

Program 7.8 The implementation file

```
1  /***************************************************************
2   * This is the implementation file that defines the definition  *
3   * of all member functions. A copy of the interface file is     *
4   * included at the top to allow compilation of this file.      *
5   ***************************************************************/
6  # include "circle.h"
7  /***************************************************************
8   * The parameter constructor with one argument that initializes *
9   * a circle with the given value. It uses the assert function to *
10  * validate that the radius is a positive double value. If not, *
11  * the program is aborted.                                      *
12  ***************************************************************/
```

(continued)

Program 7.8 The implementation file (Continued)

```
Circle :: Circle (double rds)
: radius (rds)
{
    if (radius < 0.0)
    {
        assert (false);
    }
}
/****************************************************************
 * The default constructor that initializes a circle set to 0.0.    *
 * It does not need an assertion.                                    *
 ****************************************************************/
Circle :: Circle ()
: radius (0.0)
{
}
/****************************************************************
 * The copy constructor that copies the radius of another circle     *
 * to create a new one. The source circle is already validated,      *
 * which means that we do not need validation.                       *
 ****************************************************************/
Circle :: Circle (const Circle& circle)
: radius (circle.radius)
{
}
/****************************************************************
 * A destructor that cleans up an object when the application is     *
 * terminated.                                                       *
 ****************************************************************/
Circle :: ~Circle ()
{
}
/****************************************************************
 * The setRadius function is defined to change the circle            *
 * by decreasing or increasing the size of the radius. It needs      *
 * validation because the new size of must be a positive value.      *
 ****************************************************************/
void Circle :: setRadius (double value)
{
    radius = value;
    if (radius < 0.0)
    {
        assert (false);
```

(continued)

Program 7.8 The implementation file (Continued)

```
    }
}
/***************************************************************
 * The getRadius is a function that returns the radius        *
 * of an object. It needs the const modifier to prevent the   *
 * accidental change of the host object.                      *
 ***************************************************************/
double Circle :: getRadius () const
{
   return radius;
}
/***************************************************************
 * The getArea accessor function returns the area of the host *
 * object. It needs the const modifier to prevent the accidental *
 * change of the host object.                                 *
 ***************************************************************/
double Circle :: getArea () const
{
   const double PI = 3.14;
   return (PI * radius * radius);
}
/***************************************************************
 * The getPerimeter accessor function returns the perimeter of *
 * the host object. It needs the const modifier to prevent the *
 * accidental change of the host object.                      *
 ***************************************************************/
double Circle :: getPerimeter () const
{
   const double PI = 3.14;
   return (2 * PI * radius);
}
```

Creating the Application File Program 7.9 is the same as we have seen before with one exception: The contents of the interface file is added at the beginning using the include macro.

Program 7.9 The application file

```
/***************************************************************
 * This is the application file that instantiates objects and *
 * lets the object operate on themselves using member functions. *
 * To be to compiled, it needs a copy of the interface file.  *
 ***************************************************************/
# include "circle.h"
```

(continued)

Program 7.9 The application file (Continued)

```
int main ( )
{
    // Instantiation of first object and applying operations
    Circle circle1 (5.2);
    cout << "Radius: " << circle1.getRadius() << endl;
    cout << "Area: " << circle1.getArea() << endl;
    cout << "Perimeter: " << circle1.getPerimeter() << endl;
    cout << endl;
    // Instantiation of second object and applying operations
    Circle circle2 (circle1);
    cout << "Radius: " << circle2.getRadius() << endl;
    cout << "Area: " << circle2.getArea() << endl;
    cout << "Perimeter: " << circle2.getPerimeter() << endl;
    cout << endl;
    // Instantiation of third object and applying operations
    Circle circle3;
    cout << "Radius: " << circle3.getRadius() << endl;
    cout << "Area: " << circle3.getArea() << endl;
    cout << "Perimeter: " << circle3.getPerimeter() << endl;
    cout << endl;
    return 0;
}
```

Compiling, Linking, and Running The following shows the compiling, the linking, and the running processes. Note that these processes are separate from the creation of other files.

```
c++ -c circle.cpp                          // Compilation of implementation file
c++ -c app.cpp                             // Compilation of application file
c++ -o application circle.o app.o          // Linking of two compiled object files
application                                // Running the executable file
```

```
Radius: 5.2
Area: 84.9056
Perimeter: 32.656

Radius: 5.2
Area: 84.9056
Perimeter: 32.656

Radius: 0
Area: 0
Perimeter: 0
```

7.6.3 Preventing Multiple Inclusion

If we include the contents of the same header file more than once in a compilation file, the compiler issues an error and the compilation is aborted. To prevent this, we use the

```
#ifndef  CIRCLE_H
#define  CIRCLE_H

    // contents of the circle.h file

#endif
```

circle.h

Figure 7.16 The contents of the header file after adding three directives

following preprocessor directives: *define, ifndef* (if not defined), and *endif.* In this section we learn how to use these three preprocessor directives to ignore a duplicate inclusion of a header file. In the file that will be included in another file, such as the interface file, we add these three directives as shown in Figure 7.16.

These three directives work with a flag (a constant). The flag we have used in the figure is the name of the file with an underscore followed by the letter H, all in uppercase. This is a convention; any name can be used if consistent. The directive *ifndef* follows the rule of the *if* statement. If the directive constant has not been defined, the body of *ifndef* is included. In other words, the code in CIRCLE_H is included in the file. If the flag is already defined, the pre-process ignores the rest of the text and jumps to the *endif* directive.

Now let us see what happens when we include the file *cirlce.h* more than once in our program or include another file that also has the include directive. What we get is two copies of the *circle.h* contents in our file as shown in Figure 7.17.

When the pre-processor encounters the first *ifndef* directive, since the flag is not defined yet, it defines it (next line) and adds the rest of code until it encounters the *endif* directive, which means that the contents of the header file are added to the source file. When the pre-processor encounters the second *ifndef* directive, since the flag is already defined, it immediately jumps to the *endif* directive and does not include the contents of the header file again. That is what we need to accomplish. You may be wondering how a file gets included twice. Generally this happens when two different files, each with the same include file, are added to a third file.

7.6.4 Encapsulation

You may wonder why we need separate compilations. Separate compilations allow us to achieve one of the goals of object-oriented programming, encapsulation. **Encapsulation** in

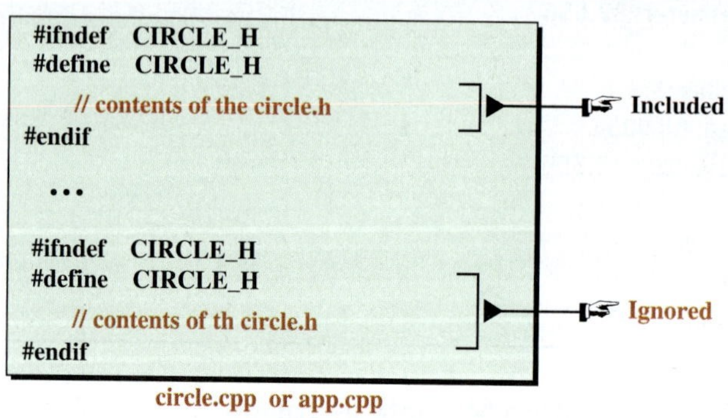

Figure 7.17 How conditional directives ignore duplicate inclusion

object-oriented programming allows us to distinguish between the design of a class and the use of the class.

Design of the Class

The designer creates the interface file and the implementation file. The designer makes the interface file public. The implementation file is compiled, but only the compiled version is made public; the source code remains private. The designer can change the implementation file at any time, re-compile it, and re-announce it.

Use of the Class

The user receives a copy of the interface file and the compiled version of the implementation file. The user adds the interface to her application file and compiles it. He then links his own compiled file and the compiled file received from the designer to create an executable file.

Effect

The effective result is that the designer protects both the interface file and the implementation file from any changes by the user as follows:

- The interface file is protected from change because there are two copies of it used in the process. The designer uses one copy and the user uses another copy. If the user changes the copy he received publicly, the separate-compilation process does not work.
- The implementation file is protected from change because the designer sends the compiled version of the file to the user. Compilation is a one-way process. The user cannot get the original file from the compiled file to change it.

This means the whole design is *encapsulated* in a box and cannot be changed by the user; the user can only create instances and let the instances operate on themselves.

Public Interface

There is one more step before users can effectively instantiate objects and use them. Although users can print and look at the interface created by the designer, the designer normally creates what is called a **public interface,** which is the declaration of the member functions with some explanation so users will understand how to call the member functions in their applications.

The public interface is a text file based on the function declaration that tells the user of the class how to use it.

Compared with a real-life object such as a product, the *public interface* is the manual we receive from the manufacturer that states how to use the product.

EXAMPLE 7.6

Table 7.5 shows an example of the public interface for our *Circle* class (as developed so far). We can always add more explanation if needed to make the user comfortable.

Table 7.5 The public interface for the Circle class

Constructors and Destructor
Circle :: Circle () A default constructor to build a circle with length = 0.0 and height = 0.0.
Circle :: Circle (double radius) A parameter constructor to build a circle with the given radius.
Circle :: Circle (const Circle& circle) A copy constructor to build a circle the same as an existing circle.
Circle :: ~Circle (). The destructor to clean up the circle object that goes out of scope.
Accessor Functions
Circle :: double getRadius () const An accessor function that returns the radius of the host object.
Circle :: double getArea () const An accessor function that returns the area of the host object.
Circle:: double getPerimeter () const An accessor function that returns the perimeter of the host object.
Mutator Functions
Circle:: void setRadius (double radius) A mutator function that changes the radius of the host object.

7.7 DESIGNING CLASSES

In this section we create two new types using classes: one to represent a *fraction* and one to represent a *timer.*

7.7.1 Fraction Class

A **fraction,** also called a *rational number,* is a ratio of two integers such as 3/4, 1/2, 7/5, and so on. There is no built-in type in C++ that can represent a fraction; we need to create a new type for it with two data members of type integer. We call the first the *numer* (abbreviation for *numerator*) and the second the *denom* (abbreviation for *denominator*).

We create three constructors, one destructor, some accessors, and some mutators. We also add a private member function called *normalize*, which is used to handle class invariants. We add a private member function called *gcd* that finds the greatest common divisor, as discussed in Chapter 5. This function is called by the *normalize* function.

Note that we play the roles of both the designer and the user, but in real life these two roles are performed by different people.

Invariants

The first things we must consider when defining a new class are the invariants, as we discussed earlier in the chapter. The invariants that concern us in the fraction objects are three conditions:

- The numerator and the denominator should not have a common factor. For example 6/9 should be reduced to 2/3.
- The denominator cannot be 0. A fraction such as 2/0 is undefined.
- The sign of the fraction is the product of the sign of the numerator and denominator and should be set as the sign of the numerator.

We create two private member functions to take care of the invariants. The *gcd* function finds the greatest common divisor between the numerator and denominator. The *normalized* function takes care of the three invariants using the *gcd* function.

Interface File

We now create the interface file, *fraction.h*. The interface file is the definition of the class. Although the declarations of private data members and private member functions (if any) are not part of the public interface, they must be in this file because we will need them when this file is included in the other two compiled files.

Data Members Our fraction objects will have only two data members: the numerator, which we call *numer*; and the denominator, which we call *denom*. Both of these data members can be of type *int* because we normally do not use fractions with a very large numerator or denominator.

Member Functions We have many member functions that can be applied to the data members. We can also have member functions that operate on multiple objects created from the class, such as compare two fractions or add two fractions. We postpone the second category until the next chapter.

Code Program 7.10 shows the interface file. Note that the instance member functions are all public and accessible through the class instances, but we also have two helper functions

Program 7.10 The fraction.h file

```
/***************************************************************
 * The interface file fraction.h defining the class Fraction      *
 ***************************************************************/
#include <iostream>
using namespace std;

#ifndef FRACTION_H
#define FRACTION_H

class Fraction
{
```

(continued)

Program 7.10 The fraction.h file (Continued)

```
    // Data members
    private:
        int numer;
        int denom;

    // Public member functions
    public:
        // Constructors
        Fraction (int num, int den);
        Fraction ();
        Fraction (const Fraction& fract);
        ~Fraction ();
        // Accessors
        int getNumer () const;
        int getDenom () const;
        void print () const;
        // Mutators
        void setNumer (int num);
        void setDenom (int den);

    // Helping private member functions
    private:
        void normalize ();
        int gcd (int n, int m);
};
#endif
```

to handle the class invariants (*normalize* and *gcd*). They are declared private so that they are only accessible through the class parameter constructor.

Implementation File

We now write the function definition for all member functions (public and private) defined in the interface file. Note that we have added the interface file as a header file in this program (the compiler needs to see the declarations before compiling the definitions). Program 7.11 shows the implementation file.

- We have added the <cassert> header file in line 7 to allow the use of the *assert* macro in line 101, which is needed to abort the program if the denominator is 0.
- Lines 104 to 108 take care of second condition of the class invariant. If the denominator is negative, we change both numerator and denominator to move the negative sign to the numerator.
- Lines 110 to 112 take care of the third condition of the class invariant. We use the greatest common divisor function, as discussed in previous chapters, to find the greatest divisor between numerator and denominator and then divide both by this divisor. Note that we use the absolute values of numerator and denominator when computing *gcd*.

Program 7.11 The fraction.cpp file

```
/****************************************************************
 * The implementation file fraction.cpp defining the instance     *
 * member functions and helper functions for the Fraction class   *
 ****************************************************************/
#include <iostream>
#include <cmath>
#include <cassert>
#include "fraction.h"
using namespace std;

/****************************************************************
 * The parameter constructor gets values for the numerator        *
 * and denominator, initializes the object, and normalizes the    *
 * value of the numerator and the denominator according to the    *
 * conditions defined in the class invariant.                     *
 ****************************************************************/
Fraction :: Fraction (int num, int den = 1)
: numer (num), denom (den)
{
   normalize ();
}
/****************************************************************
 * The default constructor creates a fraction as 0/1. It does     *
 * not need validation.                                           *
 ****************************************************************/
Fraction :: Fraction ( )
: numer (0), denom (1)
{
}
/****************************************************************
 * The copy constructor creates a new fraction from an exisiting  *
 * object. It does not need normalization because the source      *
 * object is already normalized.                                  *
 ****************************************************************/
Fraction :: Fraction (const Fraction& fract )
: numer (fract.numer), denom (fract.denom)
{
}
/****************************************************************
 * The destructor simply cleans up a fraction for recycling.      *
 ****************************************************************/
Fraction :: ~Fraction ()
{
}
```

(continued)

Program 7.11 The fraction.cpp file (Continued)

```
/*****************************************************************
 * The getNumer function is an accessor function returning the   *
 * numerator of the host object. It needs the const modifier.    *
 *****************************************************************/
int Fraction :: getNumer () const
{
  return numer;
}
/*****************************************************************
 * The getDenum function is an accessor function returns the     *
 * denominator of the host object. It needs the const modifier.  *
 *****************************************************************/
int Fraction :: getDenom () const
{
  return denom;
}
/*****************************************************************
 * The print function is an accessor function with a side effect *
 * that display the fraction object in the form x/y.             *
 *****************************************************************/
void Fraction :: print () const
{
  cout << numer << "/" << denom << endl;
}
/*****************************************************************
 * The setNumer is a mutator function that changes the numerator *
 * of an existing object. The object needs normalization.        *
 *****************************************************************/
void Fraction :: setNumer (int num)
{
  numer = num;
  normalize();
}
/*****************************************************************
 * The setDenom is a mutator function that changes the denominator *
 * of an existing object. The object needs normalization.        *
 *****************************************************************/
void Fraction :: setDenom (int den)
{
  denom = den;
  normalize();
}
```

(continued)

Program 7.11 The fraction.cpp file (Continued)

```
/*****************************************************************
 * Normalize function takes care of three fraction invariants.   *
 *****************************************************************/
void Fraction :: normalize ()
{
   // Handling a denominator of zero
   if (denom == 0)
   {
       cout << "Invalid denomination. Need to quit." << endl;
       assert (false);
   }
   // Changing the sign of denominator
   if (denom < 0)
   {
       denom = - denom;
       numer = - numer;
   }
   // Dividing numerator and denominator by gcd
   int divisor = gcd (abs(numer), abs (denom));
   numer = numer / divisor;
   denom = denom / divisor;
}
/*****************************************************************
 * The gcd function finds the greatest common divisor between    *
 * the numerator and the denominator.                            *
 *****************************************************************/
int Fraction :: gcd (int n, int m)
{
   int gcd = 1;
   for (int k = 1; k <= n && k <= m; k++)
   {
       if (n % k == 0 && m % k == 0)
       {
           gcd = k;
       }
   }
   return gcd;
}
```

Application File

The application file is created by the user. Program 7.12 is an example to show what it looks like. The only thing the user needs to include is a copy of the interface file (line 4). We ran the program once and entered a zero for the denominator; it was aborted (not shown here).

Program 7.12 Application file (app.cpp)

```
/*****************************************************************
  * The application file app.cpp uses the Fraction objects.           *
  *****************************************************************/
#include "fraction.h"
#include <iostream>
using namespace std;

int main ( )
{
  // Instantiation of some objects
  Fraction fract1 ;
  Fraction fract2 (14, 21);
  Fraction fract3 (11, -8);
  Fraction fract4 (fract3);
  // Printing the object
  cout << "Printing four fractions after constructed: " << endl;
  cout << "fract1: ";
  fract1. print();
  cout << "fract2: ";
  fract2. print();
  cout << "fract3: ";
  fract3. print();
  cout << "fract4: ";
  fract4. print();
  // Using mutators
  cout << "Changing the first two fractions and printing them:" << endl;
  fract1.setNumer(4);
  cout << "fract1: ";
  fract1.print();
  fract2.setDenom(-5);
  cout << "fract2: ";
  fract2.print();
  // Using accessors
  cout << "Testing the changes in two fractions:" << endl;
  cout << "fract1 numerator: " << fract1.getNumer() << endl;
  cout << "fract2 numerator: " << fract2.getDenom() << endl;
  return 0;
}
```

Compiling, Linking, and Running

The following shows the compiling, the linking, and the running processes. Note that this process is separate from the creation of other files.

```
c++ -c fraction.cpp                        // Compilation of implementation file
c++ -c app.cpp                             // Compilation of application file
c++ -o application fraction.o app.o        // Linking of two compiled object files
application                                // Running the executable file
```

```
Run:
Printing four fractions after constructed:
fract1: 0/1
fract2: 2/3
fract3: -11/8
fract4: -11/8
Changing the first two fractions and printing them:
fract1: 4/1
fract2:-2/5
Testing the changes in two fractions:
Numerator of fract1: 4
Denominator of fract2: 5
```

The second object is normalized; 14/21 is changed to 2/3. The third object is also normalized; 11/−8 is changed to −11/8. The numerator of the first object is changed and reprinted as 4/1. The denominator of second object is changed to −5, but it was normalized and printed as −2/5. Finally, we use the accessor functions to get the numerator of the first object and denominator of the second object.

7.7.2 Time Class

We now add a *Time* class. This class, like time used in real life, has three data members: *hours*, *minutes*, and *seconds*. We have a parameter constructor and a default constructor, but we do not need a copy constructor (it does not make sense to have two objects showing the same time). We have three accessor functions to get hours, minutes, and seconds, respectively. We use only one mutator function, which we call *tick*, that, each time it is called, moves the time object 1 second forward.

Invariants

Before writing the code for this class, we must consider the invariants of the class. We must focus on the following two conditions:

- All three data members must be nonnegative; otherwise, the program is aborted. We cannot have a negative time.
- The hours should be between 0 and 23 (we assume military time), the minutes should be between 0 and 59, and the seconds should also be between 0 and 59. We use modulo arithmetic to keep these values in the range. If the value of the seconds is greater than 59, we must extract the corresponding minutes from it and add them to the minutes. We do the same with the seconds. In the case of the hours, the extracted values are discarded.

We create a private member function called *normalize* to take care of the invariants.

Interface File

We now create the interface file, *time.h*. The interface file is the definition of the class.

Program 7.13 The interface file (time.cpp)

```
/***************************************************************
 * The interface file for time.h class                        *
 ***************************************************************/
#include <iostream>
using namespace std;

#ifndef TIME_H
#define TIME_H

class Time
{
   private:
        int hours;
        int minutes;
        int seconds;
   public:
        Time (int hours, int minutes, int seconds);
        Time ();
        ~Time ();
        void print() const;
        void tick();

   private:
   void normalize ();                      // Helping function
};
#endif
```

Data Members We need three private data members: *hours*, *minutes*, and *seconds*. All are of type *int*.

Member Functions There are many member functions that could be applied not only on data members but also on the objects created from the class. For example, we can compare two times, determine the time elapsed between two times, and so on. We defer defining these operations to future chapters. In this chapter, we use member functions that act as constructors, destructor, accessors of data members, and mutators of data members.

Code Program 7.13 shows the interface file. This is just a header file and will be included in both the application file and the user file.

Implementation File

We now write the function definition for all member functions (public and private) defined in the interface file. Note that we have added the interface file as a header file in this program. Program 7.14 shows the implementation file.

Program 7.14 The implementation file (time.cpp)

```
/******************************************************************
 * The impletation file time.cpp for functions in Time class      *
 ******************************************************************/
#include <cmath>
#include <cassert>
#include "time.h"

/******************************************************************
 * The parameter constructor accepts three values corresponding   *
 * to the data members from the user and initializes and object.  *
 * It uses the normalize function to ensure that hours, minutes,  *
 * and seconds are in the predefined ranges.                      *
 ******************************************************************/
Time :: Time (int hr, int mi, int se )
: hours (hr), minutes (mi), seconds (se)
{
   normalize ();
}
/******************************************************************
 * The default constructor creates a time object.                 *
 ******************************************************************/
Time :: Time ( )
: hours (0), minutes (0), seconds (0)
{
}
/******************************************************************
 * The destructor just cleans up the object(s) before recycling.  *
 ******************************************************************/
Time :: ~Time ()
{
}
/******************************************************************
 * The print function is an accessor function that has a side     *
 * effect: it displays the time.                                  *
 ******************************************************************/
void Time :: print () const
{
   cout << hours << ":" << minutes << ":" << seconds << endl;
}
/******************************************************************
 * The tick function is a mutator function that increments the    *
 * number of seconds.                                             *
 ******************************************************************/
```

(continued)

Program 7.14 The implementation file (time.cpp) (Continued)

```
void Time :: tick ()
{
   seconds++;
   normalize();
}
/****************************************************************
 * The normalize function checks the invariants of the class.    *
 * It either aborts the creation of the class or normalizes the  *
 * the hours, minutes, and the seconds.                          *
 ****************************************************************/
void Time :: normalize ()
{
   // Handling negative data members
   if ((hours < 0) || (minutes < 0) || (seconds < 0))
   {
        cout << "Data are not valid. Need to quit!" << endl;
        assert (false);
   }
   // Handling out of range values
   if (seconds > 59)
   {
        int temp = seconds / 60;
        seconds = seconds % 60;
        minutes = minutes + temp;
   }
   if (minutes > 59)
   {
        int temp = minutes / 60;
        minutes = minutes % 60;
        hours = hours + temp;
   }
   if (hours > 23)
   {
        hours = hours % 24;
   }
}
```

Please note the following about this program:

- We have added the <cassert> header file so we can use the assert macro and thereby prevent negative values for hours, minutes, and seconds.
- In the *normalize* function, we have used three *if* statements to take care of values out of range.

Program 7.15 Application file (app.cpp) to test the Time class

```
/**************************************************************
 * The application file app.cc to use the Time class          *
 **************************************************************/
#include "time.h"

int main ( )
{
  // Instantiation of a time object
  Time time (4, 5, 27);
  // Printing the original time
  cout << "Original time: " ;
  time.print();
  // adding 143500 seconds to the original time
  for (int i = 0; i < 143500; i++)
  {
      time.tick ();
  }
  // Printing the time after 143500 ticks
  cout << "Time after 143500 ticks " ;
  time.print();
  return 0;
}
```

Application File

The user creates the application file. Program 7.15 is just one example of an application file. The only thing the user must do is include a copy of the interface file.

Compiling, Linking, and Running

The following shows the compiling, the linking, and the running processes.

```
c++ -c time.cpp                        // Compilation of implementation file
c++ -c app.cpp                         // Compilation of application file
c++ -o application time.o app.o        // Linking of two object files
application                            // Running the executable file
```

```
Run:
Original time: 4:5:27
Time after 143500 ticks: 19:57:7
```

Note that after ticking for 143500 seconds, one day passes and we move to hour 19, minute 57, and seconds. We can verify this easily.

Key Terms

- access modifier
- accessor member function
- application file
- attribute
- behavior
- class
- class body
- class definition
- class header
- class invariant
- constructor
- data member
- destructor
- encapsulation
- explicit inline function
- fraction
- host object
- implementation file
- implicit inline function
- inline function
- instance
- instance data member
- instance member function
- interface file
- member function
- member selector operator
- mutator member function
- object
- parameter constructor
- public interface
- separate compilation
- static data member
- static member function
- struct
- this pointer

Summary

Object-oriented concepts include types and instances, attributes and behaviors, and data members and member functions. A type is a concept (abstraction) from which an instance (concrete entity) is created. Attributes are the characteristics of an object, such as name and address, that we are interested in. A behavior is an action of an object. A data member of an object is a variable whose value represents an attribute. A member function, then, represents one of the behaviors of an object.

A class definition is made up of the reserved word *class* followed by its name and the body, which is a block that holds the declaration of data members and member functions. There are three access modifiers that determine who can see a data member or member function: *private, protected,* and *public.* Private data members can be accessed only through member functions. Member functions, on the other hand, are usually public and can be accessed through an instance. Constructors and destructors are special member functions that construct or destroy a class instance. The state of an object is the combination of the values stored in its data members.

In object-oriented programming, instantiation of an object is done by a special member function called a constructor, and the cleanup is done by a special member function called a destructor.

The instance data members define the attributes of each instance, which means that each instance needs to encapsulate all instance data members. An instance member function defines one of the behaviors of an instance.

A *static* data member is one that belongs to all instances and the class. It cannot be initialized by a constructor; it needs to be initialized in the global area of the program.

In object-oriented programming, we divide the three sections of a program into three separate files: interface file, implementation file, and application file. The interface file is included at the beginning of the implementation file and the application file. These two files are compiled separately and linked together. Separate compilation allows us to reveal the interface of the class to the user but to hide the implementation from the user. The principle is called encapsulation.

Problems

PR-1. Which of the following is the declaration of a parameter constructor? Which is the declaration of a default constructor? Which is the declaration of a copy constructor?

```
Fun ();
Fun (int x);
Fun (const Fun& fun);
```

PR-2. What is the error in the following declaration of a constructor for the class *Rectangle*?

```
int Rectangle (int length, int height);
```

PR-3. What is the error in the following declaration of a destructor for the class *Rectangle*?

```
int ~Rectangle ();
```

PR-4. Change the definition of the following constructor to use initialization instead of assignment.

```
Rectangle :: Rectangle (int len, int wid)
{
        length = len;
        height = wid;
}
```

PR-5. Given the following class definition:

```
class Sample
{
        private:
            int x;
        public:
            int getX () const;
};
```

Find the error (if any) in each of the following constructor calls.

```
Sample first  (4):
Sample second ( );
Sample third;
```

PR-6. Given the following class definition:

```
class Sample
{
        private:
          int x;
        public:
            Sample (int x);
            int getX () const;
};
```

Find the error in each of the following instantiations.

```
Sample first (4);
Sample second (4, 8);
Sample third;
```

PR-7. Find the error(s) in the following class definition.

```
class First
    private:
        double x;
        double y;
    public:
        double getX () const;
        double getY () const;
```

PR-8. Find the error (s) in the following class definition.

```
class Second
{
    private:
        double x;
        double y;
    public:
        bool Second (int x, int y);
        double getX () const;
        double getY () const;
};
```

PR-9. Find the error(s) in the following class definition.

```
class Third
{
    private:
        int x;
        int y;
    public:
        ~Third (int z);
        int getX () const;
        int getY () const;
};
```

PR-10. If *x* is a data member of the class, find the error in the following member function definition of the class:

```
Fun :: int getX ( ) const
{
    return x;
}
```

PR-11. Which of the following is the proper definition of an accessor function of the class *Sample*?

```
type Sample :: getValue ( ) const          type Sample :: getValue ( )
{                                          {
```

```
    return ...;                          return ...;
}                                    }
```

PR-12. Which of the following can be a mutator function for the class *Sample*?

```
void Sample :: setValue ( ) const        void Sample :: setValue ( )
{                                        {
    ...;                                     ...;
}                                        }
```

PR-13. Assume we have the following class definition. Write the definition of the two member functions.

```
class Fun
{
    private:
        int x;
    pubic:
        Fun (int);
        Fun (const Fun&);
};
```

PR-14. Show how an application can use the parameter constructor and the copy constructor defined in PR-13.

Programs

PRG-1. Create a class named One with two integer data members, *x* and *y*, and two member functions *getX* and *getY*. Define the interface file, the implementation file, and an application file that instantiates one object from the class and prints the values of *x* and *y*.

PRG-2. Create a class named Two with one integer data member named *x* and one character data member named *a*. Define four member functions *getX*, *getA*, *setX*, and *setA*. Define the interface file, the implementation file, and an application file that instantiates one object from the class and prints the values of data members. Then set the values of data members through the mutator functions and print their values again.

PRG-3. A point in planar Cartesian coordinates is normally defined with two integer values (*x* and *y*). Define a class named Point with two data members. Define a print function that returns the coordinates of a Point object. Define functions to tell the user if a point is on the left side, right side, above, or below another point. Define a function to find the distance between two points as shown below:

$$distance = sqrt\ (\ (x_2 - x_1)^2 + (y_2 - y_1)^2)$$

PRG-4. Code the interface file, the implementation file, and the application file for a class name *Person* with the following members:

a. Data members are *name* and *age*.
b. Accessor member functions are *getName* and *getAge*.

c. Mutator member functions are *setName* and *setAge*.
d. There is a parameter constructor and a destructor.

PRG-5. Define a class named *Triangle* as follows:

a. Data members are *firstSide*, *secondSide*, and *thirdSide*.
b. Use a constructor that asserts that the sum of any two sides to be greater than the third one.
c. Accessor member functions are *getSides,getPerimeter, and getArea.* To find the perimeter and area of a triangle, use the following.

perimeter = a + b + c
area = sqrt ((p) * (p - a) * (p - b) * (p - c)) // **p = perimeter / 2**

d. Define a constructor for the class.

PRG-6. Define a class name *Address* as follows:

a. Data members are *houseNo* and *streetName, cityName, stateName*, and *zipcode*.
b. Define a parameter constructor and a destructor.
c. Define an accessor member function to print the address.

PRG-7. Define a class name *Employee* as follows:

a. Data members are *name, age, serviceYear, salary.*
b. Define a parameter constructor and a destructor.
c. Accessor member functions are *getName, getAge, getServiceYear, and getSalary.*

PRG-8. In object-oriented programming, we can create a class that helps to find the solution to a mathematical equation. One of the equations we often need to solve in algebra is the *quadratic equation* as shown below:

$$ax^2 + bx + c = 0$$

The roots of this equation are:

$$x_1 = -b + \text{sqrt}(b^2 - 4 * a * c) \qquad x_2 = -b - \text{sqrt}(b^2 - 4 * a * c)$$

The phrase inside the parentheses is called the *discriminant*. If the value of the discriminant is positive, the equation has two roots. If it is zero, the equation has one root. If it is negative, the equation has no roots. Create a class named Quadratic that finds the roots of a quadratic equation when the coefficients *a*, *b*, and *c* are given.

PRG-9. We wrote a program in Chapter 4 to find the day of the week for any given date using Zeller's congruence:

weekday = (day + 26 * (month + 1) / 10 +
year + year / 4 – year /100 + year /400) % 7

To show that any program written in the procedural paradigm can be written in the object-oriented paradigm, design a class Zeller with three data members—*day*, *month*, and *year*—to find the corresponding week day (Saturday to Sunday).

PRG-10. Design a Complex class representing complex numbers. A complex number in mathematics is defined as $x + i\,y$ where x defines the real part of the number and y is the imaginary part. The letter i represents the square root of -1 (which means i^2 is -1). Include functions to add one complex number to the host object, to subtract one complex number from the host object, to multiply one complex number by the host object, and to divide one complex number by the host object:

$$(x_1 + i\,y_1) + (x_2 + i\,y_2) = (x_1 + x_2) + i\,(y_1 + y_2)$$

$$(x_1 + i\,y_1) - (x_2 + i\,y_2) = (x_1 - x_2) + i\,(y_1 - y_1)$$

$$(x_1 + i\,y_1) * (x_2 + i\,y_2) = (x_1x_2 - y_1y_2\,) + i\,(x_1y_2 + x_2y_1)$$

$$(x_1 + i\,y_1) \,/\, (x_2 + i\,y_2) = ((x_1x_2 + y_1y_2\,) + i\, -x_1y_2 + x_2y_1)) \,/\, \textbf{denominator}$$

In which denominator $= x_2^{\,2} + y_2^{\,2}$

After discussing most of the fundamental built-in data types and the user defined type, it is time to discuss the first compound data type: the array. We will discuss other compound data types in the next chapter.

Objectives

After you have read and studied this chapter, you should be able to:

- Introduce a one-dimensional array as a sequence of elements in which all elements must be of the same type (fundamental or user-defined).
- Discuss the three attributes of a one-dimensional array: type, capacity, and size.
- Show how to declare and initialize a one-dimensional array.
- Discuss how we can access the elements of a one-dimensional array using the subscript expression.
- Discuss nonmodifying and modifying operations on one-dimensional arrays.
- Discuss how we can use functions to apply both nonmodifying and modifying operations on one-dimensional arrays.
- Discuss parallel one-dimensional arrays and their application.
- Discuss two-dimensional arrays and how they are declared and initialized.
- Discuss operations on two dimensional arrays that create another two-dimensional array.
- Show how to change a two-dimensional array to a one-dimensional array using the linear operation or the zigzag operation.

8.1 ONE-DIMENSIONAL ARRAYS

A **one-dimensional array** is a sequence of data items of the same built-in or user-defined type. A compound type is a structure that contains two types; the array is the first type and the data type in the array is the second type.

An array is a compound type that defines a sequence of data items of the same type.

8.1.1 Array Attributes

Arrays have three attributes—*type*, *capacity*, and *size*—as shown in Figure 8.1. The figure shows three arrays, each with different attributes. We discuss each attribute next.

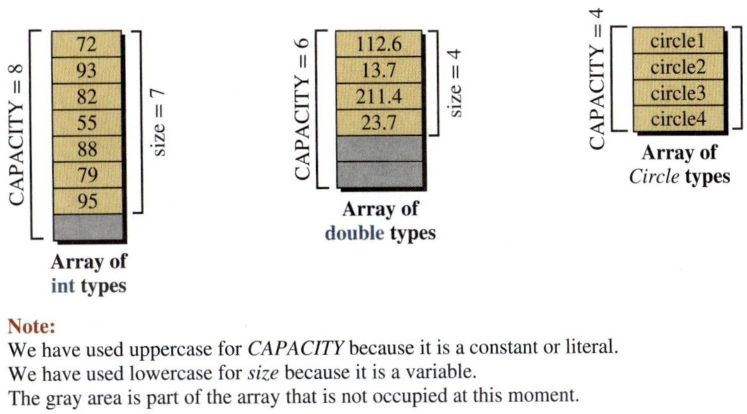

Figure 8.1 Attributes of arrays

Type

The *type* of an array is the type of data items (elements) in the array. For example, we can have an *int* array, a *double* array, a *char* array, and a *Circle* array.

The type of all data items in an array must be the same; the array type is the type of the elements.

Capacity

The *capacity* of an array is the maximum number of elements it can hold. This attribute is either a literal or a constant value that cannot be changed after the array is declared. We normally use uppercase letters for the name of the capacity.

We cannot change the capacity of the array after it has been declared.

Size

The *size* of an array defines how many elements are valid at each moment; that is, how many contain valid data. We may create an array of capacity 10, but at one moment we may have only three valid elements; at another moment, we may have eight valid elements. In other words, *size* is a controlling attribute of the array.

Array size defines the number of valid elements at each moment.

8.1.2 Declaration, Allocation, and Initialization

An array must be declared before being used. The compiler allocates memory locations for the array when it is declared. The elements of an array can also be initialized at the time the array is declared.

Array Declaration

Array declaration gives an array a name, sets the type of the elements, sets the capacity of the array, and allocates memory locations for the array. In other words, declaration of an

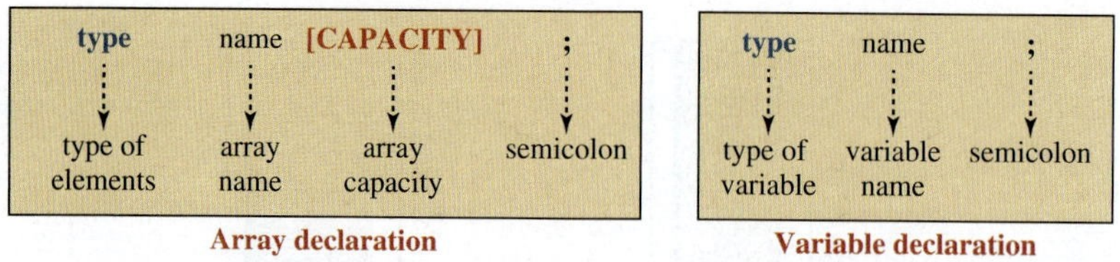

Figure 8.2 Array declaration compared with variable declaration

array is also a definition. Figure 8.2 shows the syntax for declaring an array and compares it with the declaration of a variable.

There are three important points about the above syntax shown in Figure 8.2:

1. The declaration consists of four sections: type, name, capacity, and the terminating semicolon.
2. If we compare an array declaration with a variable declaration, we see that the only difference is the addition of the capacity enclosed in two brackets.
3. The capacity of an array must be either a constant or a literal.

EXAMPLE 8.1

The following shows how we declare the arrays shown in Figure 8.1 using literal values for capacity.

```
int scores [8];          double nums [6];          Circle crls [4];
```

EXAMPLE 8.2

The following shows the same declarations defining capacity.

```
const int CAPACITY = 8;      const int CAPACITY = 6;       const int CAPACITY = 4;
int scores [CAPACITY];       double nums [CAPACITY];       Circle crls [CAPACITY];
```

The advantage of this practice is that we can refer to the capacity of the array using the constant identifier (CAPACITY). As we discussed previously, it is customary to use uppercase letters to define constants.

Memory Allocation

After an array has been declared, the compiler allocates memory locations for the array. Allocation depends on the type and capacity of the array. Each element of the array is accessible through an index enclosed in two brackets. The index, however, starts from [0] and goes to [CAPACITY – 1]. Figure 8.3 shows declarations and allocation of memory for three arrays: *scores*, *nums*, and *crls*.

Note that elements in an array use zero-indexing, which means the indexes start from [0] and go to [CAPACITY – 1].

The array elements are referenced using zero indexing.

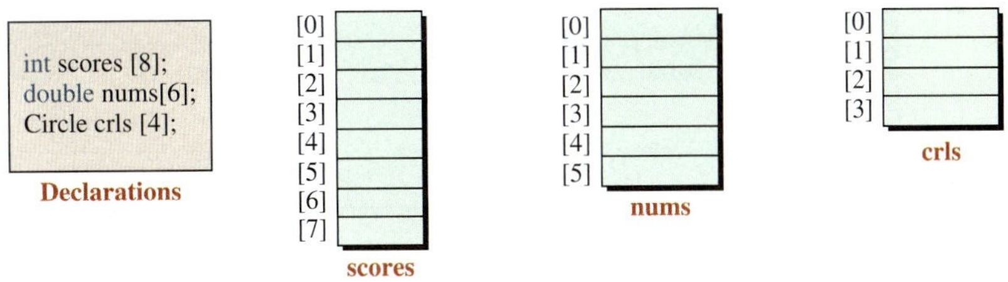

Figure 8.3 Three arrays of different types

Initialization

Each element of an array is like an individual variable. When we declare an array, the compiler allocates memory locations for each element according to the array type. As with individual variables, we have two cases:

1. If the array is declared in the global area of the program, each element is given a default value according to the array type. The default value for the Boolean type is *false*, for the character type is the *nul* character, for the integer type is 0, for the floating type is 0.0, and for the object type is the object created by the default constructor.
2. If the array is declared inside a function (including *main*), the elements are filled with garbage values (what is left from the previous use of the memory location).

Explicit Initialization To better control the initial values stored in the array elements, we can explicitly initialize the elements of the array. The initial values, however, must be enclosed in braces and separated by commas. The following shows how we can declare and, at the same time, initialize the elements of the array *scores* of eight elements.

```
const int CAPACITY = 8;
int scores [CAPACITY] = {87, 92, 100, 65, 70, 10, 96, 77};
```

We can also initialize an array of class objects in this way when each element in the initialization is a call to a constructor as shown below:

```
const int CAPACITY = 4;
Circle circles [CAPACITY] = {Circle (4.0), Circle (5.0), Circle (6.0), Circle (7.0)};
```

The declaration initializes the array of *Circle* object to four circles of radii 4.0, 5.0, 6.0, and 7.0, respectively.

Implicit Capacity When the number of the initialization elements is exactly the capacity of the array, we do not have to define the array capacity, as shown below. The compiler counts the initial values and sets the capacity of the array accordingly. However, we do not have the advantage of a constant that refers to the array's capacity.

```
int scores [ ] = {87, 92, 100, 65, 70, 10, 96, 77};
```

Partial Default Filling The number of initialization values cannot be larger than the capacity of the array (compilation error), but it can be less than the capacity of the array. In this

Table 8.1					
Group	**Name**	**Operator**	**Expression**	**Pred**	**Assoc**
postfix	subscript	[...]	name [expr]	18	→

case, the rest of elements are filled with default values regardless if the array is declared in the global area or inside a function.

```
const int CAPACITY = 10;
int scores [CAPACITY] = {87, 92, 100};
```

The first three elements are set to 87, 92, and 100, respectively; the rest of the elements are set to 0.

The following shows how we can explicitly initialize all elements of an array of 100 elements to 0.0.

```
const int CAPACITY = 100;
double anArray [CAPACITY] = {0.0};
```

The first element is set to 0.0; the rest of the elements are set to the default value, which is also 0.0 for a floating-point type.

8.1.3 Accessing Array Elements

We have learned that if we want to access the contents of a variable, we must use an expression. In the case of a single variable, the name of the variable is a *primary expression* and we can use it to get the value stored in the variable. In the case of an array, we must use a *postfix expression* called **subscript.** The subscript expression uses the subscript operator ([...]), with one operand. The operand is the name of the array. In Chapter 9 we show that the name of an array is actually the name of a pointer pointing to the first element. Table 8.1 provides an example of C++ expressions as shown in Appendix C.

Figure 8.4 shows how we can access an element of the array using the subscript expression.

The following shows how we can access one of the elements of each of three arrays we declared previously in Figure 8.3.

```
scores [4]                              // Accessing element at location 4
nums [5]                                // Accessing element at location 5
crls [3]                                // Accessing element at location 3
```

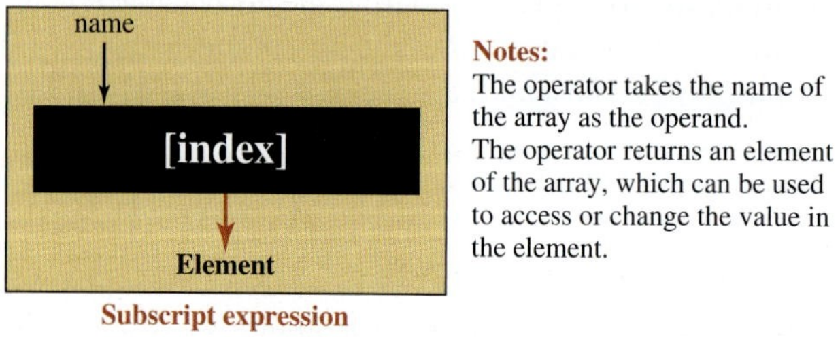

Figure 8.4 Accessing an array element using a subscript expression

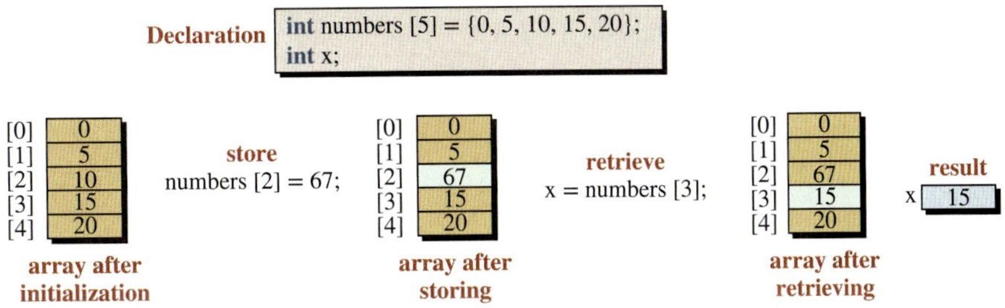

Figure 8.5 Storing and retrieving an element of an array

Note that the subscript expression returns the element. We can use the element wherever a variable can be used. For example, we can use the element as an *lvalue* or an *rvalue*. Figure 8.5 shows how we can store (change or set) and retrieve (get) the value of an element.

Out-of-Range Error

One of the hidden errors that cannot be caught during compilation or run time is accessing an element of an array that is not bounded by the capacity of the array. The index used in the subscript expression, *arrayName* [index], must be in the range between 0 and CAPACITY – 1. If we use a subscript expression to retrieve the value of an element that is out of range, we will get a garbage value because the location is not part of the array. The more dangerous situation is when we try to store a value in an element that is out of range. In this case, we may unintentionally destroy data or program code. When the program runs, the result is unpredictable: The program may fail or it may produce invalid results. C++ implementations do not give a compile-time or run-time warning when these errors occur. We will discuss the reason for this strange behavior when we discuss pointers in the next section.

Out-of-range error is a serious issue that must be avoided.

Two Uses of Brackets

We have seen two uses of brackets in an array, as shown in Figure 8.6.

EXAMPLE 8.3

An array is very useful for holding a list of items of the same type when all of the items need to be in memory for processing. Assume we want to read a list of items and print them in the reverse order. We use an array whose capacity is large enough to hold all elements in the list. Program 8.1 shows how we use a validation loop to ensure that the projected size of the array is not greater than the capacity of the array.

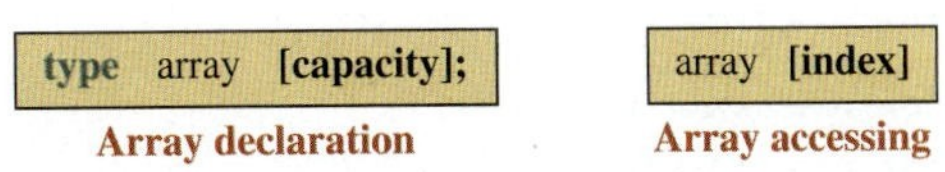

Figure 8.6 Two uses of brackets

Program 8.1 Printing a list in reverse order

```
/***************************************************************
 * Use of an array to read a list of integers and output them  *
 * in the reverse order of reading.                            *
 ***************************************************************/
```

(*continued*)

Program 8.1 Printing a list in reverse order (Continued)

```
#include <iostream>
using namespace std;

int main ( )
{
    // Declarations
    const int CAPACITY = 10;
    int numbers [CAPACITY];
    int size;
    // Getting the size from user and validate it
    do
    {
        cout << "Enter the size (1 and 10) ";
        cin >> size;
    } while (size < 1 || size > CAPACITY);
    // Inputting Integers
    cout << "Enter " << size << " integer(s): " ;
    for (int i = 0 ; i < size ; i++)
    {
        cin >> numbers [i] ;
    }
    // Outputting Integers in reverse order of inputting
    cout << "Integer(s) in reversed order: ";
    for (int i = size - 1 ; i >= 0 ; i--)
    {
        cout << numbers[i] << "  " ;
    }
    return 0;
}
```

```
Run:
Enter the size (1 to 10): 10
Enter 10 integer(s): 2 3 4 5 6 7 8 9 10 11
Integer(s) in reversed order: 11 10 9 8 7 6 5 4 3 2
```

```
Run:
Enter the size (1 to 10): 0
Enter the size (1 to 10): 11
Enter the size (1 to 10): 7
Enter 7 integer(s): 4 11 78 2 5 3 8 9          // The last integer is ignored.
Integer(s) in reversed order: 8 3 5 2 78 11 4
```

There are two important points about Program 8.1.

1. We do not have the out-of-range problem in this array because we forced the value of the *size* variable to be between 1 and CAPACITY in the validation loop. For example, when we have set the CAPACITY to 10, we can have between 1 and 10 integers, which

fills elements with index 0 to 9; no integer goes out of the array boundaries (see the second run).

2. The keyboard is treated as a file in which the numbers are keyed one after another with at least one space between them. As long as the read loop is not terminated, the numbers are read one by one. Even if the user enters a return key before inputting the number of integers defined by the *size* variable, the program waits for the user to enter the rest of the integers (the return key is taken as a space). On the other hand, if the user enters more numbers than defined by the *size* variable, only the predefined number of integers is read and the rest are ignored (as in the second run, in which the last entered number, integer 9, is ignored).

EXAMPLE 8.4

Instead of reading array elements from the keyboard, we can use an input file. A keyboard and an input file behave similarly (each acts as a source of sequential items). Also, instead of writing the array elements on the monitor after processing, we can store them in an output file. A monitor and an output file behave similarly (each acts as a destination for a sequence of data items). Program 8.2 shows how we can repeat Program 8.1, reading the original numbers from a file and writing the processed number to another file.

Program 8.2 Reversing the order of a list of numbers using files

```
/***************************************************************
 * Use of an array to read a list of integers from a file, to  *
 * reverse the order of elements, and to write the reversed    *
 * elements to another file                                    *
 ***************************************************************/
#include <iostream>
#include <fstream>
using namespace std;

int main ( )
{
   // Declarations
   const int CAPACITY = 50;
   int numbers [CAPACITY];
   int size = 0;
   ifstream inputFile;
   ofstream outputFile;
   // Openning the input file
   inputFile.open ("inFile.dat");
   if (!inputFile)
   {
       cout << "Error. Input file cannot be opened." << endl;
       cout << "The program is terminated";
```

(*continued*)

Program 8.2 Reversing the order of a list of numbers using files (Continued)

```
24            return 0;
25        }
26        // Reading the list of numbers from the input file into array
27        while (inputFile >> numbers [size] && size <= 50)
28        {
29            size++;
30        }
31        // Closing the input file
32        inputFile.close();
33        // Opening the output file
34        outputFile.open ("outFile.dat");
35        if (!outputFile)
36        {
37            cout << "Error. Output file cannot be opened." << endl;
38            cout << "The program is terminated.";
39            return 0;
40        }
41        // Writing the elements of the reversed array into the output file
42        for (int i = size - 1 ; i >= 0 ; i--)
43        {
44            outputFile << numbers[i] << " ";
45        }
46        // Closing the output file
47        outputFile.close();
48        return 0;
49    }
```

When we open the input file and the output file in a text editor, we get the following contents, in which the lists are inverse of each other.

Input file	Output file
12 56 72 89 11 71 61 92 34 13	13 34 92 61 71 11 89 72 56 12

There are several important points about Program 8.2:

1. We have included the <fstream> header file so we can use operations on files.
2. Since we do not know the count of the numbers in the input file, we must be cautious and select a large number (50 in this case) for the capacity.
3. If the input file is not successfully opened, we terminate the program with a message (lines 19 to 25). Similarly, if the output file is not opened successfully, we terminate the program with a message (lines 34 to 40).
4. The size of the array is automatically set when we reach the end of the input file (line 29).
5. When we run the program, we see nothing unless there is a problem with opening the input or output file.
6. The program never reads more than 50 integers (see line 27).

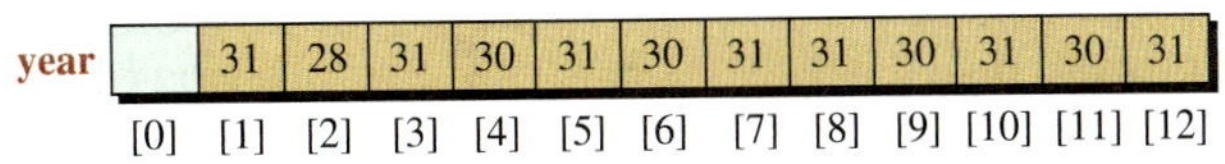

Figure 8.7 An array representing the number of days in a year

EXAMPLE 8.5

Although most of the time we use zero indexing in the array, sometimes it is convenient to create an array of one extra element and ignore the element at index 0. In this case, our indexing starts from 1. For example, we can create an array of 12 elements to hold the number of days in each month (for a non–leap year). However, it is convenient to create an array of 13 elements and not use the element at index 0, as shown in Figure 8.7. (Note that we have shown the array horizontally to save space.)

Program 8.3 shows how we can write a short program to use the array shown in Figure 8.7. This can serve the same purpose as the *switch* statement.

Program 8.3 Finding the number of days in a month of year

```
/***************************************************************
 * Use of an array to get the number of days in each month        *
 ***************************************************************/
#include <iostream>
using namespace std;

int main ( )
{
   // Declarations
   int numberOfDays [13] = {0, 31, 28, 31, 30, 31, 30,
                              31, 31, 30, 31, 30, 31};
   int month;
   // Getting input and validate
   do
   {
      cout << "Enter the month number (1 to 12): ";
      cin >> month;
   } while (month < 1 || month > 12);
   // Output
   cout << "There are " << numberOfDays[month];
   cout << " days in this month.";
   return 0;
}
```

```
Run:
Enter the month number (1 to 12): 1
There are 31 days in this month.
```

```
Run:
Enter the month number (1 to 12): 6
There are 30 days in this month.
```

(continued)

Program 8.3 Finding the number of days in a month of year (Continued)

```
Run:
Enter the month number (1 to 12): 0
Enter the month number (1 to 12): 13
Enter the month number (1 to 12): 3
There are 31 days in this month.
```

Note that the third run rejects the months less than 1 and greater than 12.

EXAMPLE 8.6

In Chapter 7 we created a *Circle* class. Using the *Circle* implementation file, we can create an application program that uses the compiled version of the *Circle* class to create an array of three circles (Program 8.4).

The following shows how we can compile and link the implementation and application files to see the radius, area, and perimeter of each circle.

Program 8.4 Creating an array of three circles

```
/***************************************************************
 * A program that uses the compiled version of the Circle class  *
 * to create an array of three circles.                          *
 ***************************************************************/
#include <iostream>
#include "circle.h"
using namespace std;

int main ( )
{
  // Declaration of array
  Circle circles [3];
  // Instantiation of objects
  circles [0] = Circle (3.0);
  circles [1] = Circle (4.0);
  circles [2] = Circle (5.0);
  // Printing information
  for (int i = 0; i < 3 ; i++)
  {
      cout << "Information about circle [" << i << "]" << endl;
      cout << "Radius: " << circles[i].getRadius() << "  ";
      cout << "Area: " << circles[i].getArea() << "  ";
      cout << "perimeter: " << circles[i].getPerimeter() << "  ";
      cout << endl;
  }
  return 0;
}
```

```
c++ -c circle.cpp
c++ -c app.cpp
c++ -o application circle.o app.o
application
```

```
Run:
Information about circle [0]
Radius: 3 Area: 28.26   perimeter: 18.84

Information about circle [1]
Radius: 4 Area: 50.24   perimeter: 25.12

Information about circle [2]
Radius: 5 Area: 78.5   perimeter: 31.4
```

8.2 MORE ON ARRAYS

In this section, we discuss some operations that we can apply on one-dimensional arrays. We divide these operations into two categories: those that access the elements of the array without changing their values or modifying their order and those that either change the value or change the structure of the array. We also explain how to use functions with arrays to simulate operations. Finally, we discuss parallel arrays and their applications.

8.2.1 Accessing Operations

The accessing operations are those that neither change the value of the elements nor the structure of the array (order of the elements). We discuss some of these operations.

Finding the Sum and Average

Assume we want to find the sum and average of the elements in an array named *numbers*. The following shows how to do this using a *for* loop. We assume that the capacity of the array is greater than or equal to the size.

```
double average;
int sum = 0;
for (int i = 0; i < size; i++)
{
   sum += numbers [i];
}
average = static_cast <double> (sum) / size;
```

Finding the Smallest and Largest

In previous chapters, we learned how to find the smallest and largest of a list of numbers. If the numbers are encapsulated in an array, we can use the same strategy to find the smallest and the largest values in the array.

```
int smallest = + 1000000;
int largest = - 1000000;
for (int i = 0; i < size; i++)
```

```
{
   if (numbers [i] < smallest)
   {
      smallest = numbers [i];
   }
   if (numbers [i] > largest)
   {
      largest = numbers [i];
   }
}
```

EXAMPLE 8.7

In this example, we write a program to read a list of integers from an input file *(numFile.dat)* whose contents are shown below:

```
14 76 80 33 21 95 22 88 16 39
```

Program 8.5 finds and prints the sum, the average, the smallest, and the largest of the numbers and displays them on the monitor.

Program 8.5 Finding the sum, average, smallest, and largest in a sequence

```
/***************************************************************
 * Use of an array to read a list of integers from a file and      *
 * prints the sum, the average, the smallest, and largest of       *
 * the numbers in the file.                                        *
 ***************************************************************/
#include <iostream>
#include <fstream>
using namespace std;

int main ( )
{
  // File declaration
  ifstream inputFile;
  // Array and variable declarations
  const int CAPACITY = 50;
  int numbers [CAPACITY];
  int size = 0;
  // Initialization
  int sum = 0;
  double average;
  int smallest = 1000000;
  int largest = -1000000;
```

(continued)

Program 8.5 Finding the sum, average, smallest, and largest in a sequence (Continued)

```
    // Opening input file with opening validation
    inputFile.open ("numFile.dat");
    if (!inputFile)
    {
        cout << "Error. Input file cannot be opened." << endl;
        cout << "The program is terminated.";
        return 0;
    }
    // Reading (copying) numbers from the file
    while (inputFile >> numbers [size])
    {
        size++;
    }
    // Closing input file
    inputFile.close();
    // Finding sum, average, smallest, and the largest
    for (int i = 0; i < size; i++)
    {
        sum += numbers[i];
        if (numbers[i] < smallest)
        {
            smallest = numbers[i];
        }
        if (numbers[i] > largest)
        {
            largest = numbers[i];
        }
    }
    average = static_cast <double> (sum) / size;
    // Printing results
    cout << "There are " << size << " numbers in the list" << endl;
    cout << "The sum of them is: " << sum << endl;
    cout << "The average of them is: " << average << endl;
    cout << "The smallest number is: " << smallest << endl;
    cout << "The largest number is: " << largest << endl;
    return 0;
}
```

Run:

```
There are 10 numbers in the list.
The sum of them is: 484
The average of them is: 48.4
The smallest number is: 14
The largest number is: 95
```

Searching for a Value

In array processing, we often need to search for a value. Although there are advanced and efficient algorithms to search an array, they require that the array is sorted. We show an elementary search here that can be used even when the array is not sorted. It is sometimes called a *linear search*. The value we are testing for is known as the *search argument*.

EXAMPLE 8.8

Assume we want to find if any value in an array of size 100 is equal to a value entered at run time. We can use a *for* loop with two terminating conditions. The first assures that we do not go beyond the size of the array; the second tests if we have found the element we are looking for. If the search is successful, we have found the index of the element, which is what we are looking for.

```
bool found = false;
for (int i = 0; (i < size) && (!found); i++)
{
   if (numbers [i] == value)
   {
       index = i;
       found = true;
   }
}
if (found)
{
   cout >> "The value was found at index: " << index;
}
else
{
   cout >> "The value was not found".;
}
```

8.2.2 Modifying Operations

There are operations that may change the value of elements, the order of elements, or both.

Swapping

The first operation we discuss is the one that swaps (exchanges) the contents of two elements. This exchange is often used in other operations such as sorting. Figure 8.8 shows the wrong approach and the right approach in swapping elements 1 and 3.

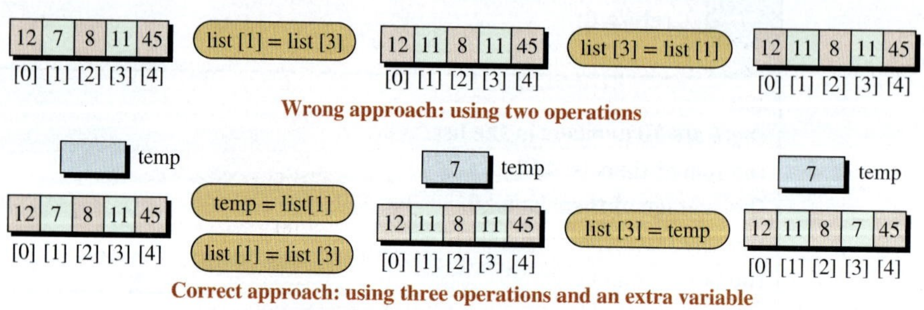

Figure 8.8 Wrong way and right way to swap two elements in an array

In the wrong approach, we use only two operations. As Figure 8.8 shows, after the two operations, both *list* [1] and *list* [3] contain the integer 11 because we lose the contents of *list* [1] in the first operation.

```
list [1] = list [3];                    // Copy list[3] into list[1]
list [3] = list [1];                    // Copy value of list [3] to list [1]
```

The solution is to use a temporary variable to store the value of *list* [1] before losing it. Figure 8.8 shows that this must be done before the other two operations. After the second operation, we lose the value of *list* [1], but we have saved a copy of it in *temp*. We retrieve this value in the third operation.

```
temp = list [1];                        // Save original value of list [1]
list [1] = list [3];                    // Copy value of list [3] to list [1]
list [3] = temp;                        // Copy value of temp to list [3]
```

Note each of the three variables, *temp*, *list* [1], *list* [3], is used once in the left-hand side and once in the right-hand side of the three operations.

Sorting an Array

An operation that only changes the order of elements is called *sorting*. Sorting is a very involved operation that uses swapping of elements until the elements in the array are in order. We discuss sorting techniques in Chapters 17 and 19.

Deleting an Element

One of the operations that is not very efficient in an array is to delete an element. Let us assume that we want to delete the element at index 3. The way to delete an element in the array is to copy (move) all elements after the target index one element toward the beginning of the array, as shown in Figure 8.9.

The figure shows that we need three movements. We cannot delete the element at index 6, but we can reduce the size of the array to make the element unavailable.

EXAMPLE 8.9

Assume we want to delete the element at index *pos*. We can use a *for* loop to move elements up and then decrement the size of the array.

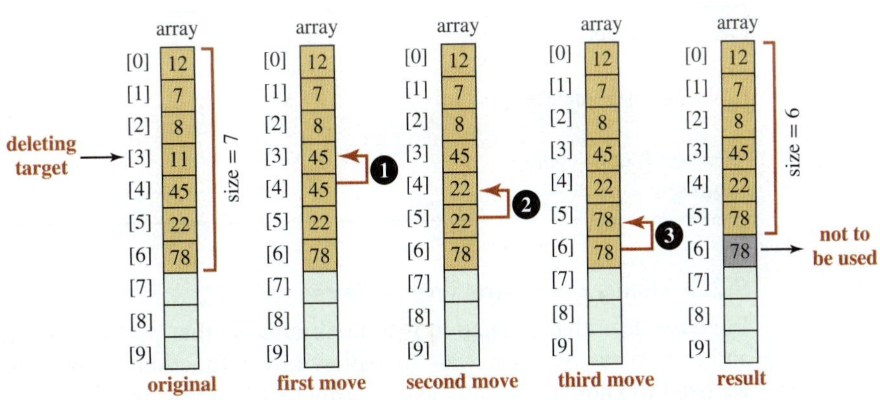

Figure 8.9 Deleting an element in an array

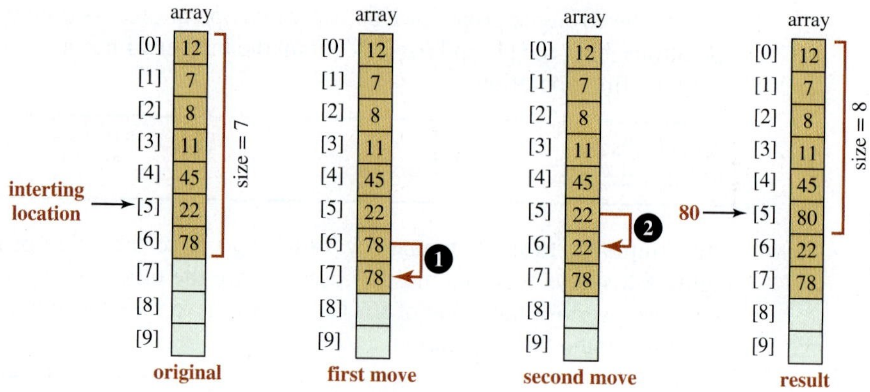

Figure 8.10 Inserting an element into an array

```
for (int i = pos + 1; i < size; i++)
{
   array [i – 1] = array [i]                    // Movement
}
size––;
```

Inserting an Element

Another inefficient operation is inserting an element into the middle of an array. This operation can be done only if the array is partially filled; otherwise, we go out of the boundary of the array. Figure 8.10 shows how we can insert an element of value 80 at index 5. All elements must be moved one position toward the end to make space for the insertion. However, this time we need to start movements from the last element.

EXAMPLE 8.10

Assume we want to insert an item (*value*) at a specific index (*pos*) in an array whose current size is defined by the variable *size*. If the size of the array is less than its capacity, we move all elements from the index (*size*) up to index (*pos*) one element toward the end of the array and make space for the new element to be inserted.

```
for (int i = size; i > pos; i––)
{
   numbers[i] = number [i –1];                  // Movement
}
numbers [pos] = value;
size++;
```

8.2.3 Using Functions with Arrays

We have seen that a function is a block of code that performs operations on fundamental and class types. We now want to explore how a function can operate on an array. To do so, we need to know if we can pass an array to a function as an argument and if we can return an array from a function.

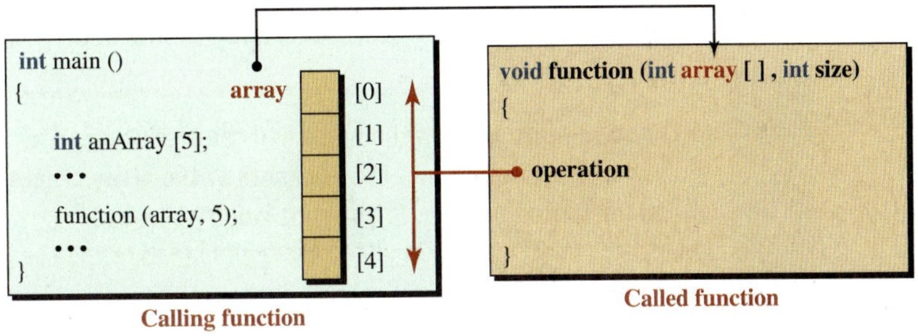

Figure 8.11 Passing an array to a function

Passing Arrays to Functions

As we will discuss later in the chapter, the name of the array is a constant pointer (address) to the first element. In other words, the name defines a fixed point in memory. When we pass the name of an array to a function, we are passing this address to the function. In other words, the array is still stored in the area belonging to the calling function, but the called function can access it or modify it. Figure 8.11 shows the situation. The figure shows that the memory allocation is done only through the calling function, but the called function is allowed to access or modify the element of the array. To access the array that belongs to the calling function, the called function must know the beginning address and the size of the array. The beginning address is defined using a parameter that contains the type, the name of the array, and an empty bracket *(int array [])*. The size of the array is defined as a separate parameter.

We can have two situations. If we want the called function to access only the elements of the array without being able to modify it, we must use the *const* modifier in front of the array name. On the other hand, if we want the called function to be able to modify the array, we do not use the *const* modifier. The following shows the prototype of the called function in both cases:

```
void function (const type array [], int size);      // Only for accessing
void function ( type array [], int size);            // For modifying
```

In other words, we add the *const* modifier to the name of the array to protect the array from changes by the called function.

EXAMPLE 8.11

As a simple example, we create a small array and then call a function named *print* to print the value of the elements. This is an example in which the called function is not supposed to change the array passed to the function (Program 8.6).

Program 8.6 Using a function to access an array

```
/***************************************************************
 * Passing array name and size to a function to let it print the      *
 * element of the array                                               *
 ***************************************************************/
#include <iostream>
using namespace std;
```

(continued)

Program 8.6 Using a function to access an array (Continued)

```
/***************************************************************
 * Function print accepts the name and the size of an array.    *
 * The function then prints the elements of the array created   *
 * and initialized in main. It does not modify the array.       *
 ***************************************************************/
void print (const int numbers [], int size)
{
  for (int i = 0; i < size; i++)
  {
      cout << numbers [i] <<" ";
  }
  return;
}

int main( )
{
  // Declaration and initialization of the array
  int numbers [15] = {5, 7, 9, 11, 13};
  // Calling the print function
  print (numbers, 5);
  return 0;
}
```

Run:

```
5 7 9 11 13
```

EXAMPLE 8.12

As another simple example, we create a small array and then call a function named *multiplyByTwo* to multiply the elements of the array by 2. This is an example in which the called function modifies the array created in *main*. Note that we also use the print function defined in the previous program. We call this function two times, before modifying the array and after modifying the array (Program 8.7).

Program 8.7 Using a function to modify an array

```
/***************************************************************
 * Passing array name and size to a function to let it modify  *
 * the elements of the array                                    *
 ***************************************************************/
#include <iostream>
using namespace std;

```

(continued)

Program 8.7 Using a function to modify an array (Continued)

```
/*******************************************************************
 * Function multiplyByTwo is a modifying function that changes      *
 * the array in main. There is no const modifier here.              *
 * The function accesses the array in main and modifies it.         *
 *******************************************************************/
void multiplyByTwo (int numbers [ ], int size)
{
  for (int i = 0; i < size; i++)
  {
      numbers [i]  *= 2;
  }
  return;
}

/*******************************************************************
 * Function print accepts the name and the size of an array.        *
 * The function then prints the elements of the array created       *
 * and initialized in main. It does not modify the array.           *
 *******************************************************************/
void print (const int numbers [ ], int size)
{
  for (int i = 0; i < size; i++)
  {
      cout << numbers [i] << " ";
  }
  cout << endl;
  return;
}

int main( )
{
  // Declaration and initialization of an array
  int numbers [5] = {150, 170, 190, 110, 130};
  // Printing the array before being modified
  print (numbers, 5);
  // Modifying the array in multiplyByTwo function
  multiplyByTwo (numbers , 5);
  // Printing the array after being modified
  print (numbers, 5);
  return 0;
}
```

Run:

```
150 170 190 110 130
300 340 380 220 260
```

The first line of output shows the original array; the second line shows the array after modification.

No Returning Array from Function

C++ does not allow us to return an array from a function. In other words, we cannot have a function prototype such as the following.

```
type [ ] function (const type array [], int size);      // It is not allowed in C++
```

When passing arrays to function, we have three choices as shown below:

```
// array will not change.
void (const type array [ ], int size);
// array will change.
void (type array [ ], int size);
// array1 will not change, but array 2 can be modified version of array1.
void (const type array1 [ ], type array2 [ ], int size);
```

To simulate returning an array from a function, we can use two arrays (one constant and one nonconstant).

EXAMPLE 8.13

Assume we want to write a function to reverse the contents of an array without changing the original array. This is possible if we create two similar arrays, the original and the modified one (which can originally be empty) as shown in Program 8.8. Note that we print both the original and modified arrays.

Program 8.8 Simulating array return by passing two arrays

```
/*****************************************************************
 * Passing two array to a function simulating returning an array.   *
 *****************************************************************/
#include <iostream>
using namespace std;
/*****************************************************************
 * Function reverse is a function that takes two arrays. It uses     *
 * the first array to reverse the element in the second array.       *
 *****************************************************************/
void reverse (const int array1[], int array2[], int size)
{
  for (int i = 0, j = size – 1; i < size; i++, j––)
  {
      array2 [j] = array1 [i];
  }
  return;
}
```

(continued)

Program 8.8 Simulating array return by passing two arrays (Continued)

```
/*****************************************************************
 * Function print accepts the name and the size of an array.    *
 * It then prints the elements of the array without modifying it.    *
 *****************************************************************/
void print (const int array [], int size)
{
  for (int i = 0; i < size; i++)
  {
      cout << array [i] << " ";
  }
  cout << endl;
  return;
}

int main ( )
{
  // Declaration of two arrays
  int array1 [5] = {150, 170, 190, 110, 130};
  int array2 [5];
  // Calling reverse function to modify array2 to be the reverse of array1
  reverse (array1, array2 , 5);
  // Printing both arrays
  print (array1, 5);
  print (array2, 5);
  return 0;
}
```

Run:

```
150 170 190 110 130
130 110 190 170 150
```

8.2.4 Parallel Arrays

Sometimes we need a list in which each row is made of more than one data item, possibly of different types. For example, we may need to keep *name*, *score*, and *grade* information about each student in a course. This can be done using three **parallel arrays** as shown in Figure 8.12.

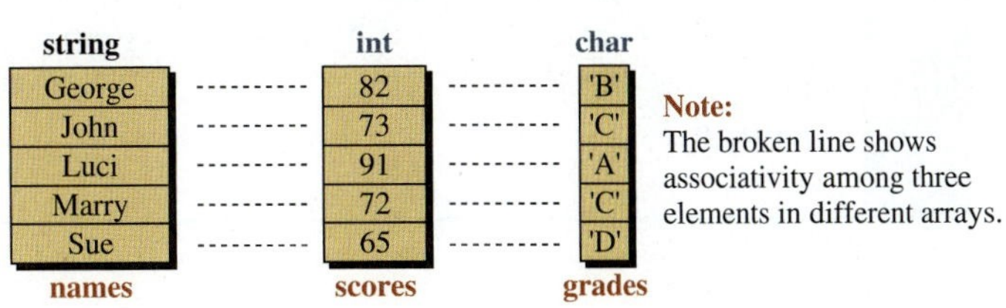

Figure 8.12 Three parallel arrays of different types

EXAMPLE 8.14

Program 8.9 creates and initializes two parallel arrays, *names* and *scores*, in *main*. It then calls a function to determine the student's grades and stores them in a third parallel array, called *grades*. It then prints the arrays.

Program 8.9 Using three parallel arrays

```
/*****************************************************************
 * The program uses three parallel arrays to create a list of      *
 * names, scores, and grades of five students in a course.         *
 *****************************************************************/
#include <iostream>
#include <iomanip>
using namespace std;
/*****************************************************************
 * The function findGrades accepts the constant array score, the   *
 * non-constant array grades, and the common size of the arrays.   *
 * It uses the first array to create the second array.             *
 *****************************************************************/
void findGrades (const int scores [], char grades [], int size)
{
  char temp [ ] = {'F', 'F', 'F', 'F', 'F', 'F', 'D', 'C', 'B', 'A', 'A'};
  for (int i = 0; i < size; i++)
  {
           grades [i] = temp [scores [i] / 10];
  }
  return ;
}
int main( )
{
  // Declaration of three arrays and initialization of two
  string names [4] = {"George", "John", "Luci", "Mary"};
  int scores [4] = {82, 73, 91, 72};
  char grades [4];
  // Function call
  findGrades (scores, grades, 5);
  // Printing values in all three arrows with headers
  for (int i = 0; i < 4; i++)
  {
     cout << setw (10) << left << names[i] << "    " << setw (2) ;
     cout << scores[i] << "     " << setw(2) << grades[i] << endl;
  }
  return 0;
}
```

(continued)

Program 8.9 Using three parallel arrays (Continued)

```
Run:
George    82    B
John      73    C
Luci      91    A
Mary      72    C
```

EXAMPLE 8.15

A better approach to parallel arrays is the use of an array of objects. For example, we can create a class named *Student* with three data members—*name*, *score*, and *grade*—to solve the problem presented in Example 8.14. We then create an array of objects in which each element is an instance of the class *Student*. In this way, we can create the class and make it available to each professor using separate compilation. The professors can then create their customized applications (*main* function) to use the class with any number of students. Program 8.10 shows the *Student* interface.

Program 8.10 The interface for the *Student* class

```
/*****************************************************************
 * This is the interface file for a Student class with three      *
 * private data members and four public member functions.         *
 *****************************************************************/
#ifndef STUDENT_H
#define STUDENT_H
#include <iostream>
#include <string>
using namespace std;

class Student
{
  private:
      string name;
      int score;
      char grade;
  public:
      Student ();
      Student (string name, int score);
      ~Student ();
      void print();
};
#endif
```

Program 8.11 The implementation file for the *Student* class

```
/***************************************************************
 * This the implementation for the Student class whose interface     *
 * file is given in Program 8-11.                                    *
 ***************************************************************/
#include "student.h"

// Default constructor
Student :: Student()
{
}
// Parameter Constructor
Student :: Student (string nm, int sc)
:name (nm), score (sc)
{
  char temp [ ] = {'F', 'F', 'F', 'F', 'F', 'F', 'D', 'C', 'B', 'A', 'A'};
  grade = temp [score / 10];
}
// Destructor
Student :: ~Student()
{
}
// Print member function
void Student :: print()
{
  cout << setw (12) << left << name;
  cout << setw (8) << right << score;
  cout << setw (8) << right << grade << endl;
}
```

Program 8.11 shows the implementation.
Program 8.12 shows the application.

Program 8.12 The application file for *Student* class

```
/***************************************************************
 * The application file to create objects from the Student           *
 * class and print the name, score, and grade of each student        *
 ***************************************************************/
#include "student.h"
#include "iomanip"

int main ( )
{
```

(*continued*)

Program 8.12 The application file for *Student* class (Continued)

```
    // Declaration of an array of Students using default constructors
    Student students [5];
    // Instantiation of five objects using parameter constructors
    students[0] = Student ("George", 82);
    students[1] = Student ("John", 73);
    students[2] = Student ("Luci", 91);
    students[3] = Student ("Mary", 72);
    students[4] = Student ("Sue", 65);
    // Printing students' name, score, and grade
    for (int i = 0; i < 5; i++)
    {
        students[i].print();
    }
    return 0;
}
```

The following shows the separate compilation and running of the application program for creating and displaying students' information.

```
c++ - c students.cpp                          // Compilation of implementation file
c++ - c app.cpp                               // Compilation of application file
c++ - o application student.o app.o           // Linking of two compiled object files
application                                   // Running the executable file
```

```
Run:
George    82    B
John      73    C
Luci      91    A
Mary      72    C
Sue       65    D
```

Although the approach may look more involved and uses more lines of code, it has the advantage that when the *Student* class is created, it can be used by any professor by just downloading the interface and the implementation. Each professor can customize her own application based on her need.

8.3 MULTIDIMENSIONAL ARRAYS

Some applications require that a set of values be arranged in a **multidimensional array.** The most common are two-dimensional arrays, but we may occasionally encounter three-dimensional arrays.

8.3.1 Two-Dimensional Arrays

A **two-dimensional array** defines a structured data type in which two indices are used to define the location of elements in rows and columns. The first index defines the row; the second index defines the column. Figure 8.13 shows a two-dimensional array, named *scores*, with five rows and three columns.

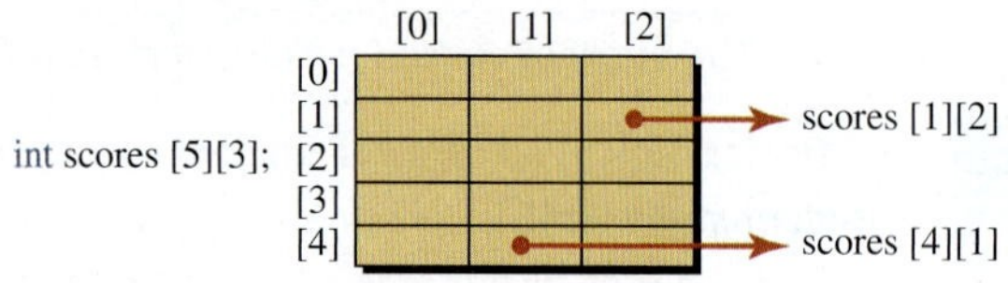

Figure 8.13 Two-dimensional array (scores of five students in three tests)

Note that just like one-dimensional arrays, the first row is row 0 and the first column is column 0. The scores for student 1 occupy row 0; The scores for test 1 for all students occupy column 0.

Declaration and Initialization

We declare and define a two-dimensional array like we did with a one-dimensional array, but we must define two dimensions, rows and columns. We define the number of rows first and the number of columns second. The following shows how we define an array of *scores* of five students in three tests.

```
int score [5][3];
```

Subscript Operators In one-dimensional arrays, we need to use one subscript operator. In two-dimensional arrays, we need to use two subscript operators.

Initialization Initializing the elements in the array is done row by row. However, the initialization list is more readable if we separate the rows using braces, as shown below.

```
int scores [5][3] = { {82, 65, 72},
                      {73, 70, 80},
                      {91, 76, 40},
                      {72, 72, 68},
                      {65, 90, 80} };
```

To initialize the whole array to zeros (when array is declared locally), we specify only the first value, as follows:

```
int scores [5][3] = {0};
```

Accessing Elements We can access each element in the array using the exact location of the element defined by the two indexes. Accessing can be used to store a value in an individual element or retrieve the value of an element.

```
scores[1][0] = 5;           // Storing 5 in row 1 column 0
cin >> scores[2][1];        // Inputting value for row 2 column 1
x = scores [1][2];          // Copying the value of row 1 column 2 into variable x
cout << scores [0][0];      // Outputting value of row 0 column 0
```

Passing Two-Dimensional Arrays to Functions

Passing a two-dimensional array to a function uses the same principle we discussed for one-dimensional arrays. As shown below, the first parameter defines the array. Here, the first

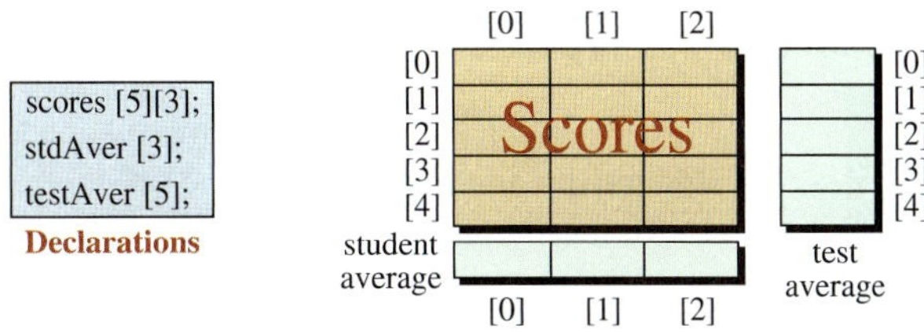

Figure 8.14 One two-dimensional and two one-dimensional arrays

bracket is empty, but the second bracket must literally define the size of the second dimension. The size of the first dimension must be passed to the array as a separate parameter.

```
void function (int array[ ] [3] , int rowSize);
```

EXAMPLE 8.16

Figure 8.14 shows the relationship between the two-dimensional array and the two one-dimensional arrays.

Program 8.13 shows how we can find the student average and the test average using two functions. Each function accepts a two-dimensional array and a one-dimensional array.

Program 8.13 Using three arrays

```
/**************************************************************
 * The program creates student average and test average from the    *
 * two-dimensional test scores.                                      *
 **************************************************************/
#include <iostream>
#include <iomanip>
using namespace std;

/**************************************************************
 * The function takes a two-dimensional array of test scores        *
 * for six students in three tests. It then modifies an array       *
 * in main representing student average.                            *
 **************************************************************/
void findStudentAverage (int const scores [ ][3],
                         double stdAver [ ], int rowSize, int colSize)
{
   for (int i = 0; i < rowSize; i++)
   {
        int sum = 0;
        for (int j = 0; j < colSize; j++)
        {
              sum += scores[i][j];
        }
```

(*continued*)

Program 8.13 Using three arrays (Continued)

```
        double average = static_cast <double> (sum) / colSize;
        stdAver[i] = average;
    }
    return;
}
/***************************************************************
 * The function takes a two-dimensional array of test scores    *
 * for six students in three tests. It then modifies an array   *
 * in main representing test averages.                           *
 ***************************************************************/
void findTestAverage (int const scores [][3],
                                    double tstAver [], int rowSize , int colSize)
{
    for (int j = 0; j< colSize; j++)
    {
        int sum = 0;
        for (int i = 0; i < rowSize; i++)
        {
            sum += scores [i][j];
        }
        double average = static_cast <double> (sum) / rowSize;
        tstAver[j] = average;
    }
}

int main( )
{
    // Declarations of three arrays and some variables
    const int rowSize = 5;
    const int colSize = 3;
    int scores [rowSize][colSize] = {{82, 65, 72},
                                     {73, 70, 80},
                                     {91, 67, 40},
                                     {72, 72, 68},
                                     {65, 90, 80}};
    double stdAver [rowSize];
    double tstAver [colSize];
    // Calling two functions to modify two average arrays
    findStudentAverage (scores, stdAver, rowSize, colSize);
    findTestAverage (scores, tstAver, rowSize, colSize);
    // Print headings
    cout << "                Test Scores                  stdAver" << endl;
    cout << "     --------------------------  -------  " << endl;
```

(continued)

Program 8.13 Using three arrays (Continued)

```
67      // Print test scores and student averages
68      for (int i = 0; i < rowSize ; i++)
69      {
70          for (int j = 0 ; j < colSize; j++)
71          {
72                  cout << setw (12) << scores[i][j];
73          }
74          cout << fixed << setprecision (2) << "     " << stdAver[i] << endl;
75      }
76      // Print test averages
77      cout << "tstAver ";
78      cout << "---------------------------- ";
79      for (int j = 0 ; j < colSize; j++)
80      {
81          cout << fixed << setprecision (2) << stdAver[j] << "     ";
82      }
83      return 0;
84  }
```

Run:

```
                  Test Scores                  stdAver
           ------------------------           -------
           82          65          72          73.00
           73          70          80          74.33
           91          67          40          66.00
           72          72          68          70.67
           65          90          80          78.33
tstAver    73.00       74.33       66.00
```

We use the indexes *i* and *j* to represent rows and columns in the loops. In lines 14 and 34, we pass the two-dimensional array as a constant entity with the second index set to literal 3 (number of columns). In lines 15 and 35, we pass a one-dimensional array as a nonconstant entity to allow each function to store the average. In lines 15 and 35, we pass both *rowSize* and *colSize* to be used by the loops.

Operations

Some of the operations we defined previously for a one-dimensional array can be used with two-dimension arrays. Others must be modified to be applicable to two-dimensional arrays. For example, searching and sorting should be applied to each dimension separately. However, there are some operations that can be applied specifically to two-dimensional arrays.

Folding We can fold a two-dimensional array around a horizontal axis (row folding) or a vertical axis (column folding) as shown in Figure 8.15.

EXAMPLE 8.17

The following shows how we can use a nested loop to do row folding. We leave the code for column folding as an exercise.

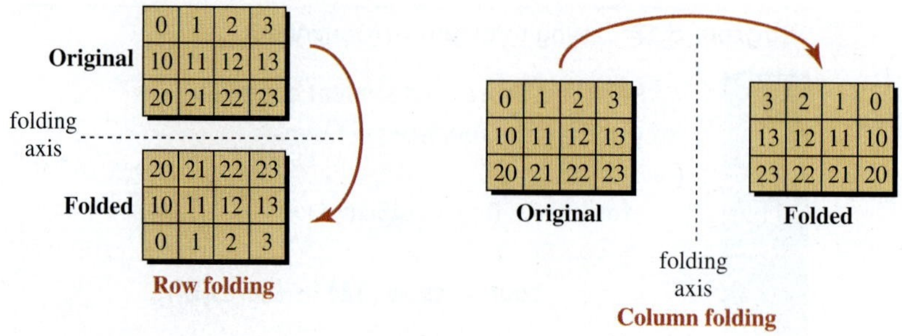

Figure 8.15 Folding a two-dimensional array

```
for (int i = 0 ; i < rowSize ; i++)
{
   for (int j = 0 ; j < colSize ; j++)
   {
      foldedArray [rowSize - 1 - i][j] = originalArray [i][j];
   }
}
```

Transposing When working with a two-dimensional array, we may need to *transpose* it. For example, transposition is necessary if we want to solve a set of equations using matrixes. Transposing means changing the role of the rows and columns. A row becomes a column; a column becomes a row. Figure 8.16 shows the idea applied to a 3 × 4 array. The result is a 4 × 3 array. To transpose an array, we need to change the row index to a column index and vice versa.

EXAMPLE 8.18

The following shows how we can use a nested loop to do transposing.

```
for (int i = 0 ; i < orgRowSize ; i++)
{
   for (int j = 0 ; j < orgColSize ; j++)
   {
      trasposedArray [j][i] = originalArray [i][j];
   }
}
```

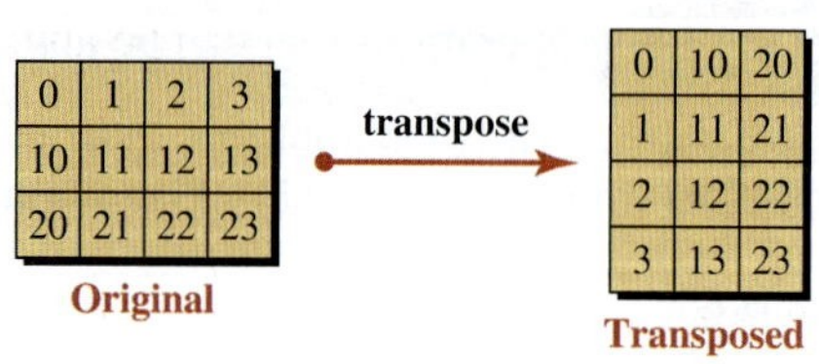

Figure 8.16 Transpose operation on a two-dimensional array

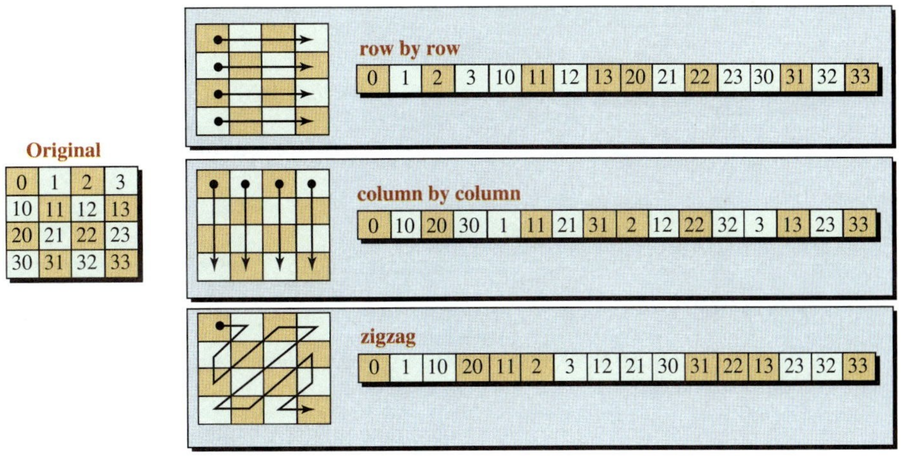

Figure 8.17 Linearizing an array

Linearizing We may need to send the contents of a two-dimensional array through a network (for example, when we send a video). Before transmission, the array must be changed to a one-dimensional array (through a process known as **linearization**). Figure 8.17 shows three ways to do so: row by row, column by column, and zigzag.

8.3.2 Three-Dimensional Arrays

C++ does not limit arrays to two dimensions. However, arrays with more than three dimensions are rare. Figure 8.18 shows how we can represent a **three-dimensional array.** The business shown in Figure 8.18 operates in three states, has up to four offices in each state, and has up to 12 employees in each office. We leave writing a program to handle a three-dimensional array as an exercise.

8.4 PROGRAM DESIGN

In this section, we show how to use arrays to solve classical problems in computer science.

8.4.1 Frequency Array and Histogram

Arrays can be used to create a **frequency array** that shows the distribution of elements in a list of integers. The array can then be used to create a **histogram,** which is a graphical representation of the table. Figure 8.19 shows typical data and the frequency array created from the data.

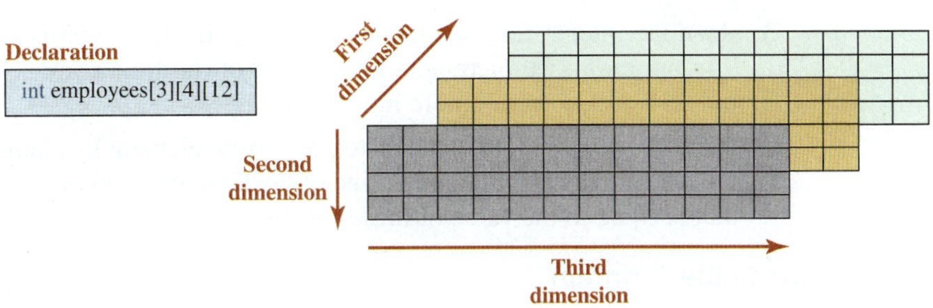

Figure 8.18 A three-dimensional array

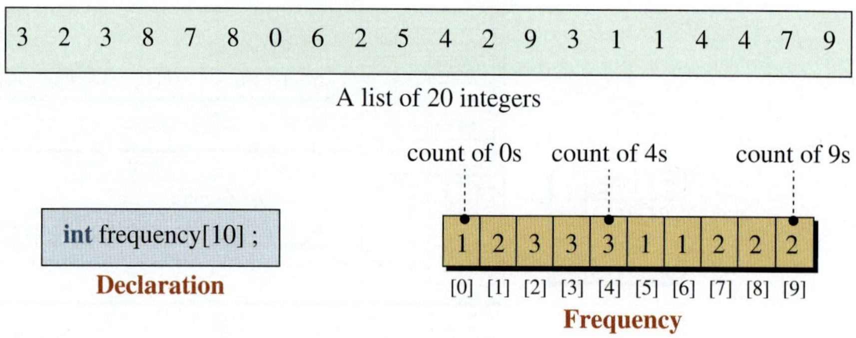

Figure 8.19 List of integers and frequency array

Assume we have collected a sequence of integers in which each integer is between 0 and 9 inclusive (Figure 8.19 shows only 20 integers, but the list can be of any length). We want to know the number of 0s, the number of 1s, the number of 2s, and so on. We create an array of 10 elements to hold the count of each value. We call the array *frequency*. Note that if we add all values in the *frequency* array, we come up with the number of integers in the list. The number of integers and range of numbers are normally large, and the integers are read from a file. The list in the figure can be thought of as the contents of a file. We read the integers one by one from the file and create a *frequency* array. For example, each time we read an integer 4, we add one to the frequency[4]. Note that we can only use a list of integers because an index of the frequency array is an integer.

Understand the Problem

We need to create an array *frequency*, in which each integer read from the list is related to the *index* of the array. In other words, if we encounter a 6 in the list, we need to increment the value of the element in *frequency*[6]. For this reason, the size of the *frequency* array is equal to the range of the values in the data array. The values in the data array are between 0 and 9; the indexes of the frequency array are [0] to [9]. To create the frequency array, we go through the list, element by element, and when we see an element of value x, we add 1 to *frequency*[*x*]. Once the array is built, we create a histogram that graphically shows it. Note that some literature creates two arrays for this problem: *data* and *frequencies*. The *data* array is not needed unless we want to keep all of the data items in memory during program execution for other purposes.

Develop the Algorithm

The following steps are necessary:

1. Declare and initialize the frequency array to all 0s.
2. Open the integer file and make sure that the file is opened correctly; otherwise, the program should be terminated.
3. Read the integer file, one integer at a time. If the integer is in the desired range (0 to 9 in our case), we increment the content of the frequency array at the corresponding index. If it is not, we ignore it.
4. Print the values stored in the histogram array, element by element. At the same time we must create the corresponding line of the histogram (in our case, a number of asterisks that is equal to the value of that element).

Write the Program

Program 8.14 shows the code based on the five-step algorithm.

Program 8.14 Creating a frequency array and a histogram

```
/**************************************************************
 * The program reads a list of integers from a file and creates a    *
 * frequency array and histogram for the list of integers between    *
 * 0 and 9 (inclusive).                                              *
 **************************************************************/
#include <iostream>
#include <fstream>
#include <iomanip>
using namespace std;

int main ( )
{
   // Declaration and initialization
   const int CAPACITY = 10;
   int frequencies [CAPACITY] = {0};
   ifstream integerFile;
   // Opening integer file
   integerFile.open ("integerFile.dat");
   if (!integerFile)
   {
        cout << "Error. Integer file cannot be opened." << endl;
        cout << "The program is terminated.";
        return 0;
   }
   // Reading from the integer file and creating frequency array
   int data;
   int size = 0;
   while (integerFile >> data )
   {
        if (data >= 0 && data <= 9)
        {
                size++;
                frequencies[data]++;
        }
   }
   // Closing integer file
   integerFile.close();
   // Printing frequencies and histogram
   cout << "There are " << size << " valid data items." << endl;

   for (int i = 0; i < 10 ; i++)
   {
        cout << setw (3) << i << " ";
```

(continued)

Program 8.14 Creating a frequency array and a histogram (Continued)

```

        for (int f = 1; f <= frequencies [i] ; f++)
        {
            cout << '*' ;
        }
        cout << " " << frequencies [i] << endl;
    }
    return 0;
}
```

```
Run:
There are 202 valid data items.
0 ********************** 22
1 **** 4
2 ******************* 19
3 ************* 13
4 ******************** 20
5 ********************************* 33
6 **************************** 28
7 **************************** 28
8 ************************* 25
9 ********** 10
```

The number of asterisks in each line is actually the count of the corresponding integer.

The following shows the contents of the integer file we used. Note that there are 205 integers in the list, but three of them (shown in color) are not in the range 0 to 9. This means that the program reads all 205 integers, but the frequency array is formed with only 202 integers.

```
1 3 2 2 5 7 3 2 8 0 6 4 6 7 0 7 8 5 4 2 3 0 6 7 5 8 5 4 8 9 6 5 5 9 2 3 5 2 6 7 8
0 6 4 6 7 0 7 8 5 4 2 13 0 6 7 5 8 5 4 8 9 6 7 0 7 8 5 4 2 3 0 6 7 5 8 5 4 8 9 6 5
2 7 0 7 8 5 4 2 3 0 6 7 5 8 5 4 8 9 6 15 5 9 7 0 7 8 5 4 2 3 0 6 7 5 8 9 6 5 6 6 4
5 9 7 0 7 8 5 4 2 3 0 6 7 5 8 9 6 5 6 6 4 2 7 0 7 8 5 4 2 3 0 6 7 5 8 5 4 8 9 6 5
1 3 2 2 5 7 3 2 8 0 6 4 6 17 0 7 8 5 4 2 3 0 0 6 4 6 7 0 7 8 5 4 2 3 0 6 7 5 8 1 1
```

8.4.2 Linear Transformation

We mentioned earlier that in the linear transformation of a two-dimensional array to a one-dimensional array, we have two choices: row transformation and column transformation. In the first, the transformation is done row by row; in the second, it is done column by column (Figure 8.20).

Understand the Problem

We must find the logic that will allow us to change the data in an array of N rows and M columns of elements to a line with N × M elements.

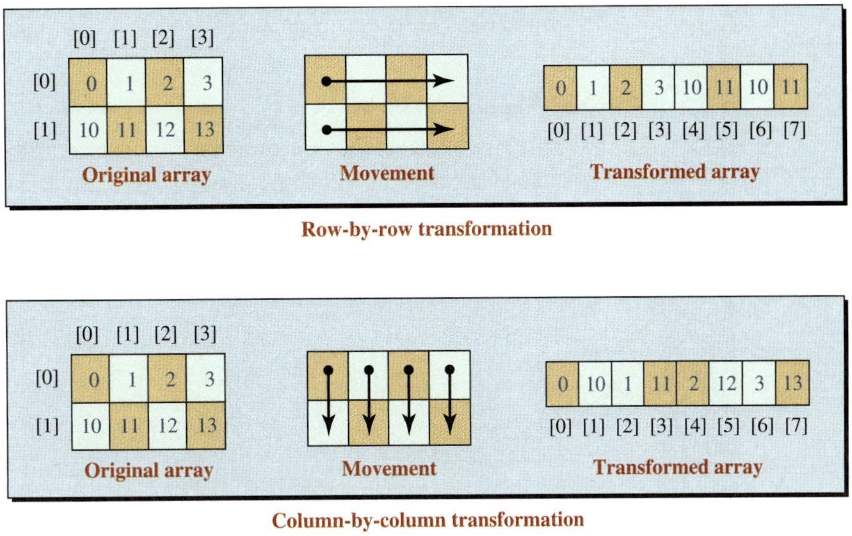

Figure 8.20 Linear transformation

Develop the Algorithm

We declare and initialize a two-dimensional array. For a small array, we can simply enter the values; for a large array, we would read the data from a file. We define four functions:

1. The first function transforms the array row by row and creates an array we call the *rowArray*.
2. The second function transforms the array column by column and creates an array we call the *colArray*.
3. The third function prints the two-dimensional array.
4. The fourth function prints either of the one-dimensional arrays.

The job of the *main* function is very simple. After declaration and initialization of the two-dimensional array, it calls the first function and the second function to create one-dimensional arrays. It then calls the corresponding functions to print the two-dimensional and each of the one-dimensional arrays.

Write the Program

Program 8.15 shows the code based on the explanations we provided.

Program 8.15 Array transformation

```
/*****************************************************************
 * The program shows how to transform a two-dimensional array to  *
 * two one-dimensional arrays using row-by-row or column-by-column *
 * transformation.                                                *
 *****************************************************************/
#include <iostream>
#include <iomanip>
using namespace std;
```

(continued)

Program 8.15 Array transformation (Continued)

```

/***************************************************************
 * The rowTransform function creates a one-dimensional array from   *
 * a two-dimensional array using row-by-row transformation. The     *
 * first array is passed as a const to prevent changes.             *
 ***************************************************************/
void rowTransform (const int originArray [][4], int rowSize,
                                                   int rowArray[])
{
  int i = 0;
  int j = 0;
  for (int k = 0 ; k < 8; k++)
  {
      rowArray [k] = originArray [i] [j];
      j++;
      if (j > 3)
      {
            i++;
            j = 0;
      }
  }
}
/***************************************************************
 * The colTransform function creates a one-dimensional array from   *
 * a two-dimensional array using column-by-column transformation.   *
 * The first array is passed as a constant to prevent changes.      *
 ***************************************************************/
void colTransform (const int originArray [][4], int rowSize,
                                                   int colArray[])
{
  int i = 0;
  int j = 0;
  for (int k = 0 ; k < 8; k++)
  {
      colArray[k] = originArray [i][j];
      i++;
      if (i > 1)
      {
            j++;
            i = 0;
      }
  }
}
```

(continued)

Program 8.15 Array transformation (Continued)

```
/****************************************************************
 * The function prints the contents of a two-dimensional array  *
 * passed to it as a constant argument.                         *
 ****************************************************************/
void printTwoDimensional (const int twoDimensional [][4],
                                            int rowSize)
{
  for (int i = 0; i < rowSize; i++)
  {
      for (int j = 0; j < 4; j++)
      {
            cout << setw (4) << twoDimensional [i][j];
      }
      cout << endl;
  }
  cout << endl;
}

/****************************************************************
 * The function prints the contents of a one-dimensional array  *
 * passed to it as a constant argument.                         *
 ****************************************************************/
void printOneDimensional (const int oneDimensional[], int size)
{
  for (int i = 0; i < size; i++)
  {
      cout << setw (4) << oneDimensional[i];
  }
  cout << endl;
}

int main ( )
{
  // Declaration of three arrays and initialization of the first
  int originArray [2][4] = {{0, 1, 2, 3}, {10, 11, 12, 13}};
  int rowArray [8];
  int colArray [8];
  // Calling two functions to transform arrays
  rowTransform (originArray, 2, rowArray);
  colTransform (originArray, 2, colArray);
  // Printing the two-dimensional array
  cout << "   Original Array   " << endl;
  printTwoDimensional (originArray, 2);
```

(continued)

Program 8.15 Array transformation (Continued)

```
    // Printing the row-transformed one-dimensional array
    cout << "Row-Transformed Array:     ";
    printOneDimensional (rowArray, 8);
    // Printing the col-transformed one-dimensional array
    cout << "Column-Transformed Array:  ";
    printOneDimensional (colArray, 8);
    return 0;
}
```

Run:

```
  Original Array
   0   1   2   3
  10  11  12  13

Row-Transformed Array:      0   1  2   3 10  11 12  13
Column-Transformed Array:   0  10  1  11  2  12  3  13
```

Key Terms

array declaration
frequency array
histogram
linearization
multidimensional array
one-dimensional array
parallel arrays
subscript
three-dimensional array
two-dimensional array

Summary

Arrays are sequences of data items of the same type. An array is a compound type; we can have an array of any type other than *void*. An array has three attributes: *type, size* and *capacity*. To declare an array, we specify its type, name, and capacity enclosed in square brackets. Arrays declared in the global area of a program are initialized with default values. Arrays declared inside of functions are initialized with garbage values left over from the previous operations.

In a one-dimensional array, each element can be accessed using a single index. Accessing an element in a two-dimensional array requires two indexes, representing the row and the column. Several operations are common on two-dimensional arrays: folding, transposing, and linearizing, We are not limited to two dimensions; however more than three dimensional arrays are very rare.

Problems

PR-1. Given the following declarations, write the code that prints the array elements with an even index.

```
int arr [10] = {0, 1, 2, 3, 4, 5, 6, 7, 8, 9};
```

PR-2. Given the following declaration, write the code that prints the first five elements of the array.

```
int arr [12] = {0, 10, 20, 39, 40, 50, 60, 70, 80, 90};
```

PR-3. Write the code that fills the elements with an even index with integer 0 and the elements with an odd index with integer 1 using the following declaration.

```
int arr [10];
```

PR-4. Write the code that fills the first five elements with integer 5 and the last five elements with integer 10 given the following array declarations.

```
int arr [10];
```

PR-5. What is the output from the following code segment?

```
int arr [10] = {0, 1, 2, 3, 4, 5, 6, 7, 8, 9};
for (int i = 0; i < 5; i++)
{
    cout << arr [i * 2] << " ";
}
```

PR-6. What is the output from the following code segment?

```
int arr [10] = {0, 1, 2, 3, 4, 5, 6, 7, 8, 9};
for (int i = 0; i < 5; i++)
{
    arr [i ] = arr [i * 2 + 1];
    cout << arr [i] << endl;
}
```

PR-7. What is the output from the following code segment?

```
int arr1 [5] = {0, 1, 2, 3, 4};
int arr2 [5];
for (int i = 0; i < 5; i++)
{
    arr2 [i] = arr1 [i];
    cout << arr1 [i] + arr2 [i] << endl;
}
```

PR-8. What is the output from the following code segment?

```
int arr [5] = {0, 1, 2, 3, 4};
for (int i = 1; i <= 4; i++)
{
    cout << arr [i] << " ";
}
cout << endl;
```

PR-9. Write the code that creates another array, *arr2*, whose elements are in the reverse order of the following array named *arr1*.

```
int arr1 [10] = {0, 10, 20, 39, 40, 50, 60, 70, 80, 90};
```

PR-10. Write the definition of a function that, given two arrays of integers, *arr1* and *arr2*, as parameters, compares the two arrays for equality and returns *true* or *false*. Assume that the capacity of both arrays is the same.

PR-11. Write the definition of a function that, given an array of integers, *arr1* with capacity *n*, creates another array *arr2*. Each element in *arr2* should be two times the corresponding element in *arr1*. Assume that the capacity of *arr2* is the same as *arr1*.

PR-12. Write the definition of a function that, given an array of integers, *arr,* with size *n*, checks to see if the elements of the array are in increasing order (value of each element is greater than or equal to the previous element). The function should return *true* or *false.*

PR-13. Write the definition of a function that, given an array of integers, *arr* with size *n*, searches the array for the given value. The function returns *true* or *false.*

PR-14. Write the definition of a function that, given an array of integers named *arr*, swaps the two elements of the array with the given indexes. Note that the function should check the validity of the given indexes.

PR-15. Write the definition of a function that, given an array of integers named *arr*, deletes the element at the given index. Note that the function should assert the validity of the given index.

PR-16. Write the definition of a function that, given an array of integers named *arr*, inserts a given value at the given index. Note that the function should check the validity of the given index.

PR-17. Write the declarations and initialization of two arrays of capacity 10 in which the first holds the name and the second the salary of employees in a company.

PR-18. Write the definition of a function that, given a two-dimensional array named *table*, of *n* rows and 3 columns, prints the elements in row *r*. Check the validity of *r* passed as a parameter.

PR-19. Write the definition of a function that takes a two-dimensional array, named *table,* of *n* rows and 3 columns, and prints the elements in column *c*. Check the validity of *c* passed as a parameter.

PR-20. Show the values of the elements in the following array, which is created by linear row transformation of the array.

```
int sample [2][4] = {{1, 2, 3, 4} , {5, 6, 7, 8}};
```

PR-21. Show the values of the elements in the following array, which is created by linear column transformation of the following array initialization:

```
int sample [2][4] = {{1, 2, 3, 4} , {5, 6, 7, 8}};
```

PR-22. Show the values of the elements in the array that is created by zigzag transformation of the following array.

```
int sample [3][3] = {{1, 2, 3},{4, 5, 6},{7, 8, 9}};
```

Programs

PRG-1. Write a program that randomly creates an array of 100 elements and fills the elements with random integers between 100 and 200. The program prints the elements in 10 rows by calling a print function.

PRG-2. Write a program that creates a list of 10 random integers between 1 and 100 and then prints the elements of array, the smallest element, and the largest element.

PRG-3. Write a program that creates a list of 10 random integers between 1 and 100 and then prints the elements of the array, the average of the elements, and the standard deviation of them using the formula shown below, in which *n* defines the size of the list and *aver* defines the average value:

```
stdDev = sqrt ( (num[0] - aver)² + ··· + (num [n-1] - aver)² ) / n
```

PRG-4. Write a program that creates a list of 10 random integers between 1 and 100 and a function to round shift the elements one element toward the end of the array such that the first element becomes the second, the second element becomes the third, …, and the last element becomes the first. The program prints the original array and the shifted array.

PRG-5. Write a program that creates an array of 10 integers filled randomly with values from 1 to 100. The program then removes the largest and the smallest elements from the array and prints the original array and the array after the two elements have been removed.

PRG-6. Write a program that creates an array of 10 integers filled randomly with values from 1 to 100; then creates another array in which the order of elements is reversed; and then prints the contents of both arrays.

PRG-7. Write a program that creates an array of 20 integers in which each element is between 1 and 100. The program then creates two arrays: one holding odd values and the other holding even values.

PRG-8. Write a program that randomly creates a two-dimensional array of size 6 by 6; the array contains integers from 100 to 199. The program then creates two functions. The first creates an array that contains the diagonal elements from left to right, and the second creates the diagonal elements from right to left. The program prints the two-dimensional array and both one-dimensional arrays.

PRG-9. Write a program that creates two one-dimensional arrays of size 5 and fills them with random values between 100 and 199. The program then uses a function to merge the two arrays to create a new one. Merging takes one element from each array in sequence. The program prints the contents of all arrays.

PRG-10. Write a program that initializes two arrays of size 5 with random values between 100 and 199 and then writes a function to create a two-dimensional array of size 2 by 5 in which each row is the copy of one of the original arrays. The program prints the contents of the three arrays.

PRG-11. Write a program that initializes two arrays of size 5 with random values between 100 and 199 and then writes a function to create a two-dimensional array of size 5 by 2 in which each column is the copy of one of the original arrays. The program prints the contents of the three arrays.

In Chapter 8 we discussed one of the compound data types: arrays. In this chapter we discuss the other two compound data types: references and pointers. We also discuss memory management related to storing pointed objects in heap memory.

Objectives

After you have read and studied this chapter, you should be able to:

- Discuss reference types and reference variables.
- Discuss how to create a permanent binding between a reference variable and the original variable.
- Discuss how to retrieve and change data in the original variable through the reference variable.
- Show the application of references in relation to functions: pass-by-reference and return-by-reference.
- Discuss pointer types and pointer variables.
- Discuss how to create a permanent or temporary binding between a pointer variable and a data variable.
- Discuss how to retrieve and change data in a data variable through the pointer variable.
- Show the application of pointers in relation to functions: pass-by-pointer and return-by-pointer.
- Discuss relations between arrays and pointers, and discuss array arithmetic.
- Discuss four areas of memory available to programmers and their applications.
- Discuss when an object can be stored in stack memory and when it needs to be stored in heap memory.
- Discuss dynamic memory allocation.

9.1 REFERENCES

A *reference* is an alternative name for an object. References have been added to C++ to simplify communication between entities such as functions, as we will see later in the chapter.

9.1.1 Introduction

A variable declared as *type&* is an alternative name for a variable declared as *type.* When we declare a **reference variable,** we do not create a new object in memory; we just declare an alternative name for an existing variable. The original variable and the reference variable

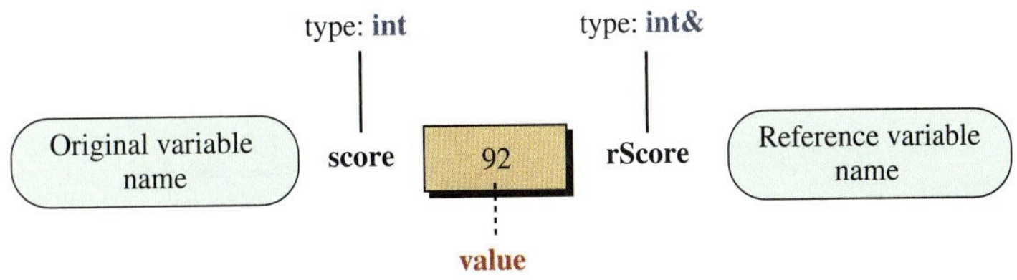

Figure 9.1 Original variable and reference variable

are in fact the same memory location called by different names. For this reason, we need to *bind* a reference variable to the original variable immediately when we declare it. Binding is done through initializing the reference variable with the name of the original variable. The following shows the creation of an original variable of type *int* named *score* and the binding of a reference variable of type *int&* to it.

```
int score = 92;                  // Declaring and initializing variable score of type int
int& rScore = score;             // Declaring variable rScore of type int& and binding it
```

Figure 9.1 shows the situation in memory. We have only one memory location, but with two names. One of the names defines the original variable; the other name defines a reference to that variable.

The interesting point is that the same value, 92, is seen as an *int* type when accessed through the *score* variable; it is seen as an *int&* type when accessed through the *rScore* variable.

The name we have used for a reference variable is the same as the original name, but we add an *r* at the beginning and make the first letter of the original name uppercase. This is not a mandate. This is our convention and helps us remember to which original variable our reference variable is bound.

Compound Type

Although the original variable and the reference variable define the same location in memory with the same value seen by both of them, the types of the original variable and the reference variable are different. For example, in Figure 9.1, the type of variable *score* is *int*, but the type of variable *rScore* is *int&*. In other words, the use of reference variables creates a new compound type: **reference type.** A reference type is a compound type because we can have a reference to an *int* (*int&*), a reference to a *double* (*double&*), a reference to a *bool* (*bool&*), and so on. When we bind a variable to a reference variable, the type of the reference variable should be a reference to the type of the original variable. The following is a compilation error. We cannot initialize a reference variable of *double&* to refer to a variable of type *int*.

```
int num = 100;
double& rNum = num;              // Compilation error. Type mismatch
```

Permanent Binding

After a reference variable has been declared and bound to a variable name, a *reference* relationship has been created between them and cannot be broken until the variables are destroyed (go out of scope). In C++ parlance, we say that the relationship between a variable and the corresponding reference variable is a constant relation. Figure 9.2 shows that we cannot change the reference relation after it has been created.

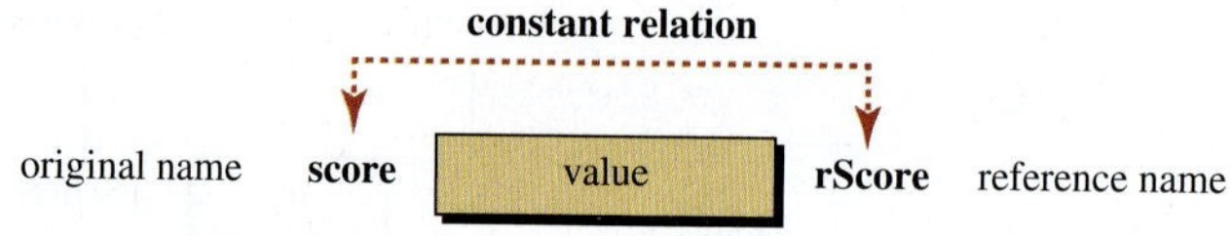

Figure 9.2 The reference relation as a constant relation

We discuss more about the constantness in reference relationships later in this chapter.

After the reference relationship is established, it cannot be changed.

EXAMPLE 9.1

We will get a compilation error if we first bind *rScore* to *score* and then try to break this relationship and bind *rScore* to *num*, as shown below:

```
int score = 92;
int& rScore = score;
int num = 80;
int& rScore = num;      // Compilation error, breaking the reference relationship
```

EXAMPLE 9.2

Sometimes we see statements that should not be confused with breaking the reference relationship. For example, consider the following:

```
int score = 92;
int& rScore = score;
int num = 80;
rScore = num;
```

In this code segment, we are not breaking the relationship. We are storing a copy of value in *num* to the common memory location established by the reference relationship. In other words, the last statement is not binding; it is an assignment to the common variable. We could have used the statement score = num with the same effect.

Multiplicity

We can have multiple reference variables bound to the same variable, but the reverse is not possible. We cannot have a reference variable bound to more than one variable.

EXAMPLE 9.3

The following shows how to bind three reference variables (*rNum1*, *rNum2*, and *rNum3*) to a single variable *num*.

```
int num = 100;
num& rNum1 = num;              // rNum1 is bound to num
num& rNum2 = num;              // rNum2 is bound to num
num& rNum3 = num;              // rNum3 is bound to num
```

This means that a memory location can be called using four names: *num*, *rNum1*, *rNum2*, and *rNum3*, as shown in Figure 9.3.

Figure 9.3 Multiple references to the same variable are allowed.

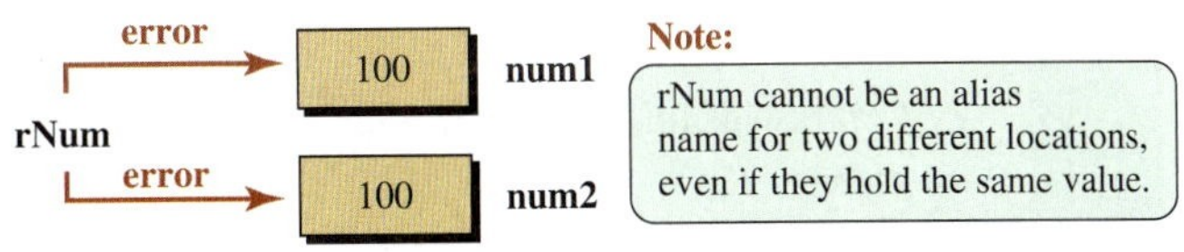

Figure 9.4 A reference to multiple variables is not allowed.

EXAMPLE 9.4

We get a compilation error if we try to bind one reference variable to more than one variable because doing so means breaking the constant reference relation and creating a new one, which is not allowed.

```
int num1 = 100;
int num2 = 200;
num& rNum = num1;          // rNum is bound to num1
num& rNum = num2;          // Compilation error. rNum cannot be bound to num2
```

Figure 9.4 shows this unacceptable relationship.

No Binding to Values

Note that a reference variable cannot be bound to a value. For example, we get a compilation error in the following statement.

```
int& x = 92;               // Compilation error: no binding to values
```

9.1.2 Retrieving Value

When the reference relationship is established, the value stored in the common memory locations can be retrieved either through the original variable or reference variable.

EXAMPLE 9.5

Program 9.1 shows the use of an original variable and its reference. However, this application is only for demonstration; the actual relationship between a variable and its reference is beneficial when we use them in two different functions, as we will see later in the chapter.

Program 9.1 Accessing value

```
/***************************************************************
 * The program shows how to declare and initialize the original   *
 * and reference variables and then access the common value       *
```

(continued)

Program 9.1 Accessing value (Continued)

```
 * through either of them.                                            *
 ***********************************************************************/
#include <iostream>
using namespace std;

int main ( )
{
   // Creation of reference relations
   int score = 92;
   int& rScore = score;
   // Using data variable
   cout << "Accessing value through data variable." << endl;
   cout << "score: " << score << endl;
   // Using reference variable
   cout << "Accessing value through reference variable." << endl;
   cout << "rScore: " << rScore;
   return 0;
}
```

```
Run:
Accessing value through data variable.
score: 92
Accessing value through reference variable.
rScore: 92
```

9.1.3 Changing Value

There is only one value in a reference relationship, but the value can be changed either through the original variable or through any of the reference variables, unless we use *const* modifiers (Figure 9.5).

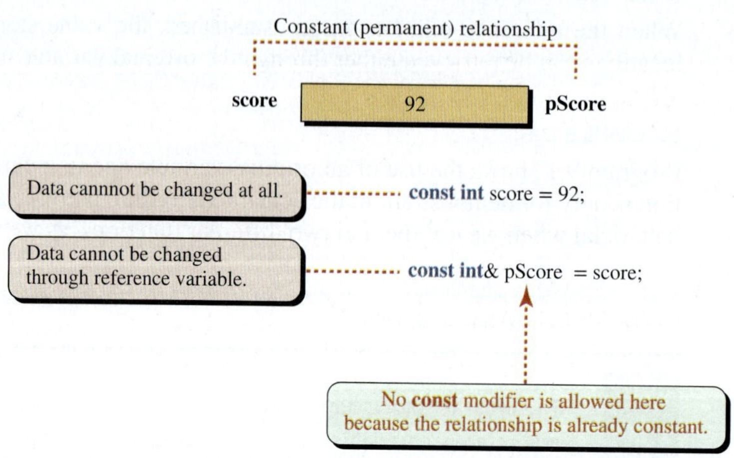

Figure 9.5 Preventing change in a reference relation

Table 9.1 Four possible combinations

Case	Data variable	Reference variable	Status
1	int name = value;	int& rName = name;	OK
2	const int name = value;	int& rName = name;	Error
3	int name = value;	const int& rName = name;	OK
4	const int name = value;	const int& rName = name;	OK

The constant modifier can be put in front of the original variable or in front of the reference variable. The relationship (binding) is by nature constant and cannot be broken. Figure 9.5 shows the use of a *const* modifier for both the original and the reference variables.

Table 9.1 shows the four possible combinations, but the second one creates a compilation error, as we describe shortly.

First Case

In the first case, there is no restriction to changing the value either through the original variable or through the reference variable.

Second Case

The second case creates a compilation error because we try to bind a nonconstant reference variable to a constant variable. Since the original variable is already constant, there is no way that we can change its value through the reference variable.

Third Case

In the third case, the data can be changed through the data variable, but we want to restrict it from being changed through the reference variable.

Fourth Case

In the fourth case, we want to create an original variable and a reference variable in a way that neither the original variable nor the reference variable can change the common value. This case has little application because the data variable and the reference variables can only be used to retrieve data, not to change them.

9.1.4 Applications

Using references in the same namespace, such as in the same function, is unnecessary because we can always use the original variable instead of the reference variable. Both variables use the same memory location. The idea of references is beneficial when the two variables are in different scopes, like in a calling function and the called function. We can save memory by using one memory location and accessing it in two functions using the original variable and the reference variable.

In this section we discuss the use of references in the communication between two functions. We discuss using references in passing data to a function and in returning data from a function. The first application is called pass-by-reference; the second is called return-by-reference.

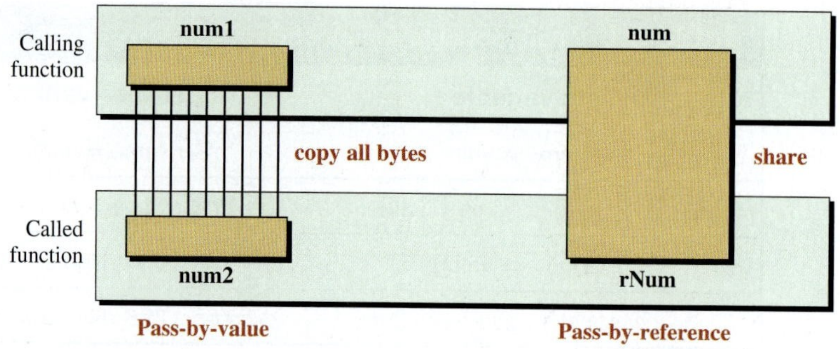

Figure 9.6 Comparing pass-by-value and pass-by-reference

Pass-by-Reference

In the first case, **pass-by-reference,** a calling function has an object (or objects) that it needs to send to the called function for processing. In Chapter 6 we used pass-by-value; now we use pass-by-reference. Both methods are shown in Figure 9.6.

We write two small programs, side by side, to compare the two methods. Assume we want a function that processes integers passed to it. The function can be designed as pass-by-value or pass-by-reference as shown below:

```
#include <iostream>
using namespace std;
// Prototype
void doIt (int);

int main ()
{
   int num = 10;
   doIt (num);
   return 0;
}
// Pass-by-value
void doIt (int num)
{
   // Code
}
```

```
#include <iostream>
using namespace std;
// Prototype
void doIt (int&);

int main ()
{
   int num = 10;
   doIt (num);
   return 0;
}
// Pass-by-reference
void doIt (int& rNum)
{
   // Code
}
```

Characteristics of Pass-by-Value In the pass-by-value method, the calling function sends a copy of its argument to the called function. The copy becomes the parameter in the called function. In other words, the following statement is done in the background:

```
int num2 = num1;
```

- In pass-by-value, we have two independent objects: the argument and the parameter. This means that changes in the parameter, intentional or accidental, cannot affect the argument. This may be an advantage in one situation and a disadvantage in another situation.

- Another issue in using pass-by-value is the cost of copying. Copying all bytes of the argument can be costly if the object to be copied is large. This means that if the object to be passed is of a fundamental type, we should not worry because the number of bytes to be copied is small (normally less that eight). However, if we need to copy an object of class type with thousands of bytes, we should consider other methods.

Characteristics of Pass-by-Reference In the pass-by-reference method, the parameter is only a reference to the argument. The binding between the two occurs in the background as part of the running environment, as shown below:

```
int& rNum = num;
```

- In pass-by-reference, the argument and the parameter are exactly the same object; we are saving memory allocation. Any change in the parameter means the same change in the argument unless we use a constant reference, as we discussed previously.
- It is obvious that pass-by-reference eliminates the cost of copying. The argument and the parameter are the same object. We must consider this method when we want to pass a large object, such as an object of class type, to a called function.

Recommendation Now that we have discussed the pros and cons of each method of passing an argument to a function, we consider the following recommendations, which will help us decide which method to use.

1. If we need to prevent change, we should use

   a. pass-by-value for small objects.
   b. pass-by-constant reference for large objects.

2. If there is a need for change, we should use pass-by-reference.

Warning We cannot bind a reference parameter to a value argument. For example, the following code creates a compilation error.

```
void fun (int& rX) { ... }          // Function definition
fun (5);                            // Function call (compilation error)
```

The parameter rX is a reference parameter. The argument of the function call must be a variable name, not a value.

EXAMPLE 9.6

Assume we want to write a function to print the value of a fundamental data type. We do not want to change the value of the data in the calling function. This is the first case in our recommendation; we can use either pass-by-value or pass-by-constant reference. Since the object is small, we can use pass-by-value. We have given several examples of this situation previously.

EXAMPLE 9.7

Assume we want to write a copy constructor for a class. This is also the first case in our recommendation because we do not want the function to change the original object. However, pass-by-value is costly (the object can be large) and, more important, it is impossible because pass-by-value needs the call to the copy constructor to copy the object, which means we need the copy constructor to create a copy constructor (vicious circle). The C++ standard says we must use pass-by-constant reference as shown below:

```
// Pass-by-reference in copy constructor
Circle :: Circle (const Circle& circle)
: radius (circle.radius)
{
}
```

EXAMPLE 9.8

Assume we want to write a function to swap two data items. This is the second case in our recommendation. We need change, so we use pass-by-reference as shown in Program 9.2.

Program 9.2 Using a swap function with pass-by-reference

```
/***************************************************************
 * The program shows how to use pass-by-reference to allow a    *
 * called function to swap two values in the calling function.  *
 ***************************************************************/
#include <iostream>
using namespace std;

void swap (int& first, int& second) ; // Prototype

int main ( )
{
   // Definition of two variables
   int x = 10;
   int y = 20;
   // Printing the value of x and y before swapping
   cout << "Values of x and y before swapping." << endl;
   cout << "x: " << x << "   " << "y: " << y << endl;
   // Calling swap function to swap the values of x and y
   swap (x , y);
   // Printing the value of x and y after swapping
   cout << "Values of x and y after swapping." << endl;
   cout << "x: " << x << "   " << "y: " << y;
   return 0;
}
/***************************************************************
 * The swap function swaps the values of the parameters and     *
 * pass-by-reference allows the corresponding arguments in main *
 * to be swapped accordingly.                                   *
 ***************************************************************/
void swap (int& rX, int& rY)
{
```

(continued)

Program 9.2 Using a swap function with pass-by-reference (Continued)

```
    int temp = rX;
    rX = rY;
    rY = temp;
}
```

Run:

```
Values of x and y before swapping.
x: 10  y: 20
Values of x and y after swapping.
x: 20  y: 10
```

Return-by-Reference

In the second case, **return-by-reference,** a called function has an object that must be returned to the calling function.

Characteristics of Return-by-Value In **return-by-value,** the called function returns an object of the desired type using the following prototype.

```
type function (...);
```

Return-by-value is simple and can be used anywhere. We can return the value of a parameter or a local variable. The only drawback is the cost of copying. If the object to be returned is a fundamental type, we should not worry; if it is an object of a class type, we know that the copy constructor will be called and the cost may be high.

Characteristics of Return-by-Reference In **return-by-reference,** the type of the object to be returned is a reference to another object, as shown in the following prototype.

```
type& function (...);
```

This method eliminates the cost of copying, but it has a drawback: We cannot return an object by reference if it is a value parameter or a local variable (except static). The reason, as we will discuss later in the chapter, is that when a function is terminated all local variables and value parameters are destroyed. When an object is destroyed, we cannot have an alias name to it, but we can return a reference to a reference parameter.

EXAMPLE 9.9

Assume we want to write a function to find the larger between two integers. We could use either the combination of pass-by-value and return-by-value or the combination of pass-by-reference and return-by-reference. The following shows the two programs side by side for comparison.

```
#include <iostream>
using namespace std;
```

```
#include <iostream>
using namespace std;
```

```
// Return-by-value
int larger (int x, int y )
{
   if (x > y)
   {
        return x;
   }
   return y;
}
int main ()
{
   int x = 10;
   int y = 20;
   int z = larger (x, y);
   cout << z;
   return 0;
}
```

Run:
20

```
// Return-by-reference
int& larger (int& x, int& y )
{
   if (x > y)
   {
        return x;
   }
   return y;
}
int main ()
{
   int x = 10;
   int y = 20;
   int z = larger (x, y);
   cout << z;
   return 0;
}
```

Run:
20

We see examples of both practices in cases like this because the cost of copying is small in pass-by-value and return-by-value.

EXAMPLE 9.10

In this example we find the larger between two objects of class types. In Chapter 7 we created a *fraction* class. We do not repeat the interface and the implementation file here (separate compilation). We just create an application file that uses pass-by-reference and return-by-reference to find the smaller of two fractions. Program 9.3 shows the application file.

Program 9.3 Finding the larger of two fractions

```
/*****************************************************************
 * The program creates two pairs of fractions and then calls a      *
 * function named larger to find the larger in each pair            *
 *****************************************************************/
#include "fraction.h"

Fraction& larger (Fraction&, Fraction&); // Prototype

int main ( )
{
  // Creating first pair of fractions and finding the larger
  Fraction fract1 (3, 13);
  Fraction fract2 (5, 17);
  cout << "Larger of the first pair of fraction: " ;
  larger (fract1, fract2).print ();
  // Creating second pair of fractions and finding the larger
```

(continued)

Program 9.3 Finding the larger of two fractions (Continued)

```
17      Fraction fract3 (4, 9);
18      Fraction fract4 (1, 6);
19      cout << "Larger of the second pair of fractions: " ;
20      larger (fract3, fract4).print ();
21      return 0;
22  }
23  /****************************************************************
24   * The function gets two fractions by reference, compares them  *
25   * and returns the larger.                                      *
26   ****************************************************************/
27  Fraction& larger (Fraction& fract1, Fraction& fract2)
28  {
29      if (fract1.getNumer() * fract2.getDenom() >
30                              fract2.getNumer() * fract1.getDenom())
31      {
32          return fract1;
33      }
34      return fract2;
35  }
```

```
Run:
Larger of first pair of fractions: 5/17
Larger of second pair of fractions: 4/9
```

The interesting point is that in each call, the returned item is an *lvalue*, one of the objects that was sent to the function. This is why we can apply the *print* function defined in the class to the object (lines 17 and 22).

9.2 POINTERS

A **pointer type** is a compound type representing the address of a memory location. A pointer variable is a variable whose contents are of pointer type. In this section, we discuss addresses, pointer types, pointer variables, and some related issues.

9.2.1 Addresses

When we talk about addresses, we must consider two separate concepts: addresses in memory and the address of a variable.

Addresses in Memory

As we discussed briefly in Chapter 1, computer memory is a sequence of bytes. In other words, the smallest accessible unit is a *byte*. When we say that a computer has a memory (random access memory, or RAM) of 1 kilobyte, we mean that memory is made of 2^{10} or 1024 bytes. Today's computers have memories in the range of megabytes (2^{20}), gigabytes (2^{30}), or even terabytes (2^{40}).

Each byte of memory has an address. The addresses are shown in hexadecimal format. For example, in a computer with 1 kilobyte of memory, the bytes are numbered from 0x000 to 0x3ff (0 to 1023 in decimal) as shown in Figure 9.7.

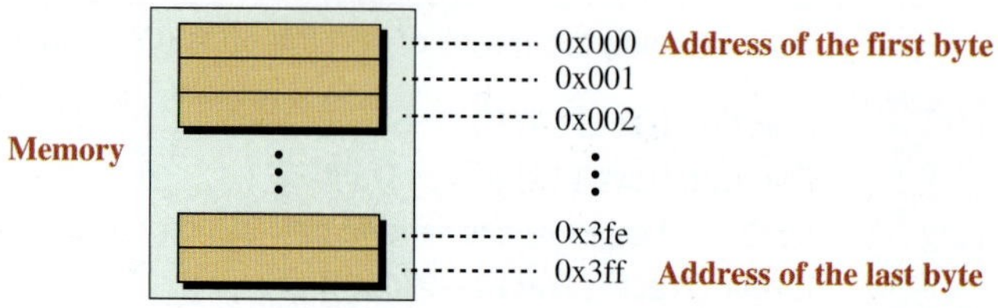

Figure 9.7 Addresses in 1 kilobyte of RAM

Address of a Variable

In our programs, we define variables of different types: Boolean, character, integer, floating point, and class. Each variable occupies one or more bytes of memory. A variable of type *bool* or *char* normally occupies one byte of memory. A variable of type *int* may occupy four or more bytes of memory. A variable of type *double* may also occupy four or more bytes of memory (the *sizeof* operator can be used to determine the number of bytes). The address of a variable is the address of the first byte it occupies. This is an important point we must remember when we are working with addresses or pointers, as we will see. To get the address of a variable, we use the **address operator** (&) in front of the variable.

> **The address of a variable is the address of the first byte occupied by that variable.**

EXAMPLE 9.11

In this example we write a simple program that prints the addresses of three variables: *bool*, *int*, and *double* (Program 9.4).

Program 9.4 Printing size, value, and addresses

```
/***************************************************************
 * The program to define three variables and to print their    *
 * values and their addresses in the memory                    *
 ***************************************************************/
#include <iostream>
using namespace std;

int main ( )
{
   // Declaration of three data variables
   bool flag = true;
   int score = 92;
   double average = 82.56;
   // Printing size, value, and address of the flag variable
   cout << "A variable of type bool" << endl;
   cout << "Size: " << sizeof (flag) << "  ";
   cout << "Value: " << flag << "  ";
   cout << "Address: "<< &flag << endl << endl;
```

(continued)

Program 9.4 Printing size, value, and addresses (Continued)

```
    // Printing size, value, and address of the score variable
    cout << "A variable of type int" << endl;
    cout << "Size: " << sizeof (score) << "  ";
    cout << "Value: " << score << "  ";
    cout << "Address: "<< &score << endl << endl;
    // Printing size, value, and address of the average variable
    cout << "A variable of type double" << endl;
    cout << "Size: " << sizeof (average) << "  ";
    cout << "Value: " << average << "  ";
    cout << "Address: "<< &average << endl;
    return 0;
}
```

Run:

```
A variable of type bool
Size: 1  Value: 1   Address: 0x28fef0

A variable of type int
Size: 4  Value: 92   Address: 0x28fef1

A variable of type double
Size: 8  Value: 82.56   Address: 0x28fef5
```

There are three important points about Program 9.4:

- The extraction operator (<<) is overloaded so that it can accept an address. Therefore, we can use the expression *cout << &score* to print the address of the variables.
- The addresses are displayed using hexadecimal notation. The addresses are not integers; they are pointer types, as we will see shortly.
- The sizes and addresses may be different in different systems. The addresses may start from the smallest to largest or vice versa. There may be some gaps in the addresses.

Figure 9.8 shows the addresses as printed in Program 9.5.

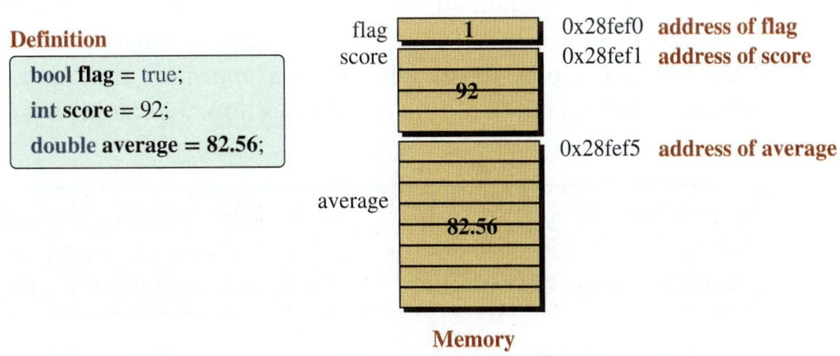

Figure 9.8 Memory situation declared and defined in Program 9.5

9.2.2 Pointer Types and Pointer Variables

We can manipulate addresses because C++ defines the *pointer type* and allows us to use pointer variables.

Pointer Types

The pointer type is a compound type whose literal values are addresses. It is a compound type in the sense that we have pointer to *char* (address of a *char* variable), pointer to *int* (address of an *int* variable), pointer to *double* (address of a *double* variable), and so on. Note that we only talk about the address of a variable, not a value, because a value is always stored in a variable in memory. To create a pointer to a type, we add the asterisk symbol after the type. The following shows some pointer types.

```
bool*                                   // A pointer to an object of bool type
int*                                    // A pointer to an object of int type
double*                                 // A pointer to an object of double type
Circle*                                 // A pointer to an object of Circle type
```

To create a pointer to a type, we add the asterisk symbol to the type.

Pointer Variables

We can store the value of a pointer type in a pointer variable. Although we can have different pointer types, what is stored in a pointer variable is a 4-byte address. In other words, the size of a pointer variable is fixed in C++, which means that a pointer variable can have an address from 0x00000000 to 0xFFFFFFFF.

Declaration To use pointers, we need pointer variables. To declare a pointer variable, we need to tell the computer that it is a pointer to a specific type. The following are declaration examples. The selection of names is our choice because we later bind these pointer variables to the corresponding data variables.

```
bool* pFlag;                      // pFlag is variable of pointer type to bool
int* pScore;                      // pScore is variable of pointer type to int
double* pAverage;                 // pAverage is variable of pointer type to double
```

We read the declaration from right to left (*pFlag* is a pointer to a *bool*).

Initialization A pointer variable, like a data variable, must be initialized before being used. It must be initialized with a valid address in memory, which means that we cannot initialize it with a literal address; the address must be that of an existing variable. To meet this criterion, we use the *address operator*, the ampersand. We will discuss this operator shortly, but the following shows how we can initialize our three declared pointer variables.

```
bool* pFlag = &flag;              // Initialize pFlag with address of flag
int* pScore = &score;             // Initialize pScore with address of score
double* pAverage = &average;      // Initialize pAverage with address of average
```

Pointer initialization has some restrictions. Since *pFlag* is a pointer to a variable of type *bool*, it must be initialized with the address of a variable of type *bool*. Similarly, since

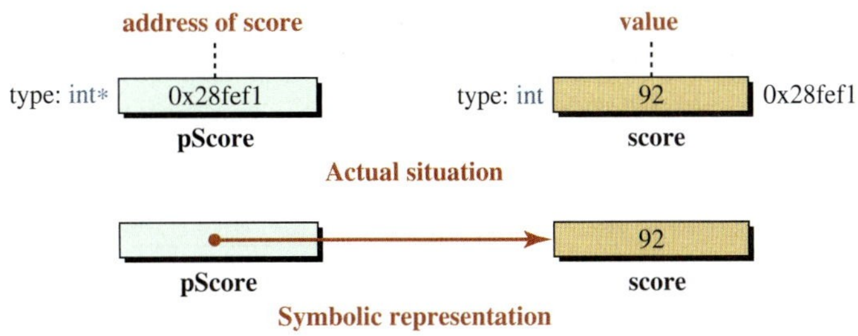

Figure 9.9 The pointed and the pointer variables

pScore is a pointer to a variable of type *int*, it must be initialized with the address of a type *int*. Figure 9.9 shows the actual and symbolic relationship between a pointer variable (*pScore*) and the corresponding pointed variable (*score*).

EXAMPLE 9.12

The following is a compilation error. We cannot assign pointer literals to pointer variables.

```
double* pAverage = 0x123467;          // Compilation Error. No literal addresses
```

EXAMPLE 9.13

The following is a compilation error. We cannot assign the address of an *int* variable to a pointer of type *double*.

```
int num;
double* p = &num;                     // Compilation Error. Variable p is of type double*
```

Indirection (Dereference)

Declaration and initialization of pointer variables allows us to use the address stored in the pointer variable to access the value stored in the pointed variable. This is done through the **indirection operator** (also called the dereference operator) using the asterisk symbol as shown below:

```
*pFlage;                              // value stored in flag
*pScore;                              // value stored in score
*pAverage;                            // value stored in average
```

You may ask why we need to use the indirection operator to retrieve or change the value of the variable *flag* when we can do so directly. The answer, as we will see later in the section, is that we use different approaches (direct and indirect accesses) in different domains. For example, we use the direct approach in a calling function and the indirect approach in the corresponding called function.

Two Related Operators

The two operators we use in this section are the *address-of operator* and the *indirection operator*. These two operators are unary operators defined in Appendix C and shown in Table 9.2.

Table 9.2 The address expression

Group	Name	Operator	Expression	Pred	Assoc
Unary	address-of indirection	& *	&lvalue * pointer	17	←

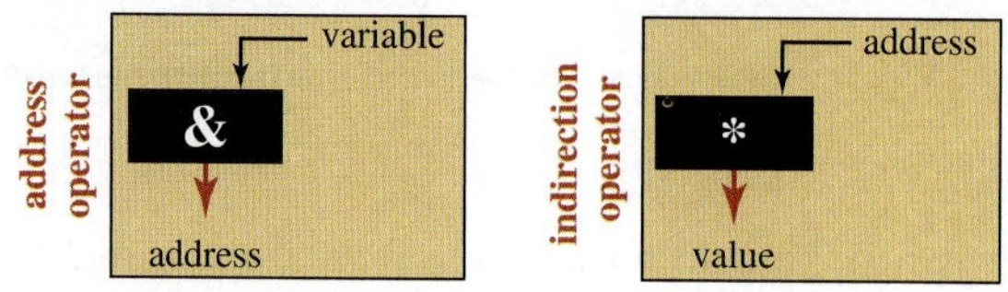

Figure 9.10 Address-of operator and indirection operator

Figure 9.10 shows how these two operators are used. The address-of operator takes a variable and returns its address; the indirection operator takes an address and returns the value of the corresponding pointed variable.

C++ uses the ampersand and the asterisk symbols for three purposes as shown in Table 9.3.

The **ampersand symbol** is used to define a reference type. It can also be used as a unary operator to get the address of a variable. It is also used as a binary bitwise AND operator (discussed in Appendix C). When it is used to define a reference type, it is put after the type (*int&*). When it is used to get the address of a variable, it is put before the variable name (&score). When it is used as a binary operator, it is used between the two operands.

The asterisk symbol can also be used in three situations: as a pointer type, as a unary operator to get the value of a pointed variable, and as a binary multiplication operator. When it is used to define a pointer type, it is put after the type (*int**). When it is used to indirectly access a value, it is put before the pointer (*pScore). When it is used as a binary operator, it is used between the two operands.

9.2.3 Retrieving Value

After the pointer relationship is established, we can retrieve the value stored in the memory location either through the data variable or pointer variable.

EXAMPLE 9.14

In this example we write a simple program that accesses the values of a data variable directly and indirectly (Program 9.5).

Table 9.3 Uses of ampersand and asterisk operators

Symbol	Type definition	Unary operator	Binary operator
&	type&	&variable	x & y
*	type*	*pointer	x * y

Program 9.5 Direct and indirect retrieval of data

```
/*****************************************************************
 * The program shows how to access (retrieve or change) the value      *
 * of a data variable both directly and indirectly.                     *
 *****************************************************************/
#include <iostream>
using namespace std;

int main ( )
{
   // Declaration and initialization of variables
   int score = 92;
   int* pScore = &score;
   // Retrieving value of data variable directly and indirectly
   cout << "Direct retrieve of score: " << score << endl;
   cout << "Indirect retrieve of score: " << *pScore;
   return 0;
}
```

```
Run:
Direct retrieve of score: 92
Indirect retrieve of score 92
```

9.2.4 Using Constant Modifiers

One of the issues that is a source of confusion and error is how to control changes to a data variable and a pointer. Changes are controlled through the use of *const* modifiers. We can use up to three *const* modifiers, each with a different purpose, as shown in Figure 9.11. The first two are related to changing data; the third is related to changing the relationship between the data variable and the pointer variable.

Controlling Data Change

Table 9.4 shows the four possible combinations that we can use to control data change.

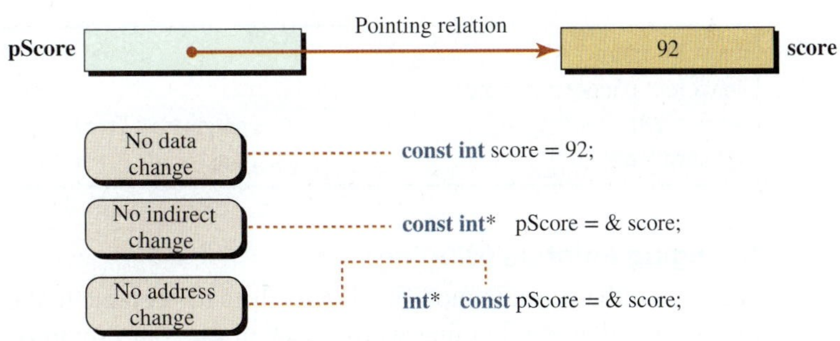

Figure 9.11 Three uses of constant modifiers in relation to pointers

Table 9.4 Four possible combinations

Case	Data variable	Pointer variable
1	int name = value;	int* pName = &name;
2 (forbidden)	const int name = value;	int* pName = &name;
3	int name = value;	const int& pName = &name;
4	const int name = value;	const int& pName= &name;

First Case In the first case, there is no restriction on changing the value either through the data variable or through the pointer variable.

```
int score = 92;
int* pScore = &score;
score = 80;                          // Change through data variable
*pScore = 70;                        // Change through pointer variable
```

Second Case The second case is a forbidden case. We get a compilation error when we try to bind the data variable to the pointer variable. Since the data variable is already constant, there is no way that we can bind it to a nonconstant pointer type.

```
const int score = 92;
int* pScore = &score;                // Compilation error
```

Third Case In the third case, the data can be changed through the data variable, but we want to prevent it from being changed through the pointer variable. If we try to change it through the pointer variable, we get a compilation error.

```
int score = 92;
const int* pScore = &score;
score = 80;
*pScore = 80;                        // Compilation Error
```

Fourth Case In the fourth case, we want to create both a data variable and a pointer variable that cannot be changed. This case has little application because data variables and pointer variables can only be used to retrieve data, not to change them.

```
const int score = 92;
const int* pScore = &score;
score = 80;                          // Compilation Error
*pScore = 80;                        // Compilation Error
```

Changing Pointers (Binding)

We can use the constant modifier to bind the data variable to the pointer variable for the lifetime of the program. In other words, each of the four previous cases can be combined with either a nonconstant or a constant pointer (Table 9.5).

Table 9.5 Eight possible combinations

Changing relationship between the data variable and the pointer variable	
any-of-four-previous-cases pName = &name;	// Changeable
any-of-four-previous-cases const pName = &name;	// Unchangeable

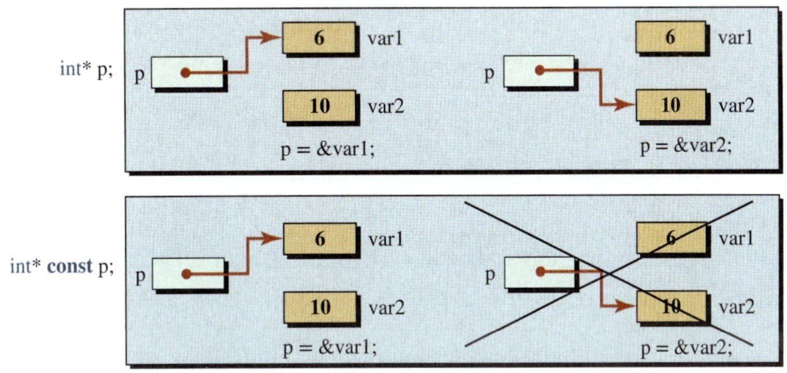

Figure 9.12 Constant pointing relationship cannot be broken.

Figure 9.12 shows that if the pointing relationship is constant, we cannot break the relationship and make the pointer point to another data variable. Note that in this case, the *const* modifier must be put in front of the name of the pointer variable.

9.2.5 Pointer to Pointer

A pointer variable is a location in memory. Can we store the address of this memory location in another memory location? The answer is yes. We can have new types: *pointer to pointer to int*, *pointer to pointer to double*, and so on. We can even go further and have a *pointer to pointer to pointer to int* and so on. But more than two levels are rarely seen in practice. When we use double asterisks after a type, we mean pointer to pointer to type, as shown below:

```
int score = 92;                  // Declaration and initialization of score
const int* pScore = &score;      // Binding pScore to score
int** ppScore = &pscore;         // Binding ppScore to pscore
```

Figure 9.13 shows the concept of pointer to pointer.

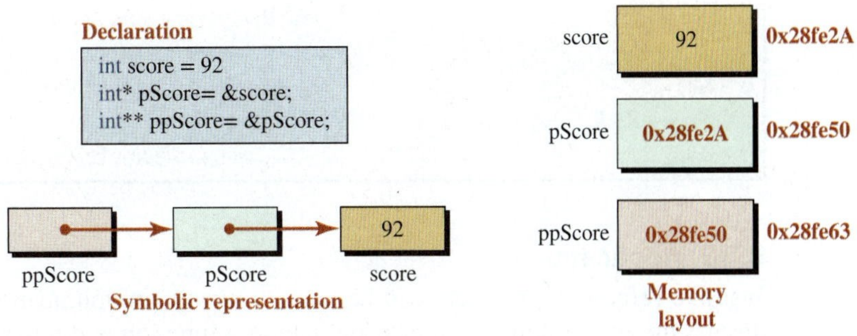

Figure 9.13 A pointer to pointer to *int*

9.2.6 Two Special Pointers

Sometimes we see two special pointers: pointer to nowhere and pointer to void. We briefly explain these two pointers; we will see more applications in future chapters.

Pointer to Nowhere: Null Pointer

A pointer to nowhere (sometimes called a **null pointer**) is a pointer that points to no memory location. Although the C language used the word NULL to define such a pointer, the C++ language prefers to use the literal 0. In other words, if we want to show that a pointer is not pointing to any memory location at this moment, we can bind it to 0 as shown below.

```
int* p1 = 0;
double* p2 = 0;
```

Note that neither of the previous two statements means that *p1* or *p2* is pointing to the memory location at 0x0. The byte at this address is used for the system and is not available to the user. The literal value 0 simply means that the pointer at this moment is pointing to nowhere.

The programmer assigns 0 to a pointer to show that the pointer cannot be used until it is bound to a valid address. Note that when a name is declared, it cannot become invalid until it goes out of scope. Assigning 0 to a pointer variable means that declaration is still valid, but we cannot use it. If a logic error does try use the pointer, the program aborts.

When a pointer is not null, its value can be interpreted as true; when it is null, its value can be interpreted as false. This means we can always check to see if a pointer is null or not as shown below:

```
int x = 7;
int* p = &x;
if (p) {...}                          // Test is true here (p is not null)
p = 0;
if (p) {...}                          // Test is false here (p null)
```

Pointer to Void: Generic Pointer

A *void* pointer is a **generic pointer.** It can point to an object of any type. The following shows how we can use a generic pointer to point to any type. Assume that we first need to point it to an *int* object and later to a *double* object. Note that a *void* pointer cannot be redirected until it is cast to an appropriate type.

```
void* p;                              // Declaring a void pointer
int x = 10;
p = &x;                               // Make p to point to an int type
double y = 23.4;
p = &y;                               // Make p to point to a double type
```

9.2.7 Applications

Just like references, pointers can be used to create communication between functions. We discuss the use of pointers in passing data to a function and returning data from a function. The first application is called pass-by-pointer; the second is called return-by-pointer.

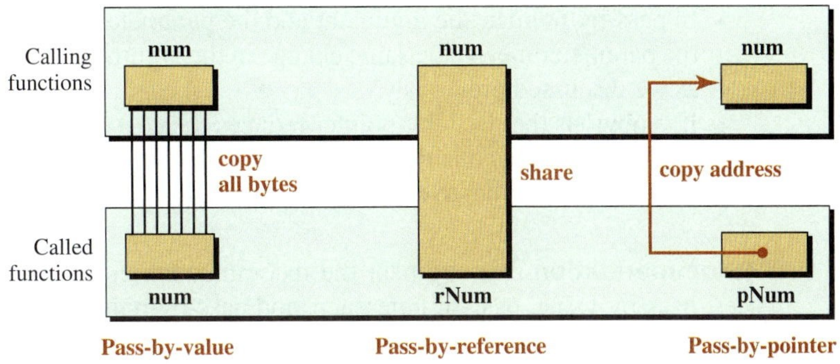

Figure 9.14 Comparing three methods of passing data to a function

Pass-by-Pointer

Pointers can be used to send data from a calling function to a called function. We show pass-by-value, pass-by-reference, and pass-by-pointer in Figure 9.14. In the third case, **pass-by-pointer,** the calling function sends the address of the object (argument) to the called function and the called function stores it in a pointer (parameter). Unlike the case of pass-by-reference, there is no sharing here. The run-time system must copy the address of the argument in the calling function and send it to the called function. However, the cost of copying is not as high in the case of pass-by-value. It is a fixed cost of copying a 4-byte address.

We write two small programs, side by side, to compare the two methods. Assume we want to have a function that does something to an integer passed to it. The function can be designed as pass-by-value or pass-by-pointer, as shown below:

```
#include <iostream>
using namespace std;
// Prototype
void doIt (int);

int main ()
{
   int num1 = 10;
   doIt (num1);
   return 0;
}
// Pass-by-value
void doIt (int num2)
{
   // Code
}
```

```
#include <iostream>
using namespace std;
// Prototype
void doIt (int*);

int main ()
{
   int num = 10;
   doIt (&num);
   return 0;
}
// Pass-by-pointer
void doIt (int* pNum)
{
   // Code
}
```

Characteristics of Pass-by-Pointer We discussed the characteristics of pass-by-value and pass-by-reference previously. In the pass-by-pointer method, the parameter is the address of the argument. The binding between the two occurs in the background as part of the running environment, as shown below:

```
int* pNum = &num;
```

- In pass-by-pointer, the argument and the parameter are bound together. Any change in the parameter means the same change in the argument unless we use a constant pointer, as we discussed previously.
- It is obvious that pass-by-pointer reduces the cost of copying. Only a 4-byte address is copied. We must consider this method when we want to pass a large object, such as an object of class type, to a called function.

Recommendation We augment the recommendation we made previously to three practices: pass-by-value, pass-by-reference, and pass-by-pointer.

1. If we need to prevent change, we must use
   a. pass-by-value for small objects.
   b. pass-by-constant reference or pass-by-constant pointer for large objects.
2. If there is a need for change, we must use pass-by-reference or pass-by-pointer.

EXAMPLE 9.15

Assume we want to write a function to print the value of a fundamental data type. We do not want to change the value of the data in the calling function. This is the first case in our recommendation. Since the object is small, we can use pass-by-value.

EXAMPLE 9.16

Assume we want to write a function to swap two data items. This is the second case in our recommendation. We showed how to use pass-by-reference previously; in Program 9.6 we show how to use pass-by-pointer.

Program 9.6 Using a swap function with pass-by-pointer

```
/***************************************************************
  * The program shows how to use pass-by-pointer to allow a         *
  * called function to swap two values in the calling function.     *
  ***************************************************************/
#include <iostream>
using namespace std;

void swap (int* first, int* second) ; // Prototype

int main ( )
{
   // Definition of two variables
   int x = 10;
   int y = 20;
   // Printing the value of x and y before swapping
   cout << "Values of x and y before swapping." << endl;
   cout << "x: " << x << "   " << "y: " << y << endl;
```

(continued)

Program 9.6 Using a swap function with pass-by-pointer (Continued)

```
    // Calling swap function to swap the values of x and y
    swap (&x , &y);
    // Printing the value of x and y after swapping
    cout << "Values of x and y after swapping." << endl;
    cout << "x: " << x << "   " << "y: " << y;
    return 0;
}
/*************************************************************
 * The swap function swaps the values of parameters and      *
 * pass-by-pointer allows the corresponding arguments in main *
 * to be swapped accordingly.                                  *
 *************************************************************/
void swap (int* pX, int* pY)
{
    int temp = *pX;
    *pX= *pY;
    *pY = temp;
}
```

```
Run:
Values of x and y before swapping.
x: 10  y: 20
Values of x and y after swapping.
x: 20  y: 10
```

Return-by-Pointer

In the second case, **return-by-pointer,** a called function has an object that must be returned to the calling function. We can use return-by-pointer.

Characteristics of Return-by-Pointer

In this case, the type of the object to be returned is a pointer to a function parameter, which itself is a pointer to an object in the calling function, as shown in the following prototype:

```
type* function (type* ...);
```

As we discussed in the case of return-by-reference, this practice has some drawbacks, most notable the following: We cannot return a pointer to a value parameter or to a local variable. When the called function is terminated, all local objects and value parameters are destroyed and there is no longer an object to point to.

EXAMPLE 9.17

Assume we want to write a function to find the larger of two integers. We could use either the combination of pass-by-value and return-by-value or the combination of pass-by-pointer and return-by-pointer. The following shows the two programs side by side for comparison.

```
#include <iostream>
using namespace std;

int larger (int x, int y )
{
   if (x > y)
   {
        return x;
   }
   return y;
}
int main ()
{
   int x = 10;
   int y = 20;
   int z = larger (x, y);
   cout << z;
   return 0;
}
```

Run:
20

```
#include <iostream>
using namespace std;

int* larger (int* x, int* y )
{
   if (*x > *y)
   {
        return x;
   }
   return y;
}
int main ()
{
   int x = 10;
   int y = 20;
   int z = *larger (&x, &y);
   cout << z;
   return 0;
}
```

Run:
20

We will see examples of both practices in cases like this because the cost of copying is not large in pass-by-pointer and return-by-pointer.

EXAMPLE 9.18

In this example we find the larger of two objects of class type. We used return-by-reference previously; now we use return-by-pointer. We create an application file that uses pass-by-pointer and return-by-pointer to find the smaller of two fractions. Program 9.7 shows the application file.

Note that the member select expression, (*object -> member*), is in fact a shortcut for the expression (**object.member*). Both were discussed in Chapter 7. Also note that the object returned by a pointer is an lvalue, which means we can apply the member function *print* to the returned object as shown in lines 17 and 22.

Program 9.7 Finding the larger between two objects

```
1  /*********************************************************************
2   * The program creates two pairs of fractions and then calls a        *
3   * function named larger to find the larger in each pair.             *
4   *********************************************************************/
5  #include "fraction.h"
6  #include <iostream>
7  using namespace std;
8
9  Fraction* larger (Fraction*, Fraction*); // Prototype
```

(*continued*)

Program 9.7 Finding the larger between two objects (Continued)

```

int main ( )
{
   // Creating the first pair of fractions
   Fraction fract1 (3, 13);
   Fraction fract2 (5, 17);
   cout << "Larger of the first pair of fraction: " ;
   larger (&fract1, &fract2) -> print ();
   // Creating the second pair of fractions
   Fraction fract3 (4, 9);
   Fraction fract4 (1, 6);
   cout << "Larger of the second pair of fractions: " ;
   larger (&fract3, &fract4) -> print ();
   return 0;
}
/*************************************************************
  * The function gets two fractions by pointer, compares them     *
  * and returns the larger of the two.                             *
  *************************************************************/
Fraction* larger (Fraction* fract1, Fraction* fract2)
{
   if (fract1 -> getNumer() * fract2 -> getDenom() >
                          fract2 -> getNumer() * fract1 ->getDenom())
   {
        return fract1;
   }
   return fract2;
}
```

```
Run:
Larger of first pair of fractions: 5/17
Larger of second pair of fractions: 4/9
```

9.3 ARRAYS AND POINTERS

In C++, arrays and pointers are intertwined with each other. In this section we learn how one-dimensional and two-dimensional arrays can be represented by pointers.

9.3.1 One-Dimensional Arrays and Pointers

When we declare an array named *arr* of type t and of capacity N, the system creates N memory locations of type t. The system then creates a constant pointer of type t that is pointed to the first element, as shown in Figure 9.15.

That the pointer is constant means its contents (address) cannot be changed. It is always pointing to the first element. Since the address of the first element is fixed, we know

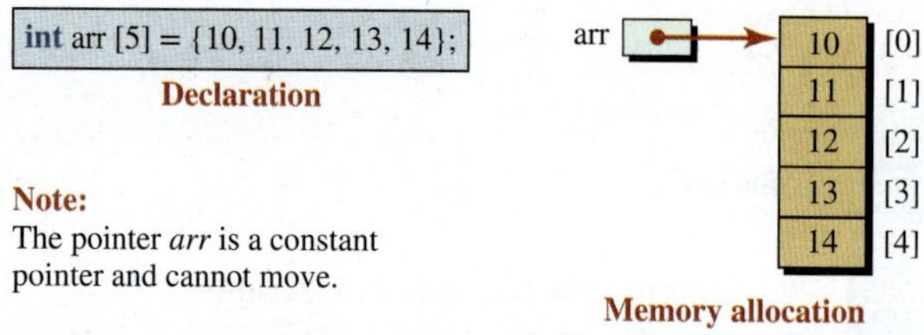

Figure 9.15 Relationship between an array and a pointer

the address of all the elements. The address of the element at index 0 is *arr* (or *arr* + 0); the address of the element at index 1 is *arr* + 1; and so on.

The name of the array is a constant pointer to the first element.

To demonstrate, we write a program and print the addresses of the array elements defined in Figure 9.15. We use the value of both the pointers and the address operator to prove that they are the same (Program 9.8). The program demonstrates that we can access the address of each element using either constant pointers or indexes. In fact, the indexes are

Program 9.8 A program to check the address of each array element

```
/***************************************************************
 * The program proves that the system stores the address of each   *
 * element in the array in a constant pointer.                      *
 ***************************************************************/
#include <iostream>
using namespace std;

int main ()
{
  // Declaration of an array of five int
  int arr [5];
  // Printing the addresses through pointers and the & operator
  for (int i = 0; i < 5; i++)
  {
      cout << "Address of cell " << i << " Using pointer: ";
      cout << arr + i << endl;
      cout << "Address of cell " << i << " Using & operator: ";
      cout << &arr [i] << endl << endl;
  }
  return 0;
}
```

Run:

```
Address of cell 0 Using pointer: 0x28fee8
Address of cell 0 Using address operator: 0x28fee8
```

(*continued*)

Program 9.8 A program to check the address of each array element (Continued)

```
Address of cell 1 Using pointer: 0x28feec
Address of cell 1 Using address operator: 0x28feec

Address of cell 2 Using pointer: 0x28fef0
Address of cell 2 Using address operator: 0x28fef0

Address of cell 3 Using pointer: 0x28fef4
Address of cell 3 Using address operator: 0x28fef4

Address of cell 4 Using pointer: 0x28fef8
Address of cell 4 Using address operator: 0x28fef8
```

symbolic representations that make it easier to access elements. This means that arr[0] is the same as *(arr + 0), but we must be careful to use parentheses because the asterisk operator has priority over the addition operator, and using parentheses will allow us to change this. It is also interesting that each address increases by 4 bytes, which demonstrates that the size of an integer is 4.

When referring to array elements using pointers, we need parentheses to give priority to the addition operator.

EXAMPLE 9.19

Program 9.9 shows that we can get the same result by referring to the elements of an array using indexes and pointers.

Program 9.9 Using indexes and pointers with an array

```
/*******************************************************************
 * The program shows how to access the elements of an array        *
 * using either the indexes or pointers to elements.               *
 *******************************************************************/
#include <iostream>
using namespace std;

int main ( )
{
   // Declaration and initialization of an array
   int numbers [5] = {10, 11, 12,13, 14};
   // Accessing elements through the indexes
   cout << "Accessing elements through indexes" << endl;
   for (int i = 0; i < 5; i++)
   {
       cout << numbers [i] << "  ";
```

(continued)

Program 9.9 Using indexes and pointers with an array (Continued)

```
    }
    cout << endl;
    // Accessing elements through the pointers
    cout << "Accessing elements through pointers" << endl;
    for (int i = 0; i < 5; i++)
    {
        cout << *(numbers + i) << "  ";
    }
    return 0;
}
```

```
Run:
Accessing elements through indexes
10  11  12  13  14
Accessing elements through pointers
10  11  12  13  14
```

Pointer Arithmetic

Pointer types are not integer types. However, **pointer arithmetic** allows a limited number of arithmetic operators to be applied to pointer types. We must look at these operators with a new definition in mind. When we use these operators, we must remember that because the result is another pointer value, that value must point to a memory location in our control; otherwise, the result is nonsense. This is why using these operators makes sense when we apply them to pointers to the elements of the array: When we declare an array, the memory locations involved are in our control.

Integer Addition or Subtraction We can use the addition operator to add an integer to, or the subtraction operator to subtract an integer from, a pointer:

```
Addition: ptr1 = ptr + n                    Subtraction: ptr2 = ptr - n
```

Using the addition and subtraction operators this way creates a new definition for them. It creates a new pointer $n \times m$ bytes forward or backward; m is the size of the pointed variable, where m is the number of bytes occupied by each element. So the operation moves the pointer n elements forward or backward as shown in Figure 9.16. Addition creates a pointer

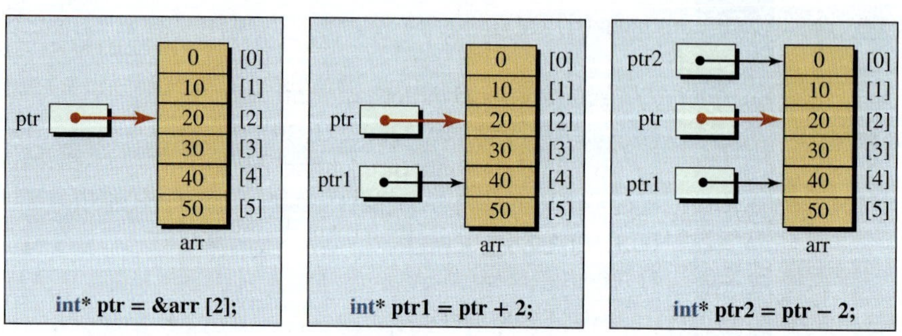

After creation of ptr After creation of ptr1 After creation of ptr2

Figure 9.16 Integer addition and subtraction of pointers

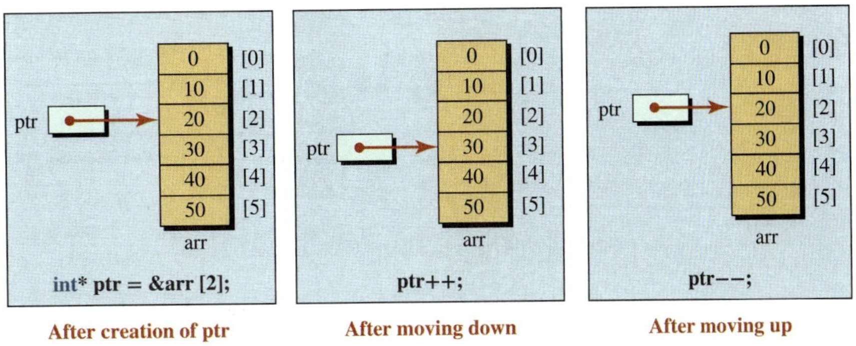

Figure 9.17 Increment and decrement operators apply to pointers

farther from the beginning of the array; subtraction creates a pointer closer to the beginning of the array. The red arrow shows the original pointer.

Increment and Decrement These two operators are designed to be used with variables (*lvalues*). They cannot be used with the name of the array because the name is a constant value. The meaning of ptr++ is the same as ptr = ptr + 1, and the meaning of ptr−− is the same as ptr = ptr − 1. In these cases the original pointer moves as shown in Figure 9.17. After the increment operation, the original pointer is pointing to the *arr*[3]. After the decrement operation, it is pointing back to *arr*[2].

Compound Addition and Subtraction We can also use compound addition and subtraction operators on pointer variables. If *ptr* is a pointer variable, the expression (ptr += 3) is equivalent to (ptr = ptr + 3) and the expression (ptr −= 3) is equivalent to (ptr = ptr − 3). These operations, like the increment and decrement operators, move the pointer toward the beginning or toward the end, as shown in Figure 9.18.

Pointer Subtraction We can subtract one pointer from another. If *ptr1* and *ptr2* are pointers in which *ptr1* points to an element of a lower index and *ptr2* to an element of a higher index, then the expression (ptr2 − ptr1) returns a positive integer and (ptr1 − ptr2) returns a negative integer as shown in Figure 9.19. In other words, the results of these operations are integers, not pointers.

No Pointer Addition The addition of pointer values is not allowed in C++ because it does not make sense.

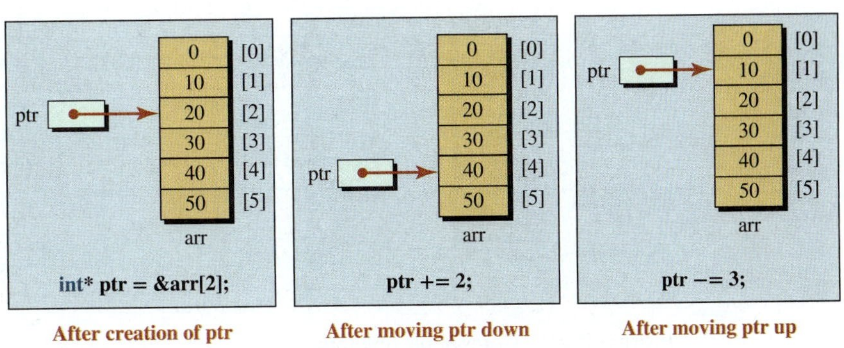

Figure 9.18 Compound addition and subtraction

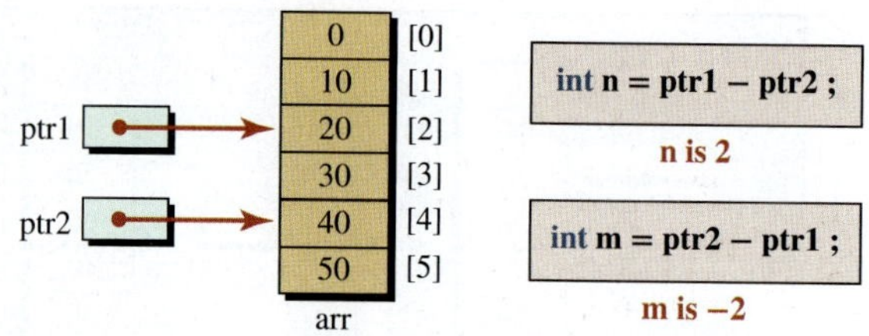

Figure 9.19 Pointer subtraction

We cannot add two pointers.

Comparing Pointers We can compare two pointers as shown in Figure 9.20. If *ptr1* and *ptr2* are pointers to elements of an array, the expression (*ptr1* == *ptr2*) is *true* when *ptr1* and *ptr2* point to the same element. The expression (*ptr1* != *ptr2*) is *true* when *ptr1* and *ptr2* point to different elements. The expression (*ptr1* < *ptr2*) is *true* if *ptr1* points to an element with a lower index than pointer *ptr2*. The expression (*ptr1* > *ptr2*) is *true* if *ptr1* points to a higher index than *ptr2*. The expression (*ptr1* <= *ptr2*) is true if the two pointers point to the same element or *ptr1* points to an element closer to the beginning of the array than *ptr2*. The expression (*ptr1* >= *ptr2*) is true if the two pointers point to the same element or *ptr1* points to an element closer to the end of the array than *ptr2*.

No Other Operations We cannot use any other arithmetic operations on pointers. For example, multiplication, division, and modulo operators are not defined for pointer types.

A Warning We must use pointer arithmetic with caution. If the operation causes access outside the array territory, we may destroy memory locations that are not part of the array.

Functions with Array Parameters

A pointer in a function can be used to represent an array. We discuss two cases.

Passing a Pointer to a Function for an Array We can pass a pointer to a function instead of passing the array. In other words, the following two prototypes are the same.

```
int getSum (const array [ ], int size);        // Using array
int getSum (const int* p, int size);           // Using pointer
```

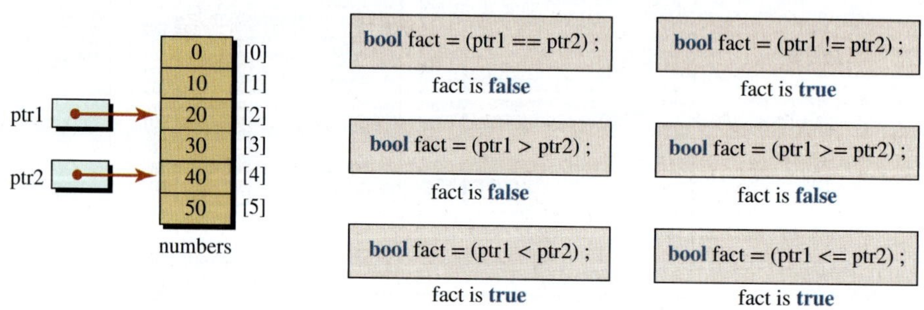

Figure 9.20 Comparing pointers

We have used the constant modifier to prevent the function *getSum* from changing the value of the elements.

EXAMPLE 9.20

Program 9.10 shows how we can use the second version in the code above to find the sum of the elements in an array.

In Program 9.10, the first parameter of the *getSum* function is a constant to integer (so that the function cannot change the values of the elements). However, this does not mean that it is a constant pointer. We can move it. If we had made the parameter a constant pointer with the prototype (*const int* const, int*), then we could not use p++ in line 27. We would have to use *(p + 1) instead.

Program 9.10 Finding the sum of elements in an array

```
1  /*****************************************************************
2   * The program shows how to access the elements of an array      *
3   * using pointers.                                               *
4   *****************************************************************/
5  #include <iostream>
6  using namespace std;
7
8  int getSum (const int*, int); // Prototype
9
10 int main ()
11 {
12    // Array declaration and initialization
13    int arr [5] = {10, 11, 12, 13, 14};
14    // Function call
15    cout << "Sum of elements: " << getSum (arr, 5);
16    return 0;
17 }
18 /*****************************************************************
19  * The function gets a pointer to the first element of an       *
20  * array and calculates and returns the sum of the elements.    *
21  *****************************************************************/
22 int getSum (const int* p, int size)
23 {
24    int sum = 0;
25    for (int i = 0; i < size ; i++)
26    {
27         sum += *(p++);
28    }
29    return sum;
30 }
```

```
Run:
Sum of elements: 60
```

EXAMPLE 9.21

Assume we want to write a function that reverses the elements of the array using pointers. Program 9.11shows an example.

Program 9.11 Reversing the elements of an array

```
/****************************************************************
 * The program shows how a function can reverse the elements    *
 * of an array using a pointer.                                 *
 ****************************************************************/
#include <iostream>
using namespace std;

void reverse (int* , int );

int main ()
{
  // Array declaration and initialization
  int arr [5] = {10, 11, 12, 13, 14};
  // Calling function
  reverse (arr, 5);
  // Printing array after reversed
  cout << "Reversed array: ";
  for (int i = 0; i < 5; i++)
  {
       cout << *(arr + i) << "  ";
  }
  return 0;
}
/****************************************************************
 * The function uses a pointer to the first element of the array *
 * and the size of the array to reverse the elements in place.   *
 ****************************************************************/
void reverse (int* pArr, int size)
{
  int i = 0;
  int j = size - 1;
  while (i < size / 2)
  {
       int temp = *(pArr + i);
       *(pArr + i) = *(pArr + j);
       *(pArr + j) = temp;
       i++;
       j--;
  }
}
```

Run:

```
Reversed array: 14 13 12 11 10
```

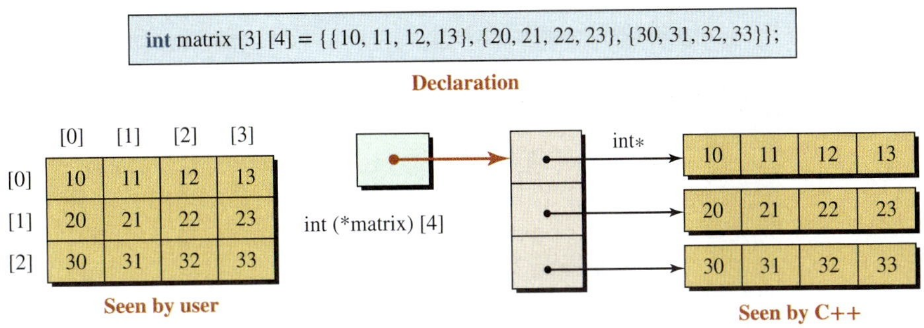

Figure 9.21 A two-dimensional array seen by user and C++

Although *arr* is a constant pointer and cannot move, *pArr* does not have to be a constant pointer; it is a separate pointer variable. Also note that *pArr* cannot be a pointer to a constant integer because it is supposed to change the pointed element in swapping. We swap only half of the elements. When half of the elements are swapped, we are done.

Returning an Array from a Function Although we may think about returning an array from a function, we must remember that an array is a combination of two pieces of information: the pointer to the first element and the size of the array. A function can return only one piece of information (unless we bundle the pointer and the size in an object). As we mentioned in Chapter 8, we cannot return an array from a function.

9.3.2 Two-Dimensional Arrays and Pointers

A two-dimensional array in C++ is an array of arrays. If we keep this fact in mind, then it is easy to use pointers with two-dimensional arrays. Figure 9.21 shows what we see as a two-dimensional array and what C++ sees.

Contrary to some beliefs, the name of a two-dimensional array is not a pointer to pointer to integer; it is a pointer to an array of four integers or *int* (matrix*) [4]. The parentheses around the array name mean that the array is read as "matrix is a pointer to an array of four integers." We must remember this fact when we pass a two-dimensional array to a function. As usual, the column size must be given with the pointer; the row size should be given separately as an integer.

EXAMPLE 9.22

In this example we write a short program and pass the array defined in Figure 9.21 to a function that will print the elements as shown in Program 9.12.

Program 9.12 Passing a two-dimensional array to a function

```
/***************************************************************
 * The program to show how to pass a two-dimensional array to a   *
 * function using pointer notations.                               *
 ***************************************************************/
#include <iostream>
using namespace std;

void print (int (*) [4], int);  // Prototype

```

(continued)

Program 9.12 Passing a two-dimensional array to a function (Continued)

```
int main ()
{
   int matrix [3][4] = {{10, 11, 12, 13}, {20, 21, 22, 23},
                                          {31, 32, 33, 34}};
   // Calling print function
   print (matrix, 3);
   return 0;
}
/***************************************************************
  * The function accepts a pointer to any array of four integers   *
  * with the number of rows.                                       *
  ***************************************************************/
void print (int (*m) [4], int rows)
{
   for (int i = 0; i < rows; i++)
   {
        for (int j = 0 ; j < 4; j++)
        {
                cout << m[i][j] << "  ";
        }
        cout << endl;
   }
}
```

Run:

```
10 11 12 13
20 21 22 23
31 32 33 34
```

9.4 MEMORY MANAGEMENT

When a program in C++ is running, it uses memory locations. The code must be stored in memory and every object, fundamental or user-defined, must also be stored in memory. However, the C++ environment divides memory into different areas, as shown in Figure 9.22, to make memory management more efficient. Note that the figure does not show the order of different memory areas in the computer.

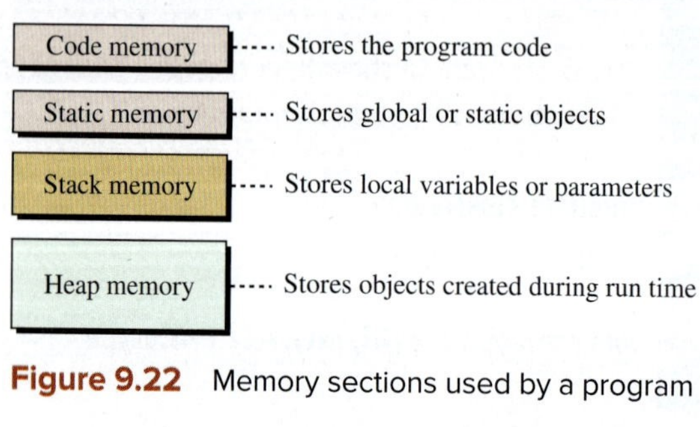

Figure 9.22 Memory sections used by a program

In this section we discuss these areas of memory and how we can use them. Understanding the characteristics and knowing how to use each area enables us to write better programs.

9.4.1 Code Memory

Code memory holds the program code. When the program is running, the running environment of C++ executes each statement, one after another, or branches to another statement. No objects are stored in this area of memory. Code memory is released when the program is terminated.

> **Code memory stores the program code;**
> **it is released when the program terminates.**

9.4.2 Static Memory

Static memory is used to hold **global objects** (those that are not part of any function, including *main*) and **static objects** created anywhere in the program (in the global area or inside functions). These objects are automatically destroyed and their memory is released when the program is terminated.

> **Static memory stores the global and static objects;**
> **it is released when the program terminates.**

EXAMPLE 9.23

Program 9.13 shows a very simple program. The memory locations for three data variables, *first*, *second*, and *third*, are created in static memory. The first is a global variable; the second and the third are static variables.

Program 9.13 Using static memory

```
/**********************************************************************
 * The program shows how global and static objects are visible        *
 * at any point in the program. They last through the life of the     *
 * the program.                                                       *
 **********************************************************************/
#include <iostream>
using namespace std;

int first = 20;                 // Global variable in static memory
static int second = 30 ;        // Static variable created in static memory

int main ()
{
  static int third = 50;  // Static variable in static memory

  cout << "Value of Global variable: " << first << endl;
```

(*continued*)

Program 9.13 Using static memory (Continued)

```
    cout << "Value of Global static variable: " << second << endl;
    cout << "Value of local static variable: " << third;
    return 0;
}
```

Run:

```
Value of Global variable: 20
Value of Global static variable: 30
Value of local static variable: 50
```

9.4.3 Stack Memory

The part of memory used by a program to hold local or parameter objects of functions is **stack memory.** As we know from daily life, a *stack* is a last-in-first-out container. Whatever is pushed last is popped first. This characteristic of a stack is well suited for storing parameters and local variables in functions. When we call a function, the system pushes the parameters and local variables into stack memory. When the function is terminated, the system pops these variables and throws them away. Figure 9.23 shows the functions calls and the behavior of stack memory for a simple program that calls the function *first*, which in turn calls the function *second.*

Figure 9.23 shows pushing and popping at the right-hand side. The stack memory is empty at the beginning.When the running environment calls the *main* function, it pushes its only local variable (*x*) into the stack (*main* has no parameter). When *main* calls the function *first*, the system pushes its only parameter (*a*) into the stack. When the function *first* calls *second,* the system pushes its only parameter (*b*) into the stack.

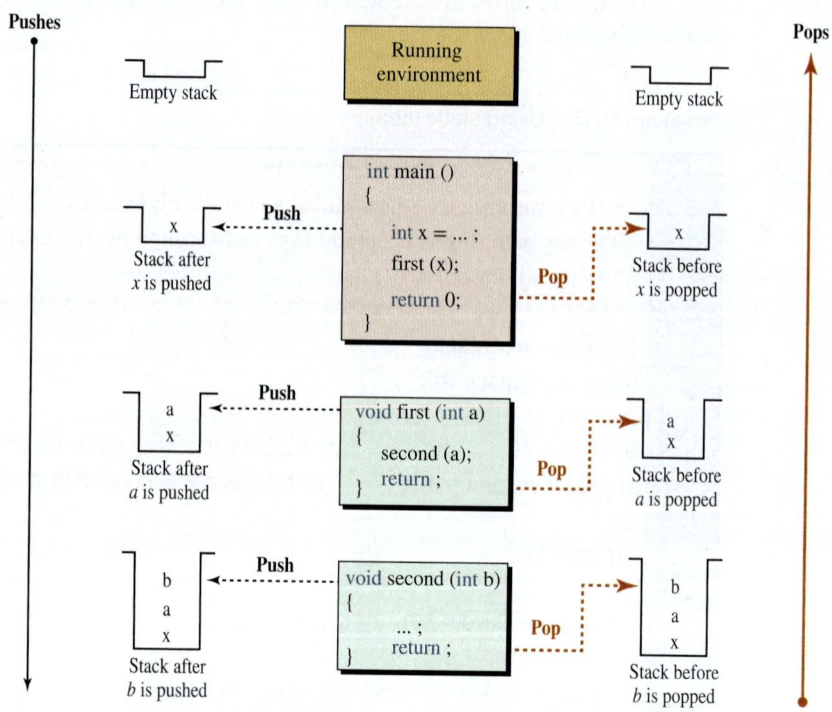

Figure 9.23 Using stack memory

When the function *second* returns, the system pops its only parameter (*b*) and throws it away (not needed anymore). When the function *first* returns, the system pops its only parameter (*a*) and throws it away (not needed anymore). When the function *main* returns, the system pops its only local variable (*x*) and throws it away (not needed anymore). The stack memory is empty again at the end when the program is terminated. For the sake of simplicity, we have not used local variables in function *first* or *second*; otherwise, those local variables would also be pushed and popped from the stack.

Advantage

The system uses stack memory in every program. The last-in first-out operation of stack memory makes it very efficient. Objects are stored and remain in stack memory only when they are in a function's scope. When an object goes out of the function's scope, it is popped and thrown away; it is not accessible anymore.

Limitations

The efficiency of using stack memory creates two restrictions on its use:

- The objects must have a name at compilation time. No unnamed object can be stored in a stack.
- The size of the object must be defined at compilation time. The system cannot allocate stack memory for an object unless it knows the exact size of the object. For a single object, the size can be inferred from the type; for a list of objects (such as an array), the number of elements must be defined at compilation time.

Based on the preceding discussion, we can call *stack memory* the *compile-time memory*. Every object stored in stack memory must be clearly defined during compilation time.

> **An object created in stack memory must be given a name and have a size during compilation.**

EXAMPLE 9.24

Assume that we need a variable-size array, which means that every time we run the program, the array size must be defined by the user as shown below:

```
#include <iostream>
using namespace std;

int main ()
{
   int size;
   cin >> size;
   double array [size];              // Compilation error
   ...
   return 0;
}
```

We get the compilation error shown above because the compiler must know the size of the array before it can allocate memory in the stack. We solve this problem in the next section.

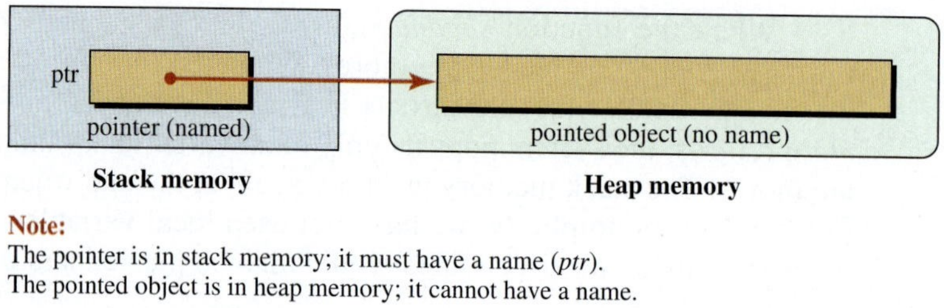

Figure 9.24 A pointer in the stack and a pointed object in the heap

9.4.4 Heap Memory

Sometimes we need to create objects in memory during run time. This happens when we do not know the size of the object when we create and compile the program. **Heap memory** (also called *free* memory or *dynamic* memory) is used to store objects created during run time. This situation occurs when an object, or a collection of objects, needs a lot of memory or when the amount of memory cannot be calculated during the compilation. The objects created in heap memory cannot have a name, so to access them, we need a pointer in stack memory that can be pointed to them. In other words, we need both stack and heap memory for this purpose. Stack memory is used to hold the pointer (a small object of 4 bytes); heap memory is used to store the pointed object (usually a large object) as shown in Figure 9.24.

The pointed object in heap memory cannot have a name; it is referred to by the pointer that is pointing to it. On the other hand, the pointer object is in the stack; it must have a name. In other words, the name of the pointer helps us refer to it; the address of the pointed object enables us to access it.

An object created in heap memory cannot have a name; it can be accessed only through its address, which is reached by a pointer in stack memory.

Two Operators: new and delete

Now the questions are how we can create an object in the heap during run time, and how we can destroy it when it is not needed, if the object has no name. This is done through four operators. These operators are defined in Appendix C and are shown in Table 9.6 for quick reference.

The first operator in Table 9.6 is used to create memory in the heap for a single object. The second operator is used to create an array of objects in the heap. The third operator is used to delete the single object using its pointer. The fourth operator is used to delete

Table 9.6 Operators for memory allocation and release in the heap

Group	Name	Operator	Expression	Pred	Assoc
Unary	allocate object allocate array delete object delete array	new new [ ] delete delete [ ]	new type new type [size] delete ptr delete [ ] ptr	17	←

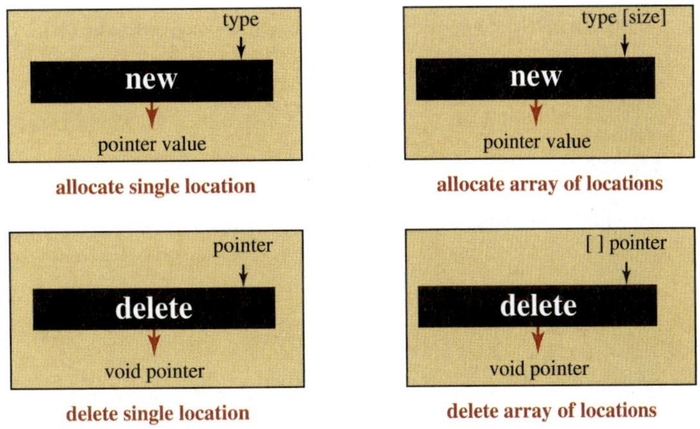

Figure 9.25 The new and delete operators

allocated memory for an array in the heap. Figure 9.25 shows the four operators that create the *new* and *delete* expressions.

Note that after delete, the pointer is a dangling pointer, which we discuss later in this section. It cannot be used until the *new* operator is applied to it again.

EXAMPLE 9.25

In this example, we create an object in the heap. Assume we want to write a program that creates a variable-size array each time the user runs the program. This array cannot be created in stack memory because the size of the array is not defined during compilation time; it is only defined during run time. Figure 9.26 shows this situation.

Program 9.14 show how we can achieve this situation. Before terminating the program, we must delete the array created in the heap (line 34).

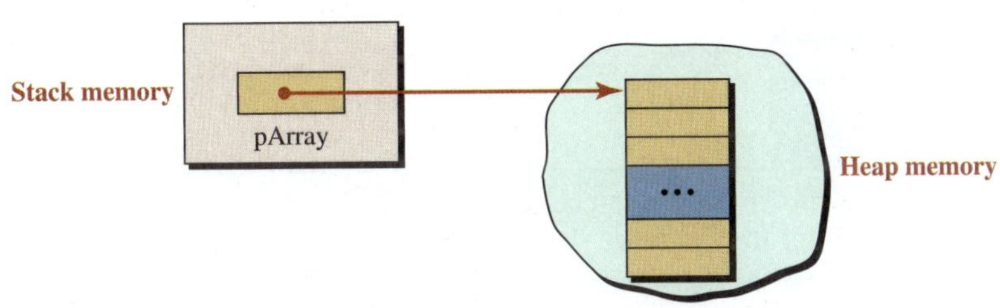

Figure 9.26 A pointer in the stack and an array in the heap

Program 9.14 Using heap memory to store a variable-size array

```
1  /***************************************************************
2   * The program shows how to create and access a variable-size   *
3   * array in the heap and use pointers to access elements.       *
4   ***************************************************************/
5  #include <iostream>
6  using namespace std;
```

(continued)

Program 9.14 Using heap memory to store a variable-size array (Continued)

```

int main ( )
{
  // Declaration of array size and the pointer in the stack
  int size;
  int* pArray;
  // Validation of the size to be greater than zero
  do
  {
      cout << "Enter the array size (larger than zero): ";
      cin >> size;
  } while (size <= 0);
  // Creation of array in the heap
  pArray = new int [size];
  // Inputting the values of array
  for (int i = 0; i < size ; i++)
  {
      cout << "Enter the value for element " << i << ": ";
      cin >> *(pArray + i);
  }
  // Outputting the values of the array
  cout << "The elements in the array are: " << endl;
  for (int i = 0; i < size ; i++)
  {
      cout << *(pArray + i) << "  ";
  }
  // Deleting the array in the heap
  delete [ ] pArray;
  return 0;
}
```

```
Run:
Enter the array size (larger than zero): 3
Enter the value for element 0: 6
Enter the value for element 1: 12
Enter the value for element 2: 5
The elements in the array are:
6  12  5
```

Issues Related to Heap Memory

When we work with heap memory and use the related operators (*new* and *delete*), we must be aware of some problems that may occur.

Deleting without Allocating One of the errors that may occur in programming is that we try to use the *delete* operator without using the *new* operator first. This means we try to delete an object in the heap without allocating it. This normally occurs when the object is allocated in the stack but we try to delete it from the heap, as shown below:

```
double x = 23.4;
double* pX = &x;  // Allocation in the stack
delete pX;  // Deletion in the heap may create run-time error
```

Allocating without Deleting (Memory Leak) A more serious problem, known as **memory leak,** occurs when we allocate an object in the heap but we do not delete it, as shown below:

```
double* pX = new double;
... // using the allocated memory
```

This means that we have created a memory location in the heap and we have not deleted it. Most of the operating systems delete the memory location when the pointer that is pointing to it goes out of the scope. There is, however, a serious problem if the pointer is re-pointed to another memory location (in the stack or the heap). In this case, there is no pointer pointed to the object that goes out of scope and alerts the operating system to delete the allocated memory. This serious problem is referred to as memory leak and should be avoided. A memory leak makes the undeleted memory location unusable and may result in the collapse of the computer system if it runs out of memory.

Dangling Pointer Another problem is a **dangling pointer** that, which may occur that may occur when we delete the pointed object and then try to use it again, as shown below:

```
double* pX = new double;
... // using the allocated memory
delete pX;
*pX = 35.3;  // Dangling pointer
```

The last line creates an unexpected error because the pointer is null and cannot be indirected.

When we work with heap memory, we must pair each *new* operator with the *delete* operator and avoid dangling pointers.

Recommendation

Always explicitly delete any memory locations created in the heap.

9.4.5 Two-Dimensional Arrays

As we discussed previously, a two-dimensional array is made of rows and columns. We have three choices when creating a two-dimensional array. We discuss these choices in this section.

Using Only Stack Memory

If both the row size and the column size are known before compilation, we can create the array totally in the stack as we have done previously.

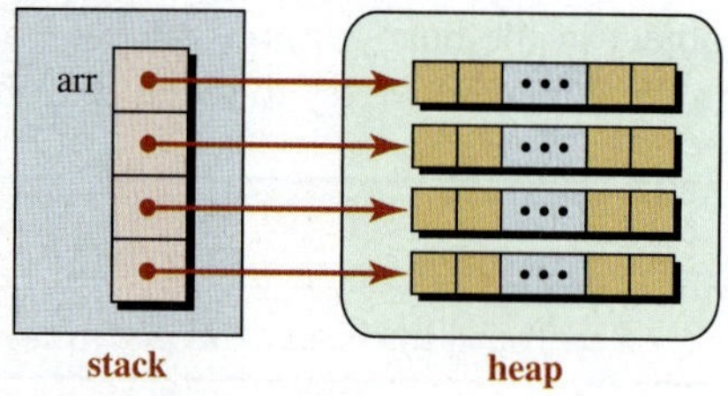

Figure 9.27 A two-dimensional array in the stack and in the heap

Using Both Stack and Heap Memory

If the row dimension is know before the compilation, we can create an array of pointers in the stack and then create each row in the heap as shown in Figure 9.27.

The following shows the code to create such an array. The number of rows is fixed before compilation (4); the number of columns must be entered during run time.

```
int* arr [4]; // This is an array of four pointers to integers in the stack
cin >> colNums;
for (int i = 0; i < 4 ; i++)
{
   arr[i] = new int [colNums]; // an array of colNums in the heap
}
```

Using Only Heap Memory

If neither of the dimensions is known before the compilation, we must create the whole two-dimensional array in the heap as shown in Figure 9.28.

The following code creates such an array. The value of both dimensions is not known during compilation.

```
cin >> rowNums;
cin >> colNums;
int** arr = new int* [rowNums];
for (int i = 0; i < n + 1 ; i++)
{
   arr[i] = new int [colNums];
}
```

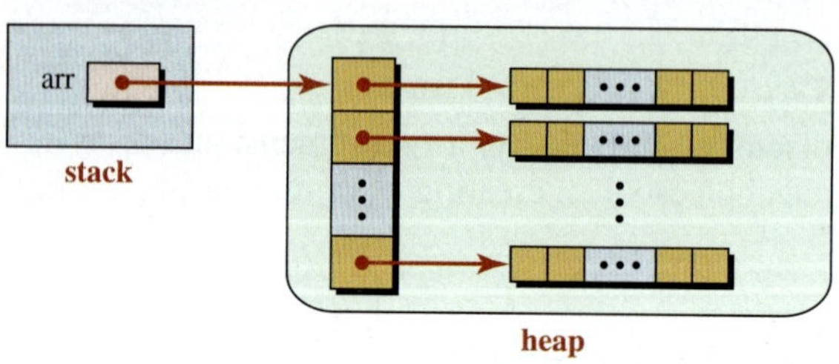

Figure 9.28 A two-dimensional array totally in the heap

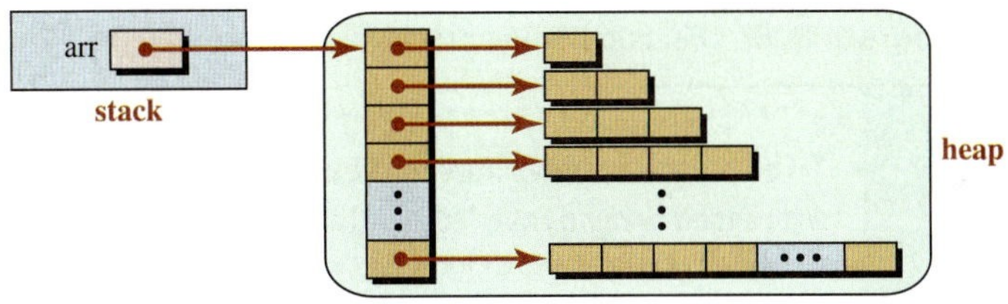

Figure 9.29 Ragged array

An Example: Ragged Array

We can create a two-dimensional array in which the number of elements in one row is different from the number of elements in another row, as shown in Figure 9.29.

In other words, can we have an array in which the first row has, for example, three elements, and the second row has four elements. This is referred to as a **ragged array.** This is possible, but we cannot allocate the elements in stack memory; they must be created in the heap. In other words, we must think about an array of pointers in which each pointer points to an array of the desired size, as shown in Figure 9.29. This design is more memory efficient than using a two-dimensional array, which leaves some of the elements empty.

EXAMPLE 9.26

Pascal's triangle determines the coefficients of a binomial expansion. When a binomial like $(x + y)$ is raised to a positive integer power, we have:

$$(x + y)^n = a_0 x^n + a_1 x^{n-1}y + a_2 x^{n-2}y^2 + \ \dots \ + a_{n-1} x\, y^{n-1} + a_n y^n$$

The coefficient of each term (a_0, a_1, a_2, ..., a_{n-1}, a_n) can be calculated using a triangle of $n + 1$ rows and $n + 1$ columns. Each cell in the array holds the coefficient for a term. The number of rows is one more than the power value (n). Each element in the triangle is calculated by adding the element in the previous row and the previous column with the element in the previous row and the same column, as shown below (when $n = 4$). It is obvious that to calculate the coefficients for any value of n (beyond 0 and 1), we must know the value of the coefficients for the previous n. This justifies the use of a two-dimensional array. We can use an array of pointers to dynamically create the array and calculate the coefficients.

n = 0	1				
n = 1	1	1			
n = 2	1	2	1		
n = 3	1	3	3	1	
n = 4	1	4	6	4	1

EXAMPLE 9.27

Program 9.15 finds the coefficients for any n between 0 and 9. The number of allocated locations for each row is one greater than the row number. For example, when $i = 0$, we must allocate one location from the heap. When $i = 9$, we must allocate 10 locations from the heap.

Program 9.15 Finding the Pascal coefficients

```
/*******************************************************************
 * The program shows how to create Pascal coefficients using       *
 * a ragged array dynamically allocated on the heap.               *
 *******************************************************************/
#include <iostream>
#include <iomanip>
using namespace std;

int main ( )
{
  // Declaration
  int maxPower = 10;
  int n;
  // Input validation
  do
  {
      cout << "Enter the power of binomial : ";
      cin >> n;
  } while (n < 0 || n > maxPower);
  // Allocate memory from heap
  int** pascal = new int* [n + 1];
  for (int i = 0; i < n + 1 ; i++)
  {
      pascal[i] = new int [i];
  }
  // Formation of the coefficient
  for (int i = 0; i <= n ; i++)
  {
      for (int j = 0; j < i + 1; j++)
      {
            if (j == 0 || i == j)
            {
                pascal [i][j] = 1;
            }
            else
            {
                pascal [i][j] = pascal [i - 1] [j - 1] + pascal [i - 1][j];
            }
      }
  }
  // Print coefficients
  cout << endl;
  cout << "Coefficients for (x + y)^" << n << " are:";
  for (int j = 0; j <= n  ; j++)
```

(continued)

Program 9.15 Finding the Pascal coefficients (Continued)

```
45     {
46         cout << setw (5) << pascal [n][j] ;
47     }
48     cout << endl;
49     // Delete allocated memory
50     for (int i = 0; i < n + 1 ; i++)
51     {
52         delete [ ] pascal [i];
53     }
54     delete [ ] pascal;
55     return 0;
56 }
```

```
Run:
Enter the power of binomial : 5
Coefficients for (x + y)^5 are: 1   5  10  10   5   1
```

In line 22 of this program, we created a variable named *pascal* of type *int*** in stack memory. In the same line, we created an array of pointers in the heap and stored the returned pointer in the variable *pascal*. The variable *pascal* now points to an array of pointers. We then used a loop to create $(n + 1)$ arrays, each of a different size in the heap. Each array is pointed to by a pointer in the array *pascal* [i]. In lines 51–55, we first deleted the $(n + 1)$ arrays of integer in the heap. We then deleted the array pointed by the Pascal variable. Locations in the heap must be deleted in the reverse order of allocations.

9.5 PROGRAM DESIGN

In this section, we create two classes in which some of the data members are created in the heap.

9.5.1 Course Class

We create a *Course* class whose objects can be used by a professor in a school to create statistics about each of her courses. Since each course may have a different number of students, we must have an array of variable size in each course to keep track of the scores. To save each professor from having to write a program, the *Course* class has been created and saved by the programmers in administration. Each professor is given the public interface with which to create the application and run it. In this section, we show what has been done by the programmer in administration and what should be done by the professors.

Data Members

Figure 9.30 shows the arrangement of data member in the *Course* class.

We must keep four pieces of information for each student: identity, score, grade, and deviation from average. Instead of creating four parallel arrays in the heap, we have packed these four pieces of information in a *struct* and created an array of structs in the heap.

Member Functions

Several private member functions are called by the constructor automatically when an object of the class is instantiated. The two public member functions are the constructor and destructor.

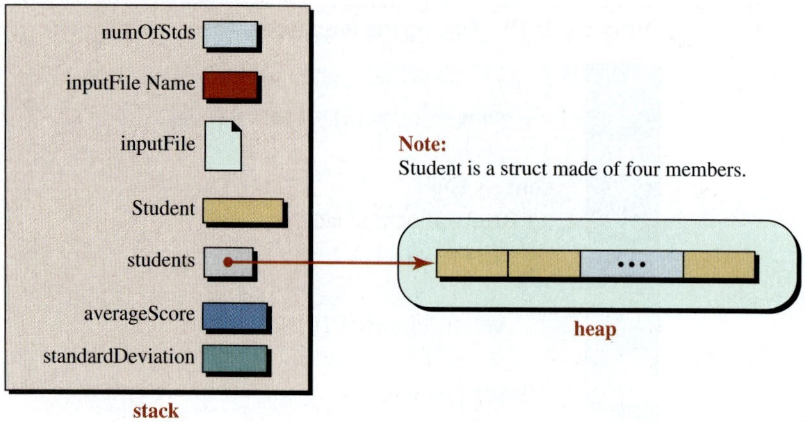

Figure 9.30 Data members of the Course class

Input File

We assume that the input file contains the following data, in which the first column represents the student identity and the second column defines the score in the course.

```
1000   88
1001   100
1002   92
1003   77
1004   54
1005   82
1006   67
1007   95
1008   93
1009   100
```

Interface, Implementation, and Application Files

Programs 9.16, 9.17, and 9.18 show the files.

Program 9.16 Interface file for the Course class

```
/*********************************************************************
 * We have private data members and public member functions.         *
 * The private member functions are helper functions called          *
 * by the constructor to do its job. The constructor is              *
 * responsible for everything. The destructor deletes arrays         *
 * created in the heap and closes the input file.                    *
 *********************************************************************/
#ifndef COURSE_H
#define COURSE_H
#include <iostream>
```

(continued)

Program 9.16 Interface file for the Course class (Continued)

```
#include <fstream>
using namespace std;

class Course
{
   private:
       int numOfStds;
       const char* inputFileName;
       ifstream inputFile;
       struct Student {int id; int score; char grade;
                                        double deviation;};
       Student* students;
       double averageScore;
       double standardDeviation;
       // Private member functions
       void getInput ();
       void setGrades ();
       void setAverage ();
       void setDeviations();
       void printResult() const;
   public:
       Course (int numOfStds, const char* inputFileName);
       ~Course ();
};
#endif
```

Program 9.17 Implementation file

```
/*******************************************************************
 * The implementation file gives the definitions of all private    *
 * and public member functions.                                    *
 *******************************************************************/
#include "course.h"
#include <iomanip>
#include <cmath>

/*******************************************************************
 * The constructor is responsible for initializing student's       *
 * number and the name of the input file containing scores.        *
 * The constructor then opens the input file and creates           *
 * an array in the heap. The rest of the job is done by helper     *
 * functions that set the scores, the grades, the average and      *
 * deviations, and prints the results.                             *
 *******************************************************************/
```

(continued)

Program 9.17 Implementation file (Continued)

```
Course :: Course (int num, const char* ifn)
:numOfStds (num), inputFileName (ifn)
{
   inputFile.open (inputFileName);
   students = new Student [numOfStds];
   getInput ();
   setGrades ();
   setAverage ();
   setDeviations();
   printResult();
}
/*****************************************************************
 * The destructor is responsible for deleting the array created   *
 * in the heap using the corresponding pointer. It also closes    *
 * the input file opened by the constructor.                      *
 *****************************************************************/
Course :: ~Course ()
{
   delete [ ] students;
   inputFile.close ();
}
/*****************************************************************
 * The getInput function is responsible for reading the input     *
 * file containg the identity and score of students.              *
 *****************************************************************/
void Course :: getInput()
{
   for (int i = 0; i < numOfStds; i++)
   {
        inputFile >> students [i].id;
        inputFile >> students [i].score;
   }
}
/*****************************************************************
 * The getGrades function uses the score for each student and     *
 * changes it to the grade using an array of chars.               *
 *****************************************************************/
void Course :: setGrades()
{
   char charGrades [ ] =
                  {'F', 'F', 'F' , 'F' , 'F' , 'F', 'D' , 'C' , 'B' , 'A' , 'A'};
   for (int i = 0; i < numOfStds; i++)
   {
        int index = students[i].score / 10;
```

(continued)

Program 9.17 Implementation file (Continued)

```
        students[i].grade = charGrades [index];
    }
}
/**************************************************************
 * The setAverage function processes scores in the array and  *
 * creates the average for the class.                         *
 **************************************************************/
void Course :: setAverage()
{
    int sum = 0;
    for (int i = 0; i < numOfStds; i++)
    {
        sum += students[i].score;
    }
    averageScore = static_cast <double> (sum) / numOfStds;
}
/**************************************************************
 * The setDeviation function reprocesses the scores to determine *
 * the deviation of each student's score from the average.    *
 **************************************************************/
void Course :: setDeviations()
{
    standardDeviation = 0.0;
    for (int i = 0; i < numOfStds; i++)
    {
        students[i].deviation = students[i].score - averageScore;
        standardDeviation += pow(students[i].deviation , 2);
    }
    standardDeviation = sqrt (standardDeviation) / numOfStds;
}
/**************************************************************
 * The printResult function prints all information about the  *
 * the course.                                                *
 **************************************************************/
void Course :: printResult() const
{
    cout << endl;
    cout << "Identity    Score    Grade        Deviation" << endl;
    cout << "--------    -----    -----        ---------" << endl;
    for (int i = 0; i < numOfStds ; i++)
    {
        cout << setw (4) << noshowpoint << noshowpos;
        cout << right << students[i].id;
        cout << setw (14) << noshowpoint << noshowpos;
```

(continued)

Program 9.17 Implementation file (Continued)

```
        cout << right << students[i].score;
        cout << setw (10) << right << students[i].grade;
        cout << fixed << setw (20) << right << setprecision (2);
        cout << showpoint << showpos;
        cout << students[i].deviation << endl;
    }
    cout << "Average score: " << fixed << setw (4);
    cout << setprecision (2) <<averageScore << endl;
    cout << "Standard Deviation: " << standardDeviation;
}
```

Program 9.18 Application file

```
/****************************************************************
 * The application program is very simple. The user instantiates   *
 * an object of the class and passes the number of students and    *
 * name of the input file where the scores are stored.             *
 * Everything is done by the constructor of the class.             *
 ****************************************************************/
#include "course.h"

int main ( )
{
    // Instantiation of the Course object
    Course course (10, "scores.dat");
    return 0;
}
```

```
Run:
Identity        Score        Grade        Deviation
--------        -----        -----        ---------
1000             88            B           +3.20
1001             100           A           +15.20
1002             92            A           +7.20
1003             77            C           -7.80
1004             54            F           -30.80
1005             82            B           -2.80
1006             67            D           -17.80
1007             95            A           +10.20
1008             93            A           +8.20
1009             100           A           +15.20
Average score: +84.80
Standard Deviation: +4.51
```

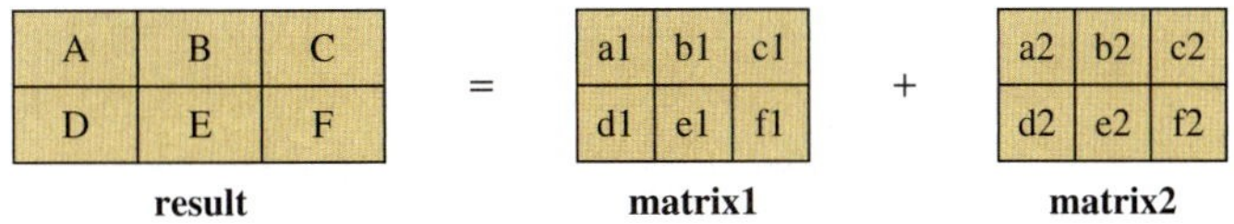

Figure 9.31 Adding two matrices

9.5.2 A Matrix Class

A matrix is a table of values in mathematics. In computer programming, we can simulate a matrix with a two-dimensional array. In this section, we define a *Matrix* class to show how to apply selected operations on matrices.

Operation

We define three operations on matrices: addition, subtraction, and multiplication. Division of matrices is very complex and requires the inversion of matrices.

Addition We can add two matrices if the number of rows in the first is the same as the number of rows in the second and the number of columns in the first is the same as the number of columns in the second. In other words, $r1 == r2$ and $c2 == c2$. The resulting matrix consists of r rows and c columns (Figure 9.31). Note that letters are symbolic values.

Each element in the resulting matrix is the sum of the corresponding elements in the two matrices, as shown below:

```
A = a1 + a2
...
F = f1 + f2
```

Subtraction Subtraction is the same as addition but the values of the corresponding cells are subtracted. (Figure 9.32).

Each element in the resulting matrix is the difference of the corresponding element in the two matrices, as shown below:

```
A = a1 - a2
...
F = f1 - f2
```

Multiplication We can multiply two matrices if the number of columns in the first matrix is the same as the number of rows in the second matrix ($c1 == r2$). The result is a matrix with the number of rows equal to r1 and the number of columns equal to c2 as shown in Figure 9.33.

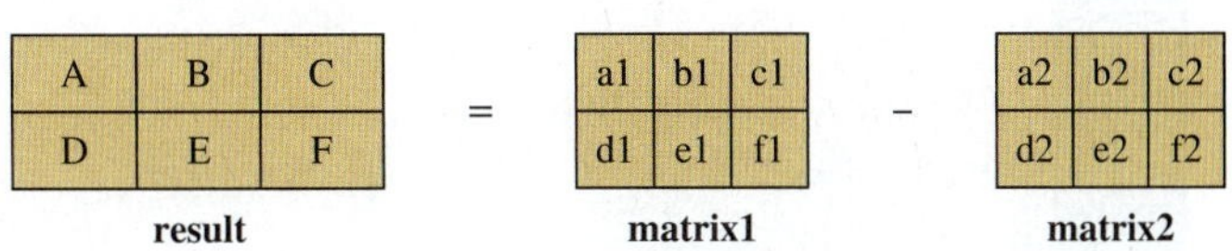

Figure 9.32 Subtracting two matrices

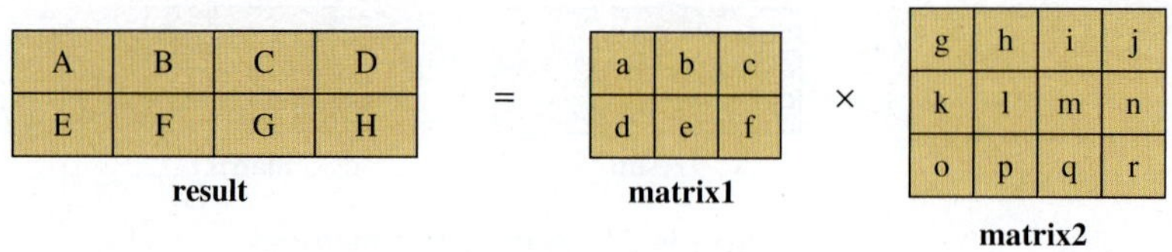

Figure 9.33 Multiplying two matrices

Each element in the resulting cell is the sum of the product of the corresponding row and column.

```
A = a * g + b * k + c * o
B = a * h + b * l + c * p
...
H = d * j + e * n + f * r
```

Code

Now we define the interface, implementation, and application files.

Interface File Program 9.19 shows the interface file.

Program 9.19 The interface file for the *Matrix* class

```
/***************************************************************
 * The interface file for the Matrix class. The only private data     *
 * members are the sizes of the matrix and the pointer that           *
 * points to the matrix in the heap.                                  *
 * The constructor creates a matrix in the heap and the destructor    *
 * deletes the allocated memory in the heap.                          *
 * The setup member function fills the matrices randomly.             *
 * We have addition, subtraction, multiplication, and print           *
 * member functions.                                                  *
 ***************************************************************/
#include <iostream>
#ifndef MATRIX_H
#define MATRIX_H
#include <cmath>
#include <cstdlib>
#include <iomanip>
#include <cassert>
using namespace std;

// Matrix class definition
class Matrix
{
  private:
```

(*continued*)

Program 9.19 The interface file for the *Matrix* class (Continued)

```
        int rowSize;
        int colSize;
        int** ptr;
    public:
    Matrix (int rowSize, int colSize);
        ~Matrix ();
        void setup ();
        void add (const Matrix& second, Matrix& result) const;
        void subtract (const Matrix& second, Matrix& result) const;
        void multiply (const Matrix& second, Matrix& result) const;
        void print () const;
};
#endif
```

Implementation File Program 9.20 shows the implementation file. Note that the setup member function randomly fills the matrix, but in real-life situations, we can read the values from a file.

Program 9.20 The implementation file for the *Matrix* class

```
/*****************************************************************
 * We have implemented all member functions declared in the       *
 * interface file.                                                *
 * The implementation follows the description of operations       *
 * discussed before.                                              *
 *****************************************************************/
#include "matrix.h"

// Constructor: creates a matrix in the heap
Matrix :: Matrix (int r, int c)
: rowSize (r), colSize ©
{
    ptr = new int* [rowSize];
    for (int i = 0; i < rowSize; i++)
    {
        ptr [i] = new int [colSize];
    }
}
// Destructor: deletes memory locations in the heap
Matrix :: ~Matrix ()
{
    for (int i = 0; i < rowSize ; i++)
    {
        delete [] ptr [i];
```

(*continued*)

Program 9.20 The implementation file for the *Matrix* class (Continued)

```
    }
    delete [] ptr;
}
// The setup fills the cells with random values between 1 and 5.
void Matrix :: setup ()
{
    for (int i = 0; i < rowSize; i++)
    {
        for (int j = 0; j < colSize ; j++)
        {
                ptr [i][j] = rand () % 5 + 1;
        }
    }
}
// The add function adds second to the host and creates result.
void Matrix :: add (const Matrix& second, Matrix& result) const
{
    assert (second.rowSize == rowSize && second.colSize == colSize);
    assert (result.rowSize == rowSize && result.colSize == colSize);

    for (int i = 0; i < rowSize ; i++)
    {
        for (int j = 0; j < second.colSize; j++)
        {
                result.ptr[i][j] = ptr[i][j] + second.ptr[i][j];
        }
    }
}
// The subtract function subtracts second from host.
void Matrix :: subtract (const Matrix& second, Matrix& result) const
{
    assert (second.rowSize == rowSize && second.colSize == colSize);
    assert (result.rowSize == rowSize && result.colSize == colSize);
    for (int i = 0; i < rowSize ; i++)
    {
        for (int j = 0; j < second.colSize; j++)
        {
                result.ptr[i][j] = ptr[i][j] - second.ptr[i][j];
        }
    }
}
// The multiply function multiplies second by host.
void Matrix :: multiply (const Matrix& second, Matrix& result) const
{
```

(*continued*)

Program 9.20 The implementation file for the *Matrix* class (Continued)

```
    assert (colSize == second.rowSize);
    assert (result.rowSize = rowSize);
    assert (result.colSize = second.colSize);
    for (int i = 0; i < rowSize ; i++)
    {
        for (int j = 0; j < second.colSize; j++)
        {
                result.ptr[i][j] = 0;
                for (int k = 0 ; k < colSize; k++)
                {
                    result.ptr[i][j] += ptr[i][k] * second.ptr[k][j];
                }
        }
    }
}
// The print function prints the values of cells.
void Matrix :: print () const
{
    for (int i = 0 ; i < rowSize; i++)
    {
        for (int j = 0; j < colSize ; j++)
        {
                cout << setw (5) << ptr [i][j];
        }
        cout << endl;
    }
    cout << endl;
}
```

Application File Program 9.21 shows the application for using the *Matrix* class.

Program 9.21 Application to test the *Matrix* class

```
/*****************************************************************
 * We create several matrix objects in the heap, and we apply   *
 * some operations on them.                                      *
 *****************************************************************/
#include "matrix.h"

int main ()
{
    // Instantiation and setup of matrix1
    cout << "matrix1" << endl;
```

(continued)

Program 9.21 Application to test the *Matrix* class (Continued)

```
    Matrix matrix1 (3, 4);
    matrix1.setup ();
    matrix1.print();
    // Instantiation and setup of matrix2
    cout << "matrix2" << endl;
    Matrix matrix2 (3, 4);
    matrix2.setup ();
    matrix2.print ();
    // Instantiation and setup of matrix3
    cout << "A new matrix3" << endl;
    Matrix matrix3 (4, 2);
    matrix3.setup ();
    matrix3.print ();
    // Adding matrix2 to matrix1 and printing the resulting matrix
    cout << "Result of matrix1 + matrix2" << endl;
    Matrix addResult (3, 4);
    matrix1.add (matrix2, addResult);
    addResult.print ();
    // Subtracting matrix2 from matrix1 and printing the resulting matrix
    cout << "   Result of matrix1 - matrix2" << endl;
    Matrix subResult (3, 4);
    matrix1.subtract (matrix2, subResult);
    subResult.print ();
    // Multiplying matrix1 and matrix3 and printing the resulting matrix
    cout << "Result of matrix1 * matrix3" << endl;
    Matrix mulResult (3, 2);
    matrix1.multiply (matrix3, mulResult);
    mulResult.print();
    return 0;
}
```

Run:

```
matrix1
    3    2    3    1
    4    4    5    1
    4    1    1    5
matrix2
    4    3    1    3
    3    5    1    5
    4    5    1    4
matrix3
    4    1
    5    5
    3    4
    2    1
```

(continued)

Program 9.21 Application to test the *Matrix* class (Continued)

```
Result of matrix1 + matrix2
         7        5        4        4
         7        9        6        6
         8        6        2        9
Result of matrix1 - matrix2
        -1       -1        2       -2
         1       -1        4       -4
         0       -4        0        1
Result of matrix1 * matrix3
        33       26
        53       45
        34       18
```

Key Terms

address operator
ampersand symbol
code memory
dangling pointer
generic pointer
global object
heap memory
indirection operator
memory leak
null pointer
pass-by-pointer
pass-by-reference
pointer arithmetic
pointer type
ragged array
reference type
reference variable
return-by-pointer
return-by-reference
return-by-value
static memory
stack memory
static object

Summary

A reference type is a compound type that allows a memory location to be used with different names.

A pointer type is a compound type representing an address in memory. A pointer variable is a variable that contains an address.

The memory used by a C++ program is made of four distinct areas: code memory (holding programs), static memory (holding global and static objects), stack memory (holding the parameter and local objects), and heap memory (holding the object created during runtime).

Problems

PR-1. Given the following lines of code, show what would be printed.

```
int x = 10;
int& y = x;
cout << x << " " << y;
```

PR-2. Given the following lines of code, show what would be printed.

```
int x = 100;
int& y = x;
int& z = x;
cout << x << " " << y << " " << z;
```

PR-3. What is wrong with the following lines of code?

```
int x = 1000;
int& y = 2000;
```

PR-4. What is printed from the following lines of code?

```
int x = 1;
int y = 2;
int& z = x;
z = y;
cout << x << " " << y << "  " << z;
```

PR-5. What is wrong with the following lines of code?

```
const int x = 100;
double& y = x;
```

PR-6. What is wrong with the following lines of code?

```
const int x = 100;
int& y = x;
```

PR-7. What is wrong with the following lines of code?

```
int x = 1000;
const int& y = x;
```

PR-8. What is printed from the following program?

```
#include <iostream>
using namespace std;

void fun (int& y);

int main ()
{
	int x = 10;
	fun (x) ;
	cout << x << endl;
	return 0;
}

void fun (int& y)
{
	y++;
}
```

PR-9. What is printed from the following program?

```
#include <iostream>
using namespace std;

void fun (int& y);

int main ()
{
      fun (10) ;

      cout << x << endl;
      return 0;
}

void fun (int& y)
{
      y++;
}
```

PR-10. What is printed from the following program?

```
#include <iostream>
using namespace std;

int& fun (int& yy, int& zz);

int main ()
{
      int x = 120;
      int y = 80;
      cout << fun (x , y);
      return 0;
}

int& fun (int& yy, int& zz)
{
      if (yy > zz)
      {
            return yy;
      }
      return zz;
}
```

PR-11. What is printed from the following program?

```
#include <iostream>
using namespace std;

int& fun (int yy, int zz);
```

```
int main ()
{
    int x = 120;
    int y = 80;
    cout << fun (x , y);
    return 0;
}

int& fun (int yy, int zz)
{
    if (yy > zz)
    {
        return yy;
    }
    return zz;
}
```

PR-12. What is printed from the following program?

```
#include <iostream>
using namespace std;

int& fun (int& yy, int& zz)
{
    if (yy > zz)
    {
        return yy;
    }
    return zz;
}
int main ()
{
    cout << fun (120 , 80);
    return 0;
}
```

PR-13. Given the following lines of code, show what would be printed.

```
int x = 10;
int* y = &x;
cout << x << " " << *y;
```

PR-14. Given the following lines of code, show what would be printed.

```
int x = 100;
int* y = &x;
int* z = &x;
cout << x << "  " << *y << "  " << *z;
```

PR-15. What is wrong with the following line of code?

```
int* x = 25;
```

PR-16. What is wrong with the following lines of code?

```
const int x = 100;
double* y = &x;
```

PR-17. What is wrong with the following lines of code?

```
const int x = 100;
int* y = &x;
```

PR-18. What is wrong with the following lines of code?

```
const int x = 100;
const int* y = &x;
int* y = &x;
```

PR-19. What is wrong with the following lines of code?

```
int x = 1000;
int y = 2000;
int* const z = &x;
z = &y;
```

PR-20. What is printed from the following lines of code?

```
int sample [5] = {0, 10, 20, 30, 40};
cout << *(sample + 2);
```

PR-21. What is printed from the following lines of code?

```
int sample [5] = {5, 10, 15, 20, 25};
cout << *sample + 2 << endl;
cout << *(sample + 2);
```

PR-22. What is printed from the following lines of code?

```
int sample [5] = {0, 10, 20, 30, 40};
cout << *(sample + 7);
```

PR-23. What is printed from the following program?

```
#include <iostream>
using namespace std;

void fun (int* x)
{
    cout << *(x + 2);
}

int main ()
{
    int sample [5] = {0, 10, 20, 30, 40};
    fun (sample);
    return 0;
}
```

PR-24. What is created in the heap from the following statement? Draw a picture to show the object in the heap.

```
int** arr = new int* [3];
```

PR-25. What is created in the heap from the following statements? Draw a picture to show the object in the heap.

```
int** arr = new int* [3];
for (int i = 0; i < 3; i++)
{
    arr[i] = new int [5];
}
```

PR-26. Write the code to fill the two-dimensional array created in PR-25 with values entered at the keyboard.

PR-27. How should the *delete* operator be used to delete the array created in PR-25?

Programs

PRG-1. Write a function that finds the largest of three integers using pass-by-reference and return-by-reference. Your design can use the function we wrote for finding the larger between two integers. Test your function in a program.

PRG-2. Write a function that finds the largest of three fractions using pass-by-reference and return-by-reference. Your design can use the design we wrote to find the largest between two fractions. Test your function in a program.

PRG-3. Write a function that multiplies two fractions and returns the result using pass-by-reference and return-by-reference. Test your function in a program.

PRG-4. For greater control over how an array can be used, we can create an array class. Design a class named Array with the data members *capacity*, *size*, and *arr* (a pointer that points to the first element of the array in the heap). Also design a member function named *insert* that adds elements to the end of the array, and a function named *print* that prints the element of the array. Test your program with different lists of array elements.

PRG-5. Redesign the Array class from PRG-4 to be a sorted array (with possible duplicate values). In a sorted array, we may need to move some elements toward the end of the array to insert a new elements at the correct position. We also may need to move some elements toward the front of the array when we delete an element.

PRG-6. In object-oriented programming, we can always create a class for the problem to be solved and let the user instantiate objects from the class and use them. Define a class that creates a multiplication table of any size up to 10. Then use an application program to instantiate any multiplication table.

PRG-7. Redesign the Pascal triangle as a class in which we can create a list of coefficients of a binomial of any size that is passed to the constructor. For example, Pascal (5) prints the coefficients for $(x + y)^5$.

This chapter explores the topic of strings, something that we use in virtually every program. The C++ language inherits the C string from the C language; we discuss this in the first section of this chapter. C++ defines a richer and more secure string that we discuss in the second section of the chapter. The C-string is an array of null-terminated characters; the C++ string is a class that matches the idea of object-oriented programming.

Objectives

After you have read and studied this chapter, you should be able to:

- Describe the general concepts and use of C strings.
- Provide a brief list of the C string library in the <cstring> header file.
- Demonstrate the use of C strings in programs.
- Explain the operations defined for C strings in the library.
- Provide a brief list of the C++ string library in the <string> header file.
- Explain the operations defined for C++ strings in the library.
- Demonstrate the use of C++ strings in programs.

10.1 C STRINGS

Although the C++ language contains the C++ string class type, which we will discuss in the second section of this chapter, we briefly discuss the C string (or C-style string as it is sometimes called) for two reasons. First, there are some programs (including some libraries) that still use C strings. Second, the C++ string class uses some C strings in its definitions, so a basic knowledge of C-strings is necessary to understand C++ strings. To use C strings, we need the <cstring> library header file.

The <cstring> header file is needed to use C strings.

A **C string** is not a class type. It is an array of characters, but this does not mean that any array of characters is a C string. To be a C string, the last character in the array must be the null character ('\0'). In other words, a C string is a null-terminated array of characters. Figure 10.1 shows a C string.

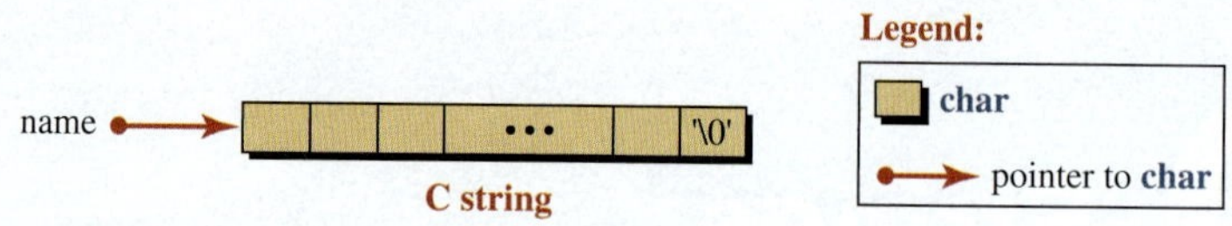

Figure 10.1 General idea behind a C string

Since the name of an array is a pointer to the first element in the array, the name of a C string is a pointer to the first character in the string. However, we must remember that the name of a C string does not define a variable; it defines a pointer value (like the name of any array). In other words, it is not an *lvalue*; it is an *rvalue*. It is a constant pointer, which means that the pointer cannot be moved to point to any other element.

The C string name is a constant pointer to the first character.

10.1.1 C String Library

Before we discuss how to use C strings, we list the common operations with their prototypes (if applicable) in Table 10.1.

Table 10.1 Prototypes for functions in the <cstring> header

// Construction
There is no constructor. User needs to create an array of characters.
// Destruction
There is no destructor. The user needs to destroy the array if created in the heap.
// Copy construction (two member functions are designed for copying a string)
char* strcpy (char* *str1*, const char* *str2*)
char* strncpy (char* *str1*, const char* *str2*, size_t *n*)
// Finding the length
size_t strlen (const char* *str*)
// Input / output
There is no input/output operation in the library, but the >> and << operators are overloaded for input and output. The user can also use the getline () function defined in the *istream* class to input a line of characters.
// Accessing characters
There is no member function to access individual characters, but the user can use the index operator [...] to do so.
// Searching for a character (forward and backward)
char* strchr (const char* *str*, int *c*)
char* strrchr (const char* *str*, int *c*)
// Searching for a substring
char* strstr (const char* *str*, const char* *substr*)

(continued)

Table 10.1 Prototypes for functions in the <cstring> header (Continued)

// Searching for a character in a set (only forward search)
char* strpbrk (const char* *str*, const char* *set*)
// Comparing two strings
int strcmp (char* *str1*, const char* *str2*)
int strncmp (char* *str1*, const char* *str2*, size_t *n*)
// Concatenation (appending a string at the back of another)
char* strcat (char* *str1*, const char* *str2*)
char* strncat (char* *str1*, const char* *str2*, size_t *n*)
// Tokenizing
char* strtok (char* *str*, const char* *delimit*)

10.1.2 Operation on C Strings

In this section, we explain how we can use the member functions defined in Table 10.1.

Construction

As we said, a C string is not a class type, which means there is no constructor defined in the library. To construct a C string, we must create an array of characters and set the last element to the null character '\0'.

We can create two types of C strings: nonconstant and constant. In a nonconstant C string, the value of the characters can be changed after creation; in a constant C string, the value of the characters cannot be changed. The following shows how we can create and initialize a C string.

```
char str [ ] = {'A', 'B', 'C', 'D', '\0'};          // Nonconstant
char str [ ] = "ABCD";                              // Nonconstant compact
const char str [ ] = {'A', 'B', 'C', 'D', '\0'};    // Constant
const char str [ ] = "ABCD";                        // Constant compact
```

The first form of initialization is what we have seen in the past for any array of characters. The second form, which is sometimes referred to as the compact form, uses a compact initialization in which the characters are enclosed in double quotes and no null character is included. The compiler extracts the characters one by one and stores them in the corresponding array cells. The null character is added automatically. Figure 10.2 shows the idea behind the compact form.

We recommend using the compact form to avoid omitting the null character.

```
char str [ ] = "ABCD" ;

const char str [ ] = "ABCD" ;
```

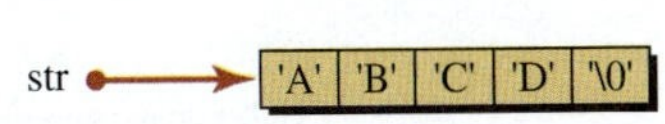

Figure 10.2 The effect of using compact initialization

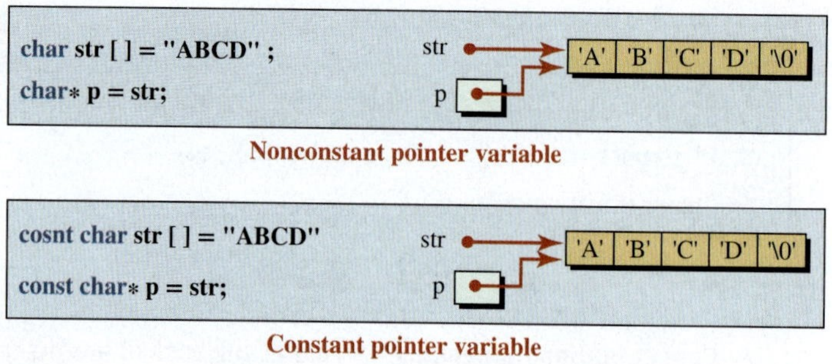

Figure 10.3 Creation of pointer variable from a string

As we mentioned, the name of the string created in Table 10.1 or Figure 10.2 is an *rvalue* pointer, not a variable. If we want to create a variable, we must declare a variable of type *char** or *const char** and assign the name of the string to that variable, as shown in Figure 10.3.

In Chapter 8 we mentioned that we cannot return an array from a function because an array requires a pointer to the first element and its size. The design of the C string eliminates the second requirement. The size is not needed because the last character is a null character and implicitly defines the size. This means that we can return a pointer variable pointing to a C string from a function.

String Literal We have seen literals of data types, such as integer, floating point, or character. For example, 3 is an integer literal, 23.7 is a floating-pointing literal, and `'A'` is a character literal. We can also have a string literal. A **string literal** is a null-terminated array of characters whose name is the sequence of characters in the array enclosed by two quotation marks, as shown in Figure 10.4.

A string literal is a constant string that is part of the C++ language and is used with both C strings and C++ strings. When it is created, it can be used anywhere that a string literal can be used. We have used a string literal to print messages. However, we must remember that a string literal is a constant entity and cannot be changed after it has been created.

A string literal is a constant entity; it cannot be changed.

EXAMPLE 10.1

The following code fragment shows that we can use a string literal like other literals. For example, we can use the *cout* object and the insertion operator to print the value of an integer literal, a floating-point literal, a character literal, and a string literal.

```
cout << 5 << endl;                 // Printing an integer literal
cout << 21.3 << endl;              // Printing a floating-point literal
cout << 'A' << endl;               // Printing a character literal
cout << "Hello dear" << endl;      // Printing a string literal
```

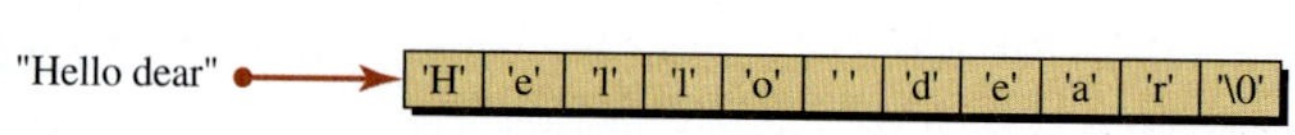

Figure 10.4 A string literal

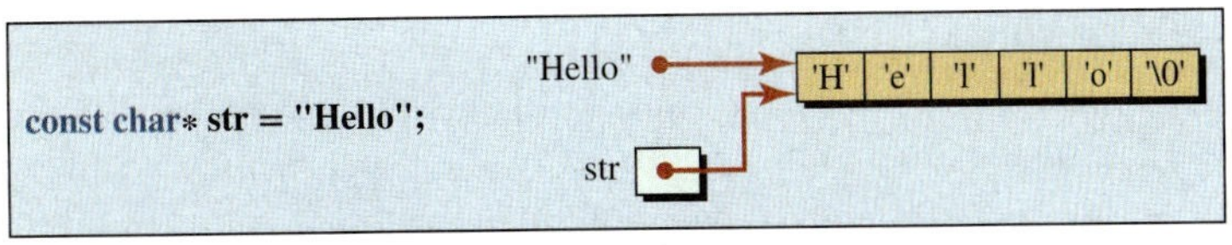

Pointer assignment by a literal

Figure 10.5 Assignment of a string literal to a pointer

Creating Strings Using String Literals The string literal makes it easy to create a C string by first creating the desired string literal and then assigning it to a pointer to a constant character. Figure 10.5 shows the process.

C++ forbids assigning a string literal to a nonconstant pointer to a character, as shown below:

```
char* str = "Hello";                    // Error. Literal is a constant
const char* str = "Hello";              // OK.
```

Assigning a string literal to a nonconstant pointer results in a compilation error.

Compact Initializer and String Literal We must distinguish between a compact initializer and a string literal, although both look the same. The difference is where they are used. A compact initializer is a simple form of a regular initializer that we have seen. When used, the compiler takes out the characters one by one and stores them in the character array. A string literal is already a constant string that can be used wherever a string can be used. It is a pointer to a string created in memory and can be assigned to a pointer to a constant character. The following shows the difference in use:

```
char str1 [ ] = "Hello";                // "Hello" is a compact initializer
const char str2 [ ] = "Hello";          // "Hello" is a compact initializer
const char* str3 = "Hello";             // "Hello" is a literal string
```

Construction in Heap Memory Since a C string is an array, we can create it in heap memory. However, since the name of the string in this case is a pointer to a character, we cannot use compact initialization. If it is a nonconstant string, we must initialize it character by character; if it is a constant string, we must use a string literal to do so.

```
char* str = new char [3];               // Nonconstant string of two characters
const char* str = new char [3];         // Constant string of two characters
```

Destruction

As mentioned in Table 10.1, a C string is not a class type, which means no destructor is defined in the library. If a C string is created in stack memory, it is automatically deleted when the *main* function terminates. When the string is created in the heap, we must use the delete operator to delete it; in doing so we avoid a memory leak.

```
const char* str = new char [3];         // Creation
delete [ ] str;                         // Deletion
```

Copying

Since a C string is not defined as a class, there is no copy constructor. However, the designers of the library have defined two member functions: *strcpy* and *strncpy*. The function *strcpy* replaces the first string with the whole second string; the function *strncpy* replaces the first *n* characters in the first string with the first *n* characters of the second string. Note that the copying changes the destination string, but not the source string.

```
strcpy (str1, str2);                    // Using the whole str2
strncopy (str1, str2, n);               // Using part of str2
```

The two functions *strcpy* (...) and *strncpy* (...) can be used to replace one string with another.

EXAMPLE 10.2

In Program 10.1 the first function totally erases *str1* and replaces it with *str2*. The second function replaces the first *n* character of *str1* with the first *n* characters of *str2* and leaves the rest of *str1* unchanged.

Program 10.1 Copying in a C string library

```
/***************************************************************
 * The program shows how to use strcpy and strncpy to replace  *
 * the whole string or part of it with the whole or part of    *
 * another string.                                             *
 ***************************************************************/
#include <cstring>
#include <iostream>
using namespace std;

int main ( )
{
  // Copy the whole str2 to str1. String str1 is erased.
  char str1 [] = "This is the first string.";
  char str2 [] = "This is the second string.";
  strcpy (str1, str2);
  cout << "str1: " << str1 << endl;
  // Copy part of str4 to str3. str3 is partially erased.
  char str3 [] = "abcdefghijk.";
  const char* str4 = "ABCDEFGHIJK";
  strncpy (str3, str4, 4);
  cout << "str3: " << str3 << endl;
  return 0;
}
```

```
Run:
str1: This is the second string.
str3: ABCDefghijk.
```

String Length

Each C string has a size (length) that is the number of characters in the string without counting the null character. The C string library defines the *strlen* function to find the length of the string. The function accepts a C string and returns its length as a *size_t* type, which is defined as an *unsigned int* in the library.

```
size_t n = strlen (str);                    // Finding the length of str
```

The *strlen* (...) function returns the number of characters in a C string without counting the null character.

EXAMPLE 10.3

Program 10.2 shows how we can find the length of a C string.

Input and Output

In addition to initialization with a compact form or assignment using a literal string, we can read the characters into a C string that is declared as an array of characters. We cannot do so when the string is declared as a type (*char** or *const char**) because the compiler must allocate memory before reading the characters.

Overloaded Extraction and Insertion Operators Consider the situation in which a <cstring> library has overloaded the extraction operator (>>) and the insertion operator

Program 10.2 Finding the length of two strings

```
/***************************************************************
 * The program shows how to get the length of a C-string, which   *
 * is the number of characters before the null character          *
 ***************************************************************/
#include <cstring>
#include <iostream>
using namespace std;

int main ( )
{
  // Declaration and definition of four strings
  const char* str1 = "Hello my friends.";
  char str2 [] = {'H', 'e', 'l', 'l', 'o', '\0'} ;
  // Finding and printing the length of each string
  cout << "Length of str1: " << strlen (str1) << endl;
  cout << "Length of str2: " << strlen (str2);
  return 0;
}
```

Run:

```
Length of str1: 17
Length of str2: 5
```

(<<) to be used for string input and output. The extraction operator extracts characters one by one from an input object (keyboard or a file) and stores them in the array until a whitespace character is encountered. It then adds the null character at the end. The problem is that the character array that stores the input must have allocated enough memory locations to store all characters entered (before a whitespace) plus one for the *null* character. If the allocation is not large enough, the result is unpredictable. The insertion operator writes characters in the array to an output device until a *null* character is encountered.

```
cin >> str;                          // Input
cout << str;                         // Output
```

EXAMPLE 10.4

Program 10.3 includes a null character in the literal string for *str4* just to show that the literal string is terminated by the null character and the rest of the characters are not part of the literal string (line 15). In other words, the string has only 8 characters instead of 19. We have input the characters for *str5*, but note that only the first word is stored in the string; the rest are ignored because the extraction operator stops at the first whitespace.

Program 10.3 Using C strings

```
1   /***************************************************************
2    * The program shows how to create C-strings and use input and   *
3    * output operations with them.                                  *
4    ***************************************************************/
5   #include <iostream>
6   using namespace std;
7
8   int main ( )
9   {
10     // Create one constant and one non-constant string.
11     char str1 [] = {'H', 'e', 'l', 'l', 'o', '\0'} ;
12     const char str2 [] = {'H', 'e', 'l', 'l', 'o', '\0'};
13     // Create two constant string types and use string literals.
14     const char* str3 = "Goodbye";
15     const char* str4 = "Goodbye\0 my friend";
16     // Printing four strings
17     cout << "str1: " << str1 << endl;
18     cout << "str2: " << str2 << endl;
19     cout << "str3: " << str3 << endl;
20     cout << "str4: " << str4 << endl << endl;
21     // Create and input a fifth string.
22     char str5 [20];
23     cout << "Enter the characters for str5: " ;
24     cin >> str5;
25     cout << "str5: " << str5;
```

(continued)

Program 10.3 Using C strings (Continued)

```
    return 0;
}
```

```
Run:
str1: Hello
str2: Hello
str3: Goodbye
str4: Goodbye

Enter the characters for str5: This is the one.
str5: This
```

The getline Function To read a line of characters that includes whitespace, we must use the function defined for this purpose, the *getline* function. The *getline* function is a member of the *istream* class, which means that we must have an object of type *cin*. If the *delim* parameter is missing, we use the `'\n'` character.

```
cin.getline (str, n);                    // Using '\n' as the delimiter
cin.get (str, n, 'delimeter');           // Using a specific delimiter
```

EXAMPLE 10.5

Program 10.4 creates an array of strings, reads lines into the array, and prints the lines.

Program 10.4 Using an array of strings

```
/***************************************************************
 * The program shows how to read a set of lines using the        *
 * getline function and print them.                              *
 ***************************************************************/
#include <iostream>
#include <cstring>
using namespace std;

int main ()
{
   // Declaration of an array of strings
   char lines [3][80];
   // Inputting three lines
   for (int i = 0; i < 3; i++)
   {
        cout << "Enter a line of characters: ";
        cin.getline (lines [i], 80);
   }
```

(continued)

Program 10.4 Using an array of strings (Continued)

```
    // Outputting three lines
    cout << endl;
    cout << "Output: " << endl;
    for (int i = 0; i < 3; i++)
    {
        cout << lines [i] << endl;
    }
    return 0;
}
```

```
Run:
Enter a line of characters: This is the first line.
Enter a line of characters: This is the second line.
Enter a line of characters: This is the third line.

Output:
This is the first line.
This is the second line.
This is the third line.
```

Accessing Characters

The next operation we discuss is how to access any character in a string. We can use the subscript operator to access a character if we know its position in the string. Accessing means retrieving only if the string is constant. Accessing can mean retrieving or changing if the string is nonconstant.

```
char c = str [i];                    // The string str is a constant
str[i] = c;                          // The string str is nonconstant
```

EXAMPLE 10.6

Program 10.5 shows how to access characters in constant and nonconstant strings.

Program 10.5 Accessing characters in a C string

```
/****************************************************************
 * The program shows how to access a character in a string     *
 * using the subscript operator.                                *
 ****************************************************************/
#include <cstring>
#include <iostream>
using namespace std;

int main ( )
{
```

(continued)

Program 10.5 Accessing characters in a C string (Continued)

```
    // Creation of two C-strings
    const char* str1 = "Hello my friends.";
    char str2 [ ] = "This is the second string.";
    // Retrieving character at a given position
    cout << "Character at index 6 in str1: " << str1[6] << endl;
    // Changing character at a given position
    str2 [0] = 't';
    cout << "str2 after change: " << str2;
    return 0;
}
```

```
Run:
Character at index 6 in str1: m
str2 after change: this is the second string.
```

Searching for a Character

We can search a string to find a character. The search can return a pointer of the first occurrence (forward search) or the last occurrence (backward search). The first search uses the *strchr* function; the second uses the *strrchr* function. After a pointer to the character is set, we can use it to change the character if the string is not constant. If the character cannot be found, a null pointer is returned.

```
char* ptr = strchr (str, 'c');          // Forward search
char* ptr = strrchr (str, 'c');         // Backward search
```

We can use strchr (...) and strrchr (...) member functions to create a pointer to a character.

EXAMPLE 10.7

Program 10.6 shows how to search for a character.

Program 10.6 Finding the start of a substring

```
/***********************************************************************
 * A program to search for a given character using forward            *
 * search to find the first occurrence or backward search to          *
 * to find the last occurrence                                        *
 ***********************************************************************/
#include <cstring>
#include <iostream>
using namespace std;

int main ( )
{
```

(continued)

Program 10.6 Finding the start of a substring (Continued)

```
    // Declaration of a string
    char str [ ] = "Hello friends.";
    // Capitalizing the first occurrence of character e
    char* cPtr = strchr (str, 'e');
    *cPtr = 'E' ;
    cout << "str after first change: " << str << endl;
    // Capitalizing the last occurrence of character e
    cPtr = strrchr (str, 'e');
    *cPtr = 'E' ;
    cout << "str after last change: " << str << endl;
    return 0;
}
```

```
Run:
str after first change: HEllo friends.
str after last change: HEllo friEnds.
```

Searching for a Substring

We can search a string to find the position of a substring using the *strstr* function. The function returns a pointer to the first character in the substring. If the substring cannot be found in the string, a null pointer is returned.

```
char* ptr = strstr (str, substr);                    // Searching for a substring
```

EXAMPLE 10.8

Program 10.7 shows how to find a substring.

Program 10.7 Finding a substring

```
/***************************************************************
 * The program shows how to use the strstr member function to  *
 * find the occurrence of a substring in a string.             *
 ***************************************************************/
#include <cstring>
#include <iostream>
using namespace std;

int main ( )
{
    // Creating a string
    char str [ ] = "Hello friends of mine.";
    // Finding the location of the substring
    char* sPtr = strstr (str, "friends");
    cout << "The substring starts at index: " << sPtr - str;
```

(*continued*)

Program 10.7 Finding a substring (Continued)

```
   return 0;
}
```

Run:

```
The substring starts at index: 6
```

Searching for Any Character in a Set

Sometimes we need to search a string to find the position of any character defined in a set of characters. In other words, we do not want to find the position of a specified character in the string; we want to find the first position of any character in the set. Later in this chapter we learn that this operation is used to tokenize a string. The set is also defined as a string. The function *strpbrk* is used for this purpose. If no character can be found, a null pointer is returned.

```
char* p = strpbrk (str, set);                    // Searching for character in a set
```

The member function strpbrk (...) allows us to find the position of the first occurance of any character in a set of characters.

EXAMPLE 10.9

Program 10.8 shows how to use the *strpbrk* (...) function.

Program 10.8 Searching for a character in a set

```
/*****************************************************************
 * The program shows how we can use the strpbrk function to      *
 * find the location of any character in a set of characters.    *
 *****************************************************************/
#include <cstring>
#include <iostream>
using namespace std;

int main ( )
{
   // Creation of a string
   char str [ ] = "Hello friends of mine.";
   // Finding the first occurance of any character in a set
   char* pPtr = strpbrk (str, "pfmd");
   cout << "The character " << *pPtr << " was found." << endl ;
   cout << "It is at index: " << pPtr - str;
   return 0;
}
```

Run:

```
The character f was found.
It is at index: 6
```

Comparing

We can compare two strings using the *strcmp* and *strncmp* functions. The first compares the two strings; the second compares only the first *n* characters of the two strings. Comparison is done character by character until a character that is not the same is reached (note that the null character is also used in the comparison). When unequal characters are found, the comparison stops and the functions return a negative number if the character in the first string is smaller than the second. It returns a positive integer if the character in the first string is larger than the second. If different characters were not found, the functions return 0.

```
int value = (str1, str2);          // Comparing str1 with the whole str2
int value = (str1, str2, n);       // Comparing str1 with the first n characters of str2
```

Two strings can be compared with *strcmp* (...) and *strncmp* (...) member functions.

EXAMPLE 10.10

Program 10.9 uses these two functions. Note that the compare function does not modify any of the two strings.

Program 10.9 Comparing C strings

```
/***************************************************************
 * The program shows how we can compare two strings using the  *
 * strcmp and strncmp functions.                               *
 ***************************************************************/
#include <cstring>
#include <iostream>
using namespace std;

int main ( )
{
  // Declaration of two C-strings
  const char* str1 = "Hello Alice.";
  const char* str2 = "Hello John.";
  const char* str3 = "Hello Betsy.";
  // Comparison use the whole length
  cout << "Comparing str1 and str2: ";
  cout  << strcmp (str1, str2) << endl;
  cout << "Comparing str2 and str3: ";
  cout << strcmp (str2, str3) << endl;
  // Comparison using one the first characters
  cout << "Comparing first 5 characters of str1 and str2: ";
  cout << strncmp (str1, str2, 5);
```

(continued)

Program 10.9 Comparing C strings (Continued)

```
    return 0;
}
```

```
Run:
Comparing str1 and str2: -1
Comparing str2 and str3: 1
Comparing first 5 characters of str1 and str2: 0
```

Concatenation (Appending)

We can add a string at the end of another string. In this case the destination string will be changed, but the source remains unchanged. The library defines two member functions for this purpose: the *strcat* and *strncat* functions. The first function concatenates all characters in *str2* at the end of *str1*. The second function concatenates only the first *n* characters of the second string at the end of the first string. However, we must be sure that *str1* has enough memory allocation to accept the concatenation (Program 10.10).

```
strcat (str1, str2);             // Appending the whole str2 to str1
strncat (str1, str2, n);         // Appending the first n characters of str2 to str1
```

The member functions *strcat* (...) and *strncat* (...) can be used to concatenate one string at the end of the other.

EXAMPLE 10.11

Program 10.10 uses the two member functions related to concatenation.

Program 10.10 Using strcat and strncat

```
/****************************************************************
 * We use strcat and strncast to concatenate a string at the    *
 * end of another string.                                       *
 ****************************************************************/
#include <cstring>
#include <iostream>
using namespace std;

int main ( )
{
    // Using strcat function
    char str1 [20] = "This is ";
    const char* str2 = "a string.";
    strcat (str1, str2);
    cout << "str1: " << str1 << endl;
    // Using strncat function
```

(continued)

Program 10.10 Using strcat and strncat (Continued)

```
    char str3 [20] = "abcdefghijk";
    const char* str4 = "ABCDEFGHIJK";
    strncat (str3, str4, 4);
    cout << "str3: " << str3 << endl;
    return 0;
}
```

Run:
```
str1: This is a string.
str3: abcdefghijkABCD
```

Tokenizing

One of the common operations on a string is to find tokens embedded in a string. **String Tokens** are substrings separated by delimiters (such as whitespace). The library defines the *strtok* function. To find all tokens in a string, we must call the *strtok* function multiple times. When the *strtok* function is called, it performs three specific tasks:

1. It searches the string for the first occurrence of a character not in the delimiter set. The search starts from the character pointed to by the first parameter. If a character is found, it sets the pointer *p* to that character. If not found, it does nothing.
2. It then searches for the first occurrence of a character in the delimiter set. If the character is found, it changes that character to a null character.
3. It returns the pointer set in the first task.

In Figure 10.6, the *strtok* function finds the first character not in the delimiter set and points *p* to that character. It then finds a character in the delimiter set and changes that

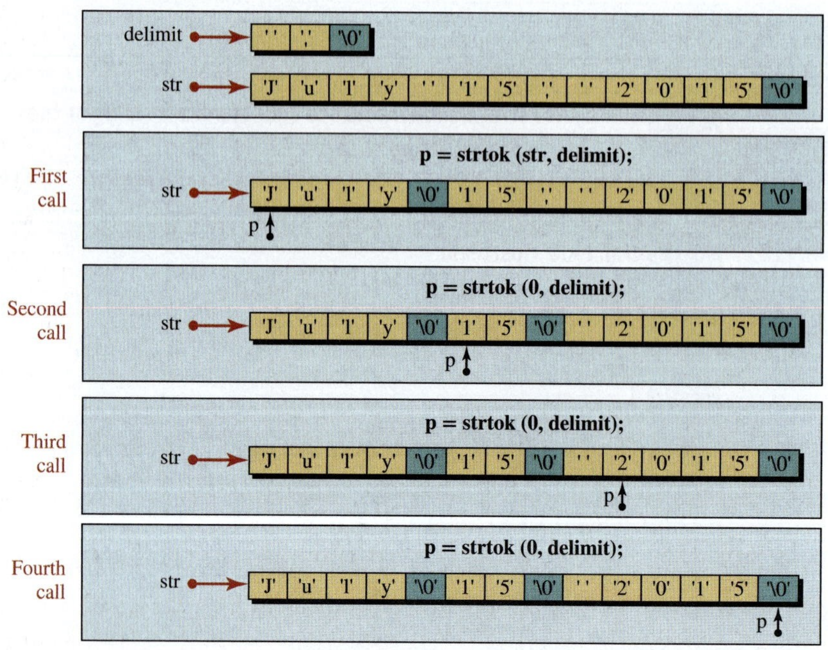

Figure 10.6 Tokenizing using space and comma as delimiters

character to a null character. This means a string has been created by *p* that spans from *p* to the null character. In the second and the following calls, the first parameter is the null pointer and the *strtok* function starts its search from the null pointer created in the previous call. When the function reaches the end of the string, *p* is null.

```
char* p = strtok (str, delimiter);                    // Tokenizing str using a delimiter
```

The strtok (...) function can be used to split a string into tokens using delimiter characters.

EXAMPLE 10.12

Program 10.11 uses the *strtok* (...) function to split a string into tokens. The program loops to repeatedly call *strtok* until *p* points to a null character (end of original string). Note that the original string is changed in this process, which means it cannot be a constant string.

Note that Program 10.11 handles two other conditions. First, if the string is empty, *p* in line 15 is set to null and the *while* is skipped, which means nothing is printed. Second, if the string is made of only one word, after the only word is printed in line 18 in the first iteration, *p* is pointed to a null character and the loop is terminated.

Program 10.11 Tokenizing a string

```
1  /***************************************************************
2   * The program shows how we can use the strtok function to extract  *
3   * tokens from a date.                                              *
4   ***************************************************************/
5  #include <cstring>
6  #include <iostream>
7  using namespace std;
8
9  int main ( )
10 {
11    // Declaration of a sentence and a pointer
12    char str [ ] = "July 15, 2015";
13    char* p;
14    // Use strtok to extract all words
15    p = strtok (str, ", ");  // first call
16    while (p)
17    {
18        cout << p << endl;
19        p = strtok (0, ", "); // second, third, and fourth calls
20    }
21    return 0;
22 }
```

```
Run:
July
15
2015
```

Problems with C Strings

Although C strings provide a way to use strings, they are more error prone and not as robust as C++ strings. We therefore recommend C++ strings be used as much as possible. We discuss C++ strings in the next section.

10.2 THE C++ STRING CLASS

The C++ library provides a class named *string*, whose objects are normally referred to as **C++ string** objects as compared to C string arrays of characters. To use the objects and member functions of this class, we must include the header file <string> in our program.

The C++ string library defines a class type whereas the C string library defines an array of characters. When working with a C string, we must create an array of characters and apply functions defined in the <cstring> library. When using a C++ string, we can construct a string object and apply the predefined member functions in the <string> library to it. We strongly recommend using the C++ string as much as possible.

To use C++ strings, we need the <string> header file.

10.2.1 General Design Idea

To better understand how the string class works, we must consider general concepts that designers use in designing the string class. The string class has private data members and public member functions. The user calls the public member functions to manipulate string objects. In general, the data members include a pointer to an array of characters. Other data members keep information about the character array. The data members are normally created in stack memory, but the character array itself is allocated in the heap because its size is not defined until run time. While the C++ string can be visualized as a character array, it is not null terminated as we saw in C strings. Figure 10.7 shows the general picture of a C++ string.

A C++ string is an array of characters, but it is not null terminated.

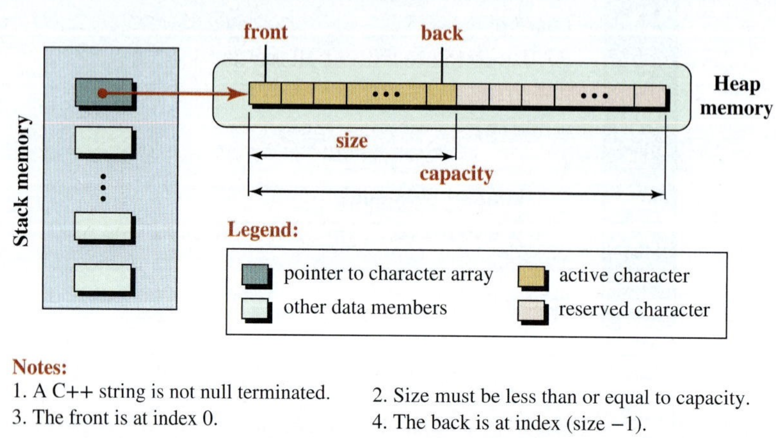

Figure 10.7 General idea behind the C++ string object

Before discussing each of the member functions, we discuss a metadata type and a constant that are used in the library: *size_type* and *npos*. We show them in a different color to emphasize that they are not fundamental data types; they are type definitions created in the library using fundamental types. The *size_type* is an *unsigned int*. It is defined as unsigned to prevent a negative integer because size must always be positive. It has two purposes: It is the index of the character array, and it contains the count of a set of characters; in both cases, the value cannot be negative. The constant *npos* has the type *size_type*, and its value is set to −1. The *npos* constant is used to show that we have passed the last element in forward movement or the first element in backward movement. In other words, it is an index that does not exist. These two identifiers are defined in the std :: string namespace. When we use them in our program, we must qualify them with their namespace as shown below:

```
string :: size-type length;
string :: npos;
```

10.2.2 C++ String Library

Before we discuss member functions in the library, we give their prototypes (Table 10.2).

Table 10.2 Selected members of C++ library

```
// Constructors
string :: string ()
string :: string (size_type count, char c)
string :: string (const char* cstr)
string :: string (const char* cstr, size_type count)
// Destructor
string :: ~string ()
// Copy constructors
string :: string (const string& strg)
string :: string (const string& strg, size_type index, size_type length = npos)
// Operations related to size and capacity
size_type string :: size ( ) const
size_type string :: max_size ( ) const
void string :: resize (size_type n, char c )
size_type string :: capacity ( ) const
void string :: reserve (size_type n = 0)
bool string :: empty ( ) const
// Input and output
istream&  operator>> (istream& in, string& strg)
ostream& operator<< (ostream& out, const string& strg)
```

(continued)

Table 10.2 Selected members of C++ library (Continued)

```
istream& getline (istream& in, string& strg)
istream& getline (istream& in, string& strg, char delimit)
// Accessing a character given its position
const char& string :: operator[ ] (size_type pos) const
char& string :: operator[ ] (size_type pos)
const char& string :: at (size_type pos) const
char& string :: at (size_type pos)
// Accessing a substring given the position of the first character and length
string string :: substr (size_type pos = 0, size_typ length = npos) const
// Finding the position of a given character (forward or backward search)
size_type string :: find (char c, size_type index = 0) const
size_type string :: rfind (char c, size_type index = npos) const
// Finding the position of a character in a set (forward or backward search)
size_type string :: find_first_of (const string& temp, size_type pos = 0)
size_type string :: find_last_of (const string& temp, size_type pos = npos)
// Finding the position of a character not in a set (forward or backward search)
size_type string :: find_first_not_of (const string& temp, size_type pos = 0)
size_type string :: find_last_not_of (const string& temp, size_type pos = npos)
// Comparing two strings
int string :: compare (size_type pos1, size_type n1,const string strg2,
                      size_type pos2, size_type n2) const
int string :: compare (size_type pos1, size_type n1,
                      const char* cstr, size_type n2) const
// Logical comparison of two strings (oper can be <, <=, >, >=, ==, !=)
bool string :: operatorOper (const string strg1, const string strg2)
bool string :: operatorOper (const string strg1, const char* cstr)
bool string :: operatorOper (const char* cstr, const string strg1)
// Pushing a character at the end of a string
void string :: push_back (char c)
// Modifying a string using another string (append, insert, replace, and assign)
string& string :: append (const string& temp)
string& string :: insert (size_type pos, const string& temp)
string& string :: replace (size_type pos, size_type n, const string& temp)
string& string :: assign (size_type pos, size_type n, const string& temp)
// Clearing and erasing a string
void string :: clear ()
```

(continued)

Table 10.2 Selected members of C++ library (Continued)

```
string& string :: erase (size_type pos = 0, size_type n = npos)
// Using the assignment operator
string& string :: operator= (const string& strg)
string& string :: operator= (const char* cstr)
string& string :: operator= (char c)
// Using the compound assignment (addition)
string& string :: operator+= (const string& strg)
string& string :: operator+= (const char* cstr)
string& string :: operator+= (char c)
// Using the addition operator
string& string :: operator+ (const string& strg1, const string& strg2)
string& string :: operator+ (const string& strg1, const char* cstr2)
string& string :: operator+ (const char* cstr1, const string& strg2)
string& string :: operator+ (const string& strg1, char c)
// Conversion to a character array
const char* string :: data ( ) const
// Conversion to a C-string
const char* string :: c_str () const
```

10.2.3 Operations Defined for C++ Strings

We briefly describe the operations defined in Table 10.2.

Construction

The C++ string defines one default constructor and three parameter constructors.

Default Constructor The default constructor shown in Table 10.2 is straight forward. It creates an empty string by setting the pointer data member in Figure 10.7 (green box) to 0 (null pointer). The following shows how we can create an empty string.

```
string strg;                                    // Creating an empty string object
```

Parameter Constructors In addition to the default constructor, the string class allows us to create a string object in three different ways, as shown in Table 10.2. We can use a set of characters of the same value, a string literal, and part of a string literal. The following shows how we can create these objects:

```
string strg1 (5 , 'a');                         // The string "aaaaa"
string strg2 ("hello");                         // The string "hello"
string strg3 ("hello", 2);                      // The string "he"
```

The string *strg*1 is made of the same five characters (the size_type here defines the length). The string *strg*2 is made of a string literal. In this case, the function copies all characters in the literal (except the null character at the end) to the string object. The string *strg*3 is part of a string literal. If we want to use a part of the C-string object (here and later in other member functions), we must start at the beginning of the string because the pointer to a string literal is a constant pointer and cannot be moved. However, we can define the number of characters that should be copied. In this case, we have said we want only two characters, which means only "he" is used to create a C++ string object.

Destruction

The destructor of the string class simply deletes the character array created in the heap and pops all data members allocated in the stack. In other words, calling the delete operator to free allocated memory is done by the destructor, which helps prevent memory leaks.

Copy Construction

The string class allows us to use two different copy constructors: a copy constructor comprised of a full existing object or a copy constructor comprised of part of an existing object.

```
string strg (oldStrg);                          // Using the whole oldStrg
string strg (oldstrg1, index, length);          // Using part of the oldStrg
```

Size and Capacity

A C++ string object uses an array of characters in the heap. If the size of the array must be decreased during an operation, the value of the *size* member function is changed. However, if the size of the string must be increased during an operation, reallocation is needed. A bigger array must be created in the heap, the value of the existing elements must be copied, the new elements must be filled, and the original memory recycled. This is done by the private member functions in the background. However, this process can create a huge overhead for the system if many small incremental changes in the size are needed. To prevent this overhead, the system allows the user to make a reservation, which leads to a larger array than needed when the array is created.

Size and Maximum Size There are two functions that return values of the string size. The *size* function returns the number of characters currently in the string object. The *max_size* function returns the maximum number of characters that a string object can have; it is normally a very big number that is system dependent.

```
size_type n = strg.size ();                     // Getting the size
size_type n = strg.max_size ();                 // Getting the maximum size
```

Resizing The *resize* function changes the size of the string. If $n < size$, characters are deleted from the end of the string to make the size equal to n; if $n > size$, copies of character c are added to the end of the string to make the size n.

```
strg.resize (n, 'c');          //Resizing and filling the rest of string with 'c'
```

Capacity and Reserve The capacity function returns the current capacity of the character array. If we have not made a reservation, the capacity is the same as the size. We can call the *reserve* function to make the capacity larger than the size.

```
size_type n = strg.capacity ();           // Getting the capacity
strg.reserve (n);                         // Reserving a larger array
```

However, there are some restrictions. If the argument of the function is less than the size, nothing happens (capacity cannot be less than the size). If the argument defines a small increase, the system may augment it.

Emptiness The *empty* function returns *true* if the size is 0; *false* otherwise.

```
bool fact = strg.empty();                 // Checking emptiness
```

EXAMPLE 10.13

Program 10.12 uses the member functions related to size, capacity, emptiness, and reservation.

Program 10.12 Testing functions related to size and capacity

```
/***************************************************************
 * The program creates a string object and then tests the size,  *
 * maximum size, and capacity before and after reservation.      *
 ***************************************************************/
#include <string>
#include <iostream>
using namespace std;

int main ( )
{
  // Creating a string object
  string strg ("Hello my friends");
  // Test size, maximum size and capacity
  cout << "Size: " << strg.size () << endl;
  cout << "Maximum size: " << strg.max_size() << endl;
  cout << "Capacity: " << strg.capacity() << endl;
  cout << "Empty? " << boolalpha << strg.empty() << endl;
  cout << endl;
  // Making reservation and test again
  strg.reserve (20);
  cout << "Size: " << strg.size () << endl;
  cout << "Maximum size: " << strg.max_size() << endl;
  cout << "Capacity: " << strg.capacity() << endl;
  cout << "Empty? " << boolalpha << strg.empty();
  return 0;
}
```

(*continued*)

Program 10.12 Testing functions related to size and capacity (Continued)

```
Run:
Size: 16
Maximum size: 1073741820
Capacity: 16
Empty? false

Size: 16
Maximum size: 1073741820
Capacity: 32
Empty? false
```

In Program 10.12 we tried to reserve a total of 20 characters, but the system reserved 32 characters (16 more than the current size). The system thinks that if we have created the original string with 16 characters, an extra four locations probably would not be enough.

Input and Output

We discuss more about input/output of class objects in Chapters 13 and 16. In this section, we briefly discuss how we input a string object and how we output a string object.

Input/Output Operators The input and output operators that we have used so far with fundamental data types are member functions of the input object (*istream*) and output object (*ostream*). The object to be input or output is the parameter. If we want to input or output a string, the parameter must be an instance of the string class.

The *in* object is connected to the keyboard (*cin*) or a file; the *out* object is connected to the monitor (*cout*) or a file. The second parameter for the output operator is a constant string because outputting should not change the string object, but the second parameter for the input operator is not constant because the input read from the keyboard or file changes the string.

The input operator reads from an input stream character by character. It needs to know when it should stop reading. The designer of the function has decided that it will stop when a whitespace character is encountered. This means that if there is a space, or a new line character in the input stream, the reading will stop when it is read.

The output operator writes the string object to an output stream from the beginning to the end. It does not have the limitations of the input operator.

```
cin >> strg;                    // inputting characters for a string
cout << strg;                   // outputing the character of a string
```

EXAMPLE 10.14

Program 10.13 shows how we can use the input/output operators with a string object.

Program 10.13 Using input/output operators

```
/***************************************************************
 * A program to test input/output operators with string objects.   *
 ***************************************************************/
#include <string>
#include <iostream>
using namespace std;

int main ( )
{
  // Constructing a default object
  string strg;
  // Inputting and outputting values for the strg object
  cout << "Input the string: " ;
  cin >> strg;
  cout << strg << endl;
  return 0;
}
```

```
Run:
Input the string: Hello
Hello
```

```
Run:
Input the string: Hi my friends
Hi
```

In the first run, we just type the string "Hello". All characters are input and output. In the second run, we type the string "Hi my friends", and the input stops when the first space is encountered. Only the string "Hi" is stored in the string object and printed.

The getline Function As we said, input operators have predefined delimiters that stop the reading from an input stream. To give users more control, the *istream* object has a function named *getline* with two versions. The first version uses '\n' as the delimiter, which means it can read the whole line; the second version allows users to define their own delimiter character.

```
getline (in, strg);                    // The input stops with '\n'
getline (in, strg, 'c');               // The input stops with character c
```

EXAMPLE 10.15

Program 10.14 shows how we input single-line and multiple-line strings.

Program 10.14 Using getline for input

```
/***************************************************************
 * A program to test the getline function with strings.        *
 ***************************************************************/
#include <string>
#include <iostream>
using namespace std;

int main ( )
{
  // Constructing a default object
  string strg;
  // Creating a string made of a single line
  cout << "Enter a line of characters: " << endl;
  getline (cin, strg);
  cout << strg << endl << endl;
  // Creating a string made of multiple lines
  cout << "Enter lines of characters ended with $: " << endl;
  getline (cin, strg, '$');
  cout << strg;
  return 0;
}
```

```
Run:
Enter a line of characters:
This is a line of text.
This is a line of text.

Enter lines of characters ended with $:
This is a multi-line set of
characters to be
stored in a string.$
This is a multi-line set of
characters to be
stored in a string.
```

Note that the input is shown in red; the output is in black. In the first section, we use the default delimiter, which is the `'\n'` character (enter key). In the second section, we use the `'$'` character as the delimiter. Neither of the delimiter characters is printed.

Accessing Characters

After a string object has been instantiated, we can access an individual character to retrieve or change it if we know its index (its position in the string relative to zero). The string class provides four member functions for this purpose. The first two use the overloaded subscript *operator* [ ] to return a character as an *rvalue* or *lvalue*. We discuss operator overloading in Chapter 13; for the moment, the operator [ ] gives the name of a function that allows us to use the operator [ ] as we did with an array. The second two members use the *at* function to select a character.

```
char c = strg [pos];              // The character c can be modified
char c = strg.at (pos);           // The character c can be modified
const char c = strg [pos];        // The character c cannot be modified
const char c = strg.at (pos);     // The character c cannot be modified
```

The subscript operator does not check the size of the string and may create an unpredictable result and termination of the program if the subscript is out of range; the *at* functions checks the size and throws an exception if the position parameter is not within the range of the array. We learn how to handle exceptions in Chapter 14.

Accessing character functions allows us to provide the position of the character to be returned.

EXAMPLE 10.16

Program 10.15 shows how we can retrieve individual characters in a string.

EXAMPLE 10.17

Program 10.16 shows how we can change all lowercase characters in a line to uppercase. We first use the subscript operator ([ ]) to retrieve the character (as an *rvalue*). We then use the same operator as an *lvalue* to store the uppercase version of the character.

Program 10.15 Retrieving and changing characters

```
/***************************************************************
 * The program shows how to retrieve a single character in a   *
 * string.                                                     *
 ***************************************************************/
#include <string>
#include <iostream>
using namespace std;

int main ( )
{
  // Construction of a string
  string strg ("A short string");
  // Retrieving and printing characters at index 5 and 8
  cout << "Character at index 5: " << strg [5] << endl ;;
  cout << "Character at index 8: " << strg.at(8) << endl;
  return 0;
}
```

```
Run:
Character at index 5: r
Character at index 8: s
```

Program 10.16 Changing all characters to uppercase

```
/***************************************************************
 * The program shows how we can capitalize a line of text using  *
 * the operator [] as an lvalue and rvalue.                      *
 ***************************************************************/
#include <string>
#include <iostream>

using namespace std;
int main ( )
{
  string line;

  cout << "Enter a line of text: " << endl;
  getline (cin, line);
  for (int i = 0; i < line.size(); i++)
  {
      line[i] = toupper (line[i]);
  }
  cout << line;
  return 0;
}
```

```
Run:
Enter a line of text:
This is a line of text to be capitalized.
THIS IS A LINE OF TEXT TO BE CAPITALIZED.
```

EXAMPLE 10.18

Program 10.17 creates and tests a function that reverses the characters in a string. The function uses pass-by-reference to reverse the same string object passed to it. Inside the function, we create a temporary string using the copy constructor to create and then reverse the string. We use this function for problems that we discuss later in the chapter.

Program 10.17 Reversing a string object

```
/***************************************************************
 * The program uses a function to reverse a string object.       *
 ***************************************************************/
#include <string>
#include <iostream>
using namespace std;

void reverse (string& strg);    // Function declaration

```

(continued)

Program 10.17 Reversing a string object (Continued)

```
int main ( )
{
  // Declaration of string object
  string strg;
  // Input the original object and print it
  cout << "Enter a string: ";
  getline (cin, strg);
  cout << "Original string: " << strg << endl;
  // Reverse the object and print it
  reverse (strg);
  cout << "Reversed string: " << strg;
  return 0;
}
/***************************************************************
 * The function reverses a string passed by reference to it.   *
 ***************************************************************/
void reverse (string& strg)
{
  string temp (strg);
  int size = strg.size () ;
  for (int i = 0; i < size; i++)
  {
      strg [i] = temp [size - 1 - i];
  }
}
```

```
Run:
Enter a string: Hello my friends.
Original string: Hello my friends.
Reversed string: .sdneirf ym olleH
```

Retrieving a Substring

We can retrieve a substring, a set of consecutive characters, from a string by giving the index of the first character and the number of characters to be retrieved (length). Since only the left-most parameters can be set to default, if only one parameter is given, it is taken as *pos*. If both parameters are missing, the whole string is returned. Note that the function is defined as constant, which means that the host object cannot be changed. The following result contains a string that is created in the process.

```
string result = strg.substr (pos, n);          // Result contains n characters
```

EXAMPLE 10.19

Program 10.18 shows the two uses of a substring function.

Program 10.18 Retrieving two substrings

```
/***************************************************************
 * The program shows how to retrieve two substrings from a     *
 * string object.                                              *
 ***************************************************************/
#include <string>
#include <iostream>
using namespace std;

int main ( )
{
  // Construction of a string
  string strg ("The C++ language is fun to work with.");
  // Retrieving two substrings.
  cout << strg.substr(8) << endl ;
  cout << strg.substr(4,12) << endl;
  return 0;
}
```

```
Run:
language is fun to work with.
C++ language
```

Searching for a Character

Searching in a C++ string is very broad and covers many cases. In specific searching, we are given a search argument consisting of a specific character that we want to find in the host string object. However, it may happen that there is more than one copy of the search argument in the host object. In a forward search, we are looking for the first copy; in a backward search, we are looking for the last copy. Note that searching does not retrieve or change the object being searched; it only finds the position of the search argument. If we want to retrieve or change the located character or string, we must use other member functions that we discussed earlier.

Forward and Backward Search for a Given Character In character searches, we can use two member functions (*find* and *rfind*) to search for a specific character in the forward or backward direction as shown in Figure 10.8.

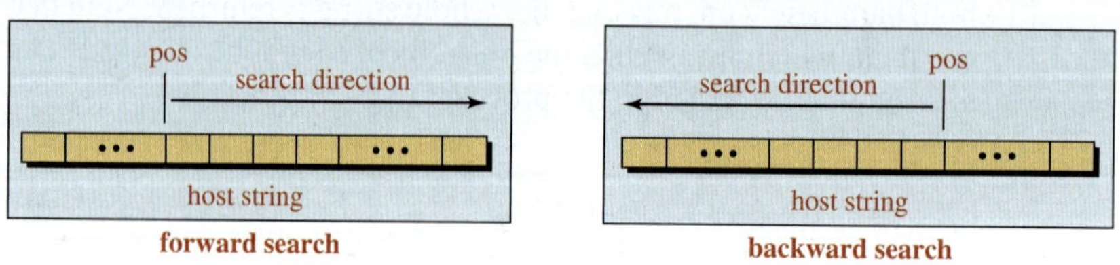

Note:
If the character is not found (in either direction), the constant *npos* (−1) is returnd.

Figure 10.8 Searching for a character in a string

Table 10.2 shows the function definitions for the character searches. The host string is searched. The first parameter defines the character to be found; the second parameter defines the starting index. If the second parameter is missing, the character defaults to 0 in forward searches or npos in backward searches. If the search is successful, the index of the corresponding character is returned; otherwise the constant npos (−1) is returned.

Warning: Both functions return an unsigned integer (size_type). However, when the character is not found, both functions return the constant npos, which is an integer with value −1. Since −1 cannot be returned as an unsigned integer, the value is wrapped and a very large number (maximum integer −1) is returned. We must be aware of this issue and handle it properly in our programs.

```
size_type pos = strg.find (c, index);          // forward search
size_type pos = strg.rfind (c, index);         // backward search
```

Forward or Backward Search for a Character Belonging to a Set A more interesting search is when need to find any character in a set. For example, assume we want to find the first vowel in the host string. A vowel belongs to the set "aeiou". We look for any one of these characters, and we return the index of the first vowel in forward search or the index of last vowel in backward search. Another alternative is that we want to look for a character not in a set. For example, we want to find the first or last nonvowel character in the host string.

We can have a variety of search sets: a C++ string, a C string, part of a C string, or even a single character. To make the format of the functions easier to understand, we create a temporary host object defining the set and then use the temporary object in the search function. Figure 10.9 shows the idea. We have four functions that we can combine with each of the four sets.

- The *find_first_of* function does a forward search to find the first character in the string that matches any character in the given set. If found, it returns the corresponding index; otherwise, it returns npos.
- The *find_first_not_of* function does a forward search to find the first character in the string that does not match any given character in the set. If found, it returns the corresponding index; otherwise, it returns npos.
- The *find_last_of* function does a backward search to find the last character in the string that matches any character in the given set. If found, it returns the corresponding index; otherwise, it returns npos.

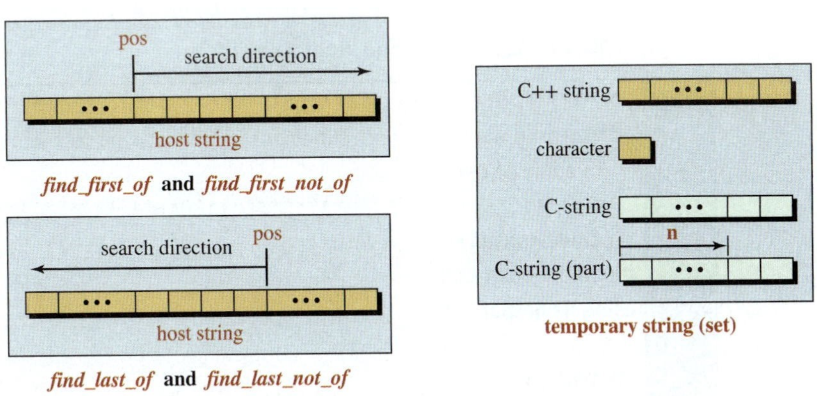

Figure 10.9 The idea behind four find functions

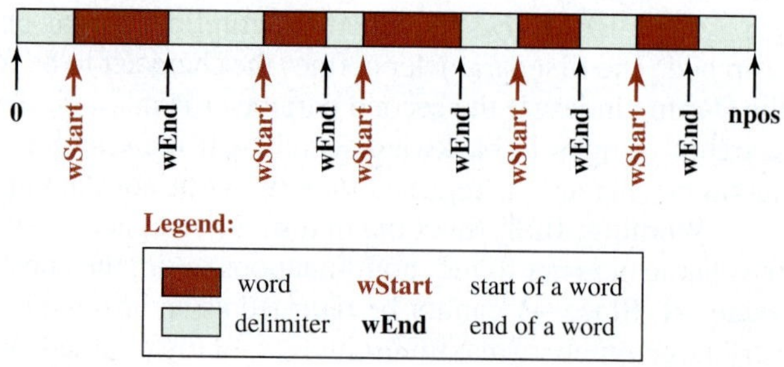

Figure 10.10 Strategy to extract words from a line of text

- The *find_last_not_of* function does a backward search to find the last character in the string that does not match any character in the given set. If found, it returns the corresponding index; otherwise, it returns `npos`.

The following shows how we can use these functions. Note that the set is the temporary string we need to create in one of the four ways defined in Figure 10.9, and the index defines the starting point of the search.

```
size_type pos = strg.find_first_of (set, index);        // forward search
size_type pos = strg.find_last_of (set, index);         // backward search
size_type pos = strg.find_first_not_of (set, index);    // forward search
size_type pos = strg.find_last_not_of (set, index);     // backward search
```

Tokenizing

We can use the search functions to find the beginning and end of substrings and then extract the substrings from the string. For example, assume we are looking to find words in a text. The words in a text are normally separated by a space or a new line character (`'\n'`). If we create a set of these two characters as the delimiters of the words, we can extracts words from the text. Figure 10.10 shows how we can use a strategy to do so.

Program 10.19 extracts words using two search functions and a loop. We use the function *find_first_not_of* to find the beginning of a word (a word cannot have a character in the set); we use *find_first_of* to find the end of a word (a character in the set comes after a word). The delimiter is made of two characters in this case: space and new line. We could have more, such as comma, semicolon, and so on, but we ignore them to keep the program simple.

Program 10.19 Retrieving words from a line of text

```
/***************************************************************
 * The program uses search functions to find and extract words     *
 * in a line of text.                                              *
 ***************************************************************/
#include <string>
#include <iostream>
using namespace std;

int main ( )
```

(*continued*)

Program 10.19 Retrieving words from a line of text (Continued)

```
10 {
11     // Declaration of variables, types, and constants
12     string text, word;
13     string delimiter (" \n");
14     string:: size_type wStart, wEnd;
15     string :: size_type npos;
16     // Input a line of text from keyboard
17     cout << "Enter a line of text: " << endl ;
18     getline (cin, text);
19     // Search, find, and print words
20     cout << "Words in the text:" << endl;
21     wStart = text.find_first_not_of (delimiter, 0);
22     while (wStart < npos)
23     {
24         wEnd = text.find_first_of (delimiter, wStart);
25         cout << text.substr (wStart, wEnd - wStart) << endl;
26         wStart = text.find_first_not_of (delimiter, wEnd);
27     }
28     return 0;
29 }
```

```
Run:
Enter a line of text:
This is a line of text.
Words in the text:
This
is
a
line
of
text.
```

Before the loop in Program 10.19, we set *wStart* to point to the beginning of the current word, which is the first word in the text (line 21). In each iteration of the loop

a. We set *wEnd* to the end of the current word (line 24).
b. We retrieve the substring between *wStart* and *wEnd* (line 25).
c. We update the value of *wStart* to point to the beginning of the next word for the next iteration (line 26).

When we come out of the loop, all words have been retrieved and printed. Analyze the loop to determine what happens if two or three spaces are found between words.

Comparing Strings

The C++ string provides two ways to compare two strings: integral and Boolean.

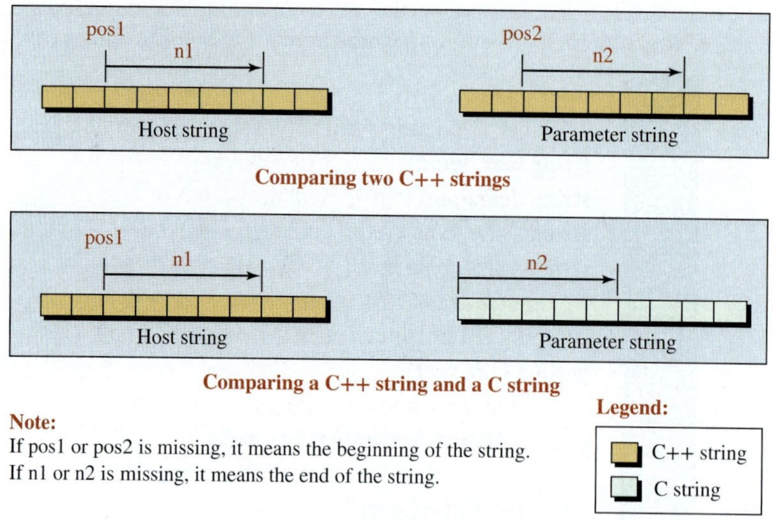

Figure 10.11 Comparing two strings

Integral Comparison The integral comparison compares two strings and returns one of three integral values: zero when the two strings are equal, a positive number when the first string is greater than the second, and a negative number when the first string is less than the second. There are a few syntax rules. The first string is the host string. The string parameter can be a C++ string or a C string. Each can be a string or a substring. The substring of a C++ string can be defined by giving the beginning index and the length; the substring of a C string must start from the first character. Figure 10.11 shows the idea.

```
int result = strg.compare (pos1, n1, strg2, pos2, n2);      // Two C++ strings
int result = strg.compare (pos1, n1, str, n2);              // C++ string and C string
```

Table 10.2 gives two member functions to compare two strings. The first compares the host string with another C++ string; the second compares the host string with a C string. Note that the C string does not use the *pos* parameter because it must always start from the beginning.

As usual, *pos1* and *n1* define the beginning index and the length of the first string; *pos2* and *n2* define the beginning index and the length of the second string. Figure 10.11 shows how we can use these member functions.

EXAMPLE 10.20

Program 10.20 compares strings.

Program 10.20 Integral comparison of strings

```
/***************************************************************
 * The program to test integral comparison.                    *
 ***************************************************************/
#include <string>
#include <iostream>
using namespace std;

```

(continued)

Program 10.20 Integral comparison of strings (Continued)

```
8   int main ( )
9   {
10      // Declaration of two C++ strings
11      string strg1 ("Hello my friends");
12      string strg2 ("Hello friends");
13      // Comparing two C++ strings
14      cout << strg1 << " compared with " << strg2 << ": ";
15      cout << strg1.compare (strg2) << endl;
16      // Comparing part of the two C++ strings
17      cout << "Hello compared with Hello: ";
18      cout << strg1.compare( 0, 5, strg2, 0, 5) << endl;
19      // Comparing part of the first C++ string and a C-string
20      cout << "Hello compared with Hello: ";
21      cout << strg1.compare (0, 5, strg2) << endl;
22      // Comparing part of a C++ string and part of a C-string
23      cout << "Hel compared with Hell: ";
24      cout << strg2.compare (0, 3, "Hello" ,4);
25      return 0;
26  }
```

```
Run:
Hello my friends compared with Hello friends: 1
Hello compared with Hello: 0
Hello compared with Hello: -8
Hel compared with Hell: -1
```

We check the results:

1. In the first comparison (line 15), we are comparing "Hello my friends" with "Hello friends". The comparison goes character by character until we compare the 'm' character with the 'f' character. The 'm' character is larger than the 'f' character, the comparison stops, and the function returns 1 (a positive number).
2. In the second comparison (line 18), we are comparing "Hello" with "Hello". The two substrings are equal; the result is 0.
3. In the third comparison (line 21), we are comparing "Hello" and "Hello friends". A null character is compared to a space. The result is a negative number (−8).
4. In the fourth comparison (line 24), we are comparing "Hel" with "Hell". When we reach the fourth character, we are comparing a null character with 'l'. The result is a negative number (−1).

We must be careful that we do not convert the integral result to a Boolean type in integral comparison because both 1 and −1 are converted to true, which is not correct.

Logical Comparison The logical comparison compares two strings and returns a Boolean value (*true* or *false*). Just like the integral comparison, two strings are compared. The first is always the host, and the second is a C++ string or a C string. Unlike the integral comparison, we cannot compare two substrings. If we want to do so, we must make temporary C++ strings out of the substrings and then compare them.

The prototypes use operator overloading, which we will discuss in Chapter 13. The term Oper in the prototypes can be one of the relational or equality operators (<, <=, >, >=, ==, or !=). We can compare the two strings as though they are fundamental types using these operators. You may wonder if we can compare two C strings. We can do that, but they are considered fundamental types, and normal relational and equality operators are applied to them (we do not need the <string> header). Note that in logical comparisons, one of the two strings must be a C++ string.

The following shows how we can use these member functions.

```
bool result = strg1 oper strg2;          // Comparing two C++ strings
bool result = strg oper str;             // Comparing a C++ string and a C string
bool result = str oper strg;             // Comparing a C string and a C++ string
```

EXAMPLE 10.21

Program 10.21 compares strings.

Program 10.21 Using logical operators to compare strings

```
/***************************************************************
 * The program to test logical operators to compare two strings.     *
 ***************************************************************/
#include <string>
#include <iostream>
using namespace std;

int main ( )
{
   // Creation of four C++ strings
   string strg1;
   string strg2 (5, 'a');
   string strg3 ("Hello Friends");
   string strg4 ("Hi People", 4);
   // Using six logical operators (relational and equality)
   cout << "strg1 < strg2 : " << boolalpha << (strg1 < strg2);
   cout << endl;
   cout << "strg2 >= strg3: " << boolalpha << (strg2 >= strg3);
   cout << endl;
   cout << "strg1 == strg2: " <<  boolalpha << (strg1 == strg2);
   cout << endl;
   cout << "Hi P != strg4: " << boolalpha << ("Hi P" != strg4);
   return 0;
}
```

```
Run:
strg1 < strg2 : true
strg2 >= strg3: true
strg2 < strg3: false
strg1 == strg2: false
Hi P != strg4: false
```

EXAMPLE 10.22

A string is a palindrome if it reads the same forward and backward. The strings “rotor,” “dad,” and “noon” are all palindromes. Examples of more complex palindromes are “Madam, I am Adam” and “Able was I ere I saw Elba.” We can easily check if a string is a palindrome by comparing it with its own reverse. In some cases, we must remove the punctuation and make the characters all the same before reversing the string. Program 10.22 shows how to check a string for palindrome.

Program 10.22 Testing for a palindrome

```
/***************************************************************
 * The program checks to see if an input string is a palindrome.   *
 ***************************************************************/
#include <string>
#include <iostream>
using namespace std;

// Declaration of two functions
void reverse (string& strg);
bool isPalindrome (string& strg);

int main ( )
{
  // Construction of a default string object
  string strg;
  // Inputting
  cout << "Enter a string: ";
  getline (cin, strg);
  // Checking for palindrome
  if (isPalindrome (strg))
  {
      cout << strg << " is a palindrome.";
  }
  else
  {
      cout << strg << " is not a palindrome.";
  }
  return 0;
}
/***************************************************************
 * The isPalindrome function calls the reverse function           *
 * to compare its parameter with its reversed parameter.          *
 ***************************************************************/
bool isPalindrome (string& strg)
{
  string temp (strg);
  reverse (temp);
```

(continued)

Program 10.22 Testing for a palindrome (Continued)

```
    return (temp == strg);
}
/***************************************************************
 * The reverse function reverses the string parameter.         *
 ***************************************************************/
void reverse (string& strg)
{
    string temp (strg);
    int size = strg.size () ;
    for (int i = 0; i < size; i++)
    {
        strg[i] = temp [size - 1 - i];
    }
}
```

```
Run:
Enter a string: rotor
rotor is a palindrome.
```

```
Run:
Enter a string: mom
mom is a palindrome.
```

```
Run:
Enter a string: son
son is not a palindrome.
```

Push_Back

We often need to add a character to a string. The string library defines the *push_back* function that adds a character at the end of the string. The library member function can be used as shown below:

```
strg.push_back (c);          // Append character c at the end of strg
```

In our programming design section, we show how we can push a character in front of the string. We also show how we can pop a character from the front or the back.

Modifying Operations

The C++ string library gives a set of different function definitions for modifying operations. However, if we construct a temporary string as the parameter, the number of member functions can be reduced to four. The *temp* string is the set of characters that we are looking for.

```
temp (strg);                 // A complete C++ string
temp (strg, pos2, n2);       // A part of C++ string
temp (1, c);                 // A string made of one character
temp (cstr);                 // A complete C-String
temp (cstr, n);              // The first n characters of a C-string
```

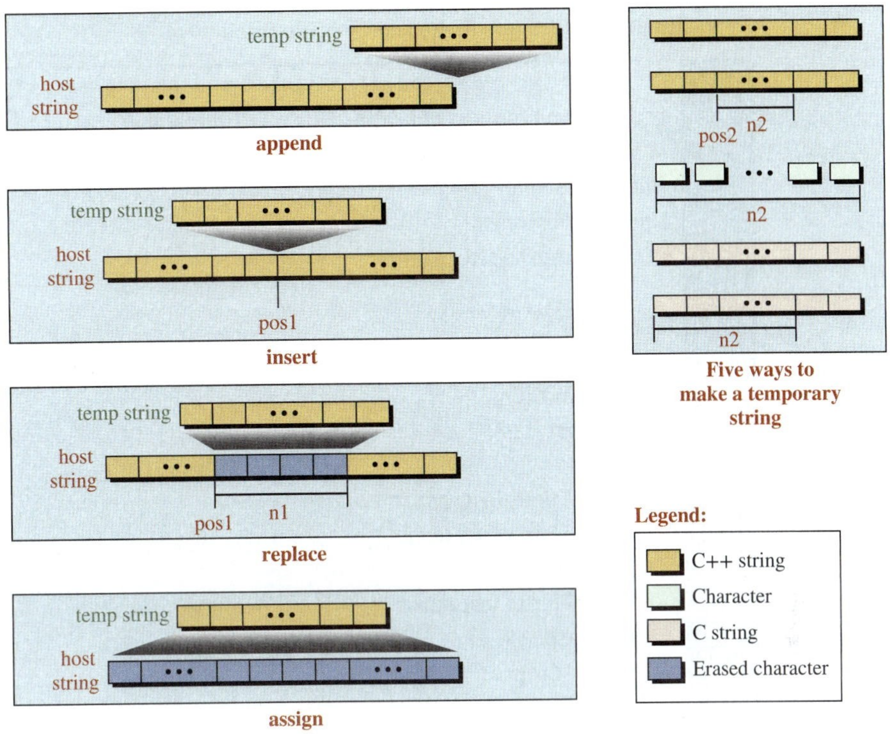

Figure 10.12 General idea behind append, insert, replace, and assign

Figure 10.12 shows how four groups of functions use the temporary string to modify the host string.

The following shows how we use these four categories of functions:

```
strg.append (temp);                // Append
strg.insert (pos1, temp);          // Insert
strg.replace (pos1, n1, temp);     // Replace
strg.assign (temp);                // Assign
```

Partial or Total Erasure

There are two functions that can totally or partially erase the characters in the string without destructing the string. The object still exists, but it is partially or totally devoid of its characters.

```
strg.clear ();                     // Erase all character in the string
strg.erase (pos, n);               // Erase part of the string
```

Overloaded Operators

Some of the modifying operations are achieved using overloaded operators. C++ overloads the assignment operator (=), the compound assignment operator (+=), and the addition operator (+) as shown below. The *temp*, *temp1*, and *temp2* are instances of the *string* class.

```
string strg = temp;                // Assignment
string strg += temp;               // Compound Assignment
string strg = temp1 + temp2;       // Addition
```

Program 10.23 Printing the full name of a person

```
/***************************************************************
 * A program to show concatenation of strings and characters.  *
 ***************************************************************/
#include <string>
#include <iostream>
using namespace std;

int main ( )
{
  // Declarations
  string first, last;
  char init;
  // Input first, last, and initial
  cout << "Enter first name: ";
  cin >> first;
  cout << "Enter last name: ";
  cin >> last;
  cout << "Enter initial: ";
  cin >> init;
  // Printing the full name in one format
  cout << endl;
  cout << "Full name in first format: ";
  cout << first + " " + init + "." + " " + last << endl << endl;
  // Printing the full name in another format
  cout << "Full name in second format: ";
  cout << last + ", " + first + " " + init + ".";
  return 0;
}
```

```
Run:
Enter first name: John
Enter last name: Brown
Enter initial: A

Full name in first format: John A. Brown

Full name in second format: Brown, John A.
```

EXAMPLE 10.23

Program 10.23 shows how we can read the first name, last name, and initial of a person to create the full name in two formats.

EXAMPLE 10.24

In this example we show how we can change a file with left-justified text to a file with right-justified text. There are several approaches to this problem, depending on how much information we have about the file. If we know the maximum line size, the problem is very simple. Otherwise, we need to find the maximum line size. To find the maximum line size, we can use two approaches. In the first, we can read the lines in the input file into an array of strings, find the maximum line size, and then write the array into the output file. The problem is that we need to create an array in stack memory. In the second approach, we can read the input file two times. The first time, we just find the maximum line size. We then close the file and read it again to change the size of the line and store it in the output file. Program 10.24 uses the second approach.

Program 10.24 Writing justified lines in a file

```
/***************************************************************
 * The program reads a left-justified file and creates a new    *
 * right-justified file.                                        *
 ***************************************************************/
#include <string>
#include <iostream>
#include <fstream>
#include <cassert>
using namespace std;

int main ()
{
   // Declaration of files and a string object
   ifstream inputFile;
   ofstream outputFile;
   string line;
   // Read the input file just to find the maximum line size
   inputFile.open ("inFile.dat");
   assert (inputFile);
   int maxSize = 0;
   while (!inputFile.eof())
   {
       getline (inputFile, line);
       if (line.size() > maxSize)
       {
             maxSize = line.size();
       }
   }
   inputFile.close ();
   // Read the input file and create the output file.
   inputFile.open ("inFile.dat");
   assert (inputFile);
   outputFile.open ("outFile.dat");
   assert (outputFile);
   while (!inputFile.eof())
}
```

(continued)

Program 10.24 Writing justified lines in a file (Continued)

```
        getline (inputFile, line);
        string temp (maxSize - line.size() , ' ');
        line.insert (0, temp);
        line.append ("\n");
        outputFile << line;
    }
    inputFile.close();
    outputFile.close();
    return 0;
}
```

The following shows the contents of the input file and output file set side by side after the program is run.

Contents of input file	Contents of output file
This is a line.	This is a line.
This is the second line.	This is the second line.
This is a new longer line.	This is a new longer line.
This is a shorter one.	This is a shorter one.
This is the longest line by far.	This is the longest line by far.

Conversion

We can convert a C++ object to a character array or to a C string.

```
const char* arr = strg.data ();        // Conversion to a character array
const char* str = strg.c_str ();       // Conversion to a C string
```

10.3 PROGRAM DESIGN

In this section, we first create four customized functions using member functions in the string class. We then use these functions to solve some of the classic problems in string processing.

10.3.1 Four Customized Functions

A library class defines a set of member functions, but we can always create functions customized to our need. The functions we add cannot be class member functions, but they can use class types as parameters. We demonstrate this capability by defining four new functions related to the C++ string class. We create these functions in terms of member functions defined in the C++ string class. To use them in any program, we collect them in a header file called *customized.h* and include the file everywhere we need to use them. We have called these functions: *pushBack*, *pushFront*, *popBack*, and *popFront*. In later chapters, we will see that these functions are defined for other class libraries (although by different names), but only one of them, under the name *push_back,* is defined for the string class. Figure 10.13 shows the behavior of these four customized functions.

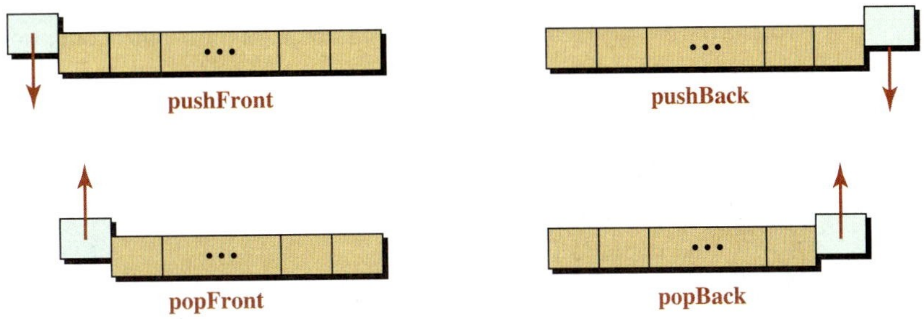

Figure 10.13 Effect of four customized functions

Program 10.25 shows the header file that creates our four customized functions. Program 10.26 shows how we test our customized function using a trivial string.

Program 10.25 Header file for our customized functions

```
/*****************************************************************
 * A header file to define our four customized functions.       *
 * The pushFront function adds the given character at the front. *
 * The pushBack function adds the given character at the back.   *
 * The popFront function removes the character at the front.     *
 * The popBack function removes the character at the back.       *
 *****************************************************************/
#ifndef custom_H
#define custom_H
#include <iostream>
#include <string>
using namespace std;

// Definition of pushFront function
void pushFront (string& strg, char c)
{
  string temp (1, c);
  strg.insert (0, temp);
}
// Definition of pushBack function
void pushBack (string& strg, char c)
{
  string temp (1, c);
  strg.append (temp);
}
// Definition of popFront function
char popFront (string& strg)
{
  int index = 0;
  char temp = strg [index];
```

(*continued*)

Program 10.25 Header file for our customized functions (Continued)

```
    strg.erase (index, 1);
    return temp;
}
// Definition of popBack function
char popBack (string& strg)
{
    int index = strg.size () – 1;
    char temp = strg [index];
    strg.erase (index, 1);
    return temp;
}
#endif
```

Program 10.26 Testing four customized functions

```
/***************************************************************
 * A program that tests the customized functions defined in the      *
 * customized header file.                                           *
 ***************************************************************/
#include "customized.h"
#include <string>
#include <iostream>
using namespace std;

int main ( )
{
    // Declaration of original string
    string strg ("abcdefgh");
    // Testing pushFront function
    cout << "String before calling pushFront: " << strg << endl;
    pushFront (strg, 'A');
    cout << "String after calling pushFront: " << strg << endl;
    cout << endl;
    // Testing pushBack function
    cout << "String before calling pushBack: " << strg << endl;
    pushBack (strg, 'Z');
    cout << "String after calling pushBack: " << strg << endl;
    cout << endl;
    // Testing popFront function
    cout << "String before calling popFront: " << strg << endl;
    char c1 = popFront (strg);
    cout << "String after calling popFront: " << strg << endl;
    cout << "The popped character: " << c1 << endl;
```

(continued)

Program 10.26 Testing four customized functions (Continued)

```
    cout << endl;
    // Testing popBack function
    cout << "String before calling popBack: " << strg << endl;
    char c2 = popBack (strg);
    cout << "String after calling popBack: " << strg << endl;
    cout << "The popped character: " << c2 << endl;
    cout << endl;
    return 0;
}
```

```
Run:
String before calling pushFront: abcdefgh
String after calling pushFront: Aabcdefgh

String before calling pushBack: Aabcdefgh
String after calling pushBack: AabcdefghZ

String before calling popFront: AabcdefghZ
String after calling popFront: abcdefghZ
The popped character: A

String before calling popBack: abcdefghZ
String after calling popBack: abcdefgh
The popped character: Z
```

10.3.2 Conversion in Positional Number Systems

In computer science we use different positional numbering systems; these are described in Appendix B: binary, octal, decimal, and hexadecimal. Each positional numbering system uses a set of symbols and a base. The *base* defines the total number of symbols used in the system. Table 10.3 shows the base and the symbols we work with in programming. Note that the values of symbols A, B, C, D, E, F are 10, 11, 12, 13, 14, and 15, respectively.

Although all of these number systems represent an integer using different notations, the decimal system is the only one that can be directly used as an integer in a program. A number in other systems must be represented as a string of characters.

Table 10.3 Positional numbering system

System	Base	Symbols
binary	2	0, 1
octal	8	0, 1, 2, 3, 4, 5, 6, 7
decimal	10	0, 1, 2, 3, 4, 5, 6, 7, 8, 9
hexadecimal	16	0, 1, 2, 3, 4, 5, 6, 7, 8, 9, A, B, C, D, E, F

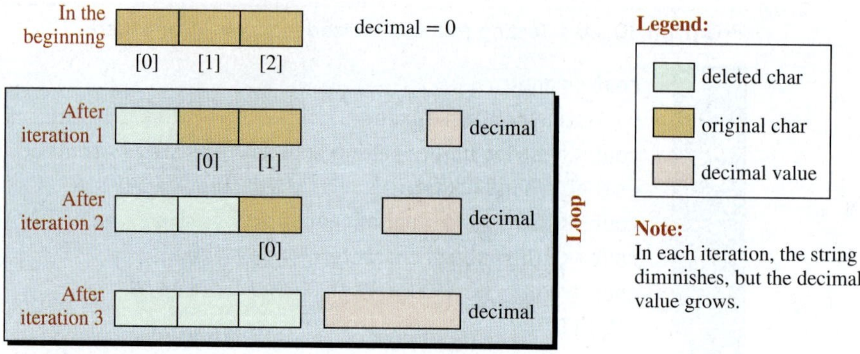

Figure 10.14 Converting from any base to decimal

In C++, a number in the decimal system is used as an integer; numbers in other systems are used as a string of characters.

This means that when we are working with different numbering systems, we must change a string to an integer or vice versa. In this section we give a general design for doing so. Before studying the rest of this section, we recommend that you review Appendix B.

Conversion from Any Other Base to Decimal

Figure 10.14 shows how we convert a string of three characters to an integer.

We use a loop that is controlled by the size of the string. When the string is empty, we exit the loop. Before starting the loop, we set the value of the *decimal* variable to 0. In each iteration, we multiply the previous value of *decimal* by its base. We then pop the front character, convert it to decimal, and add it to the value of *decimal*. Note that in each iteration, the value of *decimal* is increased, but the size of the string is decreased. When we come out of the loop, the value of *decimal* is computed. Table 10.4 shows the algorithm.

Table 10.4 Algorithm for converting a string to a decimal

set base	// set base to 2, 8, 16
decimal = 0	
input string	
while (string not empty)	
{	
decimal *= base;	
ch = popFront (string)	// Use popFront function developed before
decimal += findValue (ch)	// Use a function to change ch to its value
}	
output decimal	

EXAMPLE 10.25

Program 10.27 changes a binary string to a decimal integer. In this case, base is 2. We have used the *popFront* function we developed before (included in the header file). We have written a small function named *findValue* to change the extracted character to its integer value.

Program 10.27 Changing a binary string to a decimal integer

```
/***************************************************************
 * A program to change a binary string to a decimal integer.   *
 ***************************************************************/
#include "customized.h"
#include <string>
#include <iostream>
using namespace std;
/***************************************************************
 * A function to change a numeric character to its equivalent  *
 * integer value.                                              *
 ***************************************************************/
int findValue (char ch)
{
  return static_cast <int>(ch) - 48;
}

int main ( )
{
  // Declaration, inputting, and validation of binary string
  string binary;
  do
  {
      cout << "Enter binary string: ";
      getline (cin, binary);
  } while (binary.find_first_not_of ("01") < binary.size());
  // Initialization and calculation of decimal integer
  int base = 2;
  int decimal = 0;
  while (!binary.empty())
  {
      decimal *= base;
      char ch = popFront (binary);
      decimal += findValue (ch);
  }
  cout << "Decimal value: " << decimal;
  return 0;
}
```

(continued)

Program 10.27 Changing a binary string to a decimal integer (Continued)

```
Run:
Enter binary string: 11 101
Enter binary string: 11101
Decimal value: 29
```

```
Run:
Enter binary string: 1181
Enter binary string: 11111
Decimal value: 31
```

```
Run:
Enter binary string: 111000111
Decimal value: 455
```

There are three important points about Program 10.27: First, in lines 21 to 25 we process a line of text that represents a binary string. The string we need must be made only of the characters '0' and '1', which means the input string must be validated before being used. This is done by the *find_first_not_of* function we learned earlier in the chapter. This function looks for characters that are not '0' or '1' and returns the corresponding index. If the returned index is less than the size of the string, it means that a character other than 0 or 1 was found in the string, and we loop back to read again.

Second, consider line 31. Each time we enter the loop, we must reset the value of *decimal* to *decimal* times the value of *base*, as for the algorithm given in Table 10.3.

Third, consider the *popFront* function. We know that in each iteration we must extract the next character in the string, which is correctly done by the *popFront* function defined in the header file.

Conversion from Decimal to Any Other Base

Figure 10.15 shows how we convert a decimal to a string of three characters.

We use a loop that is controlled by the value of the decimal number. When the value is 0, we stop. Before starting the loop, the string is empty. In each iteration, we divide the previous value of decimal by base and get the remainder. We then change the resulting value to a character and push it to the front of the string. Note that in each iteration, the value of the decimal decreases until it becomes 0, but the size of the string is increased. When we come out of the loop, the string is ready. Table 10.5 shows the algorithm.

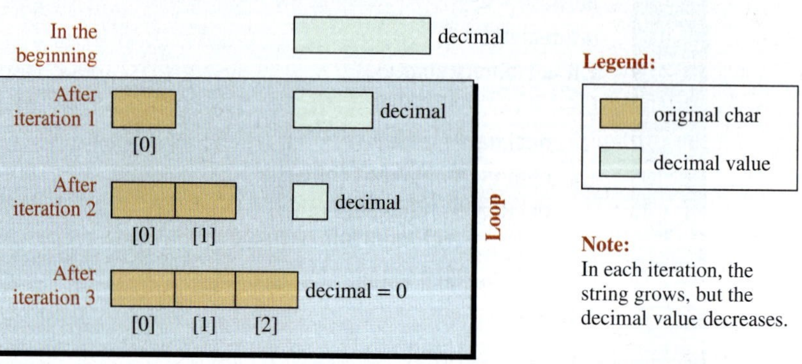

Figure 10.15 Converting from decimal to other bases

Table 10.5 Algorithm for converting a decimal to a string

set base	// set base to 2, 8, 16
input decimal	
while (decimal > 0)	
{	
value = decimal % base;	
ch = findChar (value)	// Use a function to change value to char
string.pushFront (ch)	// Use pushFront function developed before
}	
output string	

EXAMPLE 10.26

Program 10.28 shows how we convert a decimal to a binary string.

Program 10.28 Converting from decimal to binary

```
/***********************************************************************
 * A program to change a decimal numeral to a binary string            *
 ***********************************************************************/
#include <string>
#include "customized.h"
#include <iostream>
using namespace std;

/***********************************************************************
 * A function to change an integer to a character using the            *
 * char function                                                       *
 ***********************************************************************/
char findChar (int digit)
{
   return char (digit + 48);
}

int main ( )
{
   // Declaration of variables
   int decimal;
   int base = 2;
   string strg;
   // Input and validation of decimal number
   do
```

(continued)

Program 10.28 Converting from decimal to binary (Continued)

```
    {
        cout << "Enter a positive decimal: " ;
        cin >> decimal;
    } while (decimal <= 0);
    // Conversion to binary
    while (decimal > 0)
    {
        int digit = decimal % base;
        char ch = findChar (digit);
        pushFront (strg, ch);
        decimal /= base;
    }
    // Outputting binary
    cout << "Binary: " << strg;
    return 0;
}
```

```
Run:
Enter a positive decimal: 35
Binary: 100011
```

```
Run:
Enter a positive decimal: 7
Binary: 111
```

```
Run:
Enter a positive decimal: 126
Binary: 1111110
```

The validation of the input decimal value is simple and is done in a do-while loop. To insert the character in the binary string, we use the *pushFront* function we created and included in the header file.

Key Terms

C string
C++ string
string literal
string token

Summary

The C string is a null-terminated array of characters that can be created like an array. A literal string is a constant value that encloses characters in two double quotes. We can input C strings using the extraction operator or the *getline* library function. We can output C strings using the insertion operator.

The C++ string class is found in the <*string*> header file. It is a class that creates a character array that is not null-terminated and is created in heap memory. It defines data members and member functions like any other class.

Problems

PR-1. The following code fragment uses C strings. Change the code to use C++ strings.

```
const char* str = "This is a string.";
cout << strlen (str) << endl;
```

PR-2. The following code fragment uses C strings. Change the code to use C++ strings.

```
const char* str1 = "This is a string.";
const char* str2 = "This is another one.";
cout << strcmp (str1, str2) << endl;
```

PR-3. The following code fragment uses C strings. Rewrite the following code using C++ strings to achieve the same goal.

```
char str1 [ ] = "This is the first string.";
const char* str2 = "Here is another one.";
strcpy (str1, str2);
cout << str1 << endl;
```

PR-4. The following code fragment uses C strings. Rewrite the code using C++ strings to achieve the same goal.

```
char str1 [ ] = "This is the first string.";
const char* str2 = "Here is another one.";
strncpy (str1, str2, 4);
cout << str1 << endl;
```

PR-5. The following code fragment uses C strings. Change the code to use C++ strings.

```
char str1 [40] = "The time has come. ";
const char* str2 = "Are your ready?";
strcat (str1, str2);
cout << str1 << endl;
```

PR-6. The following code fragment uses C strings. Change the code to use C++ strings.

```
char str1 [40] = "The time has changed. ";
const char* str2 = "Do you know? My dear friend.";
strncat (str1, str2, 12);
cout << str1 << endl;
```

PR-7. The following code fragment uses C strings. Change the code to use C++ strings.

```
char str [ ] = "This is a long string.";
*strchr (str, 's') = 'S';
*strrchr (str, 's') = 'S';
cout << str << endl;
```

PR-8. The following code fragment uses C strings. Change the code to use C++ strings.

```
const char* str = "This is a long string.";
char* p = strstr (str, "is");
cout << *p << endl;
```

PR-9. The following code fragment uses C strings to delete the first character in the string. Change the code to use C++ strings.

```
const char* str = "ABCDEFGH";
str = str + 1;
cout << str << endl;
```

PR-10. The following code uses C strings to delete all but the last character in a string. Change the code to use C++ strings.

```
const char* str = "ABCDEFGH";
str = str + strlen (str) – 1;
cout << str << endl;
```

PR-11. The following code fragment is written using C++ strings. Change the code to use C strings.

```
string strg ("ABCDEFGH");
strg.push_back ('I');
cout << strg << endl;
```

PR-12. Write a code fragment that splits a C++ string into two equally sized strings. If the number of characters in the original string is odd, the code adds a blank character at the end of string before splitting.

PR-13. Write a code fragment to extract the first four characters of a string and the last four characters of a string. Then print the extracted strings.

Programs

PRG-1. Write a function that finds the count of a given character in a C++ string. Test the function in a program.

PRG-2. Write a function that converts all characters in a C++ string to uppercase. Test the function in a program.

PRG-3. Write a function that removes all occurrences of a given character from a C++ string. Test the function in a program.

PRG-4. Write a function that removes duplicate characters from a string (keeping only one instance of each character). Test the function in a program.

PRG-5. Write a function that, given two strings, creates another string that contains only the common characters of the two strings. One solution is to first remove the duplicate characters from each string before creating the string with common characters (PRG-4).

PRG-6. Write a function that has three C++ strings as parameters. It searches the first parameter to find the second parameter (as a substring) and replaces it with the third parameter. It returns the changed first parameter if the substring can be found; otherwise, it returns the original first parameter. Test your function in a program.

PRG-7. Write a function that inserts a given string in the middle of a second string. If the second string has an odd number of characters, the program first repeats the last character before inserting. Write a program to test your function.

PRG-8. Modify Program 10.21 to handle complex palindromes such as "Madam, I'm Adam" or "A man, a plan, a canal: Panama."

PRG-9. Write a program to change a positive integer to its corresponding octal string (base 8). For example, the integer 1234 will be changed to the string "2322." Hint: You can use a *toChar* function to change each octal digit to an octal character, the *pushFront* function we developed in the text to insert an octal character into the string, and a *toString* function that calls the other two functions repeatedly until the whole transformation is done.

PRG-10. Write a program to change a positive integer to its corresponding hexadecimal string (base 16). For example, the integer 23456 will be changed to the string "5BA0" when we use only uppercase letters. Hint: You can use a *toChar* function to change each hex digit to a hex character, the *pushFront* function we developed in the text to insert a hex character into the string, and a *toString* function that calls the other two functions repeatedly until the whole transformation is done.

PRG-11. Write a program to change an octal string to a decimal integer. An octal string uses only characters '0' to '7'. The base is 8. Hint: You can use the *popFront* function we developed in the text to extract the next character from an octal string, a *toInt* function to change an octal character into an octal digit, and a *toDecimal* function that continuously calls the other two functions to finish the task. Note that the octal string must be validated, which can be done using the *find_first_not_of* function discussed in the text.

PRG-12. Write a program to change a hexadecimal string to a decimal integer. For our purpose, a hexadecimal string uses only characters '0' to '9' and 'A' to 'F' or 'a' to 'f'. The base is 16. Hint: You can use the *popFront* function we developed in the text to extract the next character from a hexadecimal string, a *toInt* function to change a hexadecimal character into an hexadecimal digit, and a *toDecimal* function that continuously calls the other two functions to finish the task. Note that the hexadecimal string must be validated, which can be done using the *find_first_not_of* functions discussed in the text.

PRG-13. In situations where a piece of data can be represented in different forms, as shown in programming problems PRG-9 through PRG-11, we can use a class. We can declare the only data member in the most common form (such as *unsigned integer*) and then use *set* and *get* functions to *set* and *get* the value of the data as a string in four different bases (2, 8, 10, and 16). Give the interface file, the implementation file, and the application file for this class. Define some helper function, namely *toInt*, *toChar*, *pushFront*, *popFront*, and *validate,* that validates the string passed to the *set* function.

PRG-14. Create a class called Address that represents an Internet address. An Internet address in version 4 (IPv4 address) is a decimal value between 0 and 4,294,967,295. In other words, it can be the addresses of more than four billion computers connected to the Internet. The two common representations of an IP address are in binary format (base 2) or dotted decimal format (base 256) as shown below. The binary format is a string made of four 8-bit sections. The dotted-decimal format is a string made of four decimal values (0 to 255) that are separated by dots. Note that both in binary and dotted decimal notation, all elements (bits or decimal values) must be present, although some may be zero. The following shows an example of an IPv4 address.

```
Decimal format: 71832456
Binary format : 00000100 01001000 00010011 10001000
Dotted Decimal format: 4.72.19.136
```

In object-oriented programming, classes are not used in isolation. They are used in relation to each other. A program normally uses several classes with different relationships between them. Figure 11.1 shows the taxonomy of relations we discuss in this chapter.

Objectives

After you have read and studied this chapter, you should be able to:

- Define inheritance relationships between classes, including public, protected, and private inheritance.
- Learn how to write class definitions and member function definitions for several classes in an inheritance relationship.
- Define association as a relationship between classes, and define its variations: aggregation and composition.
- Learn how to write class definitions and member function definitions for several classes in an association.
- Define the dependency relationship between classes to show that one class can use the objects of another class.
- Learn how to write class definitions and member function definitions for classes in a dependency relationship.

11.1 INHERITANCE

Inheritance in object-oriented programming derives a more specific concept from a more general one. That is what we do in real life. For example, the concept of *animal* in biology is more general than the concept of *horse*. We can give the definition of an *animal*; we can then add to the definition to create the definition of a *horse*. There is an *is-a* relation from the more specific to the more general. All horses are animals, but not all animals are horses.

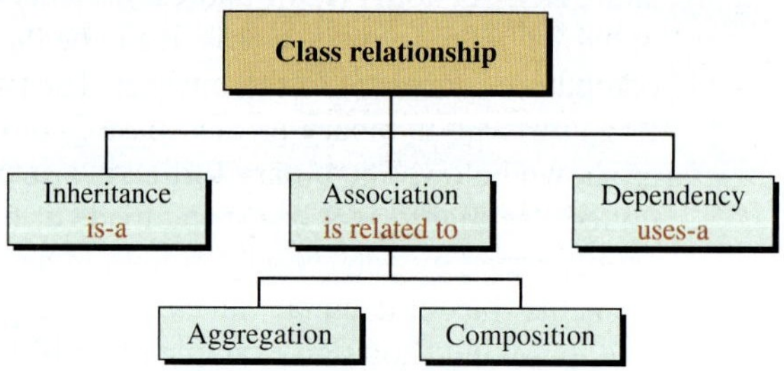

Figure 11.1 Relationship among classes

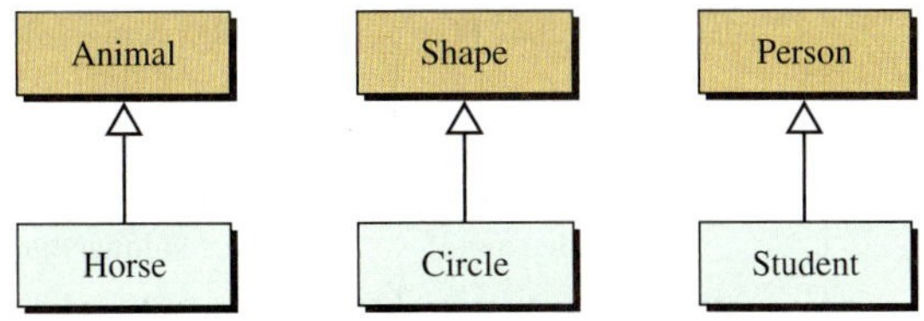

Figure 11.2 UML diagram for inheritance

11.1.1 General Idea

To show the relationship between classes in inheritance, we use the Unified Modeling Language (UML). UML is a language that shows the relationship between classes and objects graphically. We discuss UML in Appendix N in more detail, but we show some of the diagrams used in it in this chapter. The classes are shown as rectangular boxes in UML. The inheritance relation is shown by a line ending in a hollow triangle that goes from the more specific class to a more general class. Figure 11.2 shows three inheritance relationships.

In C++, the most general class is called the **base class** and a more specific class is called the **derived class.** A more general class is also known as a **superclass;** a more specific class is also known as a **subclass.**

From a UML diagram, we can derive the relationship between the set of objects in an inheritance as in Figure 11.3, which shows that the set of horses is smaller than the set of animals.

A specific concept must have the characteristics of the general concept, but it can have more. In other words, a horse should first be an animal, then a horse. That is why C++ says that a derived class extends its base class. The term *extends* here means the derived class must have all of the data members and member functions defined in the base class, but it can add to the list. In other words, the derived class inherits all of the data members and member functions of the base class (with the exception of constructors, destructor, and assignment operators that need to be redefined), and it can create new data members and member functions. We will discuss later why constructors, the destructor, and assignment operators cannot be inherited.

The derived class inherits all members (with some exceptions) from the base class, and it can add to them.

To create a derived class from a base class, we have three choices in C++: *private inheritance*, *protected inheritance*, and *public inheritance*. To show the type of the inheritance we want to use, we insert a colon after the class, followed by one of the keywords (*private,*

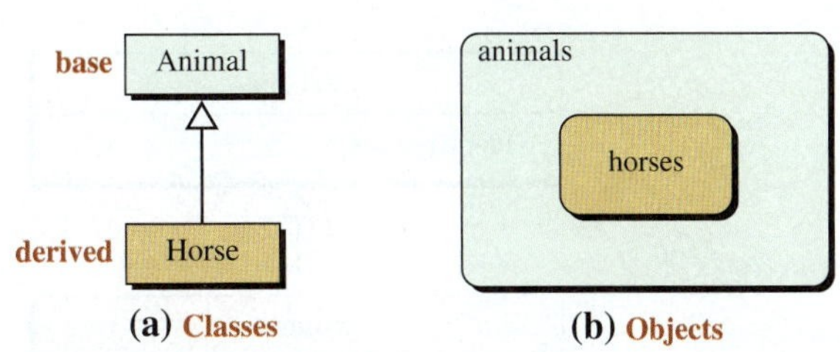

Figure 11.3 Classes and objects in an inheritance hierarchy

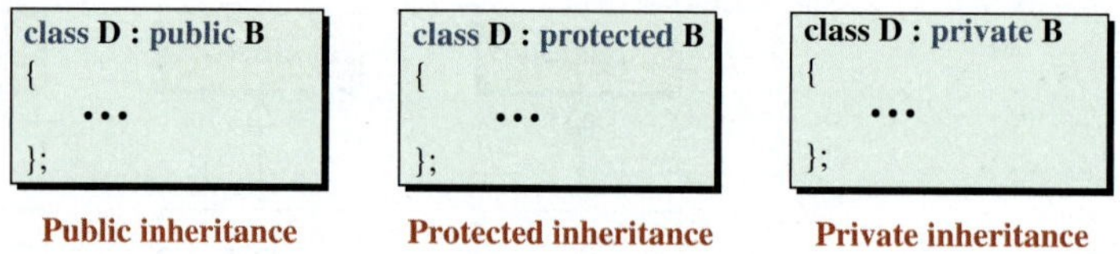

Figure 11.4 Inheritance types

protected, or *public*). Figure 11.4 shows these three types of inheritance in which B is the base class and D is the derived class.

The default type of inheritance is private. In other words, if we do not specify the type (*public, protected,* or *private*), the system assumes that we want private inheritance. Since private inheritance, as we will see later, is seldom used, we need to explicitly define the type of the inheritance. The most common is the public inheritance.

11.1.2 Public Inheritance

Although the default inheritance type is private inheritance, the most common, by far, is public inheritance. The other two types of inheritance are rarely used. We briefly discuss the other two types of inheritance later in the chapter, but in this section we concentrate on public inheritance. Some other object-oriented languages, like Java, have only public inheritance.

The most common use of inheritance is public inheritance.

EXAMPLE 11.1

In this example we design two classes, *Person* and *Student,* in which the class *Student* inherits from the class *Person*. We know that a student is a person. We assume that the *Person* class uses only one data member: *identity* (such as social security number). We also assume that the *Student* class needs two data members: *identity* and *gpa*. However, since the *identity* data member is already defined in the class *Person*, it does not need to be defined in the class *Student* because of inheritance. Figure 11.5 shows the extended UML class diagram with two compartments to accommodate the data members.

Based on Figure 11.5, we can immediately see the advantage of inheritance. The *Student* class uses the data member of the *Person* class and adds one data member of its own.

EXAMPLE 11.2

In this example we add member functions to the two classes. We ignore the constructors and destructor at this point because they are not inherited; we assume the synthetic ones are

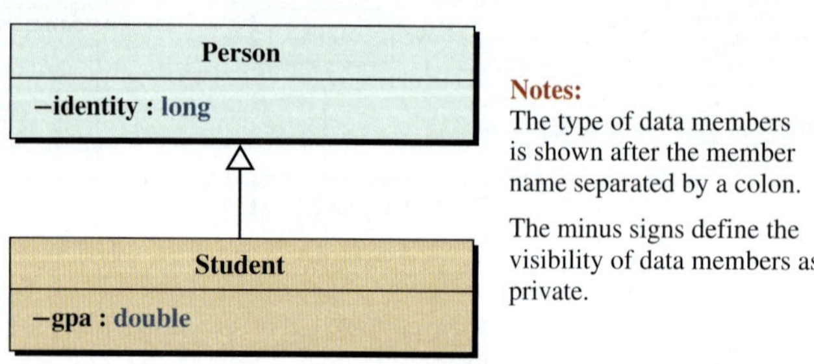

Figure 11.5 Two classes in an inheritance relationship

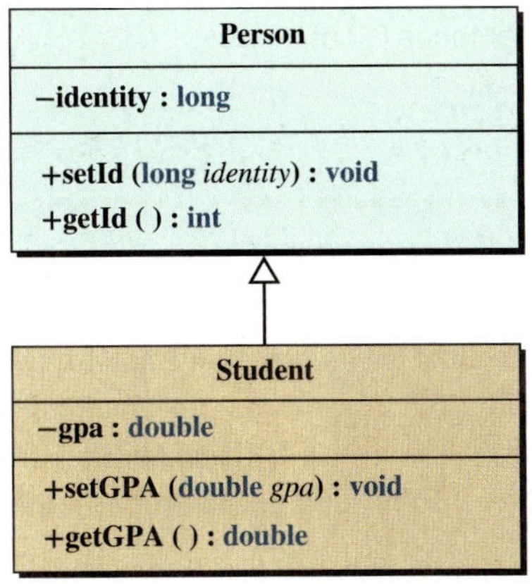

Notes:
The type of data members and member functions is shown after the member name separated by a colon.

The minus signs define the visibility of data members as private; the plus signs define the visibility of the member fuctions as public.

Figure 11.6 Classes with both data members and member functions

used. We add one getter and one setter function to each class. We use a more extended UML diagram with another compartment defining the member functions, as shown in Figure 11.6.

Based on Figure 11.6, we can see another advantage. The object of the *Student* class must set and get the *identity value*, but the *identity* is already defined in the *Person* class and the *Student* class does not need to set or get it.

EXAMPLE 11.3

Program 11.1 shows the idea in a simple program. Later we show how to use inheritance to obtain separate compilation.

Program 11.1 Public inheritance

```
/***************************************************************
 * The program shows how we can let the class Student inherit  *
 * from the class Person because a student is a person.         *
 ***************************************************************/

#include <iostream>
#include <cassert>
#include <string>
using namespace std;

/***************************************************************
 * The class definition for the Person class                    *
 ***************************************************************/
class Person
{
  private:
      long identity;
  public:
      void setId (long identity);
```

(*continued*)

Program 11.1 Public inheritance (Continued)

```
        long getId( ) const;
};
/*****************************************************************
 * The definition of setId function in the Person class          *
 *****************************************************************/
void Person :: setId (long id)
{
  identity = id;
  assert (identity >= 100000000 && identity <= 999999999) ;
}

/*****************************************************************
 * The definition of the getId function in the Person class      *
 *****************************************************************/
long Person :: getId () const
{
  return identity;
}

/*****************************************************************
 * The class definition for the Student class                    *
 *****************************************************************/

class Student : public Person
{
  private:
        double gpa;
  public:
        void setGPA (double gpa);
        double getGPA () const;
};

/*****************************************************************
 * The definition of setGPA function in Student class            *
 *****************************************************************/
void Student :: setGPA (double gp)
{
  gpa = gp;
  assert (gpa >=0 && gpa <= 4.0);
}

/*****************************************************************
 * The definition of getGPA function in Student class            *
 *****************************************************************/
```

(continued)

Program 11.1 Public inheritance (Continued)

```
double Student :: getGPA() const
{
  return gpa;
}


/*****************************************************************
 * The application function (main) that uses both classes        *
 *****************************************************************/
int main ( )
{
  // Instantiation and use of a Person object
  Person person;
  person.setId (111111111L);
  cout << "Person Information: " << endl;
  cout << "Person's identity: " << person.getId ( );
  cout << endl << endl;
  // Instantiation and use of a Student object
  Student student;
  student.setId (222222222L);
  student.setGPA (3.9);
  cout << "Student Information: " << endl;
  cout << "Student's identity: " << student.getId() << endl;
  cout << "Student's gpa: " << student.getGPA();
  return 0;
}
```

Run:

```
Person Information:
Person's Identity: 111111111

Student Information:
Student's identity: 222222222
Student's gpa: 3.9
```

There are three important points about this program:

a. There are two classes in this program. We instantiate an object of the *Person* class and we also instantiate an object of the *Student* class.

b. Although we have not defined the data member *identity* for the *Student* class, an object of this class inherits *identity* from the *Person* class.

c. We have used an *identity* instead of *name* to identity a person. We use *identity* because a name is of type *string*, which is a class type, and if we use it we are actually adding a composition relationship to the inheritance relationship, but we have not yet defined the composition relationship.

Figure 11.7 Private data members in public inheritance

Private Data Members

Before delving further into the subject of inheritance, we discuss the contents of the base class and derived class objects. As Figure 11.7 shows, the base class object has only one data member, but the derived class object has two data members: one inherited and one created.

In public inheritance, a private data member in the base class is inherited in the derived class, but it goes one step further in privacy; it becomes inaccessible (sometimes called hidden) in the derived class; it must be accessed only through its own class member functions, as we discuss shortly.

> **A private member in the base class becomes an inaccessible (hidden) member in the derived class.**

Public Member Functions

Figure 11.8 adds public member functions to Figure 11.7. We can see that the base class has only two member functions while the derived class has four member functions, two inherited and two newly defined in the derived class.

> **A public member in the base class becomes a public member in the derived class.**

Accessing Private Data Members

The following list shows how we access private data members in each class:

- In the base class, we can access the private data members through the public member functions defined in this class (*setId* and *getId*).
- In the derived class, we need two groups of public member functions:
  a. To access the inherited private data members, which are hidden, we use the public member functions defined in the base class (*setId* and *getId*).

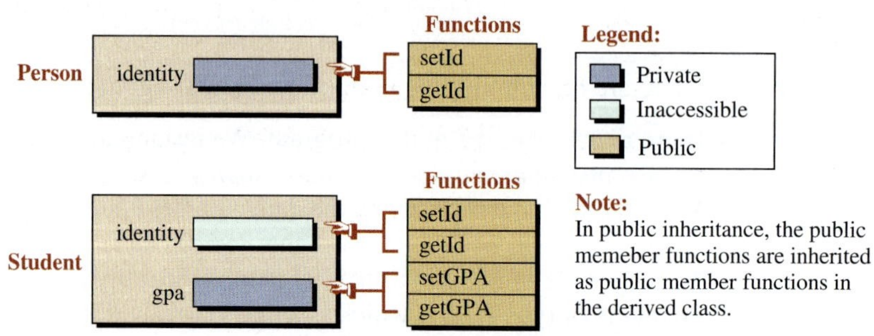

Figure 11.8 Public member functions in public inheritance

b. If we need to access a data member defined in the derived class, we use the member functions defined in the derived class (*setGPA* and *getGPA*).

Functions with the Same Names in Different Classes

In the two previous classes, *Person* and *Student*, we have used two member functions for setting data members (*setId* and *setGPA*) and two member functions for getting data members (*getId* and *getGPA*). Can we use two functions with the same name, one in the base class and the other in the derived class? In other words, can we have a function named *set* in the base class and another function also named *set* in the derived class? Similarly, can we have a function named *get* in the base class and another function also named *get* in the derived class? The answer to both questions is positive, but we need to use two different concepts: *overloaded* and *overridden* functions.

To use the same name for a function in the base and derived classes, we need overloaded or overridden member functions.

Overloaded Member Functions As we discussed in Chapter 6, overloaded functions are two functions with the same name but with two different signatures. Overloaded functions can be used in the same or different classes without being confused with each other. We can have two functions named *set*, one in the base class and the other in the derived class, with the following prototypes:

// In Person class	// In Student class
void set (long identity);	void set (double gpa);

Since the signatures are different, we can the use the first in the *Person* class and the second in the *Student* class.

Overridden Member Functions If the signature of the two functions with the same name is the same, we have *overridden* member functions as shown below.

// In Person class	// In Student class
long get ();	double get ();

Class Scope

We can better understand the rules of inheritance if we know the scope to which the base and the derived classes belong. We discussed *scope* in Chapter 6; classes in public inheritance hierarchy also have scope. The base class has its own class scope and the derived class has its own. However, the scope of the derived class is enclosed in the scope of the base class as shown in Figure 11.9. Note that although we show only two inheritance levels here, there is no limit to how many levels can be used.

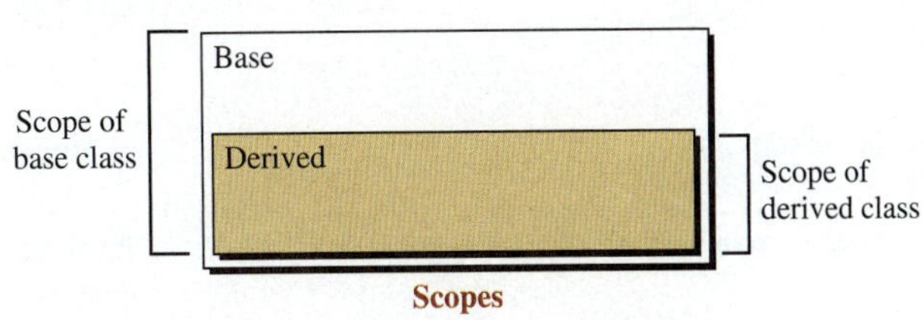

Figure 11.9 The scope of base and derived classes

In Figure 11.9, the scope of the two classes shows that every name defined in the base class is also visible in the derived class, but the reverse is not true. This concept parallels block scope within a function.

How can the system distinguish which function we are calling? We must remember that we do not call member functions in a class just by name; we let the instance call the appropriate function. In other words, if *person* and *student* are two objects of the *Person* and *Student* classes, respectively, we use the following two statements:

// Using Person object	// Using Student object
person.set (111111111L);	student.set (3.7);
person.get ();	student.get ();

Scope tells us how a compiler invokes a function based on the following rules:

a. The compiler tries to find a matching function (using names and parameters) that belongs to the class of the object that has invoked the function.
b. If no matching function is found, the compiler looks at the functions inherited from the superclass.
c. If no match is found, the search continues until the base class is reached.
d. If no match is found in any class, a compilation error is issued.

Delegation Of Duty

An overloaded or overridden member function in a derived class can delegate part of its operation to a member function in a class in a higher level by calling the corresponding member function. This is easily done with *void* member functions; it is more complicated with value-returning functions because two values must be returned, which requires a *struct* or a class object. We concentrate on the *void* member function in this case.

For example, the *set* member function in the *Student* class can be designed to set the data members of the *Person* class, *identity*, and the data member of its own class, *gpa*. However, as we said, the *identity* data member is hidden in the *Student* class and cannot be accessed by the *set* function in the *Student* class, but the set function in the *Student* class can call the set function of the *Person* class. In the same way, we can design a *print* function in the *Person* class that prints only the value of the *identity* data member. We can also design a *print* function in the *Student* class to call the print function in the *Person* class to do parts of its job. The following shows the definition of *set* function and *print* function with delegation.

```
// Using Person object
void Person :: set (long id)
{
  identity = id;
}

void Person :: print ()
{
  cout << name;
}
```

```
// Using Student object
void Student :: set (long id, double gp)
{
  Person :: set (id); // Delegation
  gpa = gp;
}

void Student :: print ()
{
  Person :: print (); // Delegation
  cout << gpa;
}
```

Note that to call the *set* function or the *print* function in the base class, we must use the class scope operator, *Person* :: *set* (...) or *Person* :: *print* ().

Members Not Inherited: Invocation

There are five member functions that are not inherited in the derived class: *default constructor, parameter constructor, copy constructor, destructor,* and the *assignment operator*. We postpone the discussion of the assignment operator until Chapter 11, but we discuss the other four in this chapter.

The constructors and the destructor are not inherited because an object of a derived class naturally has more data members than a corresponding base class. The constructor of a derived class must construct more; the destructor of a derived class must destruct more.

Constructors, destructor, and assignment operators are not inherited; they must be redefined.

However, we have a dilemma here. The constructor of the derived class cannot initialize the data members of the base class because they are hidden in the derived class. Similarly, the destructor of a derived class cannot delete the data members of the base class because they are hidden in the derived class.

The constructor problem can be solved if the constructor of the derived class *invokes* the constructor of the base class in its initialization and then initializes the data members of the derived class. Similarly, the destructor problem can be solved if the destructor of the derived class first deletes the data members of the derived class and then calls the destructor of the base class, as shown in Figure 11.10.

Note that the orders of activities in a constructor and destructor are reverse of each other. Since the destructor is called by the system, not the user, the activities are done in the background unless the object uses pointers or files that may need the intervention of the user.

EXAMPLE 11.4

Table 11.1 shows the default constructor, parameter constructor, copy constructor, and destructor for our *Person* and *Student* classes side by side. Note that the derived class section uses the base class constructor (invocation). After calling the constructor of the base class, the initializer can initialize the private member of the derived class.

The term *st* in the call to the copy constructor refers to a *Student* object. You may wonder how we can pass this object to the *Person* copy constructor, which needs a parameter of type *Person* object. The puzzle can be solved if we know that whenever we use an object of the derived class where an object of the base class is needed, the object is *sliced* and the data members belonging to the derived class are dropped. In other words, the object in the *Person* (*st*) call is only that part of the *Student* class that is inherited from the *Person* class.

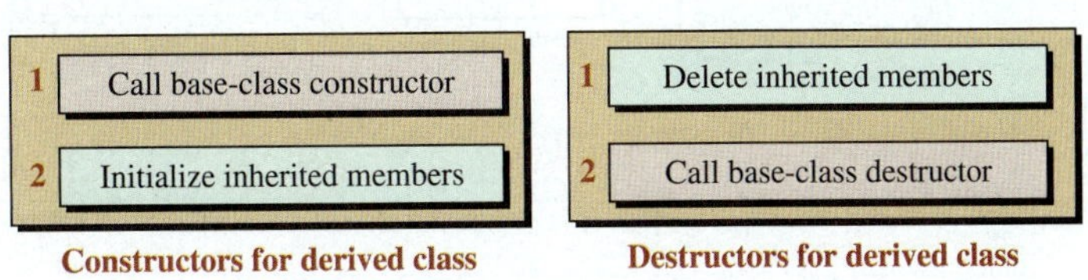

Figure 11.10 Constructors and destructor in inheritance

Table 11.1 Definition of constructors and destructor

Base class	Derived class

// Default Constructor
Person :: Person ()
: identity (0)
{
}
	// Default Constructor
	Student :: Student ()
	: Person (0), gpa (0.0)
	{
	}

// Parameter Constructor
Person :: Person (long id)
: identity (id),
{
}
	// Parameter Constructor
	Student :: Student (long id, double gp)
	: Person (id), gpa (gp)
	{
	}

// Copy Constructor
Person :: Person (const Person& obj)
: identity (obj.identity)
{
}
	// Copy Constructor
	Student :: Student (const Student& st)
	: Person (st) , gpa (std.gpa)
	{
	}

// Destructor
Person :: ~Person ()
{
}
	// Destructor
	Student :: ~Student ()
	{
	}

Figure 11.11 shows how the base class and the derived class objects are constructed using the parameter constructor. In the case of the base class (*Person*), we must initialize the only data member. In the derived class (*Student*), we can construct the inherited part by calling the constructor of the base class and then initializing the new data member. The constructor of the base class is a public member and can be accessed in the derived class.

Delegation versus Invocation

Delegation and invocation are different concepts and are done differently. In delegation, a derived member function delegates part of its duty to the base class using the class resolution operator (::). In invocation, the constructor of a derived class calls the constructor of the base class during initialization, which does not require the class resolution operator.

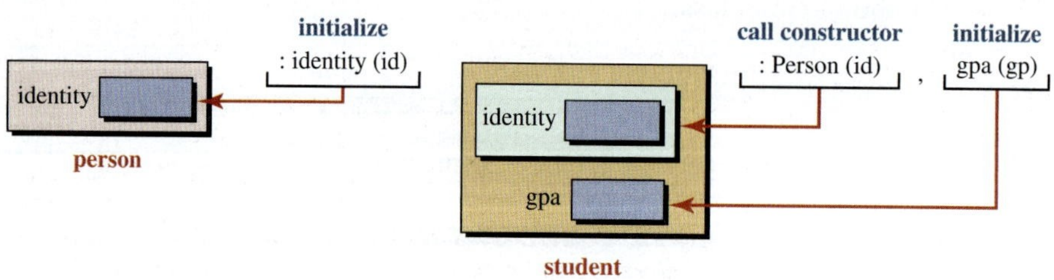

Figure 11.11 Constructing an object of type Person and Student

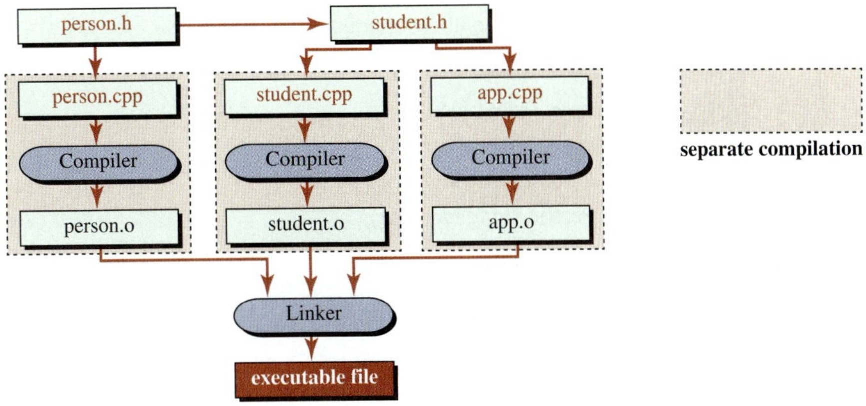

Figure 11.12 Separate compilation

Separate Compilation

We discussed separate compilation before, but it is interesting to see how it works in the case of inheritance, as shown in Figure 11.12.

The figure reveals several points. The *Person* class is compiled and sent to anyone who wants to use only that class. The *Person* and the *Student* classes are compiled by two different entities if the *Student* class has access to the interface file for the *Person* class because the interface file for the *Student* class must include the interface file for the *Person* class.

An Example Using Separate Compilation

We now give the interface, implementation, and application files for our simple inheritance example with constructors, destructor, and other functions. We have added more data fields, but we have eliminated the *set* and *get* functions and used only the *print* function to print the information for a person or a student.

The Interface and Implementation Files for the Person Class We first give the interface and implementation files for the *Person* class. This class is independent and can be used in conjunction with an application file. Program11.2 shows the interface file for the *Person* class.

Program 11.2 File person.h

```
/***************************************************************
 * The interface file for the Person class                     *
 ***************************************************************/

#ifndef PERSON_H
#define PERSON_H
#include <cassert>
#include <iostream>
#include <iomanip>
using namespace std;

class Person
{
```

(continued)

Program 11.2 File person.h (Continued)

```
    private:
        long identity;
    public:
        Person ();
        Person (long identity);
        ~Person();
        Person (const Person& person);
        void print () const;
};
#endif
```

Program 11.3 shows the implementation file for the *Person* class.

Program 11.3 File person.cpp

```
/***************************************************************
 * The implementation file for the Person class                *
 ***************************************************************/
#include "person.h"

// Default constructor
Person :: Person ()
: identity (0)
{
}
// Parameter constructor
Person :: Person (long id)
: identity (id)
{
   assert (identity >= 100000000 && identity <= 999999999);
}
// Copy constructor
Person :: Person (const Person& person)
: identity (person.identity)
{
}
// Destructor
Person:: ~Person()
{
}
// Accessor member function
void Person :: print () const
{
   cout << "Identity: " << identity << endl;
}
```

Program 11.4 File student.h

```
/***************************************************************
 * The interface file for the Student class                   *
 ***************************************************************/
#ifndef STUDENT_H
#define STUDENT_H
#include "person.h"

class Student: public Person
{
  private:
       double gpa;
  public:
       Student ( );
       Student (long identity, double gpa);
       ~Student();
       Student (const Student& student);
       void print () const;
};
#endif
```

The Interface and Implementation Files for the Student Class Now we show the interface and implementation files for the *Student* class, which is inherited from the *Person* class.

Program 11.5 shows the implementation file for the *Student* class.

Program 11.5 File student.cpp

```
/***************************************************************
 * The implementation file for the Student class              *
 ***************************************************************/
#include "student.h"

// Default constructor
Student :: Student ()
: Person (), gpa (0.0)
{
}
// Parameter constructor
Student :: Student (long id, double gp)
: Person (id), gpa (gp)
{
   assert (gpa >= 0.0 && gpa <= 4.0);
}
// Copy constructor
Student :: Student (const Student& student)
```

(continued)

Program 11.5 File student.cpp (Continued)

```
: Person (student), gpa (student.gpa)
{
}
// Destructor
Student :: ~Student()
{
}
// Accessor member function
void Student ::print () const
{
  Person :: print ();
  cout << "GPA: " << fixed << setprecision (2) << gpa << endl;
}
```

Application File for Using the Classes Program 11.6 shows a simple example of the application file. The client can create any application file and use the *Person* and *Student* classes.

Program 11.6 File app.cpp

```
/*****************************************************************
 * The application to test the Person and Student classes        *
 *****************************************************************/
#include "student.h"

int main ( )
{
  // Instantiation and using a Person object
  Person person (111111111);
  cout << "Information about person: " << endl;
  person.print ();
  cout << endl;
  // Instantiation and using a Student object
  Student student (222222222, 3.9);
  cout << "Information about student: " << endl;
  student.print ();
  cout << endl;
  return 0;
}
```

```
Run:
Information about person:
Identity: 111111111

Information about student:
Identity: 222222222
GPA: 3.90
```

11.1.3 More about Public Inheritance

In this section we discuss additional issues about public inheritance.

Protected Members

So far we have only discussed the private and the public members in a class. C++ also defines another specifier for a member, *protected*. A **protected member** acts like a private member in the base class (or when there is no derivation). When we extend a class, then the role of a protected member manifests itself. A protected member is accessible in the derived class and all classes derived from the derived class. In other words, a protected member is inherited like a private member, but it is not hidden in the derived class. The functions defined in the derived class can easily access a protected member without having to call a function inherited from the base class. Figure 11.13 shows the difference.

Figure 11.13 shows two cases. In the first case, we have only one private data member and one public member function. When we use derivation, the private member *x* is hidden. Although the function *set* (*x*) is public and seen in the derived class, it cannot be called directly because the parameter *x* cannot be seen. We need to create another function, with another dummy variable *y* to access *x*, as shown below:

```
void Derived :: set (int y)
{
   Base :: set (y);              // Calling the inherited function
}
```

If we have defined the data member as protected, it is seen in the derived class and we can use *set* (*x*) directly without having to create another function with a dummy variable. The question is which approach we should take: using private data members or the protected data members. We discuss the advantage and disadvantage of both approaches next.

Using Private Data Members Using private data members enforces the concept of encapsulation. As we discussed in previous chapters, encapsulation means hiding the data

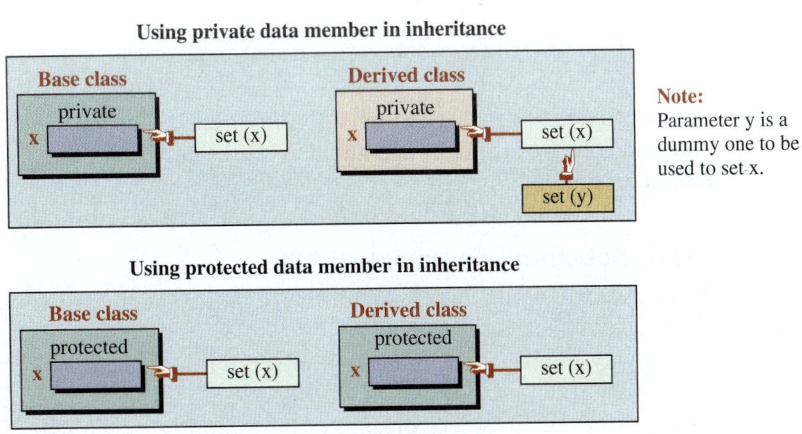

Figure 11.13 Private versus protected member

members of a class. When we use private data members, data are hidden to entities outside of the class and also to derived classes. On the other hand, using private data members means creating more code in the derived class. Therefore, the advantage of private data members is stronger encapsulation; its disadvantage is creating more code in the derived class. If we are the designer of the base class and want to protect our data members from direct access, we should use private data members.

Using Protected Data Members Using protected data members makes the coding of the derived classes simpler. However, it breaks the idea of encapsulation. We will see that sometimes we must use protected data members because the coding becomes very complicated if we use private data members.

Blocking Inheritance

Sometimes we may want to block inheritance—for example, when we have defined a class (as a designer) and do not want users to inherit from this class and create derived classes. The C++ standard allows us to do so using the `final` modifier, as shown below.

```
class First final
{
   ...
}
```

We can also use the final modifier to stop the inheritance anywhere in the hierarchy. For example, we may have a derived class from a base class, but we do not want the hierarchy to continue, as shown below.

```
class First
{
   ...
}
class Second final : public First
{
   ...
}
```

The *Second* class is inherited from the *First* class, but inheritance is blocked here. We do not want someone try to create another subclass from the *Second* class. The final modifier blocks further inheritance.

Liskov Substitution Principle (LSP)

A design principle that is sometimes ignored is the **Liskov substitution principle** (LSP), developed by Barbara Liskov. This principle says that an object of a superclass must always be substitutable by an object of a subclass without altering any of the properties of the superclass. We may think of an object as a special kind of another object in real life, but in object-oriented programming, we must check LSP before writing the code.

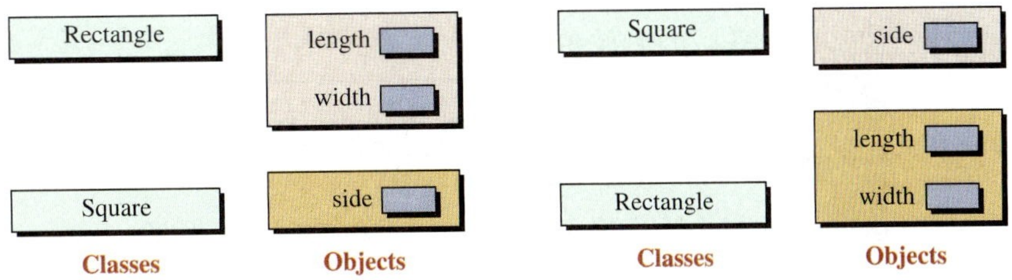

Figure 11.14 Liskov substitution principle

EXAMPLE 11.5

To better understand the Liskov substitution principle, we consider two objects: *square* and *rectangle*. In real life, we may say that a square is a special kind of a rectangle in which the length and the width are the same. We may also say that a rectangle is a square in which the length and sides are not of the same size. Neither of these two definitions complies with the *is-a* relationship in object-oriented programming. To understand the reason, we examine both approaches as shown in Figure 11.14.

In Figure 11.14, in the case on the left, we may think that the *Square* class can be derived from the *Rectangle* class because a square is a special kind of a rectangle. However, we see that an object of type *Square* has only one data member instead of two. An object of type *Square* cannot encapsulate an object of type *Rectangle* so it is not substitutable.

Also in Figure 11.14, in the case on the right, an object of the *Rectangle* class has more data members than an object of the *Square* class, but none of them can be copied from the *Square* class. In other words an object of *Rectangle* class has no relationship with an object of *Square* class and cannot be substituted for it.

This does not mean that we cannot have a *Square* class and a *Rectangle* class in an inheritance hierarchy. It means that they cannot inherit from each other; they can be at the same level and inherit from a common base class.

Inheritance Tree

In C++, we can have an **inheritance tree.** For example, we can have two classes that inherit from the *Person* class: *Student* and *Employee*. It is clear that a student is a person and an employee is also a person. Figure 11.15 shows this inheritance tree. Later in this chapter we define other classes, such as *Undergraduate* class and *Graduate* students class, that inherit from the *Student* class. We also define *Staff* and *Professor* classes that inherit from the *Employee* class.

Example 11.6

In this example we create interface files, implementation files, and application files for the classes shown in Figure 11.15. See Programs 11.7 through 11.13.

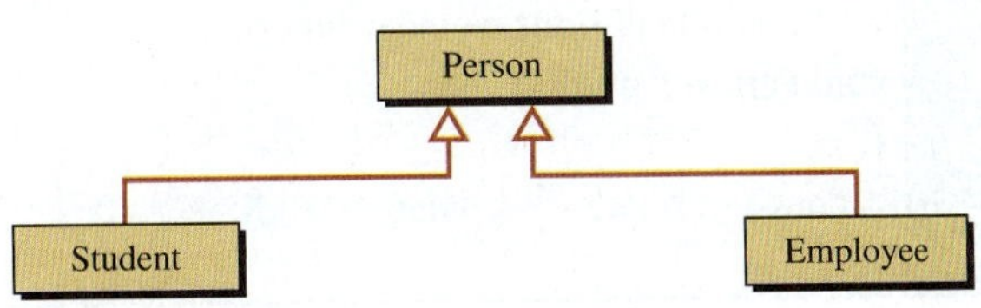

Figure 11.15 Inheritance tree

Program 11.7 File person.h

```
/***************************************************************
 * The interface file to define the Person class               *
 ***************************************************************/
#ifndef PERSON_H
#define PERSON_H
#include <iostream>
#include <string>
using namespace std;

// Definition of Person class
class Person
{
  private:
       string name;
  public:
       Person (string nme);
       ~Person();
       void print () const;
};
#endif
```

Program 11.8 File person.cpp

```
/***************************************************************
 * The implementation file for the Person class                *
 ***************************************************************/
#include "person.h"

// Constructor for Person class
Person :: Person (string nm)
:name (nm)
{
}
// Destructor for Person class
Person :: ~Person()
{
}
// Definition of print member function
void Person :: print () const
{
  cout << "Name: " << name << endl;
}
```

Program 11.9 File student.h

```
/*****************************************************************
 * The interface file to define the Student class                *
 *****************************************************************/
#ifndef STUDENT_H
#define STUDENT_H
#include "person.h"

// Definition of the Student class
class Student : public Person
{
   private:
         string name;
         double gpa;
   public:
         Student (string name, double gpa);
         ~Student ( );
         void print () const;
};
#endif
```

Program 11.10 File student.cpp

```
/*****************************************************************
 * The interface file to define the Employee class               *
 *****************************************************************/
#include "student.h"

// Constructor for Student class
Student :: Student (string nm, double gp)
:Person (nm), gpa (gp)
{
}
// Destructor for Student class
Student :: ~Student ()
{
}
// Definition of the print member function
void Student :: print () const
{
   Person :: print();
   cout << "GPA: " << gpa << endl;
}
```

Program 11.11 File employee.h

```
/*****************************************************************
 * The interface file to define the Student class               *
 *****************************************************************/
#ifndef EMPLOYEE_H
#define EMPLOYEE_H
#include "person.h"

// Definition of the Employee class
class Employee : public Person
{
  private:
       string name;
       double salary;
  public:
       Employee (string name, double salary);
       ~Employee ( );
       void print () const;
};
#endif
```

Program 11.12 File employee.cpp

```
/*****************************************************************
 * The implementation file for the Employee class               *
 *****************************************************************/
#include "employee.h"

// Constructor for Employee class
Employee :: Employee (string nm, double sa)
:Person (nm), salary (sa)
{
}
// Destructor for Employee class
Employee :: ~Employee()
{
}
// Definition of print member function
void Employee :: print () const
{
  Person :: print();
  cout << "Salary: " << salary << endl;
}
```

Program 11.13 File application.cpp

```
/************************************************************
 * The application file to use classes                      *
 ************************************************************/
#include "student.h"
#include "employee.h"

int main ()
{
  // Instantiation and using an object of the Person class
  cout << "Person: " << endl;
  Person person ("John");
  person.print ();
  cout << endl << endl;
  // Instantiation and using an object of the Student class
  cout << "Student: " << endl;
  Student student ("Mary", 3.9);
  student.print ();
  cout << endl << endl;
  // Instantiation and using an object of the Employee class
  cout << "Employee: " << endl;
  Employee employee ("Juan", 78000.00);
  employee.print ();
  cout << endl << endl;
  return 0;
}
```

```
Run:
Person:
Name: John

Student:
Name: Mary
GPA: 3.9

Employee:
Name: Juan
Salary: 78000
```

11.1.4 Three Types of Inheritance

Although *public* inheritance is by far the most common type of derivation, C++ allows us to use two other types of derivation: *private* and *protected*. Before we discuss the application of these two derivations, we show the status of elements in each derivation using Figure 11.16. The term *hidden* in the table means that the member is not accessible to the public member functions of the derived class. It must be accessed by the public member function of the base class.

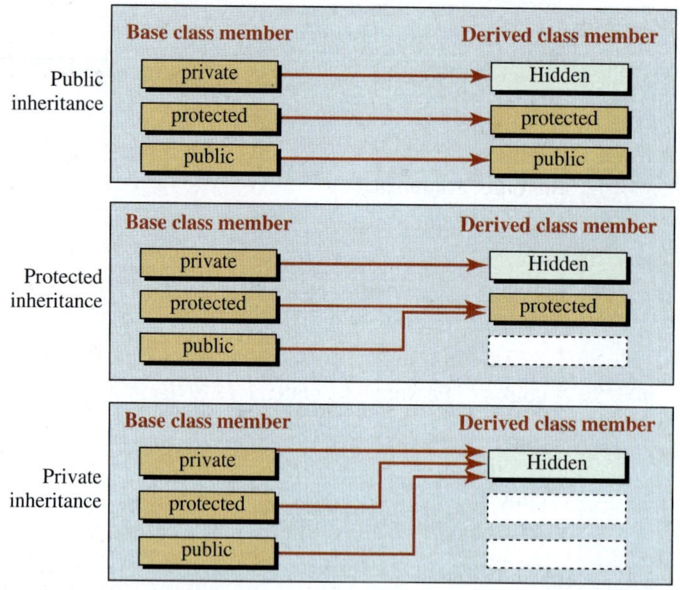

Figure 11.16 Inheritance types

Public Inheritance

Public inheritance is what we use most of the time. This type of derivation defines an *is-a* relationship between the base class object and the derived class object because the public interface of the base class becomes a public interface of the derived class. In other words, an object of a derived class is an object of the base class. Note that the private members of the base class remain private in the derived class, and they cannot be accessed through the public functions of the derived class; they must be accessed through the member functions of the base class.

Protected Inheritance

Protected inheritance is rare and virtually never used.

Private Inheritance

Private inheritance is much less common than public inheritance, but it has some applications. In Figure 11.16, we see that the public members of the base class become private members in the derived class. This property allows inherited implementation (code reuse). Assume that we have written the code for a class. Now we want to write the code for another class, but there is no *is-a* relationship between the two. However, we notice that some of the public members of the first class can help us code some of the public members of the new class. We inherit the second class privately from the first class to use some of its functions. The following is example. We do not need to specify that the inheritance is private because private inheritance is by default.

```
void First :: functionFirst ( )
{
   ... ;
}
```

```
void Second :: functionSecond( )
{
    First : FunctionFirst()              // Use FunctionFirst to do some of the job
    ...;                                 // Add more code to the rest of the job
}
```

We will see examples of private inheritance when we discuss data structures in future chapters. For example, a *stack* is not a *linked-list*, but it can inherit code from a linked list.

Private inheritance does not define a type inheritance; it defines an implementation inheritance.

11.2 ASSOCIATION

Not all relationships between classes can be defined as inheritance. We encounter classes in object-oriented programming that have other types of relationships with each other. The second type of relationship we discuss here is **association.** More programs are being developed today that use association rather than inheritance. An association between two classes shows a relationship. For example, we can define a class named *Person* and another class named *Address*. An object of the type *Person* may be related to an object of type *Address*: A person lives in an address and the address is occupied by a person. The *Address* class is not inherited from the *Person* class; neither the other way. In other words, a person *is not* an address; an address *is not* a person. We cannot define either class as a subclass of the other one. A relationship of this type is shown in UML diagrams as a solid line between two classes, as shown in Figure 11.17.

An association diagram also shows the type of relationship between the classes. This is shown by an arrow and text in the direction of the corresponding class. Another piece of information represented in an association diagram is **multiplicity.** Multiplicity defines the number of objects that take part in the association. Multiplicity is shown at the end of the line next to the class. Figure 11.17 shows that one person can have only one address, but one address can belong to any number of occupants (all people who live in that address). Table 11.2 shows different types of multiplicity.

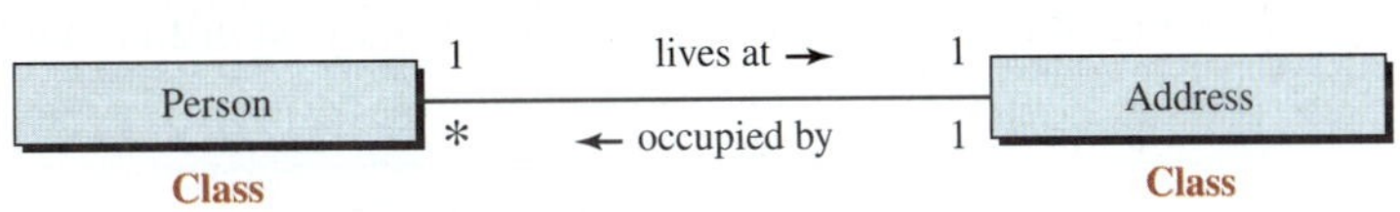

Figure 11.17 An association relationship

Table 11.2 Multiplicity in association diagrams

Key	Interpretation
n	Exactly *n* objects
*	Any number of objects including none
0 ... 1	Zero or one object
n ... *m*	A range from *n* to *m* objects
n, *m*	*n* or *m* objects

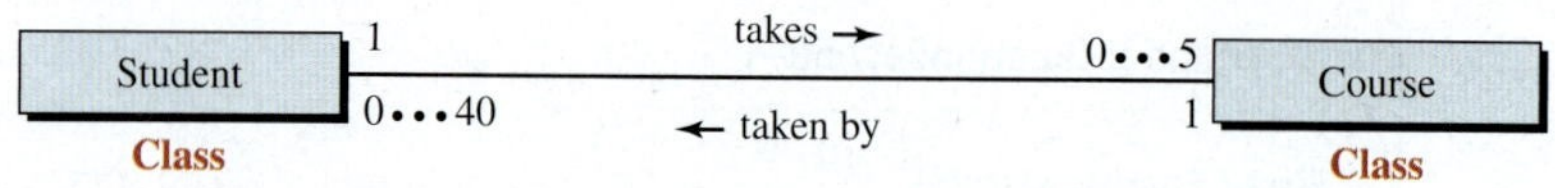

Figure 11.18 Association between courses and students

As another example, assume we need to define the association relationship between students and courses they take. We can define two classes: *Course* and *Student*. If we assume that at each semester a student can take up to five courses, and a course can be taken by up to forty students, we can depict these relationships in an association diagram, as shown in Figure 11.18.

The association relationship in Figure 11.18 defines a many-to-many relationship. An association representing a many-to-many relationship cannot be implemented directly because it creates an infinite number of objects in the program (circular relationship). Usually this type of association is implemented in a such a way that this circular infinity is avoided. For example, a *Student* object can have a list of five course names (not a complete *Course* object), and a *Course* object can have a list of forty student names (not a complete *Student* object). Later in this chapter we present a program that shows this type of relationship.

11.2.1 Aggregation

Aggregation is a special kind of association in which the relationship involves ownership. In other words, it models the "has-a" relationship. One class is called an aggregator and the other an aggregatee. An object of the aggregator class contains one or more objects of the aggregatee class. Figure 11.19 shows the UML diagram for aggregation. Note that the symbol for aggregation is a hollow diamond placed at the site of the aggregator.

The aggregation relationship is one-way; it cannot be two way because that would create an infinite number of objects. As Figure 11.19 shows, a *Person* can have a birth date (an object of the class *Date*), but a *Date* object can be related to multiple events, not only the birth date of a person.

An aggregation is a one-to-may relationship from the aggregator to the aggregatee.

We must remember that in this type of relationship, the life of an aggregatee is independent of the life of its aggregator. An aggregatee may be instantiated before the instantiation of the aggregator and may live after it.

In an aggregation, the lifetime of the aggregatee is independent of the lifetime of the aggregator.

Example 11.7

In this example we create a *Person* class and a *Date* class. The *Date* class is independent and can be used to represent any event. The *Person* class uses an object of the *Date* class to define the birthday of a person.

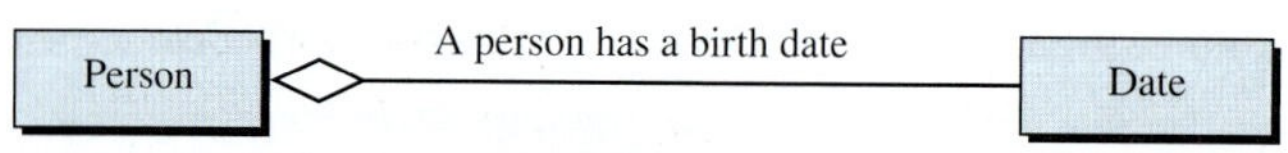

Figure 11.19 Example of aggregation relationship

Program 11.14 The file date.h

```
/*****************************************************************
 * The interface file for date.h class                           *
 *****************************************************************/
#ifndef DATE_H
#define DATE_H
#include <iostream>
#include <cassert>
using namespace std;

class Date
{
  private:
       int month;
       int day;
       int year;
  public:
       Date (int month, int day, int year);
       ~Date ();
       void print() const;
};
#endif
```

The Date Class Program 11.14 show the interface file for the *Date* class.

Program 11.15 shows the implementation of the *Date* class.

Program 11.15 File date.cpp

```
/*****************************************************************
 * The implementation of functions in the Date class             *
 *****************************************************************/
#include "date.h"

// Parameter constructor
Date :: Date (int m, int d, int y)
: month (m), day (d), year (y)
{
  if ((month < 1) || (month > 12))
  {
       cout << "Month is out of range. ";
       assert (false);
  }
  int daysInMonths [13] = {0, 31, 28, 31, 30, 31, 30, 31,
                                 31, 30, 31, 30 ,31};
```

(continued)

Program 11.15 File date.cpp (Continued)

```
    if ((day < 1) || (day > daysInMonths [month]))
    {
        cout << "Day out of range! ";
        assert (false);
    }
    if ((year < 1900) || (year > 2099))
    {
        cout << "Year out of range! " ;
        assert (false);
    }
}
// Destructor
Date :: ~Date ()
{
}
// Print member function
void Date :: print() const
{
  cout << month << "/" << day << "/" << year << endl;
}
```

The Person Class Program 11.16 shows the interface file for the *Person* class.

Program 11.16 File person.h

```
/***************************************************************
 * The interface file for the Person class                    *
 ***************************************************************/
#ifndef PERSON_H
#define PERSON_H
#include "date.h"

// Definition of the Person class
class Person
{
  private:
      long identity;
      Date birthDate;
  public:
      Person (long identity, Date birthDate);
      ~Person ( );
      void print ( ) const;
};
#endif
```

Program 11.17 File person.cpp

```
/***************************************************************
 * The implementation file for Person concrete class          *
 ***************************************************************/
#include "person.h"

// Constructor
Person :: Person (long id, Date bd)
: identity (id), birthDate (bd)
{
  assert (identity > 111111111 && identity < 999999999);
}
// Destructor
Person :: ~Person ( )
{
}
// Print function
void Person :: print ( ) const
{
  cout << "Person Identity: " << identity << endl;
  cout << "Person date of birth: ";
  birthDate.print ();
  cout << endl << endl;
}
```

Program 11.17 shows the implementation file for the *Person* class that aggregates the *Date* class.

The Application Class Program 11.18 shows the implementation of the application class that uses the *Person* class.

Program 11.18 File app.cpp

```
/***************************************************************
 * The application file to test the Person class              *
 ***************************************************************/
#include "person.h"

int main ( )
{
  // Instantiation
  Date date1 (5, 6, 1980);
  Person person1 (111111456, date1);
  Date date2 (4, 23, 1978);
  Person person2 (345332446, date2);
```

(continued)

Program 11.18 File app.cpp (Continued)

```
    // Output
    person1.print ( );
    person2.print ( );
    return 0;
}
```

```
Run:
Person Identity: 111111456
Person date of birth: 5/6/1980

Person Identity: 345332446
Person date of birth: 4/23/1978
```

11.2.2 Composition

Composition is a special kind of aggregation in which the lifetime of the containee depends on the lifetime of the container. For example, the relationship between a person and her name is an example of composition. The name cannot exist without being the name of a person. Figure 11.20 shows the relationship between an employee and her name. The name itself is composed of three string objects. Note that the symbol for composition is a solid diamond placed at the side of the composer. In the case of the relationship between the *Employee* and the *Name*, the composer is the *Employee.* In the case of the relationship between *Name* and string, the *Name* is the composer.

The distinction between aggregation and composition is normally conceptual; it depends on how the designer thinks about the relationship. For example, a designer may think that a name must always belong to a person and cannot have a life of its own. Another designer may think that a name continues to exist even if the person dies. The distinction also depends on the environment in which we are designing our classes. For example, in a car factory, the relationship between a car and its engine is composition; we cannot use the engine without installing it in a car. In an engine factory, each engine has its own life cycle.

Like the aggregation relationship, the composition relationship is implemented as classes in which the container class has a data member (or list of data members) of the containee type. However, containee objects are created inside the container objects; they do not have independent lives.

Example 11.8

We create an employee class in which an employee object has two data members: salary and name. The name itself is an object of a class with three fields: first name, initial, and last name.

Name Class Program 11.19 shows the interface file for *Name* class.

Figure 11.20 Example of the composition relationship

Program 11.19 File name.h

```
/*****************************************************************
 * The interface file for the Name class                         *
 *****************************************************************/

#ifndef NAME_H
#define NAME_H
#include <string>
#include <iostream>
#include <cassert>
using namespace std;

class Name
{
  private:
            string first;
            string init;
            string last;
  public:
        Name (string first, string init, string last);
        ~Name ( );
        void print ( ) const;
};
#endif
```

Program 11.20 shows the implementation file for the *Name* class.

Program 11.20 File name.cpp

```
/*****************************************************************
 * The implementation file for Name class                        *
 *****************************************************************/
#include "name.h"

// Constructor
Name :: Name (string fst, string i, string lst)
:first (fst), init (i), last (lst)
{
  assert (init.size () == 1);
  toupper (first[0]);
  toupper (init [0]);
  toupper (last[0]);
}
 // Destructor
Name :: ~Name ( )
```

(*continued*)

Program 11.20 File name.cpp (Continued)

```
{
}
// Print member function
void Name :: print ( ) const
{
   cout << "Emplyee name: " << first << " " << init << ". ";
   cout << last << endl;
}
```

Employee Class Program 11.21 shows the interface file for the *Employee* class Program 11.22 shows the implementation file for the *Employee* class.

Program 11.21 File employee.h

```
/*****************************************************************
  * The interface file for the employee class                    *
  *****************************************************************/
#ifndef EMPLOYEE_H
#define EMPLOYEE_H
#include "name.h"

class Employee
{
   private:
         Name name;
         double salary;
   public:
         Employee (string first, string init, string last,
                                          double salary);
         ~Employee ( );
         void print ( ) const;
};
#endif
```

Program 11.22 File employee.cpp

```
/*****************************************************************
  * The implementation file for Employee class                   *
  *****************************************************************/

#include "employee.h"

// Constructor
Employee :: Employee (string fst, string i, string lst,
                                          double sal)
```

(continued)

Program 11.22 File employee.cpp (Continued)

```
: name (fst, i, lst), salary (sal)
{
   assert (salary > 0.0 and salary < 100000.0);
}
// Destructor
Employee :: ~Employee ( )
{
}
// Print member function
void Employee :: print ( ) const
{
   name.print();
   cout << "Salary: " << salary << endl << endl;
}
```

Application Program 11.23 shows the application file for testing the *Employee* class.

Program 11.23 The file appl.cpp

```
/*****************************************************************
 * The application file to test the Employee class              *
 *****************************************************************/
#include "employee.h"

int main ( )
{
   // Instantiation
   Employee employee1 ("Mary", "B", "White", 22120.00);
   Employee employee2 ("William", "S", "Black", 46700.00);
   Employee employee3 ("Ryan", "A", "Brown", 12500.00);
   // Output
   employee1.print ( );
   employee2.print ( );
   employee3.print ( );
   return 0;
}
```

```
Run:
Emplyee name: Mary B. White
Salary: 22120

Emplyee name: William S. Black
Salary: 46700

Emplyee name: Ryan A. Brown
Salary: 12500
```

11.3 DEPENDENCY

The third type of relationship that we can define between two classes is **dependency.** Dependency is a weaker relationship than inheritance or association. Although there are several definitions for dependency, we use the one that is most prevalent. We say that dependency models the "uses" relationship. Class A depends on class B if class A somehow *uses* class B. It other words, class A depends on class B if A cannot perform its complete task without knowing that class B exists. This happens when

- Class A uses an object of type B as a parameter in a member function.
- Class A has a member function that returns an object of type B.
- Class A has a member function that has a local variable of type B.

11.3.1 UML Diagrams

We use both UML class diagrams and UML sequence diagrams to show dependencies (see Appendix Q).

UML Class Diagram

Although there are many variations of the UML class diagram for dependency, we use the one that shows the dependency with a dashed line and arrow from the depending class to the depended class. Figure 11.21 shows an example of a dependency relationship in which class A depends on class B.

UML Sequence Diagram

A sequence diagram shows the interaction between objects. The *main* function and each object have lifelines that show the passing of time. The objects can be instantiated and their member function can be called.

As a simple example, we have two classes, *First* and *Second*. Class *First* has a member function called *fun*() that the user cannot call directly in the application (for some reason such as security). We want to use another function in the *Second* class called *funny*() to call the function *fun*() in the *First* class. However, we must pass an instance of the *First* class inside *funny*() so the *First* class can use it when it calls its *fun*() class (Figure 11.22).

In Figure 11.22 the *main* function instantiates an object of the class *First* and an object of the class *Second*. The *main* function calls the *funny*(...) member function of the class *Second* and passes an object of the class *First* as a parameter. An object of the class *Second* can then call the *fun*() function of the class *First* using the name of the object that received from *main*. Note that the relationship between objects *First* and *Second* is dependency. Object *Second* uses class *First* in its member function *funny*(...), and object *Second* calls the member function of object *First*.

11.3.2 A Comprehensive Example

We use a comprehensive example to demonstrate the basics of dependency relationships. Assume we want to create an invoice for the list of products sold. We have a class named *Invoice* and a class named *Product*. The class *Invoice* uses instances of the class *Product* as a parameter in one of its member functions (*add*). Figure 11.23 shows the UML class diagram.

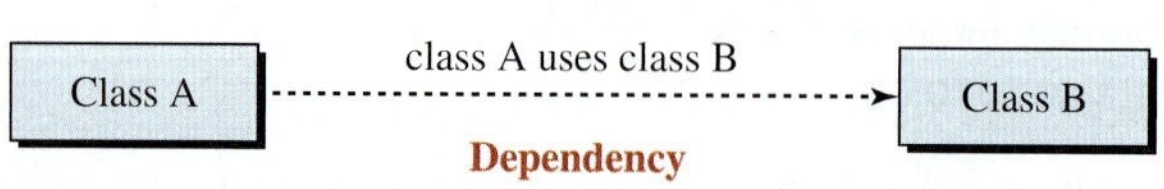

Figure 11.21 UML class diagram for dependency

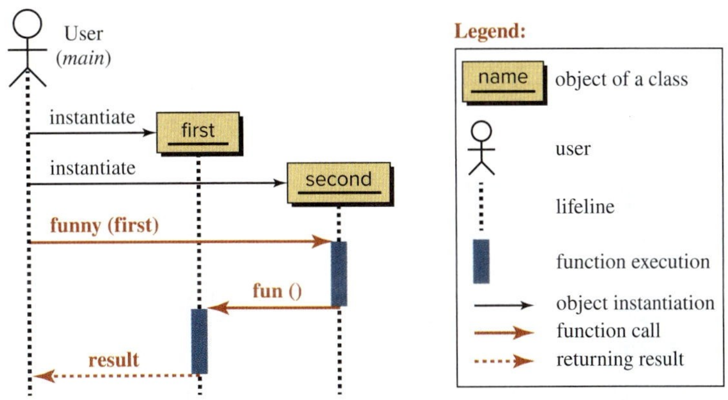

Figure 11.22 Sequence diagram for the *First* and *Second* classes

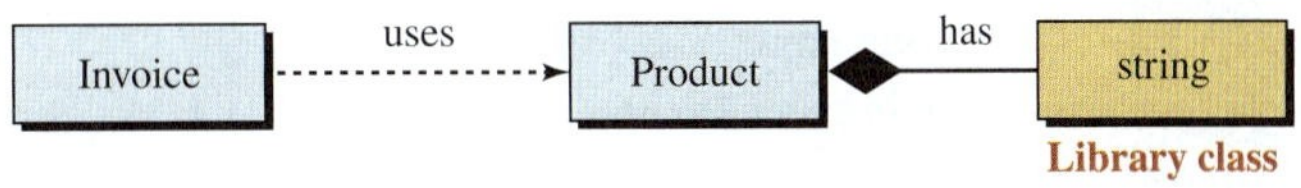

Figure 11.23 UML class diagram for *Invoice* and *Product* classes

We show the sequence diagram for two products in Figure 11.24. Note that the *main* function must instantiate two objects of type *Product* and one object of type *Invoice*. The *main* function then calls the add function in the *Invoice* class to add the products to the invoice, but it must get the price of each product from the corresponding object.

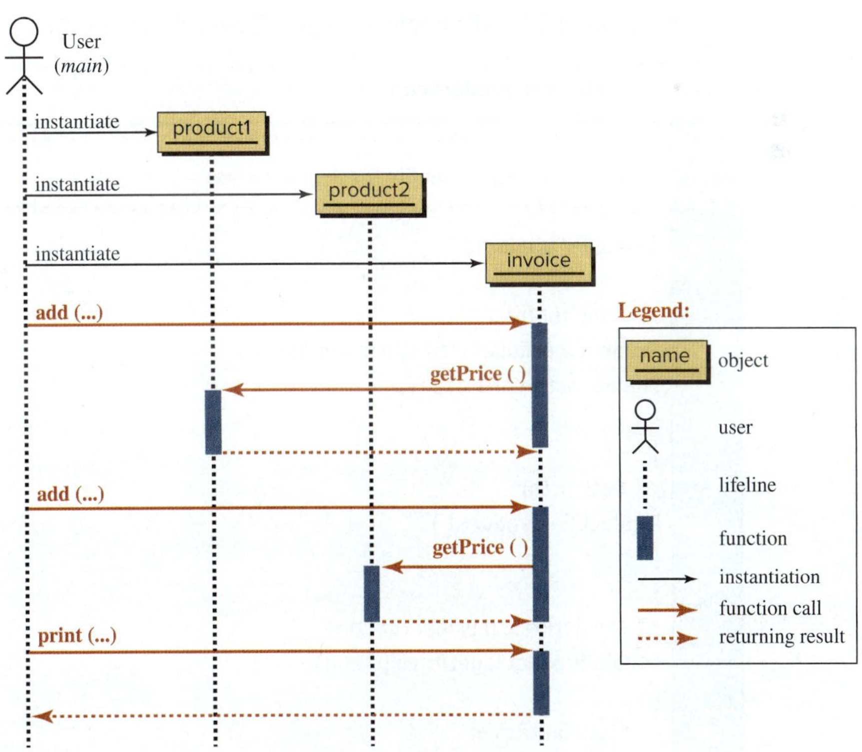

Figure 11.24 Sequence diagram for the Invoice program

Program 11.24 File product.h

```
/***************************************************************
 * The interface file for the Product class                    *
 ***************************************************************/
#ifndef PRODUCT_H
#define PRODUCT_H
#include <string>
#include <iostream>
using namespace std;

class Product
{
  private:
       string name;
       double unitPrice;
  public:
       Product (string name, double unitPrice);
       ~Product ( );
       double getPrice ( ) const;
};
#endif
```

Product Class Program 11.24 is the interface for the *Product* class.

Program 11.25 is the implementation file for the *Product* class.

Program 11.25 File product.cpp

```
/***************************************************************
 * The implementation file for Product class                   *
 ***************************************************************/
#include "product.h"

// Constructor
Product :: Product (string nm, double up)
: name (nm), unitPrice (up)
{
}
// Destructor
Product :: ~Product ( )
{
}
// The getPrice member function
double Product :: getPrice ( ) const
{
  return unitPrice;
}
```

Program 11.26 File Invoice.h

```
/***************************************************************
 * The interface file for the Invoice class                    *
 ***************************************************************/
#ifndef INVOICE_H
#define INVOICE_H
#include "product.h"

class Invoice
{
  private:
       int invoiceNumber;
       double invoiceTotal;
  public:
       Invoice (int invoiceNumber);
       ~Invoice ( );
       void add (int quantity, Product product);
       void print ( ) const;
};
#endif
```

Invoice Class Program 11.26 is the interface file for the *Invoice* class.

Program 11.27 shows the implementation file for the *Invoice* class.

Program 11.27 File invoice.cpp

```
/***************************************************************
 * The implementation file for Invoice class                   *
 ***************************************************************/
#include "invoice.h"

// Constructor
Invoice :: Invoice (int invNum)
: invoiceNumber (invNum), invoiceTotal (0.0)
{
}
// Destructor
Invoice :: ~Invoice ( )
{
}
// Add member function
void Invoice :: add (int quantity, Product product)
{
  invoiceTotal += quantity * product.getPrice ();
}
```

(continued)

Program 11.27 File invoice.cpp (Continued)

```
// Print member function
void Invoice :: print ( ) const
{
   cout << "Invoice Number: " << invoiceNumber << endl;
   cout << "Invoice Total: " << invoiceTotal << endl;
}
```

Application Program 11.28 is the application file for testing the *Invoice* class.

Program 11.28 File application.cpp

```
/***************************************************************
 * The application file to test the Invoice class              *
 ***************************************************************/
#include "invoice.h"

int main ( )
{
   // Instantiation of two products
   Product product1 ("Table", 150.00);
   Product product2 ("Chair", 80.00);
   // Creation of invoice for the two products
   Invoice invoice (1001);
   invoice.add (1, product1);
   invoice.add (6, product2);
   invoice.print ();
   return 0;
}
```

```
Run:
Invoice Number: 1001
Invoice Total: 630
```

11.4 PROGRAM DESIGN

In this section we discuss two projects. The first shows how to create a *Tokenizer* class; the second shows how to simulate the registration process at a university.

11.4.1 A Tokenizer Class

A common problem is to tokenize a string of characters using a list of delimiters. For example, we may need to extract words from a text. The words in a text are separated by spaces and new-line characters. The words in this case are called *tokens,* and the characters that separate the words are *delimiters*. For example, the following string has seven tokens (words) in it.

```
"This is a book about C++ language"
```

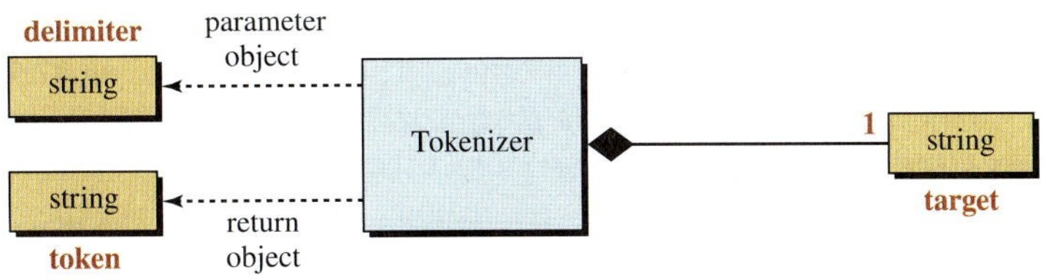

Figure 11.25 Relationship between classes

The C++ language has no class whose objects can tokenize a string, but we can create a class to do so. The string library class has member functions that search a string to find a character in a string or to find a character which is not in a string. We can use these functions in the string library to create a *Tokenizer* class.

Relationship Among Classes

Before writing the code for the *Tokenizer* class, we show the UML class diagram that depicts the relationship between classes. We use only two classes in this task: *Tokenizer* class and *string* class. Figure 11.25 shows the relationship between these two classes.

In Figure 11.25 the *Tokenizer* class uses the *string* class three times. It uses it to create the target string (the text to be tokenized), to create the delimiter string, and finally to create tokens. We have one string as a target and one string as a delimiter, but we create many strings as tokens. The relationship between the tokenizer object and the target or delimiter object is composition. The relationship between the tokenizer object and tokens is dependency (the tokens are returned objects from functions in the *Tokenizer* class).

Sequence Diagram

Figure 11.26 shows the interaction between objects in a sequence diagram.

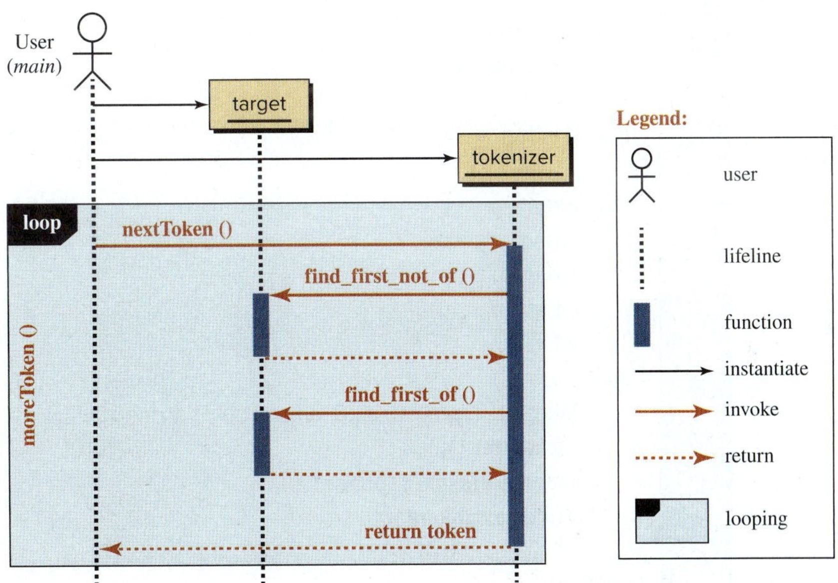

Figure 11.26 Sequence diagram for the Tokenizer design

After the *target* and *tokenizer* objects have been instantiated, the program uses a loop to extract tokens from the *target* object. The user calls the *nextToken*() function in the *tokenizer* object, which in turn calls *find_first_not_of*() and *find_first_of*() member functions in the *target* object. The *tokenizer* object then returns an instance of the *token* object to the user. Note that we do not use the token objects in the sequence diagram because they are used only as a returning object (dependency).

Programs

Since the *string* class is a library class with predefined public interfaces, we must create only one class, *Tokenizer*. Its interface file is shown in Program 11.29. The class has only two data members, *target* and *delim*, which are of type *string*. However, the class returns a token of type string (line 21). The class has only two member functions (besides the constructor and destructor): the first checks to see if there are any tokens in the target string; the second returns the next token in the target string.

We also have one implementation file that implements the *Tokenizer* class. There are four functions in this file: constructor, destructor, the function that checks if there are more tokens, and the function that returns the next token (Program 11.30).

We can create an application file to create and use objects of the *Tokenizer* class. Program 11.31 is an example.

Program 11.29 File tokenizer.h

```
1  /***************************************************************
2   * The interface file for the Tokenizer class                  *
3   ***************************************************************/
4  #ifndef TOKENIZER_H
5  #define TOKENIZER_H
6  #include <iostream>
7  #include <string>
8  using namespace std;
9  
10 class Tokenizer
11 {
12   private:
13       string target;
14       string delim;
15       int begin;
16       int end;
17   public:
18       Tokenizer (const string& target, const string& delim);
19       ~Tokenizer ();
20       bool moreToken() const;
21       string nextToken();
22 };
23 #endif
```

Program 11.30 File tokenizer.cpp

```
/***************************************************************
 * The implementation file for the Tokenizer class             *
 ***************************************************************/
#include "tokenizer.h"

// Constructor
Tokenizer :: Tokenizer (const string& tar, const string& del)
: target (tar), delim (del)
{
   begin = target.find_first_not_of (delim, 0);
   end = target.find_first_of (delim, begin);
}
// Destructor
Tokenizer :: ~Tokenizer()
{
}
// Checks for more tokens
bool Tokenizer :: moreToken ( ) const
{
   return (begin != - 1);
}
// Returns the next token
string Tokenizer :: nextToken ( )
{
   string token = target.substr (begin, end - begin);
   begin = target.find_first_not_of (delim, end);
   end = target.find_first_of(delim, begin);
   return token;
}
```

Program 11.31 File app.cpp

```
/***************************************************************
 * The application file to test the Tokenizer class            *
 ***************************************************************/
#include "tokenizer.h"

int main ( )
{
   // The target string that needs to be tokenized
   string target ("This is the string to be tokenized. \n");
   // The delimit string defines the set of separators
   string delimit (" \n");     // Delimiter made of ' ' and '\n'
```

(continued)

Program 11.31 File app.cpp (Continued)

```
    // Instantiation of tokenizer object
    Tokenizer tokenizer (target, delimit);
    // Traversing the target string to find tokens
    while (tokenizer.moreToken ())
    {
        cout << tokenizer.nextToken () << endl;
    }
    return 0;
}
```

```
Run:
This
is
the
string
to
be
tokenize.
```

11.4.2 Registration

In this section we use association and dependency between classes to design a simple registration system for a small department in a college or university.

UML Class Diagram

We use six classes as shown in Figure 11.27.

Each *student* object composes a *string* object (as student name) and composes a *schedule* object, which in turn composes an array of student names (strings). Each *course* object composes a *string* object (as course name) and composes a *roster* object, which in turn composes an array of course names (strings). The registrar class just uses the *student* and *course* objects.

UML Sequence Diagram

Before writing the code for the five user-defined classes involved, we show the sequence diagram and the interaction between the classes (Figure 11.28). Note that the *roster* object

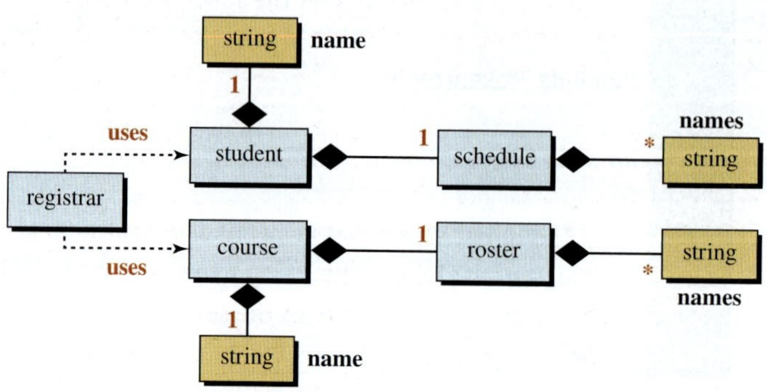

Figure 11.27 Relationship among classes in registration project

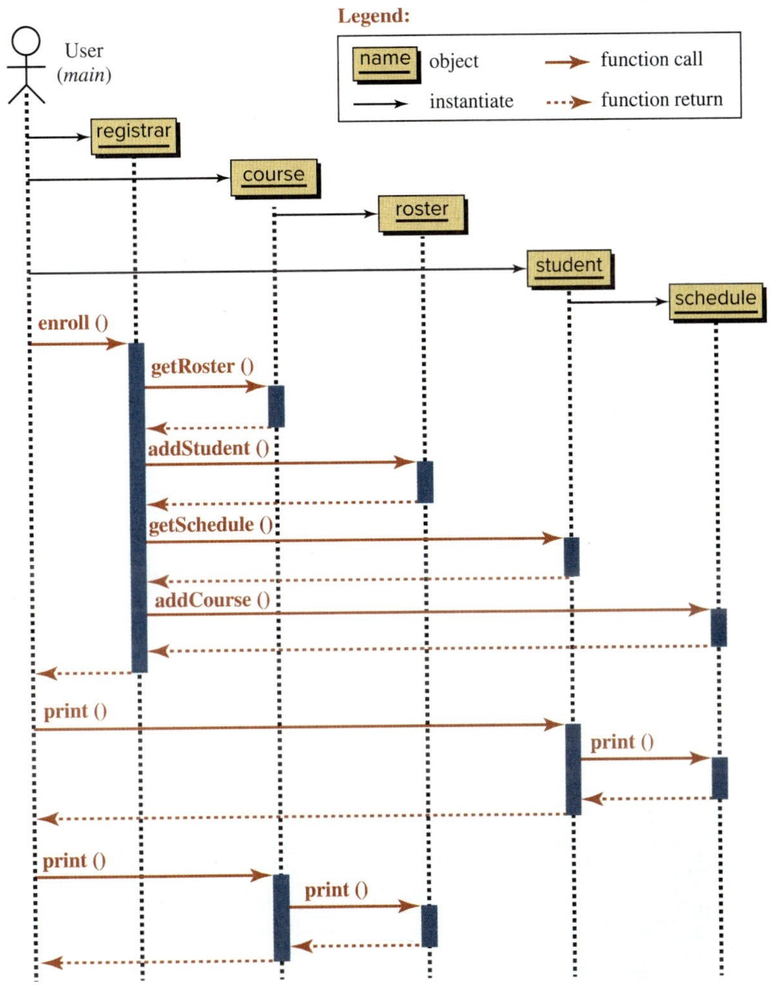

Figure 11.28 Sequence diagram for the registrar project

is created by the *course* object, and the schedule object is created by the *student* object. The *registrar*, *course*, and *student* objects are created by *main*. We show the case for one single student and one single course to make the diagram simpler.

Programs

Program 11.32 is the interface file. Program 11.33 is the implementation file.

Program 11.32 File courseRoster.h

```
/***********************************************************************
 * The interface file for the class CourseRoster                       *
 ***********************************************************************/
#ifndef COURSEROSTER_H
#define COURSEROSTER_H
```

(*continued*)

Program 11.32 File courseRoster.h (Continued)

```
#include <string>
#include <iostream>
#include <cassert>
using namespace std;

// Class Definition
class CourseRoster
{
   private:
         int size;
         string* stdNames;
   public:
         CourseRoster ();
         ~CourseRoster();
         void addStudent (string studentName);
         void print () const;
};
#endif
```

Program 11.33 File courseRoster.cpp

```
/*****************************************************************
 * The implementation file for class CourseRoster               *
 *****************************************************************/
#include "courseRoster.h"

// Constructor
CourseRoster :: CourseRoster ()
:size (0)
{
        stdNames = new string [20];
}
// Destructor
CourseRoster :: ~CourseRoster ( )
{
        delete [ ] stdNames;
}
// Definition of addStudent function
void CourseRoster :: addStudent (string studentName)
{
   stdNames [size] = studentName;
   size++;
```

(continued)

Program 11.33 File courseRoster.cpp (Continued)

```
}
// Definition of print function
void CourseRoster :: print () const
{
   cout << "List of Students" << endl;
   for (int i = 0; i < size; i++)
   {
        cout << stdNames[i] << endl;
   }
   cout << endl;
}
```

Class Course

Program 11.34 is the interface file. Program 11.35 is the implementation file.

Program 11.34 File course.h

```
/**************************************************************
 * The interface file for the class Course                    *
 **************************************************************/
#ifndef COURSE_H
#define COURSE_H
#include <cassert>
#include <string>
#include <iostream>
#include "courseRoster.h"
using namespace std;

// Class Definition
class Course
{
  private:
        string name;
        int units;
        CourseRoster* roster;
  public:
        Course (string name, int units);
        ~Course ();
        string getName() const;
        CourseRoster* getRoster () const;
        void addStudent (string name);
        void print () const;
};
#endif
```

Program 11.35 File course.cpp

```
/*************************************************************
 * The implementation file for the class Course              *
 *************************************************************/
#include "course.h"

// Constructor
Course :: Course (string nm, int ut)
: name (nm), units (ut)
{
  roster = new CourseRoster;
}
// Destructor
Course :: ~Course ()
{
}
// Definition of getName function
string Course :: getName() const
{
  return name;
}
// Definition of addStudent function
void Course :: addStudent (string name)
{
  roster - >addStudent (name);
}
// Definition of getRoster function
CourseRoster* Course :: getRoster () const
{
  return roster;
}
// Definition of print function
void Course :: print () const
{
  cout << "Course Name: " << name << endl;
  cout << "Number of Units: " << units << endl;
  roster - > print ();
}
```

StudentSchedule Class

Program 11.36 is the interface file.

Program 11.36 File studentSchedule.h

```
/*************************************************************
 * The interface file for the class StudentSchedule          *
 *************************************************************/
#ifndef STUDENTSCHEDULE_H
#define STUDENTSCHEDULE_H
#include <string>
#include <iostream>
#include <cassert>
using namespace std;

// Class Definition
class StudentSchedule
{
  private:
       int size;
       string* courseNames;
  public:
       StudentSchedule ();
       ~StudentSchedule();
       void addCourse (string course);
       void print () const;
};
#endif
```

Program 11.37 is the implementation file.

Program 11.37 File studentSchedule.cpp

```
/*************************************************************
 * The implementation file for the class StudentSchedule     *
 *************************************************************/
#include "studentSchedule.h"

// Constructor
StudentSchedule :: StudentSchedule ()
:size (0)
{
  courseNames = new string [5];
}
// Destructor
StudentSchedule :: ~StudentSchedule ()
```

(continued)

Program 11.37 File studentSchedule.cpp (Continued)

```
{
    delete [ ] courseNames;
}
// Definition of addCourse function
void StudentSchedule :: addCourse (string name)
{
    courseNames [size] = name;
    size++;
}
// Definition of print function
void StudentSchedule :: print () const
{
    cout << "List of Courses" << endl;
    for (int i = 0; i < size; i++)
    {
        cout << courseNames[i] << endl;
    }
    cout << endl;
}
```

Program 11.38 is the interface file.

Program 11.38 File student.h

```
/*****************************************************************
 * The interface file for the class Student                       *
 *****************************************************************/
#ifndef STUDENT_H
#define STUDENT_H
#include <cassert>
#include <string>
#include <iostream>
#include "studentSchedule.h"
using namespace std;

// Class Definition
class Student
{
  private:
      string name;
      StudentSchedule* schedule;
  public:
      Student (string name);
      ~Student ();
      string getName () const;
      StudentSchedule* getSchedule () const;
```

(continued)

Program 11.38 File student.h (Continued)

```
        void addCourse (string name);
        void print () const;
};
#endif
```

Program 11.39 is the implementation file.

Program 11.39 File student.cpp

```
/*****************************************************************
 * The implementation file for the class Student                 *
 *****************************************************************/
#include "student.h"

// Constructor
Student :: Student (string nm)
:name (nm)
{
  schedule = new StudentSchedule;
}
// Destructor
Student :: ~Student ()
{
}
// Definition of getName function
string Student :: getName () const
{
  return name;
}
// Definition of getSchedule function
StudentSchedule* Student :: getSchedule () const
{
  return schedule;
}
// Definition of addCourse function
void Student :: addCourse (string name)
{
  schedule -> addCourse (name);
}
// Definition of print function
void Student :: print () const
{
  cout << "Student name: " << name << endl;
  schedule - >print ();
}
```

Program 11.40 File registrar.h

```
/***************************************************************
 * The interface file for the class Registrar                  *
 ***************************************************************/
#ifndef REGISTRAR_H
#define REGISTRAR_H
#include "course.h"
#include "student.h"

// Class Definition
class Registrar
{
  public:
       Registrar ();
       ~Registrar();
       void enroll (Student student, Course course);
};
#endif
```

Program 11.40 is the interface file.

Program 11.41 is the implementation file.

Program 11.42 is the application file. Note that the application creates one registrar object. In Chapter 20, we learn how to control the Registrar object so that it is unique

Program 11.41 File registrar.cpp

```
/***************************************************************
 * The implementation file for the class Registrar             *
 ***************************************************************/
#include "registrar.h"

// Constructor
Registrar :: Registrar ()
{
}
// Destructor
Registrar :: ~Registrar ()
{
}
// Enroll function
void Registrar :: enroll (Student student, Course course)
{
  (course.getRoster ()) -> addStudent (student.getName());
  (student.getSchedule()) -> addCourse (course.getName());
}
```

(Singleton pattern), but for the moment we assume only one registrar object is created. The Program 11.42 then creates three Student objects and three Course objects. The registrar object is responsible for enrolling the students in the courses they want. Note that we do not instantiate any object from the *StudentSchedule* or *CourseRoster* class. The first is instantiated in the *Student* class and the second in the *Course* class.

Program 11.42 File application.cpp

```
/***************************************************************
 * The application file to test classes in Registration project   *
 ***************************************************************/
#include "registrar.h"

int main ( )
{
  // Instantiation of a Registrar object
  Registrar registrar;
  // Instantiation of three student objects
  Student student1 ("John");
  Student student2 ("Mary");
  Student student3 ("Ann");
  // Instantiation of three course objects
  Course course1 ("CIS101", 4);
  Course course2 ("CIS102", 3);
  Course course3 ("CIS103", 3);
  // Let the registrar object enroll students in the courses
  registrar.enroll (student1, course1);
  registrar.enroll (student1, course2);
  registrar.enroll (student2, course1);
  registrar.enroll (student2, course3);
  registrar.enroll (student3, course1);
  // Printing the information about each student
  student1.print();
  student2.print();
  student3.print();
  // Printing information about each course
  course1.print();
  course2.print();
  course3.print();
  return 0;
}
```

Run:

```
Student name: John
List of Courses
CIS101
CIS102
```

(continued)

Program 11.42 File application.cpp (Continued)

```
Student name: Mary
List of Courses
CIS101
CIS103

Student name: Ann
List of Courses
CIS101

Course Name: CIS101
Number of Units: 4
List of Students
John
Mary
Ann

Course Name: CIS102
Number of Units: 3
List of Students
John

Course Name: CIS103
Number of Units: 3
List of Students
Mary
```

Key Terms

aggregation
association
base class
composition
dependency
derived class
inheritance
inheritance tree
Liskov substitution principle
multiplicity
private inheritance
protected inheritance
protected member
public inheritance
subclass
superclass

Summary

Inheritance in object-oriented programming derives a more specific concept from a more general one. The more general class is called the base class and a more specific one is called the derived class. The derived class inherits all of the base class members except parameter constructors, the default constructor, copy constructor(s), the destructor, and the assignment operator. There are three inheritance types, public, protected, and private; the default is private but the most common is public.

An *association* between two classes shows the relationship between them. *Aggregation* is a special kind of association in which the relationship involves ownership, a "has-a" relationship. A *composition* is a special kind of aggregation in which the lifetime of the containee depends on the lifetime of the container.

Dependency is a weak relationship between classes. It models the "uses" relationship.

Problems

PR-1. Assume we have defined the following two classes. Write the definition of the *set* and *print* functions for both classes using delegation.

```
// Declaration of the class First
class First
{
    private:
        int a;
    public:
        void set (int a);
        void print () const;
};
// Declaration of the class Second
class Second : public First
{
    private:
        int b;
    public:
        void set (int a, int b);
        void print () const;
};
```

PR-2. Assume we have defined the following two classes. Write the definition of the *set* and *print* functions for both classes without using delegation.

```
// Declaration of the class First
class First
{
    protected:
        int a;
    public:
        void set (int a);
        void print () const;
};
// Declaration of the class Second
class Second : public First
{
    private:
        int b;
    public:
        void set (int a, int b);
        void print () const;
};
```

PR-3. Assume we have a class *First* defined as follows. If class *Second* is a public derivative from class *First*, what is the accessibility of members *one*, *two*, and *set* in class *Second*?

```
class First
{
    private:
        int one;
    protected:
        int two;
    public:
        void set (int one, int two);
}
```

PR-4. Repeat PR-3 but assume class *Second* is a protected derivative of class *First*.

PR-5. Repeat PR-4 but assume class *Second* is a private derivative of class *First*.

PR-6. We have the following three class definitions. Write the definition for the constructor and the print functions for all three classes.

```
// Definition of class First
class First
{
    private:
        int a;
    public:
        First (int a);
        void print ( ) const;
};
// Definition of class Second
class Second : public First
{
    private:
        int b;
    public:
        Second (int a, int b);
        void print ( ) const;
};
// Definition of class Third
class Third : public Second
{
    private:
        int c;
    public:
        Third (int a, int b, int c);
        void print () const;
};
```

PR-7. We have the following three class definitions. Write the definition for the constructor and the print functions for all three classes.

```
// Definition of class First
class First
```

```
{
    private:
        int a;
    public:
        First (int a);
        void print ( ) const;
};
// Definition of class Second
class Second : public First
{
    private:
        int b;
    public:
        Second (int a, int b);
        void print ( ) const;
};
// Definition of class Third
class Third : public First
{
    private:
        int c;
    public:
        Third (int a, int c);
        void print () const;
};
```

PR-8. We have the following two class definitions. Write the definition for the constructor and the print functions for both classes.

```
// Definition of class First
class First
{
    private:
        int a;
        double b;
    public:
        First (int a, double b);
        void print ( ) const;
};
// Definition of class Second
class Second
{
    private:
        First f;
        char c;
    public:
        Second (First f, char c);
        void print ( ) const;
};
```

PR-9. Draw a sequence diagram for the interaction of *main* with the Person and Student objects in Program 11.6.

PR-10. Draw a sequence diagram for the interaction of *main* with the Person and Date objects in Program 11.6. Note that we have two instances of the *Person* class and two instances of *Date* class.

PR-11. Draw a sequence diagram for the interaction of objects in Program 11.21.

Programs

PRG-1. Design a class name *Square* that defines a square geometric shape. The class must have a data member named *side* that defines the length of each side. Then define two member functions, *getPeri* and *getArea*, to find the perimeter and area of the square shape. Now define a *Cube* that defines a cubic shape and inherits from the *Square* class. The class *Cube* needs no new data members, but it needs the member functions *getArea* and *getVolume*. Provide the appropriate constructors and destructors for both classes.

PRG-2. Design a class named *Rectangle* with two private data members: *length* and *width.* Define constructors and a destructor for the class and write member functions to find the perimeter and area of a rectangle. Then define a class named *Cuboid* (representing a box) that inherits from the class *Rectangle* with an extra data member: *height.* Then write constructors and a destructor for the *Cuboid* class, and write member functions to find the surface and volume of the *Cuboid* objects.

PRG-3. Create a *Sphere* class that inherits from a *Circle* class. We know that we can create a sphere object by turning a circle around its diameter.

a. Design an interface for a class named *circle* with one private data member: *radius.* Define a parameter constructor and a destructor for the class and write member functions to find the perimeter and area of a circle using the following relationships.

```
perimeter = 2 * π * radius                    area = π * radius * radius
```

b. Define an interface file for a class named *Sphere*. Also define a parameter constructor and a destructor for the class and write member functions to find the surface and volume of a sphere.

c. Define an implementation file for the class *Sphere* using the following formulas to find the surface and the volume of a sphere; in the formulas, *perimeter* is the perimeter of the circle and *area* is the area of the circle defined in part (b).

```
surface = 2 * radius * perimeter              volume = (4 / 3) * radius * area
```

d. Write an application file to test the *Circle* and *Sphere* classes.

PRG-4. Create a *Cylinder* class that inherits from a *Circle* class. We know that we can create a cylinder object by adding a height to the circle object.

a. Design an interface for a class named *circle* as done in PRG-3.

b. Define an interface file for a class named *Cylinder.* Also define a parameter constructor and a destructor for the class, and write member functions to find the surface and volume of a sphere.

c. Define an implementation file for the class *Cylinder* using the following formulas to find the surface and the volume of a cylinder; in these formulas, *perimeter* is the perimeter of the circle and *area* is the area of the circle defined in part (b).

```
surface = height * perimeter                volume = height * area
```

d. Write an application file to test the *Circle* and *Cylinder* class.

PRG-5. Create a simple employee class that supports two classifications of employees, salaried and hourly. All employees have four data members: *name*, *employee number*, *birth date*, and *date hired*. Salaried employees have a monthly salary and an annual bonus, which is stated as a percentage in the range of 0 to 10 percent. Hourly employees have an hourly wage and an overtime rate which ranges from 50 to 100 percent.

PRG-6. Design a class named *Student* with two data members: *name* and *gpa*. Then define a class named *Course* whose data member capacity holds the number of students in the course and an array of students created in heap memory. The *Student* class must have a member function to print information about the student object. The *Course* class must have information about enrolling students in the course and must print information about all students enrolled.

PRG-7. Design a class named *Course* with two data members: *name* and *units*. Then design a class named *Student* with three data members: *name*, *gpa*, and a *list* of courses taken. The list must be implemented as an array in heap memory. Create constructors, destructor, and all necessary member functions for the operation of the *Course* and *Student* class. Test both classes in an application program.

PRG-8. Write a program that simulates the three classes defined as shown below:

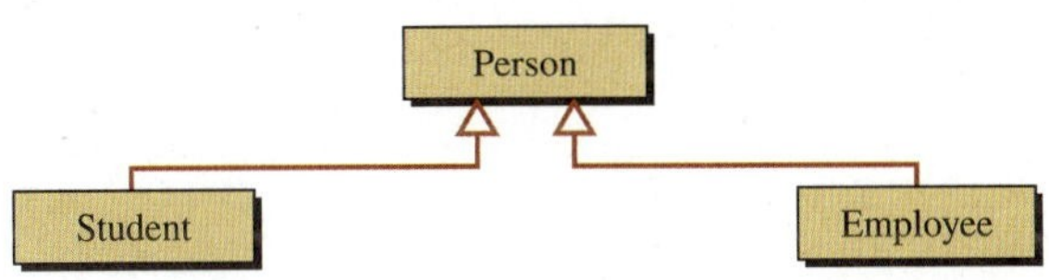

a. Use *name* as the only data member for the *Person* class.
b. Use *name* and *gpa* as data members for the *Student* class.
c. Use *name* and *salary* as data members for the *Employee* class.

PRG-9. Write a program that simulates the seven classes defined as shown below. The first three classes (*Person, Student,* and *Employee*) have been defined in PRG-8. Create codes to define the other four classes.

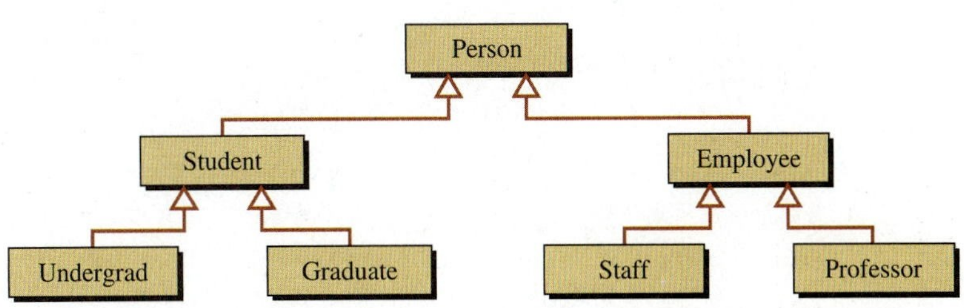

a. Use *year* (1, 2, 3, 4) for the *Undergraduate* class.
b. Use *goal* (master, phd) for the *Graduate* class.
c. Use *status* (manager, nonmanager) for the *Staff* class.
d. Use *status* (part-time, full-time) for the *Professor* class.

We recommend to use the *enum* construct to define any of the four statuses and thus to avoid value checking.

PRG-10. Define a class named *Point* that represents a point with coordinates *x* and *y*. Then write member functions that use the *Point* class to find the distances between two points. Use the dependency relationship as shown below:

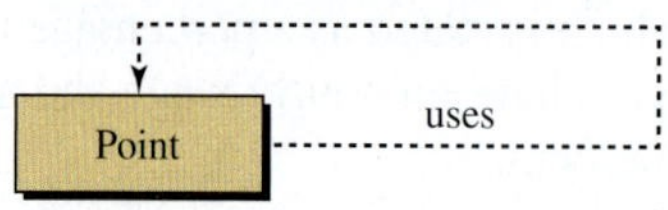

PRG-11. Redesign the *Fraction* class that we defined in Chapter 7 to make the *Fraction* class dependent on itself for four operations: *add*, *subtract*, *multiply*, and *divide*, as shown in the following figure:

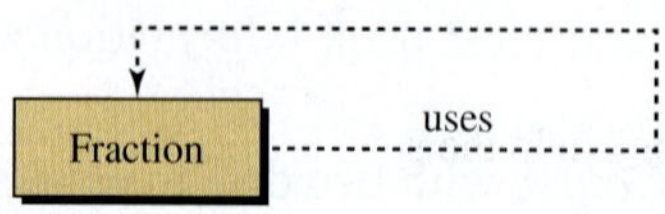

In this chapter we discuss polymorphism and other issues related to object-oriented programming. Polymorphism gives us the ability to write several versions of a function in different classes. We also discuss two other issues that are related to polymorphism: abstract classes and multiple inheritance.

Objectives

After you have read and studied this chapter, you should be able to:

- Define polymorphism and describe three necessary conditions to achieve it.
- Define virtual tables and how they help the system decide which virtual function to use during run time.
- Discuss virtual destructors and why they are needed for the proper use of polymorphism.
- Distinguish between static and dynamic binding in inheritance.
- Discuss Run Time Type Information (RTTI) and how it is used.
- Discuss abstract classes and their use.
- Discuss interface classes and their use.
- Discuss multiple inheritance and its associated problems.
- Show how the use of virtual base inheritance and class mixing can eliminate the problem of duplicated data members in multiple inheritance.

12.1 POLYMORPHISM

In previous chapters, we mentioned that one of the main pillars of object-oriented programming is **polymorphism.** Polymorphism gives us the ability to write several versions of a function, each in a separate class. Then, when we call the function, the version appropriate for the object being referenced is executed. We see the same concept in our everyday language. We use one verb (*function*) to mean different things. For example, we say "open," meaning to open a door, a jar, or a book; which one is determined by the context. Similarly, in C++, we can call a function named *printArea* to print the area of a triangle or the area of a rectangle.

To better understand the concept of polymorphism, we must first understand the concept of plug-compatible objects. An analogy with electrical devices may help, as shown in Figure 12.1.

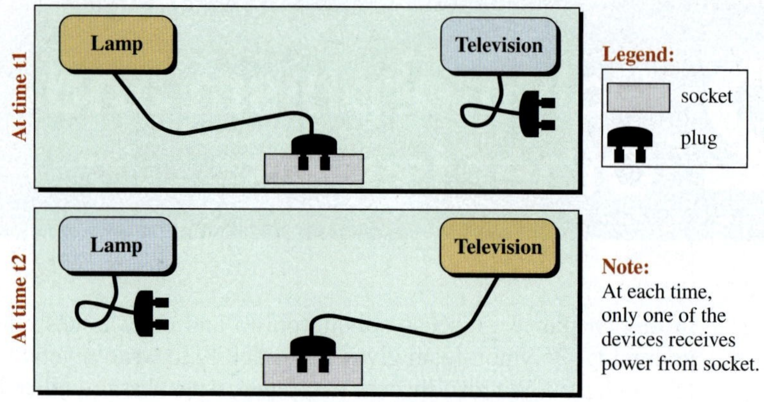

Figure 12.1 A socket and plug-compatible devices

Assume we have two electrical devices (such as a table lamp and a television set). We have only one socket that can supply power to one of these devices at a time. Each device has a plug that can be inserted in the only socket. At time t1, we plug the lamp into the socket. At time t2, we unplug the lamp and plug the TV set in the socket. We can do so because the two devices are plug-compatible; their plugs follow the same standard. The interesting point about plug-compatible devices is that all get the same thing (electrical power) from the socket, but each does a different task.

12.1.1 Condition for Polymorphism

We define the conditions for polymorphism in inheritance by comparing polymorphism with a plug.

Pointers or References

For comparison, we need something that plays the role of a socket that, once created, can accept plug-compatible objects. In C++, a pointer or a reference can play this role. We can define a pointer (or a reference) that can point to the base class; we can then let the pointer point to any object in the hierarchy. For this reason, the pointer and reference variables are sometimes referred to as polymorphic variables.

Exchangeable Objects

We need plug-compatible objects that play the role of the devices. An object in an inheritance hierarchy plays this role.

Virtual Functions

We need something to play the role of power given to different devices that perform different tasks. This is done in C++ using virtual functions, which are modified by the keyword **virtual**. For example, we can have a print function in all classes, all named the same but each printing differently.

For polymorphism, we need pointers (or references), we need exchangeable objects, and we need virtual functions.

EXAMPLE 12.1

Program 12.1 shows an incomplete polymorphic program using only the first two conditions. We define two classes. We then create a pointer (simulating a socket) that can accept an object of each class at different times (plug-compatible object). For simplicity, we define only one public member function for each class and let the system add default constructors.

Program 12.1 An incomplete polymorphic program

```
/***************************************************************
 * A simple program to show the first two conditions for      *
 * polymorphism                                                *
 ***************************************************************/
#include <iostream>
#include <string>
using namespace std;

// Definition of Base class and in-line print function
class Base
{
  public:
      void print () const {cout << "In the Base" << endl;}
};
// Definition of Derived class and in-line print function
class Derived : public Base
{
  public:
      void print () const {cout << "In the Derive" << endl;}
};

int main ( )
{
   // Creation of a pointer to the Base class (simulating socket)
   Base* ptr;
   // Let ptr point to an object of the Base class
   ptr = new Base ();
   ptr -> print();
   delete ptr;
   // Let ptr point to an object of the Derived class
   ptr = new Derived();
   ptr -> print();
   delete ptr;
   return 0;
}
```

```
Run:
In the Base
In the Base
```

At line 27, *ptr* is pointing to an object of the *Base* class, and at line 28, we call the function defined in the *Base* class. At line 31, we make the same pointer point to an object of the *Derived* class, and at line 32, we tried to call the function defined in the *Derived* class, but the result shows that the function defined for the *Base* class is called. The first two conditions of polymorphism are accomplished in the program, but the third condition (virtual functions) is not fulfilled. The print function is not a *virtual* function.

The result should be expected because the variable *ptr* is defined as a pointer to *Base*. It can accept being pointed to an object of the *Derived* type because a derived object is a *Base* object (inheritance defines an *is-a* relationship). However, when it wants to call the print function, it is still a pointer to *Base*, so it calls the *print* function defined in the *Base* class. We have not changed the type of the pointer; we have just forced it to point to the *Derived* class.

EXAMPLE 12.2

We repeat the previous example, but we make the print function *virtual*. The result is that the correct function is activated in each call as shown in Program 12.2. In lines 13 and 19, we added the modifier *virtual* to the *print* function. Line 28 calls the appropriate *print* function for the *Base* class, and line 32 calls the appropriate *print* function for the *Derived* class.

Program 12.2 A valid polymorphic program using all three conditions

```
1  /*****************************************************************
2   * A simple program to show that if all three necessary          *
3   * conditions are fulfilled, we have polymorphism.               *
4   *****************************************************************/
5  #include <iostream>
6  #include <string>
7  using namespace std;
8
9  // Definition of Base class and in-line definition for print function
10 class Base
11 {
12   public:
13       virtual void print () const {cout << "In the Base" << endl;}
14 };
15 // Definition of Derived class and in-line definition for print function
16 class Derived : public Base
17 {
18   public:
19       virtual void print () const {cout << "In the Derive" << endl;}
20 };
21
22 int main ( )
23 {
24   // Creation of a pointer to the Base class (simulating socket)
25   Base* ptr;
```

(continued)

Program 12.2 A valid polymorphic program using all three conditions (Continued)

```
    // Let ptr point to an object of the Base class
    ptr = new Base ();
    ptr -> print();
    delete ptr;
    // Let ptr point to an object of the Derived class
    ptr = new Derived();
    ptr -> print();
    delete ptr;
    return 0;
}
```

```
Run:
In the Base
In the Derived
```

Virtual Modifier Not Necessary

Although we have added the **virtual** modifier to both *print* functions, it is not needed. When a function is defined as virtual, all functions in the hierarchy of classes with the same signature are automatically virtual.

Mechanism

To understand how virtual functions take part in polymorphic behavior, we must understand virtual tables (*vtables*). In polymorphism, the system creates a virtual table for each class in the hierarchy of classes. Each entry in each *vtable* has a pointer to the corresponding virtual function. Each object created in an application will have an extra data member that is a pointer to the corresponding *vtable*. In the case of our simple program, there are two objects and two *vtables,* each with one entry as shown in Figure 12.2.

When *ptr* is pointing to the *Base* object, the *VPTR* pointer added to the *Base* class object is reached, which is pointing to the *vtable* of the *Base* class. In this case, the *vtable* has only one entry, which invokes the only virtual function in *Base* class. When *ptr* is pointing to the *Derived* object, the *vtable* of the *Derived* object is reached, and the print function defined in the *Derived* class is invoked.

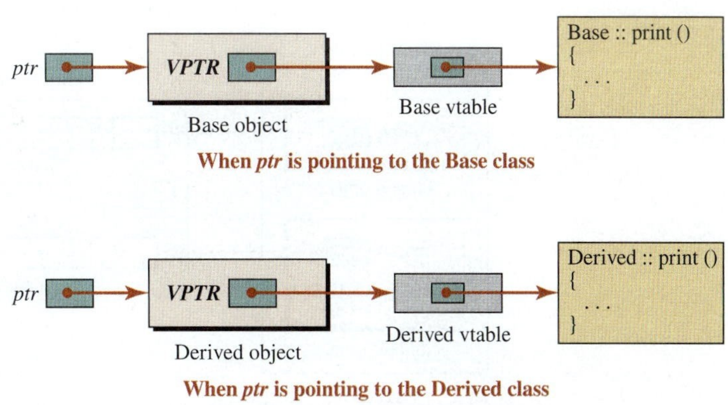

Figure 12.2 Virtual tables for Base and Derived classes

12.1.2 Constructors and Destructors

Constructors and destructors in a class hierarchy are also member functions, although special ones. Do they need to be declared virtual? We discuss the cases of constructors and destructors separately.

Constructors Cannot Be Virtual

Constructors cannot be virtual because although constructors are member functions, the names of the constructors are different for the base and derived classes (different signatures).

Virtual Destructors

Although the names of the destructors differ in the base and derived classes, the destructors are not normally called by their name. When there is a virtual member function anywhere in the design, we should also make the destructors virtual to avoid memory leaks. To understand the situation, we discuss two cases: (1) when we are not using polymorphism, and (2) when we are using polymorphism.

Case 1: No Polymorphism Assume that the base class has a data member of type string allocated in heap memory. Since the derived class inherits the string data member, the derived class also has a data member allocated in heap memory. Figure 12.3 shows the situation when we are not using polymorphism. We create a *Person* class and a *Student* class. The *Person* class has a *name* data member of type string in which the characters are created in the heap. The *Student* class inherits *name* from the *Person* class, but it also adds another data member, *gpa*.

We cannot have a memory leak in this situation. When the program terminates, the destructors for *Person* class and *Student* class are called, which automatically calls the destructors of the *string* class, which delete the allocated memory in the heap.

Case 2: Polymorphism Now assume we use polymorphism. The situation is different. The *Person* object and the *Student* object are created in the heap. The string objects are also created in the heap. We must apply the *delete* operator to the polymorphic variable, *ptr*, in stack memory to delete the objects in heap memory. When the objects are deleted, their destructors are called and the string objects are deleted. Figure 12.4 shows the situation.

Is it guaranteed that both objects are deleted when we apply the *delete* operator on the *ptr* pointer? To answer the question, let us look at the *delete* operator when applied to the pointer in two different situations.

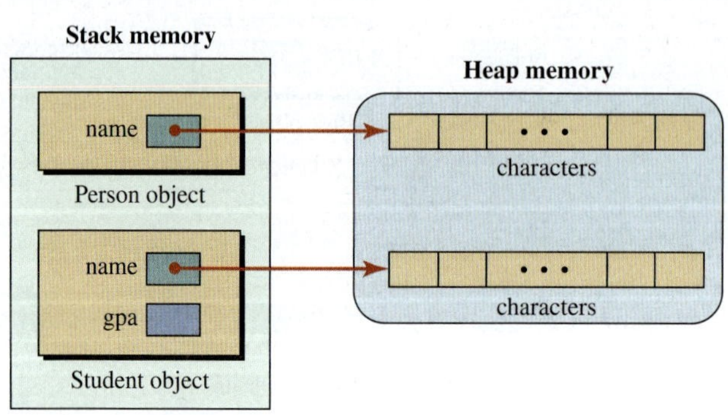

Figure 12.3 Two objects in a program when polymorphism is not used

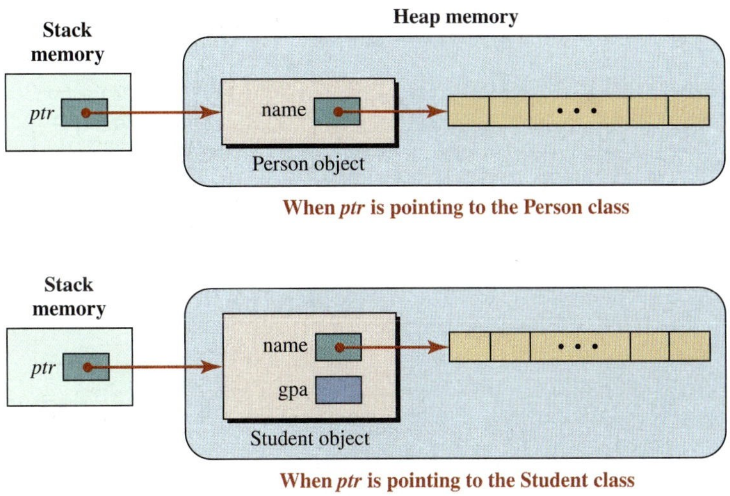

Figure 12.4 Two objects in a program when polymorphism is used

```
ptr = new Person (...);
...
delete ptr;          // It deletes Person because ptr is of type Person*.
```

```
ptr = new Student (...);
...
delete ptr;          // It does not delete Student  because ptr is of type Person*.
```

In the first case, the pointer *ptr* is a pointer to *Person* type and the *delete* operator can delete the *Person* object. When the *Person* object is deleted, its destructor is called, which in turn calls the destructor of the string class. The characters created in the heap are de-allocated. There is no memory leak.

In the second case, the pointer *ptr* is still a pointer to *Person* type, which means it can delete an object of a *Person* class (which does not exist and nothing happens), but it cannot delete the object of the *Student* class. When the object of the *Student* class is not deleted, its destructor is not called, which means that the destructor of the string class is not called, which means the characters in the heap are not de-allocated. We have memory leak. Note that the memory occupied by the *Student* object will be eventually deallocated when the program goes out of scope, but the pointer pointing to characters becomes a dangling pointer and the system can never delete the memory location created by the characters in the string.

The solution is to make the destructor of the base class virtual, which automatically makes the destructor of the derived class virtual. In this case, the system allows two different member functions with different names to be virtual, and they are both added to the virtual table. Figure 12.5 shows that we have two entries in the virtual table, and when an object in the heap is deleted, the program knows which destructor should be called.

C++ recommends that we always define an explicit destructor for the base class in polymorphism and make it virtual. Use of virtual destructors prevents possible memory leaks in polymorphism.

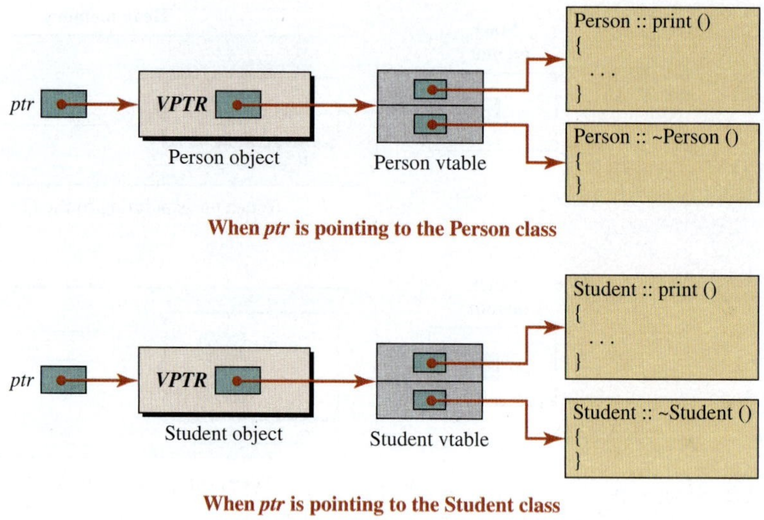

Figure 12.5 Virtual tables when using virtual destructors

Example 12.3

We show how we can use polymorphism to print the information in the *Student* class through a pointer pointing to the *Person* class.

Person Class Program 12.3 shows the interface file for the *Person* class .

Program 12.3 File person.h

```
/***************************************************************
 * The interface file for the Person class                     *
 ***************************************************************/
#ifndef PERSON_H
#define PERSON_H
#include <iostream>
#include <string>
using namespace std;

class Person
{
  private:
      string name;
  public:
      Person (string name);
      virtual ~Person ();
      virtual void print () const;
};
#endif
```

Program 12.4 File person.cpp

```
/*****************************************************************
 * The implementation file for the Person class                  *
 *****************************************************************/
#include "Person.h"

// Definition of the Person constructor
Person :: Person (string nm)
: name (nm)
{
}
// Definition of the Person destructor (virtual)
Person :: ~Person ()
{
}
// Definition of the print function (virtual)
void Person :: print () const
{
   cout << "Name: " << name << endl;
}
```

Program 12.4 shows the implementation file for the *Person* class.

Student Class Program 12.5 shows the interface file for the *Student* class. Program 12.6 shows the implementation file for the *Student* class.

Program 12.5 File student.h

```
/*****************************************************************
 * The interface file for the Student class                      *
 *****************************************************************/
#ifndef STUDENT_H
#define STUDENT_H
#include "person.h"

class Student: public Person
{
   private:
         double gpa;
   public:
         Student (string name, double gpa);
         virtual void print () const;
};
#endif
```

Program 12.6 File student.cpp

```
/***************************************************************
 * The implementation file for the Student class              *
 ***************************************************************/
#include "Student.h"

// Definition of Constructor for Student class
Student :: Student (string nm, double gp)
: Person (nm), gpa (gp)
{
}
// Definition of virtual print function for Student class
void Student :: print () const
{
   Person :: print ();
   cout << "GPA: " << gpa << endl;
}
```

Application Program 12.7 shows the application file.

Program 12.7 File app.cpp

```
/***************************************************************
 * The application file to test Person and Student classes    *
 ***************************************************************/
#include "Student.h"

int main ( )
{
   // Creation of ptr as polymorphic variable
   Person* ptr;
   // Instantiation Person object in the heap
   ptr = new Person ("Lucie");
   cout << "Person Information";
   ptr -> print();
   cout << endl;
   delete ptr;
   // Instantiation Student object in the heap
   ptr = new Student ("John", 3.9);
   cout << "Student Information";
   ptr -> print();
   cout << endl;
   delete ptr;
   return 0;
}
```

(continued)

Program 12.7 File app.cpp (Continued)

```
Run:
Person Information
Name: Lucie
Student Information
Name: John
GPA: 3.9
```

A Better Use of Polymorphism

As you may have noticed, we did not need polymorphism in Program 12.3. We can achieve the same result without using a pointer to point to different objects. We can use *person.print( )* instead of *ptr –> print()* and we can use *student.print( )* instead of *ptr –> print()*. However, the program shows the idea of polymorphism with only one pointer that can point to different objects.

A better demonstration is when we have to use polymorphism. Assume we need to have an array of objects. We know that all elements of an array must be of the same type; this means we cannot use an array of objects if the objects are of different types. However, we can use an array of pointers, in which each pointer can point to an object of the base class (*Person* in the previous example). In other words, we can have an array of *polymorphic variables* instead of one. Program 12.8 is the same as Program 12.7 except that we have used an array of pointers.

Program 12.8 Using an array of pointers in polymorphism

```
/****************************************************************
 * Modification of application file to show the actual use of  *
 * polymorphism with an array of pointers.                      *
 ****************************************************************/
#include "student.h"

int main ( )
{
  // Declaration of an array of polymorphic variables (pointers)
  Person* ptr [4];
  // Instantiation of four objects in the heap memory
  ptr[0] = new Student ("Joe", 3.7);
  ptr[1] = new Student ("John", 3.9);
  ptr[2] = new Person ("Bruce");
  ptr[3] = new Person ("Sue");
  // Calling the virtual print function for each object
  for (int i = 0; i < 4; i++)
  {
      ptr[i] -> print ();
      cout << endl;
  }
```

(continued)

Program 12.8 Using an array of pointers in polymorphism (Continued)

```
    // Deleting the objects in the heap
    for (int i = 0; i < 4; i++)
    {
        delete ptr [i];
    }
    return 0;
}
```

```
Run:
Name: Joe
GPA: 3.70

Name: John
GPA: 3.90

Name: Bruce

Name: Sue
```

Figure 12.6 shows the virtual tables for Program 12.8 with four objects, two of each type.

In Figure 12.6 we have only one virtual table for each class, but both objects of type *Person* have a VPTR pointer that points to the *Person vtable*, and both objects of the *Student* class have a pointer that points to the *Student vtable*.

Polymorphism in Other Languages

If you know other object-oriented languages, you might wonder why you cannot find all of aforementioned conditions in other languages even though polymorphism is often mentioned in discussions of those languages. These three conditions always exist in

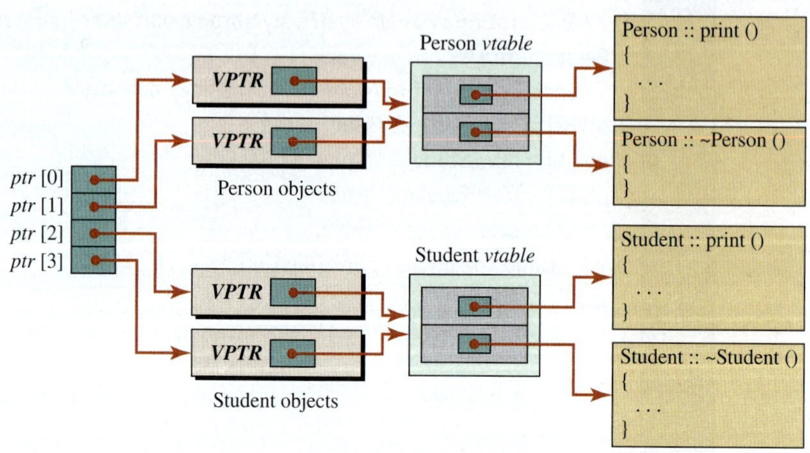

Figure 12.6 Virtual tables for objects in Program 12.8

other languages, but they may be hidden. For example, in the Java language, which was designed after C++, polymorphism occurs with all of the three conditions as follows:

1. Java supports public inheritance (in fact, Java has only one type of inheritance, public), which means we have interchangeable objects through inheritance.
2. Although there are no pointers or references in Java at the user level, class objects are always created in the heap and there are variables (called reference types) that point to these objects; each class object is accessible through polymorphic variables (sockets).
3. All member functions in Java are virtual functions by default, which means that the third condition, existence of polymorphic functions, is also fulfilled.

12.1.3 Binding

Binding is an issue related to polymorphism. While there is no extra code required to assure that binding is correct, we should understand what happens. As mentioned in previous chapters, a function is split into two entities: function call and function definition. Binding here means the association between the function call—for example, *print*()—and the function body—for example, *void print* {…}.

We know that the function definition is created somewhere and the function call occurs somewhere else. If we have only one single definition for a function, there is no confusion. Whenever we call a function, the corresponding definition is executed.

However, we have seen in inheritance that we may have two functions with the same signature (overriding functions). This means that the function has only one form of call but may have more than one definition. If a *Person* object calls the *print* function, one definition is executed; if a *Student* object calls the *print* function, a different definition is executed. Binding here means how the program binds (associates) a function call to a function definition. There are two cases: *static binding* and *dynamic binding*.

Static Binding

The term **static binding** (sometimes called *compile-time binding* or *early binding*) occurs when we have more than one definition for a function, but the compiler knows which version of the definition is to be used when the program is compiled. We know that each definition of the function is stored somewhere in memory, and the compiler knows where it is when it encounters the function call. This may happen, for example, when the function is called by its corresponding object, as shown below.

```
person.print ();
student.print ();
```

When the compiler encounters the first call, it knows that the call should be for the definition of *print* function that prints the data member of the *Person* object (only *name*). When the compiler encounters the second call, it knows that the call should be to the definition of the print function that prints the data members of the *Student* object (*name* and *gpa*).

There is no ambiguity and there is no need for polymorphism. Everything is defined earlier; binding is established during compilation time and the compiler establishes the association.

Dynamic Binding

Static binding is simple, but it is not always possible. We use polymorphism for **dynamic binding** (also called *late binding* or *run-time binding*), which means that we must bind a call to the corresponding definition during run time. This is needed when the object is not known

Table 12.1 Operation on type_info objects

t1 == t2	// Return true if t1 and t2 are of the same type
t1 != t2	// Return true if t1 and t2 are of different types
t1.name ( )	// Returns a C-type string (name of the t1)
t1.before (t2)	// Returns true if t1 comes before t2 (in inheritance)

during the compilation. For example, when, during program execution, different objects are being inserted into a polymorphic variable and the program needs to call the appropriate function, then the binding must be done during run time. For this reason, we need a virtual function to force the run-time system to create a table that shows which object needs which function and to bind the call to the appropriate function. Polymorphism is closely tied to dynamic binding because we want to be able to execute the appropriate function definition.

12.1.4 Run-Time Type Information (RTTI)

When working with hierarchy of classes, sometimes we need to know the type of the object we are dealing with or sometimes we want to change the type of the object.

Using typeid Operator

If we want to find the type of the object at run time, we can use the <typeinfo> header to access an object of the class *type_info* (note that the class name has an underscore, but the header name does not). The class *type_info* has no constructor, destructor, or copy constructor. The only way to create an object of *type_info* is by using an overloaded operator named *typeid.* We can create an object of *type_info* by passing an expression to the operator *typeid* that can be evaluated as a type; for example, *typeid* (5), *typeid* (object_name), *typeid* (6 + 2), and so on. We can then use one of the four member functions or operators that are defined in the *type_info* class as shown in Table 12.1, in which *t1* and *t2* are objects of *type_info* class.

Program 12.9 shows how we can find the type of two objects.

Program 12.9 Testing typeid operator

```
/***************************************************************
 * A program to use typeid operator to find the name of classes    *
 ***************************************************************/
#include <iostream>
#include <string>
#include <typeinfo>
using namespace std;

class Animal {};
class Horse {};

int main ( )
{
```

(continued)

Program 12.9 Testing typeid operator (Continued)

```
    Animal a;
    Horse h;
    cout << typeid(a).name() << endl;
    cout << typeid(h).name();
    return 0;
}
```

Run:

```
6Animal
5Horse
```

Note that the name of the class is preceded by the number of characters in each case (6 and 5).

Using a Dynamic-Cast Operator

We have seen that in a polymorphic relationship we can *upcast* a pointer, which means that we make a pointer in the derived class so that it points to the base class as shown below:

```
Person* ptr1 = new Student
```

Here, the pointer returned from the **new** operator is a pointer to a *Student* object, but we assign it to a pointer that points to a *Person* object (the pointer is upcast).

C++ also allows us to downcast a pointer to make it point to an object in the lower order of hierarchy. This can be done using a **dynamic_cast** operator as shown below:

```
Student* ptr2 = dynamic_cast <Student*) (ptr1)
```

This casting proves that the *Student* class is a class derived from the *Person* class because *ptr1* can be downcast to *ptr2*. Some programmers consider this to be a form of type checking. However, we do not recommend that programmers use the *dynamic_cast* operator for type checking because it involves a lot of overhead.

12.2 OTHER ISSUES

In this section we discuss abstract classes and multiple inheritance. We include a project that uses several levels of inherited classes.

12.2.1 Abstract Classes

The classes we have designed so far are called concrete classes. A **concrete class** can be instantiated and create objects of its type. When we create a set of classes, sometimes we find that there is a list of behaviors that are identical to all classes. For example, assume we define two classes named *Rectangle* and *Square*. Both of these classes have at least two common behaviors: *getArea*() and *getPerimeter*(). How can we force the creator of these two classes (in particular when each class is created by a different entity) to provide the definition of both member functions for each class? We know that the formulas to find the area and perimeter of these geometrical shapes differ, which means that each class must create its own version of *getArea* and *getPerimeter*.

The solution in object-oriented programming is to create an **abstract class,** which forces the designers of all derived classes to add these two definitions to their classes. A set of classes with one abstract class must have the declaration and definition for the *pure virtual functions*.

An *abstract class* is a class with at least one *pure virtual function*.

Declaration of Pure Virtual Functions

An **abstract class** is a class with at least one *pure virtual function*. A **pure virtual function** is a virtual function in which the declaration is set to zero and there is no definition in the abstract class. The following shows two *virtual member functions* for the *Shape* class:

```
virtual double getArea (0) = 0;
virtual double getPerimeter (0) = 0;
```

Definition of Pure Virtual Functions

The abstract class does not define its pure virtual function, but every class that inherits from the abstract class must provide the definition of each pure virtual function or declare it as a pure virtual to be defined in the next lower level of the hierarchy.

No Instantiation

We cannot instantiate an object from an abstract class because it does not have the definition of its pure virtual functions. For an object to be instantiated from a class, the class must have the definitions of all member functions. This means that an abstract class must be polymorphically inherited if we are to define concrete classes for instantiation.

An abstract class cannot be instantiated because there is no definition for the pure virtual member functions.

Interfaces

An abstract class can have both virtual and pure virtual functions. In some cases, however, we may need to create a blueprint for inherited classes. We can define a class with all pure virtual functions. This class is sometimes referred to as an *interface*; we cannot create any implementation file from this class, only the interface file.

An interface is a special case of an abstract class in which all member functions are pure virtual functions.

Shape Class

To show the use of an abstract class, we create five concrete classes to represent shapes. All classes are inherited from an abstract class *Shape,* as shown in Figure 12.7.

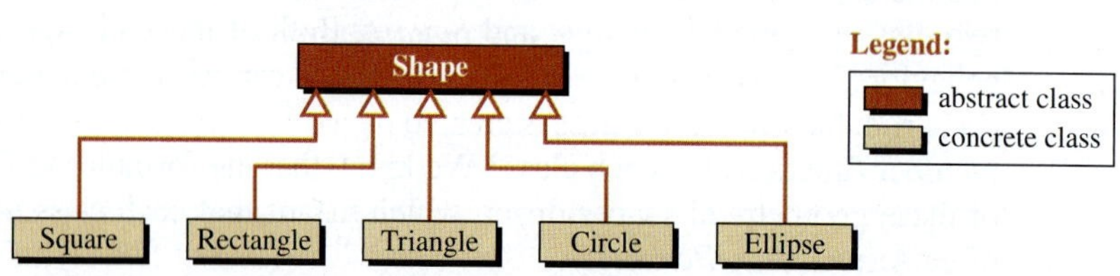

Figure 12.7 Adding an abstract class to a set of classes

Program 12.10 File shape.h

```
/*****************************************************************
 * The interface for the abstract Shape class                   *
 *****************************************************************/
#ifndef SHAPE_H
#define SHAPE_H
#include <iostream>
#include <cassert>
#include <cmath>
using namespace std;

// Class definition
class Shape
{
  protected:
       virtual bool isValid () const = 0;
  public:
       virtual void print () const = 0 ;
       virtual double getArea () const = 0 ;
       virtual double getPerimeter () const = 0;
};
#endif
```

Program 12.10 is the interface file for the *Shape* class.

Note that we have no data members and only pure virtual member functions in this program. The reason is that we do not want objects instantiated from this class; its purpose is only to force the derived classes to implement the pure virtual member functions. The first pure member function forces all classes to implement an *isValid*() member function and thus validate their data members during the construction of objects. The other two pure member functions force each derived class to have at least two member functions to calculate the area and perimeter of the corresponding shape.

Program 12.11 is the interface file for the *Square* class. It has only one data member, one private member function to validate the only data member, and three public member functions.

Program 12.11 File square.h

```
/*****************************************************************
 * The interface file of the Square class                       *
 *****************************************************************/
#ifndef SQUARE_H
#define SQUARE_H
#include "shape.h"

```

(continued)

Program 12.11 File square.h (Continued)

```
// Class Definition
class Square : public Shape
{
  private:
        double side;
        bool isValid() const;
  public:
        Square (double side);
        ~Square ();
        void print() const;
        double getArea () const;
        double getPerimeter () const;
};
#endif
```

Program 12.12 is the implementation file for the *Square* class.

Program 12.12 File square.cpp

```
/*****************************************************************
  * The implementation file of the Square class                  *
  *****************************************************************/
#include "square.h"

// Constructor
Square :: Square (double s)
:side (s)
{
   if (!isValid ())
   {
        cout << "Invalid square!";
        assert (false);
   }
}
// Destructor
Square :: ~Square ()
{
}
// Definition of print function
void Square :: print () const
{
   cout << "Square of side " << side << endl;
}
```

(continued)

Program 12.12 File square.cpp (Continued)

```
// Finding the area
double Square :: getArea () const
{
  return (side * side);
}
// Finding the perimeter
double Square :: getPerimeter () const
{
  return (4 * side);
}
// Private isValid function
bool Square :: isValid () const
{
  return (side > 0.0);
}
```

Program 12.13 is the interface file for the *Rectangle* class. It has two data members, one private member function, and three public member functions.

Program 12.13 File rectangle.h

```
/*****************************************************************
  * The interface file for the Rectangle class                    *
  *****************************************************************/
#ifndef RECTANGLE_H
#define RECTANGLE_H
#include "shape.h"

// Class definition
class Rectangle : public Shape
{
  private:
       double length;
       double width;
       bool isValid() const;
  public:
       Rectangle (double length, double width);
       ~Rectangle ();
       void print () const;
       double getArea() const;
       double getPerimeter() const;
};
#endif
```

Program 12.14 File rectangle.cpp

```
/***************************************************************
 * The implementation file the Rectangle class                 *
 ***************************************************************/
#include "rectangle.h"

// Constructor
Rectangle :: Rectangle (double lg, double wd)
: length (lg), width (wd)
{
   if (!isValid())
   {
        cout << "Invalid rectangle!";
        assert (false);
   }
}
// Destructor
Rectangle :: ~Rectangle ()
{
}
// Definition of print function
void Rectangle :: print () const
{
   cout << "Rectangle of " << length << " X " << width << endl;
}
// Finding the area
double Rectangle :: getArea() const
{
   return length * width;
}
// Finding the perimeter
double Rectangle :: getPerimeter() const
{
   return 2 * (length + width);
}
// Private isValid function
bool Rectangle :: isValid () const
{
   return (length > 0.0 && width > 0.0);
}
```

Program 12.14 is the implementation file for the *Rectangle* class.

Program 12.15 is the interface file for the *Triangle* class. It has three private data members, one private member function, and three public member functions.

Program 12.15 File triangle.h

```
/*****************************************************************
 * The interface file for the Triangle class                     *
 *****************************************************************/
#ifndef TRIANGLE_H
#define TRIANGLE_H
#include "shape.h"

// Class definition
class Triangle : public Shape
{
  private:
      double side1;
      double side2;
      double side3;
      bool isValid () const;
  public:
      Triangle (double side1, double side2, double side3);
      ~Triangle ();
      void print() const;
      double getArea() const;
      double getPerimeter() const;
};
#endif
```

Program 12.16 is the implementation file for the *Triangle* class.

Program 12.16 File triangle.cpp

```
/*****************************************************************
 * The implementation file the Triangle class                    *
 *****************************************************************/
#include "triangle.h"

// Constructor
Triangle :: Triangle (double s1, double s2, double s3)
: side1(s1), side2(s2), side3 (s3)
{
  if (!isValid())
  {
      cout << "Invalid triangle!";
      assert (false);
  }
}
```

(continued)

Program 12.16 File triangle.cpp (Continued)

```
// Destructor
Triangle :: ~Triangle ()
{
}
// Definition of print function
void Triangle :: print() const
{
   cout << "Triangle of : " << side1 << " X " << side2 << " X ";
   cout << side3 << endl;
}
// Finding the area
double Triangle :: getArea() const
{
   double s = (side1 + side2 + side3) / 2;
   return (sqrt (s * (s – side1) * (s – side2) * (s – side3)));
}
// Finding the perimeter
double Triangle :: getPerimeter() const
{
   return (side1 +  side2 + side3);
}
// Private isValid function
bool Triangle :: isValid () const
{
   bool fact1 = (side1 + side2) >  side3;
   bool fact2 = (side1 + side3) >  side2;
   bool fact3 = (side2 + side3) >  side1;
   return (fact1 && fact2 && fact3);
}
```

Program 12.17 is the interface file for the *Circle* class. It has only one private data member (the radius).

Program 12.17 File circle.h

```
/*******************************************************************
 * The interface file for the Circle class                         *
 *******************************************************************/
#ifndef CIRCLE_H
#define CIRCLE_H
#include "shape.h"

```

(continued)

Program 12.17 File circle.h (Continued)

```
// Class definition
class Circle : public Shape
{
  private:
      double radius;
      bool isValid () const;
  public:
      Circle (double radius);
      ~Circle ();
      void print() const;
      double getArea() const;
      double getPerimeter() const;
};
#endif
```

Program 12.18 is the implementation file for the *Circle* class. Program 12.19 is the interface file for the *Ellipse* class. It is similar to the one for the Circle class, but it needs two radii.

Program 12.18 File circle.cpp

```
/****************************************************************
 * The implementation file the Circle class                     *
 ****************************************************************/
#include "circle.h"

// Constructor
Circle :: Circle (double r)
: radius (r)
{
  if (!isValid())
  {
      cout << "Invalid circle!";
      assert (false);
  }
}
// Destructor
Circle :: ~Circle ()
{
}
// Definition of print function
void Circle :: print() const
{
```

(continued)

Program 12.18 File circle.cpp (Continued)

```
    cout << "Circle of radius : " << radius << endl;
}
// Finding the area
double Circle :: getArea() const
{
    return (3.14 * radius * radius);
}
// Finding the perimeter
double Circle :: getPerimeter() const
{
    return 2 * 3.14 * radius;
}
// Private isValid function
bool Circle :: isValid () const
{
    return (radius > 0);
}
```

Program 12.19 File ellipse.h

```
/*****************************************************************
 * The interface file for the Ellipse class                      *
 *****************************************************************/
#ifndef ELLIPSE_H
#define ELLIPSE_H
#include "shape.h"

// Class definition
class Ellipse : public Shape
{
  private:
        double radius1;
        double radius2;
        bool isValid () const;
  public:
        Ellipse (double radius1, double radius2);
        ~Ellipse ();
        void print() const;
        double getArea () const;
        double getPerimeter () const;
};
#endif
```

Program 12.20 is the implementation file for the *Ellipse* class.

Program 12.20 File ellipse.cpp

```
/*****************************************************************
 * The interface file for the Ellipse class                      *
 *****************************************************************/
#include "ellipse.h"

// Constructor
Ellipse :: Ellipse (double r1, double r2)
: radius1 (r1), radius2 (r2)
{
  if (!isValid())
  {
       cout << "Invalid ellipse!";
       assert (false);
  }
}
// Destructor
Ellipse :: ~Ellipse ()
{
}
// Definition of print function
void Ellipse :: print() const
{
  cout << "Ellipse of radii: " << radius1 << " X " <<;
  cout << radius2 << endl;
}
// Finding the area
double Ellipse :: getArea () const
{
  return (3.14 * radius1 * radius2);
}
// Finding the perimeter
double Ellipse ::getPerimeter () const
{
  double temp = (radius1 * radius1 + radius2 * radius2) / 2;
  return (2 * 3.14 * temp);
}
// Private isValid function
bool Ellipse :: isValid () const
{
  return (radius1 > 0 && radius2 > 0);
}
```

Program 12.21 is the application for testing one instance of each class.

Program 12.21 File app.cpp

```
/*****************************************************************
 * The application file to test all classes                      *
 *****************************************************************/
#include "square.h"
#include "rectangle.h"
#include "triangle.h"
#include "circle.h"
#include "ellipse.h"

int main ( )
{
  // Instantiation and testing the Square class
  cout << "Information about a square" << endl;
  Square square (5);
  square.print ();
  cout << "area: " << square.getArea () << endl;
  cout << "Perimeter: " << square.getPerimeter () << endl;
  cout << endl;
  // Instantiation and testing the Rectangle class
  cout << "Information about a rectangle" << endl;
  Rectangle rectangle (5, 4);
  rectangle.print ();
  cout << "area: " << rectangle.getArea () << endl;
  cout << "Perimeter: " << rectangle.getPerimeter () << endl;
  cout << endl;
  // Instantiation and testing the Triangle class
  cout << "Information about a triangle" << endl;
  Triangle triangle (3, 4, 5);
  triangle.print ();
  cout << "area: " << triangle.getArea () << endl;
  cout << "Perimeter: " << triangle.getPerimeter () << endl;
  cout << endl;
  // Instantiation and testing the Circle class
  cout << "Information about a circle" << endl;
  Circle circle (5);
  circle.print ();
  cout << "area: " << circle.getArea () << endl;
  cout << "Perimeter: " << circle.getPerimeter () << endl;
  cout << endl;
  // Instantiation and testing the Ellipse class
  cout << "Information about an ellipse" << endl;
  Ellipse ellipse (5, 4);
```

(continued)

Program 12.21 File app.cpp (Continued)

```
    ellipse.print ();
    cout << "area: " << ellipse.getArea () << endl;;
    cout << "Perimeter: " << ellipse.getPerimeter ()<< endl;
    return 0;
}
```

Run:

```
Information about a square
Square of size 5
area: 25
Perimeter: 20

Information about a rectangle
Rectangle of 5 X 4
area: 20
Perimeter: 18

Information about a triangle
Triangle of : 3 X 4 X 5
area: 6
Perimeter: 12

Information about a circle
Circle of radius : 5
area: 78.5
Perimeter: 31.4

Information about an ellipse
Ellipse of radii: 5 X 4
area: 62.8
Perimeter 28.4339
```

12.2.2 Multiple Inheritance

C++ allows **multiple inheritance,** the derivation of a class from more than one class. As a simple example, we can have a class named TA (teaching assistant) that is inherited from two classes: Student and Professor (Figure 12.8). The figure shows the UML diagram and the object of each class.

Unfortunately, the inheritance fails when we code these classes because the TA class inherits the data member *name* from both the *Student* and *Professor* classes. In the object of the *TA* class, we have two copies of this data member, which is not acceptable in C++.

The *Person* class defines one single data member, *name*. This data member is inherited in both the *Student* object and the *Professor* object. Since the *TA* (teaching assistant) class inherits the *Student* and *Professor* classes, the data member name is duplicated in the *TA* class. We cannot use inheritance in this case without removing the duplicate data member.

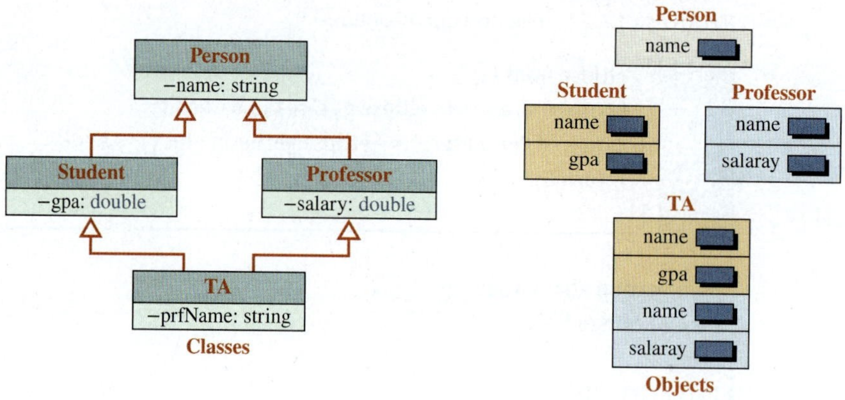

Figure 12.8 Classes and objects in multiple inheritance

Virtual Base

One solution for the problem of duplicated shared data members in multiple inheritance is to use **virtual base inheritance.** In this type of inheritance, two classes can inherit from a common base using the *virtual* keyword. Figure 12.9 shows this approach.

In this case, we have the following four classes.

```
class Person {...};
class Student: virtual public Person {...};
class Professor: virtual public Person {...};
class TA: public Student, public Professor {...};
```

When we use virtual base inheritance, the object of the virtual base class is not stored in each object of the derived class. The object of the virtual base class is stored separately, and each derived class has a pointer to this object.

When using the virtual base technique, we must avoid *delegation*, as discussed in Chapter 11. In other words, we cannot define a *print* function in the TA class by calling the corresponding *print* functions in the *Student* and *Professor* classes because the data member *name* would be printed three times. There is more than one solution to this dilemma; the one that we recommend is to make the common data members protected and thus seen in all derived classes and to avoid using delegated member functions.

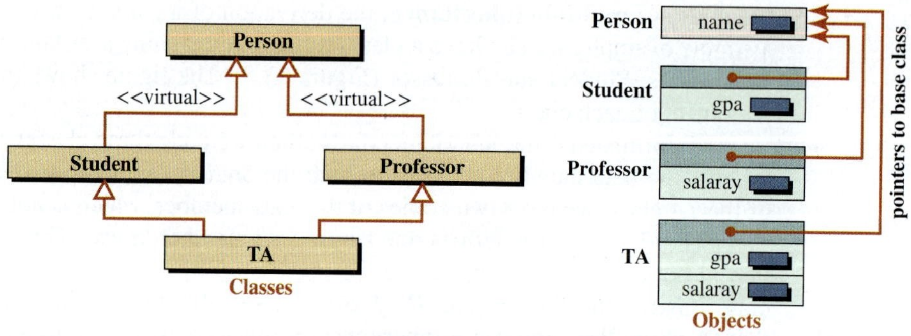

Figure 12.9 Classes and objects in virtual base inheritance

EXAMPLE 12.4

In this example we give the interface files, the implementation files, and the application file for the class in Figure 12.9.

Program 12.22 shows the interface file for the *Person* class. Note that the data member *name* has a protected accessibility.

Program 12.23 shows the implementation file for the *Person* class.

Program 12.22 File person.h

```
/***************************************************************
 * The interface file for the Person class                    *
 ***************************************************************/
#ifndef PERSON_H
#define PERSON_H
#include <iostream>
#include <cassert>
using namespace std;

class Person
{
  protected:
      string name; // Protected data member
  public:
      Person (string name);
      ~Person ();
      void print ();
};
#endif
```

Program 12.23 File person.cpp

```
/***************************************************************
 * The implementation file for the Person class               *
 ***************************************************************/
#include "person.h"

// Constructor
Person :: Person (string nm)
: name (nm)
{
}
// Destructor
Person :: ~Person ()
{
}
```

(continued)

Program 12.23 File person.cpp (Continued)

```
// Print member function
void Person :: print ()
{
   cout << "Person" << endl;
   cout << "Name: " << name << endl << endl;
}
```

Program 12.24 shows the interface file for the *Student* class that is virtually inherited from the Person class. Note that the data member *gpa* has a protected accessibility.

Program 12.25 shows the implementation of the *Student* class. Note that the print function does not call the *print* function of the *Person* class (no delegation).

Program 12.24 File student.h

```
/***************************************************************
 * The interface file for the Student class                    *
 ***************************************************************/
#ifndef STUDENT_H
#define STUDENT_H
#include "person.h"

class Student: virtual public Person   // Virtual inheritance
{
  protected:
      double gpa; // Protected data member
  public:
      Student (string name, double gpa);
      ~Student ();
      void print ();
};
#endif
```

Program 12.25 File student.cpp

```
/***************************************************************
 * The implementation file for the Student class               *
 ***************************************************************/
#include "Student.h"

// Constructor
Student :: Student (string name, double gp)
: Person (name), gpa (gp)
{
```

(continued)

Program 12.25 File student.cpp (Continued)

```
	assert (gpa <= 4.0);
}
// Destructor
Student :: ~Student()
{
}
// Print member function uses a protected data member (name)
void Student :: print ()
{
	cout << "Student " << endl;
	cout << "Name: " << name << " ";
	cout << "GPA: " << gpa << endl << endl;
}
```

Program 12.26 shows the interface file for the *Professor* class. Note that the data member *salary* has a protected accessibility.

Program 12.27 shows the implementation for the *Professor* class. Note that the *print* function does not call the *print* function of the *Person* class (no delegation).

Program 12.26 File professor.h

```
/***************************************************************
 * The interface file for the Professor class                  *
 ***************************************************************/
#ifndef PROFESSOR_H
#define PROFESSOR_H
#include "person.h"

class Professor: virtual public Person    // Virtual inheritance
{
	protected:
		double salary; // Protected data member
	public:
		Professor (string name, double salary);
		~Professor ();
		void print ();
};
#endif
```

Program 12.27 File professor.cpp

```
/***************************************************************
 * The implementation file for the Professor class             *
 ***************************************************************/
#include "professor.h"
```

(continued)

Program 12.27 File professor.cpp (Continued)

```

// Constructor
Professor :: Professor (string nm, double sal)
: Person (nm), salary (sal)
{
}
// Destructor
Professor :: ~Professor ()
{
}
// Print member function
void Professor :: print ()
{
   cout << "Professor " << endl;
   cout << "Name: " << name << " ";
   cout << "Salary: " << salary << endl << endl;
}
```

Program 12.28 shows the interface file for the *Teaching Assistance* class. Note that this class has no data member.

Program 12.29 shows the implementation file for the TA class. Note that the *print* function does not call the *print* function of the Student class (no delegation) or the *print* function of the *Professor* class (no delegation).

Program 12.28 File ta.h

```
/***************************************************************
 * The interface file for the TA class                         *
 ***************************************************************/
#ifndef TA_H
#define TA_H
#include "student.h"
#include "professor.h"

class TA: public Professor, public Student  // Double inheritance
{
   public:
       TA (string name, double gpa, double sal);
       ~TA ();
       void print ();
};
#endif
```

Program 12.29 File ta.cpp

```
/*****************************************************************
 * The implementation file for the TA class                       *
 *****************************************************************/
#include "ta.h"

// Constructor
TA :: TA (string nm, double gp, double sal)
: Person (nm), Student (nm, gp), Professor (nm, sal)
{
}
// Destructor
TA :: ~TA ()
{
}
// Print member function
void TA :: print ()
{
   cout << "Teaching Assistance: " << endl;
   cout << "Name: " << name << " ";
   cout << "GPA: " << gpa << " ";
   cout << "Salary: " << salary << endl << endl;
}
```

Program 12.30 shows the application file for testing all four classes.

Program 12.30 File application.cpp

```
/*****************************************************************
 * The application to test all four classes (Person, Student,     *
 * Professor, and TA).                                            *
 *****************************************************************/
#include "ta.h"

int main ( )
{
   // Testing Person class
   Person person ("John");
   person.print ();
   // Testing Student class
   Student student ("Anne", 3.9);
   student.print ();
   // Testing Professor class
   Professor professor ("Lucie", 78000);
   professor.print ();
```

(continued)

Program 12.30 File application.cpp (Continued)

```
    // Testing TA class
    TA ta ("George", 3.2, 20000);
    ta.print ();
    return 0;
}
```

```
Run:
Person
Name: John

Student
Name: Anne  GPA: 3.9

Professor
Name: Lucie  Salary: 78000

Teaching Assistance:
Name: George  GPA: 3.2  Salary: 20000
```

Mixin Classes

Another solution for the problem of common base classes in multiple inheritance is the use of **mixin classes.** A *mixin* class is never instantiated (it has some pure virtual functions), but it can add data members to other classes. For example, we can think of a *Student* object as a *Person* object with one extra data member, *gpa*. We can think of a *Professor* object as a *Person* object with one extra data member, *salary*. We can also think about a *TA* object as a person with two extra data members, *gpa* and *salary*. These extra data members can be added to these classes with the help of *mixin* classes, as shown in Figure 12.10.

Figure 12.10 shows us that a student, a professor, and a teaching assistant are all instances of the *Person* class. A *Student* object has one more qualification (taking courses), a *Professor* object has one more qualification (teaching courses), and a *TA* object has two qualifications (taking courses and teaching courses). Note that there is still multiple inheritance

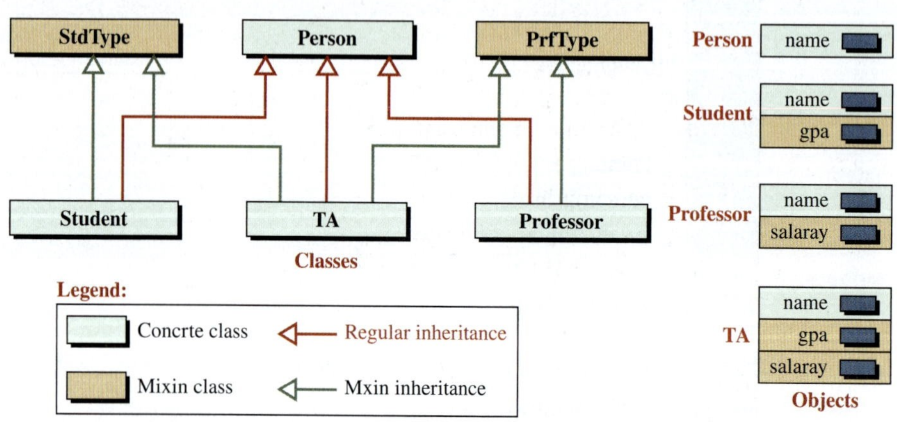

Figure 12.10 Multiple inheritance using mixin classes

in this case (*TA* class inherits from *StdType* and *PrfType*), but there is no common base class and *StdType* and *PrfType* are not instantiated to create the problem we mentioned for multiple inheritance.

An analogy may help here. Consider an ice cream parlor that sells one type of ice cream and that allows customers to buy up to two extra toppings. A person object gets no topping, a student or a professor object gets one topping, and a teaching assistant object gets two toppings. We assume toppings are not sold without ice cream.

EXAMPLE 12.5

In this example we develop the code for the *mixin* classes shown in Figure 12.10. We give the code for five interface files, three implementation files, and one application file. Note that the *mixin* classes are abstract classes (interfaces) and have no implementations. Program 12.31 shows the interface file the *StdType* class.

Program 12.32 shows the interface file the *PrfType* class.

Program 12.31 File stdtype.h

```
/***************************************************************
 * The interface file for StdType abstract class               *
 ***************************************************************/
#ifndef STDTYPE_H
#define STDTYPE_H
#include <iostream>
using namespace std;

class StdType
{
  protected:
      double gpa;
  public:
      virtual void printGPA( ) = 0 ;
};
#endif
```

Program 12.32 File prftype.h

```
/***************************************************************
 * The interface file for PrfType abstract class               *
 ***************************************************************/
#ifndef PRFTYPE_H
#define PRFTYPE_H
#include <iostream>
using namespace std;

class PrfType
{
```

(continued)

Program 12.32 File prftype.h (Continued)

```
    protected:
        double salary;
    public:
        virtual void printSalary () = 0;
};
#endif
```

Program 12.33 shows the interface file the *Person* class.

Program 12.34 shows the interface file the *Student* class. Note that this class has no data members of its own; it only inherits data members from the *Person* class and *StdType* class.

Program 12.33 File person.h

```
/***************************************************************
 * The interface file for Person concrete class                *
 ***************************************************************/
#ifndef PERSON_H
#define PERSON_H
#include <iostream>
#include <string>
#include <iomanip>
using namespace std;

class Person
{
    private:
        string name;
    public:
        Person (string name);
        void print ();
};
#endif
```

Program 12.34 File student.h

```
/***************************************************************
 * The interface file for Student concrete class. This class   *
 * inherits from two classes: Person and StdType.              *
 ***************************************************************/
#ifndef STUDENT_H
#define STUDENT_H
#include "person.h"
```

(continued)

Program 12.34 File student.h (Continued)

```
#include "stdtype.h"

class Student: public Person, public StdType
{
  public:
      Student (string name, double gpa);
      void printGPA();
      void print();
};
#endif
```

Program 12.35 shows the interface file the *Professor* class. Note that this class has no data members of its own; it only inherits data members from the *Person* class and *PrfType* class.

Program 12.36 shows the interface file for the TA class. Note that this class has no data members of its own; it only inherits data members from the *Person* class, *StdType* class, and *PrfType* class.

Program 12.35 File professor.h

```
/*****************************************************************
 * The interface file for Professor concrete class. This class       *
 * inherits from two classes: Person and PrfType.                    *
 *****************************************************************/
#ifndef PROFESSOR_H
#define PROFESSOR_H
#include "person.h"
#include "prftype.h"

class Professor : public Person, public PrfType
{
  public:
      Professor (string name, double salary);
      void printSalary();
      void print ();
};
#endif
```

Program 12.36 File ta.h

```
/*****************************************************************
 * The interface file for TA concrete class. This class              *
 * inherits from tree classes: Person and StdType and PrfType.       *
 *****************************************************************/
```

(continued)

Program 12.36 File ta.h (Continued)

```
#ifndef TA_H
#define TA_H
#include "person.h"
#include "stdtype.h"
#include "prftype.h"

class TA: public Person, public StdType, public PrfType
{
  public:
      TA (string name, double gpa, double salary);
      void printGPA ();
      void printSalary();
      void print ();
};
#endif
```

Program 12.37 shows the implementation file for the *Person* class.

Program 12.38 shows the implementation file for the *Student* class. Note that it inherits the *gpa* data member as a protected data member from the *StdType* class. This data member is accessible in the *Student* class but cannot be initialized in this class. We must assign a value to it in the constructor.

Program 12.37 File person.cpp

```
/***************************************************************
 * The implementation file for Person concrete class           *
 ***************************************************************/
#include "person.h"

// Constructor
Person :: Person (string nm)
: name(nm)
{
}
// Print member function
void Person :: print ( )
{
  cout << "Name: " << name << endl;
}
```

Program 12.38 File student.cpp

```
/***************************************************************
 * The implementation file for Student concrete class          *
 ***************************************************************/
```

(continued)

Program 12.38 File student.cpp (Continued)

```
#include "student.h"

// Constructor
Student :: Student (string na, double gp)
:Person (na)
{
    gpa = gp;                        // Assignment, not initialization
}
// PrintGPA member function
void Student :: printGPA ()
{
    cout << "GPA: " << fixed << setprecision (2) << gpa << endl;
}
// Print member function
void Student :: print ()
{
    Person :: print();
    printGPA ();
}
```

Program 12.39 shows the implementation file for the *Professor* class. Note that it inherits the *salary* data member as a protected data member from the *PrfType* class. This data member is accessible in the *Professor* class but cannot be initialized in this class; we must assign a value to it in the constructor.

Program 12.39 File professor.cpp

```
/***************************************************************
 * The implementation file for Professor concrete class         *
 ***************************************************************/
#include "professor.h"

// Constructor
Professor :: Professor (string nm, double sal)
: Person (nm)
{
    salary = sal;                    // Assignment, not initialization
}
// PrintSalary member function
void Professor :: printSalary ()
{
    cout << "Salary: ";
    cout << fixed << setprecision (2) << salary << endl;
}
```

(continued)

Program 12.39 File professor.cpp (Continued)

```
// General print function
void Professor :: print ()
{
   Person :: print();
   printSalary();
}
```

Program 12.40 shows the implementation file for the *TA* class. Note that it inherits the *salary* data member as a protected data member from the *PrfType* class and the *gpa* data member as a protected data member from the *StdType* class. These data members are accessible in the *TA* class but cannot be initialized in this class. We must assign values to them in the constructor.

Program 12.40 File ta.cpp

```
/***************************************************************
 * The implementation file for TA concrete class               *
 ***************************************************************/
#include "ta.h"

// Constructor
TA :: TA (string nm, double gp, double sal)
: Person (nm)
{
   gpa = gp;                  // Assignment, not initialization
   salary = sal;              // Assignment, not initialization
}
// member function to print GPA
void TA :: printGPA ()
{
   cout << "GPA: " << gpa << endl;
}
// member function to print salary
void TA :: printSalary ()
{
   cout << "Salary: ";
   cout << fixed << setprecision (2) << salary << endl;
}
// General print function
void TA :: print ()
{
   Person :: print();
   printGPA ();
   printSalary();
}
```

Program 12.41 shows a very simple application file for testing the idea of mixin classes. The user defines the application program.

Program 12.41 File application.cpp

```
/***************************************************************
 * The application file to test the three classes               *
 ***************************************************************/
#include "student.h"
#include "professor.h"
#include "ta.h"

int main ( )
{
  // Instantiation of four objects
  Person per ("John");
  Student std ("Linda", 3.9);
  Professor prf("George", 89000);
  TA ta ("Lucien", 3.8, 23000);
  // Printing information about a person
  cout << "Information about person" << endl;
  per.print();
  cout << endl << endl;
  // Printing information about a student
  cout << "Information about student" << endl;
  std.print ();
  cout << endl << endl;
  // Printing information about a professor
  cout << "Information about professor" << endl;
  prf.print();
  cout << endl << endl;
  // Printing information about a teaching assistant
  cout << "Information about teaching assistance " << endl;
  ta.print();
  cout << endl << endl;
  return 0;
}
```

```
Run:
Information about person
Name: John

Information about student
Name: Linda
GPA: 3.90
```

(continued)

Program 12.41 File application.cpp (Continued)

```
Information about professor
Name: George
Salary: 89000.00

Information about teaching assistance
Name: Lucien
GPA: 3.80
Salary: 23000.00
```

Key Terms

abstract class
concrete class
dynamic binding
mixin class
multiple inheritance
polymorphism
pure virtual function
static binding
virtual base inheritance

Summary

Polymorphism gives us the ability to write several versions of a function, each in a separate class. Then, when we call the function, the version appropriate for the object being referenced is executed. We need three conditions for polymorphism: pointers or references, inheritance hierarchy, and virtual functions. An issue related to polymorphism is *binding*: We can have *static binding* and *dynamic binding*.

In C++ we can have *concrete* classes and *abstract* classes. A concrete class can be instantiated and can create objects of its type.

An abstract class can be used as a general base for concrete classes to follow. An abstract class must have at least one pure virtual function whose declaration is set to 0 and there is no definition for it. We cannot instantiate an object from an abstract class, but it can be inherited. An interface is a special case of an abstract class in which all member functions are pure virtual functions.

Problems

PR-1. Assume we have a class named *Base* and two classes named *Derived1* and *Derived2* that are inherited from the *Base* class. We want to use these classes in a polymorphic relationship. If each class has a virtual *print* function and a virtual destructor, show the virtual table entries for these classes.

PR-2. Assume we have the following two classes. Show how we can use stack memory to instantiate objects of these two classes polymorphically.

```
class First                              class Second : public First
{                                        {
    private:                                 private:
        int fr;                                  int se;
    public:                                  public:
        First (int fr);                          Second (int fr, int se);
        virtual ~First ();                       ~Second ();
        virtual void print () const;             void print () const;
};                                       };
```

PR-3. Repeat PR-2, but let the objects be created in heap memory.

PR-4. Assume we have a class named *Base* and a class named *Derived*. The base class composes another class named *Base1* as a private data member. Show the UML diagram for these classes.

PR-5. Consider the following lines of code. What do we need to impose on function *print* () so that classes A and B can be used polymorphically?

```
class A {...};
class B: public A {...};

int main()
{
    A* ptr
    ptr = new A ();
    ptr -> print ();
    ptr = new B ();
    ptr -> print ();
    return 0;
}
```

PR-6. Assume we have the following classes. Do we need to use virtual base or mixin classes in this case? Explain your answer.

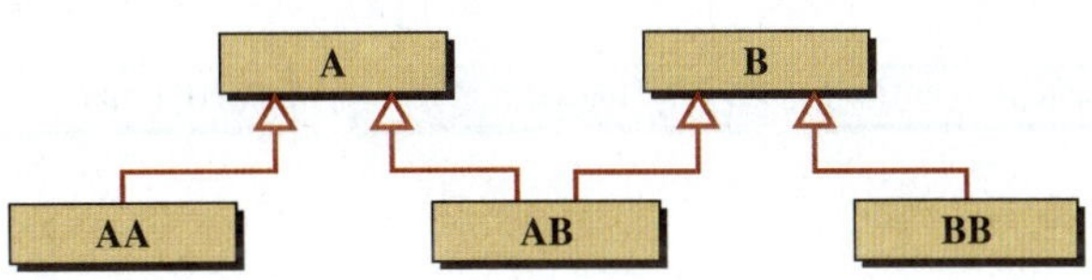

PR-7. Assume we have the following classes. Do we have the problem of multiple inheritance in this case?

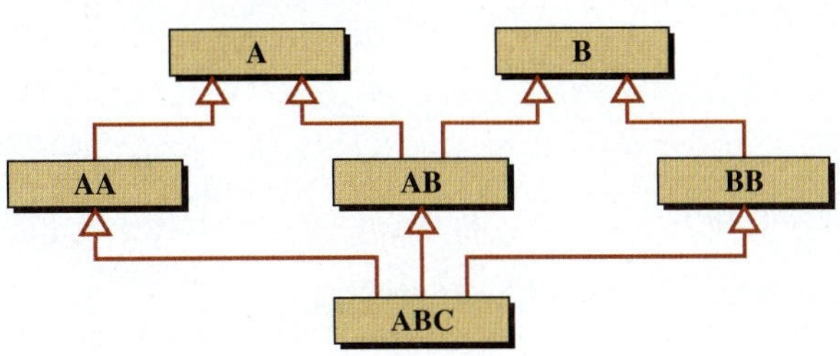

Programs

PRG-1. Modify Program 12.10 through Program 12.14 so they can be used polymorphically.

PRG-2. Modify Program 12.25 through Program 12.35 so they can be used polymorphically.

PRG-3. Assume we have the following classes in a polymorphic relationship.

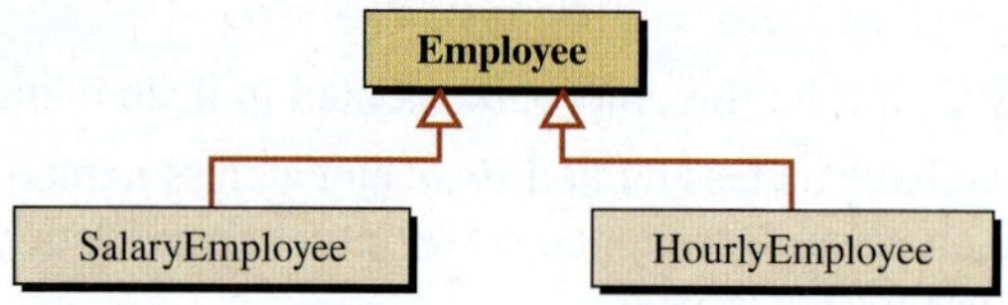

The *Employee* class is an abstract class. An employee has a first name, an initial, and a last name. A salary employee receives a fixed salary per month. An hourly employee receives wages based on the number of hours worked per month and a fixed rate/hour. Write the interface files and the implementation files for all three classes and then test them in an application file.

PRG-4. Modify PRG-4 to add another class named SalaryHourlyEmployee whose object receives a fixed amount of salary per month and extra pay if she works more than 180 hours per month using the same rate received by an hourly employee. Use two more abstract classes, SalaryType and HourlyType, to avoid multiple inheritance (mixin classes) as shown below. Write the interface files and the implementation files for all classes and then test them in an application file.

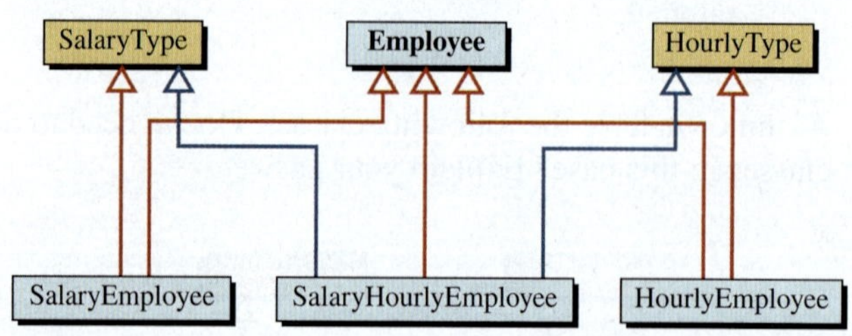

We have defined and used several classes in the last few chapters. If we want to treat the user-defined types the same as fundamental types, we must use on them the same operations we used on fundamental types. For example, we know that we can add two objects of fundamental type such as $(x + y)$ when both x and y are variables of type integer or floating point. We should be able to add two fractions (*fract1* + *fract2*) if both are of type *Fraction*. Of course the operations on objects of user-defined types should make sense. We know from mathematics that we can add two fractions; on the other hand, adding two loans does not make sense.

Objectives

After you have read and studied this chapter, you should be able to:

- Explain how host objects, parameter objects, and returned objects are handled during operator overloading.
- Distinguish between overloadable and non-overloadable operators.
- Understand the role of operator functions and how they can be used as member and nonmember functions.
- Show how to overload unary operators as member operator functions in which the only operand becomes the host object.
- Show how to overload combined binary operators as member operator functions.
- Show how to overload binary operators as friend functions.
- Show how to convert from a fundamental type to a user-defined type using a constructor.
- Show how to convert from a user-defined type to a fundamental type using a conversion function.

13.1 THREE ROLES OF AN OBJECT

Objects of user-defined types can play three different roles in a function: *host object*, *parameter object*, and *returned object*. We must carefully study the issues related to objects in each role to understand the process of writing a function or overloading operators.

13.1.1 Host Object

When we define a nonstatic member function for a class, the function must be called through an instance of the class. For example, we can have *functionOne* as a nonstatic member function of the class *Fun* as shown in Table 13.1.

Table 13.1 Example of host objects

```
void Fun :: functionOne (...)
{
    ...
}
int main ()
{
    fun1.functionOne (...);       // fun1 is the object affected by functionOne
    fun2.functionOne (...);       // fun2 is the object affected by functionOne
    fun3.functionOne (...);       // fun3 is the object affected by functionOne
    ...
}
```

The member function *functionOne* operates on *fun1* in the first call, on *fun2* in the second call, and on *fun3* in the third call. The object the function operates on in each case is called the **host object.** The host object in the first call is *fun1*, in the second call is *fun2*, and in the third call is *fun3*.

If you have written instance member functions, you may be wondering why there was no reference to the host object inside the body of the function. The reason is that the host object, as mentioned above, is changing all of the time. In the first call it is *fun1*; in the second call it is *fun2*; and in the third call it is *fun3*. This means that the definition of the function cannot include the name of the host object because it is changing. The solution is to use a pointer, named *this*, as we discussed in Chapter 7, to point to the host object. In other words, the member function accesses the host object indirectly through the **this pointer.** In the first call, the system makes the *this* pointer point to *fun1*, in the second call to *fun2*, and in the third call to *fun3*. In other words, in each call the host object is `*this` object.

The host object is the one that is pointed to by the *this* pointer.

EXAMPLE 13.1

Assume that the Fun class has only one integer member function named *num*. In Table 13.2, the left section shows how we normally define the *multiplyByTwo* function; the right section shows how the compiler changes it to access the host object pointed to by the *this* pointer.

We can directly use the code on the right-hand side to define this function, but it is easier to write it as shown on the left-hand side. In other words, the host object is always the object pointed to by the *this* pointer. We can access the host function using the asterisk operator (or the –> operator).

Table 13.2 Two formats for a member function

// Written by the user	// Changed by the compiler

void Fun :: multiplyByTwo ()
{
  cout << num * 2;
}
	void Fun :: multiplyByTwo ()
	{
	  cout << (this -> num) * 2;
	}

Protection

The nature of some member functions requires change in the host object; some other functions should not change the host object. For example, if we are writing a member function to input values for data members, the host object must be changed (mutator function). On the other hand, if we are writing a member function that outputs the values of data members, the host object should not change (accessor function). To prevent a member function from changing the host object, we must show that we want the host object to be constant. Since the host object is invisible in the member function, we must use the *const* modifier at the end of the function header to warn the compiler that we do not want the host object to be changed. We must do this in both the function declaration and function definition, but the function call is the same in both cases.

The host object must be constant if the function is not supposed to change it; it must be nonconstant otherwise.

EXAMPLE 13.2

Table 13.3 shows two cases of a host object: one nonconstant and the other constant.

The *input* function is supposed to get values for the data member of the host object, which means the host object will be changed by the function. On the other hand, the *output* function is supposed to print the copy of the members of the host object, which means the host object should not be changed.

13.1.2 Parameter Objects

A **parameter object** is different from a host object. The host object is the hidden part of the member function; a parameter object must be passed to the member function.

Three Ways to Pass

As we have discussed in Chapter 6, a parameter can be passed to a function in three ways: pass-by-value, pass-by-reference, and pass-by-pointer.

Pass-by-Value The first method, **pass-by-value,** is normally not used when the parameter is an object of a user-defined type because it involves calling the copy constructor, making a copy of the object, and then passing it to the function. It is very inefficient.

Table 13.3 Two cases of host objects

// The host object can be changed	//The host object cannot be changed

`// Declaration`
`void input (...);`
`// Definition`
`void Fun :: input (...)`
`{`
`  ...;`
`}`
	`// Declaration`
	`void output (...) const;`
	`// Definition`
	`void Fun :: output (...) const`
	`{`
	`  ...;`
	`}`

`// Call` `fun1.input (...);`	`// Call` `fun1.output (...);`

Pass-by-Reference The second method, **pass-by-reference,** is the most common method we encounter in practice. We do not copy the object; we just define an alias name in the function header so we can access the object. The function can use this name to access the original object and operate on it. There is no cost of copying.

Pass-by-Pointer The third method, **pass-by-pointer,** is not very common unless we already have a pointer pointed to the object (such as when the object was created in the heap) and we pass the pointer to the function.

The most common way to pass a user-defined object to a function is pass-by-reference.

Protection

Since we normally use pass-by-reference to pass an object of user-defined type to a function, the function can change the original object. If we want to prevent this change (most of the time), we should insert the *const* modifier in front of the parameter, which means that the function cannot change the original object. There are occasions, however, when the function needs to change the parameter (such as a stream that is passed to an input function). In this case, the parameter object should not be constant (Table 13.4).

13.1.3 Returned Objects

A constructor and a destructor do not return an object; they create or destroy the host object. Other functions may return an object. We can have a function that returns an instance of an object.

Three Ways to Return

We can return an object from a function in three ways: return-by-value, return-by-reference, and return-by-pointer.

Return-by-Value In **return-by-value,** the function calls the copy constructor, creates a copy of object, and returns the copy. As we know, this is expensive, but we have no choice if the object to be returned is created inside the function because the other two methods (return-by-reference and return-by-pointer) do not work in this case.

Table 13.4 Two types of parameter objects

// The parameter can be changed	// The parameter cannot be changed
// Declaration void one (Type& para);	// Declaration void two (const Type& para);
// Definition	// Definition

void Fun :: one (Type& para)
{
  ... ;
}
	void Fun :: two (const Type& para)
	{
	  ... ;
	}

// Call fun1.one (para);	// Call fun1.two (para);

We must use return-by-value if the returned object is created in the body of the function.

Return-by-Reference **Return-by-reference** eliminates the cost of copying, but it is not possible to use it when the object is created inside the body of the function. When the function terminates, the object created inside the body is destroyed, and we cannot make a reference to a destroyed object. However, we can do so when the object to be returned is a parameter object passed by reference (or pointer) or it is the host object. The origin of an object passed by reference (or by pointer) exists even when the object is terminated. We can make a reference to it. A host object also exists when the function terminates.

Return-by-Pointer **Return-by-pointer** has the same limitation and advantage of pass-by-reference but is seldom used unless the original object is created in the heap.

We must use return-by-reference or by pointer if the returned object is passed as the parameter to the function.

Protection

The next issue is to allow or prevent a returned object from being changed after it is returned to the application program. The answer depends on how we want to use the returned object. If the returned object is to be used only as an *rvalue*, it should be protected from change by using the *const* specifier. On the other hand, if the returned object is to be used as an *lvalue*, there should not be a *const* specifier. When the returned object can be used in both cases, we must make two versions of the function: one with and one without the *const* modifier.

EXAMPLE 13.3

Table 13.5 shows an example of returning by value using two approaches: return-by-constant-value and return-by-value.

EXAMPLE 13.4

Table 13.6 shows two examples of return-by-reference in which the host object is returned.

Table 13.5 Two types of return-by-value

//The object can be changed	//The object cannot be changed

// Declaration
Fun one (int value);
// Definition
Fun Fun :: one (int value)
{
  ...
  Fun fun (value);
  return fun;
}
	// Declaration
	const Fun functOne (int value);
	// Definition
	const Fun Fun :: two (int value)
	{
	  ...
	  Fun fun (value);
	  return fun;
	}

// Call	// Call
fun1.one (value) = ...;	fun1.two (value);

Table 13.6 Two examples of return-by-reference

// The object can be changed	// The object cannot be changed

// Declaration
Fun& one ();
// Definition
Fun& Fun :: one()
{
  ...
  return *this;
}
	// Declaration
	const Fun& two ();
	// Definition
	const Fun& Fun :: two ()
	{
	  ...
	  return *this;
	}

// Call fun1.one () = ...;	// Call fun1.two ();

13.2 OVERLOADING PRINCIPLES

Operator overloading is the definition of two or more operations using the same operator. C++ uses a set of symbols called operators to manipulate fundamental data types such as integers and floating points. Most of these symbols are *overloaded* to handle several data types. For example, the symbol for the addition operator of two fundamental data types (x + y) can be used to add two values of type *int, long, longlong, double,* and *long double.* This means that the following two expressions in C++ use the same symbol with two distinct interpretations. The first symbol means add two integers; the second symbol means add two reals.

```
14 + 20                    14.21 + 20.45
```

If we think about how C++ uses two different processes for adding two integers and two floating-point types, we can better understand the meaning of overloading. The addition symbol in each expression means a different process. In the following example, the compiler changes the first operand to 14.0 to do the operation:

```
14 + 20.35
```

The C++ language goes one step further when it uses the symbol << to mean two different things when applied to an integer data type and the *ostream* class. The following two expressions give two different interpretations for this symbol:

```
x << 5;                    cout << 5;
```

In the expression on the left, the symbol << means to shift the bits in the integer object five positions to the left (we discuss bit operations in Appendix D); in the expression on the right, it means apply the insertion operator on the *cout* object to print the value of the fundamental data type 5 (the *cout* object overloaded in the class *ostream* that we discuss later in the chapter).

Overloading is a powerful capability of the C++ language that allows the user to redefine operators for user-defined data types, possibly with a new interpretation. For example, instead of using a function call to add two fractions, we can overload the addition symbol (+) to do the same thing.

add (fr1, fr2)	fr1 + fr2

The expression on the right looks more concise and more natural. However, we must carefully redefine the interpretation of the addition symbol (+) for our fraction objects.

13.2.1 Three Categories of Operators

We can divide the operators in C++ (see Appendix D) into three categories: non-overloadable, not recommended for overloading, and overloadable, as shown in Table 13.7.

Table 13.7 Operators in C++ and their overloadability

Operator	Arity	Name	Overloadability
::	primary	scope	Non-overloadable
[ ]	postfix	array subscript	Overloadable
( )	postfix	function call	Overloadable
.	postfix	member selector	Non-overloadable
->	postfix	member selector	Overloadable
++	postfix	postfix increment	Overloadable
--	postfix	postfix decrement	Overloadable
++	prefix	prefix increment	Overloadable
--	prefix	prefix decrement	Overloadable
~	unary	bitwise not	Overloadable
!	unary	logical not	Overloadable
+	unary	plus	Overloadable
-	unary	minus	Overloadable
*	unary	dereference	Overloadable
&	unary	address-of	Not recommended
new	unary	allocate object	Overloadable
new [ ]	unary	allocate array	Overloadable
delete	unary	delete object	Overloadable
delete[ ]	unary	delete array	Overloadable
type	unary	Type conversion	Overloadable
.*	unary	ptr to member select	Non-overloadable
-> *	unary	ptr to member select	Overloadable
*	binary	multiply	Overloadable
/	binary	divide	Overloadable
%	binary	modulo (remainder)	Overloadable
+	binary	add	Overloadable
-	binary	subtract	Overloadable
<<	binary	bitwise shift left	Overloadable
>>	binary	bitwise shift right	Overloadable
<	binary	less than	Overloadable
<=	binary	less or equal	Overloadable
>	binary	greater	Overloadable
>=	binary	greater or equal	Overloadable

(continued)

Table 13.7 Operator in C++ and their overloadability (Continued)

Operator	Arity	Name	Overloadability
==	binary	equal	Overloadable
!=	binary	not equal	Overloadable
&	binary	bitwise and	Not recommended
^	binary	bitwise ex or	Overloadable
|	binary	bitwise or	Not recommended
&&	binary	logical and	Not recommended
||	binary	logical or	Not recommended
? :	binary	conditional	Not overloadable
=	binary	simple assignment	Overloadable
oper=	binary	comp. assignment	Overloadable
,	ternary	comma	Not recommended

Non-Overloadable Operators

The C++ language does not allow us to overload the operators marked as *not overloadable* in Table 13.7. The reason behind this decision is beyond the scope of this book, but we must try not to overload them.

Not Recommended for Overloading

There are six operators that can be overloaded, but C++ strongly recommends that we do not overload them. The reason for not overloading the *address-of* operation is that C++ defines a very special meaning to this operator and there is no guarantee that this special meaning will be implemented by the user. The reason for the next five recommendations is that the built-in version of these operators evaluates the two operands in predefined order (left operand first and right operand next). A member function cannot guarantee this order. In addition, the fourth and fifth operators have *short-circuit* behavior, as we discussed in Chapter 4, which also cannot be guaranteed by a member function.

Overloadable Operators

The rest of the operators as defined in Table 13.7 can be overloaded, and the overloading follows the natural behavior of the operators as defined in C++. We do not discuss all of the operators; here; we discuss only the most common ones.

13.2.2 Rules of Overloading

Before we try to overload operators for our user-defined data types, we must be aware of the rules for and restrictions on overloading:

- **Precedence.** Overloading cannot change the precedence of the operator. Good examples are the *insertion* (<<) and the *extraction* (>>) operators. These are actually bitwise operators and have a very low-level precedence (2). When we use an operator for our user-defined classes, we must pay attention to the precedence of the operator as defined in the precedence list.
- **Associativity.** Overloading cannot change the associativity of the operator. Most operators have left-to-right associativity, but there are a few with right-to-left associativity. When we overload an operator, the operator keeps its associativity.

return_type **operator symbol** (parameter lists)

function name

Figure 13.1 Format of the function operator

- **Commutativity.** Overloading cannot change the commutativity of the operator. For example, the addition operator (+) is commutative: (a + b) is the same as (b + a); while the subtraction operator is not: (a – b) is not the same as (b – a). When we overload the operator, we must pay careful attention to this rule.
- **Arity.** Overloading cannot change the *arity* of the operator. If a native operator is unary (taking only one operand), then the overloaded definition must also be unary. If the native operator is binary (taking two operands), then the overloaded definition must also be binary. We don't need to worry about the only ternary operator (? :) because it is not overloadable.
- **No new operators.** We cannot invent operators; we can only overload the existing overloadable operators. For example, we cannot use the symbol # as a new operator because this symbol is not defined in the list of operators for the C++ language.
- **No combination.** We cannot combine two operator symbols to create a new one. For example, we cannot use the combination of two asterisks (**) to define a new operator, such as the one used in some other languages for power.

13.2.3 Operator Function

To overload an operator for a user-defined data type, we must write a function named **operator function,** a function that acts as an operator. The name of this function starts with the reserved word *operator* and is followed by the symbol of the operator that we need to overload. Figure 13.1 shows the general form of an operator function prototype.

Member versus Nonmember Functions

Most of the overloadable operators can be defined either as a member function or a nonmember function. A few can be overloaded only as member functions; a few need to be overloaded only as nonmember functions. Since the syntax for member and nonmember operator functions is different, we discuss the functions separately.

Using Operators or Operator Functions

After overloading, we can either use the operator itself or the function operator. For example, imagine we have overloaded the unary minus operator for our *Fraction* class as a member function. We can then apply the operator on a fraction object or invoke the fraction operator as shown below. The version on the left is more concise and intuitive. The whole purpose of operator overloading is to use the operator itself to mimic the behavior of built-in types.

```
-fr //operator                          fr.operator- ( ) // function
```

13.3 OVERLOADING AS A MEMBER

Although all overloadable operators (except for *insertion* and *extraction*) can be overloaded as member functions, some operators are better suited to being overloaded as member functions than others.

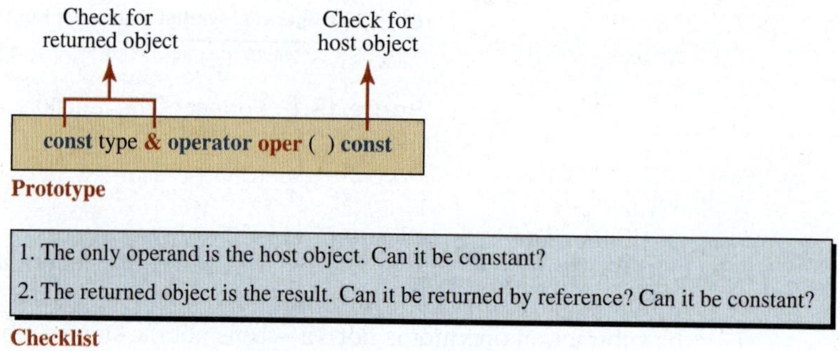

Figure 13.2 Guidelines for overloading unary operators

13.3.1 Unary Operators

In a unary operator, the only operand becomes the host object of the *operator function*. We have no parameter object. This means that we should only think about two objects: the host object and the returned object, as shown in Figure 13.2.

Plus and Minus Operators

We first overload the *plus* and *minus* operators as shown in Figure 13.3.

Example

To define the plus and minus operators for a class, we must first define the meaning of these operators when applied to an object of a class. Although these two operators make sense when applied to a Fraction object, they do not make sense when applied to a Loan object. Based on this guideline, we can define the declaration and the definition of the plus/minus overloaded operator for our *Fraction* class that we defined in Chapter 7, as shown in Table 13.8.

We need to know that there is no parameter object in this case. Both operators are unary operators, and the host object serves as the only operand. The host object is not supposed to be changed (no side effect) and the returned object is the host object after modification.

As 13.8 shows, the meaning of plus and minus operators for the Fraction class means to apply the plus or minus operator to the nominator. We can construct a new object in the body of the function and apply these operators to the numerator data member of the host object. The function then returns the temporary function as a constant value. We return the object as a value because the returning object is created inside the body of the function and

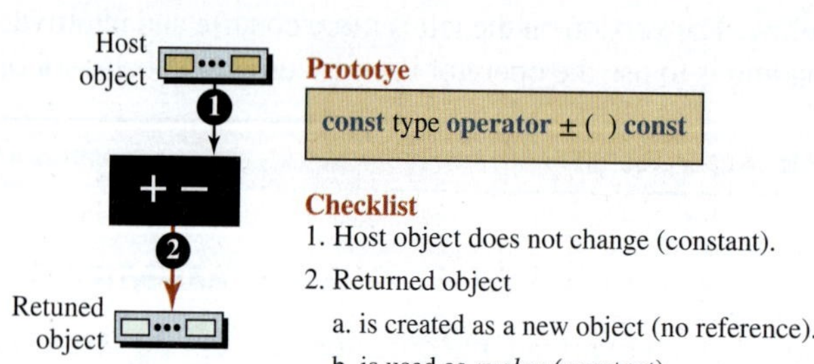

Figure 13.3 Overloading plus/minus operators

Table 13.8 Unary operator plus or minus

$+\frac{a}{b} \rightarrow \frac{+a}{b}$ $\quad$ $-\frac{a}{b} \rightarrow \frac{-a}{b}$

```
// Declarations
const Fraction operator+( ) const;
const Fraction operator-( ) const;
// Definition of plus operator
const Fraction  Fraction :: operator+ ( ) const
{
   Fraction temp (+numer, denum);               // a new object
   return temp;
}
// Definition of minus operator
const Fraction Fraction :: operator- ( ) const
{
   Fraction temp (-numer, denum);               // a new object
   return temp;
}
```

does not exist when the function terminates (we cannot return it as a reference). We also return the object with a constant modifier because the returning object can only be used as an *rvalue* (we cannot uses it as an *lvalue* such as at the left-hand side of the assignment operator). An object with a constant modifier cannot be chained either.

Pre-Increment and Pre-Decrement Operators

We now overload the pre-increment and the pre-decrement operators. Each operator has a side effect that changes its operand; the returned object is a copy of the changed object. C++ allows the chaining of these two operators, which means that we can have ++++*x* or −−−−*x*. This means that the returned value must be an *lvalue* (Figure 13.4).

Based on the checklist in Figure 13.4, we can define the declaration and the definition of the pre-increment/pre-decrement overloaded operators for our *Fraction* class in Table 13.9. Each of these two operators has two tasks to perform. The operator must change

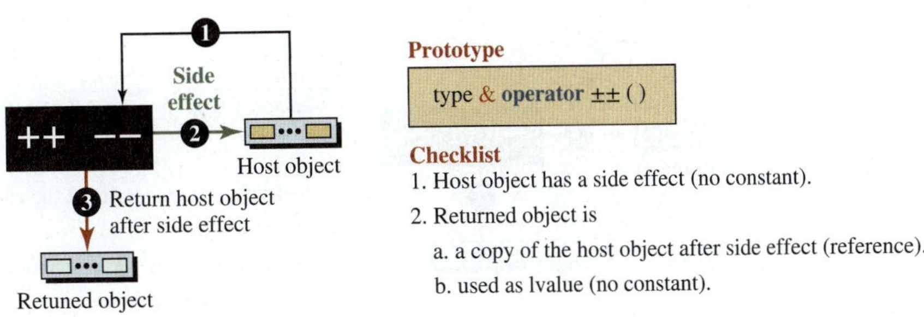

Figure 13.4 Overloading the pre-increment and pre-decrement operators

Table 13.9 Pre-increment/pre-decrement operators

$$++\frac{a}{b} \rightarrow \frac{a}{b} + 1 \rightarrow \frac{a+b}{b}$$

$$--\frac{a}{b} \rightarrow \frac{a}{b} - 1 \rightarrow \frac{a-b}{b}$$

```
// Declaration of pre-increment operator
Fraction& operator++ ( );
// Definition of pre-increment operator
Fraction& Fraction :: operator++ ( )
{
   numer = numer + denom;
   this -> normalize ();
   return *this;
}
// Declaration of pre-decrement operator
Fraction& operator-- ( );
// Definition of pre-decrement operator
Fraction& Fraction :: operator-- ( )
{
   numer = numer - denom;
   this -> normalize ();
   return *this;
}
```

the host object and then return the changed host object (host object cannot be constant). This means that instead of creating a new object from the host object, we should change the host object and then return it. Since the returned object is the changed version of the host object, we can return by reference instead of by value (which is more expensive). The C++ allows chaining of this operator (++++x and −−−−x), which means that the return object cannot be constant.

Post-Increment and Post-Decrement Operators

We now overload the post-increment and the post-decrement operators. The returned object is created before the side effect (Figure 13.5).

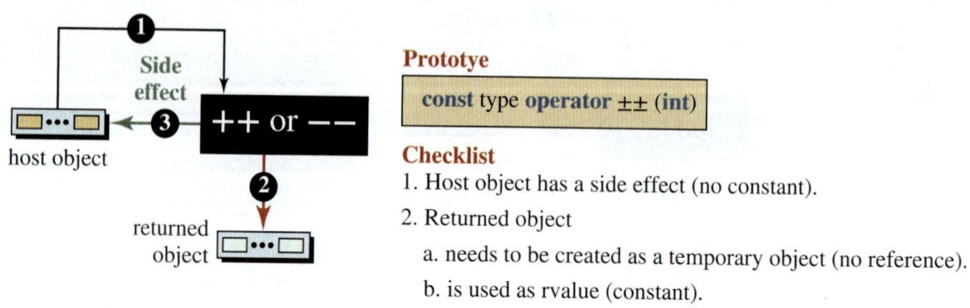

Figure 13.5 Overloading the post-increment and post-decrement operators

Table 13.10 Post-increment/post-decrement operators

$$\frac{a}{b}{++} \rightarrow \frac{a}{b}+1 \rightarrow \frac{a+b}{b}$$

$$\frac{a}{b}{--} \rightarrow \frac{a}{b}-1 \rightarrow \frac{a-b}{b}$$

```
// Declaration of post-increment operator
const Fraction operator++ (int);
// Definition of post-increment operator
const Fraction Fraction :: operator++ (int dummy)
{
   Fraction temp (numer, denom);
   ++(*this);
   return temp;
}
// Declaration of post-increment operator
const Fraction operator-- (int);
// Definition of post-decrement operator
const Fraction Fraction :: operator-- (int dummy)
{
   Fraction temp (numer, denom);
   --(*this);
   return temp;
}
```

Since we cannot return the host object before changing it, we need to create a temporary object out of the host object, apply the side effect to the host object, and then return the temporary object. The dummy integer parameter creates a unique signature to distinguish between the prototype of the pre-operator and post-operator; it is ignored.

Based on the checklist in Figure 13.5, we can define the declaration and the definition of the post-increment/post-decrement overloaded operators for our *Fraction* class in Table 13.10. The returned object is the temporary object created before change, which means that we cannot return it by reference. The returned object is constant because C++ does not allow chaining of the operation such as (*x*++++) or (*x*−−−−). Also note that since the side effect of a prefix and a postfix operator is the same, we can call the postfix operator to change the host object.

13.3.2 Binary Operators

A binary operator has two operands (left operand and right operand). If we want to overload a binary operator as a member function, we must consider one of the operands as the host object and the other as the parameter object. It is more natural to use the left operand as the host object and the right operand as the parameter object. For this reason, it is common to overload only those binary operators as member functions in which the left operand (which becomes the host object) has a different role than the right operand (which becomes the parameter object). Among the binary operators, the assignment and compound assignment operators (= , += , −= , *= , /= , and %=) are the best candidate for this purpose. In each

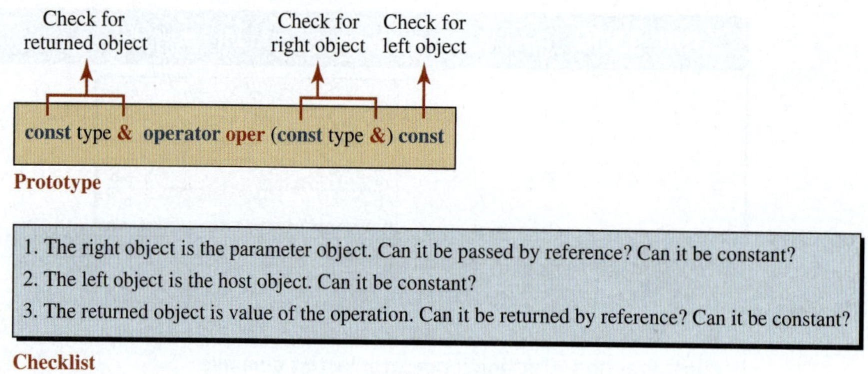

Figure 13.6 Guidelines for binary operators

of these operators, the left operand plays a different role from the right operand. The left operand represent an *lvalue*, but the right operand is an *rvalue*. This means that we have three objects to consider. The left operand becomes the host object, the right operand becomes the parameter object, and the returned value of the operation is the value of the host object after the side effect. Figure 13.6 shows the general prototype for the binary operator implemented as a member function.

Assignment Operator

The first candidate in this category is the assignment operator. This is an asymmetric operation in which the nature of the left and right operands is different. The left operand is an lvalue object that receives the side effect of the operation; the right operand is an rvalue object that should not be changed in the process. Before we proceed with this operator, we must mention that to use this operator, the left and the right operands must already exist. In other words, this operator is different from the copy constructor, which creates a new object from an existing object. Both objects must exist; we only change the left object so it is an exact copy of the right object.

In an assignment operator, both the left object (host) and right object (parameter) must already exist.

Figure 13.7 shows the simple assignment operator. First, the host object (left operand) cannot be constant because of the side effect. Second, the returned object cannot be constant because we can chain this operator ($x = y = z$).

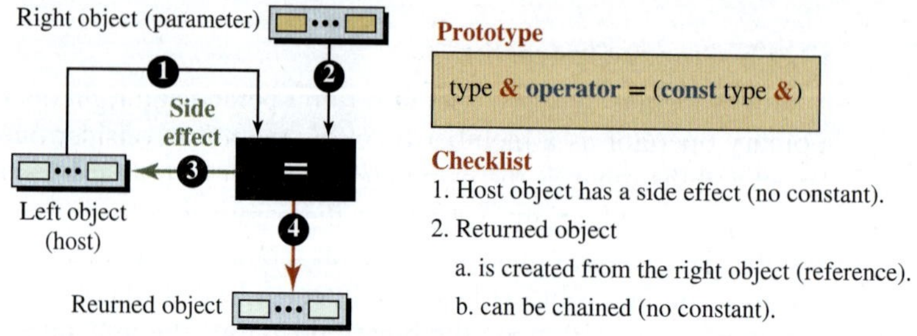

Figure 13.7 Overloading the assignment operator

There is another important point we must mention about this operator. If we do not define an assignment operator for our class, the system provides one (synthetic assignment operator). However, the synthetic operator may not be the one we need. Furthermore, the following warnings apply to overloaded operators:

- We should verify that the host and the parameter objects are not the same object (do not have the same address). This is particularly important if the objects are created in heap memory. Since we must delete the host object before we copy the contents of the parameter object, if the two objects are the same, the parameter object, which is physically the same as the host object, is deleted and there is nothing to be copied.
- We know that the assignment object is associative from right to left. In other words, if we have $y = x$, then we can assign the result of operation to another object $z = y = x$, which is interpreted as $z = (y = x)$. However, C++, requires that z be considered as a reference to y. This is why the returned object must be returned by reference.

EXAMPLE 13.5

Table 13.11 shows the declaration and definition of the assignment operator for the *Fraction* class.

Compound Assignment Operators

Another set of operators that we can overload is the compound assignment operators (+=, −=, *=, /=, and %=). We know the meanings of the compound assignments.

fract1 += fract2	means	fract1 = fract1 + fract2
fract1 -= fract2	means	fract1 = fract1 - fract2
fract1 *= fract2	means	fract1 = fract1 * fract2
fract1 /= fract2	means	fract1 = fract1 / fract2
fract1 %= fract2	means	fract1 = fract1 % fract2

Table 13.11 Assignment operator

$$\frac{a}{b} = \frac{c}{d} \rightarrow \frac{c}{d}$$

```
// Declaration of assignment operator
Fraction& operator= (const Fraction& right)
// Definition of assignment operator
Fraction& Fraction :: operator= (const Fraction& right)
{
  if (*this != right) // or check inequality in another way
  {
      numer = right.numer;
      denom = right.denom;
  }
  return *this;
}
```

In this operation, *fract1* is the host object and *fract2* is the parameter object. The process is the same as for the assignment operator except that we must define carefully the numerator and denominator of the host object. The returned object is the host object after change.

EXAMPLE 13.6

Table 13.12 shows the declaration and definition of the compound assignment operator for the *Fraction* class.

Table 13.12 Overloading compound assignment operators

$$\frac{a}{b} \mathrel{+}= \frac{c}{d} \rightarrow \frac{a}{b} = \frac{a}{b} + \frac{c}{d} \rightarrow \frac{a*d+b*c}{b*d}$$

$$\frac{a}{b} \mathrel{-}= \frac{c}{d} \rightarrow \frac{a}{b} = \frac{a}{b} - \frac{c}{d} \rightarrow \frac{a*d-b*c}{b*d}$$

$$\frac{a}{b} \mathrel{*}= \frac{c}{d} \rightarrow \frac{a}{b} = \frac{a}{b} * \frac{c}{d} \rightarrow \frac{a*c}{b*d}$$

$$\frac{a}{b} \mathrel{/}= \frac{c}{d} \rightarrow \frac{a}{b} = \frac{a}{b} \,/\, \frac{c}{d} \rightarrow \frac{a*d}{b*c}$$

```
// Declaration of += operator
Fraction& operator+= (const Fraction& right)
// Definition of += operator
Fraction& Fraction :: operator+= (const Fraction& right)
{
   numer = numer * right.denom + denom * right.numer;
   denom = denom * right.denom;
   normalize ();
   return *this;
}
// Declaration of -= operator
Fraction& operator-= (const Fraction& right)
// Definition of -= operator
Fraction& Fraction :: operator-= (const Fraction& right)
{
   numer = numer * right.denom - denom * right.numer;
   denom = denom * right.denom;
   normalize ();
   return *this;
}
// Declaration of *= operator
Fraction& operator*= (const Fraction& right)
// Definition of *= operator
Fraction& Fraction :: operator*= (const Fraction& right)
{
```

(*continued*)

Table 13.12 Overloading compound assignment operators (Continued)

```
    numer = numer * right.numer;
    denom = denom * right.denom;
    normalize ();
    return *this;
}
```

```
// Declaration of /= operator
Fraction& operator/= (const Fraction& right)
// Definition of /= operator
Fraction& Fraction :: operator/= (const Fraction& right)
{
    numer = numer * right.denom;
    denom = denom * right.numer;
    normalize ();
    return *this;
}
```

In Table 13.12, the right operand does not need to be of the same object type as the left operand as long as the operation is well defined. For example, we can use any compound assignment operator to add, subtract, multiply, or divide a fraction by an integer. The operation is well defined. The rules of overloading do not require that the host object and the parameter object are of the same type.

13.3.3 Other Operators

There are other operators that can be implemented as member functions. We discuss some of them next.

Indirection and Member-Selector Operators

In C++, we often use the indirection (*) or the member-selector (->) operator to access an object or a member of an object stored in stack memory or heap memory. Before overloading these two operators, we must mention some points about them.

- Both operators are unary operators, which means both have only one operand, which must be a pointer to the corresponding object. The *indirection* operator returns the object pointed to by the operand; the *member-selector* operator changes the pointer operand to a pointer that can point to any member of the corresponding object and returns the member. In the first, the operator comes before the operand (prefix); in the second, the operator comes after the operand (suffix) as shown below:

// Returns object	// Returns member
`*ptr`	`ptr ->`

- If we want to overload these two operators, we need a class that acts as a pointer because the operand (host object) must be a pointer.

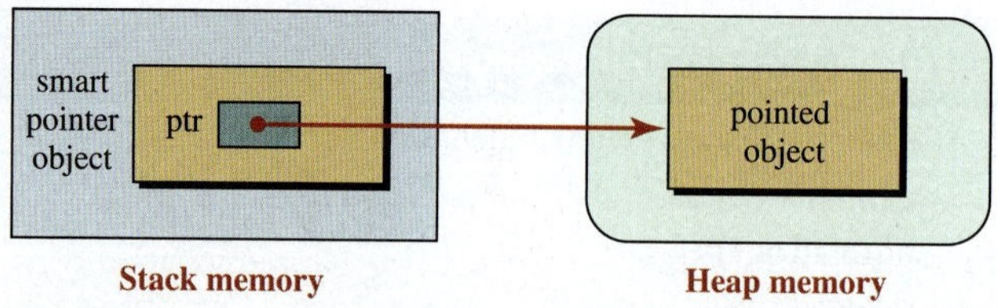

Figure 13.8 Smart pointer

Smart Pointers When we use a pointer to point to an object in the stack, we do not need to overload the indirection and member-selector operators (∗ and ->). We can use a pointer, as a compound data type, to point to our object. When the object goes out of scope, it is automatically popped out of the stack and there is no memory leak. However, when we create an object in the heap, we must remember to delete it to avoid a memory leak, as we discussed in Chapter 9. To do this, we create a **smart pointer** as shown in Figure 13.8.

The smart pointer object is an object with one single data member: a pointer to the desired type (such as *Fraction*). When the constructor of this object is called, it creates a pointer to the desired type. The two operators ∗ and -> are also overloaded for the class *SmartPtr*, which can point to the desired object and to a member of the desired object.

EXAMPLE 13.7

We create a smart pointer class called *SmartPtr* whose interface is shown in Program 13.1.

Program 13.1 File smartptr.h

```
/***************************************************************
 * The interface file for the SmartPtr class                   *
 ***************************************************************/
#ifndef SMARTPTR_H
#define SMARTPTR_H
#include <iostream>
using namespace std;

class Fraction;    // Forward declaration
class SmartPtr
{
  private:
       Fraction* ptr;
  public:
       SmartPtr (Fraction* ptr);
       ~SmartPtr ( );
       Fraction& operator* ( ) const;
       Fraction* operator->( ) const;
};
#endif
```

Note that we added a forward declaration in line 9 to tell the header file that the name *Fraction* in the declaration of *SmartPtr* is a type. The declaration and the definition of the *Fraction* class are in other files, as we discussed in Chapter 7 regarding in the principle of separate compilation.

Now we create the implementation for the *SmartPtr* class (Program 13.2). Note that the destructor deletes the memory allocated by *ptr* member (line 15).

Now we create our application program to test the class SmartPtr (Program 13.3).

Program 13.2 File smartptr.cpp

```
1  /***************************************************************
2   * The implementation file for the SmartPtr class              *
3   ***************************************************************/
4  #include "smartptr.h"
5
6  // Constructor
7  SmartPtr :: SmartPtr (Fraction* p)
8  : ptr (p)
9  {
10 }
11 // Destructor
12 SmartPtr :: ~SmartPtr ( )
13 {
14   delete ptr;
15 }
16 // Overloading of indirection operator
17 Fraction& SmartPtr :: operator* ( ) const
18 {
19   return *ptr;
20 }
21 // Overloading of the arrow operator
22 Fraction* SmartPtr :: operator-> ( ) const
23 {
24   return ptr;
25 }
```

Program 13.3 File app.cpp

```
/***************************************************************
 * The application file to test the SmartPtr class             *
 ***************************************************************/
#include "smartptr.h"
#include "fraction.h"

```

(continued)

Program 13.3 File app.cpp (Continued)

```
int main ( )
{
   // Creating a smart Pointer object
   SmartPtr sp = new Fraction (2, 5);
   // Accessing the member through the * operator
   cout << "Fraction: " << endl;
   (*sp).print ();
   cout << endl;
   // Accessing the member through -> operator
   cout << "Fraction: " << endl;
   sp -> print ();
   cout << endl;
   return 0;
}
```

```
Run:
Fraction: 2 / 5
Fraction: 2 / 5
```

Note that we could have used the following statements in the application to create a fraction in the heap without using a smart pointer.

```
Fraction* ptr = new Fraction (2, 5);
(*ptr).print ();
ptr -> print ();
```

The difference is that the fraction object created in the heap will not automatically be deleted and we must delete it in the application program to avoid a possible memory leak. The smart pointer does this task for us.

Subscript Operator

Another operator that can be overloaded as a member function is the subscript operator ([ ]). However, we must be careful not to change the semantics of this operator. The subscript operator is a binary operator in which the left operand is the name of an array and the right operand is a type that defines the index of the element in the array. This means that we should overload this operator only when our type is an array or something behaving like an array (such as string or a list).

If we want to overload this operator correctly, we need two versions. In the first version, the operator is overloaded as an accessor function; in the second version, it is overloaded as a mutator function. Figure 13.9 shows the design of subscript operators.

Assume that we want a class named *Array* in which we have control over the size of the array and the whole array is created in the heap memory. Program 13.4 shows the interface file.

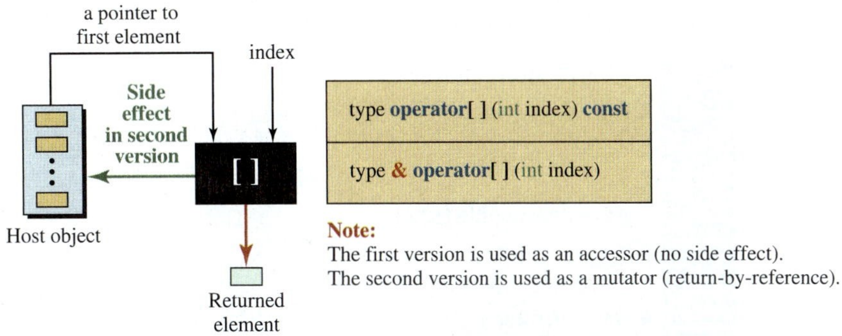

Figure 13.9 Overloading the subscript operator

Program 13.4 File array.h

```
/*****************************************************************
 * The interface file for an Array class                         *
 *****************************************************************/
#ifndef ARRAY_H
#define ARRAY_H
#include <iostream>
#include <cassert>
using namespace std;

class Array
{
  private:
        double* ptr;
        int size;
  public:
        Array (int size); // Constructor
        ~Array( ); // Destructor
        double& operator[ ] (int index) const; // Accessor
        double& operator[ ] (int index) ; // Mutator
};
#endif
```

Program 13.5 shows the implementation file.

Program 13.5 File Array.cpp

```
/*****************************************************************
 * The implementation file for Array class                       *
 *****************************************************************/
#include "array.h"

```

(continued)

Program 13.5 File Array.cpp (Continued)

```
// Constructor (allocating memory in the heap)
Array :: Array (int s)
:size (s)
{
  ptr = new double [size];
}
// Destructor (freeing memory in the heap)
Array :: ~Array( )
{
  delete [ ] ptr;
}
// Accessor subscript
double& Array :: operator[ ] (int index) const
{
  if (index < 0 || index >= size)
  {
      cout << "Index is out of range. Program terminates.";
      assert (false);
  }
  return ptr [index];
}
// Mutator subscript
double& Array :: operator[ ] (int index)
{
  if (index < 0 || index >= size)
  {
      cout << "Index is out of range. Program terminates.";
      assert (false);
  }
  return ptr [index];
}
```

Program 13.6 shows a simple application.

Program 13.6 File app.cpp

```
/*****************************************************************
 * The application file to test the Array class                 *
 *****************************************************************/
#include "array.h"

int main ( )
{
```

(*continued*)

Program 13.6 File app.cpp (Continued)

```
    // Instantiation of array object with three elements
    Array arr (3);
    // Storing values using mutator operator [ ]
    arr[0] = 22.31;
    arr[1] = 78.61;
    arr[2] = 65.22;
    // Retrieving values using accessor operator [ ]
    for (int i = 0; i < 3; i++)
    {
        cout << "Value of arr [" << i << "]: " << arr[i] << endl;
    }
    return 0;
}
```

```
Run:
Value of arr [0]: 22.31
Value of arr [1]: 78.61
Value of arr [2]: 65.22
```

Function Call Operator

Another unary operator that can be overloaded is the **function call operator,** as shown below:

```
name (list of arguments)
```

The overloading of the function call operator allows us to create a *function object* (sometimes called a *functor*): an instance of an object that acts like a function. If a class overloads the function call operator, the compiler allows us to instantiate an object of this class as though we are calling a function. We are actually wrapping a function in a class that has the benefit of being used in different applications. We can instantiate an object of the class to invoke the function embedded in the class.

The difference between a function object and a function is that the function object can hold its state (a function has no state). For example, a function object called *smallest* can hold the smallest value from the previous call (as a data member). In this way, we can call the function object as many times as we want, and it always gives us the smallest value as long as the object is in scope.

EXAMPLE 13.8

Program 13.7 shows the interface file that declares a class called *Smallest*.

Program 13.7 File smallest.h

```
/*****************************************************************
 * The implementation file for the SmartPtr class                *
 *****************************************************************/
#ifndef SMALLEST_H
```

(continued)

Program 13.7 File smallest.h (Continued)

```
#define SMALLEST_H
#include <iostream>
using namespace std;

class Smallest
{
  private:
       int current;
  public:
       Smallest ( );
       int operator ( ) (int next); // function call operator
};
#endif
```

Program 13.8 shows the implementation of the class *Smallest*. Program 13.9 shows the application file for testing the function object.

Program 13.8 File smallest.cpp

```
/****************************************************************
 * The implementation file for the Smallest class               *
 ****************************************************************/
#include "smallest.h"

// Constructor
Smallest :: Smallest ( )
{
  current = numeric_limits <int> :: max();
}
// Overloaded function call operator
int Smallest :: operator() (int next)
{
  if (next < current)
  {
       current = next;
  }
  return current;
}
```

Program 13.9 File app.cpp

```
/****************************************************************
 * The application file to test the Smallest class              *
 ****************************************************************/
```

(continued)

Program 13.9 File app.cpp (Continued)

```
#include "smallest.h"
#include <iostream>

int main ( )
{
  // Instantiation of an smallest object
  Smallest smallest;
  // Applying the function call operator to objects
  cout << "Smallest so far: " << smallest (5) << endl;
  cout << "Smallest so far: " << smallest (9) << endl;
  cout << "Smallest so far: " << smallest (4) << endl;
  return 0;
}
```

```
Run:
Smallest so far: 5
Smallest so far: 5
Smallest so far: 4
```

In Chapter 19 we discuss more about function objects (functor) when we show how C++ uses them in the Standard Template Library (STL).

An interesting point about a function object is that C++ does not limit the number of arguments in a function call. This means that we can overload this operator with more than one argument. One application is to use it to get an element in a class defining a two-dimensional array (or even an array with more dimensions). The first argument can define the index of the first dimension (row), and the second argument can define the index of the second dimensional (column).

13.4 OVERLOADING AS A NONMEMBER

When we overload a binary operator as a member function, one of the operands needs to be the host object. This is fine when each operand has a different role in the operation. However, in some operators, such as $(a + b)$ or $(a < b)$, the two operands play the same role and neither of them is related to the result. In these cases, it is better to use a nonmember function. We have two choices: global functions or friend functions.

There is nothing to prevent us from using a global function for overloading binary operators. Although there are many advocates for this strategy, there is one drawback. The definition of the operator function is longer and more complicated because it needs to use the accessor and mutator functions of the class to access data members of the class. We do not develop these types of functions.

C++ allows functions to be declared as friend functions of the class. A **friend function** has no host object, but it is granted friendship so that it can access the private data members and member functions of the class without calling the public member functions. We use friend functions to overload selected operators.

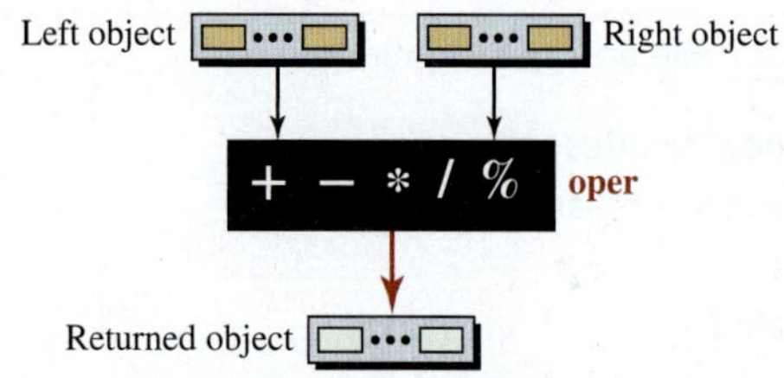

Prototye

friend const *type* operator oper (const *type* & left, const *type* & right)

Figure 13.10 Overloading binary arithmetic operators

13.4.1 Binary Arithmetic Operators

We have postponed until now our discussion of overloading binary arithmetic operators because it is more appropriate to overload them as friend functions. Figure 13.10 shows the design. The two operands must already exist. We create a new object inside the function and return it as a constant object. We can pass the two operands as reference, but the return object cannot be a reference type because it is created inside the function definition.

Table 13.13 shows arithmetic operators for the *Fraction* class. Note that the modulo operator (%) cannot be applied to the *Fraction* class, because this operation does not make sense with fractions. We give the declaration and definition for the first operator; the rest are similar. Note that *friend* qualifier is needed only for declaration.

Note that the results are *rvalues*, which means that they can only be used when *rvalues* are needed. However, we can instantiate an object and then assign the results to that object if needed (fract = fract1 + fract2). We must make sure that the assignment operator is overloaded.

Table 13.13 Binary arithmetic operators for the Fraction class

$$\frac{a}{b}+\frac{c}{d} \rightarrow \frac{a*d+b*c}{b*d} \qquad \frac{a}{b}*\frac{c}{d} \rightarrow \frac{a*c}{b*d}$$

$$\frac{a}{b}-\frac{c}{d} \rightarrow \frac{a*d-b*c}{b*d} \qquad \frac{a}{b}/\frac{c}{d} \rightarrow \frac{a*d}{b*c}$$

```
// Declarations of addition operator
friend const Fraction operator+  (const Fraction& left,
                                  const Fraction& right);
// Definition of addition operator
const Fraction operator+ (const Fraction& left,
                          const Fraction& right)
{
  int newNumer = left.numer * right.denom + right.numer* left.denom;
  int newNumer = left.numer * right.denom + right.numer* left.denom;
  int newDenom = left.denom * right.denom;
  Fraction result (newNumer, newDenom);
  return result;
}
```

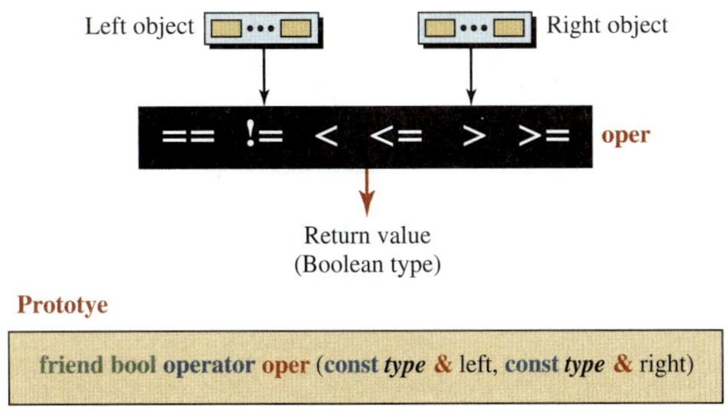

Figure 13.11 Overloading the equality and relational operators

13.4.2 Equality and Relational Operators

We can also overload the two equality (== and !=) and four relational operators (<, <=, >, and >=) using friend functions. The structure of the operator function is the same as the arithmetic operators except that the return value is of type Boolean (*true* or *false*).

Figure 13.11 shows the design. The two operands must already exist. We pass the two parameter functions as constant references. We return a Boolean value, which is automatically constant and can be used only as an *rvalue*.

Table 13.14 shows the code only for the equality operator; the code for the other five operators is similar.

13.4.3 Extraction and Insertion Operators

The value of a fundamental type can be extracted from an input stream object using the extraction operator (>>) or inserted into an output stream using the insertion operator (<<). We can overload these two operators for our class types as shown in Figure 13.12.

Table 13.14 Equality and relational operators for the Fraction class

$\frac{a}{b} == \frac{c}{d} \rightarrow a * d == b * c$	$\frac{a}{b} \mathrel{!=} \frac{c}{d} \rightarrow a * d \mathrel{!=} b * c$
$\frac{a}{b} < \frac{c}{d} \rightarrow a * d < b * c$	$\frac{a}{b} <= \frac{c}{d} \rightarrow a * d <= b * c$
$\frac{a}{b} > \frac{c}{d} \rightarrow a * d > b * c$	$\frac{a}{b} >= \frac{c}{d} \rightarrow a * d >= b * c$

```
// Declaration of equality operator
friend bool operator== (const Fraction& left, const Fraction& right);
// Definition of equality operator
bool operator== (const Fraction& left, const Fraction& right)
{
   return (left.numer * right.denom == right.numer * left.denom) ;
}
```

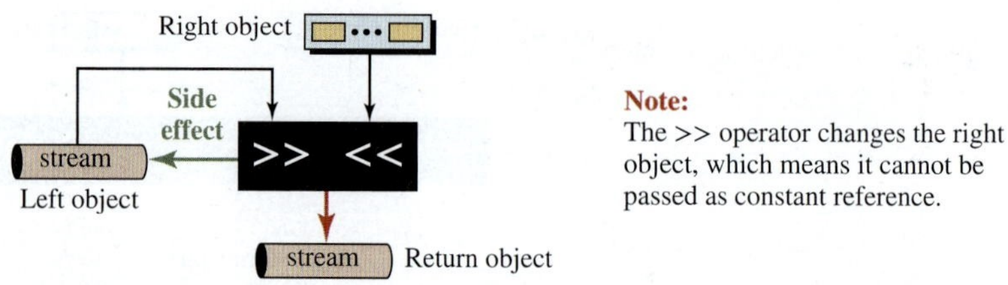

Prototyes

```
friend istream & operator >> (istream & left, type & right)
friend ostream & operator << (ostream & left, const type & right)
```

Figure 13.12 Overloading insertion or extraction operators

Each of these operators is a binary operator, but the left operand is an object of the *istream* class in the case of the extraction operator and the object of the *ostream* class in the case of the insertion operator. In other words, the left operand in both cases is an object of a library class, not the class that we want to overload for these operators. The right operand, on the other hand, is the class object. Note that if we want to use the keyboard as the input stream, the input stream object is *cin*; if we want to use the monitor as the output stream, the output stream object is *cout*. Otherwise, the left parameter should be a file declared as *istream* or *ostream* type.

EXAMPLE 13.9

In this example we create extraction and insertion assignment operators for the *Fraction* class. See Table 13.15.

Table 13.15 Overloaded extraction and insertion operator

```
// Declaration of >> operator
friend istream& operator >> (istream& left, Fraction& right) ;
// Definition of >> operator
istream& operator >> (istream& left, Fraction& right)
{
  cout << "Enter the value of numerator: " ;
  left >> right.numer;
  istream << "Enter the value of denominator: " ;
  left >> right.denom;
  right.normalized( );
  return left ;
}
// Definition of << operator
friend ostream& operator << (ostream& left, const Fraction& right) ;
// Definition of << operator
ostream& operator << (ostream& left, const Fraction& right)
{
  left << right.numer << "/" << right.denom << endl;
  return left;
}
```

13.5 TYPE CONVERSION

When we are working with fundamental data types, we sometimes use mixed types in a an expression and expect the system to make them the same type according to the rules of conversion. For example, in the following expression statement, which finds the perimeter of a circle with radius 5, the system does two conversions from integer 5 to double 5.0 and integer 2 to 2.0 to find the perimeter:

```
double perimeter = 2 * 5 * 3.1415;
```

We can do the same, with some limitation, to change a fundamental type to a user-defined type and vice versa.

13.5.1 Fundamental Type to Class Type

If we need to change a fundamental type to a class type (when it makes sense), we create a new parameter constructor (also referred to as conversion constructor). For example, we can convert an integer to a fraction and we can convert a real number to a fraction. In both cases, we create a constructor with one parameter.

Converting an Integer to a Fraction

This can be done easily using a constructor that takes one integer parameter that is set as numerator; the denominator is set to 1.

EXAMPLE 13.10

Table 13.16 shows how we can convert an integer to a Fraction object.

We can add a fraction to an integer because the compiler changes the integer 4 to the fraction 4/1 before addition.

```
Fraction fract1 (2, 5);
Fraction fract2 = fract1 + 4
```

Converting a Real Number to a Fraction

We can use a constructor to convert a real number to a fraction. A fraction can be a real number. For example, the fraction $7/4$ is the real number 1.75. This means that we can also convert a real number, such as 1.75, to its corresponding fraction representation. Given the value 1.75, we can rewrite it as 175/100 and then normalize it to get $7/4$.

Table 13.16 Converting an integer value to a fraction

```
// Declaration
Fraction (int n);
// Definition
Fraction :: Fraction (int n)
: numer (n), denom (1)
{
}
```

Table 13.17 Converting a real value to a fraction

```
// Declaration
Fraction (double value);
// Definition
Fraction :: Fraction (double value)
{
  denom = 1;
  while ((value - static_cast <int> (value)) > 0.0)
  {
      value *= 10.0;
      denom *= 10;
  }
  numer = static_cast <int> (value);
  normalize ();
}
```

Table 13.18 Converting class type to fundamental type

```
// Declaration
operator double ();
// Definition
Fraction :: operator double ()
{
  double num = static_cast <double> (numer);
  return (num / denom);
}
```

Table 13.17 shows how this is done. The constructor accepts the a real number (*value*) that becomes the numerator. We set the denominator to 1 and continuously multiply the real value and the denominator until the fraction part of the value disappears. The numerator is then the integer cast of the value. A fraction object is made after normalizing the numerator and the denominator.

13.5.2 Class Type to Fundamental Type

Sometimes we need to convert a class type into a fundamental type. We can do this using a *conversion operator*, an operator function in which the term *operator* and the operator symbol are replaced with a fundamental data type, as shown in Table 13.18.

The syntax of the operator looks strange (no return value), but we must think of it as a constructor for the **double** type. It takes a fraction and constructs a double value. We know that a constructor has no return value; it constructs a type.

13.6 DESIGNING CLASSES

In this section we create four classes to show the importance of overloading operators in some applications. We re-create the *Fraction* class using overloaded operators. We define a *Date* class by overloading appropriate operators. We design and define a *Matrix* class with some simple operators defined for a matrix. We also design and implement a *Polynomial* class that can be used in many areas of computer science.

13.6.1 Fraction Class with Overloaded Operators

We created a *Fraction* class in Chapter 7. In this section we show how we can overload several operators for this class.

Interface File

Program 13.10 shows the interface file.

Program 13.10 File fraction.h

```
/****************************************************************
 * The interface file for the Fraction file                     *
 ****************************************************************/
# ifndef Fraction_H
# define Fraction_H
# include <iostream>
# include <cassert>
# include <iomanip>
# include <cmath>
using namespace std;

// Fraction class definition
class Fraction
{
  private:
      int numer;
      int denom;
      int gcd (int n, int m = 1); // Helper function
      void normalize ();        // Helper function
  public:
      Fraction (int numer, int denom); // Parameter constructor
      Fraction (double value); // Parameter constructor
      Fraction (); // Default constructor
      Fraction (const Fraction& fract); // Copy constructor
      ~Fraction (); // Destructor
      // Member operators
      operator double (); // Conversion
      const Fraction  operator+( ) const;    // Unary plus
      const Fraction  operator-( ) const; // Unary minus
      Fraction& operator++ ( ); // Prefix increment
      Fraction& operator-- ( );   // Prefix decrement
      const Fraction operator++ (int); // Postfix increment
      const Fraction operator-- (int); // Postfix decrement
      Fraction& operator= (const Fraction& right); // Assign
      Fraction& operator+= (const Fraction& right); // Compound Assign
      Fraction& operator-= (const Fraction& right); // Compound Assign
      Fraction& operator*= (const Fraction& right); // Compound Assign
      Fraction& operator/= (const Fraction& right); // Compound Assign
```

(continued)

Program 13.10 File fraction.h (Continued)

```
        // Friend arithmetic operators
        friend const Fraction operator+
              (const Fraction& left, const Fraction& right); //Addition
        friend const Fraction operator-
              (const Fraction& left, const Fraction& right); //Subtraction
        friend const Fraction operator*
              (const Fraction& left, const Fraction& right); //Multiplication
        friend const Fraction operator/
              (const Fraction& left, const Fraction& right); //Divsion
        // Friend relational operators
        friend bool operator==
              (const Fraction& left, const Fraction& right);
        friend bool operator!=
              (const Fraction& left, const Fraction& right);
        friend bool operator<
              (const Fraction& left, const Fraction& right);
        friend bool operator<=
              (const Fraction& left, const Fraction& right);
        friend bool operator>
              (const Fraction& left, const Fraction& right);
        friend bool operator>=
              (const Fraction& left, const Fraction& right);
        // Insertion and extraction operators
        friend istream& operator >> (istream& left, Fraction& right) ;
        friend ostream& operator << (ostream& left, const Fraction& right) ;
};
#endif
```

Implementation File

Program 13.11 shows the implementation file for the *Fraction* class.

Program 13.11 File fraction.cpp

```
/****************************************************************
 * The implementation file for the Fraction class               *
 ****************************************************************/
#include "fraction.h"

// Parameter Constructor
Fraction :: Fraction (int num, int den = 1)
: numer (num), denom (den)
{
```

(*continued*)

Program 13.11 File fraction.cpp (Continued)

```
   normalize ();
}
// Parameter Constructor
Fraction :: Fraction (double value)
{
   denom = 1;
   while ((value - static_cast <int> (value)) > 0.0)
   {
        value *= 10.0;
        denom *= 10;
   }
   numer = static_cast <int> (value);
   normalize ();
}
// Default Constructor
Fraction :: Fraction ( )
: numer (0), denom (1)
{
}
// Copy Constructor
Fraction :: Fraction (const Fraction& fract)
: numer (fract.numer), denom (fract.denom)
{
}
// Destructor
Fraction :: ~Fraction ()
{
}
// Conversion operator
Fraction :: operator double ()
{
   double num = static_cast <double> (numer);
   return (num / denom);
}
// Unary plus operator
const Fraction  Fraction :: operator+ ( ) const
{
   Fraction temp (+numer, denom);
   return temp;
}
// Unary minus operator
const Fraction   Fraction :: operator- ( ) const
{
```

(continued)

Program 13.11 File fraction.cpp (Continued)

```
  Fraction temp (-numer, denom);
  return temp;
}
// Pre-increment operator
Fraction& Fraction :: operator++ ( )
{
  numer = numer + denom;
  this -> normalize ();
  return *this;
}
// Pre-decrement operator
Fraction& Fraction :: operator-- ( )
{
  numer = numer - denom;
  this -> normalize ();
  return *this;
}
// Post-increment operator
const Fraction Fraction :: operator++ (int)
{
  Fraction temp (numer, denom);
  ++(*this);
  return temp;
}
// Post-decrement operator
const Fraction Fraction :: operator-- (int)
{
  Fraction temp (numer, denom);
  --(*this);
  return temp;
}
// Assignment operator
Fraction& Fraction :: operator= (const Fraction& right)
{
  if (*this != right)
  {
      numer = right.numer;
      denom = right.denom;
  }
  return *this;
}
// Compound Assignment operator (+=)
Fraction& Fraction :: operator+= (const Fraction& right)
```

(continued)

Program 13.11 File fraction.cpp (Continued)

```
{
   numer  = numer * right.denom + denom * right.numer;
   denom = denom * right.denom;
   normalize ();
   return *this;
}
// Compound Assignment operator (-=)
Fraction& Fraction :: operator-= (const Fraction& right)
{
   numer = numer * right.denom - denom * right.numer;
   denom = denom * right.denom;
   normalize ();
   return *this;
}
// Compound Assignment operator (*=)
Fraction& Fraction :: operator*= (const Fraction& right)
{
   numer = numer * right.numer;
   denom = denom * right.denom;
   normalize ();
   return *this;
}
// Compound Assignment operator (/=)
Fraction& Fraction :: operator/= (const Fraction& right)
{
   numer = numer * right.denom;
   denom = denom * right.numer;
   normalize ();
   return *this;
}
// Addition operator (friend)
const Fraction operator+ (const Fraction& left, const Fraction& right)
{
   int newNumer = left.numer * right.denom + right.numer * left.denom;
   int newDenom = left.denom * right.denom;
   Fraction result (newNumer, newDenom);
   return result;
}
// Subtraction operator (friend)
const Fraction operator- (const Fraction& left, const Fraction& right)
{
   int newNumer = left.numer * right.denom - right.numer * left.denom;
   int newDenom = left.denom * right.denom;
```

(continued)

Program 13.11 File fraction.cpp (Continued)

```
    Fraction result (newNumer, newDenom);
    return result;
}
// Multiplication operator (friend)
const Fraction operator* (const Fraction& left, const Fraction& right)
{
    int newNumer = left.numer * right.numer;
    int newDenom = left.denom * right.denom;
    Fraction result (newNumer, newDenom);
    return result;
}
// Division operator (friend)
const Fraction operator/ (const Fraction& left, const Fraction& right)
{
    int newNumer = left.numer * right.denom;
    int newDenom = left.denom * right.numer;
    Fraction result (newNumer, newDenom);
    return result;
}
// Equality operator (friend)
bool operator== (const Fraction& left, const Fraction& right)
{
    return (left.numer * right.denom == right.numer * left.denom) ;
}
// Inequality operator (friend)
bool operator!= (const Fraction& left, const Fraction& right)
{
    return (left.numer * right.denom != right.numer * left.denom) ;
}
// Less-than operator (friend)
bool operator< (const Fraction& left, const Fraction& right)
{
    return (left.numer * right.denom < right.numer * left.denom) ;
}
// Less-than or equal operator (friend)
bool operator<= (const Fraction& left, const Fraction& right)
{
    return (left.numer * right.denom <= right.numer * left.denom) ;
}
// Greater-than operator (friend)
bool operator> (const Fraction& left, const Fraction& right)
{
    return (left.numer * right.denom > right.numer * left.denom) ;
}
```

(*continued*)

Program 13.11 File fraction.cpp (Continued)

```
// Greater-than or equal operator (friend)
bool operator>= (const Fraction& left, const Fraction& right)
{
  return (left.numer * right.denom >= right.numer * left.denom) ;
}
// Extraction operator (friend)
istream& operator >> (istream& left, Fraction& right)
{
  cout << "Enter the value of numerator: " ;
  left >> right.numer;
  cout << "Enter the value of denominator: " ;
  left >> right.denom;
  right.normalize( );
  return left ;
}
// Insertion operator (friend)
ostream& operator << (ostream& left, const Fraction& right)
{
  left << right.numer << "/" << right.denom ;
  return left;
}
// Helper function (greatest common divisor)
int Fraction :: gcd (int n, int m)
{
  int gcd = 1;
  for (int k = 1; k <= n && k <= m; k++)
  {
      if (n % k == 0 && m % k == 0)
      {
            gcd = k;
      }
  }
  return gcd;
}
// Helper function (nomalizing a fraction)
void Fraction :: normalize ()
{
  if (denom == 0)
  {
      cout << "Invalid denomination in fraction. Need to quit." << endl;
      assert (false);
  }
  if (denom < 0)
  {
```

(continued)

Program 13.11 File fraction.cpp (Continued)

```
        denom = -denom;
        numer = -numer;
    }
    int divisor = gcd (abs (numer), abs (denom));
    numer = numer / divisor;
    denom = denom / divisor;
}
```

Application File

Program 13.12 shows the application file for testing operations in the *Fraction* class.

Program 13.12 File app.cpp

```
/***************************************************************
 * The interface file date.h defining the class Date           *
 ***************************************************************/
# include "fraction.h"

int main ()
{
  // Creation of two objects and testing the plus and minus operator
  Fraction fract1 (2, 3);
  Fraction fract2 (1, 2);
  cout << "fract1: " << fract1 << endl;
  cout << "fract2: " << fract2 << endl;
  cout << "Result of +fract1: " << +fract1 << endl;
  cout << "Result of -fract2: " << -fract2 << endl << endl;
  // Creation of four objects and testing the ++ and -- operators
  Fraction fract3 (3, 4);
  Fraction fract4 (4, 5);
  Fraction fract5 (5, 6);
  Fraction fract6 (6, 7);
  cout << "fract3: " << fract3 << endl;
  cout << "fract4: " << fract4 << endl;
  cout << "fract5: " << fract5 << endl;
  cout << "fract6: " << fract6 << endl << endl;
  ++fract3;
  --fract4;
  fract5++;
  fract6--;
  cout << "Result of ++fract3: " << fract3 << endl;
  cout << "Result of --fract4: " << fract4 << endl;
  cout << "Result of fract5++: " << fract5 << endl;
  cout << "Result of fract6--: " << fract6 << endl << endl;
```

(continued)

Program 13.12 File app.cpp (Continued)

```
// Testing compound assignment operators
Fraction fract7 (3, 5);
Fraction fract8 (4, 7);
Fraction fract9 (5, 8);
Fraction fract10 (7, 9);
fract3 += 2;
fract4 -= 3;
fract5 *= 4;
fract6 /= 5;
cout << "Result of fract7 += 2: " << fract7 << endl;
cout << "Result of fract8 -= 3: " << fract8 << endl;
cout << "Result of fract9 *= 4: " << fract9 << endl;
cout << "Result of fract10 /= 5: " << fract10 << endl << endl;
// Creation of two new objects and testing friend arithmetic operations
Fraction fract11 (1, 2);
Fraction fract12 (3, 4);
cout << "fract11: " << fract11 << endl;
cout << "fract12: " << fract12 << endl;
cout << "fract11 + fract12 : " << fract11 + fract12 << endl;
cout << "fract11 - fract12 : " << fract11 - fract12 << endl;
cout << "fract11 * fract12 : " << fract11 * fract12 << endl;
cout << "fract11 / fract12 : " << fract11 / fract12 << endl << endl;
// Creation of two new objects and testing relational operators
Fraction fract13 (2, 3);
Fraction fract14 (1, 3);
cout << "fract13: " << fract13 << endl;
cout << "fract14: " << fract14 << endl;
cout << "fract13 == fract14: " << boolalpha;
cout << (fract13 == fract14) << endl;
cout << "fract13 != fract14: " << boolalpha;
cout << (fract13 != fract14) << endl;
cout << "fract13 > fract14: " << boolalpha;
cout << (fract13 > fract14) << endl;
cout << "fract13 < fract14: " << boolalpha;
cout << (fract13 < fract14) << endl << endl;
// Using convertor constructor to create two new objects
Fraction fract15 (5); // Changing an integer to a fraction
Fraction fract16 (23.45); // Changing a double value to a fraction
cout << "fract15: " << fract15 << endl;
cout << "fract16: " << fract16 << endl << endl;
// Changing a fraction to a double
Fraction fract17 (9, 13);
cout << "double value of fract17 (9, 13): ";
cout << setprecision (2) << fract17.operator double () << endl << endl;
```

(continued)

Program 13.12 File app.cpp (Continued)

```
    // Testing extraction operator
    Fraction fract18;
    cin >> fract18;
    cout << "fract18: " << fract18 << endl;
    return 0;
}
```

```
Run:
fract1: 2/3
fract2: 1/2
Result of +fract1: 2/3
Result of -fract2: -1/2

fract3: 3/4
fract4: 4/5
fract5: 5/6
fract6: 6/7

Result of ++fract3: 7/4
Result of --fract4: -1/5
Result of fract5++: 11/6
Result of fract6--: -1/7

Result of fract7+= 2: 13/5
Result of fract8 -= 3: -17/7
Result of fract9 *= 4: 5/2
Result of fract10 /= 5: 7/45

fract11: 1/2
fract12: 3/4
fract11 + fract12 : 5/4
fract11 - fract12 : -1/4
fract11 * fract12 : 3/8
fract11 /  fract12 : 2/3

fract13: 2/3
fract14: 1/3
fract3 == fract14: false
fract13 != fract14: true
fract13 >  fract14: true
fract13 <  fract14: false

fract15: 5/1
fract16: 469/20
```

(*continued*)

Program 13.12 File app.cpp (Continued)

```
double value of fract17 (9, 13): 0.69

Enter the value of numerator: 6
Enter the value of denominator: 7
Fract18 : 6/7
```

13.6.2 Date Class

We create a new class, *Date*, that represents a date as the combination of three integers: *month*, *day*, and *year* (such as 2/5/2016). Although there is a library class that can be used to find the date and time in C++, it is used to define the current date and time. We want a type that shows a date in the past or the future.

A date defines the number of days passed from an origin day, which varies from one calendar to another. In our culture, it is based on the first day of Gregorian calendar, 1/1/1. However, instead of giving the count of days (which is a number close to 800,000), a date is defined in terms of month, day, and year to make the values smaller. Since the number of days in each month is not fixed and we have leap years with 366 days instead of 365 days, the calculation of dates is complicated.

Strategies

To overcome these complications, we have used several strategies in designing this class.

a. We have set the origin of the calendar to 1/1/1900 instead of 1/1/1 because of the changes made to the calendar in the 16th century to fix leap years.

b. To follow a principle of object-oriented programming—that data members stored in an object must be independent of each other with no redundant data members that can be calculated from other data members—we store only *month*, *day*, and *year*. Although we need the total days passed from the origin to calculate dates and also to find the week day, we can use member functions to calculate the extra information.

c. To determine the day of the week for a date, we use a function called *findTotalDays*() to calculate the total number of days from the origin date. We know that the first day of January in 1900 was Monday.

d. We use the increment and decrement operators to go to the next day or previous day. However, since this may change the month or year of the date, we use two functions, called *plusReset*() and *minusReset*(), to adjust the new date when necessary.

e. To find a new date when we add or subtract days, we use compound assignment operators, but to make the adjustment easier, we define the function in terms of increment or decrement. In other words, instead of adding 20 days to a date, we increment the date 20 times.

f. To find the number of days elapsed between the two days, we apply the function *findTotalDays*() on each date and then subtract.

Invariants

Class invariants are the first thing we must consider, as we discussed Chapter 7. The invariants that we need to worry about for date objects are as follows:

a. The *month* should be between 1 and 12 (January to December).

b. The *day* in each month should be between 1 and the days in the month (28, 30, 31) and between 1 and 29 if the month is February and the year is a leap year.

c. The *year* should be greater than or equal to the starting year (the year that we set as the origin of our data calendar).

Files

We create separate interface, implementation, and application files.

Interface File We create the interface file, *date.h*, as shown in Program 13.13.

Program 13.13 File date.h

```
/***************************************************************
 * The interface file date.h defining the class Date           *
 ***************************************************************/
#ifndef DATE_H
#define DATE_H
#include <iostream>
#include <cmath>
#include <cassert>
#include <string>
using namespace std;

class Date
{
  private:
       // Instance Data Members
       int month;
       int day;
       int year;
       // Static Data Members and member functions
       static const int startWeekDay;
       static const int startYear;
       static const int daysInMonths [ ];
       static const string daysOfWeek [ ];
       static const string monthsOfYear [ ];
       static bool isLeap (int year);
       // Private helper function
       bool isValid () const;
       string findWeekDay ( );
       int findTotalDays( ) const;
       void plusReset ( );
       void minusReset ( );
  public:
       // Constructors and destructor
       Date (int month, int day, int year);
       Date ( );
       ~Date ( );
       // Member operator functions
       Date& operator++( );
       Date& operator--( );
```

(continued)

Program 13.13 File date.h (Continued)

```
        Date operator++ (int);
        Date operator--(int);
        Date& operator+= (int days);
        Date& operator-= (int days);
        bool operator== (const Date& right ) const;
        bool operator!= (const Date& right ) const;
        Date& operator= (const Date& right );
        // Friend operator functions
        friend int operator- (const Date& date1, const Date& date2);
        friend ostream& operator<< (ostream& output , const Date& date);
};
#endif
```

Implementation File We give the implementation file for all member functions defined in the interface file. We also initialize the static data members declared in the interface file. Program 13.14 shows the implementation file.

Program 13.14 File date.cpp

```
/*****************************************************************
 * The implementation file date.cpp defining the instance        *
 * member functions and helper functions for the Date class      *
 *****************************************************************/
#include "date.h"

// Parameter constructor
Date :: Date (int m, int d, int y )
: month (m), day (d), year (y)
{
    if (!isValid ())
    {
        cout << "Date is not valid; program terminates!" << endl;
        assert (false);
    }
}
// Default constructor
Date :: Date ()
: month (1), day(1), year(1900)
{
}
// Destructor
Date :: ~Date ()
{
}
```

(continued)

Program 13.14 File date.cpp (Continued)

```
// Pre-increment operator
Date& Date :: operator++()
{
  day++;
  plusReset ();
  return *this;
}
// Pre-decrement operator
Date& Date :: operator--( )
{
  day--;
  minusReset ();
  return *this;
}
// Post-increment operator
Date Date :: operator++ (int)
{
  Date temp (month, day, year);
  ++(*this);
  return temp;
}
// Post-decrement operator
Date Date :: operator--(int)
{
  Date temp (month, day, year);
  --(*this);
  return temp;
}
// Compound addition operator
Date& Date :: operator+= (int days)
{
  for (int i = 1; i <= days; i++)
  {
      ++(*this);
  }
  return *this;
}
// Compound subtraction operator
Date& Date :: operator-= (int days)
{
  for (int i = days; i >= 1; i--)
  {
      --(*this);
  }
```

(continued)

Program 13.14 File date.cpp (Continued)

```
   return *this;
}
//Operator ==
bool Date :: operator== (const Date& right ) const
{
   bool fact1 = (month == right.month);
   bool fact2 = (day == right.day);
   bool fact3 = (year == right.year);
   return (fact1 && fact2 && fact3);
}
// Operator !=
bool Date :: operator!= (const Date& right ) const
{
   return !(*this == right);
}
// Assignment operator
Date& Date :: operator= (const Date& right )
{
   if (*this != right)       // Check for self-assignment
   {
        month = right.month;
        day = right.day;
        year = right.year;
   }
   return *this;
}
// Subtraction operator (friend function)
int operator-(const Date& date1, const Date& date2)
{
   return (date1.findTotalDays() - date2.findTotalDays());
}
// Output operator (friend function)
ostream& operator<< (ostream& output , const Date& date)
{
   cout << Date :: daysOfWeek [(date.findTotalDays()
                                 + Date :: startWeekDay)% 7] << "  ";
   cout << Date :: monthsOfYear [date.month] << " ";
   cout << date.day << " ";
   cout << date.year << endl;
}
// Private function for validation
bool Date :: isValid () const
{
   bool validMonth = (month >= 1) && (month <=12);
```

(*continued*)

Program 13.14 File date.cpp (Continued)

```
    bool validYear = (year >= startYear);
    bool validDay = (day >= 1) && (day <= (Date:: daysInMonths[month]
                              + (isLeap (year) && month == 2)));
    return (validMonth && validYear && validDay);
}
// Private function for resetting after increment
void Date :: plusReset ()
{
    bool extraDay = (isLeap (year) && month == 2);
    if (day > daysInMonths[month] + extraDay)
    {
        day = 1;
        month++;
    }
    if (month > 12)
    {
        month = 1;
        year++;
    }
}
// Private function for resetting after decrement
void Date :: minusReset ()
{
    if (day < 1)
    {
        month--;
        if (month < 1)
        {
            month = 12;
            year--;
        }
        bool extraDay = isLeap (year) && (month == 2);
        day = daysInMonths[month] + extraDay ;
    }
}
// Private function to find total days
int Date :: findTotalDays() const
{
    int totalDays = 0;
    int currentYear = startYear;
    while (year > currentYear)
    {
        totalDays += 365 + isLeap(currentYear);
        currentYear++;
```

(continued)

Program 13.14 File date.cpp (Continued)

```
    }
    int currentMonth = 1;
    while (month > currentMonth)
    {
        totalDays += daysInMonths [currentMonth];
        if (currentMonth == 2)
        {
                totalDays += isLeap(year);
        }
        currentMonth++;
    }
    totalDays += day - 1;
    return totalDays;
}
// Initialization of static data members
const int Date :: startWeekDay = 1;
const int Date :: startYear = 1900;
const int Date :: daysInMonths [ ] = {0, 31, 28, 31, 30, 31,
                                     30, 31, 31, 30, 31, 30, 31};
const string Date :: daysOfWeek [ ] = {"Sun", "Mon", "Tue", "Wed",
                                       "Thr", "Fri", "Sat"};
const string Date :: monthsOfYear [ ] = {"", "Jan", "Feb", "Mar", "Apr",
                    "May", "Jun", "Jul", "Aug", "Sep", "Oct", "Nov", "Dec"};
// Definition of static member function
bool Date :: isLeap (int year)
{
    return (year % 400 == 00) || ((year % 4 == 0)&& (year % 100 != 0));
}
```

Application File The application file must create objects of the *Date* type and manipulate them. Users need to see the public interface so they can include it in their programs; they also need the compiled version of the implementation file so they can create their own version of the application file. Program 13.15 is a sample.

Program 13.15 File app.cpp

```
/**********************************************************************
 * The application file date.cpp uses the Date objects.               *
 **********************************************************************/
#include "date.h"

int main ( )
{
```

(continued)

Program 13.15 File app.cpp (Continued)

```
   // Create two dates and print them
   Date date1 (2, 8, 2014);
   Date date2 (10, 15, 1944);
   cout << "date1: " << date1;
   cout << "date2: " << date2;
   // Create two more dates, increment them, and print them
   Date date3 = date1;
   Date date4 = date2;
   date3++;
   date4++;
   cout << "date3: " << date3;
   cout << "date4: " << date4;
   // Add and subtract days to and from the previous dates
   date3 += 20;
   date4 -= 130;
   cout << "date3 after change: " << date3;
   cout << "date4 after change: " << date4;
   // Find the difference and print the number of days
   cout <<"Difference between date3 and date4: "
                                   << date3 - date4 << " days.";
   return 0;
}
```

```
Run:
date1: Sat  Feb 8 2014
date2: Sun  Oct 15 1944
date3: Sun  Feb 9 2014
date4: Mon  Oct 16 1944
date3 after change: Sat  Mar 1 2014
date4 after change: Thr  Jun 8 1944
Difference between date3 and date4: 25468 days.
```

13.6.3 Polynomials

Polynomials are one of the basic mathematical structures that we encounter in many different areas of computer science, such as networking and network security. A polynomial with one variable can be defined as shown below, in which the *n*'s are the exponents and the *a*'s are the coefficients of terms.

$$a_nx^n + a_{n-1}x^{n-1} + \ldots + a_2x^2 + a_1x + a_0$$

Representation

To perform mathematical operations on polynomials, we use two values for each term. For example, the term $3.0x^5$ has 3.0 as the coefficient and 5 as the exponent. The largest exponent is called the *degree* of the polynomial. In our implementation, we assume that the coefficient is of type *double* and the exponent is of type *unsigned int*. With these assumptions, we can store a polynomial in a computer in at least three ways.

In the first approach, we can define an array of any size to handle the largest degree of a polynomial and let the exponents be the index of the array and each coefficient the corresponding value. This approach is not very efficient. If we have multiple polynomials and they have different degrees, we create the same large array for each.

In the second approach, which is very efficient, we use a *struct* with two data members: coefficient and degree. We store only those terms in which the coefficient is not 0.0. This implementation can be done using a linked list (discussed in Chapter 18) in which each term is linked to the next through a pointer.

The third approach, which we use in this chapter, is more efficient than the first but less efficient than the second. It can be implemented as an array in which the array size is the degree plus 1 of the correspond polynomial. For example, if we want to multiply a polynomial of degree 3 by one of degree 5, we create three arrays of sizes 4, 6, and 16 instead of three arrays of size 16 (the first case). The index of the array defines the exponent. We may still have some terms with coefficient zeros, but each object has its own size. Figure 13.13 shows the heap memory at the left side of the stack to let the term with the highest exponent be at the left side and the term with the lowest exponent be at the right side. Note that the degree of the polynomial is 5; size of the array is 6 because the degree goes from 0 to 5.

Operations

We define five operations for our polynomial class as defined in mathematics: addition, subtraction, multiplication, division, and remainder. Assume we have the following two polynomials (Poly1 and Poly2):

```
Poly1 = +4.00x^5 +2.00x^3 +5.00x^2 +1.00x^1 +4.00
poly2 = +2.00x^2 + 6.00
```

Mathematics defines five operations on these polynomials as shown below:

```
Poly1 + poly2 = +4.00x^5 +2.00x^3 +7.00x^2 +1.00x^1 +10.00
poly1 - poly2 = +4.00x^5 +2.00x^3 +3.00x^2 +1.00x^1 -2.00
poly1 * poly2 = +8.00x^7 +28.00x^5 +10.00x^4 +14.00x^3 +38.00x^2 +6.00x^1 +24.00
poly1 / poly2 = +2.00x^3 -5.00x^1 +2.50
poly1 % poly2 = +31.00x^1 -11.00
```

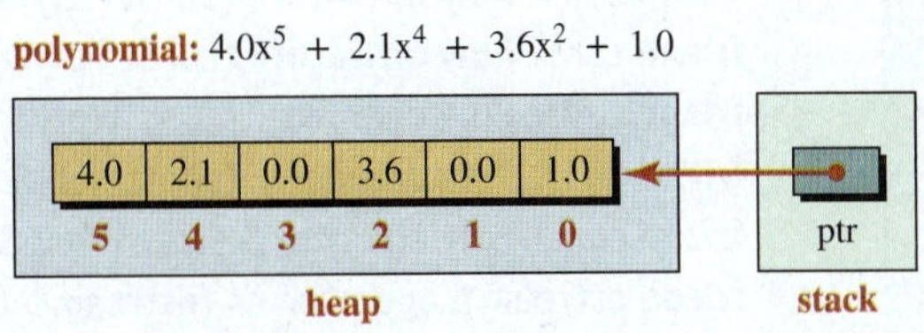

Figure 13.13 Representation of a polynomial with degree 5

Polynomial Class

We define a *Polynomial* class based on the preceding discussion.

Interface File Program 13.16 shows the interface file for the *Poly* class. We define three constructors (the third is a one-term constructor used in division), a destructor, a copy constructor, and an assignment operator. We overload the addition, subtraction, multiplication, division, and quotient operators for this class. We also overload the extraction operator. We use one member function that allows us to enter the coefficient of a constructed polynomial. The *max* function is used to find the maximum degree of two polynomials.

Program 13.16 File poly.h

```
/***************************************************************
 * The interface file for the Poly class                       *
 ***************************************************************/
#ifndef POLY_H
#define POLY_H
#include <iostream>
#include <string>
#include <cassert>
#include <iomanip>
using namespace std;

// Definition for the Poly class
class Poly
{
  private:
       int degree;
       double* ptr;
  public:
       Poly ();
       Poly (int degree);
       Poly (int degree, double coef); // One-term polynomial
       ~Poly ();
       Poly (const Poly& origin);
       Poly& operator= (const Poly& right );
       void fill ();
       int max (int x, int y);
       friend const Poly operator+ (const Poly& left, const Poly& right);
       friend const Poly operator- (const Poly& left, const Poly& right);
       friend const Poly operator* (const Poly& left, const Poly& right);
       friend const Poly operator/ (const Poly& left, const Poly& right);
       friend const Poly operator% (const Poly& left, const Poly& right);
       friend ostream& operator << (ostream& left, const Poly& poly);
};
#endif
```

Implementation Program 13.17 shows the implementation for functions declared in the *Poly* class.

Program 13.17 File poly.cpp

```
/*****************************************************************
 * The implementation file for the Poly class                    *
 *****************************************************************/
#include "poly.h"

// Default constructor
Poly :: Poly ()
:degree (0)
{
   ptr = 0;
}
// Parameter constructor
Poly :: Poly (int deg)
:degree (deg)
{
   ptr = new double [degree + 1];
   for (int i = degree; i >=0 ; i--)
   {
        ptr [i] = 0.0;
   }
}
// A constructor that creates an object of one term
Poly :: Poly (int deg, double coef)
:degree (deg)
{
   ptr = new double [degree + 1];
   for (int i = degree; i >=0 ; i--)
   {
        ptr [i] = 0.0;
   }
   ptr [degree] = coef;
}
// Destructor
Poly :: ~Poly ()
{
   delete [ ] ptr;
}
// Copy constructor
Poly :: Poly (const Poly& origin)
{
   ptr = new double [degree + 1];
```

(*continued*)

Program 13.17 File poly.cpp (Continued)

```
    for (int i = origin.degree ; i >= 0 ; i--)
    {
        ptr [i] = origin.ptr [i];
    }
}
// Assignment operator
Poly& Poly :: operator= (const Poly& right )
{
    this -> degree = right.degree;
    this -> ptr = new double [degree + 1];
    for (int i = right.degree; i >= 0; i--)
    {
        (this -> ptr) [i] = right.ptr [i];
    }
    return *this;
}
// Addition operator
const Poly operator+ (const Poly& left, const Poly& right)
{
    Poly result (max (left.degree , right.degree));
    for (int i = result.degree; i >= 0; i--)
    {
        if (i <= left.degree && i <= right.degree)
        {
                result.ptr [i] = left.ptr [i] + right.ptr[i];
        }
        else if (i <= left.degree && i > right.degree)
        {
                result.ptr [i] = left.ptr [i];
        }
        else
        {
                result.ptr [i] = right.ptr [i];
        }
    }
    return result;
}
// Subtraction operator
const Poly operator- (const Poly& left, const Poly& right)
{
    Poly result (max (left.degree , right.degree));
    for (int i = result.degree; i >= 0; i--)
    {
        if (i <= left.degree && i <= right.degree)
```

(*continued*)

Program 13.17 File poly.cpp (Continued)

```
        {
            result.ptr [i] = left.ptr [i] - right.ptr[i];
        }
        else if (i <= left.degree && i > right.degree)
        {
            result.ptr [i] = left.ptr [i];
        }
        else
        {
            result.ptr [i] = -right.ptr [i];
        }
    }
    return result;
}
// Multiplication operator
const Poly operator* (const Poly& left, const Poly& right)
{
    int degree = left.degree + right.degree;
    Poly result (degree);
    for (int i = result.degree ; i >= 0; i--)
    {
        result.ptr [i] = 0;
    }
    for (int i = left.degree; i >= 0; i--)
    {
        for (int j = right.degree; j >= 0; j--)
        {
            result.ptr [i + j] += (left.ptr [i] * right.ptr [j]);
        }
    }
    return result;
}
// Quotient operator
const Poly operator/ (const Poly& left, const Poly& right)
{
    Poly result (left.degree – right.degree);
    Poly temp (left.degree);
    temp = left;
    int i = temp.degree;
    int j = right.degree;
    int k = i – j;
    while (i >= j)
    {
        double coef = temp.ptr [i] / right.ptr [j];
```

(continued)

Program 13.17 File poly.cpp (Continued)

```
            Poly poly (k , coef);
            temp = temp - ( poly * right);
            result = result + poly;
            i--;
            k = i - j;
      }
      return result;
}
// Remainder operator
const Poly operator% (const Poly& left, const Poly& right)
{
      Poly result (left.degree - right.degree - 1);
      Poly temp (left.degree);
      temp = left;
      result = temp - (temp /right) * right;
      return result;
}
// The << operator
ostream& operator<< (ostream& output, const Poly& poly)
{
      string sign;
      for (int i = poly.degree; i >= 0 ; i--)
      {
            if (poly.ptr[i] > 0.0 || poly.ptr[i] < 0.0)
            {
                  cout << fixed << showpos << setprecision (2);
                  cout << poly.ptr[i];
                  cout << noshowpos;
                  if (i != 0)
                  {
                        cout << "x^";
                        cout << i;
                  }
                  cout << " " ;
            }
      }
      cout << endl;
      return output;
}
// Helper function
int max (int x, int y)
{
      if (x >= y)
      {
```

(continued)

Program 13.17 File poly.cpp (Continued)

```
            return x;
    }
    return y;
}
// A function to fill the coefficient of a polynomial
void Poly :: fill ()
{
    for (int i = degree; i >= 0 ; i--)
    {
        cout << "Enter coefficient for exponent " << i << ": " ;
        cin >> ptr[i];
    }
    cout << endl;
}
```

Application Program 13.18 shows an application for testing the operations we defined for polynomials.

Program 13.18 File app.cpp

```
/***************************************************************
 * The application file to test the Poly class                 *
 ***************************************************************/
#include "poly.h"

int main ()
{
    // Constructing and filling two polynomials
    Poly poly1 (5);
    poly1.fill ();
    Poly poly2 (2);
    poly2.fill ();
    // Printing the value of the two polynomials
    cout << "Printing the first two polynomials: " << endl;
    cout << "Poly1 : " << poly1 << endl;
    cout << "Poly2 : " << poly2 << endl;
    // Applying five operations to the two created polynomials
    Poly poly3 = poly1 + poly2;
    Poly poly4 = poly1 - poly2;
    Poly poly5 = poly1 * poly2;
    Poly poly6 = poly1 / poly2;
    Poly poly7 = poly1 % poly2;
    // Printing the result of operations
```

(continued)

Program 13.18 File app.cpp

```
    cout << "Printing the results of operations: " << endl;
    cout << "Poly1 + Poly2: " << poly3 << endl;
    cout << "Poly1 - Poly2: " << poly4 << endl
    cout << "Poly1 * Poly2: " << poly5 << endl;
    cout << "Poly1 / Poly2: " << poly6 << endl;
    cout << "Poly1 % Poly2: " << poly7 << endl;
    return 0;
}
```

```
Run:
Enter coefficient for degree 5: 4
Enter coefficient for degree 4: 0
Enter coefficient for degree 3: 2
Enter coefficient for degree 2: 5
Enter coefficient for degree 1: 1
Enter coefficient for degree 0: 4

Enter coefficient for degree 2: 2
Enter coefficient for degree 1: 0
Enter coefficient for degree 0: 6

Printing the first two polynomials:
Poly1 : +4.00x^5 +2.00x^3 +5.00x^2 +1.00x^1 +4.00
Poly2 : +2.00x^2 +6.00

Printing the result of operations:
Poly1 + Poly2: +4.00x^5 +2.00x^3 +7.00x^2 +1.00x^1 +10.00
Poly1 - Poly2: +4.00x^5 +2.00x^3 +3.00x^2 +1.00x^1 -2.00
Poly1 * Poly2: +8.00x^7 +28.00x^5 +10.00x^4 +14.00x^3 +38.00x^2 +6.00x^1 +24.00
Poly1 / Poly2: +2.00x^3 -5.00x^1 +2.50
Poly1 % Poly2: +31.00x^1 -11.00
```

Note that multiplying the quotient (Poly1 / Poly2) by divisor (Poly2) and adding the result to remainder (Poly1 % Poly2) should give us the dividend (Poly1).

Key Terms

friend function
function call operator
host object
operator function
operator overloading
parameter object
pass-by-pointer
pass-by-reference
pass-by-value
return-by-pointer
return-by-reference
return-by-value
smart pointer
this pointer

Summary

Objects of user-defined types can play three different roles in a function: *host object*, *parameter object*, and *returned object*. A non-static member function needs to be called through an instance of the class, which is named the *host* object. A parameter object can be passed to the member function using pass-by-value, pass-by-reference, or pass-by-pointer. A member function can also return an object.

We can divide the operators in C++ into three categories: non-overloadable, not recommended for overloading, and overloadable. We need be aware that we cannot change the precedence, the associativity, the commutativity, and the arity of the operator to be overloaded. We also need to know that we cannot create new operator symbols or combine the symbols of existing operators to create a new one. To overload an operator for a user-defined data type, we need to write a function named *operator function*, a function that acts as an operator.

We showed how to overload some operators as a member function. To overload an operator as a non-member function, we have two choices: overloading as a global function or as a friend function. We used the second option. A friend function is a function that is granted friendship from a class; it can access the private data members of the class.

Problems

PR-1. Given that *Fun* is the name of a class, identify any errors in the following prototype unary operator function:

```
Fun operator+ ( );
```

PR-2. Given that *Fun* is the name of a class, identify any errors in the following prototype unary function:

```
Fun operator? (int x, int y, int z)
```

PR-3. Given that *Fun* is the name of a class, identify any errors in the following prototype binary operator function:

```
void operator+ (const Fun& fun, const Fun& fun);
```

PR-4. Given that *Fun* is the name of a class, identify any errors in the following operator overloading prototype:

```
double operator [ ] (int x, int y);
```

PR-5. Given that *Fun* is the name of a class, identify any errors in the following operator overloading prototype:

```
void operator( ) (int x, int y);
```

PR-6. Given that *Fun* is the name of a class, what is the difference between the prototypes of two overloaded operators shown below? Can they both be present in the *Fun* class?

```
Fun operator += (const Fun& fun);
Fun operator += (int x);
```

PR-7. Assume that *fun*1, *fun*2 are objects defined in class *Fun*. Write the operator function declaration for the following operations.

a. fun1 += fun2
b. fun2 = fun1
c. fun1++
d. fun1 (a)

PR-8. Write a function that overloads the compound addition operator (+=) for the following class.

```
class Sample
{
    private:
        int value;
    public:
        Sample (int value);
        ~Sample();
        ...
}
```

PR-9. Write the declarations for the interface file in the class Matrix (Program 13.16) to overload the +=, −=, *= operators. The first operator adds a given integer to each element. The second operator subtracts the given integer from each element. The third operator multiplies each element by the given integer.

PR-10. Give the extra code for the implementation file in the class Matrix (Program 13.17) to add the operators defined in PR-9.

PR-11. Write the code for the application file in the class Matrix (Program 13.18) to add the operators defined in PR-10.

Programs

PRG-1. Create a class named *Time* that defines a point in time in terms of hours, minutes, and seconds and specifies AM or PM. Hours can be between 1 and 12, minutes can be between 1 and 59, and seconds can also be between 1 and 59. Also define an integer that can be 0 or 1 to represent AM or PM. Create a default constructor that sets the time to midnight. Overload the prefix ++ to add one second to the time (representing each tick of the clock). Overload the *operator*() to find the duration of time from midnight in seconds. Overload the operator += to add a duration of times (in seconds) to get a new point of time.

PRG-2. Design a *Complex* class representing complex numbers. A complex number in mathematics is defined as $x + iy$ where x defines the real part of the number and y is the imaginary part. The letter i represents the square root of −1 (which means i^2 is −1). Include operator functions to overload the operators +=, −=, *=, /= and the << operator for the class. Note that the following relationships exist between two complex numbers:

$$(x_1 + iy_1) + (x_2 + iy_2) = (x_1 + x_2) + i(y_1 + y_2)$$
$$(x_1 + iy_1) - (x_2 + iy_2) = (x_1 - x_2) + i(y_1 - y_2)$$
$$(x_1 + iy_1) * (x_2 + iy_2) = (x_1x_2 - y_1y_2) + i(x_1y_2 + x_2y_1)$$
$$(x_1 + iy_1) / (x_2 + iy_2) = ((x_1x_2 + y_1y_2) + i(-x_1y_2 + x_2y_1)) / \text{denominator}$$
$$\text{denominator} = x_2^2 + y_2^2$$

PRG-3. Redesign the Complex class (see PRG-2), but overload only the operators +, −, *, /, and << for the class.

PRG-4. Declare and define a class Set representing a set of integers. A set is a collection of data without repetition or ordering. The class should have only private data members: a pointer to a dynamically allocated array of integers and an integer that holds the size of the set. The following shows the operators to be defined for a set.

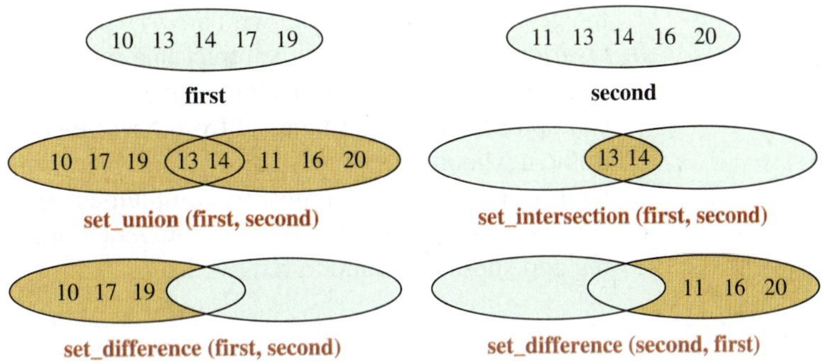

Your solution must include an interface file, an implementation file, and an application file. It should have the following methods:

a. A constructor to create an empty set.
b. A destructor.
c. A function to add an element to the set (overload the += operator).
d. A function to remove an element from the set (overload the −= operator).
e. A binary friend function to get the intersection of two sets (overload the * operator).
f. A binary friend function to get the union of two sets (overload the + operator).
g. A binary friend function to determine the difference of two sets (overload the – operator).
h. A function to print the contents of a set.

PRG-5. Create a class *Money* that represents a money valuer (combination of dollars and cents). Overload the binary plus operator to add two money values to get a new one. Overload the binary minus operator to subtract a money value from a larger value to get a new one. Also overload the *= operator to multiply a money value by an integer and /= operator to divide a money value by an integer.

PRG-6. Redesign the *Money* class by overloading only the relational operators (<, >, ==, and !=) to compare the two Money objects.

PRG-7. In Chapter 9 we designed a class *Pascal* to define the value of all terms for a given *n*. Another approach is to overload the function call operator to find the coefficient of any term. For example, the coefficient of x^5y^3 can be found using the call to *operator*() (5, 3). Use the fact that the coefficient of a term can be found as shown below:

```
coefficient of x^i y^j = factorial (i + j) / (factorial (i) * factorial (j))
```

PRG-8. Design a *BigInteger* class that handles integers of arbitrary sizes given as a string of digits such as "345672134579098765". Use the following guide lines:

a. Use the *popBack* and *pushFront* functions we defined for strings in Chapter 10 to extract the rightmost digit of a big integer or to insert a digit at the left of an integer.
b. Overload the << operator to print a big integer.
c. Overload the + operator to add two big integers. Note that when we add two digits in mathematics, we may have a *carry* (digit 1). For example, adding integers 7 and 8 results in 5 with a *carry* to be added to the next column.
d. Overload the − operator to subtract one integer from another. Note that when we subtract one digit from another one, we may have a *borrow* (digit 1). For example, subtracting integers 7 from 5 results in 8 with a borrow to be used in the next column. Note that if the first integer is smaller than the second, the result of subtraction must be complemented to give a negative integer.
e. It is easier to add leading zeros to integers to make their size the same in adding and subtracting and to remove leading zeros when printing the result.

In this chapter we concentrate on *exception handling*, which is the C++ terminology for error handling. We define the concept and then show how it can be implemented using classes. We also discuss library exceptional classes, which can be used in our programs.

Objectives

After you have read and studied this chapter, you should be able to:

- Discuss traditional approaches to error handling.
- Discuss exception handling in a function using three different patterns that use *try-catch* block and *throw* statements.
- Discuss exception specifications to define what type of an exception a function can throw, including any exception, predefined exceptions, and no exception.
- Discuss the process of stack unwinding and its effect on catching exceptions.
- Discuss exceptions in classes and how exceptions should be handled in constructors using a version of *try-catch* block called *function-try* block.
- Emphasize that we should avoid exceptions in destructors because they undermine the process of stack unwinding.
- Discuss the general layout and format of standard exception classes in C++, and discuss their public interfaces and their purposes.
- Show how we can create our own exception classes that are inherited from the standard exception classes.

14.1 INTRODUCTION

When we write source code, we expect that there could be some errors during the compilation. Many new programmers, however, think that if a program compiles successfully, everything is fine. Experienced programmers, on the other hand, are not happy until they test each program with a predetermined set of test data. Even when a complete scheduled testing phase is used, an occasional error can occur when the program is run. An error like this is referred to as an exception because it is rare. The subject of this chapter is how to handle these exceptions.

14.1.1 Traditional Approaches to Error Handling

Run-time errors are problematic. If there are no syntactical errors, the program will be compiled, but a run-time error occurs that prevents the continuation of the program with the result that the program must be aborted. There are several approaches that are often used to deal with run-time errors. We discuss four here.

Let Run-Time Environment Abort the Program

The first approach is to do nothing and let the program terminate when there is an exception.

EXAMPLE 14.1

In this example we write a simple program that takes two integers from the user, divides the first by the second, and prints the result. The program repeats the calculations up to five times, as shown in Program 14.1.

The program compiles with no errors because there are no compile-time errors. When we run the program, the loop is supposed to repeat five times, taking five pairs of integers, dividing the first by the second, and printing the result. Everything goes well with the first and second iterations, but in the third iteration, the program aborted (without an error message) because we entered 0 for the second integer and the C++ run-time system does not allow division by 0. The loop is prematurely terminated and the program is aborted.

Program 14.1 Dividing two integers

```
/***************************************************************
 * The program shows how division by zero aborts the program.   *
 ***************************************************************/
#include <iostream>
using namespace std;

int main ()
{
   int num1, num2, result;
   for (int i = 0; i < 5; i++)
   {
        cout << "Enter an integer: ";
        cin >> num1;
        cout << "Enter another integer: ";
        cin >> num2;
        result = num1 / num2;  // The statement that may create exception.
        cout << "The result of division is: " << result << endl;
   }
   return 0;
}
```

```
Run:
Enter an integer: 12
Enter another integer: 5
The result of division is: 2
Enter an integer: 10
Enter another integer: 3
The result of division is: 3
Enter an integer: 6
Enter another integer: 0
```

Ask Run-Time Environment to Abort the Program

A second approach is to test for possible errors. The advantage of this approach is that a message can be printed to explain what caused the program to abort.

EXAMPLE 14.2

In this example we repeat the previous program but check the value of the divisor in each iteration and abort the program with a message if the divisor is zero (Program 14.2).

Program 14.2 Forcing abortion in division

```
/***************************************************************
 * A program that aborts with an error message                 *
 ***************************************************************/
#include <iostream>
#include <cassert>
using namespace std;

int main ()
{
   int num1, num2, result;
   for (int i = 0; i < 5; i++)
   {
       cout << "Enter an integer: ";
       cin >> num1;
       cout << "Enter another integer: ";
       cin >> num2;
       if (num2 == 0)
       {
             cout << "No division by zero!. Program is aborted." << endl;
             assert (false);
       }
       result = num1 / num2;
       cout << "The result of division is: " << result << endl;
   }
   return 0;
}
```

```
Run:
Enter an integer: 8
Enter another integer: 3
The result of division is: 2
Enter an integer: 9
Enter another integer: 6
The result of division is: 1
Enter an integer: 7
Enter another integer: 0
No division by zero. Program is aborted.
```

After two iterations, the program is aborted, but we print a message that explains what happened. Again the program is aborted by the run-time environment, but we told the run-time system to abort it by using the *assert* macro.

Use Error Checking

A third approach is to check the value of the second number in each iteration and skip the division if it is zero. This is preferred to the previous two methods because we can skip the cases in which the second number is zero and continue with the other cases.

EXAMPLE 14.3

Since we know that the program will be aborted if the divisor is zero, we can use an *ifelse* statement and perform the division only if the divisor is not zero. Program 14.3 shows this approach.

Program 14.3 A traditional error-checking program

```
/***************************************************************
 * A program that uses traditional error checking to prevent      *
 * program abortion                                               *
 ***************************************************************/
#include <iostream>
using namespace std;

int main ( )
{
   int num1, num2, result;
   for (int i = 0; i < 4; i++)
   {
        cout << "Enter an integer: ";
        cin >> num1;
        cout << "Enter another integer: ";
        cin >> num2;
        if (num2 == 0)
        {
                cout << "Division cannot be done in this case." << endl;
        }
        else
        {
                result = num1 / num2;
                cout << "The result of division is: " << result << endl;
        }
   }
   return 0;
}
```

(continued)

Program 14.3 A traditional error-checking program (Continued)

```
Run:
Enter an integer: 8
Enter another integer: 2
The result of division is: 4
Enter an integer: 7
Enter another integer: 1
The result of division is: 7
Enter an integer: 8
Enter another integer: 0
Division cannot be done in this case.
Enter an integer: 9
Enter another integer: 7
The result of division is: 1
```

The calculation is done in the highlighted section of the program (lines 17 to 25). If the calculation cannot be done, it is skipped. The loop continues with the rest of the data.

Using Function Return Value for Error Checking

A fourth approach involves functions. Execution of a statement in a C++ program always occurs in a function, not outside a function. We may initialize variables outside a function (in the global area), but initialization is not execution; if there is a problem with the initialization, it is detected by the compiler. Since execution always occurs in a function, we can say that the run-time error always occurs in a function. In procedural programming in the past, it was customary to perform each calculation in a function and to check for errors by checking the return value of the function. An example is the *main* function, which returns 0 if there is no problem and returns other values if there is a problem. Programmers in the past used this idea and designed programs in which each function returned a specific value if there was an error.

EXAMPLE 14.4

In this example we rewrite out previous program using the return value of a function for error checking, as shown in Program 14.4.

Program 14.4 Error checking using a function

```
/*****************************************************************
 * A program that uses the return value of a function to show     *
 * the occurrence of a run-time error                             *
 *****************************************************************/
#include <iostream>
using namespace std;

// Function declaration
int quotient (int first, int second);

```

(continued)

Program 14.4 Error checking using a function (Continued)

```
int main ()
{
   int num1, num2, result;
   for (int i = 0; i < 3; i++)
   {
        cout << "Enter an integer: ";
        cin >> num1;
        cout << "Enter another integer: ";
        cin >> num2;
        result = quotient (num1, num2);
        if (result == -1)
        {
              cout << "Error, division by zero." << endl;
        }
        else
        {
              cout << "Result of division is: " << result << endl;
        }
   }
   return 0;
}

// Function definition
int quotient (int first, int second)
{
   if (second == 0)
   {
        return -1;
   }
   return (first / second);
}
```

```
Run:
Enter an integer: 6
Enter another integer: 5
The result of division is: 1
Enter an integer: 7
Enter another integer: 0
Error, division by zero.
Enter an integer: 8
Enter another integer: 2
The result of division is: 4
```

Note that when the quotient is zero, the program prints an error message instead of printing the result of the calculation.

Problems with Traditional Approaches

We analyze these approaches to see why we need a new approach (exception handling).

1. The first approach is the worst. We let the program abort without any warning.
2. The second approach is better; the program will still abort, but the user will be notified.
3. The third approach is better than the first two because the pair that would cause the program to abort is ignored, and the program continues with the rest of the data. The problem with this approach is that the code for handling an error is mingled with the productive code of the program. In other words, the problem here is *coupling*. The error-handling code is so coupled with the code to do the job that it is difficult to distinguish between them.
4. The fourth approach is the best, but it cannot be applied in all cases. In addition, the principle of modular programming dictates that the return value of a function be used only for one purpose, not two. In this case, one value (−1) is used to report an error; other values are used to return the result of the calculation.

14.1.2 Exception Handling Approach

To avoid the four problems mentioned in the previous section, C++ developed the *exception handling approach*. In this approach, the run-time system detects the error, but it does not abort the program. It lets the program handle the error.

In the exception handling approach, the run-time error is detected, but the program handles the error and aborts the program only if necessary.

When using this approach, we still need to add extra code, but the code for error handling is not coupled with code that helps us follow the logic of the program. The code to detect and handle errors has a standard pattern that must be followed, and every C++ programmer should know how to handle it.

Try-Catch Block

The exception handling approach in C++ uses what is called the **try-catch block.** This block is made of two clauses. The first clause, which is called the *try* clause, includes the code that may cause the program to abort. The run-time environment tries to execute the code. If the code can be executed, the program flow continues. If the code cannot be executed, the system *throws* an exception (an object of a fundamental type or a class), but it does not abort the program. The second clause, called the **catch clause,** lets the program handle the exception and continue with the rest of program if possible.

Figure 14.1 shows the simple *try-catch* block. Later in the chapter, we will see that *try-catch* blocks can have more than one *catch* clause.

Figure 14.2 shows the two versions of the *throw* operator. The first is used to throw an exception; the second is used to rethrow an exception (we will discuss the second version later in this chapter).

Note that the expression shown in Figure 14.2 has no return value. It is called only for its side effect, which is throwing an exception. It is usually changed to an expression statement by adding a semicolon after the expression.

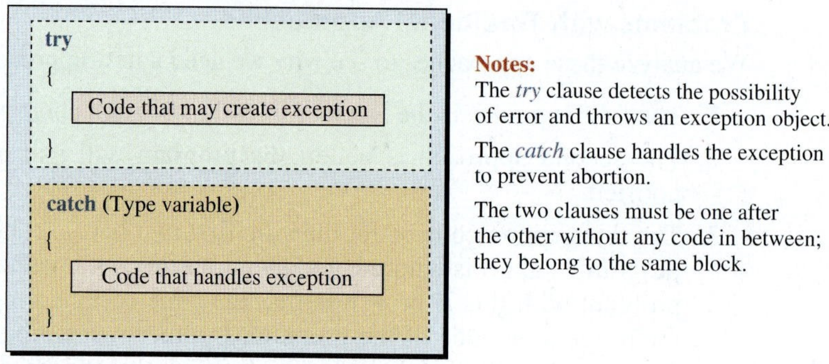

Figure 14.1 A simple try-catch block

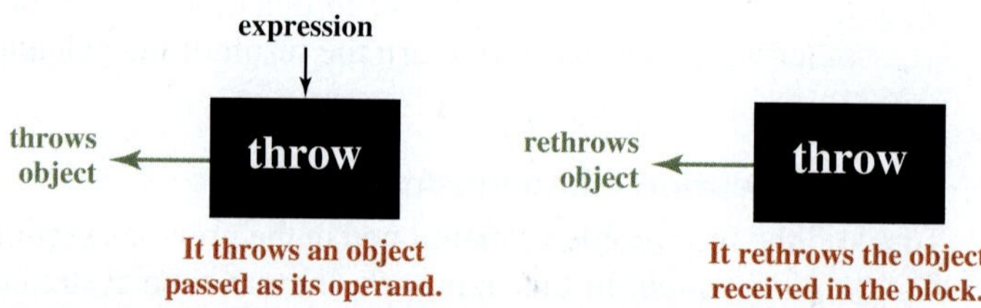

Figure 14.2 Using a throw expression to throw an object (exception)

Three Patterns

There are three patterns commonly used with exception handling approaches.

First Pattern In the first pattern, the *try-catch* block is completely contained in one function. If an exception is thrown, the rest of the *try* clause after the *throw* statement is ignored and control moves to the *catch* clause. The function continues after the *catch* clause unless the program is aborted in the *catch* clause. Figure 14.3 shows this pattern.

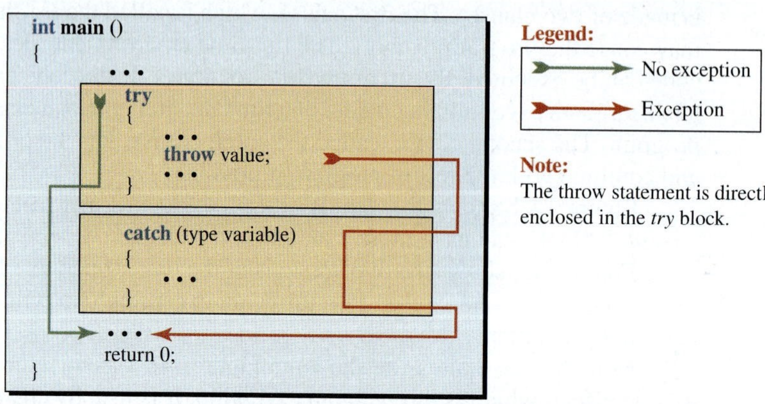

Figure 14.3 Try-catch block in the calling function

Note that in this case the throw statement is enclosed in a *try* clause. This pattern is rare.

EXAMPLE 14.5

We repeat Program 14.3 using the *try-catch* block to see the similarity between the traditional error checking and the exception handling approach (Program 14.5). Note that exception handling in this case means ignoring only the pair of integers that caused exception and continuing with the program. Later in this chapter we see that exception handling may need other actions.

Program 14.5 Using a try-catch block

```
/***************************************************************
 * A program that uses the try-catch block to detect an error   *
 * and throw it to be caught and handled by the program         *
 ***************************************************************/
#include <iostream>
using namespace std;

int main ()
{
  int num1, num2, result;
  for (int i = 0; i < 3; i++)
  {
      cout << "Enter an integer: ";
      cin >> num1;
      cout << "Enter another integer: ";
      cin >> num2;
      // The try-catch block
      try
      {
            if (num2 == 0)
            {
                throw 0;        // An object of type integer is thrown
            }
            result = num1 /num2;
            cout << "The result is: " << result << endl;
      }
      catch (int x)
      {
            cout << "Division by zero cannot be performed." << endl;
      }
  }
  return 0;
}
```

(*continued*)

Program 14.5 Using a try-catch block (Continued)

```
Run:
Enter an integer: 6
Enter another integer: 5
The result is: 1
Enter an integer: 7
Enter another integer: 0
Division by zero cannot be performed.
Enter an integer: 8
Enter another integer: 2
The result is: 4
```

In this program, the *try-catch* block (lines 18 to 30) is highlighted. There are several points that we must explain. The *try* clause includes the code that we suspect will create a run-time error. We provide the logic, in this case a decision statement, to *throw* the exception. If an exception is thrown, control transfers to the *catch* clause. If this happens. the exception must be an object of a built-in type or user-defined type. We have decided to throw an object of type *int* in this case (of value 0). If no exception is thrown, lines 24 and 25 are executed and the *catch* clause is ignored. Also note that the *catch* clause looks like a function with one parameter of the type of the exception object, but it is not a function. It is a clause in the *try-catch* block. Its parameter (*x*) is a variable of type integer. The program output follows Program 14.4.

Second Pattern In the second pattern, the *try-catch* block is still in *main*, but the exception is thrown in another function that is called in the *try* clause. The *throw* statement in this case is in the called function. When an exception is thrown, the rest of the code in the called function is ignored and the program flow moves to the *catch* block in the calling function. Figure 14.4 shows this pattern.

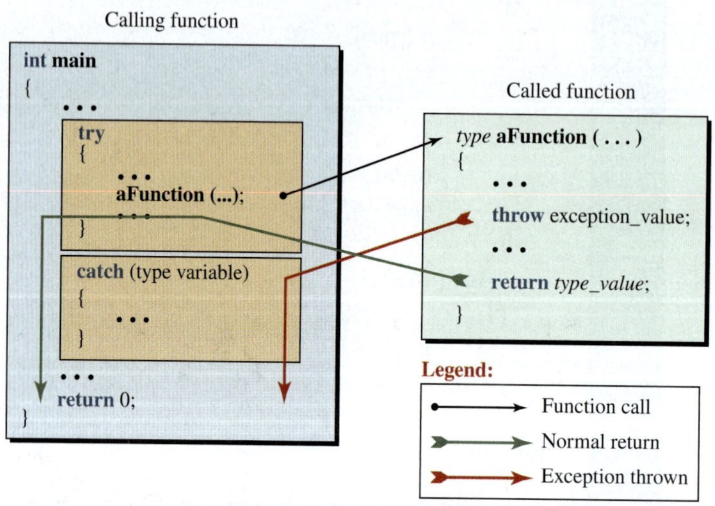

Figure 14.4 Second pattern (throw in called function)

The second pattern is preferred because it follows the structural programming principle of dividing the tasks. The task of the operation is defined in the called function, and it will throw an exception if there is a problem. The task of exception handling is in the calling function.

When we put the *throw* statement in a function, we create two different return points in the called function. If no exception is thrown, the called function will return when it reaches the return statement and the program flow goes back to the calling function. In this case, the *catch* clause is ignored. If an exception is thrown, the called function is terminated prematurely and the program flow returns to the *catch* clause in the calling function.

Figure 14.4 demonstrates another advantage of using exception handlers. We do not have to return two values from a function, one for success and one for error. In the case of an error, the exception is thrown and the function is terminated.

Is the throw statement in this pattern also enclosed in a *try* clause? The answer is yes, but the inclusion is indirect. The *try* clause encloses the called function, and the called function encloses the throw statement.

EXAMPLE 14.6

In this example we rewrite the previous program using the second pattern. The task of calculating the quotient belongs to a function called *quotient*, which throws an exception of type `int` if there is a problem. The *main* function is only responsible for calling the quotient and catching and handling the exception if thrown. Note that in this case catching the exception just means ignoring the pair of integers and continuing with the next pair. Program 14.6 shows the case.

Program 14.6 Detecting an exception thrown by a function

```
/*****************************************************************
 * A program that uses the try-catch block to detect an error      *
 * thrown by a function                                            *
 *****************************************************************/
#include <iostream>
using namespace std;

int quotient (int first, int second);    // Function declaration

int main ()
{
   int num1, num2, result;
   for (int i = 0; i < 3; i++)
   {
       cout << "Enter an integer: ";
       cin >> num1;
       cout << "Enter another integer: ";
       cin >> num2;
       // The try-catch block
       try
       {
           cout << "Result: " << quotient (num1, num2) << endl;
```

(*continued*)

Program 14.6 Detecting an exception thrown by a function (Continued)

```
        }
        catch (int ex)
        {
            cout << "Division by zero cannot be performed." << endl;
        }
    }
    return 0;
}
// Function definition
int quotient (int first, int second)
{
    if (second == 0)
    {
        throw 0;
    }
    return first / second;
}
```

```
Run:
Enter an integer: 12
Enter another integer: 4
Result: 3
Enter an integer: 16
Enter another integer: 0
Division by zero cannot be performed.
Enter an integer: 7
Enter another integer: 2
Result: 3
```

This pattern allows a function to throw an exception to its caller. In other words, the responsibility for throwing an exception and handling an exception is divided between the called function and the calling function. We create a function; we do not need to reveal its code; we can just tell users what it does (public interface) and tell them what possible exceptions it may throw. The responsibility of the users is to catch and handle the exception. This benefit is evident in the case of library functions.

One of the advantages of the exception handling approach is that we can design functions that can throw an exception. It is the responsibility of the caller to handle the exception.

Third Pattern Sometimes we need a *try-catch* block in the called function. This may occur when the called function belongs to an independent entity (such as a member function in a class). When a function is called by another function, if an exception is caught and handled, we have two cases.

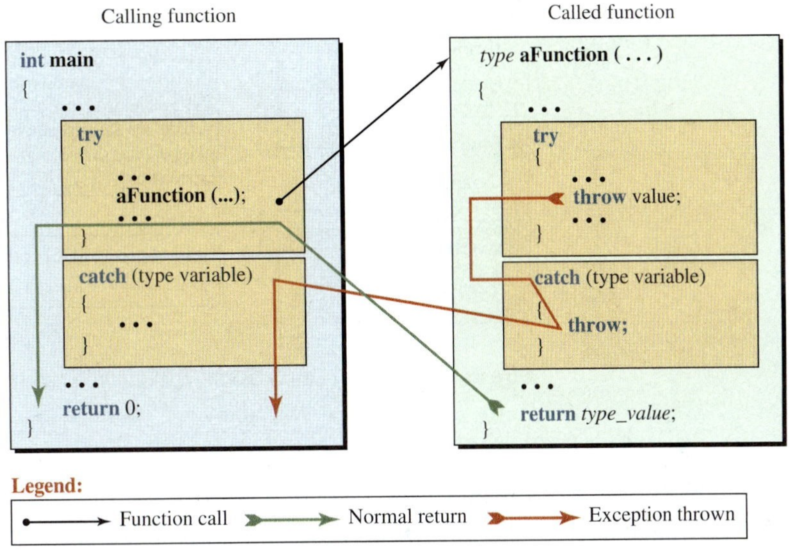

Note:
We have only one actual throw statement, which is enclosed in its own try block.
The second throw statement simply rethrows the previous one.

Figure 14.5 Third pattern (try-catch block in both the calling and called functions)

1. The called function can continue with the rest of its code and return to the calling function when it is finished. This is the first pattern in which the called function acts independently with relation to exception handling.
2. The called function cannot continue with the rest of its code. The control, however, must return to the calling function. Otherwise, the program must be aborted. This is the third pattern. We need to have the *try-catch* block in both functions. The *catch* clause rethrows the exception to the calling function so it can be caught there. Figure 14.5 shows this pattern.

Position of Throw Statement

A *throw* statement must be enclosed in a *try* clause, either directly or indirectly, to catch the exception. When the *throw* statement is explicitly inside a *try* clause, the enclosure is direct (first pattern); when it is inside a function that is called in a *try* clause, the enclosure is indirect (second pattern). The third pattern we discussed is a special case in which there are two *throw* statements. Figure 14.6 shows the difference between the direct and indirect *try* clauses.

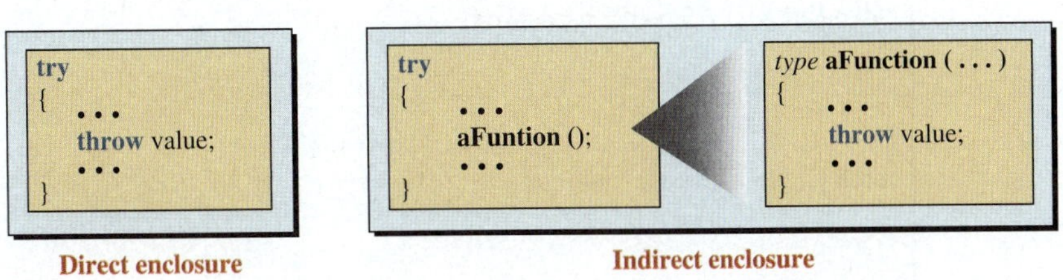

Figure 14.6 Direct and indirect enclosure of the throw statement

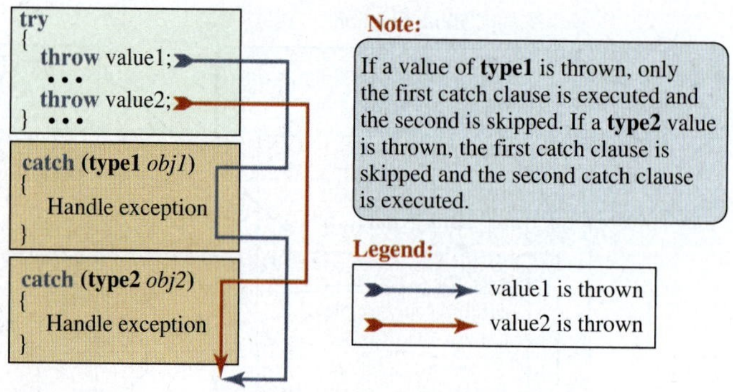

Figure 14.7 A try-catch block with multiple catch clauses

Hidden Throw Statement

Sometimes we see a *try-catch* block, but we cannot see the *throw* statement. This happens when we use a predefined or a library function whose definition we cannot see. We just see the function call in a *try* clause, but the function definition contains a *throw* statement. For example, some string member functions, such as the *at*() function, throws an exception if the index is out of range. When we call this function in our program, we may need to enclose the call in a *try-catch* block to catch the exception and prevent program abortion.

Multiple Catch Clauses

Figure 14.7 shows a situation in which a function may throw two different types of exceptions. Since the handling for each type may be different, we can have two types of *catch* clauses.

Generic Catch Clause

A *catch* clause may only catch exceptions of its parameter type. A *catch* clause of an integer type cannot catch an exception of a floating-point type when it is thrown. If we want to catch any type of exception, we can use an ellipsis as the parameter in the *catch* clause. In this case, if specific exception types need to be handled differently, the generic (any type) *catch* clause is coded as the last *catch* clause. The following shows such a *try-catch* block.

```
try
{
   ...
}
catch (int x) // Specific type catch
{
   ...
}
catch (...) // Ellipsis means any exception type
{
   ...
}
```

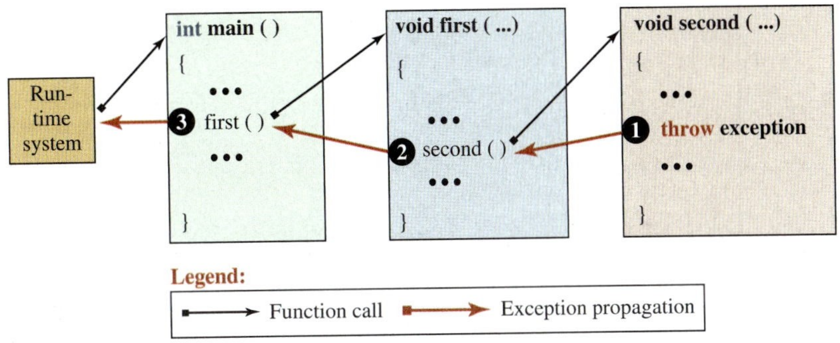

Figure 14.8 Exception propagation

Exception Propagation

A function may throw an exception, but this does not mean that the exception should be necessarily caught and handled in the same function where it has been thrown. If an exception is not caught and handled where it has been thrown, it will be automatically propagated to the previous function in the hierarchy of function calls until one of the functions in the path captures and handles it. The last function in which a thrown exception can be caught and handled is the *main* function. If the exception is not caught and handled by the *main* function, it will be propagated to the run-time system, where it is caught and causes the *main* function to be aborted, which aborts the whole program. This process is known as **exception propagation.** Figure 14.8 shows the path of function calls and the path of exception propagation in three functions: *main* is called by run-time system, *first* is called by *main*, and *second* is called by *first.*

An exception is thrown (explicitly or implicitly) in *second* and is not caught. The exception is propagated to *first,* where it is not caught. The exception is finally propagated to the run-time system, where it is caught and the program is terminated. If any of the functions (*second*, *first*, or *main*) use the *try-catch* block and handle the propagation, the exception does not reach the run-time system and the program is not aborted.

Note that *second* is terminated where the exception is thrown, *first* is terminated at the point where *second* is called, and *main* is terminated where *first* is called. This means that somewhere in the backward path we must have the *try-catch* block to handle the exception before it reaches the run-time system. That is exactly what we did in Program 14.6. The exception was thrown in the *quotient* function, but we caught and handled it in the *main* function before it reached the run-time systems, which would have aborted the program.

Rethrowing an Exception

We briefly discussed rethrowing an exception in Pattern 3. It is possible that a *catch* clause cannot or does not want to handle the exception either partially or totally. In this case, the exception can be rethrown to the function one level up. This may happen when we need to free memory, close a network connection, or perform another maintenance activity before handling the exception. We perform the maintenance and then rethrow the exception to be handled by the calling function. To rethrow an exception, we use the throw operator without any operand. The following is an example of rethrowing an exception.

```
try
{
  ...
}
catch (type variable)
{
  ... // Some work
  throw; // Re-throw the exception to the calling function
}
```

14.1.3 Exception Specification

When we write a function for our own use, we know what type of exception can be thrown in the function and we can create the appropriate *try-catch* block in the calling function. However, if we write a function to be used by others, we normally give the user only the signature of the function as the public interface. In other words, the user has no knowledge of the body of the function and what exceptions can be thrown. In this case, it is recommended that an expression in the function header be added to tell the user what type of thrown objects to use if she wants to catch an exception in the calling function. For this purpose, we can say that a function can be designed in one of three ways: *any exception, predefined exceptions.*

Any Exception

If there is no specification, the function looks like the ones we have written so far. This means that the function can throw any exception. To find out what exception is thrown, we look at the body of the function. This is not suitable for functions that are designed by one entity and used by another such as a library function. The following shows the format of the prototype for this type of a function.

```
type functionName (parameters);  // Prototype with no specification
```

In Program 14.6 we used this type of function. The quotient function can throw any exception. Since we have designed and used the function, we know that it throws an exception of type *int*.

```
int quotient (int first, int second);  // Function declaration
```

Predefined Exceptions

If the designer and the user of the function are different, we must define the exceptions thrown by the function in the header of the function (which is copied in the declaration). The syntax for this type of a function is shown below. The header of the function defines the types of all exception objects that may be thrown from the function.

```
type functionName (parameters) throw (type1, type2, ..., typen);
```

We could have added a predefined specification to show that our quotient function may throw an exception of type *int* as shown below:

```
int quotient (int first, int second) throw (int);  // Function declaration
```

No Exception

The third possibility is to declare to the user that this function does not throw an exception, which means that the user does not need to use a *try-catch* block. The syntax for this type of a function is shown below. The header of the function uses the *throw* keyword, but the parentheses are empty.

```
type functionName (parameters) throw ();
```

The following shows an example of this specification. If a function is supposed to print two integers, there are no error conditions and exception handling is unnecessary.

```
int print (int first, int second) throw ();   // Function declaration
```

14.1.4 Stack Unwinding

One of the most important concepts in exception handling is **stack unwinding.** Stack unwinding is closely related to managing the memory assigned to a program.

Program Memory

In Chapter 9 we discussed that when a C++ program starts running, the runtime system designates four areas of memory for the program: *code memory*, *static memory*, *stack memory*, and *heap memory*. The *code memory* (program memory) holds the instructions of the program executed during the program run time. The *static memory* stores the value of static variables and global variables. These values are separated from the local variables. The *stack memory* is a last-in-first-out memory similar to the stacks of trays we see in a restaurant. The last tray pushed into the stack is the first one to be popped out. The *stack memory* is responsible for keeping track of three types of information about each function: values of parameters, values of local variables, and the return address of the calling function in code memory. The *heap memory* is free memory that is used by a program to store information that may outlast the life of a function.

Pushing and Popping Stack Memory

Exception handling is based on the behavior of stack memory. Each program is made of a set of functions that may call each other. During a function call, data about the calling function, such as parameters, local variables, and the return address, are pushed into stack memory. The return address is used when the function terminates normally or abnormally (by throwing an exception). Figure 14.9 shows how data are pushed into the stack during a function call.

In the example shown in Figure 14.9, the *main* function is pushed into the stack, there are no parameters except the local variable (*x*), and the address of the instruction that called the *main* function in the RTE is pushed in the stack. When the *main* function calls *function1*, the parameter of the *function1* (*xx*), the local variable (*y*), and the address of the function call instruction (107) are pushed into the stack. Similarly, when *function1* calls *function2*, the parameter of *function2* (*yy*), the local variable of *function2* (*z*), and the address of the function call (244) are stored in the stack. Now the stack has three entries because of three function calls. Note that each parameter entry can have zero or more parameters and each local-variable record can have zero or more variables.

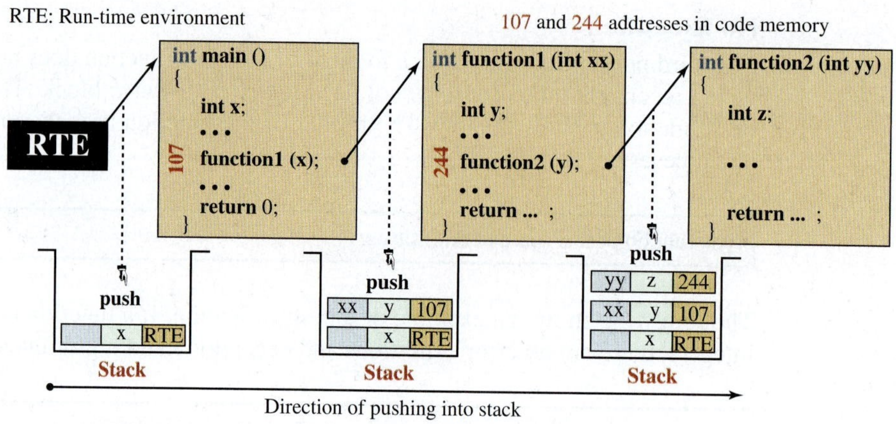

Figure 14.9 Pushing function information into the stack

Figure 14.10 shows how the information is popped from the stack during the return from each function. This is referred to as *stack unwinding*.

Stack unwinding also occurs when an exception is thrown and control returns to the calling function. In other words, the running function immediately pops the last entry on the stack when an exception is thrown instead of waiting to reach the end of the function.

Effects of Stack Unwinding

The most important effect of stack unwinding is that when a function returns or terminates, the corresponding entry is popped from the stack and the parameters and local objects are destroyed. If the parameters or objects are instances of classes, their destructors are automatically called for destruction.

This makes a big difference when we design our objects in a program. If an object is created as a parameter or local object, we do not have to worry about its destruction after a function ends or is terminated due to an exception. But if we design our object in the heap, the object may not be deleted after a termination and we will end up with a memory leak.

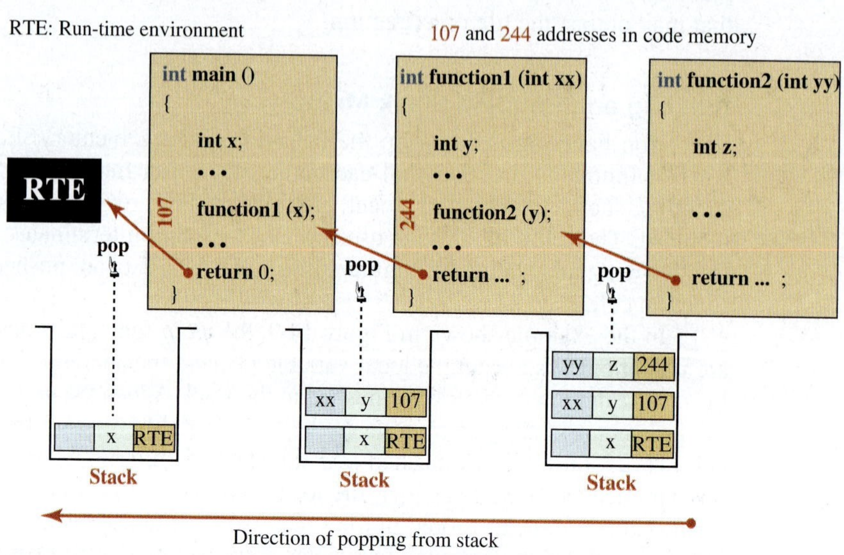

Figure 14.10 How information is popped up from the stack

Popping of entries from stack memory due to a function return or a thrown exception is referred to as stack unwinding. During stack unwinding, the parameters and local objects of the function are automatically destroyed by calling their destructors.

To avoid memory leak, we must make our objects local to the function in which they are defined.

In the next section, we will see that we wrap objects created in the heap inside a local object to ensure that heap objects are destroyed.

14.2 EXCEPTIONS IN CLASSES

An exception may be thrown in any function defined in a class. Although handling exceptions in member functions other than constructors and destructors is the same as handling the exceptions in a stand-alone function, we must be careful about exceptions in constructors and destructors.

14.2.1 Exception in Constructors

A constructor is a function, but it is different from a regular function in that it is designed to create and initialize an object. Before we learn how to catch an exception in a constructor, let us see what happens when an exception is thrown in a constructor. We consider two cases. In the first, the object is totally created in stack memory; in the second, it is partially created in heap memory.

Creation of Objects in the Stack

We consider two cases. In the first case, no exception is thrown in the constructor. In the second case, an exception is thrown in the constructor. We assume that we have a class named *Integer* that stores one single integer. This type of a class is referred to as a wrapper class and is common in object-oriented programming.

Case 1: No Exception Is Thrown in Constructor When we are using stack memory for storing an object, the object is created on the top of the stack when the constructor is called and it is destroyed when the destructor completes. Calling the constructor creates the object on the top of the stack; the execution of the constructor initializes the object and allocates resources, if any. On the other hand, when the destructor is called, the resources are released during the execution of the destructor and then the object is popped and destroyed. In other words, the object comes into existence before execution of the constructor; the object ceases to exist after the execution of the destructor, as shown in Figure 14.11. Pushing the object into the stack is the first step; popping is the last one.

Case 2: An Exception Is Thrown in the Constructor Assume that an exception is thrown in the constructor body. C++ is designed such that if the constructor of a class cannot fully do its job, the destructor for that object is never called. Figure 14.12 shows the same scenario as case 1, but the constructor throws an exception and the program terminates. All memory allocated in the stack is released.

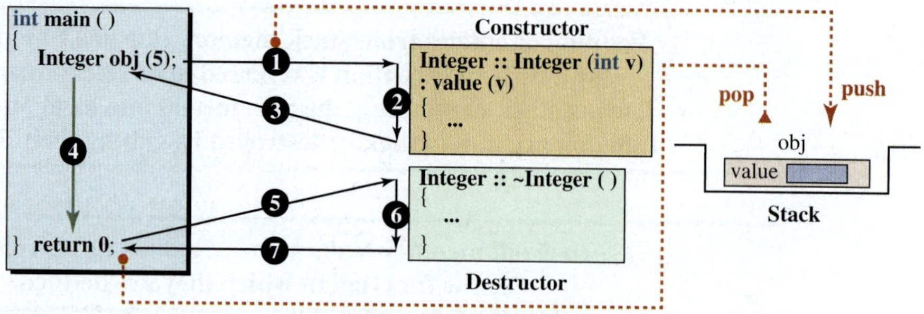

Notes:
1. An object is created and pushed into the stack when the constructor is called.
2. Execution of the constructor initializes the object and allocates resources, if any.
3. The initilized object is returned to the *main* function for use.
4. The *main* function uses the object.
5. When the object goes out of scope, the destructor is called.
6. The destructor deallocates the resources, if any.
7. The object is popped from the stack.

Figure 14.11 Construction and destruction when no exception is thrown

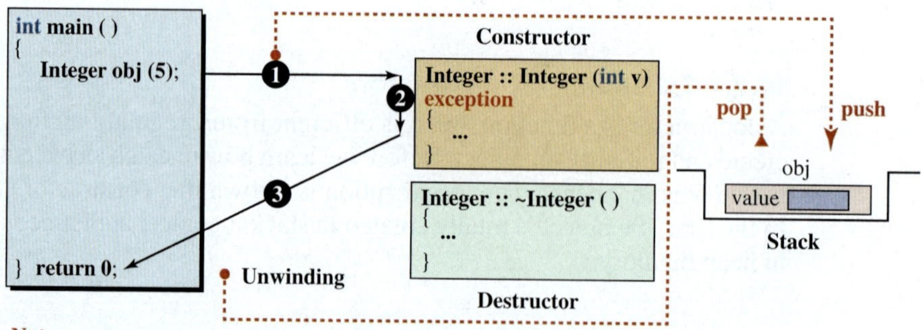

Notes:
1. An object is created and pushed into the stack when the constructor is called.
2. An exception occurs in the consturctor during initialization (or allocating resources).
3. Throwing an exception terminates the constructor. The destructor is never called, but stack unwinding pops the object and it is destroyed at this point.

Figure 14.12 When an exception is thrown in the constructor

Partial Creation of Object in the Heap

Assume that the *Integer* object has a pointer to an integer created in heap memory. Again, we consider two cases.

Case 1: No Exception Is Thrown in Constructor Figure 14.13 shows the case when no exception is thrown in the constructor. We assume that the constructor creates the object in the heap during the initialization and then stores a value in the object during the execution of the body. When the *Integer* object goes out of scope, the destructor is called and it frees the memory. After memory is freed, the *Integer* object is popped from stack memory.

Case 2: An Exception Is Thrown in Constructor Assume that an exception is thrown in the constructor body when the value is stored in the variable created in the heap. In this case, the constructor is terminated without finishing its job. Since the object is not completely

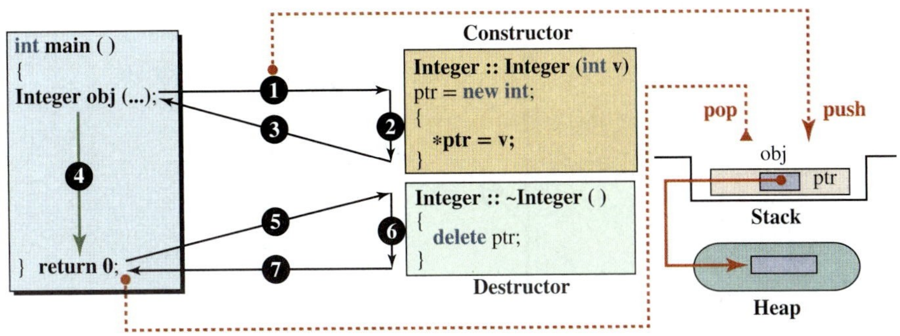

Notes:
1. An object is created and pushed in the stack when the constructor is called.
2. Initialization allocates memory in the heap and the value is stored in it during the execution of the constructor body.
3. The constructor is terminated and an object is available to the *main* function.
4. The *main* function uses the object.
5. When the object goes out of scope, the destructor is called.
6. The destructor deletes the integer in the heap.
7. The object goes out of scope after the destructor returns and the object is popped.

Figure 14.13 Construction and destruction when no exception is thrown

constructed, the destructor is not called, which means the memory allocated in the heap is never deleted. We may have memory leak. Although the *Integer* object is popped up from the stack during unwinding, the destructor is never called and the memory in the heap is never released (Figure 14.14).

The problem here is that we separated the two related tasks of allocating memory and releasing memory by another task (storing data in the allocated memory). Because this third task failed (an exception is thrown), the constructor has allocated memory, but its work is not finished. This means that the destructor is not called to release the memory. The two related tasks of allocating and releasing memory are partially done. Memory is allocated, but not released. We may have memory leak.

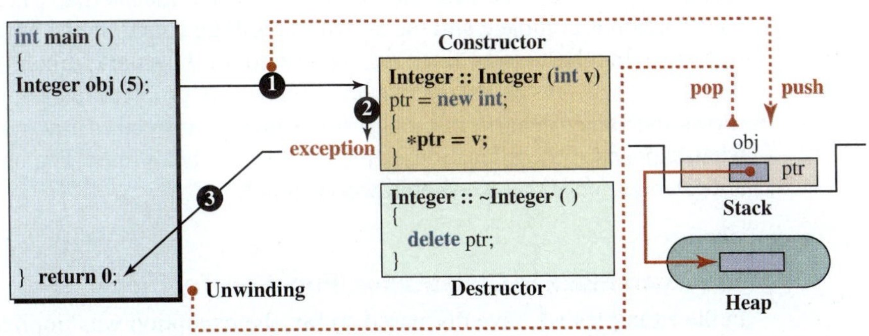

Notes:
1. An object is created and pushed into the stack when the constructor is called.
2. Allocation of the location in the heap memory is done, but an exception occurs when the constructor needs to store values in the object allocated in the heap.
3. An exception is thrown that terminates the *main* function. Stack unwinding pops the *Integer* object from the stack, but the memory in the heap is not released because the destructor is not called.

Figure 14.14 Construction and destruction when an exception is thrown

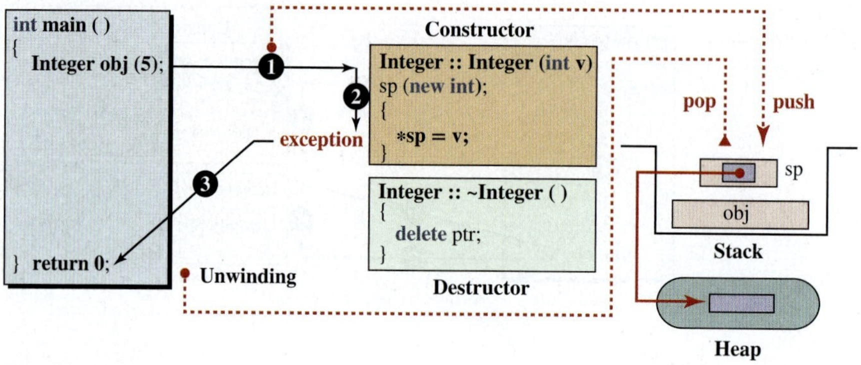

Notes:

1. An *Integer* object is created in the stack, which in turn creates an SP object and pushes it into the stack.
2. In the constructor, the SP object creates a location in the heap, but during filling the location, an exception is thrown, which means the constructor of the *Integer* class has not totally constructed the object.
3. The *main* function termainates, and unwinding pops the SP object from the stack. Since the SP object was fully constructed, the destructor of the SP object is called, which deletes the memory on the heap. The destructor of the *Integer* object is not called, but we do not have a memory leak because the SP object released the memory.

Figure 14.15 Using a smart pointer

The solution is to combine the allocation and release of memory into one atomic task and let one object be responsible for the allocation and release of memory. This is where the *smart pointers* that we discussed in Chapter 13 come to mind. We need a smart pointer to handle allocation and de-allocation without worrying about storing data in the allocated memory.

Using a Smart Pointer for Memory Management To link the allocation and release of memory, we use a smart pointer instead of a raw pointer. The smart pointer allocates memory when its constructor is called and releases memory when its destructor is called. However, the constructor has no other duty, which means that when allocation is over, the construction is complete and the destructor will be called by the unwinding if any exception is thrown. In other words, since the constructor of the smart pointer is doing only one job, its destructor is always called and we do not have any problem releasing memory. Figure 14.15 shows the same scenario but using smart pointer instead of raw pointer. You may wonder what happens if the allocation of memory in the heap fails. The answer is that there is no allocated memory that we should worry about.

Try-Catch Block in Constructor: Function-Try Block

In the examples we have discussed so far, the exception was implicitly thrown in the body of the constructor and propagated to the *main* function. We can also explicitly throw an exception and let it be caught and handled in *main*. We can also use a *try-catch* block to handle the exception in the constructor or rethrow it to *main*. What C++ does not allow us to do is to throw, implicitly or explicitly, an exception in the initializer list. To throw an exception that happens in the initializer list, we use a *function-try* block, which combines a *try-catch* block with an initialization list as shown in Figure 14.16. The *function-try* block allows the initialization to be added after the keyword *try* and a colon.

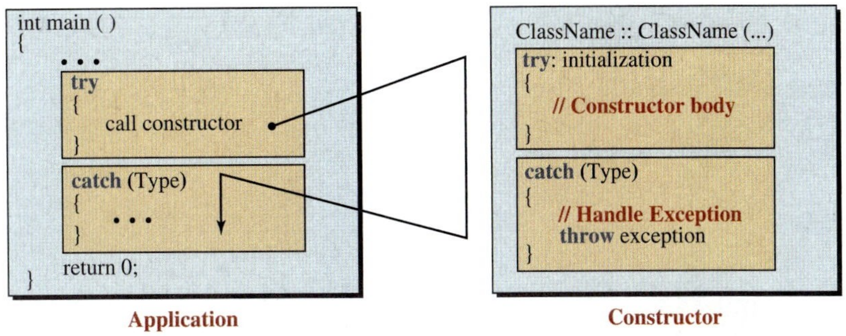

Figure 14.16 Using the function-try block

An Example

We give a simple example of the *Integer* class. Program 14.7 shows the interface file for the smart pointer (SP) class that is used in the *Integer* class.

Program 14.8 shows the implementation file for the SP class.

Program 14.7 File sp.h

```
/***************************************************************
 * The interface file for SP class                            *
 ***************************************************************/
#ifndef SP_H
#define SP_H
#include <iostream>
using namespace std;

// Definition of class SP
class SP
{
  private:
      int* ptr;
  public:
      SP (int* ptr);
      ~SP ( );
      int& operator* ( ) const;
      int* operator-> ( ) const;
};
#endif
```

Program 14.8 File sp.cpp

```
/***************************************************************
 * The implementation file for SP class                       *
 ***************************************************************/
```

(continued)

Program 14.8 File sp.cpp (Continued)

```
#include "sp.h"

// Constructor
SP :: SP (int* p)
: ptr (p)
{
}
// Destructor
SP :: ~SP ()
{
  delete ptr;
}
// Overloading of the * operator
int& SP :: operator* ( ) const
{
  return *ptr;
}
// Overloading of the -> operator
int* SP :: operator-> ( ) const
{
  return ptr;
}
```

Program 14.9 shows the interface file for the *Integer* class.

Program 14.9 File integer.h

```
/*******************************************************************
 * The interface file for the Integer class                        *
 *******************************************************************/
#ifndef INTEGER_H
#define INTEGER_H
#include "sp.h"

// Definition of the Integer class
class Integer
{
  private:
      SP sp;
  public:
      Integer (int value);
      ~Integer ();
      int getValue();
};
#endif
```

Program 14.10 File integer.cpp

```
/***************************************************************
 * The implementation file for the Integer class              *
 ***************************************************************/
#include "integer.h"

// Constructor using function-try block
Integer :: Integer (int v)
try: sp (new int)
{
   *sp = v;
}
catch (...)
{
   throw;
}
// Destructor
Integer :: ~Integer ()
{
}
// Accessor function
int Integer :: getValue()
{
   return *sp;
}
```

Program 14.10 shows the implementation file for the *Integer* class. Program 14.11 shows the application file.

Program 14.11 File app.cpp

```
/***************************************************************
 * The application to test the Integer class                  *
 ***************************************************************/
#include "integer.h"

int main ( )
{
   for (int i = 0; i < 1000000; i++)
   {
        try
        {
                Integer integer (i);
                cout << integer.getValue() << endl;
        }
```

(continued)

Program 14.11 File app.cpp (Continued)

```
        catch (...)
        {
            cout << "Exception is thrown" << endl;
        }
    }
    return 0;
}
```

```
Run:
0
1
2
3
4
5
6
...
87245
Exception is thrown
87247
...
92101
Exception is thrown
92103
...
99999
```

To save space, we have not shown all outputs, but we can see that an exception is thrown for the integers 87246 and 92102.

14.2.2 Exception in Destructors

Destructors are invoked during stack unwinding. If destructor is interrupted by throwing an exception, the unwinding process is stopped. For this reason, if any exception is thrown in the destructor, C++ calls a global function named *terminator* that terminates the whole program.

> **Exception throwing in a destructor must be avoided.**

14.3 STANDARD EXCEPTION CLASSES

The exceptions discussed in previous sections of this chapter have involved exceptions of fundamental data types. C++ defines a set of standard exception classes that are used in its library, as shown in Figure 14.17. C++ contains standard **exception classes** that are derived from a class named *exception*.

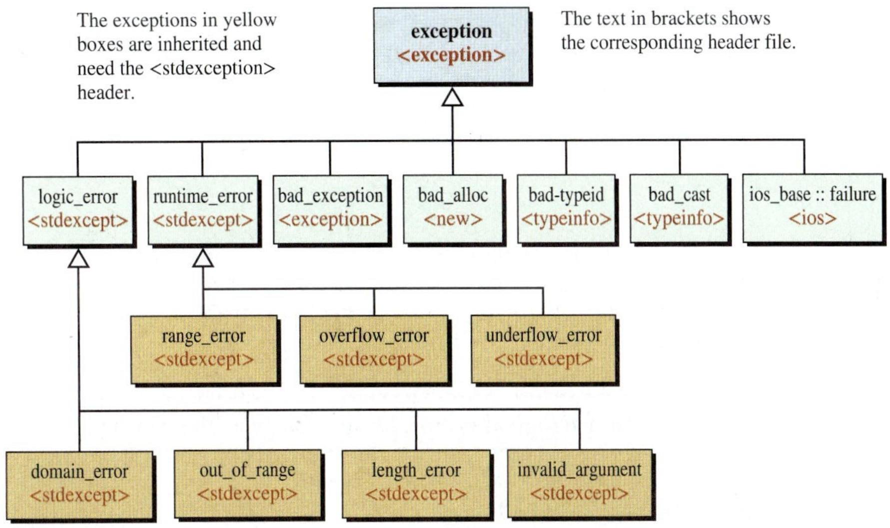

Figure 14.17 Hierarchy of standard exception classes

Studying the purposes and formats of the classes shown in Figure 14.17 can help us learn how to handle an exception when it is thrown in a library function and use them or inherit from them to create our own exception classes.

At the top of the hierarchy in Figure 14.17 is the *exception* class defined in the <exception> header. Table 14.1 shows the public interface for the *exception* class.

All of the functions defined in the *exception* class have the exception specification, which defines that no exception is thrown inside the function. The *what* member function is a virtual function that returns a C string that describes the error that occurred. The derived classes provide the implementation for this class.

14.3.1 Logical Errors

As shown in Figure 14.17, C++ defines a class named *logic_error*. This is the base class for four other classes related to logic errors, errors that are related to the precondition for a function; these errors cannot be detected during compilation time.

Logical errors are related to the preconditions of a function.

Table 14.2 shows the public interface for the *logic_error* class. These classes also inherit the *what* member function from the *exception* class.

Table 14.1 Public interface of the exception class

```
exception () throw ()  // constructor
exception (const exception&) throw ()  // copy constructor
exception&  operator = (const exception&) throw () // Assignment operator
virtual ~exception () throw ()  // destructor
virtual const char* what () const throw ()  // member function
```

Table 14.2 Public interface for the logic_error class
explicit logic_error (const string& *whatArg*) // constructor
virtual const char* what () const throw () // member function

There are four classes derived from this class: *domain_error*, *length_error*, *out_of_range,* and *invalid_argument*. The constructors of all of these classes have the same pattern as the *logic_error* class, but the names are different. Table 14.3 shows the constructor of the four exception classes inherited from the *logic_error* class.

To use logical error classes, we need the <stdexcept> header file.

The domain_error Class

The *domain_error* exception is thrown when the given data is out of domain. For example, if a function requires an argument between 0.0 and 4.0 (for example, a grade point average, GPA), then this exception is thrown if we pass a value that is not in this domain.

The length_error Class

The *length_error* exception is thrown if the length of an object is greater or smaller than the predefined length. For example, the string class throws an exception if the size of a string exceeds the value returned by the *max_size* member function. We can use this class to throw an exception if the size of the array goes beyond its predefined size.

The out_of_range Class

The *out_of_range* exception is thrown if an index goes out of range for a library class. For example, the string class has a function named *at*(…) that returns a value at the index defined as its parameter. If an integer is passed that is beyond the index of the current string object, an exception of this type is thrown. We can use this class to throw an exception if the index of array is out of range.

The invalid_argument Class

The *invalid_argument* exception normally occurs when there is a logical error but the nature of the exception does not match any of the previously defined three classes. An example is when we have a bit set in which each bit should have a value of either 0 or 1.

Table 14.3 Classes inherited from the logic_error class

class	constructor
domain_error	explicit domain_error (const string& *whatArg*)
length_error	explicit length_error (const string& *whatArg*)
out_of_range	explicit out_of_range (const string& *whatArg*)
invalid_argument	explicit invalid_argument (const string& *whatArg*)

Table 14.4 Public interface for the runtime_error class

```
explicit runtime_error (const string& whatArg) // constructor
virtual const char* what () const throw () // member function
```

14.3.2 Run-Time Errors

As shown in Figure 14.17, C++ defines a class named *runtime_error* class. A **run-time error** is normally related to the postcondition of a function such as overflow, underflow, or an out-of-range return value.

To use the run-time error classes, we need the <stdexcept> header file.

Table 14.4 shows that the public interface for the *runtime_error* class also inherits the *what* member function from the *exception* class.

Three classes are derived from this class: *underflow_error*, *overflow_error*, and *range_error* (see Figure 14.17). The constructors of all of these classes have the same pattern as the *runtime_error* class, but the names are different. The *what* function is inherited in all classes. Table 14.5 shows the constructor of the three exception class inherited from the *runtime_error* class.

Run-time errors are related to the postconditions of a function.

The underflow_error Class

We discussed the underflow concept in Chapter 3. The *underflow_error* condition occurs in arithmetic calculations. However, this type of error is not normally defined for any arithmetic operator. It can be used to throw an exception in a user-defined function.

The overflow_error Class

We also discussed the overflow concept in Chapter 3. The *overflow_error* condition also occurs in arithmetic calculations. However, this type of error is not normally defined for any arithmetic operator. It can be used to throw an exception in a user-defined function.

The range_error Class

The *range_error* exception is designed to throw an exception when the result of a function is out of the predefined range (compare with *out_of_range* error, which is related to the error in the range of a function argument). The predefined mathematical functions in the <cmath> header do not throw any of these errors, but some functions designed by other sources may.

Table 14.5 Classes inherited from runtime_error class

class	constructor
underflow_error	explicit underflow_error (const string& *whatArg*)
overflow_error	explicit overflow_error (const string& *whatArg*)
range_error	explicit range_error (const string& *whatArg*)

14.3.3 Five Other Classes

There are five other classes derived directly from the *exception* class as shown in Figure 14.17. These classes have the same member functions as the *exception* class except that the constructor, copy constructor, assignment operator, and destructor have the name of the corresponding class. The *at*() function is the same in all four.

The bad_exception Class

A *bad_exception* class object is thrown from a function with an exception specification that the function will not throw exceptions; however, something happens in the function and it throws one.

The bad_alloc Class

The <new> header defines types and functions related to dynamic memory allocation. The operator *new* throws an object of type *bad_alloc* class if the requested memory cannot be allocated.

The bad_typeid Class

The *bad_typeid* exception is thrown when we define a type that cannot be fulfilled. For example, if we *try* to dereference a pointer (*P) that is null, an exception of this type will be thrown.

The bad_cast Class

The *bad_cast* class is used to throw an exception when a dynamic cast operation fails.

The failure Class

The *<ios>* header defines a class that can be used as the base class for exceptions thrown in all input/output classes. Note that the name of the class is *failure* but its scope is *ios_base*. The only parameter in the constructor is used to customized the message shown by the *at*() function (Table 14.6).

The input/output classes in C++ were defined before the language supported exception handling. However, after the exception class was added to the language, the class *failure* was added to the hierarchy of exception classes.

The input/output classes, as we discussed before, hold states that can show if any error has occurred in the corresponding stream. To enable the use of exceptions in input/output operations, C++ added two functions named *exception*(), as shown in Table 14.7.

The first signature shown in Table 14.7 defines which flags, when triggered, will throw an exception of type *failure.* The second signature returns the flags that have been defined to throw exceptions.

Table 14.6 The interface for the failure class

```
explicit failure (const string& mesg)  // constructor
virtual ~failure ()  // destructor
virtual const char* what () const  throw ()  // member function
```

Table 14.7 Interface for input/output exception classes

```
void exception (iostate flags) // set the flags that triggered exception
iostate exception() const  // Returns flags candidate for exception
```

14.3.4 Using Standard Exception Classes

Instead of creating our own exception objects, we can use an object of one of the standard exception classes defined in the <exception> or <stdexcept> headers for this purpose.

EXAMPLE 14.7

Program 14.12 shows how we can use the *invalid_argument* class to handle the quotient problem defined in Program 14.6.

Program 14.12 Use of invalid_argument class

```
/***************************************************************
 * This program shows how to use an object of invalid_argument   *
 * to detect division by zero in a function.                     *
 ***************************************************************/
#include <stdexcept>
#include <iostream>
using namespace std;

// Function declaration
int quotient (int first, int second);

int main ()
{
  int num1, num2, result;
  for (int i = 0; i < 3; i++)
  {
      cout << "Enter an integer: ";
      cin >> num1;
      cout << "Enter another integer: ";
      cin >> num2;
      // Try-Catch block
      try
      {
            cout << "Result of division: " << quotient (num1, num2);
            cout << endl;
      }
      catch (invalid_argument ex)
      {
            cout << ex.what () << endl;
      }
```

(continued)

Program 14.12 Use of invalid_argument class (Continued)

```
    }
    return 0;
}
// Function definition
int quotient (int first, int second)
{
    if (second == 0)
    {
        throw invalid_argument ("Error! Divide by zero!");
    }
    return first / second;
}
```

```
Run:
Enter an integer: 20
Enter another integer: 4
Result of division: 5
Enter an integer: 12
Enter another integer: 0
Error! Divide by zero!
Enter an integer: 14
Enter another integer: 5
Result of division: 2
```

Key Terms

catch clause
exception classes
exception propagation
run-time error
stack unwinding
try-catch block

Summary

We discussed four approaches to traditional error handling. The first is to do nothing and let the program be aborted without any warning when there is an error. The second is to test for possible errors and print a message when an error occurs. The third is to use error checking. The fourth is to use a function return value for error checking.

To avoid problems with these four approaches, C++ has developed the *exception handling approach*. In this approach, the run-time system detects the error, but it does not abort the program. It lets the program handle the error. The exception-handling approach uses *try-catch* blocks. We discussed three patterns for the *try-catch* block. In the first pattern, the *try-catch* block is entirely in one function. In the second pattern, the *try-catch* block is in one function, but the exception is thrown in the function that is called in the *try* clause. In the third pattern, the *try-catch* block is in the called function.

We need to be careful about exceptions in constructors and destructors. If an object cannot be fully formed by the constructor, the corresponding destructor is not called. This can create a serious problem if the object is totally or partially created in the heap. Throwing an exception in this case may create a memory leak. To link the allocation and releasing of the memory together, we use a smart pointer instead of a raw pointer. The smart pointer allocates memory when its constructor is called and releases memory when its destructor is called. Standard exception classes are defined in the C++ library and are derived from the *exception* class. They are divided into *logical errors* and *run-time* errors.

Problems

PR-1. What happens when the following short program is run?

```
#include <iostream>
using namespace std;

int main ()
{
      int value = 30;
      if (value > 20) throw value;
      cout << value;
      return 0;
}
```

PR-2. What happens when we try to compile the following short program?

```
#include <iostream>
using namespace std;

int main ()
{
      int value = 30;
      try
      {
            if (value > 30) throw value;
      }
      cout << value;
      return 0;
}
```

PR-3. What happens when the following short program is run?

```
#include <iostream>
using namespace std;

int main ()
{
      int value = 30;
      try
      {
            if (value < 20) throw value;
```

```
    }
    catch (int value)
    {
        cout << "In the catch clause." << endl;
    }
    cout << value << endl;
    return 0;
}
```

PR-4. What happens when the following short program is run?

```
#include <iostream>
using namespace std;

void fun (int x )
{
    if (x < 10) throw 10.0;
}

int main ()
{
    try
    {
        fun (5);
    }
    catch (int value)
    {
        cout << value << endl;
    }
    return 0;
}
```

PR-5. What is wrong with the following function definition?

```
void fun (int x) throw ()
{
    if (x < 10) throw 10.0;
}
```

PR-6. What is wrong with the following function definition?

```
void fun (double x) throw (double)
{
    if (x < 10.0) throw 10.0;
}
```

PR-7. What is printed from the following program?

```
#include <iostream>
using namespace std;

void fun (int x ) throw (int)
{
```

```
    if (x > 1000) throw 10000;
}

int main ()
{
    try
    {
        fun (1002 );
    }
    catch (int value)
    {
        cout << value << endl;
    }
    return 0;
}
```

PR-8. What is printed from the following program?

```
#include <iostream>
using namespace std;

void second (int x ) throw (int)
{
    if (x > 1000) throw x;
}

void first (int x )
{
    try
    {
        second (1200);
    }
    catch (...)
    {
        throw x * 10;
    }
}

int main ()
{
    try
    {
        first (10);
    }
    catch (int value)
    {
        cout << value << endl;
    }
    return 0;
}
```

Programs

PRG-1. Instead of using fundamental data types as the type of exception to be thrown, we can use objects of a class type. Rewrite Program 14.5, and use a class named *DivByZero* to throw an exception object instead of an integer. The class does not need any data member or member functions.

PRG-2. Rewrite PRG-1, but define a constructor and a member function *what*() for the class DivByZero.

PRG-3. Rewrite PRG-2 with the DivByZero class inherited from the standard exception class *invalid_argument*, which is an appropriate class for this purpose. When we divide two integers, we are calling the library operator (/), in that the second argument is an integer which should not be zero.

PRG-4. Write a program that prompts the user to enter a duration of time in the form hours, minutes, and seconds. The program then calculates the duration in seconds. The program must throw three different exceptions objects: HExcept (if hours is negative), MExcept (if minutes are not between 0 and 59), and SExcept (if seconds are not between 0 and 59). Create three exceptional classes that inherit from the *out_of_range* standard exception class. Use polymorphism (catch-by-reference) and one catch clause to handle all cases.

PRG-5. The <string> library throws an exception of type *out_of_range* when the *at* function tries to access a character not in the range. Write a program that creates a string out of uppercase letters in English and prints the character when the index is given. Use the *try-catch* block to catch an error if the user enters an index less than 1 or greater than 26. Note that we do not need the *throw* statement in this case because the library throws an exception; we just need to catch it.

In this chapter we concentrate on *generalization*, which means to write a general program that can be used in several special cases. C++ calls this process *template programming*. We first discuss how to write general functions (called function templates) and then we discuss general classes (called class templates).

Objectives

After you have read and studied this chapter, you should be able to:

- Discuss *function templates* as a tool for creating a set of functions that have the same code logic but whose code can be applied to different data types.
- Give the syntax of a function template and show how the compiler generates a set of nontemplate functions during compilation.
- Discuss several issues in function templates, including nontemplate parameters, explicit type determination, predefined operations, specialization, and overloading.
- Discuss how to create separate interface and application files for a template function.
- Discuss *class templates* as a tool for creating a set of classes that differ only in the type of data members they hold.
- Discuss two methods for compiling programs that involve class templates: the inclusion approach and separate compilation.
- Discuss template friend functions and the idea of templates in inherited classes.

15.1 FUNCTION TEMPLATE

When programming in any language, we sometimes need to apply the same code to different data types. For example, we may have a function that finds the smaller of two integer data types, another function that finds the smaller of two floating-point data types, and so on. First, we should think about the code (program logic) and then about the data type to be used. We can separate these two tasks. We can write a program to solve a problem with a generic data type. We can then apply the program to the specific data type we need. This is known as generic programming or template programming.

A function in C++ is an entity that applies operations on zero or more objects and creates zero or more objects. Using **function templates,** actions can be defined when we write a program, and the data types can be defined when we compile the program. In other words, we can define a family of functions, each with one or more different data types.

15.1.1 Using a Family of Functions

If we do not use template and generic programming, we must define a family of functions. Assume we need to compare and find the smaller data item for a variety of data types in a program. For example, assume that we need to find the smaller between two characters, two integers, and two floating-point numbers. Since the types of the data are different, without templates we would need to write three functions as shown in Program 15.1. Note that in ASCII uppercase letters come before lowercase letters, which means 'B' is smaller than 'a'.

Program 15.1 Using three overloaded functions

```
/***************************************************************
 * A program to find the smaller between three types of data          *
 ***************************************************************/
#include <iostream>
using namespace std;

// Function to find the smaller between two characters
char smaller (char first, char second)
{
  if (first < second)
  {
      return first;
  }
  return second;
}
// Function to find the smaller between two integers
int smaller (int first, int second)
{
  if (first < second)
  {
      return first;
  }
  return second;
}
// Function to find the smaller between two doubles
double smaller (double first, double second)
{
  if (first < second)
  {
      return first;
  }
  return second;
}

int main ()
{
```

(continued)

Program 15.1 Using three overloaded functions (Continued)

```
    cout << "Smaller of 'a' and 'B': " << smaller ('a', 'B') << endl;
    cout << "Smaller of 12 and 15: " << smaller (12, 15) << endl;
    cout << "Smaller of 44.2 and 33.1: " << smaller (44.2, 33.1) << endl;
    return 0;
}
```

```
Run:
Smaller of 'a' and 'B': B
Smaller of 12 and 15: 12
Smaller of 44.2 and 33.1: 33.1
```

Writing three similar functions can be avoided if we use templates and write only one function.

15.1.2 Using Function Template

We first give the syntax of a function template to be defined and then the concept of instantiation, which is the way the compiler handles instantiations.

Syntax

To create a template function, we can use a placeholder for each generic type. Table 15.1 shows the general syntax for a generic function, in which T, U, …, and Z are replaced by actual types when the function is called.

As shown in Table 15.1, the template header contains the keyword *template* followed by a list of symbolic types inside two angle brackets. The template function header follows the rules for function headers except that the types are symbolic as declared in the template header. While multiple generic types are possible, a function template with more than two generic types is rare. Some older code uses the term *class* rather than *typename*. We use the keyword *typename* because it is the current standard and is used in the C++ library.

We change Program 15.1 using a function template as shown in Program 15.2. In this program we have only one generic type, but the type is used three times: twice as parameters and once as the return type. In this program the type of the parameters and the returned value are the same.

We can see that the result is the same as in Program 15.1. We have saved code by writing only one template function instead of three overloaded functions. Note that we have

Table 15.1 Syntax of a template function

```
template <typename T, typename U, ..., typename Z>
T functionName (U first, ... Z last)
{
  ...
}
```

Program 15.2 Using one function template

```
/*****************************************************************
 * A program that uses a template function to find the smaller    *
 * of two values of different types                                *
 *****************************************************************/
#include <iostream>
using namespace std;

// Definition of a template function
template <typename T>
T smaller (T first, T second)
{
   if (first < second)
   {
        return first;
   }
   return second;
}

int main ( )
{
   cout << "Smaller of a and B: " << smaller ('a', 'B') << endl;
   cout << "Smaller of 12 and 15: " << smaller (12, 15) << endl;
   cout << "Smaller of 44.2 and 33.1: " << smaller (44.2, 33.1) << endl;
   return 0;
}
```

```
Run:
Smaller of a and B: B
Smaller of 12 and 15: 12
Smaller of 44.2 and 33.1: 33.1
```

used only one single type name, *T*, which is used to define the two parameters and the return value. We did that because the type of the two parameters and the return type are the same. Note also that we have used *T&* instead of *T* to allow the objects of the user-defined type to be passed and returned by reference instead of value.

Program 15.3 shows how we can create a generic swap function to exchange two integers, two doubles, and so on. We have named the function *exchange* to avoid confusion with a library function named *swap*.

Program 15.3 Swapping two values

```
/*****************************************************************
 * A program that uses a template function to swap two values     *
 *****************************************************************/
```

(continued)

Program 15.3 Swapping two values (Continued)

```
#include <iostream>
using namespace std;

// Definition of template function
template <typename T>
void exchange (T& first, T& second)
{
  T temp = first;
  first = second;
  second = temp;
}

int main ()
{
  // Swapping two int types
  int integer1 = 5;
  int integer2 = 70;
  exchange (integer1, integer2);
  cout << "After swapping 5 and 70: ";
  cout << integer1 << "  " << integer2 << endl;
  // Swapping two double types
  double double1 = 101.5;
  double double2 = 402.7;
  exchange (double1, double2);
  cout << "After swapping 101.5 and 402.7: ";
  cout << double1 << "  " << double2 << endl;
  return 0;
}
```

```
Run:
After swapping 5 and 70: 70  5
After swapping 101.5 and 402.7: 402.7  101.5
```

Instantiation

Using template functions postpones the creation of nontemplate function definitions until compilation time. This means that when a program involving a function template is compiled, the compiler creates as many versions of the function as needed by function calls. In Program 15.2, the complier creates three versions of the function named *smaller* to handle the three function calls with their parameters, as shown in Figure 15.1. This process is referred to as *template instantiation*, but it should not be confused with instantiation of an object from a type.

15.1.3 Variations

There are several variations from the basic function template syntax that we discussed in the previous section.

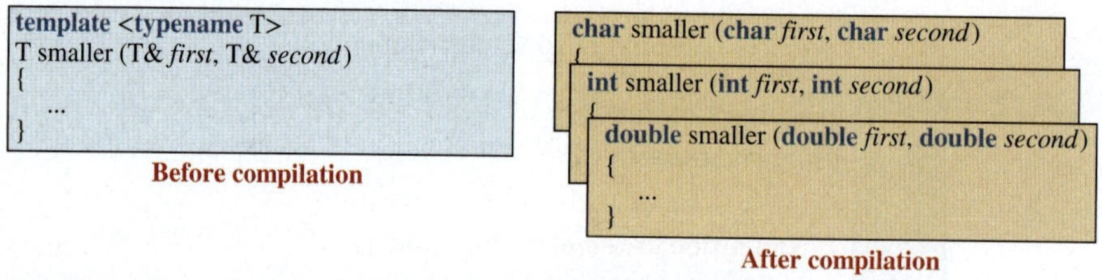

Figure 15.1 A function template is instantiated into several functions

Nontype Template Parameter

Sometimes we need to define a value instead of a type in our function template. In other words, the type of a parameter may be the same for all template functions that we want to use. In this case, we can define a template, but the type cannot be specifically defined.

Assume we want a function that prints the elements of any array regardless of the type of the element and the size of the array. We know that the type of each element can vary from one array to another, but the size of an array is always an integer (or unsigned integer). We do so using Program 15.4. We have two template parameters, *T* and *N*. The parameter *T* can be any type; the parameter *N* is a nontype (the type is predefined as integer).

Program 15.4 Printing an array

```
/***************************************************************
 * A program that uses a template function to print elements of   *
 * any array of any type                                          *
 ***************************************************************/
#include <iostream>
using namespace std;

// Definition of the print template function
template <typename T, int N>
void print (T (&array) [N])
{
  for (int i = 0; i < N ; i++)
  {
     cout << array [i] << " ";
  }
  cout << endl;
}

int main ()
{
  // Creation of two arrays
  int arr1 [4] = {7, 3, 5, 1};
  double arr2 [3] = {7.5, 6.1, 4.6};
  // Calling template function
  print (arr1);
```

(*continued*)

Program 15.4 Printing an array (Continued)

```
    print (arr2);
    return 0;
}
```

```
Run:
7 3 5 1
7.5 6.1 4.6
```

Explicit Type Determination

If we try to call the function template to find the smaller between an integer and a floating-point value such as the following, we get an error message.

```
cout << smaller (23, 67.2); // Errors! Two different types for the same template type T.
```

In other words, we are giving the compiler an integral value of 23 for the first argument of type `T` and a floating-point value of 67.2 for the second argument of type `T`. The type `T` is one template type, and the values for it must always be the same as each other. The error with the previous case can be avoided if we define the explicit type conversion during the call. This is done by defining the type inside the angle brackets as shown below:

```
cout << smaller <double> (23, 67.2); // 23 will be changed to 23.0
```

We are telling the compiler that we want to use the version of the *smaller* programs in which the value of `T` is of type *double*. The compiler then creates that version and converts 23 to 23.0 before finding the *smaller*.

Predefined Operation

We can compare two integers, two doubles, or two characters using the *smaller* function because the less-than operator (<) is defined for these types. This means that we can use a function template for any type for which the overloaded operator less than (<) is defined. For example, we know that the library *string* class has overloaded this operator. We can tell the compiler to replace `T` by a *string* and then call the function. This means that the following statement is valid and the result is the string "Bi".

```
cout << smaller ("Hello" , "Bi"); // The result is "Bi"
```

The C-string type and the *Rectangle* type have not been overloaded for this operator, and we will get a compilation error if we do overload it. The solution is specialization, as we discuss next.

Specialization

The operator less than (<) is not defined for a C-style string. This means that we cannot use the template function to find the smaller of two C-style strings. However, there is a solution, which is called **template specialization.** We can define another function with a specific type (instead of the template type), as shown in Program 15.5. There are two important points about this program.

Program 15.5 Specialization

```
/***************************************************************
 * Template function definition with specialization           *
 ***************************************************************/
#include <iostream>
#include <string>
#include <cstring>
using namespace std;

// Template Function
template <typename T>
T smaller (const T& first, const T& second)
{
  if (first < second)
  {
      return first;
  }
  return second;
}
// Specialization of template function
template <>
const char* smaller (const (const char*) & first, const (const char*) & second)
{
  if (strcmp (first, second ) < 0)
  {
      return first;
  }
  return second;
}

int main ( )
{
  // Calling template with two string objects
  string str1 = "Hello";
  string str2 = "Hi";
  cout << "Smaller (Hello , Hi): " << smaller (str1, str2) << endl;
  //Calling template function with two C-string objects
  const char* s1 = "Bye";
  const char* s2 = "Bye Bye";
  cout << "Smaller (Bye, Bye Bye)" << smaller (s1, s2) << endl;
  return 0;
}
```

Run:

```
Smaller (Hello , Hi): Hello
Smaller (Bye, Bye Bye): Bye
```

1. We must use the template <> before the header to show that this is the specialization of a template function previously defined.
2. We must be careful about replacing `T` with a specialized type. A C-style string is of type *const char**, which means every time we have `T`, we must replace it with *const char**.

Overloading

We discussed overloading of regular (nontemplate) functions in Chapter 7. We can apply the same concept to function templates. We can overload a function template to have several functions with the same name but different signatures. Normally, the template type is the same, but the number of parameters is different.

As an example, we overload the *smaller* template function to accept two or three parameters (we call it *smallest* because it uses more than two arguments). Program 15.6 shows the interface. Note that we have defined the second function in terms of the first one. This is why the second function is shorter.

Program 15.6 The program for overloaded smaller function

```
/***************************************************************
 * Overloaded version of the smaller template function         *
 ***************************************************************/
#include <iostream>
using namespace std;

// Template function with two parameters
template <typename T>
T smallest (const T& first, const T& second)
{
  if (first < second)
  {
      return first;
  }
  return second;
}
// Template function with three parameters
template <typename T>
T smallest (const T& first, const T& second, const T& third)
{
  return smallest (smallest (first, second), third);
}

int main ( )
{
  // Calling the overloaded version with three integers
  cout << "Smallest of 17, 12, and 27 is ";
  cout << smallest (17, 12, 27) << endl;
```

(continued)

Program 15.6 The program for overloaded smaller function (Continued)

```
    // Calling the overloaded version with three doubles
    cout << "Smallest of 8.5, 4.1, and 19.75 is ";
    cout << smallest (8.5, 4.1, 19.75) << endl;
    return 0;
}
```

```
Run:
Smallest of 17, 12, and 27 is 12
Smallest of 8.5, 4.1, and 19.75 is 4.1
```

15.1.4 Interface and Application Files

The definition of a template function can be put in an interface file, and the header can be included in an application file. This means that we can write one definition for a template function and then use it in different programs. The interface file in this case must include the definition of the function, not only the declaration. Program 15.7 shows how we can create an interface file, *smaller.h*, and put the definition of the function template in it. Any program can include this interface and use the function (Program 15.8).

Program 15.7 Definition of a function template

```
/***************************************************************
 * The interface file for the function template named smaller   *
 ***************************************************************/
#ifndef SMALLER_H
#define SMALLER_H
#include <iostream>
using namespace std;

template <typename T>
T smaller (const T& first, const T& second)
{
  if (first < second)
  {
       return first;
  }
  return second;
}
#endif
```

Program 15.8 Using the function template

```
/***************************************************************
 * The application file to test a function template             *
 ***************************************************************/
#include "smaller.h"

```

(continued)

Program 15.8 Using the function template (Continued)

```
int main ( )
{
   cout << "Smaller of 'a' and 'B': " << smaller ('a', 'B') << endl;
   cout << "Smaller of 12 and 15: " << smaller (12, 15) << endl;
   cout << "Smaller of 44.2 and 33.1: " << smaller (44.2, 33.1) << endl;
   return 0;
}
```

```
Run:
Smaller of a and B: B
Smaller of 12 and 15: 12
Smaller of 44.2 and 33.1: 33.1
```

15.2 CLASS TEMPLATE

The concept of a **class template** makes the C++ language very powerful. We have learned in the last few chapters that a class is a combination of data members and member functions. We may also have a class with data types and another class with the same functionality but with different data types. In these cases, we can use a class template. Templates are used in C++ libraries such as *string* and *stream* classes. They are also used in the Standard Template Library, STL, that we study in Chapter 19. To create a class template, we must make both the data members and the member functions generic.

15.2.1 Interface and Implementation

As we know, a class has an interface and an implementation. When we need to create a class template, we must have generic parameters in both the interface and the implementation.

Interface

The interface of a class must define the *typename* for both data members and member functions that use the parameterized type. Table 15.2 shows the syntax of a simple class template. We use only one data member, one default constructor, and two member functions. The constructor does not use the data member in this case. The accessor function returns a value of type T. The mutator function has one parameter of type T.

Table 15.2 Syntax of a simple class template

```
template <typename T>
class Name
{
  private:
      T data;
  public:
      Name ();                    // default constructor
      T get () const;             // accessor
      void set (T data);          // mutator function
};
```

Table 15.3 Implementation for the class defined in Table 15.2

```
// Implementation of the get function
template <typename T>
T name <T > :: get () const
{
  return data;
}
// Implementation of the set function
template <typename T>
void name < T > :: set (T d )
{
  data = d;
}
```

Implementation

In the implementation, we must mention the *typename* for each member function that uses the generic type. Table 15.3 shows the syntax of the implementation for the simple class we defined in Table 15.2.

Note that the name of the class that is used before the resolution operator (::) should be ***Name*** <T>, not just ***Name***.

To concentrate on the syntax, we define a very simple class, which we call *Fun*, with only one data member (which can be of type *int, double, char*, or even *string*). We want to show how the syntax is actually used in defining the interface, the implementation, and the application files of the class. We will present more sophisticated classes later in the chapter. At the end of this chapter, we create a more involved class (a generic array) to better show the usefulness of templates in C++.

Program 15.9 shows the interface for the *Fun* class. Note that every time we need to define a type (line 13), we must use the typename (*T* in this case). We also must use the declaration of the template <*typename* T> at the beginning of the class definition.

Program 15.9 The interface file for class Fun

```
1  /***************************************************************
2   * The interface file for a class named Fun                    *
3   ***************************************************************/
4  #ifndef FUN_H
5  #define FUN_H
6  #include <iostream>
7  using namespace std;
8
9  template <typename T>
10 class Fun
11 {
12   private:
13        T data;
```

(*continued*)

Program 15.9 The interface file for class Fun (Continued)

```
  public:
      Fun (T data);
      ~Fun ();
      T get () const;
      void set (T data);
};
#endif
```

Program 15.10 shows the implementation file for the template class *Fun*. Note that each function definition should use a template function with the template <*typename* T> declaration. Every time we need a type declaration, we use *T* as a generic type.

Program 15.10 The implementation file for class Fun

```
/*****************************************************************
 * The implementation file for the template class Fun            *
 *****************************************************************/
#ifndef FUN_CPP
#define FUN_CPP
#include "fun.h"

// Constructor
template <typename T>
Fun <T> :: Fun (T d)
: data (d)
{
}
// Destructor
template <typename T>
Fun <T> :: ~Fun ()
{
}
// Accessor Function
template <typename T>
T Fun <T> :: get () const
{
   return data;
}
// Mutator Function
template <typename T>
void Fun <T> :: set (T d)
{
   data = d;
}
#endif
```

A very important difference we notice in the implementation of a nontemplate class and the one for a template class is that the compiler needs to see the parameterized version of the template function when it compiles the application file. In other words, the application file (defined later) needs to have the implementation file as a header file, which means we need to add the macros *ifndef*, *define*, and *endif* to the implementation file.

Program 15.11 shows the application that uses the template class *Fun*. Note that we have included *fun.cpp* as a header file to help the compiler create different versions of the class. Also note that to instantiate template classes (lines 10 to 13), we must define the actual type that replaces the *typename* T.

The actual type for the data member of class *Fun1* is *int*, the one for *Fun2* is *double*, the one for *Fun3* is *char*, and the one for *Fun4* is a string.

Program 15.11 The application file using class Fun

```
1  /*****************************************************************
2   * The application file to test the template class Fun          *
3   *****************************************************************/
4  #include "fun.cpp"
5
6  int main ( )
7  {
8    // Instantiation of four classes each with different data type
9    Fun <int> Fun1 (23);
10   Fun <double> Fun2 (12.7);
11   Fun <char> Fun3 ('A');
12   Fun <string> Fun4 ("Hello");
13   // Displaying the data values for each class
14   cout << "Fun1: " << Fun1.get() << endl;
15   cout << "Fun2: " << Fun2.get() << endl;
16   cout << "Fun3: " << Fun3.get() << endl;
17   cout << "Fun4: " << Fun4.get() << endl;
18   // Setting the data values in two classes
19   Fun1.set(47);
20   Fun3.set ('B');
21   // Displaying values for newly set data
22   cout << "Fun1 after set: " << Fun1.get() << endl;
23   cout << "Fun3 after set: " << Fun3.get() << endl;
24   return 0;
25 }
```

```
Run:
Fun1: 23
Fun2: 12.7
Fun3: A
Fun4: Hello
Fun1 after set: 47
Fun3 after set: B
```

15.2.2 Compilation

We can compile and link different files related to a program when there are several function templates or class templates in our project. There are basically two ways to do so.

Inclusion Approach

The first approach is called *inclusion* and is shown in Figure 15.2. In this approach we put the declaration and definition in header files and then include the header files in the our application program. Of course, it is always recommended to use separate header files, one for the declaration and one for the definition. The separation of these two files allows us to move to other approaches quickly. We can put the declaration in a (.h) file and the definition in a (.cpp) file. We do not compile the definition file separately; we just include it in the application file and compile only the application file. Note that the declaration file must be included in the definition file and the definition file must be included in the application file. We only compile the application file.

Separate Compilation

All of the programs we have designed based on object-oriented programming have used the *separate compilation* concept that we discussed in a Chapter 7. In this model we have three different files: interface files, implementation files, and one application file, as shown in Figure 15.3. As we discussed in Chapter 7, separate compilation has the advantage of hiding the implementation from the end user and thus promotes the concept of encapsulation.

Although this approach has been used with nontemplate functions and classes, it needs modifications if our program has template functions or template classes. The problem is that the implementation file cannot be compiled independently because the compiler needs the application file to figure out which instances of each template function or template class must be used in the compilation.

The C++ standard has found the solution. We must use the keyword *export* to export each template declaration or definition. We insert the keyword *export* in front of each typename. For example, in the definition of class *Fun*, we add this keyword as shown

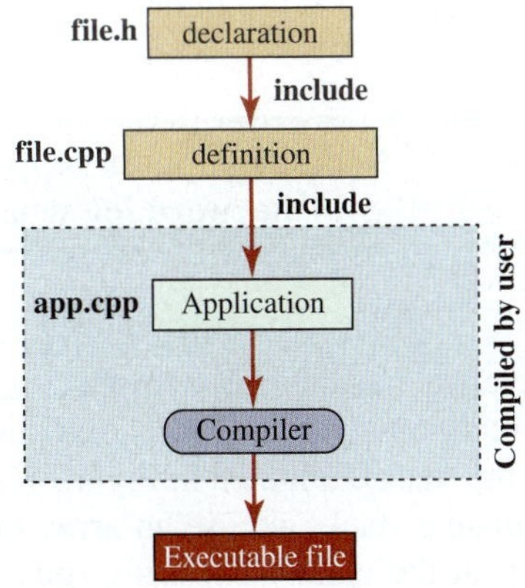

Figure 15.2 Compilation using inclusion

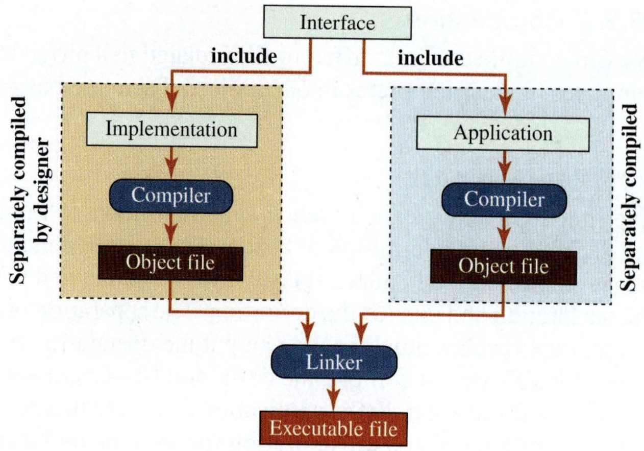

Figure 15.3 Separate compilation

below. For each member function, we also need to add the keyword as shown for the constructor below:

```
// fun.h
export template <typename T>
class Fun
{
  ...
};
```

```
// fun.cpp
export template <typename T>
Fun <T> :: Fun (T d)
: data (d)
{
}
```

If your compiler has not implemented the *export* keyword, you will have to use the inclusion approach.

> **Not all compilers support the use of the *export* keyword for separate compilation.**

Example

In this example we create a class template that simulates a stack. As we mentioned before, a stack is a structure in which the last item pushed into the stack is the first item that will be popped from the stack, as shown in Figure 15.4.

To simulate a stack, we use an array of type *T*, but we provide only the operations that can insert at the end of the array (push) and remove the element at the end of the array (pop). When an item is popped, its value can be retrieved. Program 15.12 shows the interface file.

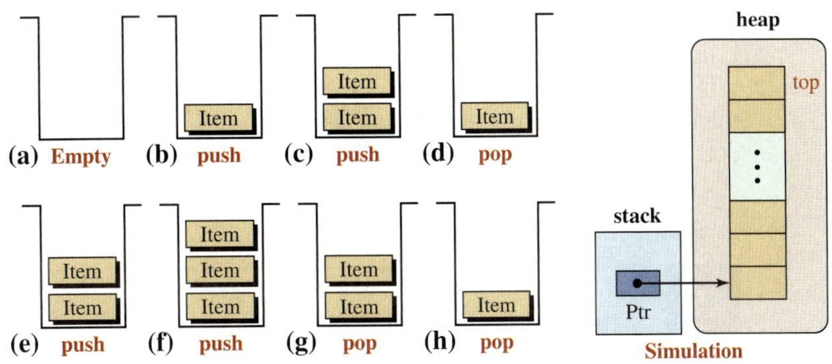

Note:
The push operation inserts an item in the stack.
The pop operation erases the item at the top of the stack.
We have simulated the stack as an upside-down array in the heap.

Figure 15.4 Operations on a stack

In this program we have defined the stack as an array (line 14), but the operations defined for the array allow only pushing and popping of the top element. Accessing or changing other elements is not allowed.

Program 15.12 File stack.h

```
1  /*******************************************************************
2   * The interface file for the class template stack                 *
3   *******************************************************************/
4  #ifndef STACK_H
5  #define STACK_H
6  #include <iostream>
7  #include <cassert>
8  using namespace std;
9  
10 template <typename T>
11 class Stack
12 {
13    private:
14        T* ptr;
15        int capacity;
16        int size;
17    public:
18        Stack (int capacity);
19        ~Stack ();
20        void push (const T& element);
21        T pop ();
22 };
23 #endif
```

Program 15.13 shows the implementation file. Note that we defined the implementation file as a separate file as though we want to use separate compilation, but in fact it is a header file. We include it in the application file. The separation of two files organizes the code, and we can always switch to separate compilation when we have a compiler that accepts the *export* keyword.

Program 15.13 File stack.cpp

```
/***************************************************************
 * The implementation file class template stack                *
 ***************************************************************/
#ifndef STACK_CPP
#define STACK_CPP
#include "stack.h"

// Constructor
template <typename T>
Stack <T> :: Stack (int cap)
: capacity (cap), size (0)
{
   ptr = new T [capacity];
}
// Destructor
template <typename T>
Stack <T> :: ~Stack ()
{
   delete [ ] ptr;
}
// Push function
template <typename T>
void Stack <T> :: push (const T& element)
{
   if (size < capacity)
   {
        ptr[size] = element;
        size++;
   }
   else
   {
        cout << "Cannot push; stack is full." << endl;
        assert (false);
   }
}
// Pop function
template <typename T>
T Stack <T> :: pop ()
```

(continued)

Program 15.13 File stack.cpp (Continued)

```
{
   if (size > 0)
   {
       T temp = ptr [size - 1];
       size--;
       return temp;
   }
   else
   {
       cout << "Cannot pop; stack is empty." << endl;
       assert (false);
   }
}
#endif
```

Program 15.14 shows the application file. We have instantiated the application file with an integer replacing the typename, but the integer can be of type `double`, `char`, or even a user-defined type.

15.2.3 Other Issues

There are other issues that we briefly discuss here. In future chapters we explore these issues in more detail.

Program 15.14 Application file to instantiate the stack class

```
/***************************************************************
 * The application file to test the stack class with integers   *
 ***************************************************************/
#include "stack.cpp"

int main ()
{
  Stack <int> stack (10);
  stack.push (5);
  stack.push (6);
  stack.push (7);
  stack.push (3);
  cout << stack.pop () << endl;
  cout << stack.pop ();
  return 0;
}
```

```
Run:
3
7
```

Friends

The declaration of a template class can include friend functions. There are three ways to implement friend functions. A template class can have a nontemplate function as a friend. A template class can have a template function as a friend. A template class can also have a specialized template function as a friend.

Aliases

It is sometimes easier to define aliases for template classes using the key term `typedef`. This allows us to use the alias as the full definition of the class in the program. For example, we can have the following aliases for the stack template stack class we defined previously:

```
typedef stack <int> iStack;
typedef stack <double> dStack;
typedef stack <string, int> siStack;
```

Then we can use the type definitions in our program as shown below:

```
iStack s1;
dStack s2;
siStack s3;
```

15.2.4 Inheritance

We can derive a template class from another template class or from a nontemplate class. For example, assume we have defined the class *First* as a template class:

```
template < typename T >
class First
{
...
}
```

We can then define another class, *Second,* which is publicly derived from the *First* class as shown below:

```
template < typename T >
class Second : public First <T>
{
   ...
}
```

There is nothing special about inherited template classes, and they are not very common. We do not discuss them further.

15.2.5 In Retrospect

We have discussed some classes that were actually template classes. In this section we look at these classes as generic classes.

String Classes

In Chapter 10 we discussed the *string* class. The string class is a specialization of a template class named *basic_string*. The following shows the general layout of this class.

```
template < typename charT >
class basic_string
{
   ...
};
```

The library class defines two specializations from this class, one for a *char* type and another for a *wchar_t* type, as shown below. In Appendix A we use the first specialization; the second is similar.

```
typedef basic_string <char> string;
typedef basic_string <wchar_t> wstring;
```

Input/Output Classes

Another set of classes that are actually generic classes are the input/output classes. All of the input classes we discussed before are actually specializations of the template classes. For example, the *istream* class is a specialization of the *basic_istream* class as shown below:

```
typedef basic_istream <char> istream;
typedef basic_istream <wchar_t> wistream;
```

Key Terms

class template
function template
template specialization

Summary

Function templates allow us to define a function but defer the definition of the types until the program is compiled. When the program is compiled, the compiler creates as many versions of the function as there are function calls with different types. The syntax includes the reserved words *template* and *typename* in angle brackets. To facilitate sharing, function templates are placed in an interface file that is included in the program being compiled. There are three rules for type determination in a function template: (1) We cannot mix the types. (2) If mixed types are required, the secondary types must be explicitly typed. (3) The operations in the function, such as compare, must be valid for the types being specified. If they are not, we can use specialization; that is, we can define another function with the specific type to handle the exception. We can overload a template function as long as the signatures are different.

Class templates can be created by using generic parameters in both the interface and the implementation. The interface of a class must define the typename for both data members and member functions that use the parameterized type. In the implementation, we must use the *typename* for each member function that involves the generic type. However, the compiler must see the parameterized version of the template function when it compiles the application file, which means that the implementation file must be included as a header file. While the implementation file can be included using either the inclusion approach or by separate compilations, separate compilation is not yet available for all compilers. Class templates can include multiple types as long as each typename is specified with a different identifier.

Problems

PR-1. How many versions of the following function are instantiated during the compilation?

```
template <typename T>
void fun (T x)
{
    ...
}
int main ()
{
    fun (7);
    fun (12.5);
    fun ("Hello");
    return 0;
}
```

PR-2. How many versions of the following function are instantiated during the compilation?

```
template <typename T>
void fun (T x)
{
    ...
}
int main ()
{
    Sample (7);
    Sample (9) ;
    return 0;
}
```

PR-3. Write a function template that computes the average of two numbers, such as integers, long integers, doubles, or long doubles.

PR-4. Overload the function written in PR-3 to find the average of three numbers.

PR-5. Write a template for a *struct* called *Pair* that creates a *struct* of any two data items of any type. We can have a pair of an integer and a double, a pair of a double and a character, and so on.

Programs

PRG-1. Write a templated function to find the index of the smallest element in an array of any type. Test the function with three arrays of type *int*, *double*, and *char*. Then print the value of the smallest element.

PRG-2. If we can find the smallest element in an array, we can sort an array using the *selection sort* algorithm. In this algorithm, we find the smallest element in the array and swap it with the first element. We then find the smallest in the rest of the array and exchange it with the second element. We continue until the array is completely sorted. Write a program that sorts three arrays of type *int*, *double*, and *char*.

PRG-3. Write a templated function to search an array for a value. Test the function with two arrays of type *int* and *char*. Note that searching for a double value may not give the correct response because the equality operator is not well defined for floating-point values.

PRG-4. Define a function to reverse the order of elements in an array of any type. Test your program with an array of integers, doubles, characters, and strings. Use a swap helper function to swap any two elements. Use a print helper function to print the contents of the arrays before and after swapping.

PRG-5. Create a templated class *Array* that can handle an array of objects of any type and any size in the heap. Define an *add* member function to add elements to the end of the array. Define a *print* function to print all elements in the array. Test your program with arrays of type *int*, *double*, and *char*.

PRG-6. A *queue* is a first-in, first-out structure. An example of a queue is a line of people waiting to be served. We can implement a queue using an array in which the items are inserted (enqueued) at the end of the array and removed (dequeued) from the front. Create a templated class and a queue of any type. Then test the queue in two separate application files: one as a queue of integers, the other as a queue of strings. Add appropriate *try-catch* blocks to catch adding to the full queue or removing from an empty queue.

C++ treats input/output operations as library classes called *streams*. In this chapter, we first introduce sources and sinks of data. We then discuss streams, which are classes that connect our programs to those sources and sinks. We discuss console streams, file streams, and string streams. Finally, we discuss data formatting as it pertains to streams.

Objectives

After you have read and studied this chapter, you should be able to:

- Discuss communication between a program and a source or sink of data using stream objects.
- Discuss the hierarchy of stream classes.
- Emphasize that the *ios* class, as a virtual base for all the classes in the hierarchy, cannot be instantiated, but it defines data members that are inherited by all classes throughout the hierarchy.
- Discuss the console streams (*istream*, *ostream*, and *iostream* classes) and emphasize that users cannot instantiate objects from these classes.
- Show that C++ has already instantiated one object from the *istream* and three objects from the *ostream* class and stored them in the <iostream> header file.
- Show that we can use the member functions defined in the console streams to read from the keyboard and write to the monitor.
- Discuss file streams (*ifstream*, *ofstream*, and *fstream*) as three classes that are used to connect to files as sources or sinks of data.
- Show that file streams are capable of both text and binary input/output.
- Show how we can access a source or sink of data both sequentially and randomly.
- Discuss string streams (*istringstream*, *ostringstream*, and *stringstream*) as adapters to be used between an application and the string class.
- Show how we use the flags and fields defined in the *ios* class to directly format data and how we can use standard or customized manipulators to do so.

16.1 INTRODUCTION

When we run a program, data must be stored in memory. The data stored in memory for processing comes from an external source and goes to an external sink. This means that we must consider the source and the sink of our data. A source can be a keyboard, a file, or a string. A sink can be a monitor, a file, or a string. Figure 16.1 shows the relationship between the input/output data and a program.

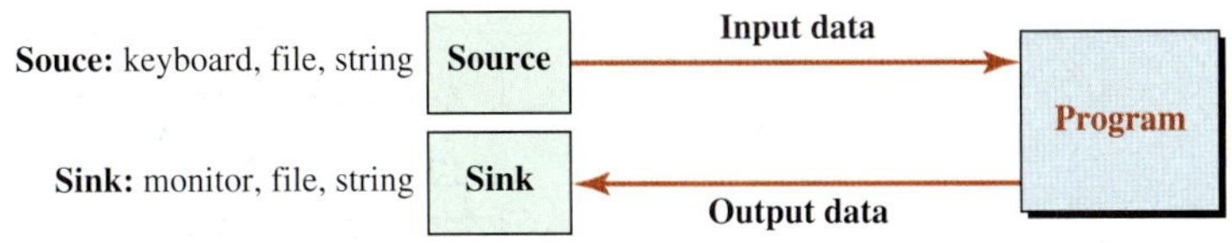

Figure 16.1 A program related to a source and a sink

So far we have used the keyboard (as the source) and the monitor (as the sink) for data. The keyboard is a temporary source and the monitor is a temporary sink of data. When we run a program, the input data must be entered again and the output data will be created anew on the monitor.

Files, on the other hand, are permanent sources and sinks of data. They can be saved. They can be physically transferred to another computer. And they can be used over and over again.

Strings as internal sources or sinks of data have been designed for special purposes, as we will see later in the chapter.

The source or sink of data can be the console, a file, or a string.

16.1.1 Streams

A source and a sink of data cannot be directly connected to a program. We need a mediator to stand between them and the program to control the flow of data and at the same time interpret data when reading or writing. We have input streams and output streams. An *input stream* stands between a source and the program; an *output stream* stands between the program and a sink.

Figure 16.2 shows the way we normally think of a **stream:** a sequence of bytes flowing in or out of a program. The bytes are *extracted* from an *input stream* and *inserted* into an *output stream*. An *input/output stream* can be bidirectional, but this not shown in the figure.

16.1.2 Data Representation

Although, we can receive data from a source and we can send data to a sink in text or binary format, the sink and source of data are part of the computer system and are organized as a sequence of *bytes* (8-bit chunks). We can only send a sequence of bytes to a sink or receive a sequence of bytes from the source. Understanding this fact makes it easier to deal with different sources and sinks.

A sink can receive only a sequence of bytes;
a source can only send a sequence of bytes.

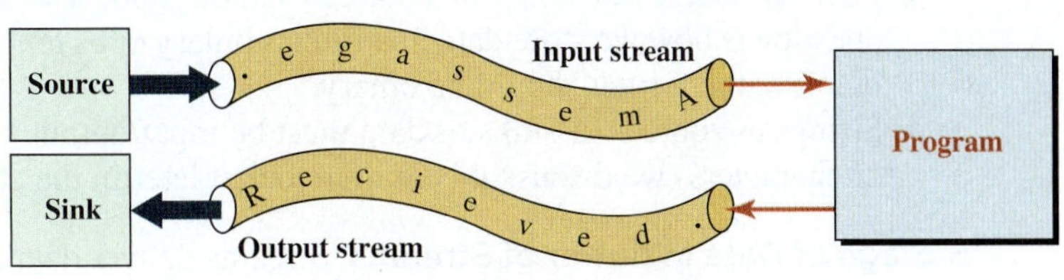

Figure 16.2 Conceptual representation of input and output streams

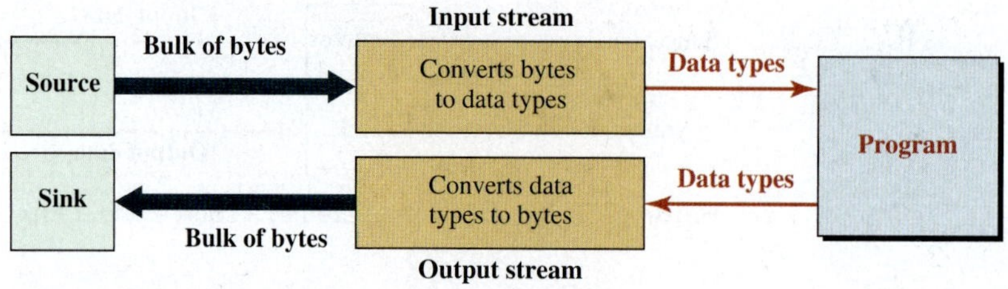

Figure 16.3 Main role of streams as convertors

Role of Streams

One of the reasons that the C++ standard created input/output streams is to change bytes of data that are received from a source to the data type the program needs and to change the data types that the program sends to a sink into bytes that the sink can store. In other words, the main job of streams can be thought of as converting bytes to data types and data types to bytes. Of course streams have other jobs, such as controlling the flow of bytes in and out of the computer, as we will see gradually in this chapter. Figure 16.3 shows this idea.

Text versus Binary Input/Output

When we input or output data, we must understand that three locations are involved: memory, a stream, and a source/sink. We now examine how data are stored in these three locations.

Storage of Data in Memory The memory of a computer is a collection of bytes (8-bit) chunks, but we do not store data as individual bytes; we store data as a set of contiguous bytes. For example, each data object of type *int* occupies 4 bytes of memory no matter what the value of the variable is. In other words, a small integer of value 23 and a large integer of value 4,294,967,294 both occupy 4 bytes of memory or 32 bits of binary data.

Data in memory are stored in binary form.

Storage of Data in Sources or Sinks Sources and sinks of data also store data in a chunk of bytes, but data can be either binary or text. If a data item is stored as binary, the type of the data defines the number of bytes; if a data item is stored as text, the value of the data defines the number of bytes. For example, the integer 23 can be stored as four bytes (binary) or it can be stored as two characters '2' and '3' (text). The integer 4294967294 can be stored as 4 bytes in binary but 10 bytes in text.

The question is which method of storage we need to use. The following considerations may help us decide.

- The keyboard as a source of data can accept data only as text. Similarly, the monitor as a sink of data shows data only as a set of characters.
- Files as sources or sinks of data can handle both text and binary input/output. The question is how we store data in a file: as binary or as text. If we want to store an object in a file, the format should be binary.
- Strings as sources or sinks of data must be input/output as text; a string is a collection of characters (we discuss this in more detail later in the chapter).

Storage of Data in Buffer of Streams Streams deliver data to a sink or receive data from a source in bulk. This means the stream buffer should exactly match the sink or source it is

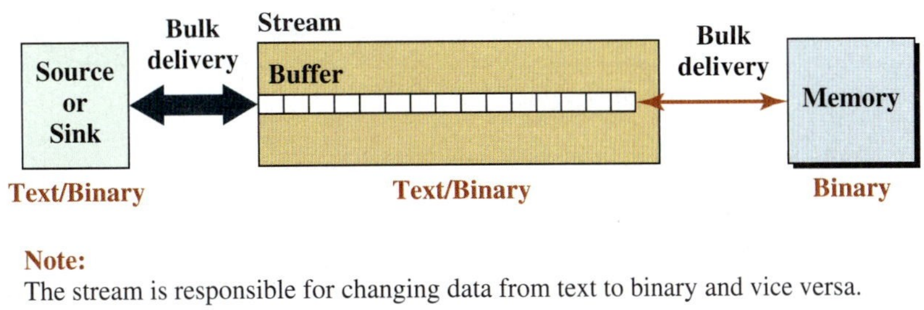

Figure 16.4 Responsibility of streams

connected to. In other words, if the source or sink is using text data, the stream must use text data; if the source or sink is using binary data, the source or the sink must use binary data. As we will see later, the streams are designed to operator in text mode by default; if we want them to operate in binary mode, the stream object must be instantiated as binary. A question: If memory operates in binary and the stream operates in text or binary (based on the source or sink it is connected to), how is this disparity resolved? This is one of the main purposes of using streams. A stream always accepts data or delivers data to memory in binary, but it converts the data as necessary to match the need of the source or sink. Figure 16.4 shows this responsibility.

16.1.3 Stream Classes

To handle input/output operations, the C++ library defines a hierarchy of classes (Figure 16.5).

The ios Class

At the top of the hierarchy is the *ios* class, which serves as a virtual base class. The ***ios* class** is the base class for all input/output classes. It defines data members and member functions that are inherited by all input/output stream classes. Since the *ios* class is never instantiated, it does not use its data members and member functions. They are used by other stream classes.

The *ios* class cannot be instantiated.

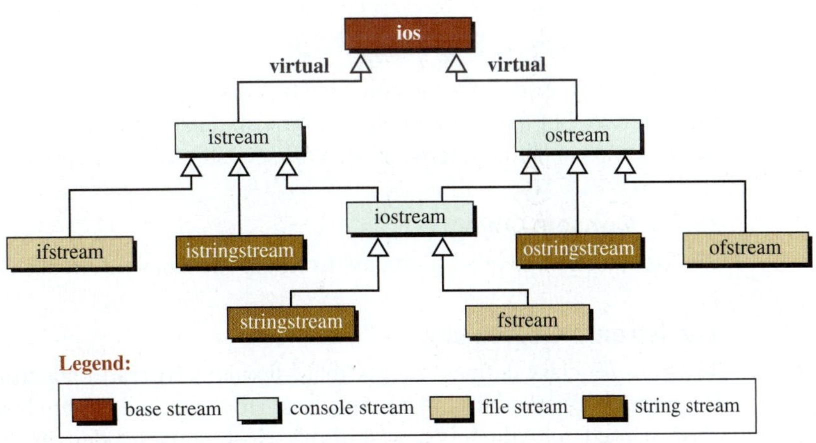

Figure 16.5 Basic stream hierarchy in C++

Table 16.1 Five steps in using a stream
1. Construct the stream
2. Connect the stream to the source or sink
3. Read or write from the stream
4. Disconnect the source or the sink
5. Destroy the stream

Other Classes

For convenience, we refer to *istream*, *ostream*, and *iostream* as console classes (they are used to connect our program to the console); we refer to *ifstream*, *ofstream*, and *fstream* as file streams (they are used to connect our program to files); and we refer to *istringstream*, *ostringstream*, and *stringstream* as string streams.

Using Streams

To use any streams, we must consider the chain of five actions shown in Table 16.1. An appropriate stream object is constructed, the object is connected to the source or sink, data are read from the source or written to the sink, the source or sink is disconnected from the stream, and the stream is destroyed.

Characteristics of Stream Objects

When we work with stream objects, we need to know that none of the classes in the hierarchy have provided a copy constructor or assignment operators. We should also know that the objects of these classes will change when they are used. This means that we should remember three facts about the objects instantiated from these classes:

- We can never pass an object of any stream class to a function by value (doing so requires a copy constructor). Passing these objects must be by reference.
- We can never return an object of any stream class from a function by value (doing so requires a copy constructor); returning must be done by reference.
- We cannot pass or return an object of any stream class using a constant modifier; the nature of these objects requires change.

16.2 CONSOLE STREAMS

In this section we discuss the **console streams:** *istream*, *ostream,* and *iostream.* We can use the first two, but the *iostream* class cannot be instantiated. It is defined as a superclass for other classes in the hierarchy, as we will see later in the chapter.

16.2.1 Console Objects

We first discuss the objects created from the two console stream classes.

The istream Object: cin

The *istream* class defines a class that allows us to read data from the keyboard into our program. We cannot instantiate this class. However, the system has created an object of this class, named *cin*, which is stored in the <iostream> header file. The system also connects the *cin* object to the keyboard as shown in Figure 16.6.

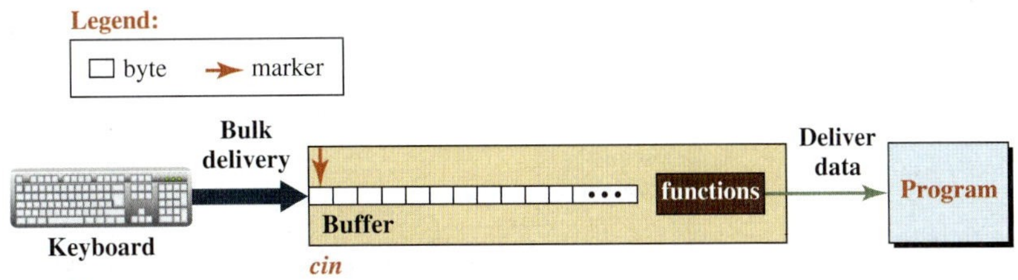

Note:
The marker is at the beginning of the buffer when the keyboard is connected to the stream.
After a read operation, the marker moves to the right.

Figure 16.6 The cin object in relation to our program and keyboard

When our program goes out of scope, the *cin* object is destroyed and is automatically disconnected from the keyboard. This means that four out of five tasks, as defined in Table 16.1, are automatically done for us by the system; we simply use the member functions defined in this class to read data from the keyboard.

> **The system has created an object from istream class, named *cin*, and stored it in the <iostream> header.**

The ostream Objects: cout, cerr, and clog

The *ostream* class defines a class that allows us to write data from our program to the monitor. We cannot instantiate this class. However, the system has created three objects of this class (named *cout*, *cerr*, and *clog*) that are stored in the <iostream> header file. The system also connects all three classes to the monitor. When our program goes out of scope, these objects are automatically destroyed and are automatically disconnected from the monitor. This means that four out of five tasks, as defined in Table 16.1, are automatically done for us by the system. We can only use the member functions defined in this class to write data to the monitor. Figure 16.7 shows the connection of these objects to the monitor and our program.

There are important points about these objects. First, *cout* is tied to the *cin* object, which means every time we want to input data through the *cin* object, the *cout* object is flushed (emptied). Second, both *cerr* and *clog* are designed to send errors to the console. The difference is that the *cerr* object flushes its contents immediately after each operation; the *clog* object collects the error messages and is flushed whenever the program terminates or when it is explicitly flushed.

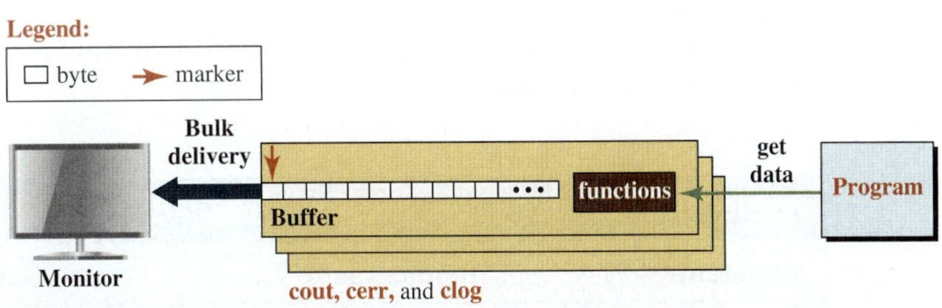

Note:
There are three simulatneous objects.
The marker is at the beginning of the buffer when the monitor is connected to the streams.
After a write operation, the marker moves to the right.

Figure 16.7 The cout, cerr, and clog objects in relation to our program and monitor

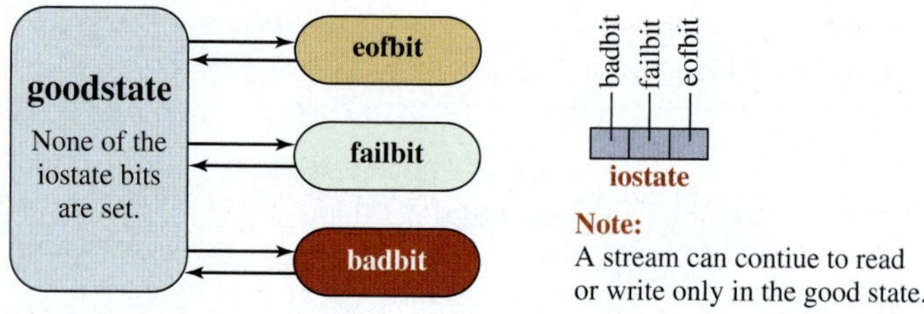

Figure 16.8 State of a stream

> **The system has created the *cout*, *cerr*, and *clog* objects from the *ostream* class and stored them in the <iostream> header.**

16.2.2 Stream State

When we read text data from the keyboard, we must use an *istream* object (*cin*); when we write text data to the monitor, we must use an *ostream* object (*cout*, *cerr*, or *clog*). These objects are different from the ones we have used so far. The member functions that we need to apply to these objects may not be able to do their job. We may try to read from an empty buffer or write to a full buffer. The current position from which we need to read a byte may not contain what we need to read (we may need to read a digit as part of an integer, but the current position may contain a character that is not a digit).

For these reasons, a stream must keep track of its *state*. The **stream state** is stored in a data member that shows the status of the stream object. The stream also needs member functions to test its state. Since the state of a stream is the same for console streams, file streams, and string streams, the state data member and the corresponding member functions are defined in the *ios* class, which is inherited by all stream classes.

> **Data members and member functions related to the state of a strem are defined in the *ios* stream class but inherited by all stream classes.**

State Data Member

The *ios* stream defines a type called *iostate* (input/output state). The implementation of this type is system dependent, but we know that it defines three constants: *eofbit*, *failbit*, and *badbit*. We can think about the *iostate* data member as a bit set made of three bits, as shown in Figure 16.8.

Table 16.2 shows the bits defined in the *iostate* type. Note that the *eofbit* does not apply to the output stream.

Table 16.2 Constant values used with iostate

Constants	Input stream	Output stream
ios :: eofbit	No more characters to extract.	Not applicable.
ios :: failbit	An invalid read operation.	An invalid write operation.
ios :: badbit	Stream integrity is lost.	Stream integrity is lost.
ios :: goodbit	Everything is fine.	Everything is fine.

The *eofbit* is set when we try to extract a byte that does not exist in the stream buffer (the stream position has reached the end of the buffer and there is no character to read). The *failbit* is set when we try to extract a byte that does not correspond to what we want. For example, if we try to read an integer, we must extract digits (or white space that defines the end of a set of digits), not any other character. Note that if one of the two bits (*eofbit* or *failbit*) is set, the *badbit* is automatically set. The *badbit* is set when the integrity of the stream is lost, such as when there is a memory shortage, when there is a conversion problem, when an exception is thrown, and so on. As is said, no news is good news: When none of the three bits are set, the stream is in a good state and can be used.

State-Related Member Functions

The *ios* class also provides member functions to check the condition of the state. Several member functions have been defined; most of them are system dependent. For example, there is a member function called *rdstate* that returns the current bit values of the *iostate* data member. We can use the member functions defined in Table 16.3 to check the input/output status.

The first four functions in Table 16.3 are straightforward. Each returns the status of the corresponding bit in the *iostate* data member. The fifth one, *clear*, resets all three bits to zero (*false*). The interesting ones are the sixth and the seventh. The sixth function is a conversion constructor, as we discussed in Chapter 6. with regard to overloaded operators. For example, we defined a conversion constructor that changes an instance of a *Fraction* object to a double value. The conversion constructor changes the host object (an instance of a stream) to a pointer to `void` (instead of a Boolean value) because a pointer to void, as we know, can be used in any expression. When the pointer is null, its value is 0, which is interpreted as *false* in a Boolean expression; when it is not null, it is interpreted as *true* in a Boolean expression. The last function is an overloaded operator that returns true if the *failbit* or *badbit* is set. It does not check the *eofbit.* The last two functions are very useful because we can apply them to the stream object (without any operator) or apply them to the returned object from an operation. Note that most operations in *istream* and *ostream,* including the extraction and insertion operators, return an object of type *stream.*

Program 16.1 shows some of the points we discussed.

Table 16.3 Member functions for checking the state of a stream

Functions	Return values
bool eof ()	true if ***eofbit*** is set; false otherwise.
bool fail ()	true if ***failbit*** or ***badbit*** is set; false otherwise.
bool bad ()	true if ***badbit*** is set; false otherwise.
bool good ()	true if the ***stream*** is in good condition; false otherwise.
clear ();	It clears all three bits (sets to zero).
operator void* ();	It returns a pointer; interpreted ***true*** if not null.
const bool operator! ();	It returns true if ***badbit*** or ***failbit*** is set.

Program 16.1 Testing the cin state

```
1  /****************************************************************
2   * A program to show how to test the state of a stream          *
3   ****************************************************************/
4  #include <iostream>
5  using namespace std;
6
7  int main ()
8  {
9     int n;
10    cout << "Enter a line of integers and eof at the end: " << endl;
11    while (cin >> n)
12    {
13        cout << n * 2 << " ";
14    }
15    return 0;
16 }
```

Run:

```
Enter a line of integers and eof at the end:
14 24 11 78 19 32 ^Z
28 48 22 156 38 64
```

In line 11 we use the expression *cin >> n*. Although we have not discussed the operator >> formally, we have used it in the past. It reads an integer from the *cin* object connected to the keyboard. We will see later that this operator reads an integer into its argument and returns a reference to the *cin* object. The expression inside the *while* statement needs to see a Boolean value, but what is returned from the statement (*cin >> n*) is an instance of the *cin* object. A conversion must occur to change the *cin* object to a Boolean value. This is done by calling *operator void**(), which returns a pointer (*true*) if the previous operation is successful and a null pointer (*false*) if it is not successful. This means that the loop continues until one of the three bits are set. When we type ^Z on the keyboard, it means that we terminate inputting data into the *cin* buffer and the *eofbit* is set.

16.2.3 Input/Output

Since the objects of the *istream* and *ostream* classes have already been instantiated for us and connected to the console, our only task is to use the member functions defined in these two stream classes to read data from the buffer or write data to the buffer. As we mentioned, the keyboard, which is connected to the only *istream* object, and the monitor, which is connected to the three *ostream* objects, can accept only text data. These means that the buffers in the *istream* and *ostream* objects store only a set of 8-bit bytes interpreted individually as characters. Since the memory of the computer stores data in binary, the member functions of the *ostream* object must change binary data to individual characters. Similarly, the member functions of the *istream* object must read a set of characters and interpret them as binary data.

Character Member Functions

The *istream* and *ostream* classes provide several character member functions and overloaded operators to read characters from the keyboard and write characters to the monitor.

Table 16.4 Reading and writing a single character

The *istream* class	The *ostream* class
int get()	None
istream& get (char& c)	ostream& put (char& c);

Reading and Writing a Single Character Table 16.4 shows two member functions to read a single character from the keyboard and one member function to write a single character to the monitor. The *istream* class provides two versions of the *get* function. The first returns an integer (the ASCII) value of the character in the buffer; this character is stored in memory as an integer (converted to 4 bytes). Since this function does not return a reference to the *istream* object, we cannot test the state of the stream at the time that we call the function. The second function reads a character that is stored in its parameter. The *ostream* object, however, provides only one *put* function, which writes a copy of a character defined in its parameter to the buffer.

Program 16.2 shows how we can use the first *get* function to print the ASCII value of five characters. Note that the loop is controlled by the value of *i,* not by the state of the stream.

Note that we type a set of five characters that are stored in the buffer of the *cin* object. The program reads them, one by one, and sends them to the monitor using the insertion operator (<<).

Program 16.2 Testing the first get function

```
/***************************************************************
 * A program to read characters and print their ASCII values   *
 ***************************************************************/
#include <iostream>
using namespace std;

int main ()
{
  int x;
  cout << "Enter five characters (no spaces): ";
  for (int i = 0; i < 5; i++)
  {
      x = cin.get ();
      cout << x << " ";
  }
  return 0;
}
```

```
Run:
Enter five characters (no spaces): ABCDE
65 66 67 68 69
```

Program 16.3 Testing the get and put functions

```
/***************************************************************
 * A program that capitalizes the first letter of each word     *
 ***************************************************************/
#include <iostream>
using namespace std;

int main ()
{
  char c;
  cout << "Enter a multi-line text and EOF as the last line." << endl;
  char pre = '\n';
  while (cin.get(c))
  {
      if (pre == ' ' || pre == '\n' )
      {
            cout.put (toupper (c));
      }
      else
      {
            cout.put (c);
      }
      pre = c;
  }
  return 0;
}
```

```
Run:
Enter a multi-line text and EOF as the last line.
This is the text that we want to capitalize
This Is The Text That We Want To Capitalize
each word.
Each Word.
^Z
```

Now we use the *get* function in the *istream* class and the *put* function in the *ostream* class to make the first letter of each word uppercase (see Program 16.3).

Note that in Program 16.3 we define two variables: the current character, *c*, and the previous character, *pre*. If the previous character is a space or return ('\n') character, we capitalize the current character. To capitalize the first word, we set *pre* to the return character. After each iteration, we store the current character as the previous character.

Reading a C String The *istream* class provides two member functions to read a set of characters and create a C string out of them. The first function, *get*, reads $n - 1$ characters from the keyboard and stores them as a C string (a *null* character is added to the end of the array). The second function, *getline*, reads $n - 1$ characters or a set of characters terminated by a delimiter, which is defaulted to '\n', whichever comes first. Note that the delimiter is

Table 16.5 Reading a C string

The *istream* class	The *ostream* class
istream& get (char* *s*, int *n*)	
istream& getline (char* *s*, int *n*, char *d* = '*n*')	

removed from the stream, but it is not added to the array. The prototypes of these functions are shown in Table 16.5.

Note that in both cases shown in the table, when *n* characters are read or the delimiter is reached, the *eofbit* is set and no more characters can be read from the stream.

We test the second function in Program 16.4. We create an array of 80 characters to accept a line. We then type a line and enter the return key. The program creates a string out of the line (without the '\n' character) and adds a null character at the end.

Input/Output of Fundamental Data Types

The *istream* and *ostream* classes are basically character stream classes, but this does not mean that we cannot extract the value of a fundamental type from an input stream or insert the value of a fundamental data type into an output stream. Inputting and outputting of fundamental data types is also considered text input/output because the function extracts several characters and puts them together to get a fundamental data type or the function creates several characters from a fundamental data type and inserts them into the output stream. This is done by two overloaded operators called the *insertion operator* and the *extraction operator*. Table 16.6 shows the general declaration of these two operators in which the type can be *bool*, *char*, *short* (signed and unsigned), `int` (signed and unsigned), `long` (signed and unsigned), *float*, *double*, *long double*, or *void**.

Program 16.4 Testing getline

```
/*****************************************************************
 * A program to test the getline functions                       *
 *****************************************************************/
#include <iostream>
using namespace std;

int main ()
{
  char str2 [80];
  cin.getline (str2, 80, '\n');
  cout << str2;
  return 0;
}
```

```
Run:
This is a line to make a string out of it.
This is a line to make a string out of it.
```

Table 16.6 Extracting and inserting a fundamental data type

```
istream& operator >> (type& x);          // Extracting next data item
ostream& operator << (type& x);          // Inserting next data item
```

The behavior of the extraction and insertion operators is different for fundamental data types. We review these operations briefly.

Extracting Fundamental Data Types The extraction operator for the fundamental data types uses the following four rules when it encounters a statement such as *cin >> variable*. The operator reads the characters one by one until it finds a character that does not belong to the syntax of the corresponding type:

a. If it is extracting a Boolean value, it must see a value that can be interpreted as 0 or 1.
b. If it is extracting a character value, it reads the next character in the input stream (including a whitespace character) and stores it in the corresponding variable.
c. If it is extracting an integral value, it reads digits until it encounters a nondigit character. It makes an integer value of the extracted characters. The unextracted characters remain in the stream.
d. If it is extracting a floating-point value, it reads digits with only one decimal point between them. If it encounters a second decimal point or a nondigit character, it stops and makes the floating-point value.

Inserting Fundamental Data Types Fundamental data types can be inserted into streams using the insertion operator (<<). The value is considered a set of characters and inserted into the stream. For example, the integer 124 is inserted as three characters (1, 2, and 4) into the stream.

Input/Output of C-Type Strings

When we use the *cin* object to input a C string, we must be careful that we do not exceed the size of array; otherwise, a run-time error occurs and the program is aborted. There is no problem when we output a C string.

Input/Output of C++ Strings

The extractor and the inserter operator are overloaded for the *string* class; they can be used as they have been defined. However, the input stops when the first whitespace is encounterd. If we want to read the whitespace characters (the whole line), we must use the *getline* function (a global function) defined in the <string> header. It has the following signature:

```
istream& getline (istream& in, string& str);
```

Other Member Functions

There are other member functions defined in *istream* and *ostream* classes, but they are not used by the objects instantiated from these classes. They are, however, inherited by the other stream classes in the hierarchy; we discuss these classes in the next sections.

16.3 FILE STREAMS

In the previous section we used the keyboard and monitor as the source and sink for data, but they are temporary. After the program terminates, the data do not exist and cannot be used again; if needed, the data must be re-created. A file is a permanent source or sink for data. After creation, it can be used by another program. Files can be saved for future use.

To use files, we must use the file stream classes defined in the <fstream> header; doing so allows us to connect the files to our program so we can read or write them.

We must include the *<fstream>* header to use file streams.

As shown in Figure 16.5, file stream classes are made from three classes: *ifstream*, *ofstream,* and *fstream*. These classes are used to input data from or output data to files or to input and output to the same file. They are inherited, respectively, from the *istream*, *ostream*, and *iostream* classes, and they inherit all member functions of these classes. The file stream classes define some new functions, mostly for instantiation and opening files.

All of the member functions defined in the console streams are inherited in the file streams.

16.3.1 File Input/Output

The source or the sink of data is always an entity that must be connected to a stream object. In the case of file input/output, the source is a file and the sink is a file. Files are entities that reside on disk (auxiliary storage). In other words, we have files and we have stream objects that must be connected to the files as shown in Figure 16.9. This means that we must construct a stream, connect the stream to the corresponding file, read or write from the file, disconnect the file, and destruct the stream.

Construct the Stream

We can instantiate any of the three streams as shown below. To do so we must include the <fstream> header file in our program.

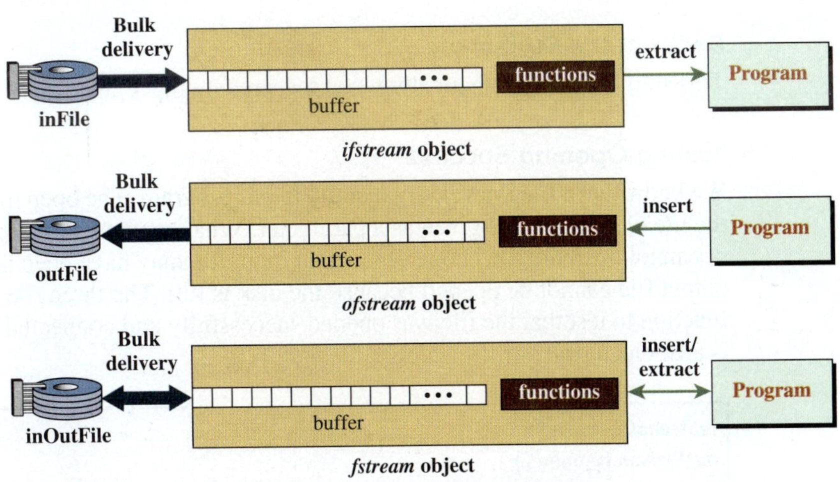

Figure 16.9 A file stream object connecting our program to a file

```
ifstream inStream ;
ofstream outStream ;
fstream inOutStream ;
```

Connect the File (Open)

Instantiation of a stream just creates an object of that type. To read from or write to a file, we must connect the instantiated stream to the corresponding file. This step is also referred to as the file-opening step because it is done using a member function named *open* in the corresponding stream class. The *open* function uses the file name (a C string) as the first parameter and an open mode as the second. For now, we ignore the open modes and use the default. The parameters *inFile*, *outFile*, and *inOutFile* are file names.

```
inStream.open (const char* inFile, ...);
outStream.open (const char* outFile, ...);
inOutStream.open (const char* inOutFile, ...);
```

Read and Write

After a stream is instantiated and the file is opened, we can read from a file opened for input or write to a file opened for output, or we can read and write to a file opened for read/write. There are no new read and write member functions defined for the file streams; these streams inherit the member functions defined for the console streams as discussed previously.

Disconnect the File (Close)

When we are done with the files, we must close them using the *close* member function defined in the file stream. Since a stream can be connected to only one file at a time, the *close* member function has no parameter.

```
inStream.close ();
outStream.close ();
inOutStream.close ();
```

Destruct the Stream

This step is done automatically when the stream object goes out of scope.

Testing Opening Success

We know that a file is an external entity to our program. The open member function connects the file whose name is given as a parameter. What happens if the operating system does not or cannot open the file? For example, an input file may have been deleted or corrupted or an output file cannot be opened because the disk is full. The three file stream classes provide a function to test that the file was opened successfully and connected to the stream. The result is a Boolean *true* or *false* value.

```
inStream.is-open ()
outStream.is-open ()
inOutStream.is-open ()
```

Program 16.5 Testing the five steps in outputting to a file

```
/***************************************************************
 * A program to create an output file and write to it          *
 ***************************************************************/
#include <iostream>
#include <fstream>
#include <cassert>
using namespace std;

int main ()
{
  // Instantiation of an ofstream object
  ofstream outStrm;
  // Creation of a file and connecting it to the ofstream object
  outStrm.open ("integerFile");
  if (!outStrm.is_open())
  {
       cout << "integerFile cannot be opened!";
       assert (false);
  }
  // Writing to the file using overloaded insertion operator
  for (int i = 1; i <= 10; i++)
  {
       outStrm << i * 10 << " ";
  }
  // Closing the file
  outStrm.close ();
  // The ofstream object is destroyed after return statement
  return 0;
}
```

Two Examples

Program 16.5 shows how we can use the steps described above to instantiate a stream, open a file and test if it is open, write to the file, and close the file (destruction of the stream object is done in the background).

In Program 16.6, we instantiate an *ifstream* class and connect it to the *integerFile* we created in Program 16.5. We then read the integers one by one and display them. Note that we are using two streams: the *ifstream*, which is connected to the *integerFile*, and the *ostream*, which is automatically connected to the monitor. As we said, the *ostream* is instantiated automatically by the system (*cout* object).

Nothing will be output to the monitor from Program 16.5 when it is run, but we can check the contents of a file named *integerFile* (a data file) with a text editor to find that the following line was stored in it.

```
10 20 30 40 50 60 70 80 90 100
```

Program 16.6 Reading from an existing file

```
/***************************************************************
 * A program to read from an existing file and display data on    *
 * the monitor                                                    *
 ***************************************************************/
#include <iostream>
#include <fstream>
#include <cassert>
using namespace std;

int main ()
{
  int data;
  // Instantiation of an ifstream object
  ifstream inStrm;
  // Connection of the existing file to the ifstream object
  inStrm.open ("IntegerFile");
  if (!inStrm.is_open())
  {
      cout << "integerFile cannot be opened!";
      assert (false);
  }
  // Reading from the ifstream object and writing to the cout object
  for (int i = 1; i <= 10; i++)
  {
      inStrm >> data ;
      cout << data << " " ;
  }
  // Disconnection of the IntegerFile from the ifstream
  inStrm.close ();
  // Destruction of the ifstream object is done after return
  return 0;
}
```

```
Run:
10 20 30 40 50 60 70 80 90 100
```

Note that this time we can see the integers printed on the monitor. We read from the *integerFile* using the extraction operator. This operator skips whitespace and reads the data. After each read, we write the data to the *cout* object (monitor).

16.3.2 Opening Modes

In Programs 16.5 and 16.6, we ignored the *opening modes*. We used the default opening mode for the *integerFile* in both cases (when connected to the *ofstream* and when connected to the *ifstream*). The opening mode is a type defined in the *ios* class and inherited by all classes in the hierarchy of stream classes. Opening modes are not used in the console streams or string streams because we do not open them; they are used only in the file

Table 16.7 The open modes used with file streams

ios :: in	open for input
ios :: out	open for output; the contents are destroyed
ios :: app	open for output and write at the end (append)
ios :: ate	move to the end immediately after opening (at end)
ios :: trunc	truncate the file to zero length
ios :: binary	read and write in binary mode (default is text)

streams. The opening mode is defined as a type, but its implementation is system dependent. Most of the time it is implemented as a *bitfield* (see Appendix E) with six bits that are used independently or in conjunction with the other bits. It is shown in Table 16.7.

Some of these modes can be combined as shown in Figure 16.10. The binary mode can be combined with all other modes (not shown in the figure).

Opening Modes for Input

Normally we use one of the two modes for an input file. The first (ios :: in) opens the file for input and puts the marker at the first byte of the buffer. This allows us to start reading the file from the first byte. With each read the marker moves to the next byte until we reach an empty position. In this case the *eofbit* is set and the file can no longer be read.

In the second mode (ios :: in | ios :: ate), the file is opened for reading, but the marker goes to the position after the last byte. This means the *eofbit* is set and we cannot read.

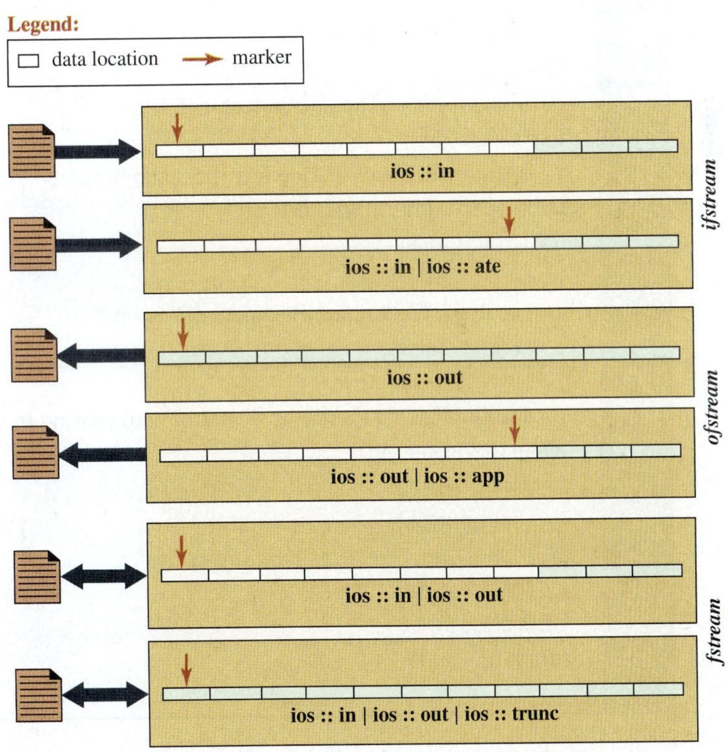

Figure 16.10 Common combinations of opening modes

However, it has other applications, such as allowing us to read the bytes in reverse by moving the marker toward the beginning. Another application is that we can find the size of the file, as we demonstrate later.

We can use the first mode (ios :: in) to read the contents of a file named *file1* whose contents are shown below:

```
This is the file that we want to open
and read its contents.
```

Program 16.7 reads the file, character by character, and writes the characters on the monitor until the *eofbit* is set.

Program 16.7 Using the first input mode to read a file

```
/***************************************************************
 * A program to open a file, read its contents, character by    *
 * by character, and write each character to the monitor        *
 ***************************************************************/
#include <iostream>
#include <fstream>
#include <cassert>
using namespace std;

int main ()
{
  // Variable declaration
  char ch;
  // Instantiation of an ifstream object
  ifstream istrm ;
  // Opening file1 and testing if it is opened properly
  istrm.open ("file1", ios :: in);
  if (!istrm.is_open())
  {
       cout << "file1 cannot be opened!" << endl;
       assert (false);
  }
  // Reading file1 character by character and writing to monitor
  while (istrm.get (ch))
  {
       cout.put(ch);
  }
  // Closing stream
  istrm.close ();
  return 0;
}
```

Run:

```
This is the file that we want to open
and read its contents.
```

Opening Modes for Output

As Figure 16.10 shows, we can use two output modes to write to a file. In the first mode (ios :: out) we open the file for output. If the file contains any data, they are deleted. In the second mode (ios :: out | ios :: app) we open the file and write at the end of the file (append). The existing data are preserved.

We create a file named *file2* and copy the contents of *file1* into it. Note that we open *file1* for input using opening mode (ios :: in), which means the marker is set on the first byte of the buffer. We open *file2* using the opening mode (ios :: out), which means the buffer is emptied and the marker is set to the first byte. In Program 16.8 we read a character at a time from *file1* and write it to *file2*. The file markers in both files are moving in sequence.

Program 16.8 Using input and output modes to copy a file

```
/***************************************************************
 * A program to open a file, read its contents character by    *
 * by character and write each character on another file       *
 ***************************************************************/
include <iostream>
#include <fstream>
#include <cassert>
using namespace std;

int main ()
{
    // Variable declaration
    char ch;
    // Instantiation of an ifstream and an ofstream object
    ifstream istr;
    ofstream ostr;
    // Opening file1 and file2 and testing if they are open
    istr.open ("file1", ios :: in);
    if (!istr.is_open())
    {
        cout << "file1 cannot be opened!" << endl;
        assert (false);
    }
    ostr.open ("file2", ios :: out);
    if (!ostr.is_open())
    {
        cout << "file2 cannot be opened!" << endl;
        assert (false);
    }
    // Reading file1 character by character and writing to file2
    while (istr.get (ch))
    {
        ostr.put(ch);
    }
```

(continued)

Program 16.8 Using input and output modes to copy a file (Continued)

```
    // Closing file1 and file2
    istr.close ();
    ostr.close ();
    return 0;
}
```

If we compare Program 16.7 and Program 16.8, we will see that both programs are doing the same thing, copying, but with some differences. Program 16.7 copies the contents of *file1* to the monitor; Program 16.8 copies the contents of *file1* to *file2*. In the first program, we have only one stream to instantiate (*cout* is already done for us); in the second program, we must instantiate two streams. In the first, we must open only one file (*cout* is done for us); in the second program, we must open two files. In the first program, we close only one file (*cout* is automatically done for us). In the second program, we must close both files. In the first program, the copy created on the monitor is temporary (but we can see the data when we run program). In the second program, we can see nothing, but we can open *file2* to see that it is the exact copy of *file1*.

The opening mode (ios :: out | ios :: app) can be used to open an existing file for appending. The contents of the file are not affected; we add at the end of the file. For example, assume that we decided to add the date at the end of *file1*. As seen in Program 16.9, we simply open the file and append the date, as a C string, at the end of the file.

Program 16.9 Appending to a file

```
/***************************************************************
 * A program to open a file, append the current date at the    *
 * end of the file and close it                                *
 ***************************************************************/
#include <iostream>
#include <fstream>
#include <cassert>
using namespace std;

int main ()
{
    // Instantiate a ostream object
    ofstream ostr;
    // Open file1 and connect it to the ostream object
    ostr.open ("file1", ios :: out | ios :: app);
    if (!ostr.is_open())
    {
        cout << "file1 cannot be opened!";
        assert (false);
    }
    // Append the date as a C-string to file1
    ostr << "\nOctober 15, 2016.";
    // Close the file
    ostr.close ();
    return 0;
}
```

When we open *file1* with a text editor, we see that the date has been added at the end of the file (in a new line) as shown below:

```
This is the file that we want to open
and read its contents.
October 15, 2015.
```

Opening for Input/Output

We can open a file for input/output if we connect our file to an *fstream* object using the mode (ios :: in | ios :: out). Assume that we have a file of integers. We decide to add the sum of the integers at the end of the file. We can open the file for both read and write (ios :: in | iso :: out). Note that this situation is different from the previous example. We must read the integers, one by one (input), and then write the sum at the end of the file (output). The contents of our file before the change is shown below:

```
12 14 17 20 21 25 32 27 56 18
```

Program 16.10 shows the solution.

Program 16.10 Opening a file for both input and output

```
/***************************************************************
 * A program that opens a file, sums its contents, and writes  *
 * the sum at the end of the file.                              *
 ***************************************************************/
#include <iostream>
#include <fstream>
#include <cassert>
using namespace std;

int main ()
{
   // Instantiate an fstream object
   fstream fstr;
   // Open the intFile and connected to the fstream object
   fstr.open ("intFile", ios :: in | ios :: out);
   if (!fstr.is_open())
   {
        cout << "intFile cannot be opened!";
        assert (false);
   }
   // Read all integers and add to the sum until end of file is detected
   int num;
   int sum = 0;
   while (fstr >> num)
   {
        sum += num;
   }
```

(continued)

Program 16.10 Opening a file for both input and output (Continued)

```
28    // Clear the file and add the message and the sum to the file
29    fstr.clear ();
30    fstr << "\nThe sum of the numbers is: ";
31    fstr << sum;
32    // Close the stream
33    fstr.close ();
34    return 0;
35  }
```

When the loop (lines 24 to 27 in Program 16.10) terminates, the *eofbit* is set and we cannot use the stream. In line 29 we clear the stream and then write the message and the sum to the end of the file. The result is a file with the following contents:

```
12 14 17 20 21 25 32 27 56 18
The sum of the numbers is: 242
```

EXAMPLE 16.1

The last file mode in Figure 16.10 (ios: in | ios: out | ios : trunc) allows us to open the file, truncate its contents, and write new data to it. This is the same as the mode (ios :: out) with one difference. In the second mode, we create a new file; in the first we delete the contents of an old file and replace it with new data. The second method is used when we want to keep the name of the file, but with new contents.

Other Opening Modes

We have not used the last three modes listed in Table 16.7, but we use them later in the chapter.

16.3.3 Other Member Functions

There are additional member functions that have been defined for the *istream* class, but they have more applications in the *ifstream* class (Table 16.8).

The function *gcount* gives the count of the number of characters extracted in the last input. The function *unget* puts the last character extracted from the stream back into the stream. The function *putback* does the same as *unget*. The function *peak* looks at the value of the next character without removing it. The function *ignore* skips over a number of characters without extracting them. We show how to use the *unget* function; we leave the rest as exercises.

Assume we have a file that includes only text and integers as shown below:

```
We have 7, 12, 23, and 442 in this file.
```

Table 16.8 Other member functions used in file streams

int gcount () const	// counts the number of characters
istream& unget ()	// put back the last character in stream
istream& putback (char c)	// same as unget
int peak ()	// look without extracting
istream& ignore (int n = 1, int d = eof)	// ignore some characters

We want to extract the integers from this file and ignore the text. Program 16.11 shows how we can use the *unget* function to do so.

The program goes through the whole file, character by character. If the character is a nondigit, it is thrown away. If the character is a digit, it is put back into the stream to be extracted again as an integer.

Program 16.11 Using the unget function

```
/***************************************************************
 * A program that extracts only integers from an input file    *
 * that contains both integer and character data types         *
 ***************************************************************/
#include <iostream>
#include <fstream>
#include <cassert>
using namespace std;

int main ()
{
  // Instantiation of an ifstream object and connection to the file
  ifstream ifstr;
  ifstr.open ("mixedFile" , ios :: in);
  if (!ifstr.is_open())
  {
      cout << "The file mixedFile cannot be opened for reading!";
      assert (false);
  }
  // Reading only integers by putting back the non-digit characters
  char ch;
  int n;
  while (ifstr.get (ch))
  {
      if (ch >= '0' && ch <= '9')
      {
            ifstr.unget();
            ifstr >> n;
            cout << n << " ";
      }
  }
  // Closing the file
  ifstr.close ();
  return 0;
}
```

Run:

```
7 12 23 442
```

16.3.4 Sequential versus Random Access

A file is a sequential collection of 8-bit bytes. We do not read or write to a file directly; we read from or write to the buffer in the stream object. In reading, the contents of the file are copied to the buffer by the system in bulk movement; in writing, the contents of the buffer are moved from the buffer to the file in bulk movement. Transferring bytes from the file to the buffer or from the buffer to the file is out of our control.

When we talk about **sequential access** or **random access,** we do not mean that the file is arranged sequentially or randomly (a file is always a sequence collection of bytes), we are referring to how we access the buffer in the stream object: sequentially or randomly. If we think about the buffer, we see that it is like an array; we can always access an array either sequentially (element after element) or randomly (any element we want). In fact, the buffer in a stream is made of elements, and the elements are indexed from 0 to $n - 1$, where n is the size of the buffer defined by the system.

The buffer in an *ifstream* has a marker that points to the next byte to be read. The buffer in an *ofstream* has a marker that points to the next byte to be written. The buffer in an *fstream* has only one marker for read or write.

Each stream has only one marker that indicates whether the next byte should be read or written.

Sequential Access

All of the examples we have shown so far have used sequential access. In sequential access, the movement of the stream marker is controlled by the read/write functions. The marker starts at the beginning of the buffer (index 0) when the file is opened. It moves toward the end of the buffer with each read or write. The marker is pointing to the next byte to be read or written, but the number of bytes in each read or write depends on the type of data. If we are reading or writing characters, movement is one byte at a time; if we are reading or writing formatted data (fundamental type or class type), the movement can be a number of bytes for each read or write.

Random Access

Reading or writing using the console system can be done only sequentially, but we can use random access when we use the file stream or stream streams. In random access, we can read data from any location and we can write data to any location. We simply move the stream marker to the corresponding character. The *istream* and *ostream* classes provide member functions that allow us to find the location of the marker and to move the marker to the desired location. Table 16.9 shows the six member functions used for this purpose.

Table 16.9 Member functions for random access

ios :: beg	ios :: cur	ios :: end

direction (dir) values

Input	output
`int tellg ();`	`int tellp ();`
`istream& seekg (int pos);`	`ostream& seekp (int pos);`
`istream& seekg (int off, ios :: dir);`	`ostream& seekp (int off, ios :: dir);`

Finding the Index of Current Location The first functions in each category, *tellg* or *tellp*, give the index of the current byte pointed to by the marker. Although there is only one marker, we must use *tellg* (*g* is for get) when we are using an *istream* object and *tellp* (*p* is for put) when we are using an *ostream* object.

Program 16.12 shows how we print the location of the marker and the value of the corresponding character in a file that has one word in it ("Hello!").

Moving the Marker Using the other four member functions in Table 16.9, we can move the marker to point to the byte we want to read or write next. Movement can be absolute or relative. If we know the index of the byte we want to move to, we can use

Program 16.12 Printing location and value of characters

```
/***************************************************************
 * A program to print characters and their locations in a file        *
 ***************************************************************/
#include <iostream>
#include <fstream>
using namespace std;

int main ()
{
  // Declaration of variables
  char ch;
  int n;
  // Instantiation of stream and opening the file
  ifstream istr;
  istr.open ("sample", ios :: in);
  // Getting characters and their locations
  n = istr.tellg ();
  while (istr.get(ch))
  {
      cout << n << " " << ch << endl;
      n = istr.tellg ();
  }
  // Closing the file
  istr.close ();
  return 0;
}
```

```
Run:
0 H
1 e
2 l
3 l
4 o
5 !
```

the two member functions with one argument: *seekg* (location) and *seekp* (location). If we want to move the marker to another position relative to the beginning, current, or the end of the buffer, we can use the relative member functions *seekg* (off, dir), or *seekp* (off, dir), where the offset (*off*) is a positive or negative integer and *dir* is the start position: *cur* for the current position, *beg* (for the beginning of the buffer), and *end* (for the end of the buffer).

Assume we have a simple file with the contents shown below:

```
There are wonderful things to do in life.
```

We want to change the contents of the file so each word is on a line by itself. Program 16.13 does the job. Note that we read a character at a time (sequential access). We then check the value of the character. If it is a space, we change it to carriage return character ('\r'), not the new line ('\n') because the new line is normally made of two characters and will replace the space and the first character of the next word. After reading a character and finding that it is a space, we must change it. However, the marker has already advanced to the beginning of the next word. We must move the marker back before putting a carriage return in place of the space character. We do this by using the *seekp* function to move the marker back one position.

Program 16.13 Changing a space to a carriage return

```
/***************************************************************
 * A program to put each word in the file on a new line        *
 ***************************************************************/
#include <iostream>
#include <fstream>
using namespace std;

int main ()
{
  fstream fstr;
  fstr.open ("file3" , ios :: in | ios :: out);

  char ch;
  while (fstr.get(ch))
  {
      if (isspace (ch))
      {
             fstr.seekp (-1 , ios :: cur);
             fstr.put ('\r');
      }
  }
  fstr.close ();
  return 0;
}
```

After running the program, the file looks like the following:

```
There
are
wonderful
things
to
do
in
life.
```

As another example, we can find the size of a file in bytes if we open the file using the *ate* (at the end) opening mode, which puts the marker after the last character in the file. We can then use the *tellg* member function to tell us the index of the character after the last character, as shown in Program 16.14.

The following shows the contents of the file we have used. Note that when we check the value returned by *tellg*, it gives the index of the character after the period in the file (43), but since the indexes start from 0 and not 1, we know that there are exactly 43 characters in the file with indexes 0 to 42.

```
This is the file whose size we want to find.
```

Program 16.14 Finding the size of a file

```
/***************************************************************
 * A program to find the length of the file                    *
 ***************************************************************/
#include <iostream>
#include <fstream>
using namespace std;

int main ()
{
   // Instantiation of stream and connection to the file
   ifstream ifstr;
   ifstr.open ("file4" , ios :: in | ios :: ate);
   // Finding the marker value after the last character
   cout << "File size: " << ifstr.tellg ();
   // Closing the file
   ifstr.close ();
   return 0;
}
```

```
Run:
File size: 44
```

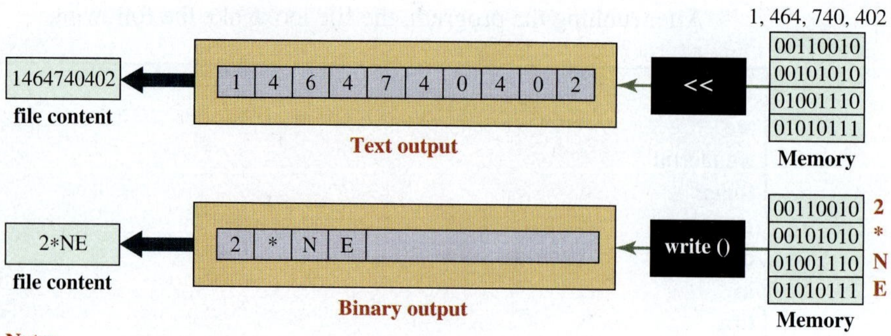

Note:
The insertion operator changes each digit to a byte.
The function *write*() copies the image of memory to the stream.

Figure 16.11 Difference between text and binary output

16.3.5 Binary Input/Output

The console streams are not used for binary data because neither the source nor the sink (keyboard or monitor) can handle them. On the other hand, files connected to a file stream can be used to input and output binary data in which 8 bits (a byte) are treated as a byte without being related to any character code (ASCII or Unicode). This is important when we want to input or output data that should be interpreted as bytes. For example, we may write a program that reads a file that has stored audio/video information. Each picture element (pixel) in a video file can be 8 bits, which may be stored as a byte. We may also need to store objects of user-defined types as a set of bytes. In these cases, we can store data in a file as a sequence of bytes. To do so, the file should be opened in the binary mode.

File streams are capable of holding text and binary data.

As we discussed at the beginning of the chapter, data are stored in 8-bit bytes in memory, in a stream, and in a file. The difference is how we interpret data stored in the stream and file (which are images of each other). In text input/output, values are converted to bytes; in binary input/output, the exact pattern of bits is converted to bytes. We show how a large integer, 1,464,740,402, is stored in memory, in a stream, and in a file both as text and binary (Figure 16.11).

Figure 16.11 shows that in text output, we must store each digit of the integer as a character (text) in the stream and in the file; in binary output we use only 4 bytes (the image of data in memory). It is obvious that in the case of text output, the file can be opened by a text editor and we can see the value of the integer; in the case of binary input, we can see the characters 2*NE, which are definitely not the value of the integer stored in memory. We can see the benefit of binary output from the figure when our integer is big. In text output, the file stores 10 bytes; in binary output, the file stores only 4 bytes.

Member Functions

To read and write binary data, the library defines three member functions as shown in Table 16.10. These member functions are defined in the *istream* and *ostream* classes, but they are not used there. The *ifstream* and *ofstream* class inherit them and use them.

In Table 16.10, the *read* function reads up to *n* characters from the stream buffer and fills an array of characters named *s*. If the number of characters available in the stream is less

Table 16.10 Read and write member functions

Input	Output
`ifstream& read (char* s, int n)` `ofstream& readsome (char* s, int n)`	`ifstream& write (char* s, int n)`

than the size of the array, the *eofbit* is set. To prevent this, the second function (*readsome*) reads characters until no character is available or *n* characters are read. None of the functions add a null character to the array, which means they cannot be used as a C string. The *write* function writes exactly *n* characters from an array of characters to the stream buffer.

Conversion of Fundamental Types

You may have noticed that the three input/output functions actually read characters into and write characters from the stream buffer; no conversion occurs between bytes stored in memory and the bytes stored in the stream buffer. We need a conversion mechanism to change the integer 1,464,740,402 to an array of four characters (2, *, N, E), and vice versa (Figure 16.12).

The conversion is done using the *reinterpret-cast* of the form:

```
reinterpret_cast <type2*> (&type1)
```

In the cast operator, *type1* is a fundamental type (or class type) and *type2* is a char type. This means that we need to rewrite the read and write functions as shown below:

```
ifstream& read (reinterpret_cast <char*> (&type), sizeof (type))
ifstream& readsome (reinterpret_cast <char*> (&type), sizeof (type))
ofstream& write (reinterpret_cast <char*> (&type), sizeof (type))
```

Program 16.15 shows how we can write the value of an *int* and a *double* to a file and read them to be sure the values are stored correctly. Note that we use the *ofstream* object to create a new file and then the *ifstream* object to check the file: in this example, we write before we read.

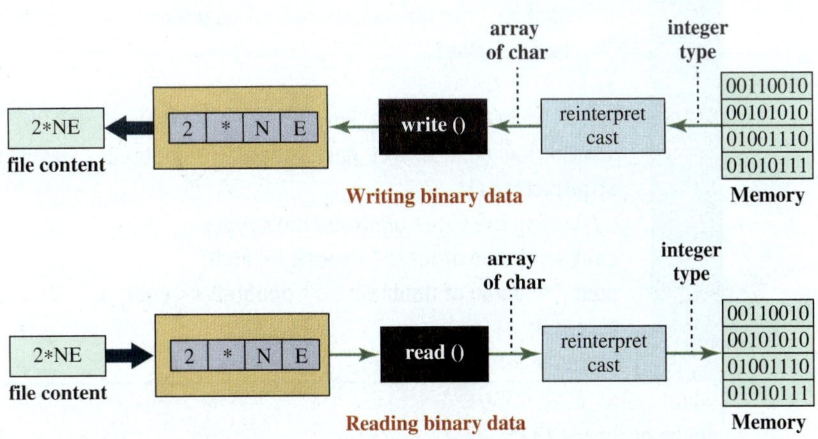

Figure 16.12 Conversion in binary input/output

Program 16.15 Writing and reading binary data

```
/****************************************************************
 * A program that shows how to write binary data to a file      *
 * and how to read the same binary data from the file           *
 ****************************************************************/
#include <iostream>
#include <string>
#include <fstream>
#include <cassert>
using namespace std;

int main ()
{
  int int1 = 12325;
  double double1 = 45.78;
  // Creating a new file for output and write the two data types
  ofstream strmOut ("Sample", ios :: out | ios :: binary);
  if (!strmOut.is_open())
  {
      cout << "The file Sample cannot be opened for writing!";
      assert (false);
  }
  strmOut.write (reinterpret_cast <char*> (&int1), sizeof (int));
  strmOut.write (reinterpret_cast <char*> (&double1), sizeof (double));
  strmOut.close ();

  int int2;
  double double2;
  // Opening the same file for input and reading the two data types
  ifstream strmIn ("Sample", ios :: in | ios :: binary);
  if (!strmIn.is_open())
  {
      cout << "The file Sample cannot be opened for reading!";
      assert (false);
  }
  strmIn.read (reinterpret_cast <char*> (&int2) , sizeof (int));
  strmIn.read (reinterpret_cast <char*> (&double2) , sizeof (double));
  strmIn.close ();
  // Testing the value of stored data types
  cout << "Value of int2: " << int2 << endl;
  cout << "Value of double2: " << double2 << endl;
  return 0;
} // End main
```

```
Run:
Value of int2: 12325
Value of double2: 45.78
```

In line 22 of Program 16.15, we take the address of a variable of type *int*, interpret it as a pointer to character, and write its contents, as characters, to the file. We do the same in line 23, but the variable is of type *double*.

In line 35, we take the address of a variable of type *int*, interpret the location reserved in memory as a pointer to character, and store characters extracted from the file in it. We do the same in line 36, but the location is of type *double*.

Note that in both cases (reading and writing), we interpret the address of a fundamental data type as a pointer to characters.

Conversion of User-Defined Objects

The conversion can be performed because an object of a fundamental data type is stored in memory as a sequence of bits (or bytes). The only thing we must do is change the read/write function to access a variable of type *class* instead of a variable of a fundamental data type.

When reading, we need an empty object (created from a default constructor) to be filled by characters from the file. When we write, we need a filled object (created from the parameter constructor) to be changed to characters and written to the file as shown below:

```
istream& read (reinterpret_cast <char*> (&object) , sizeof (class))
istream& write (reinterpret_cast <char*> (&object), sizeof (class))
```

We can create a class representing information about a student (identity, name, and GPA) and write the instances of the class to a file and then read the instances from the file. We show the interface, implementation, and the application files next. Program 16.16 shows the interface file.

Program 16.16 File student.h

```
/***************************************************************
 * The program defines the interface file for the Student class       *
 * to be used to store student records in a binary file              *
 ***************************************************************/
#ifndef STUDEN_H
#define STUDEN_H
#include <iostream>
#include <fstream>
#include <cassert>
#include <iomanip>
#include <cstring>
#include <string>
using namespace std;

class Student
{
  private:
       int stdId;
       char stdName [20];
       double stdGpa;
```

(continued)

Program 16.16 File student.h (Continued)

```
  public:
      Student (int, const string&, double);
      Student ();
      ~Student ();
      int getId() const;
      string getName() const;
      double getGpa () const;
};
#endif
```

Program 16.17 shows the implementation file for the student class. Note that we use the accessor functions to get the value of the data members, but we could have overloaded the insertion operator for the class.

Program 16.17 File student.cpp

```
/***************************************************************
 * The implementation file for Student class                   *
 ***************************************************************/
#include "student.h"

// Parameter Constructor
Student :: Student (int id, const string& name, double gpa)
: stdId (id), stdGpa (gpa)
{
strcpy (stdName, name.c_str() );
  if (stdId < 1 || stdId > 99)
  {
      cout << "Identity is out of range. Program aborted.";
      assert (false);
  }
  if (stdGpa < 0.0 || stdGpa > 4.0)
  {
      cout << "The gpa value is out of range. Program aborted.";
      assert (false);
  }
}
// Default Constructor
Student :: Student ()
{
}
// Destructor
Student :: ~Student ()
{
}
```

(continued)

Program 16.17 File student.cpp (Continued)

```
// Accessor function
int Student :: getId() const
{
  return stdId;
}
// Accessor function
string Student :: getName() const
{
  return stdName;
}
// Accessor function
double Student :: getGpa () const
{
  return stdGpa;
}
```

Program 16.18 shows the application file for writing and reading objects to a file. We first change several objects to binary data and write them to the file. We then open the same file and read student objects one after another.

Program 16.18 File app.cpp

```
/*****************************************************************
 * The application file to write students record to a binary      *
 * file and then read the records sequentially                    *
 *****************************************************************/
#include "student.h"

int main ()
{
  // Opening File.dat for binary output
  fstream stdStrm1;
  stdStrm1.open ("File.dat", ios :: binary | ios :: out);
  if (!stdStrm1.is_open())
  {
      cout << "File.dat cannot be opened for writing!";
      assert (false);
  }
  // Instantiation of five objects
  Student std1 (1 , "John", 3.91);
  Student std2 (2 , "Mary", 3.82);
  Student std3 (3 , "Lucie", 4.00);
  Student std4 (4 , "Edward", 3.71);
  Student std5 (5 , "Richard", 3.85);
```

(continued)

Program 16.18 File app.cpp (Continued)

```
    // Writing the five objects to the binary file and close it
    stdStrm1.write(reinterpret_cast <char*> (&std1), sizeof (Student));
    stdStrm1.write(reinterpret_cast <char*> (&std2), sizeof (Student));
    stdStrm1.write(reinterpret_cast <char*> (&std3), sizeof (Student));
    stdStrm1.write(reinterpret_cast <char*> (&std4), sizeof (Student));
    stdStrm1.write(reinterpret_cast <char*> (&std5), sizeof (Student));
    stdStrm1.close ();
    // Opening File.dat for input
    fstream stdStrm2;
    stdStrm2.open ("File.dat", ios :: binary | ios :: in);
    if (!stdStrm2.is_open())
    {
        cout << "File.dat cannot be opened for reading!";
        assert (false);
    }
    // Read Student objects, display them, and close the File.data
    cout << left << setw (4) << "ID" << " ";
    cout << setw(15) << left << "Name" << " ";
    cout << setw (4) << "GPA" << endl;
    Student std;
    for (int i = 0; i < 5; i++)
    {
        stdStrm2.read(reinterpret_cast <char*> (&std), sizeof (Student));
        cout << setw (4) << std.getId() << " ";
        cout << setw(15) << left << std.getName() <<" ";
        cout << fixed << setw (4) << setprecision (2) << std.getGpa ();
        cout << endl;
    }
    stdStrm2.close();
    return 0;
}
```

Run:

```
ID   Name            GPA
1    John            3.91
2    Mary            3.82
3    Lucie           4.00
4    Edward          3.71
5    Richard         3.85
```

Random Access

We can also read from or write to binary files randomly. In other words, instead of reading the record of all students, we can read the record of a specific student using her identity. However, this involves two precautions.

First, we must be sure that all of the objects stored in the file are of the same size so we can use the *seekg*() and *seekp*() functions. In the case of the object with only data members of fundamental data types, the size of each object is the sum of the size of its data members. In the case of the *Student* class, the size of array representing the name is also fixed.

Second, we must use some precautions to find the location of the object, given some information about it. For example, we can use the identity of a student in the previous example to find the location of the Student object using:

```
seekg ((id - 1) * sizeof (Student))
```

But if the identity does not start from 1, we must transform the identity to the student record number.

16.4 STRING STREAMS

String streams use three classes: *istringstream*, *ostringstream*, and *stringstream*. These classes are used to input data from or output data to strings. They are inherited, respectively, from *istream*, *ostream*, and *iostream*. With a couple of exceptions, all member functions discussed in their superclasses can be used in these classes and can add more classes. String stream classes are defined in the <sstream> header file, which must be included in our program when we use them.

To use string streams, we need the <sstream> header file.

The source or destination of string streams is different from that of console streams or file streams. In console streams, the source or destination is a physical device outside the program. In file streams, the source or destination is a file, an entity that exists outside the program. In string streams, the source or destination is in fact a string inside the program itself. In other words, we read from an existing string in the program; we write to a string in the program. For the sake of clarity, in the figures we use in this section, we show the source or sink as a string outside the program, but we must remember that it is part of the program.

We cannot open or close these streams because the source or sink entities connected to these streams are not external; they are created and destroyed inside our programs. For this reason, there are no *open*() or *close*() functions for these streams.

The *open*( ) and *close*( ) functions are not defined for string streams.

16.4.1 Instantiation

Similar to file streams, each string stream is instantiated using constructors. We show the constructors for the *istringstream*, *ostringstream*, and *stringstream* classes in Table 16.11; we show the default values for the open modes.

Each constructor instantiates an object of type *istringstream*, *ostringstream*, or *stringstream* and connects the object to the string object defined as the first parameter. Note that a string object must be included, but it can be a null string.

Table 16.11 Constructors for all three string stream classes

```
istringstream (const string strg, ios :: openmode mod = ios :: in);
ostringstream (const string strg, ios :: openmode mod = ios :: out);
stringstream (const string strg, ios :: openmode mod = ios :: in |ios :: out );
```

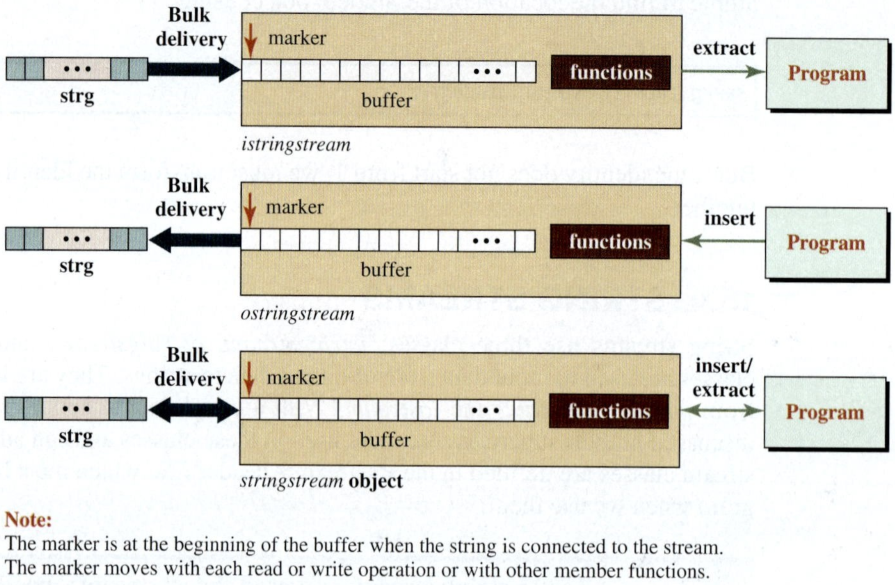

Figure 16.13 The string stream objects connected to strings and programs

Figure 16.13 shows three string stream objects graphically.

Member Functions

The *istringstream* class inherits all the member functions for sequential and random access defined in the superclass *istream* (except for the *open* and *close* functions). The *ostringstream* does the same, but it inherits from the superclass *ostream*. The *stringstream* class also does the same, but it inherits from the superclass *ostream*.

In addition, each class provides two versions of a new member function called *str*. The first version replaces the string connected to the stream; the second version returns a copy of the string connected to the stream. Table 16.12 shows the prototype for these functions.

Program 16.19 is a trivial string example. In the first section, we create an object of *istringstream* connected to a string and print the string. We then change the string connected to the same *istringstream* and print the string. In the second section, we do the same with *ostringstream*.

Table 16.12 Two versions of the str function

```
void str (string strg);        //Connect the parameter to the host object
string str () const;           // Returns the string connected to the host object
```

Program 16.19 Testing string stream classes

```
/*****************************************************************
 * A program to show how to use string stream classes           *
 *****************************************************************/
#include <iostream>
#include <string>
#include <sstream>
using namespace std;

int main ()
{
  // Using istringstream object
  istringstream iss ("Hello friends!");
  cout << iss.str () << endl;
  iss.str ("Hello world!");
  cout << iss.str () << endl << endl;
  // Using ostringstream object
  ostringstream oss ("Bye friends!");
  cout << oss.str () << endl;
  oss.str ("Bye world!");
  cout << oss.str () << endl;
  return 0;
}
```

```
Run:
Hello friends!
Hello world!

Bye friends!
Bye world!
```

16.4.2 Application: Adapter

The most common application of a string stream class is to act as an adapter for the string class. As we know, the *string* class has no constructor to wrap values of fundamental types (except *char*) and make a string out of them. It also does not have a member function to unwrap a string and take the values of fundamental data types out of it.

In programming we sometimes need to convert a fundamental data type to a string and a string to a fundamental data type. To do so we use an object of a *stringstream* class as an adapter.

In wrapping, we insert the fundamental data type(s) into an *ostringstream* object and then change the *ostringstream* object to a string object. In unwrapping, we change the string to an *istringstream* object and extract the fundamental data type from the i*stringstream* object. Both operations are shown in Figure 16.14.

We can create a function template to convert any fundamental data type to a string. We can also create a function template to return the fundamental data type embedded in a string. We include both template functions in a header file called *convert.h* as shown in

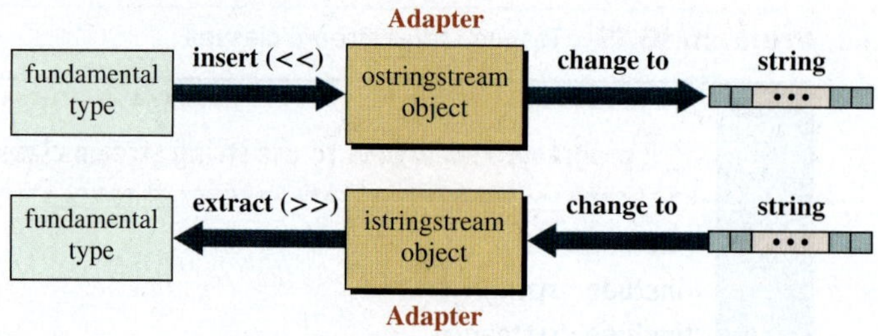

Figure 16.14 The stringstream objects as adapters

Program 16.20. Note that in line 13 we must use specialization, as discussed in Chapter 15, because the template function *toData* uses the template type only as the returned type. Without specialization, the template function cannot detect the return type.

Program 16.20 File convert.h

```
1  /***************************************************************
2   * The header file defines two template functions. The first   *
3   * inserts a fundamental type into a string. The second extracts *
4   * a fundamental type embedded in a string.                     *
5   ***************************************************************/
6  #ifndef CONVERT_H
7  #define CONVERT_H
8  #include <iostream>
9  #include <string>
10 #include <sstream>
11 using namespace std;
12 
13 // toString function changes any data type to string
14 template <typename T>
15 string toString (T data)
16 {
17   ostringstream oss ("");
18   oss << data;
19   return oss.str ();
20 }
21 // toData function takes out the data embedded in a string
22 template <typename T>
23 T toData (string strg)
24 {
25   T data;
26   istringstream iss (strg);
27   iss >> data;
28   return data;
29 }
30 #endif
```

16.21 demonstrates the use of the *convert.h* template functions.

Program 16.21 File app.cpp

```
/***************************************************************
 * A simple application program that uses toString and toData  *
 * template functions                                          *
 ***************************************************************/
#include "convert.h"

int main ( )
{
  // Converting integer 12 to a string
  string strg = toString (12);
  cout << "String: " << strg << endl;
  // Converting string "15.67" to double
  double data = toData <double> ("15.67");
  cout << "Data: " << data;
  return 0;
}
```

```
Run:
String: 12
Data: 15.67
```

16.5 FORMATTING DATA

In Chapter 3 we discussed manipulators and used some of them. Manipulators use the formatting data members (formatting flags, formatting fields, and formatting variables) defined in the *ios* class. Since all stream classes inherit from the *ios* class, they all inherit these data members and the corresponding member functions to set and unset fields and store values in variables. To create customized manipulators, we must understand how we can directly use these *flags*, *fields*, and *variables*.

16.5.1 Direct Use of Flags, Fields, and Variables

Understanding how to use flags, fields, and variables will help us create customized manipulators later in the chapter.

Formatting Flags

As we see in Table 16.13, the *ios* class defines a type named *fmtflags,* which can take a combination of any of the seven values. Each bit can be set (value 1) or unset (value 0). These flags are independent, and we can use one or more of them to format our data.

We can set or unset them using the *setf*() or *unsetf*() function as shown in Table 16.14.

Formatting Fields

The *ios* class also defines a group of three fields for formatting data. Each field has two or three fields that can be exclusively set or unset. Only one bit at a time can be set. Table 16.15 shows the three fields defined in this category.

Table 16.13 Values in fmtflags type

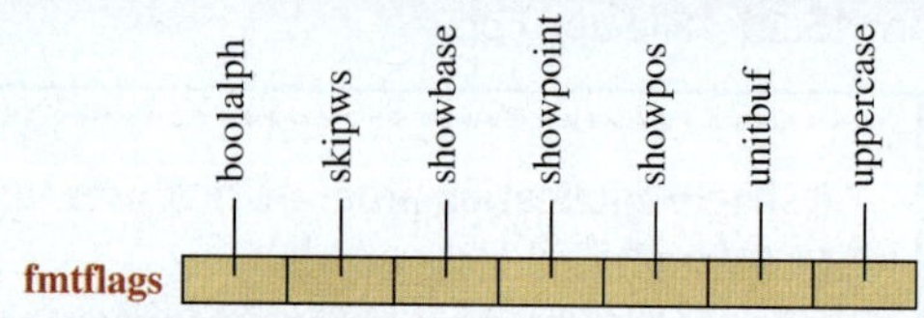

Flag	Description
ios :: boolalpha	Show representation of boolean data (*true* or *false*).
ios :: skipws	Skip white space characters (default for input).
ios :: showbase	Skip numeric base when printing integral values.
ios :: showpoint	Show the decimal point for floating-point values.
ios :: showpos	Show positive sign (plus sign) for positive values.
ios :: unitbuf	Flush the stream after each action.
ios :: uppercase	Show A-F for hexadecimal and E for scientific (in uppercase).

Table 16.14 Member functions to set or unset format flags

```
fmtflags ios :: setf (flag)        // It sets the corresponding flag
fmtflags ios :: unsetf (flag)      // It unset the corresponding flag
```

Table 16.15 Format fields working in group

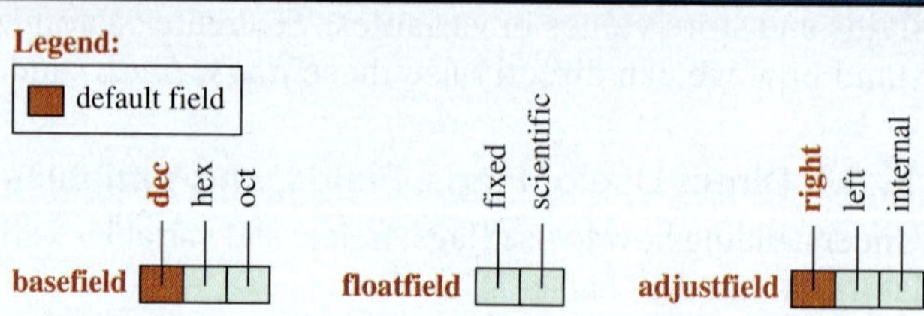

Flags	Values	Description
ios :: basefield	ios :: dec	Set integral values in decimal.
	ios :: hex	Set integral values in hexadecimal.
	ios :: oct	Set integral values in octal.
ios :: floatfield	ios :: fixed	Show the floating-value in fixed format.
	ios :: scientific	Show the floating-value in scientific format.
ios :: adjustfield	ios :: right	Right justify the data in the field.
	ios :: left	Left justify the data in the field.
	ios :: internal	Add fill character after the sign.

Table 16.16 Member function to set or unset fields

fmtField ios :: setf (*addingField, field*)	// It sets the corresponding field
fmtField ios :: unsetf (*field*)	// It unsets the corresponding field

Table 16.17 Setting and unsetting variable fields

Member function	Description
int ios :: width (int n)	Set the number of position to be used by a value.
int ios :: width ()	Reset the width field to 0.
int ios :: precision (int n)	Set the number of position after the decimal point.
int ios :: precision ()	Unset the *precision* field.
int ios :: fill (char c)	Set the type of character to fill the empty position.
int ios :: fill ()	Unset the *fill* field.

The fields in each group are not independent, and only one of them can be set at a time. The default setting is shown in color, but note that *floatfield* has no default value (the best is selected by the system if none is explicitly selected).

The setting of any of these fields is different from the methods used for *fmtflags* because it guarantees that only one of the values in each category is set (Table 16.16).

To set a field, we must use two parameters. The second parameter (field) unsets all of the fields in the field; the first parameter then sets the desired field.

Formatting Variables

The formatting variables, shown in Table 16.17, are named *width* (of type *int*), *precision* (of type *int*), and *fill* (of type *char*).

These formatting variables are used to define how many positions are set aside for a value, how many positions are set aside after a decimal point, and what character should be used to fill the unused positions. There are six member functions that are used to set and unset these flags, as shown in Table 16.17. Note that if the *fill* field is not set, the fill character defaults to a space.

Program 16.22 shows how we can directly format three data items of type *boolean*, *integer*, and *floating-point*. We have two goals in this program: (1) to show that it is possible to format data using the formatting flags, fields, and variables; and (2) to show how lengthy and involved this process is. Later, we show that we can achieve the same goal using manipulators.

Program 16.22 Printing three data items

```
/***************************************************************
 * A program to show how to format three data types using the      *
 * formatting flags, fields and variables                          *
 ***************************************************************/
#include <iostream>
```

(continued)

Program 16.22 Printing three data items (Continued)

```
using namespace std;

int main ()
{
   // Declaration and initialization of three variables
   bool b = true;
   int i = 12000;
   double d = 12467.372;
   // Printing values
   cout << "Printing without using formatting" << endl;
   cout << "Value of b: " << b << endl;
   cout << "Value of i: " << i << endl;
   cout << "Value of d: " << d << endl << endl;
   // Formatting the Boolean data and print it again
   cout << "Formatting the Boolean data" << endl;
   cout.setf (ios :: boolalpha);
   cout << b << endl << endl;
   // Formatting the integer data and print it again
   cout << "Formatting the integer data type" << endl;
   cout.setf (ios :: showbase);
   cout.setf (ios :: uppercase);
   cout.setf (ios :: hex, ios :: basefield);
   cout.setf (ios :: right, ios :: adjustfield);
   cout.width (16);
   cout.fill ('*');
   cout << i << endl << endl;
   // Formatting the floating-point data and print it again
   cout << "Formatting the floating-point data type" << endl;
   cout.setf (ios :: showpoint);
   cout.setf (ios :: right, ios :: adjustfield);
   cout.setf (ios :: fixed, ios :: floatfield);
   cout.width (16);
   cout.precision (2);
   cout.fill ('*');
   cout << d << endl;
   return 0;
}
```

Run:

```
Printing without using formatting
Value of b: 1
Value of i: 12000
Value of d: 12467.4
```

(continued)

Program 16.22 Printing three data items (Continued)

```
Formatting the Boolean data
true

Formatting the integer data type
**********0X2EE0

Formatting the floating-point data type
********12467.37
```

16.5.2 Predefined Manipulators

In this section we discuss the standard manipulators that we have used many times in this text. Our goal is to review them in more depth and find how they have been written to accomplish their goals. Doing so will help us write our own manipulators.

Manipulators Related to Formatting Flags

In Table 16.13 we listed seven formatting flags. We list them again in Table 16.18. We have exactly fourteen formatting-flag manipulators (one each for setting and unsetting) of those seven flags. The ones in color are the defaults.

Manipulators Related to Formatting Fields

In Table 16.15 we listed three formatting fields. We have exactly eight manipulators related to the flags in these fields. The ones in color are the default (Table 16.19).

Table 16.18 Manipulators using formatting flags

Flag	Manipulator	Effect	In	Out
boolalpha	noboolalpha	Show Boolean values *as* 0/1.	✓	✓
	boolalpha	Show Boolean values *false/true*.	✓	✓
skipws	noskipws	Do not skip whitespace in input.	✓	
	skipsws	Skip whitespace in input.	✓	
showbase	noshowbase	Do not show the base of decimal.		✓
	showbase	Show the base of decimal.		✓
showpoint	noshowpoint	Do not show the decimal point.		✓
	showpoint	Show the decimal point.		✓
showpos	noshowpos	Do not show the positive sign (+).		✓
	showpos	Show the positive sign (+).		✓
unitbuf	nounitbuf	Do not flush the output.		✓
	unitbuf	Flush output after write.		✓
uppercase	nouppercase	Do not show char in uppercase.		✓
	uppercase	Show char in uppercase.		✓

Table 16.19 Manipulators using formatting fields

Flag	Manipulator	Effect	In	Out
basefield	dec	Show integers in decimal.	✓	✓
	hex	Show integers in hexadecimal.	✓	✓
	oct	Show integers in octal.	✓	✓
floatfield	fixed	Show type in fixed format.		✓
	scientific	Show type in scientific format.		✓
adjustfield	right	Right justify the data in the field.		✓
	left	Left justify the data in the field.		✓
	internal	Justify data internally in the field.		✓

Manipulators Related to Formatting Variables

In Table 16.17 we mentioned three sets of member functions to set variable fields. We have three manipulators that look like a function with parameters (Table 16.20).

Manipulator Not Related to Flags or Fields

There are four manipulators that are not related to any flag or field. They perform specific actions on the stream (Table 16.21).

We repeat the program but use manipulators instead of formatting flags, fields, and variables to achieve the same goal as shown in Program 16.23. Note that we need to include the header file <iomanip> for manipulators related to the formatting variables,

16.5.3 Manipulators Definition

If we want to create new manipulators, we must first learn how predefined manipulators are defined.

Table 16.20 Manipulators using variable fields

Variables	Manipulator	Effect	In	Out
width	setw (*n*)	Set n character as the field.	✓	✓
precision	setprecision (*n*)	Set n characters for precision.		✓
fill	setfill (*c*)	Use c as the fill character.	✓	✓

Table 16.21 Manipulators using no flags or fields

Manipulator	Effect	In	Out
ws	Extract white spaces.	✓	
endl	Insert new line and flush the buffer.		✓
ends	Insert end of string character.		✓
flush	Flush stream buffer.		✓

Program 16.23 Using manipulators for formatting

```
/*****************************************************************
 * A program to show how predefined manipulators can achieve     *
 * the same goal as using flags, fields, and variables           *
 *****************************************************************/
#include <iostream>
#include <iomanip>
using namespace std;

int main ()
{
  // Declaration and initialization of three variables
  bool b = true;
  int i = 12000;
  double d = 12467.372;
  // Printing values
  cout << "Printing without using formatting" << endl;
  cout << "Value of b: " << b << endl;
  cout << "Value of i: " << i << endl;
  cout << "Value of d: " << d << endl << endl;
  // Formatting the boolean data and print it again
  cout << "Formatting the Boolean data" << endl;
  cout.setf (ios :: boolalpha);
  cout << boolalpha << b << endl << endl;
  // Formatting the integer data and print it again
  cout << "Formatting the integer data type" << endl;
  cout << showbase << uppercase << hex << right
   << setw (16) << setfill ('*') << i << endl << endl;
  // Formatting the floating-point data and print it again
  cout << "Formatting the floating-point data type" << endl;
  cout << showpoint << right << fixed << setw (16)
   << setprecision (2) << setfill ('*') << d << endl << endl;
  return 0;
}
```

Run:

```
Printing without using formatting
Value of b: 1
Value of i: 12000
Value of d: 12467.4

Formatting the Boolean data
true

Formatting the integer data type
**********0X2EE0
Formatting the floating-point data type
********12467.37
```

Manipulator without Arguments

It is not very difficult to find out how manipulators without arguments (Table 16.18, Table 16.19, and Table 16.21) are implemented. The system has two overloaded operators with one argument that takes a pointer to function as shown below:

```
istream& istream :: operator >> (istream& (*pf) (istream&));
ostream& ostream :: operator << (ostream& (*pf) (ostream&));
```

The first overloaded operator uses a pointer to a function that takes a reference to an *istream* object and returns a reference to an *istream* object (for chaining). The second overloaded operator uses a pointer to a function that takes a reference to an *ostream* object and returns a reference to an *ostream* object (for chaining).

Each manipulator without an argument can be implemented as a function as shown below. The name of the function is passed as a pointer to function to the previous overloaded operators.

```
istream& name (itream& is)
{
   action;
   return is;
}
```

```
ostream& name (ostream& os)
{
   action;
   return os;
}
```

A manipulator with no argument can be created using a function that takes a stream parameter and returns a stream.

We simulate the manipulators *boolalpha* and *noboolalpha* to see if we understand how to write a new manipulator. We call our manipulators *alpha and noalpha*. Program 16.24 defines and uses these two simulated manipulators.

Program 16.24 A program with two customized manipulators

```
/***************************************************************
 * A program to simulate boolalpha and noboolalpha manipulators     *
 ***************************************************************/
#include <iostream>
using namespace std;

// Defining a function named alpha
ostream& alpha (ostream& os)
{
   os.setf (ios :: boolalpha) ;
   return os;
}
// Defining a function named noalpha
ostream& noalpha (ostream& os)
```

(continued)

Program 16.24 A program with two customized manipulators (Continued)

```
{
   os.unsetf (ios :: boolalpha) ;
   return os;
}

int main ()
{
   // Declaration and initialization of two boolean variables
   bool b1 = false;
   bool b2 = true;
   // Printing values of variables with alpha and noalpha manipulators
   cout << alpha << b1 << " " << b2 << endl;
   cout << noalpha << b1 << " " << b2 << endl;
   return 0;
}
```

Run:

```
false true
0 1
```

Knowing how to simulate a system manipulator helps us create our own manipulators. Assume we want to have a manipulator (with no arguments) called *currency* that prints values with $, followed by the leading asterisks to fill the beginning of the field and two decimal digits after the decimal point. Program 16.25 shows such a custom manipulator.

Program 16.25 Creating and testing a customized manipulator

```
/*******************************************************************
 * A program that uses a customized manipulator                     *
 *******************************************************************/
#include <iostream>
#include <iomanip>
using namespace std;

ostream& currency (ostream& stream)
{
   cout << '$';
   stream.precision (2);
   stream.fill ('*');
   stream.setf(ios:: fixed, ios:: floatfield);
   return stream;
}
```

(continued)

Program 16.25 Creating and testing a customized manipulator (Continued)

```

int main ( )
{
   cout << currency << setw (12) << 12325.45 << endl;
   cout << currency << setw (12) << 0.36 << endl;
   return 0;
}
```

Run:

```
$****12325.45
$********0.36
```

The values are printed as normally done on checks to fill the empty spaces with asterisks and thereby prevent someone from changing the check value.

Manipulator with Arguments

Simulation of manipulators with arguments is a little more involved. A pointer to function cannot have an argument. In other words, we cannot have a pointer to a function with a parameter, such as *setw*(4); the pointer can only be named *setw*. This means we must change our strategy. Instead of a pointer to function, we can consider the phrase *setw* (4) as a call to a constructor of a class with only one data member of type integer. In other words, we interpret the statement

```
cout << setw (4);
```

as an operator with two operands. The first operand is an instance of type *ostream*; the second is an instance of type *setw*. Now we can create a manipulator with an argument using the following steps:

1. We need a class whose name is the same as the name of the manipulator and with one data member of the same type as the type of manipulator argument.
2. We need to overload the insertion or extraction operator for the class in which the first parameter is of type stream (*ostream* or *istream*) and the second parameter is the same as the class in step 1.
3. In the body of the overloaded operator, we code the action to achieve the purpose of the manipulator.

A manipulator with an argument can be created by defining a class with one data member in which the insertion or extraction operator is overloaded.

We simulate the manipulator *setw*(*n*), but we call it *length* (*n*) so it will be treated as a new manipulator. Program 16.26 shows the interface for the class *length* (we use a lowercase letter for the name of the class for consistency with the manipulator).

Program 16.26 The interface file (length.h)

```
/**********************************************************************
 * Interface file for a class named length                            *
 **********************************************************************/
#ifndef LENGTH_H
#define LENGTH_H
#include <iostream>
using namespace std;

class length
{
  private:
       int n;
  public:
       length (int n);
       friend ostream& operator << (ostream& stream, const length& len );
};
#endif
```

We also implement the class length as shown in Program 16.27. Note that we want the operator << to set the width formatting variable with the value of data member *n* in the class *length*.

We write Program 16.28 to apply the new manipulator and test it.

Program 16.27 The implementation file (length.cpp)

```
/**********************************************************************
 * Implementation of the class length                                 *
 **********************************************************************/
#include "length.h"

// Definition of the length member function
length :: length (int n1)
: n (n1)
{
}
// Overloaded operator <<
ostream& operator << (ostream& stream, const length& len )
{
  stream.width (len.n);
  return stream;
}
```

Program 16.28 The application file (application.cpp)

```
/***************************************************************
 * An application program to use the manipulator length(n)      *
 ***************************************************************/
#include "length.h"

int main ()
{
  cout << length (10) << 123 << endl;
  cout << length (20) << 234 << endl;
  return 0;
}
```

Run:

```
123
          234
```

16.6 PROGRAM DESIGN

In this section we design three programs to show the applications of the input/output streams.

16.6.1 Merging Two Sorted Files

We want to create a merge sort on two files of integers. Assume we have two files of integers in which the integers are sorted (arranged from the smallest to the largest). We want to merge the two files to create a new file in which the integers are still sorted and any duplicates are maintained. Figure 16.15 shows the contents of *infile1*, *infile2*, and *outfile*.

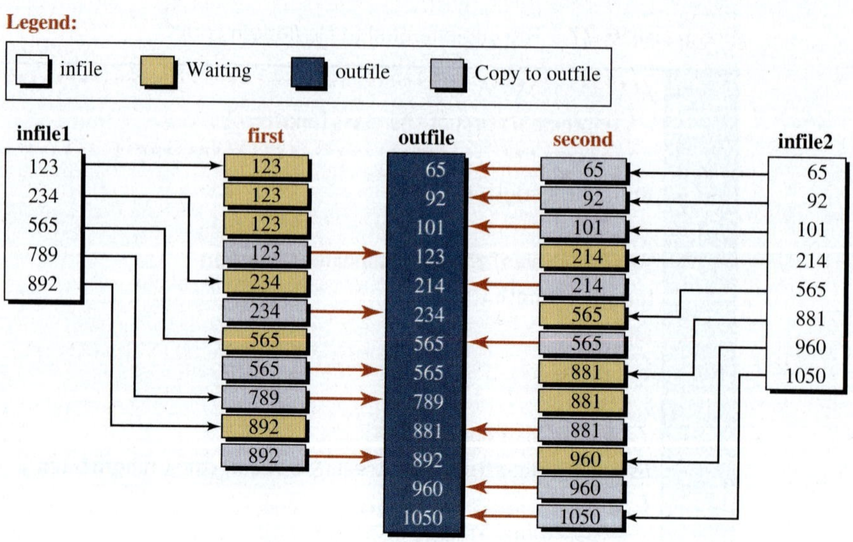

Note:
There is only one variable named *first* and one named *second*, but their values and conditions change as the sort progresses.

Figure 16.15 Data flow in a merge sort

The process of merging these files takes 13 iterations. In each iteration, either the contents of variable *first* or variable *second*, but not both, is moved to the outfile. Some integers remain in the corresponding variable for a few iterations before they can move to the output file. Note that the comparison and the decision to move an integer to the output file is always based on the contents of the variables *first* and *second*.

Program 16.29 shows the code. In line 14 we declare two variables, *first* and *second*, to hold an integer of the first and second input files during processing. In line 15 we create a sentinel (a very large integer, as we learned in previous chapters).

Program 16.29 Merge sort process applied to two files

```
1  /***************************************************************
2   * A program to merge two files of sorted integer to create    *
3   * a file of sorted integers                                    *
4   ***************************************************************/
5  #include <iostream>
6  #include <fstream>
7  #include <assert.h>
8  #include <limits>
9  using namespace std;
10
11 int main ()
12 {
13   // Declaration and Initialization
14   int first, second;
15   int sentinel = numeric_limits <int> :: max();
16   // Instantiating streams and opening files
17   ifstream strm1 ("infile1");
18   ifstream strm2 ("infile2");
19   ofstream strm3 ("outfile");
20   if (!strm1.is_open())
21   {
22       cout << "Error opening infile1!" << endl;
23       assert (false);
24   }
25   if (!strm2.is_open())
26   {
27       cout << "Error opening infile2!" << endl;
28       assert (false);
29   }
30   if (!strm3.is_open())
31   {
32       cout << "Error opening outfile!" << endl;
33       assert (false);
34   }
35   // Processing
```

(continued)

Program 16.29 Merge sort process applied to two files (Continued)

```
    strm1 >> first;
    strm2 >> second;
    while (strm1 || strm2)
    {
        if (first <= second)
        {
                strm3 << first << " ";
                strm1 >> first;
                if (!strm1)
                {
                    first = sentinel;
                }
        }
        else
        {
                strm3 << second << " ";
                strm2 >> second;
                if (!strm2)
                {
                    second = sentinel;
                }
        }
    }
    // Closing files
    strm1.close();
    strm2.close();
    strm3.close();
    return 0;
}
```

16.6.2 Symmetric Ciphers

Transmission of information using files must be handled in a secure way. One of the common techniques used for this purpose is cryptography. **Cryptography,** a word with Greek origins, means "secret writing." It involves two distinct mechanisms: symmetric-key and asymmetric-key cryptography. Cryptography uses keys to change an original message, called *plaintext*, to a secret message, called *ciphertext*.

There are two broad categories of cryptography: *symmetric* and *asymmetric*. We discuss and use an example of the first in this section; we use an example of the second in the next section.

In *symmetric-key* cryptography we use the same key for both encryption and decryption. The key can be used for bidirectional communication, which is why it is called *symmetric*. Figure 16.16 shows the general idea behind a symmetric-key cipher.

In Figure 16.16, an entity, Alice, sends a message to another entity, Bob, over an insecure channel with the assumption that an adversary cannot understand the contents of the message by simply eavesdropping over the channel.

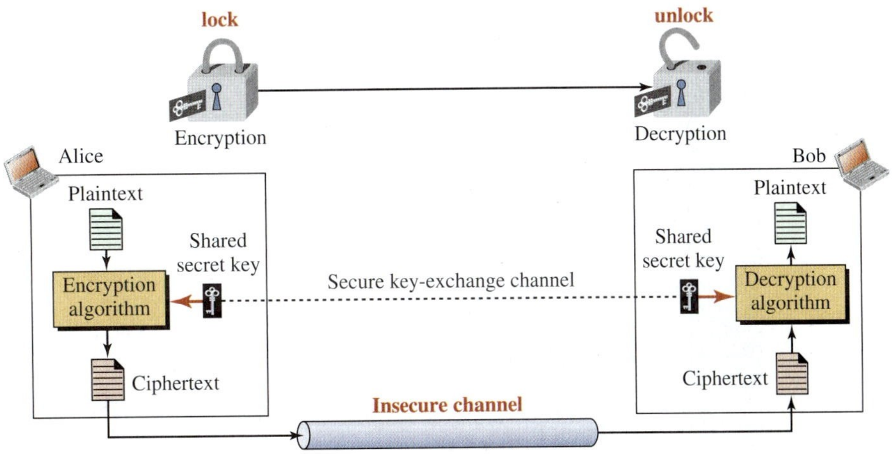

Figure 16.16 General idea of a symmetric-key cipher

The original message from Alice to Bob is *plaintext*; the message that is sent through the channel is *ciphertext*. To create the *ciphertext* from the *plaintext*, Alice uses an *encryption algorithm* and a *shared secret key*.

Symmetric-key ciphers are also called secret-key ciphers.

To create the plaintext from ciphertext, Bob uses a *decryption algorithm* and the same secret key. We refer to encryption and decryption algorithms as *ciphers*. A *key* is a value or a set of values that the cipher, as an algorithm, uses.

Symmetric-key ciphers can be divided into traditional ciphers and modern ciphers. Traditional ciphers are simple, character-oriented ciphers that are not secure based on today's standards. Modern ciphers, on the other hand, are complex, bit-oriented ciphers that are more secure. Our program uses one of the traditional ciphers. The modern ciphers, such as DES (Data Encryption Standard), are extremely involved and require a high-level of cryptography and number theory knowledge (see *Cryptography and Network Security 2008*, by Behrouz A. Forouzan, published by McGraw-Hill).

One of the traditional symmetric ciphers is called the *monoalphabetic cipher*, in which a character (or a symbol) in the *plaintext* is always changed to the same character (or symbol) in the *ciphertext* regardless of its position in the text. For example, if the algorithm says that letter A in the plaintext is changed to letter D, every letter A is changed to letter D. In other words, the relationship between letters in the plaintext and the ciphertext is one-to-one. One of the common monoalphabetic ciphers uses a two-dimensional table for encryption and decryption. Figure 16.17 shows an example of such a mapping and Program 16:30 demonstrates it use.

The key in this case is different for each character in the *plaintext* and *ciphertext*. If the character in the *plaintext* is 'a', the corresponding character in the *ciphertext* would be 'N', and so on. Note that we show the *plaintext* in lowercase and the *ciphertext* in uppercase letters.

Plaintext →	a	b	c	d	e	f	g	h	i	j	k	l	m	n	o	p	q	r	s	t	u	v	w	x	y	z
Ciphertext →	N	O	A	T	R	B	E	C	F	U	X	D	Q	G	Y	L	K	H	V	I	J	M	P	Z	S	W

Figure 16.17 An example key for a monoalphabetic substitution cipher

Program 16.30 The file monoalph.h as the interface file

```
/***************************************************************
 * The interface for the MonoAlpha class                        *
 ***************************************************************/
#ifndef MONOALPHA_H
#define MONOALPHA_H
#include <iostream>
using namespace std;

class MonoAlpha
{
   private:
        static const char key [ ][2];
        char searchEncrypt (char c);
        char searchDecrypt (char c);
   public:
        MonoAlpha ();
        ~MonoAlpha ();
        void encrypt (const char* plainFile, const char* cipherFile);
        void decrypt (const char* cipherFile, const char* plainFile);
};
#endif
```

We create a class named *MonoAlpha* that includes the secret key, a static two-dimensional array. The class has two public member functions, *encrypt* and *decrypt*. There are also two private member functions that change one character in plaintext to ciphertext and vice versa. They are called by the public encryption and decryption functions.

Implementation File The implementation file is based on the interface file. The *encrypt* function extracts characters, one by one, from the plaintext file. The function then calls the *searchEncrypt* function to change each character to a new character according to the key table. After each character is changed, it is inserted into the cipher file. The *decrypt* function reverses the process. Program 16.31 shows the implementation.

Program 16.31 The file monoalpha.cpp as the implementation

```
/***************************************************************
 * The implementation file for the MonoAlpha class              *
 ***************************************************************/
#include "monoalpha.h"
#include <fstream>

// Constructor
MonoAlpha :: MonoAlpha ()
```

(continued)

Program 16.31 The file monoalpha.cpp as the implementation (Continued)

```
{
}
// Destructor
MonoAlpha :: ~MonoAlpha ()
{
}
// Public member function
void MonoAlpha :: encrypt (const char* plainFile, const char* cipherFile)
{
  ifstream istrm (plainFile, ios :: in);
  ofstream ostrm (cipherFile, ios :: out);
  char c1, c2;
  while (istrm.get (c1))
  {
        c2 = searchEncrypt (c1);
        ostrm.put(c2);
  }
  istrm.close ();
  ostrm.close ();
}
// Public member function
void MonoAlpha :: decrypt (const char* cipherFile, const char* plainFile)
{
  ifstream istrm (cipherFile, ios :: in);
  ofstream ostrm (plainFile, ios :: out);
  char c1, c2;
  while (istrm.get (c1))
  {
        c2 = searchDecrypt (c1);
        ostrm.put(c2);
  }
  istrm.close ();
  ostrm.close ();
}
// Private member function
char MonoAlpha :: searchEncrypt (char c)
{
  int i = 0;
  while (true)
  {
        if (key[i][0] == c)
        {
                return key[i][1] ;
        }
```

(continued)

Program 16.31 The file monoalpha.cpp as the implementation (Continued)

```
            i++;
    }
}
// Private member function
char MonoAlpha :: searchDecrypt (char c)
{
    int i = 0;
    while (true)
    {
        if (key[i][1] == c)
        {
                return key[i][0];
        }
        i++;
    }
}
// Definition of the static key array
const char MonoAlpha :: key [ ][2] = {{'a', 'N'}, {'b', 'N'},
            {'c', 'A'}, {'d', 'T'}, {'e', 'R'}, {'f', 'B'}, {'g', 'E'}, {'h', 'C'},
            {'i', 'F'}, {'j', 'U'}, {'k', 'X'}, {'l', 'D'}, {'m', 'Q'}, {'n', 'G'},
            {'o', 'Y'}, {'p', 'L'}, {'q', 'K'}, {'r', 'H'}, {'s', 'V'}, {'t', 'I'},
            {'u', 'J'}, {'v', 'M'}, {'w', 'P'}, {'x', 'Z'}, {'y', 'S'}, {'z', 'W'} };
```

Application File at Encryption Site We need two application files, one at the encryption site and the other at the decryption site. Alice and Bob, however, need to share the interface and the implementation files and hide them from other people. Program 16.32 shows

Program 16.32 The file app1.cpp used at the sender site

```
/*******************************************************************
 * The application file used to encrypt the message                *
 *******************************************************************/
#include "monoalpha.h"

int main ()
{
    MonoAlpha monoalpha;
    monoalpha.encrypt ("plainFile", "cipherFile");
    return 0;
}
```

Contents of Plaintext File:

```
thisisthefiletoencrypt
```

Contents of Ciphertext File:

```
ICFVFVICRBFDRIYRGAHSLI
```

the application at the encryption site. Alice needs to change the plaintext to the ciphertext and send it to Bob. Note that we have used only lowercase letters in the plaintext and uppercase letters in the ciphertext to make the transformation easier and the code more secure. Also, the use of punctuation should be avoided because it gives more clues to hackers.

Application File at Decryption Site Program 16.33 shows the application at the decryption site. Bob must change the ciphertext received from Alice to create the plaintext.

> **The monoalphabetic program is only for educational purposes; it is not secure for use in real systems.**

Program 16.33 The file app2.cpp used at the receiver site

```
/***************************************************************
 * The application file used to decrypt the message            *
 ***************************************************************/
#include "monoalpha.h"

int main ( )
{
    MonoAlpha monoalpha;
    monoalpha.decrypt ("cipherFile", "plainFile");
    return 0;
}
```

```
Contents of Ciphertext File:
ICFVFVICRBFDRIYRGAHSLI
Contents of Plaintext File:
thisisthefiletoencrypt
```

Key Terms

console streams
cryptography
ios class
random access
sequential access
stream state

Summary

A source or a sink of data cannot be directly connected to a program. We need a mediator to stand between the sources/sinks and the program to control the flow of data and to interpret data elements when reading or writing. This is done using streams. One of the main purposes of using streams is to convert the format of data as stored in a sink or source to their format in memory. C++ defines a hierarchy of streams in which the *ios* class is the base class for all input/output classes.

Console streams are made of three classes *istream*, *ostream*, and *iostream*. We can use the first two, but the *iostream* class cannot be instantiated.

We can also read and write to files using file streams. File streams are made of three classes: *ifstream*, *ofstream*, and *fstream*. To use them, we must construct the stream, connect the file to the stream (open the file), do input or output, disconnect the file from the stream (close the file), and destruct the stream (which is done automatically).

The C++ library defines three classes to input or output strings. The most common application of a string stream class is to act as an *adapter* for the string class.

An issue in input/output is formatting data. The *ios* class defines flags, fields, and variables to be used for formatting data. They can be used directly or under the umbrella of manipulators, which are member functions or classes that use them. In addition to the predefined manipulators, we can define our own manipulators.

Problems

PR-1. Write a function, *openInput*, that opens a file in the input mode. The name of the file is passed as a parameter.

PR-2. Write a function, *openOutput*, that opens a file in the output mode. The name of the file is passed as a parameter.

PR-3. Write a function that returns a character in a file when the file name and the location of a character in the file are given as parameters.

PR-4. Write a function that changes the value of a character in a file when the file name, the location of a character in the file, and the new character to be replaced are given as parameters.

PR-5. Write a function that copies the contents of a file to a new file.

PR-6. Write a function that compares two files and returns *true* if the files are identical and *false* if their contents vary.

PR-7. Write a function that appends one file to the end of another.

PR-8. Write a function that, given a file, copies the odd-numbered characters to a second file and the even-numbered items to a third file.

PR-9. Write a function that takes a file of characters and appends the number of characters in the file to the end of the file after a blank.

PR-10. Write a function that reads items from an array of characters and creates a file of characters.

PR-11. Show how we can read a line of records of student data consisting of an *id* (integer), *name* (string), and *gpa* (double) and store the data in appropriate variables.

PR-12. Show how we can combine three variables made of an *id* (integer), a *name* (string), and a *gpa* (double) and store them in a single string.

Programs

PRG-1. Write a program that reads a text file and changes each character in the file to uppercase. Let the user enter the name of the file as a C++ string (remember to change the name to C string for opening the file). Test your program with a file of the following contents:

```
This is a file of characters to be changed.
```

PRG-2. Use a text editor to create a file of integers separated by one space character as shown below. Then use a program to find if a given integer is in the file.

```
14 17 24 32 11 72 43 88 99
```

PRG-3. Searching for a target can be faster if the elements in the file are sorted (are in order). Use a text editor to create a file of integers separated by one space character as shown below. Then use a program to find if a given integer is in the file. Note that searching time makes a lot of difference if the file is very large, although we test with a small file.

```
14 17 24 32 48 52 64 74 81 92
```

PRG-4. We can erase data elements from a random file because the connected stream in memory is in fact an array. We erase a data item by shifting the rest of the items one position toward the beginning of the stream. However, shifting creates a duplicate data item at the end. In an array, we reduce the size to avoid using that duplicate. In the case of a stream, we must change the last element to a dummy. We know that a file of characters can be accessed randomly because the size of a character is fixed. Assume that you have the following file of characters:

```
ABCDEFGHIJKLMNOPQRSTUVWXYZ
```

Write a program that erases any character in the file given its position (0 to 25). Remember to change the duplicate character in the end to a null character.

PRG-5. We can access the elements of an array randomly using an index. An array, however, is not permanent. When the program terminates, the contents of the array are destroyed. We can simulate an array with a binary file using random access. Create two programs. In the first program, store 10 different double values in a file. In the second program, randomly retrieve some of the values stored in the file by the first program. Note that we use two application programs to show that after the first program terminates, the file exists and can be accessed by the second program.

PRG-6. The question arrises, "How can we create a random-access file of strings (such as names)"? This cannot be done by simply using the *string* class because the size of a string object is not predefined. In a random-access file, the size of all items must be the same. A solution is to create a new class with only one data member of type *String*. We know that when C++ creates objects of user-defined type, it pads the objects to make them of equal size. Write a program to store some names in a binary file, and then access one of them randomly.

PRG-7. One way to create a record of information that is stored in a file and can be accessed randomly is to create a string out of it. We can use a *toString* function to change a record of variable size and different data type to a string and add padding to make the size of all strings the same. Write a program that creates records of five students in which each record is made of three parts: id (an integer between 0 and 100), name (a string of various size), and gpa (a double value less than or equal 4.0). Make the size of the strings the same (18 characters) and add a new line at the end of each record so you can read each line using *getline* function. Write a program to store five records in a file. Write another program to access records.

PRG-8. Write a program that updates a binary file for customers in a bank. The data consist of a customer identity (an integer) and customer balance (a double value). Write two application files. In the first application program, create the binary file with identity (starting with 1000) and balances for five customers. In the second application program, let the balance be changed (using deposit or withdrawal) for some customers (update the file) and then print the contents of the file after updating.

We know that computer programs involve iteration (repetition). In this chapter, we introduce a new approach called *recursion* that can make some categories of programs easier to solve. In particular, we show how recursion can be used to solve some sorting and searching problems. Finally, we show how to solve a classical problem, Towers of Hanoi, using recursion.

Objectives

After you have read and studied this chapter, you should be able to:

- Discuss the concept of recursion and compare it to repetition.
- Distinguish between a void and a value-returning recursive function.
- Show how some repetitive functions can be changed to recursive functions.
- Distinguish between tail recursion and nontail recursion and how the second can be changed to the first for efficiency.
- Discuss the use of helper functions to improve the efficiency of some recursive functions.
- Discuss list sorting and show how to write an efficient recursive sorting function such as quick sort.
- Discuss searching and show how to write a recursive search function such as a binary search.
- Discuss the Towers of Hanoi as a classical recursive algorithm.

17.1 INTRODUCTION

In previous chapters, we learned to write functions to solve problems. When the function required that we do something over and over, we used *iteration* (loops). In this chapter, we show that we can also solve repetitive problems using *recursion*.

17.1.1 Repetition versus Recursion

In a simple iteration, we use a counter to repeat a task *n* times; in recursion, the function does the task only once, but then calls itself $n - 1$ times to achieve the same goal. The approaches to void recursive functions and value-returning recursive functions are different, so we discuss them separately.

Void Recursive Functions

Assume that we need to print *n* asterisks on a line and the value of *n* is known. We can use either an iterative or a recursive solution as shown below. We have chosen the *while* loop for the iterative solution because it makes the comparison between the two easier; we have only one variable, *n*, in both functions.

```
// Iterative
void line (int n)
{
  while (n >= 1)
  {
     cout << "*";
     n--;
  }
  return;
}
```

```
// Recursive
void line (int n)
{
  if (n < 1)
  {
     return;
  }
  cout << "*";
  line (n - 1);
}
```

There is an implicit condition in the iterative version. If n is less than 1, we never enter the *while* loop and the function returns. In each iteration, we reduce the value of n by 1 until it becomes less than 1 and we return from the function.

In the recursive version, we use an explicit condition to return from the function when n is less than 1. However, instead of repeating the loop with $n - 1$, we call the function again with the parameter $n - 1$.

If we compare the two approaches, we see that they are doing the same thing. A condition, implicit or explicit, is needed to return from the function. In the iterative version, we reduce the value of the variable n one by one using the statement *n--*; in the recursive version, we call the function again with a reduced parameter ($n - 1$).

In the repetitive version, the statement (*cout* << "*") is called n times, each time in one iteration in the loop. In the recursive version, the same statement is executed once in each call to the function.

In the repetitive version, we have only one function call; in the recursive version, we have $n - 1$ function calls. In each call except the last, we print one asterisk; in the last we print nothing. The first three calls are referred to as the *general case*; the last call is referred to as the *base case*. The **general case** is related to those calls that do something; the **base case** is related to the case that terminates recursion.

Figure 17.1 symbolically shows the iterative and recursive calls.

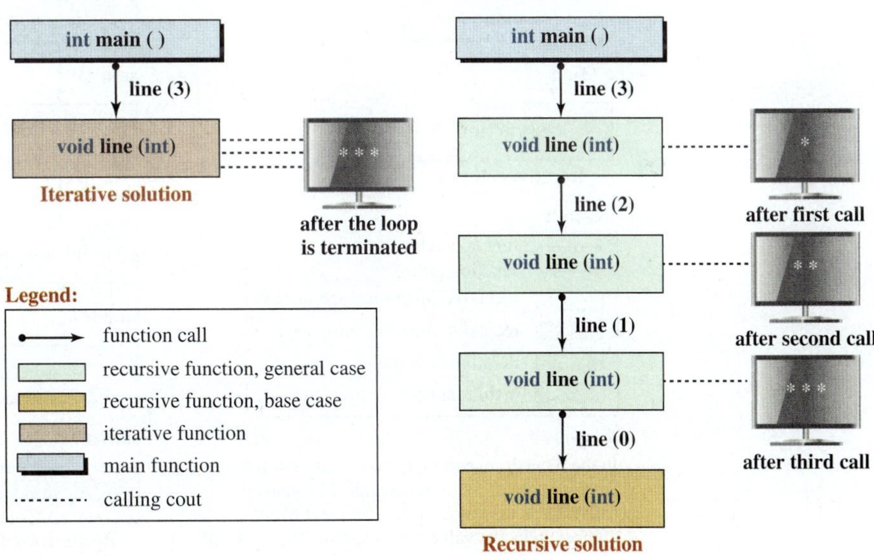

Figure 17.1 Iterative versus recursive call of a void function

Value-Returning Recursive Functions

Assume that we need to find the sum of all numbers from 0 to n (generally referred to as summation). We can write two functions, one iterative and one recursive. The functions, however, are not void functions; each must return the value of the sum.

We show two functions side by side to see the difference between the iterative version and the recursive version. Again, we use the *while* loop, which makes the comparison easier.

```
// Iterative                          // Recursive
int sum (int n)                       int sum (int n)
{                                     {
   int result = 0;                       if (n <= 0)
   while (n >= 0)                        {
   {                                         return 0;
      result += n;                       }
      n--;                               return sum (n - 1) + n;
   }                                  }
   return result;
}
```

In both cases we are summing the numbers backward, from n to 0. In other words, we are finding $sum = n + n - 1 + n - 2, + \ldots + 1 + 0$. In the case of iteration, the function skips the loop if $n < 0$ (the terminating case). In case of recursion, the function explicitly returns from the function. This means that the condition ($n <= 0$) is the base case or termination case for both functions. The iterative function reduces the value of n in each iteration; the recursive function calls the same function with value $n - 1$. Figure 17.2 symbolically shows the behavior of each function.

Comparison

When we compare the recursive *line* function (Figure 17.1) and the recursive *sum* function (Figure 17.2), we can deduce the difference between a void recursive function and a

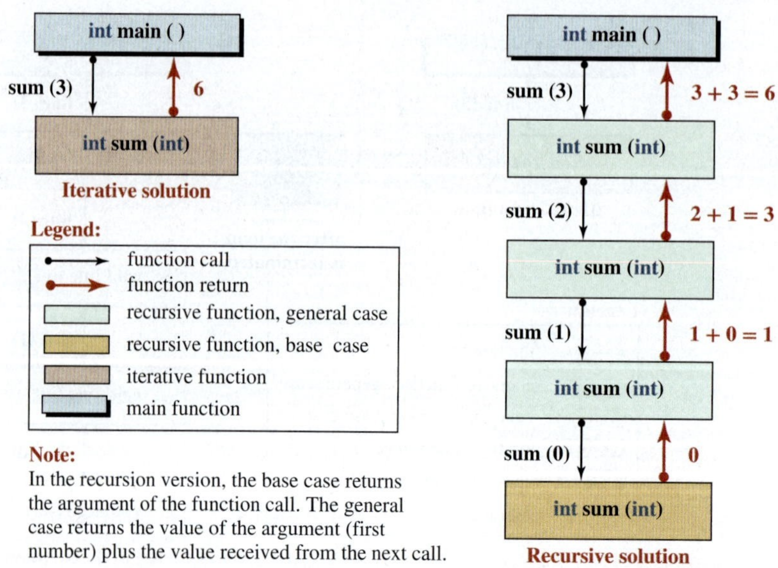

Figure 17.2 Iterative versus recursive call of a value-returning function

value-returning recursive function. In the case of a void recursive function, general cases are continuously called until a base case is reached; the general case does not have to hold any information. In the case of a value-returning function, the general cases are called until the base case is reached. Each general case must hold some information (the value of n) until the call to the next step is returned. The base case then returns the value of *sum*(0) to the previous general case, which returns the value of *sum*(1) to the previous general case, and so on.

17.1.2 Recursive Algorithms

In this section we solve simple recursive algorithms.

Sum and Factorial

We discussed how to solve the *sum*(n) problem recursively. A sibling of the *sum*(n) function is the *factorial*(n) function (also called *product*). In the *sum* function, we must add numbers from n to 0; in the *factorial* function, we must multiply numbers from n to 1.

```
// Sum function
int sum (int n)
{
   if (n =< 0)
   {
       return 0;
   }
   return sum (n - 1) + n;
}
```

```
// Factorial function
int factorial (int n)
{
   if (n =< 1)
   {
       return 1;
   }
   return factorial (n - 1) * n;
}
```

Note that *sum*(0) is 0, while *factorial*(1) is 1. In the *sum* function, we use the addition operator; in the *factorial* function, we use the multiplication operator. Note that in the *sum* function, *sum*(n − 1) is the value returned from the next call and in the factorial function, *factorial*(n − 1) is the value returned from the next call.

Program 17.1 tests the value of *sum*(n) and *factorial*(n) using the same value for n in each call. We can see that the *sum* grows slowly, but the *factorial* grows rapidly.

Program 17.1 Testing recursive sum and factorial

```
/*******************************************************************
 * A program to find the sum and factorial of an integer           *
 *******************************************************************/
#include <iostream>
using namespace std;

// Declaration of sum function
int sum (int n);
// Declaration of factorial function
int factorial (int n);

int main ( )
```

(continued)

Program 17.1 Testing recursive sum and factorial (Continued)

```
{
    // Testing sum (0) and factorial (1)
    cout << "sum (0) = " << sum (0) << endl ;
    cout << "factorial (1) = " << factorial (1) << endl << endl;
    // Testing sum (3) and factorial (3)
    cout << "sum (3) = " << sum (3) << endl;
    cout << "factorial (3) = " << factorial (3) << endl << endl;
    // Testing sum (7) and factorial (7)
    cout << "sum (7) = " << sum (7) << endl;
    cout << "factorial (7) = " << factorial (7);
    return 0;
}
// Recursive definition of sum (n)
int sum (int n)
{
    if (n <= 0)
    {
        return 0;
    }
    return n + sum (n - 1);
}
// Recursive definition of factorial (n)
int factorial (int n)
{
    if (n <= 1)
    {
        return 1;
    }
    return n * factorial (n - 1);
}
```

Run:

```
sum (0) = 0
factorial (1) = 1

sum (3) = 6
factorial (3) = 6

sum (7) = 28
factorial (7) = 5040
```

Greatest Common Divisor

One function often needed in mathematics and computer science is the *greatest common divisor*, *gcd*, of two positive integers. An integer y is a divisor of x if $x \% y = 0$. Two positive integers may have many common divisors but only one greatest common divisor.

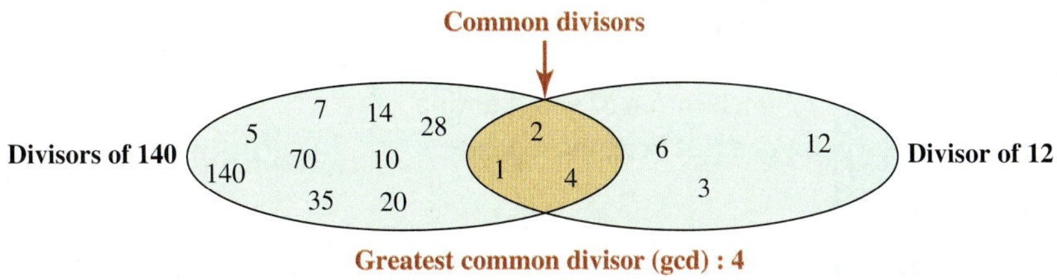

Figure 17.3 Greatest common divisor of 12 and 140

Table 17.1 The base and general cases of the Euclidean algorithm

Base case	General case
gcd (*x*, 0) = *x*	gcd (*x*, *y*) = gcd (*y*, *x* % *y*)

For example, the divisors of 12 are 1, 2, 3, 4, 6, 12. The divisors of 140 are 1, 2, 4, 7, 10, 14, 20, 28, 35, 70, and 140. The common divisors of 12 and 140 are 1, 2, 4. However, the greatest common divisor is 4. This is shown in Figure 17.3.

More than 2000 years ago, a mathematician named Euclid developed an algorithm that finds the greatest common divisor between two positive integers recursively. Table 17.1 shows the base and general case of the Euclidean algorithm.

Figure 17.4 shows how the recursive *gcd* function calls another version until it finds the greatest common divisor of its two arguments.

Program 17.2 shows how we can find the greatest common divisor of several pairs using the recursive definition.

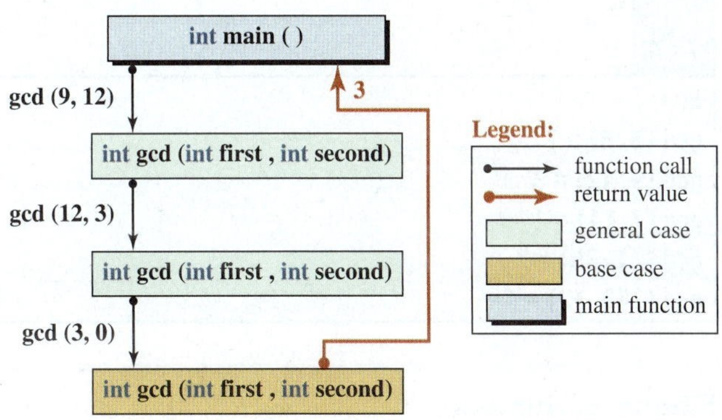

Figure 17.4 The recursive calls in gcd (9, 12)

Program 17.2 Greatest common divisor

```
/***************************************************************
 * A program to find the greatest common divisor of some pairs *
 ***************************************************************/
#include <iostream>
using namespace std;

```

(*continued*)

Program 17.2 Greatest common divisor (Continued)

```
// Declaration of gcd function
int gcd (int first, int second);

int main ()
{
   // Checking gcd of five pairs
   cout << "gcd (8, 6) = " << gcd (8, 6) << endl;
   cout << "gcd (9, 12) = " << gcd (9, 12) << endl;
   cout << "gcd (7, 11) = " << gcd (7, 11) << endl;
   cout << "gcd (21, 35) = " << gcd (21, 35) << endl;
   cout << "gcd (140, 12) = " << gcd (140, 12);
   return 0;
}
// Recursive definition of greatest common divisor
int gcd (int first, int second)
{
   if (second == 0)
   {
        return first;
   }
   else
   {
        return gcd (second, first % second);
   }
}
```

Run:

```
gcd (8, 6) = 2
gcd (9, 12) = 3
gcd (7, 11) = 1
gcd (21, 35) = 7
gcd (140, 12) = 4
```

Fibonacci Numbers

Named after an Italian mathematician, Fibonacci numbers are a series in which each number is the sum of the previous two numbers. Unlike the previous recursive problem, this problem has two bases, as shown in Table 17.2.

Figure 17.5 shows how we can calculate *fib*(4) using recursive calls. Note that we cannot find the return value of *fib*(4) until we find the return value of *fib*(3) and *fib*(2).

Table 17.2 The base and general cases of Fibonacci numbers

Base case	General case
fib (0) = 0, fib (1) = 1	fib (*n*) = fib (*n*−1) + fib (*n*−2)

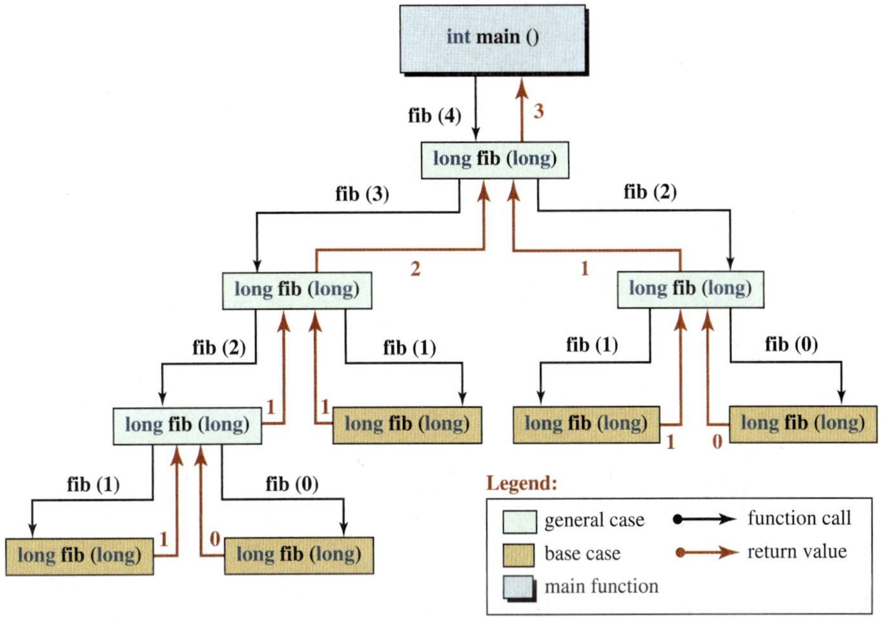

Figure 17.5 Recursive trace of Fibonacci number fib(4)

We cannot find *fib*(3) until we find *fib*(2) and *fib*(1). We cannot find *fib*(2) until we find *fib*(1) and *fib*(0). Finally, we find the answer to *fib*(0) and *fib*(1), which are the base cases.

Based on the definition of the Fibonacci numbers in Table 17.2, we write a recursive function to calculate any of them, as shown in Program 17.3.

Program 17.3 Recursive solution to Fibonacci numbers

```
/******************************************************************
 * A program to find the Fibonacci values                         *
 ******************************************************************/
#include <iostream>
using namespace std;

// Function declaration
long long fib (int n);

int main ( )
{
  // Testing Fibonocci 0 to 10
  cout << "Fibonacci numbers from 0 to 10" << endl;
  for (int i = 0; i <= 10; i++)
  {
      cout << "fib (" << i << ") = " << fib(i) << endl;
  }
  cout << endl;
```

(continued)

Program 17.3 Recursive solution to Fibonacci numbers (Continued)

```
    // Testing Fibonacci numbers of 35 and 36
    cout << "Fibonacci numbers of 35 and 36" << endl;
    cout << "fib (35) = " << fib(36) << endl;
    cout << "fib (36) = " << fib(36) << endl;
    return 0;
}
// Function Definition
long long fib (int n)
{
    if (n == 0 || n ==1)
    {
        return n;
    }
    else
    {
        return (fib (n - 2) + fib (n - 1));
    }
}
```

```
Run:
Fibonacci numbers from 0 to 10
fib (0) = 0
fib (1) = 1
fib (2) = 1
fib (3) = 2
fib (4) = 3
fib (5) = 5
fib (6) = 8
fib (7) = 13
fib (8) = 21
fib (9) = 34
fib (10) = 55

Fibonacci numbers of 35 and 36
fib (35) = 9227465
fib (36) = 14930352
```

We can see that each Fibonacci number is the sum of the two previous ones.

Reversing a String

Another problem that can be solved recursively is to reverse a string. We can define the base and general case as shown in Table 17.3. In other words, if the string is made of zero or one character, the reverse string is itself. Otherwise, we need to find the reverse of the substring

Table 17.3 The base and general cases of string reverse

Base case	General case
`if (length <= 1), return strg`	`return reverse (substr (1, length - 1)) + subtr (0, 1)`

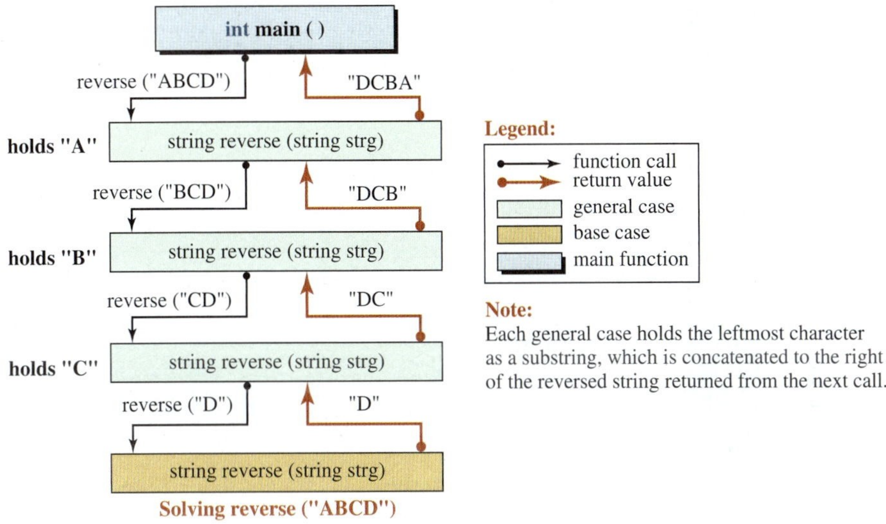

Figure 17.6 The steps involved in calling reverse ("ABCD")

minus the first character and then concatenate it with the substring that holds only the first character. Figure 17.6 shows how we find the reverse of a string recursively.

Each general case calls another general case, passing the substring of the argument (without the first character). It holds the first character in a substring until the reversed string is returned. It then concatenates the two strings and returns the result to the calling function. In other words, given the string "ABCD", the first call holds "A" as a substring and passes "BCD" to the next call. When the string "DCB" is returned, it concatenates it with the string "D" to create "DCBA".

Program 17.4 shows the recursive solution to this problem.

Program 17.4 Recursively reversing a string

```
/***********************************************************************
 * A program that reverses a string recursively                        *
 ***********************************************************************/
#include <iostream>
#include <string>
using namespace std;

// Declaration of recursive function
string reverse (string str);
```

(continued)

Program 17.4 Recursively reversing a string (Continued)

```

int main ( )
{
    // Calling reverse function using some strings
    cout << "Reverse of 'ABCD': " << reverse ("ABCD") << endl;
    cout << "Reverse of 'Hello': " << reverse ("Hello") << endl;
    cout << "Reverse of 'Bye': " << reverse ("Bye") << endl;
    return 0;
}
// Definition of recursive function
string reverse (string str)
{
    if (str.length () <= 1)
    {
        return str;
    }
    else
    {
        return reverse (str.substr (1, str.length() – 1)) + str.substr (0, 1);
    }
}
```

```
Run:
Reverse of 'ABCD': DCBA
Reverse of 'Hello': olleH
Reverse of 'Bye': eyB
```

Checking for Palindromes

A string is a palindrome if it reads the same forward and backward. We can solve this problem using a recursive function called *isPalidrome* that has two base cases and one general case, as shown in Table 17.4.

The first base case is related to an empty string or a string with only one character, which is obviously a palindrome. The second base case is related to the string in which the first character and the last character are different, which is obviously not a palindrome.

Figure 17.7 shows how we can use the base and general cases to find if a string is a palindrome.

Program 17.5 shows the code for the recursive function *isPalindrome*.

Table 17.4 The base cases and the general case of the isPalindrome function

Base case	`if (length <= 1), return true` `else if (strg[0] != strg [strg.size() - 1]) return false`
General case	`return isPalindrome (strg.substr (1, strg.size () - 2));`

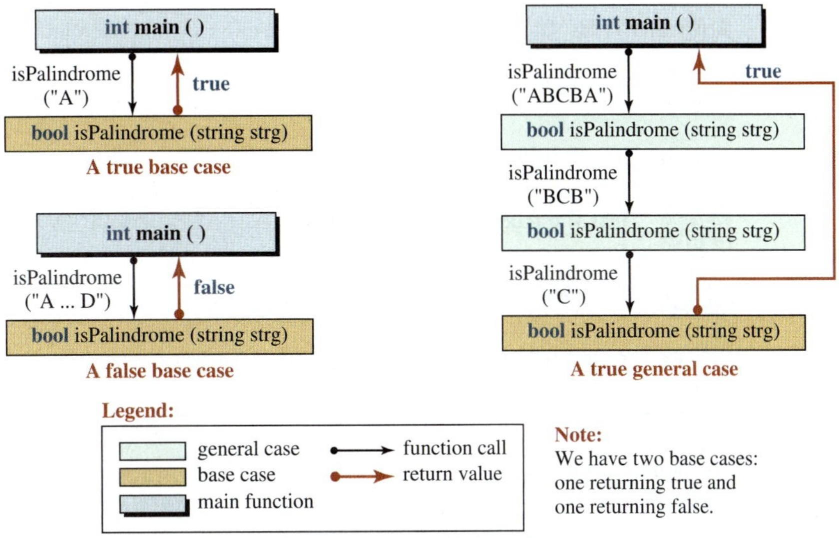

Figure 17.7 Cases of recursive isPalindrome function

Program 17.5 Using the recursive isPalindrome function

```
/*******************************************************************
 * A program that checks if a string is a palindrome                *
 *******************************************************************/
#include <iostream>
#include <string>
using namespace std;

// Declaration of recursive function
bool isPalindrome (string strg);

int main ( )
{
  // Instantiation of some strings
  string strg1 ("");
  string strg2 ("rotor");
  string strg4 ("hello");
  // Checking for palindromes
  cout << boolalpha;
  cout << "Is '' a palindrome? " << isPalindrome (strg1) << endl;
  cout << "Is 'rotor' a palindrome? " << isPalindrome (strg2) << endl;
  cout << "Is 'hello' a palindrome? " << isPalindrome (strg3);
  return 0;
}
// Definition of recursive function
bool isPalindrome(string strg)
{
```

(continued)

Program 17.5 Using the recursive isPalindrome function (Continued)

```
    if (strg.size () <= 1)
    {
        return true;
    }
    else if (strg[0] != strg [strg.size() - 1])
    {
        return false;
    }
    return isPalindrome (strg.substr (1, strg.size () - 2));
}
```

```
Run:
Is '' a palindrome? true     // empty string
Is 'rotor' a palindrome? true
Is 'hello' a palindrome? false
```

17.1.3 Tail and Nontail Recursive Functions

We encountered two types of recursion in the examples that we discussed in the previous sections: *tail recursion* and *nontail recursion* (Figure 17.8).

Tail Recursion

In **tail recursion,** each general case terminates after calling the next general case or the base case. In other words, the duty of the general case is just to call the next general function or the base function. The duty of the base case is to return the result of the whole operation to the *main* function. In tail recursion, the stack that holds the record of the next function call has only one record because when the next function is called, the current function terminates

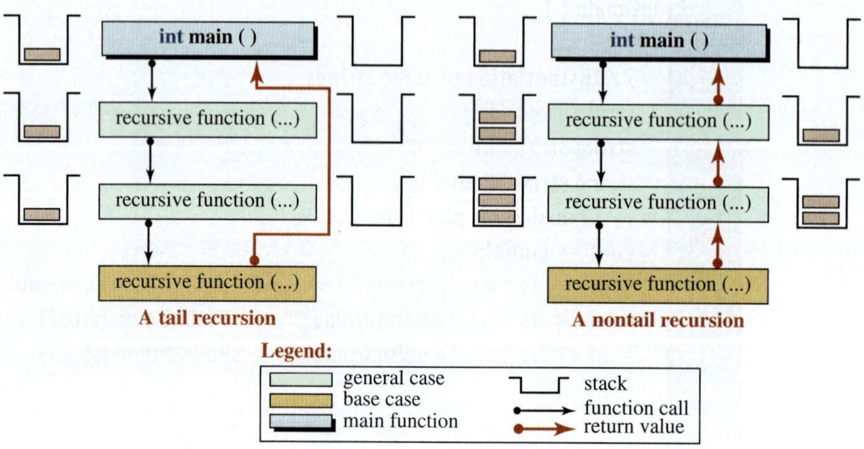

Figure 17.8 Difference between a tail and a nontail function

and its record is popped from the stack. Examples of *tail* recursive functions that we have seen so far are *gcd* and *isPalindrome*. Note that if we design a void recursive function, it is a tail recursive function in which even the base case does not return anything to the *main* function.

Nontail Recursion

In **nontail recursion,** the duty of a general-case call is not terminated until the next call returns. The current function then combines the information it is holding with what is written from the next call and passes it to the previous call. The final information is returned to the *main* function by the first general case. In nontail recursion, the stack holds the record of the next recursive call until the call is returned. Examples of nontail recursive functions that we discussed are *sum, factorial, fibonacci*, and *reverse*.

17.1.4 Helper functions

A recursive function can be inefficient. In particular, a nontail recursive function can be inefficient for two reasons. First, each general case must hold information until the result of the next call is returned. In addition, the stack eventually holds many records, which can require a large amount of memory. To improve efficiency, we can use a helper function. A **helper function** is a tail recursive function with more parameters than the nontail recursive function. We can use a nonrecursive function to call the helper function. Figure 17.9 shows the design.

We know that the *sum* function is not a tail function and is inefficient when its argument is large. We can create a tail recursive function as a helper function with an extra parameter (*result*) that holds the value of *n*, which would otherwise be held as a variable. Since each recursive call passes this parameter as a value to the next call, there is no extra usage of memory. Since the helper function is also a tail recursive function, the stack inefficiency is also removed. Program 17.6 shows this version of *sum* function.

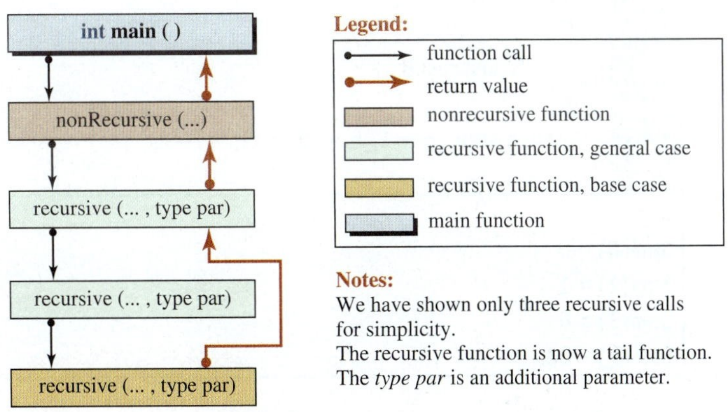

Figure 17.9 Using a helper function to remove inefficiency

Program 17.6 Using the helper function with the sum function

```
/*****************************************************************
 * A program using a helping function to create a tail recursive    *
 * function that is more efficient than a non-tail function         *
 *****************************************************************/
#include <iostream>
using namespace std;

// Functions declaration
int sum (int n);
int sum (int n, int result);

int main ( )
{
  // Calling the non-recursive function four times
  cout << "Sum (0) = " << sum (0) << endl;
  cout << "Sum (1) = " << sum (1) << endl;
  cout << "Sum (3) = " << sum (3) << endl;
  cout << "Sum (7) = " << sum (7);
  return 0;
}
// Non-recursive
int sum (int n)
{
  return sum (n, 0);
}
// Recursive
int sum (int n, int result)
{
  if (n == 0)
  {
      return result;
  }
  return sum (n - 1, n + result);
}
```

```
Run:
Sum(0) = 0
Sum(1) = 1
Sum(3) = 6
Sum(7) = 28
```

As another example, we redesign the *isPalindrome* function using a helper function. Note that *isPalindrome* is already a tail recursive function, but redesigning it removes the inefficiency of creating a substring each time we call the function.

Program 17.7 The isPalindrome function with a helper function

```
/*****************************************************************
 * A program that checks if a string is a palindrome by using     *
 * a helper function to avoid creating substring objects          *
 *****************************************************************/
#include <string>
#include <iostream>
using namespace std;

// Function declaration
bool isPalindrome (const string& strg);
bool isPalindrome (const string& strg, int left, int right);

int main ( )
{
   // Checking if the strings are palindromes
   cout << boolalpha;
   cout << "Is 'rotor" a palindrome? " << isPalindrome ("rotor") << endl;
   cout << "Is 'madam' a palindrome? "  << isPalindrome ("madam") << endl;
   cout << "Is 'Hello' a palindrome? "  << isPalindrome ("Hello");
   return 0;
}
// Function definition for non-recursive isPalindrome
bool isPalindrome(const string& strg)
{
   return isPalindrome (strg, 0, strg.size () - 1);
}
// Function definition for helper recursive isPalindrome
bool isPalindrome(const string& strg, int left, int right)
{
   if (right <= left)
   {
       return true;
   }
   else if (strg [left] != strg [right])
   {
       return false;
   }
   return isPalindrome (strg, left + 1 , right - 1);
}
```

Run:

```
Is 'rotor' a palindrome? true
Is 'madam' a palindrome? true
Is 'hello' a palindrome? false
```

17.2 RECURSIVE SORT AND SEARCH

In computer science we often need to sort a list and search a list. When a list is sorted, the search can be very fast.

17.2.1 Quick Sort

To **sort** means to rearrange the elements of a list (such as an array) so that the values are in sequence. The sorting algorithm that we introduce in this section is called *quicksort* (a recursive algorithm). This is a fast and efficient algorithm that is used in most libraries. The quicksort algorithm uses a nonrecursive algorithm called *partition,* which we discuss next.

Partition Algorithm

The partition algorithm rearranges an array around a *pivot*, one of the elements of the array, so that all elements larger than or equal to *pivot* move after it and all elements smaller than *pivot* move before it. The *pivot* is normally selected as the first element.

The following shows the partition algorithm.

```
int partition (int arr[], int i, int j) // i and j are partition indexes
{
   int p = i; // p is the pivot
   while (i < j) // outer loop
   {
      while (arr [j] > arr[p] ) // first inner loop
      {
            j--;
      }
      swap (arr[j], arr[p]);
      p = j;
      j--;
      while (arr [i] < arr [p] ) // second inner loop
      {
            i++;
      }
      swap (arr[i], arr [p]);
      p = i;
      i++;
   }
   return p;
}
```

In each execution of the outer loop, we perform the following two sets of actions.

- We move *j* to the left as long as *arr*[*j*] is larger than the *arr*[*p*]. We then swap the values of *arr*[*j*] and *arr*[*p*] and set $p = j$. Then we move *j* one more element to the left.
- We move *i* to the right as long as *arr*[*i*] is smaller than *arr*[*p*]. We then swap the values of *arr*[*i*] and *arr*[*p*] and set $p = i$. Then we move *i* one more element to the right.

The pivot *p* is set to the first element, but it moves to its final position in the array. Note that after the second iteration, *i* moves to the right of *j* and the outer loop terminates.

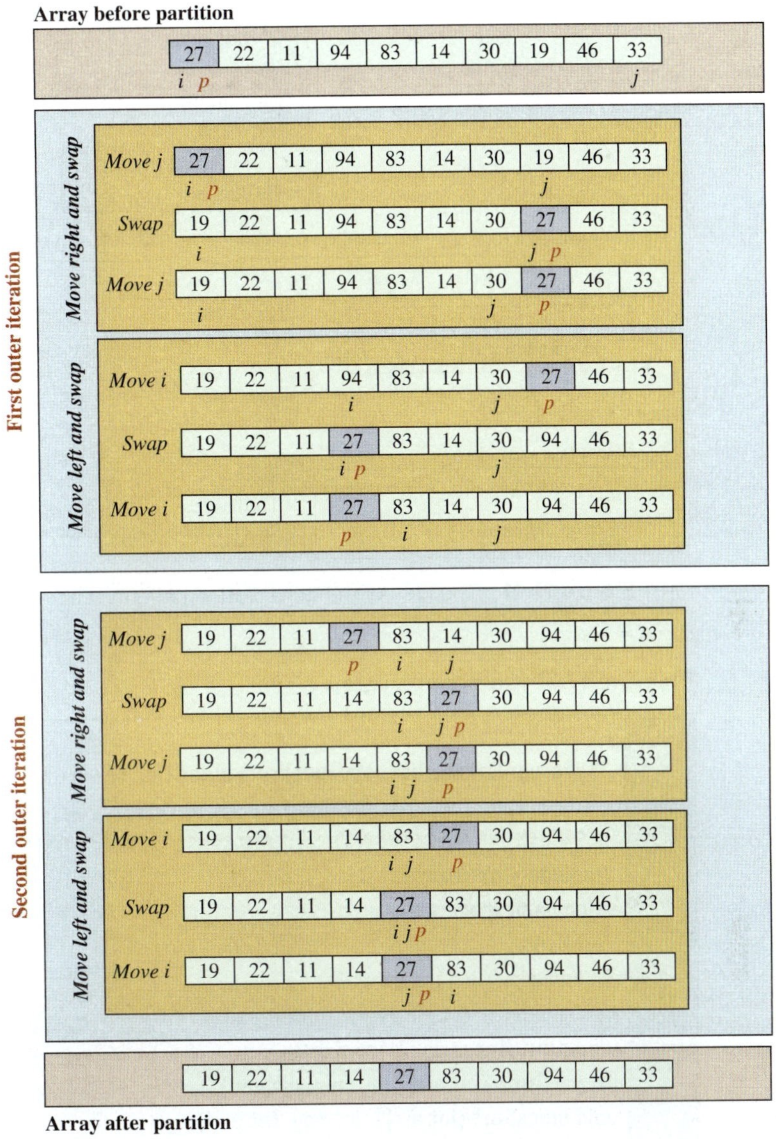

Figure 17.10 Applying the partition algorithm on an array

Figure 17.10 shows an array of 10 elements and the changes that occur during two iterations of the outer loop.

Quick Sort Algorithm

The quick sort algorithm is a void recursive algorithm, which means it does not return anything to its caller. It moves recursively down left and down right until it reaches an empty partition array. Figure 17.11 shows the idea behind the quick sort algorithm.

Program 17.8 demonstrates quick sort with a small array of 10 elements.

17.2.2 Binary Search

We often need to search an array to find the location of a element. It is much easier to search a sorted array than an unsorted array. We know that when items are in order, we can find them

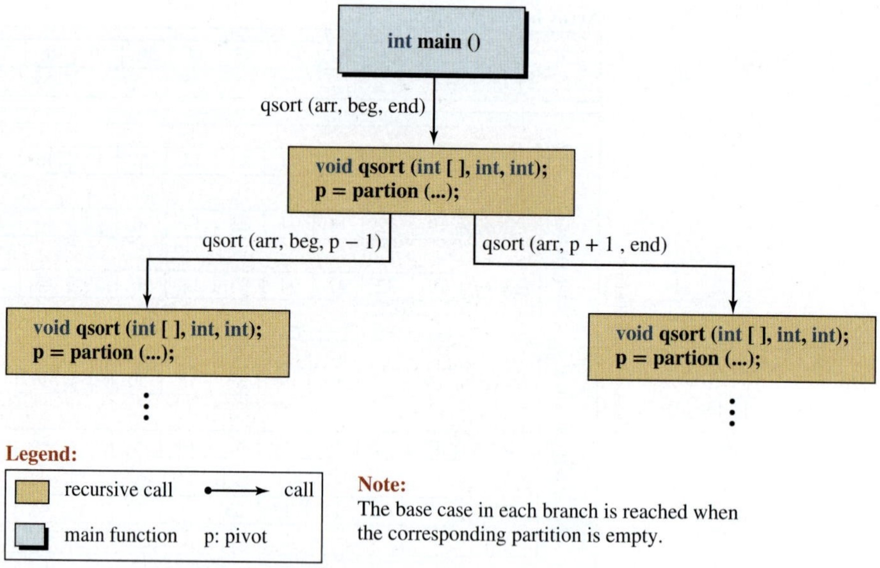

Figure 17.11 The idea of the quick sort algorithm

Program 17.8 Quick sort program

```
/***************************************************************
 * A program that uses the quicksort algorithm to sort an array    *
 * by calling the partition algorithm recursively                  *
 ***************************************************************/
#include <iostream>
using namespace std;

// Function declarations
void swap (int& x, int& y);
void print (int array[], int size);
int partition (int arr[], int beg, int end);
void quickSort (int arr[], int beg, int end);

int main ()
{
  // Declaration of an unsorted array
  int array [10] = {27, 22, 11, 94, 83, 14, 30, 19, 46, 33};
  // Printing unsorted array
  cout << "Original array: " << endl;
  print (array, 10);
  // Calling quickSort function
  quickSort (array, 0, 9);
  // Printing sorted array
  cout << "Sorted array: " << endl;
```

(continued)

Program 17.8 Quick sort program (Continued)

```
    print (array, 10);
    return 0;
}
// Swap function
void swap (int& x, int& y)
{
    int temp = x;
    x = y;
    y = temp;
}
// Print-array function
void print (int array[], int size)
    {
    for (int i = 0; i < size; i++)
    {
        cout << array [i] << "  ";
    }
    cout << endl;
}
// Partition function
int partition (int arr[], int beg, int end)
{
    int p = beg ;  // Initializing pivot
    int i = beg;   // Initializing i
    int j = end;   // Initializing j

    while (i < j)
    {
        // Moving j to the left
        while (arr [j] > arr[p] )
        {
            j--;
        }
        swap (arr[j], arr[p]);
        p = j;
        // Moving i to the right
        while (arr [i] < arr [p] )
        {
            i++;
        }
        swap (arr[i], arr [p]);
        p = i;
    }
```

(continued)

Program 17.8 Quick sort program (Continued)

```
    return p;
}
// Quick sort function
void quickSort (int arr[], int beg, int end)
{
    if (beg >= end || beg < 0)
    {
        return;
    }
    int pivot = partition (arr, beg, end);
    quickSort (arr, beg, pivot - 1);
    quickSort (arr, pivot + 1, end);
}
```

```
Run:
Original array:
27 22 11 94 83 14 30 19 46 33
Sorted array:
11 14 19 22 27 30 33 46 83 94
```

much easier. For example, it would be very difficult to search for an entry in the telephone book if the entries were not sorted. The **binary search** algorithm is designed to find a value in a sorted array. The binary search starts by looking at the middle element. We can have three cases:

- If the value is equal to the middle element, the search stops. The index has been found.
- If the value is greater than the middle element, the search continues with the right half of the array.
- If the value is less than the middle element, the search continues with the left half of the array.

Figure 17.12 shows an example of a binary search. We search for the value 30 in a sorted array of 10 elements. After three attempts, the index of the value, 5, is returned.

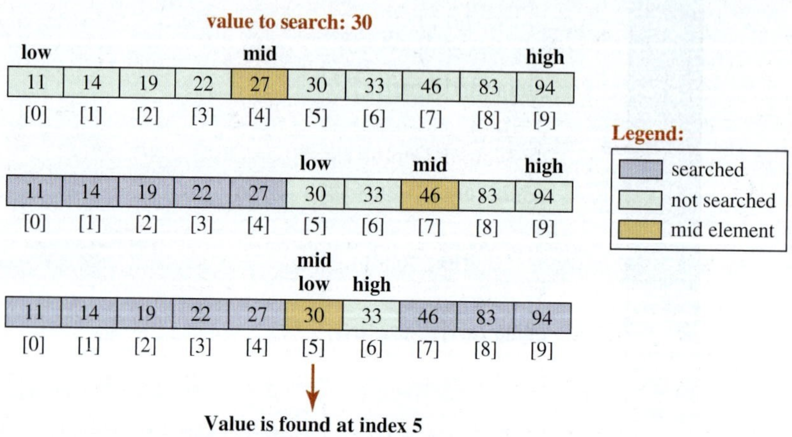

Figure 17.12 Example of a binary search

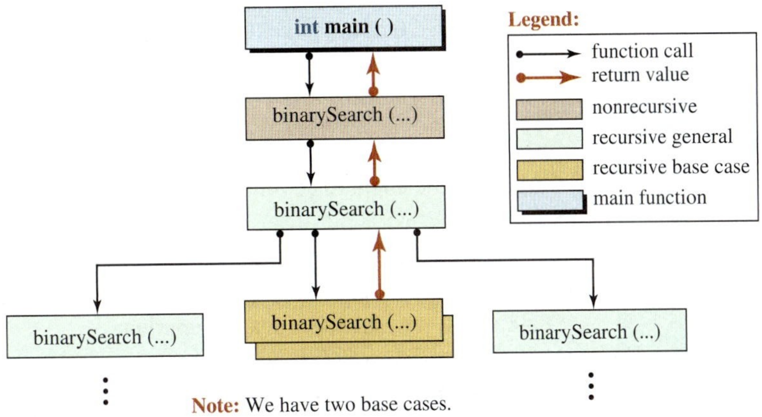

Figure 17.13 Design of binary search algorithm

Recursive Binary Search

Figure 17.13 shows the recursive binary search algorithm using a helper function.

As noted in Figure 17.13, we have two base cases. In the first, the value is not found, and in the second, it is found.

In a traditional binary search, an application calls the search function using the array name, the size, and the value to be found, such as *binarySearch* (*arr*, *size*, *value*). If the value is not the middle element, we must call again, but the new call must search only the left or right part of the array. If we want to search the left part, the array pointer does not need to be changed, but the size must be changed. If we want to search the right part, we must move the array pointer after the middle element and adjust the size. It is convenient and more efficient to use a helper function that does not move the array pointer but in each call uses a subpart of the array starting from *low* to *high*. The helper recursive call has the format *binarySearch* (*arr*, *low*, *high*, *value*). In each call only the value of *low* or *high* changes; the *arr* pointer and search arguments remain the same.

Program 17.9 shows how to implement the recursive binary search using a helper function.

Program 17.9 Recursive binary search

```
/*****************************************************************
 * A program that uses the recursive binary search to search     *
 * an array for a value                                          *
 *****************************************************************/
#include <iostream>
using namespace std;

// Declaration of non-recursive and recursive search functions
int binarySearch (const int arr[], int size, int value);
int binarySearch (const int arr[], int low, int high, int value);
// Declaration of array to be searched
const int size = 10;
int array [size] = {11, 14, 19, 22, 27, 30, 33, 46, 63, 94};
```

(continued)

Program 17.9 Recursive binary search (Continued)

```

int main ()
{
  // Inputting the value to be found
  int value;
  cout << "Enter the value to be found: ";
  cin >> value;
  // Calling the non-recursive search function
  int index = binarySearch (array, size, value);
  if (index == -1)
  {
      cout << "The value is not in the array!";
  }
  else
  {
      cout << "The value was found at index: " << index;
  }
  return 0;
}
// Definition of non-recursive search function
int binarySearch (const int arr[], int size, int value)
{
  int low = 0;
  int high = size - 1;
  return binarySearch (arr, low, high, value);
}
// Definition of recursive search function
int binarySearch (const int arr[], int low, int high, int value)
{
  int mid = (low + high) / 2;
  if (low > high)
  {
      return -1;
  }
  else if (value == arr [mid])
  {
      return mid;
  }
  else if (value < arr[mid])
  {
      return binarySearch (arr, low, mid - 1, value);
  }
  else
```

(continued)

Program 17.9 Recursive binary search (Continued)

```
    {
        return binarySearch (arr, mid + 1, high, value);
    }
}
```

```
Run:
Enter the value to be found: 11
The value was found at index: 0
```

```
Run:
Enter the value to be found: 27
The value was found at index: 4
```

```
Run:
Enter the value to be found: 94
The value was found at index: 9
```

```
Run:
Enter the value to be found: 10
The value is not in the array!
```

```
Run:
Enter the value to be found: 95
The value is not in the array!
```

17.2.3 The Towers of Hanoi

We discuss one more classic recursive problem, the Towers of Hanoi. It is normally solved using a recursive approach. In the problem, there are three pegs (towers). Stacked on the first peg is a set of disks with the smallest at the top. Figure 17.14 shows the situation with four disks.

We must move the disks from the first peg (A) to the third peg (C). The second peg (B) is used to temporarily store disks during the process. The task uses the following rules:

- Only one disk can be moved at a time.
- A larger disk must never be stacked above a smaller one.
- One temporary peg (B) is used for the intermediate storage of disks.

This problem is interesting for two reasons. First, the recursive solution is much easier to code than the iterative solution. Second, the solution pattern for this problem is different from the simple examples we have been discussing.

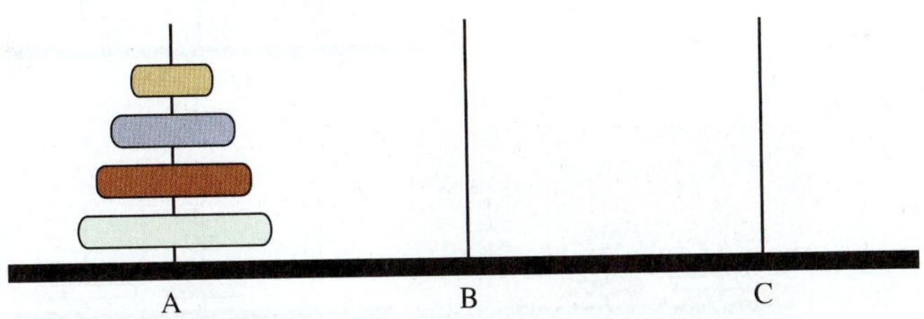

Figure 17.14 Towers of Hanoi with only four disks

Base Case

We first find the solution to the simplest case (base case). We assume that we have only one disk. The solution is simple. We move the disk from the source peg (A or B) to the destination peg (C). We do not need the auxiliary peg.

General Case

Now we see how we can solve the problem if we have n disks (general case). We can do it in three steps:

a. We must move the first $n - 1$ disks from peg A to peg B so they are out of the way and the next step is possible.
b. We move the last disk from the source peg to the destination peg (the base case).
c. We need to move $n - 1$ disks from peg B to peg C (the ones that were stored temporarily on peg B).

To fully understand the case, we show the steps graphically. Figure 17.15 shows the case with four disks.

The original call to the function knows that there are four disks, the source peg is A, the destination peg is C, and the auxiliary peg is B. In the first recursive call, we assume that the source peg is A, destination peg is B, and the auxiliary peg is C. In the second recursive call, we assume that the source peg is B, the destination peg is C, and the auxiliary peg is A.

Algorithm

The general case can be changed to a recursive algorithm easily. The signature of the function to solve the problem is `towers` (n, source, destination, auxiliary). The algorithm is shown below:

```
towers (n, source, destination, auxiliary)
{
    Call towers (n – 1, source, auxiliary, destination)
    Move one disk from source to destination            // Base case
    Call towers (n – 1, auxiliary, destination, source)
}
```

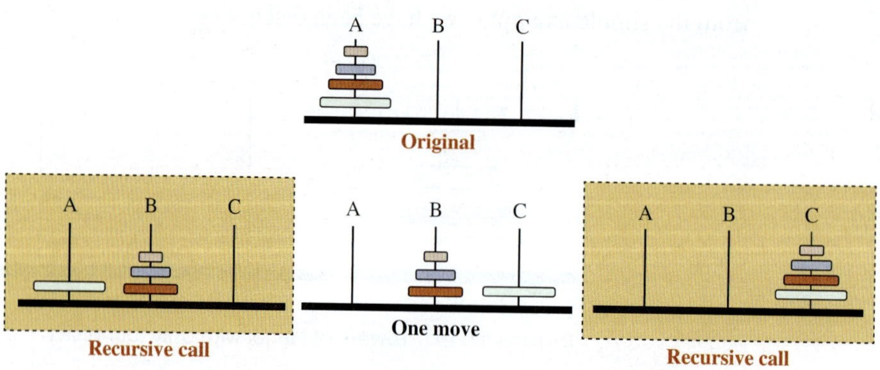

Figure 17.15 The base and recursive cases in the Towers of Hanoi

Program

Using the towers algorithm above, we have written Program 17.10 to solve this problem for any number of disks. Note that we use a separate function to handle the base case for clarity.

Program 17.10 Towers of Hanoi

```
/***************************************************************
 * A program to solve the problem of Tower of Hanoi            *
 ***************************************************************/
#include <iostream>
using namespace std;

// Function declaration
void towers (int, char, char, char);
void moveOneDisk (char, char);

int main ()
{
   // Variable declaration
   int n;
   // Input
   do
   {
        cout << "Enter number of disks (1 to 4): ";
        cin >> n;
   } while ((n < 1) || (n > 4));
   // Function call
   towers (n, 'A', 'C', 'B');
}

// Definition for towers function
void towers (int num, char source, char dest, char aux)
{
   if (num == 1)
   {
        moveOneDisk (source, dest);
   }
   else
   {
        towers (num - 1, source, aux, dest);
        moveOneDisk (source, dest);
        towers (num - 1, aux, dest, source);
   }
}
// Definition for moveOneDisk function
void moveOneDisk (char start, char end)
```

(continued)

Program 17.10 Towers of Hanoi (Continued)

```
{
    cout << "Move top disk from " << start << " to " << end << endl;
}
```

```
Run:
Enter number of disks (1 to 4): 1
Move top disk from A to C
```

```
Run:
Enter number of disks (1 to 4): 2
Move top disk from A to B
Move top disk from A to C
Move top disk from B to C
```

```
Run:
Enter number of disks (1 to 4): 3
Move top disk from A to C
Move top disk from A to B
Move top disk from C to B
Move top disk from A to C
Move top disk from B to A
Move top disk from B to C
Move top disk from A to C
```

The first run is trivial; we have one disk, which we move from A to C. The second run is simple; we move the top disk from A to B (auxiliary), we move the second disk to the destination, and we move the first disk from B to C. The third run takes seven moves. The first three steps move the top two disks from A to B (auxiliary). The fourth step moves the last disk from A to C. The last three steps move the two disks from B to C (using A as an auxiliary). Figure 17.16 shows the original and seven steps to move three disks.

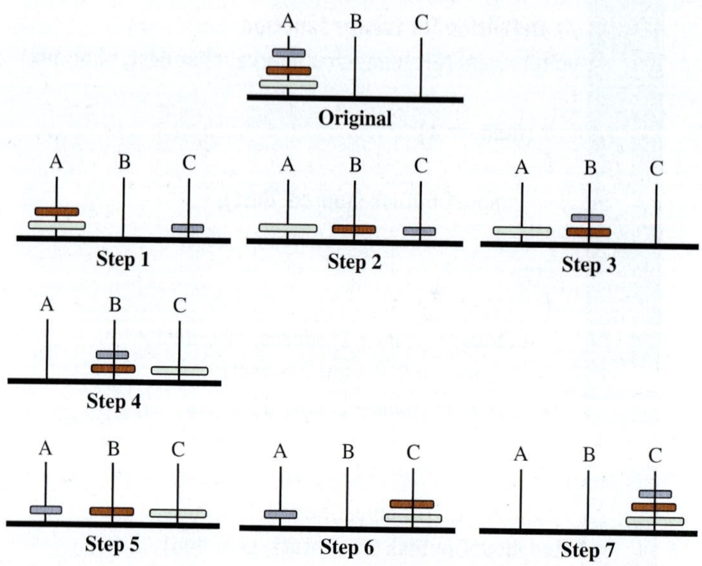

Figure 17.16 Steps to move three disks

17.3 PROGRAM DESIGN

In this section we develop recursive solutions to two problems in which recursion gives a shorter and more elegant solution than iteration.

17.3.1 String Permutation

Permutation of a string finds all possible arrangements of characters in a string. Given a string of n characters, there are *factorial*(n) permutations. For example, when $n = 3$ and the given string is "abc", we have the following six strings:

```
"abc"    "acb"    "bac"    "bca"    "cab"    "cba"
```

Permutation of any length can be solved using a combination of iteration and recursion.

Iteration

In any recursive solution for the problem, we must first choose a letter and then permute the rest. For example, in the three-character permutation, we must choose character 'a' as the first character and then apply permutation to the rest. We then need to choose character 'b' and permute the rest, and so on. Selection of the first character can be done using iteration, which first swaps the first letter with one of the letters in the string before calling the recursive solution as shown below:

```
for (int i = 0; i < str.length () ; i++)
{
   swap (str [0], str[i]);
   permute (...);
}
```

Recursive Function

Now we can define the whole recursive function that permutes a string. The recursive permute function has two parameters: the left parameter is the string to be permuted; the right parameter is the one that is partially permuted. The recursive function removes one character from the left string and adds it to the end of the right string and permutes again. The base case is called when the left string is empty. The following shows the recursive permute function:

```
void permute (string str, string p)
{
   if (str.length () == 0)
   {
      cout << p;
   }
   else
   {
      for (int i = 0; i < str.length(), i++)
      {
            swap (str[0], str[1]);
            permute ((str.substr (1, str.length() – 1), p + str.substr (0, 1);
      }
   }
}
```

Adding a Nonrecursive Function

We use the recursive function developed above as a helper function and use a nonrecursive function with only one parameter, the string to be permuted. In other words, we have a nonrecursive function that calls the recursive function with two parameters as shown below. Note that the second parameter is a null string.

```
void permute (string s)
{
  permute (s, "");
}
```

In this way, the user must call only the nonrecursive function, *permute*(*str*), to display all permutations of the function.

Program 17.11 displays the permutation of any string.

Program 17.11 Permutation of a string

```
/***************************************************************
 * A program to create all permutations of a given string      *
 ***************************************************************/
#include <iostream>
#include <string>
using namespace std;

// Function declarations
void permute (string);
void permute (string, string);
void swap (char&, char&);

int main ()
{
  // Permuting the string "xy"
  cout << "Permutation of xy: ";
  permute ("xy");
  cout << endl;
  // Permuting the string "abc"
  cout << "Permutation of abc: ";
  permute ("abc");
  cout << endl;
}
// Definition of non-recursive permute function
void permute (string s)
{
  permute (s, "");
}
```

(continued)

Program 17.11 Permutation of a string (Continued)

```
// Definition of recursive (helper) permute function
void permute (string str, string p)
{
   if (str.length () == 0)
   {
      cout << p << " ";
   }
   else
   {
      for (int i = 0; i < str.length (); i++)
      {
         swap (str[0], str[i]);
         permute (str.substr (1, str.length() - 1), p + str.substr (0, 1)) ;
      }
   }
}
// Definition of swap function
void swap (char& c1, char& c2)
{
   char temp = c1;
   c1 = c2;
   c2 = temp;
}
```

Run:

```
Permutation of xy: xy yx
Permutation of abc: abc acb bac bca cab cba
```

17.3.2 Prime Numbers

Mathematicians divide the positive integers into three groups:

1. Integer 1
2. Primes
3. Composites

The integer 1 is neither prime nor composite. A prime number is divisible by 1 and itself. A composite number is divisible by 1, itself, and other integers. In other words, the integer 1 has only one divisor (itself), a prime has two divisors (integer 1 and itself), and a composite has more than two divisors (integer 1, itself, and other integers smaller than itself). We can see that the smallest prime is integer 2. The primes less than 10 are 2, 3, 5, and 7.

Checking Primeness

Given a number n, how can we find out if it is a prime? It is axiomatic that a number is prime if it is not divisible by any prime in the range (2 ... *floor*(*sqrt*(n)).

EXAMPLE 17.1

We can check the primeness of 97 using the above rule. The *floor*(*sqrt*(97) = 9. We need only to check all primes less than or equal 9, which are 2, 3, 5, and 7. Since none of these integers divides 97, the integer 97 is a prime.

EXAMPLE 17.2

We can check the primeness of 301 using the above rule. The *floor*(*sqrt*(301) = 17. We need only to check all primes less than or equal 17, which are 2, 3, 5, 7, 11, 13, 17. The integer 7 divides 301 (301 / 7 = 43). This means that 301 is not a prime.

Recursive Function

Based on the above observations, we can write a recursive function to find out if a number is prime. We can continuously check to see if the number is divisible by its prime divisors. However, this implies that we have already created a list of prime divisors, which means that we already know how to find if a number is prime. We can relax this condition and check if the given number is divisible by all numbers in the range 2 ... *floor*(*sqrt*(number)).

The following shows the recursive function used to determine if a number is a prime. It has two base cases and one general (recursive case). The first base case returns *false* and terminates the function if the number is divisible by the first argument. The second base case returns *true* and terminates the function when all integers less than (*floor*(*sqrt*(number)) are checked and no divisor is found. The general case calls the function again with the next possible divisor in the range.

```
bool isPrime (int div, int num)
{
    if (num % div == 0)
    {
        return false;
    }
    else if (div >= floor (sqrt (num)))
    {
        return true;
    }
    return isPrime (div + 1, num);
}
```

Adding a Nonrecursive Function

You may have noticed that the previous recursive function does not correctly handle two special cases. First, if *num* is 1, it incorrectly returns *true*. Second, if *num* is 2, it incorrectly returns *false*. These two cases cannot be included in the recursive function, but they can be tested in a nonrecursive function that calls the recursive function, as shown below:

```
bool isPrime (int num)
{
    if (num <= 1)
    {
        return false;
```

```
    }
    else if (num == 2)
    {
        return true;
    }
    return isPrime (2, num);
}
```

Note that after taking care of the two special cases, the nonrecursive function calls the recursive function with divisor 2 to start.

Program 17.12 shows the complete program using the two functions.

Program 17.12 Testing the primeness of an integer

```
/*****************************************************************
 * A program to test the primeness of an integer                 *
 *****************************************************************/
#include <iostream>
#include <cmath>
using namespace std;

// Declaration of a non-recursive and a recursive function
bool isPrime (int num);
bool isPrime (int div, int num);

int main ( )
{
  // Testing the primeness of some integers
  cout << "Is 1  prime? " << boolalpha << isPrime(1)  << endl;
  cout << "Is 2  prime? " << boolalpha << isPrime(2)  << endl;
  cout << "Is 7  prime? " << boolalpha << isPrime(7)  << endl;
  cout << "Is 21 prime? " << boolalpha << isPrime(21) << endl;
  cout << "Is 59 prime? " << boolalpha << isPrime(59) << endl;
  cout << "Is 97 prime? " << boolalpha << isPrime(97) << endl;
  cout << "Is 301 prime? " << boolalpha << isPrime(301) << endl;
  return 0;
}
// Definition of non-recursive function calling the recursive function
bool isPrime (int num)
{
  if (num <= 1)
  {
      return false;
  }
  else if (num == 2)
  {
```

(continued)

Program 17.12 Testing the primeness of an integer (Continued)

```
            return true;
        }
        return isPrime (2, num);
    }
    // Definition of the recursive (helper) function
    bool isPrime (int div, int num)
    {
        if (num % div == 0)
        {
            return false;
        }
        else if (div >= floor (sqrt (num)))
        {
            return true;
        }
        return isPrime (div + 1, num);
    }
```

```
Run:
Is 1 prime? false
Is 2 prime? true
Is 7 prime? true
Is 21 prime? false
Is 59 prime? true
Is 97 prime? true
Is 301 prime? false
```

Key Terms

base case
binary search
general case
helper function
nontail recursion
Sort
tail recursion

Summary

We can solve an iteration problem using either repetition or recursion. In repetition, we let a function repeat itself until a terminating condition occurs. In recursion, we let a function call itself until the same terminating condition occurs.

We have two types of recursion: tail recursion and nontail recursion. Tail recursion is normally more efficient and uses less computer resources than nontail recursion. We can change a nontail recursion to a tail recursion by defining more parameters.

Two areas in which we encounter recursion are sorting and searching a list such as an array of items.

The Towers of Honoi is a classical recursive algorithm that uses many aspects of recursion.

Problems

PR-1. What is printed from *fun*('G') as coded below? Explain what the function does.

```
void fun (char c)
{
    if ( c < 'A' || c > 'Z')
    {
        return;
    }
    cout << c << " ";
    fun (c + 1);
}
```

PR-2. What is returned from *fun*(5, 12) and *fun*(12, 5) as coded below? Explain what the function does.

```
int fun (int n, int m)
{
    if ( n == m)
    {
        return 0;
    }
    else if ( n > m)
    {
        return 1;
    }
    else
    {
        return fun (m, n);
    }
}
```

PR-3. What is printed from *fun*(5) as coded below? Explain what the function does.

```
void fun (int n)
{
    if (n < 0)
    {
        return;
    }
    cout << n << " ";
    fun (n – 1);
}
```

PR-4. What is returned from *fun*(5) as coded below? Explain what the function does.

```
double fun (int n)
{
    if (n <= 1)
    {
        return 0;
    }
    return fun (n - 1) + 1.0 / n;
}
```

PR-5. What is returned from *fun*(4) as coded below? Explain what the function does.

```
double fun (int n)
{
    if (n <= 1)
    {
        return 0;
    }
    return fun (n - 1) + (double) n / (n + 2);
}
```

PR-6. What is returned from *fun*(4) as coded below? Explain what the function does.

```
double fun (int n)
{
    if (n <= 1)
    {
        return 0;
    }
    return fun (n – 1) + double (n) / (2 * n - 1);
}
```

PR-7. What is returned from *fun*(4) as coded below? Explain what the function does.

```
double fun (int n)
{
    if (n <= 1)
    {
        return 0;
    }
    return fun (n – 1) + double (n) / (3 * n – 1);
}
```

PR-8. What is printed from *fun*(164) as coded below? Explain what the function does.

```
int fun (int n)
{
    if (n < 10)
    {
        return n
    }
    else
    {
        cout << (n % 10);
        return fun (n / 10);
    }
}
```

PR-9. Explain what the following function does and what is returned when *n* is 3 and *m* is 4.

```
int fun (int n, int m)
{
    if (n == 0 || m == 0)
```

```
    {
        return 1;
    }
    else
    {
        return fun (n, m - 1) + fun (n - 1, m);
    }
}
```

PR-10. What is printed from *fun*(19) as coded below? Explain what the function does.

```
void fun (int n)
{
    if (n > 0)
    {
        fun (n / 2);
        cout << n % 2;
    }
}
```

Programs

PRG-1. Write a tail version of the *factorial* function and add a nonrecursive function to call it. Test the function in a program.

PRG-2. Write a recursive function to find the number of permutations of *n* objects *k* at a time and then write a program to test it. The formula is given below:

```
P (n, k) = factorial (n) / factorial (n - k)
```

PRG-3. Write a recursive function to find the combination of *n* objects *k* at a time. Then write a program to test it. The formula is given below:

```
C (n, k) = factorial (n) / ((factorial (n - k) * (factorial (k))
```

PRG-4. Write a recursive tail function that reverses the digits in its argument. For example, given the integer 12789, the function returns 98721. Then use a nonrecursive function to call it. Test the functions in a program.

PRG-5. Write a tail recursive function to convert a decimal integer to a binary string and then use a nonrecursive function to call it. For example, the decimal 78 will be changed to "1001110". Test your functions in a program.

PRG-6. Write a tail recursive function to convert a decimal integer to a string of hexadecimal characters and use a nonrecursive function to call it. For example, the decimal 78 will be changed to "4E". Test your functions in a program.

PRG-7. Write a tail recursive function to find the smallest integer in an array of integers. Then use a nonrecursive function to call it. Test your function in a program with at least three arrays of 10 integers. Note that when we look for the smallest element in an array, we must keep track of the smallest element and the next index to check. This means that your helper function must have two extra parameters.

PRG-8. Write a program that finds all the factors of a given number. A factor is a number less than or equal to the given number that divides the number with remainder zero. Note that any number has at least two factors: 1 and itself. Test your function with the factors of a few numbers and tabulate the results in a program. Write a recursive (helper) function that finds the divisor of two numbers. Then use a nonrecursive function to call it.

PRG-9. Write a tail recursive function and the corresponding nonrecursive function to test if an integer is prime. Remember that a prime number is only divisible by 1 and itself, but we can check the numbers from 1 to the square root of that number to be sure that it is prime. Remember that 1 is not a prime. Mathematicians divide the positive integers into three groups: composite, prime, and 1.

PRG-10. Write a program to find all prime factors of a given number. A prime factor is an integer that is a factor and is also a prime. Prime factors have many applications in the field of security and cryptography. In writing your program, feel free to use the ideas presented in PRG-8 and PRG-9.

PRG-11. Write a recursive function that counts and prints the number of a given character in a string. Test the function in a program.

In this chapter, we give a general view of data structures, a topic that is normally taught in a second course of C++ programming. An understanding of the basic data structures is necessary to understand the Standard Library Template (STL), which we discuss in Chapter 19.

Objectives

After you have read and studied this chapter, you should be able to:

- Discuss collections as an object of objects.
- Discuss the difference between linear and nonlinear collections.
- Explain that a collection can be implemented using an array or a linked list.
- Discuss one implementation of a linear collection, a singly linked list.
- Show how a stack class, as a last-in-first-out structure, can be implemented using a linked list class.
- Show how a queue class, as a first-in-first-out structure, can be implemented using a linked list class.
- Demonstrate a nonlinear collection by creating a binary search tree using a linked list framework.

18.1 INTRODUCTION

In previous chapters we discussed the fundamentals of object-oriented programming using the C++ language. We studied the fundamental and user-defined data types. We learned how to apply system-defined operations (operators) and user-defined operations (functions) to objects of any type. We learned how to select which operation should be applied to objects and how to repeat operations. We learned how to make user-defined objects and operations generic by using template types. In other words, we learned how handle objects in C++ individually.

In computer science, objects are often collections. This means that we need to handle a collection of objects instead of individual objects. The techniques we have learned so far can be applied to each object in the collection, but we also need to think about the collection as an *object of objects*. We have learned how to apply operations to individual objects, such as accessing or changing parts; now we learn how to apply operations to collections. We learn how to insert an object, how to erase an object, and how to access an object in a collection.

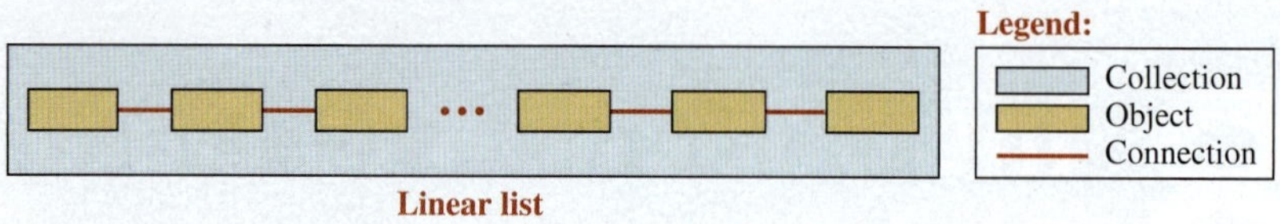

Figure 18.1 Linear collection of objects

18.1.1 Objects Relationship

Operations on a collection, as an object of objects, depend on the relationship between the objects in the collection. We normally encounter two general relationships in a collection: linear and nonlinear.

Linear Collection

A collection may impose a linear relationship between objects in a collection, which means that each object is somehow connected to the previous and next object. Figure 18.1 shows the basic concept of a linear collection.

Nonlinear Collection

In a nonlinear collection, each object can be connected to a group of objects. We do not have a collection of objects that come one after another. The objects can be related to each other in a tabular relationship, in which an object is connected to two objects in the same row and to two objects in the same column. We can also have a collection in which the objects are related to each other the way branches of a tree are connected. We can have a root and branches, each with a number of objects, in an upside-down tree. Figure 18.2 shows these two types of relationships in a nonlinear collection.

18.1.2 Interface versus Implementation

As we discussed in the case of individual objects, we need to think about two aspects of an object in object-oriented programming: interface and implementation. This statement is also true for a collection, which is an object of objects.

Interface

We learned that the interface of an individual object simply gives the list of operations that we can use without revealing how the object is created and its contents. This is true for both fundamental and user-defined objects. Since a collection is normally implemented as a template entity, we can define the type of the objects in the collection, but how the collection

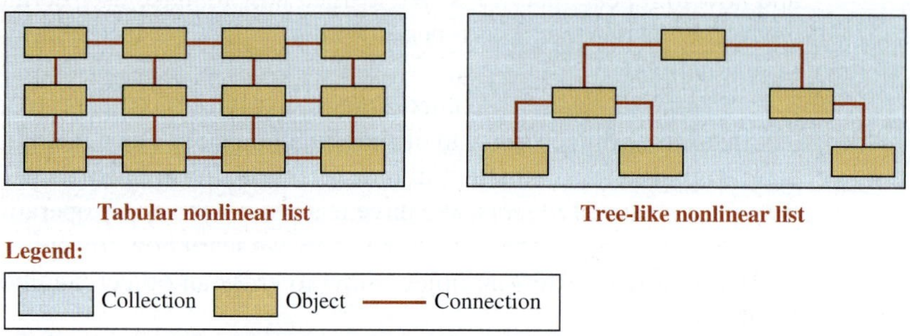

Figure 18.2 Nonlinear collection of objects

is implemented is hidden from the user. We have only the interface, which shows how to insert, how to remove, how to access, and how to rearrange the objects. This is the case with the STL. The STL provides a rich set of collections for us and gives the interface to use the collections' corresponding operations, but the implementation is hidden.

Implementation

If we want to create a personal collection with some features that are not defined in the STL, we can write our own collection class and provide the functions we need. Another solution is to inherit from the STL class and customize the operations we need.

18.1.3 Implementation Choices

Whether we create our own implementation or we use STL collections, we find out that we have two choices: using an array or using a linked list.

Array Implementation

We can use a one-dimensional array to implement a linear collection or a two-dimensional array to create a nonlinear collection. An array can be implemented in stack memory or heap memory. During execution, if the array size needs to be increased, we can create a larger array, copy the values of the previous array into the new array, and then destroy the original array. In Chapter 19, we will see that the STL uses this technique when it implements a collection as an array. In the array implementation, the connection between objects is established via the array index. An object in a higher index is located after an object of a lower index.

Linked-List Implementation

In a linked-list implementation, the connection between objects in the collection is provided through pointers instead of indexes. An object may have one or more pointers to other objects in the collection. In other words, the objects are linked through pointers. Although the linked-list implementation involves more effort from the designer, it has two major advantages over the array implementation: The size of the collection does not have to be defined during compilation, and the size can be changed without the need to copy the whole collection to a new collection.

18.1.4 Chapter Goal

Our main goal in this chapter is to learn how to implement simple collections. Although several collections have been implemented in the STL library for us, if we learn how to create our own collections, it will be easier for us to understand the relationship between objects in STL collections and how to derive our own collection from the STL. This chapter also prepares us for a second course in C++ programming: data structures, in which we design and create collections.

18.2 SINGLY LINKED LIST

In this section we develop a linear implementation collection of objects using a **singly linked list.** In this implementation, each object in the collection is related only to the next object in the collection (thus the term *singly*). The object in a singly linked list is called a node and is made of two parts: data and a pointer. The data section defines the value of the object; the pointer section points to the next node. In a singly linked list we can go to the next node from any node, but we cannot go back to the previous node. There is another implementation, called **doubly linked list,** that allows going forward and backward, but we leave it as an exercise.

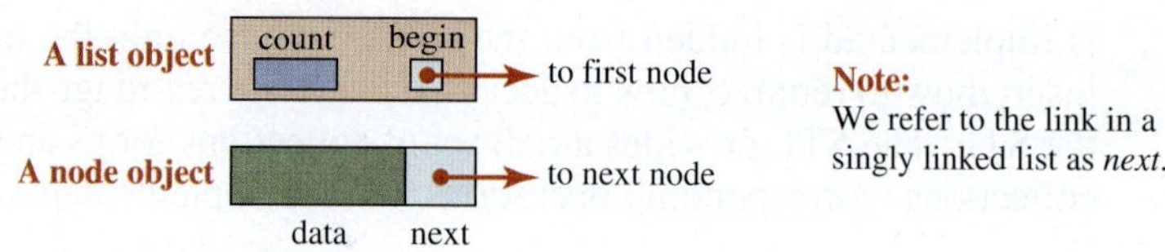

Figure 18.3 A node and a list object

18.2.1 Design

To design a container as a singly linked list, we use two different object types: *list* and *node*.

List and Node Objects

Figure 18.3 shows a list and a node object.

Creation of Objects

The list object is created in stack memory because we use only one instance of it; the nodes are created in heap memory because the number of nodes changes as we insert or erase nodes. Figure 18.4 shows the general idea behind a singly linked list.

In the design shown in Figure 18.4, the list object has a pointer, *begin,* that points to the front node and an integer data type, *count*, that holds the number of nodes in the linked list. To access the *data* and the *next* members of a *node* from the list object, we define a node as a *struct* instead of a *class* because we can access its data members from the list class directly; the members of a *struct* are public by default.

18.2.2 Implementation

We show how we implement our linear collection of objects using a singly linked list. To better understand the implementation, we first develop the code for three files and then explain the operations graphically.

The Code

The code for the interface file, implementation file, and the application file follows. In this section we develop the interface file, implementation file, and application file for our linear collection, implemented as a singly linked list. There are two definitions in the file: the definition of a Node, *struct,* and the definition of a List, *class*. The Node has only two public data members: a template data type and a pointer to the next node. The class list has two private data members, *begin* and *count*, and one private member function, *makeNode*, which is used to

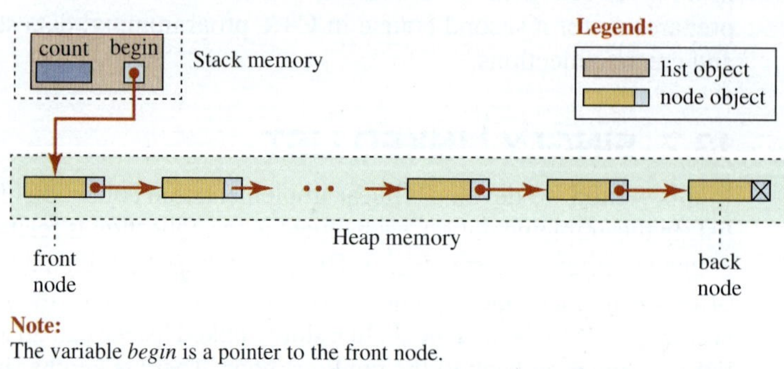

Figure 18.4 List implementation as a singly linked list.

create a new node for insertion into the list. We have created seven public member functions, including the constructor and the destructor. The public members insert a node in a list, erase a node from a list, get the data value of a node at a specific position, print the data contents of all nodes, and return to the number of nodes in the list. Our list is not a sorted list because it is not common to have a sorted list using a singly linked list; other structures, such as a *binary search tree,* are used for this purpose. Although the list structure in the STL uses specific operations, such as inserting, erasing, and retrieving data in the elements at the front and back of the list, we use only the basic operations described above at this stage. Program 18.1 contains the interface file.

Program 18.1 File list.h

```
/*****************************************************************
 * The interface file for a List class as a singly linked list    *
 *****************************************************************/
#ifndef LIST_H
#define LIST_H
#include <iostream>
#include <cassert>
using namespace std;

// Definition of the Node as a struct
template <typename T>
struct Node
{
  T data;
  Node <T>* next;
};
// Definition of the class List
template <typename T>
class List
{
  private:
      Node <T>* begin;
      int count;
      Node <T>* makeNode (const T& value);
  public:
      List ();
      ~List ();
      void insert (int pos, const T& value);
      void erase (int pos);
      T& get (int pos) const;
      void print () const;
      int size () const;
};
#endif
```

Implementation File Program 18.2 is the implementation file.

Program 18.2 File list.cpp

```
/***************************************************************
 * The implementation file for a List class                    *
 ***************************************************************/
#ifndef LIST_CPP
#define LIST_CPP
#include "List.h"

// Constructor
template <typename T>
List <T> :: List ()
:begin (0), count (0)
{
}
// Destructor
template <typename T>
List <T> :: ~List ()
{
   Node <T>* del = begin;
   while (begin)
   {
        begin = begin -> next;
        delete del;
        del = begin;
   }
}
// Insert member function
template <typename T>
void List <T> :: insert (int pos, const T& value)
{
   if (pos < 0 || pos > count)
   {
        cout << "Error! The position is out of range." << endl;
        return;
   }
   Node <T>* add  = makeNode (value);
   if (pos == 0)
   {
        add -> next = begin;
        begin = add;
   }
   else
   {
```

(continued)

Program 18.2 File list.cpp (Continued)

```
        Node <T>* cur = begin;
        for (int i = 1; i < pos; i++)
        {
                cur = cur -> next;
        }
        add -> next = cur -> next;
        cur -> next  = add;
    }
    count++;
}
// Erase member function
template <typename T>
void List <T> :: erase (int pos)
{
    if (pos < 0 || pos > count - 1)
    {
        cout << "Error! The position is out of range." << endl;
        return;
    }
    if (pos == 0)
    {
        Node <T>* del = begin;
        begin = begin -> next;
        delete del;
    }
    else
    {
        Node <T>* cur = begin;
        for (int i = 0; i < pos - 1; i++)
        {
                cur = cur -> next;
        }
        Node <T>* del = cur -> next;
        cur -> next = cur -> next -> next;
        delete del;
    }
    count--;
}
// Get member function
template <typename T>
T& List <T> :: get (int pos) const
{
    if (pos < 0 || pos > count -1)
    {
```

(*continued*)

Program 18.2 File list.cpp (Continued)

```
        cout << "Error! Position out of range.";
        assert (false);
    }
    else if (pos == 0)
    {
        return begin -> data;
    }
    else
    {
        Node <T>* cur = begin;
        for (int i = 0 ; i < pos ; i++)
        {
            cur = cur -> next;
        }
        return cur -> data;
    }
}
// Print member function
template <typename T>
void List <T> :: print () const
{
    if (count == 0)
    {
        cout << "List is empty!" << endl;
        return;
    }
    Node <T>* cur = begin;
    while (cur != 0)
    {
        cout << cur -> data << endl;
        cur = cur -> next;
    }
}
// Size member function
template <typename T>
int List <T> :: size () const
{
    return count;
}
// MakeNode member function (private)
template <typename T>
Node <T>* List <T> :: makeNode (const T& value)
{
    Node <T>* temp = new Node <T>;
```

(continued)

Program 18.2 File list.cpp (Continued)

```
    temp -> data = value;
    temp -> next = 0;
    return temp;
}
#endif
```

Application File We use a small application file to test our singly linked list. We create a list of names and test the operations defined in the implementation file. Note that we use the *inclusion process* instead of the *separate compilation process* because we want to allow compilers that do not support the *separate compilation process* of template objects to compile the file. Program 18.3 demonstrates the concept.

Program 18.3 File application.cpp

```
/***************************************************************
 * The application file to test some operations in our list        *
 ***************************************************************/
#include "list.cpp"
#include <string>

int main ( )
{
    // Instantiation of a list object
    List <string> list;
    // Inserting six nodes in the list
    list.insert (0, "Michael");
    list.insert (1, "Jane");
    list.insert (2, "Sophie");
    list.insert (3, "Thomas");
    list.insert (4, "Rose");
    list.insert (5, "Richard");
    // Printing the values of nodes
    cout << "Printing the list" << endl;
    list.print ();
    // Printing the values of three nodes
    cout << "Getting data in some nodes" << endl;
    cout << list.get (0) << endl;
    cout << list.get (3) << endl;
    cout << list.get (5) << endl;
    // Erasing three nodes from the list
    cout << "Erasing some nodes and printing after erasures" << endl ;
    list.erase (0);
    list.erase (3);
    list.print ();
```

(continued)

Program 18.3 File application.cpp (Continued)

```
    // Printing the list after erasures
    cout << "Checking the list size" << endl ;
    cout << "List size: " << list.size () ;
    return 0;
}
```

Run:

```
Printing the list
Michael
Jane
Sophie
Thomas
Rose
Richard
Getting data in some nodes
Michael
Thomas
Richard
Erasing some nodes and printing after erasures
Jane
Sophie
Thomas
Richard
Checking the list size
List size: 4
```

Explanations of Operations

Most of the operations are straightforward. Others require that we explain how the list is modified.

Constructor We have used a default constructor by storing 0 in the *count* member and a null pointer (0) in the *begin* member.

Destructor The destructor deletes all nodes one by one and frees the heap memory. Figure 18.5 shows the case of a linked list with two nodes.

Insertion Insertion is done at a specified location. We can have three cases: insertion at the front, insertion at the middle, or insertion at the end. Insertion at the beginning can be done using two operations (after making a node), as shown in Figure 18.6.

Insertion at the middle is more involved, as shown in Figure 18.7. We must have a *cur* pointer and move it to the node located before the position of insertion. We then can insert the node.

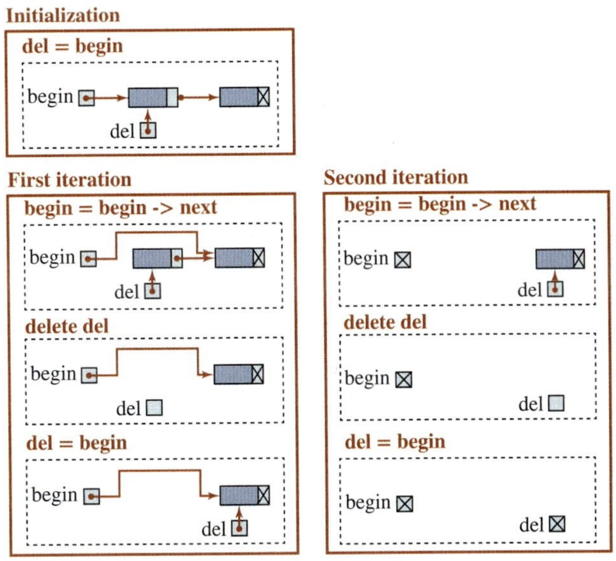

Figure 18.5 Destructor

Insertion at the end is a special case of insertion at the middle in which the *cur* pointer should move to the last node. The new node is inserted after the last node. We leave this as an exercise.

Erasure Erasure is applied to a specific node. If the list is not empty, we have three cases: erasure of the first node, erasure of a middle node, or erasure of the last node. Erasure of the first node is very simple and can be done as shown in Figure 18.8.

The erasure of a middle node is more involved. We must have a *cur* pointer to point to the node before the one to be deleted. We can then use another pointer, *del,* to point to the node to be erased. We can then erase the node. Figure 18.9 shows the operations involved in erasing a middle node.

Erasure at the end involves a similar process, but we must move the *cur* pointer to the node before the last node.

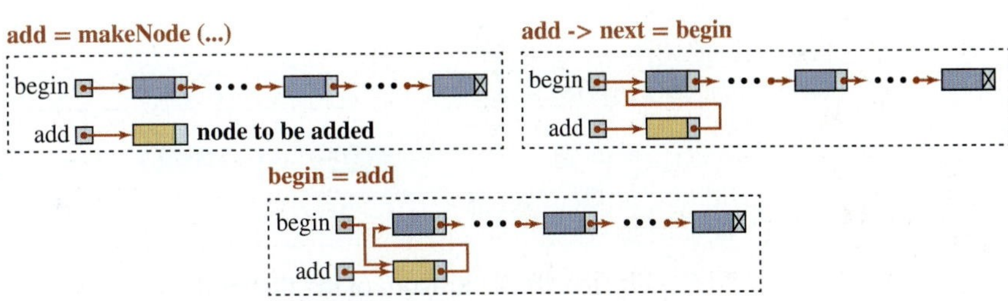

Figure 18.6 Insertion at the beginning

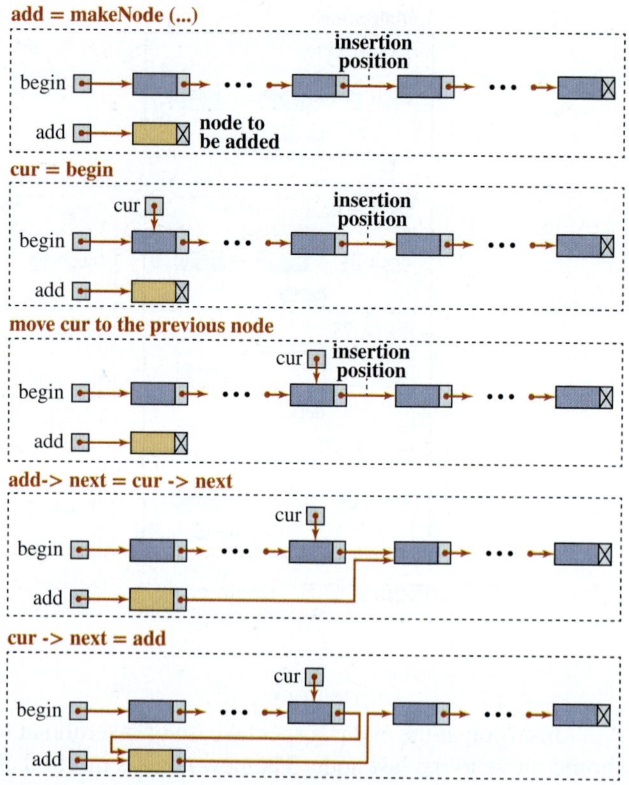

Figure 18.7 Insertion at the middle

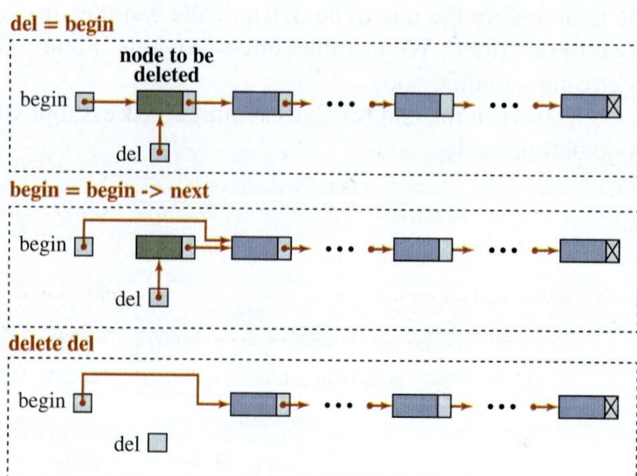

Figure 18.8 Erasure of the first node

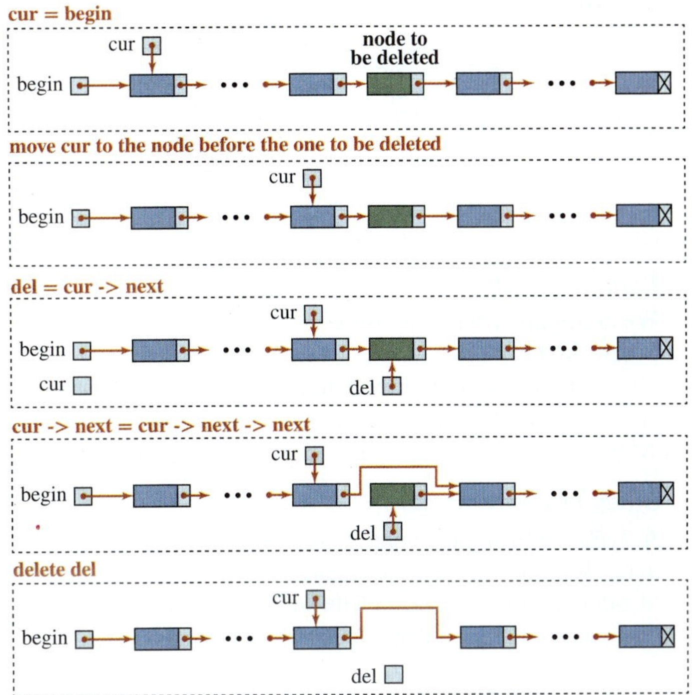

Figure 18.9 Erasure of a middle node

18.3 STACKS AND QUEUES

Often we need a linear list, but we do not need the whole interface of the linked list class we defined in the previous implementation. We can adapt the interface to our use. For example, we can adapt the linked list to create two more restricted collections called a *stack* and a *queue*. We discuss these two implementations here as a practice in adapting general collections to specific ones.

18.3.1 Stacks

A **stack** is a container implemented as a linear list in which all additions and deletions are restricted to one end, called the *top*. If we insert data items into a stack and then remove them, the order of the data items would be reversed. Data input as {5, 10, 8, 20} would be removed as {20, 8, 10, 5}. This reversing attribute is why stacks are known as a *last-in-first-out (LIFO)* data structure.

We use many different types of stacks in our daily lives. We often talk of a stack of coins or a stack of books. Any situation in which you can only add or remove an object at the top is a stack. If you want to remove any object other than the one at the top, you must first remove all objects above it. A graphic representation of stacks is shown in Figure 18.10.

Figure 18.10 Stacks

Stack Operations

We normally encounter three basic operations for a stack data structure, as shown in Figure 18.11.

The operation to insert an element at the top of the stack is referred to as *push*. The operation to delete an element from the top is referred to as *pop*. The operation that only accesses the top element without removing it is referred to as *top*.

Stack Implementation

A stack can be implemented either as an array or a linked list. Although the array implementation is easier, the size of the array must be fixed at compilation time. A linked-list implementation allows the size of the stack to grow and shrink dynamically. Figure 18.12 shows how we normally implement a stack as a linked list.

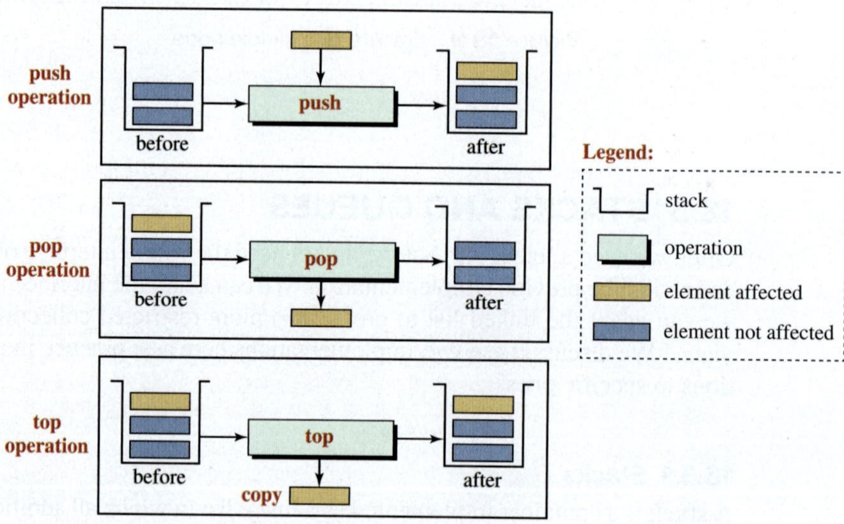

Figure 18.11 The three basic operations on stack

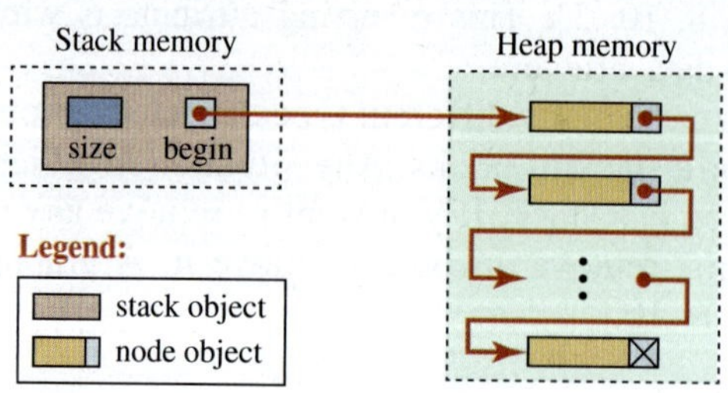

Figure 18.12 Stack implementation as a linked list

In Figure 18.12 we have one *stack* object and a number of node objects. The *stack* object is created in *stack memory*. It has one integer variable to hold the size of the stack and a pointer that points to the top node. We also have a number of node objects. Each node object has a data section and a pointer section. The data section can be of any type. The nodes are created in the heap because the number of nodes grows with each *push* operation and shrinks with each *pop* operation. Note that we have used the same terminology as we did for a linked list. We call the pointer that points to the top element *begin*. Also note that the top of the stack is the front of the underlying linked list.

The Code

We could create a new interface and implementation file for our *Stack* class, but it is more efficient to reuse the code created for the *List* class. A *Stack* class is a special List class with limited operations. However, we should remember that a *Stack* object is not a *List* object. A *Stack* object has less features than a *List* object. The Liskov substitution principle that we discussed in Chapter 11 dictates that the public and protected inheritance should not be used in this case. We can, however, use private inheritance. The private inheritance is designed for this purpose: to reuse the code. However, since we are using a template class, the private inheritance in this case may create some compilation problems. Another solution is to use composition. A stack object composes a list object and uses only limited operations defined in the list. We implement the *Stack* class using composition.

We use composition to implement the *Stack* class.

Interface File Program 18.4 shows the interface file for our *Stack* class. Note that the *Stack* class has an instance of the *List* class as a private data member. There is no constructor and destructor. The *Stack* class uses the synthesized default constructor and destructor, which use the constructor and destructor of the *List* class. Since we have already provided the constructor and destructor for our *List* class, we call them to initialize the object of the *List* class as the only data member.

Program 18.4 The interface file for the *Stack* class

```
/***************************************************************
 * The interface file for the Stack that composes an object    *
 * of the List class                                           *
 ***************************************************************/
#ifndef STACK_H
#define STACK_H
#include "list.cpp"

// Stack class definition composing a list object
template <typename T>
class Stack
{
  private:
      List <T> list;
```

(continued)

Program 18.4 The interface file for the *Stack* class (Continued)

```
 public:
     void push (const T& data);
     void pop ();
     T& top() const;
     int size() const;
};
#endif
```

Implementation File In the implementation file, we define the public member functions of the *Stack* class in terms of the *List* class as shown in Program 18.5.

Program 18.5 Implementation file for the *Stack* class

```
/***************************************************************
 * The implementation file for the Stack using the definition          *
 * of member function defined in the list class                        *
 ***************************************************************/
#ifndef STACK_CPP
#define STACK_CPP
#include "stack.h"

// Definition of the push member function
template <typename T>
void Stack <T> :: push (const T& value)
{
  list.insert (0, value);
}
// Definition of the pop member function
template <typename T>
void Stack <T> :: pop ()
{
  list.erase (0);
}
// Definition of the top member function
template <typename T>
T& Stack <T> :: top () const
{
  return list.get(0);
}
// Definition of the size member function
template <typename T>
int Stack <T> :: size () const
{
  return list.size ();
}
#endif
```

Program 18.6 A simple application for testing the *Stack* class

```
/*****************************************************************
 * The application file to test the operations in the Stack       *
 *****************************************************************/
#include "stack.cpp"

int main ( )
{
   // Instantiation of a Stack object
   Stack <string> stack;
   // Pushing four nodes into the stack
   stack.push ("Henry");
   stack.push ("William");
   stack.push ("Tara");
   stack.push ("Richard");
   // Testing the size of the stack after four push
   cout << "Stack size: " << stack.size () << endl;
   // Continuously get the value of the top node and pop it from the stack
   while (stack.size () > 0)
   {
        cout << "Node value at the top: " << stack.top () << endl;
        stack.pop ();
   }
   // Recheck the size after all elements are popped out
   cout << "Stack size: " << stack.size ();
   return 0;
}
```

```
Run:
Stack size: 4
Node value at the top: Richard
Node value at the top: Tara
Node value at the top: William
Node value at the top: Henry
Stack size: 0
```

Application File Program 18.6 is a simple application file for testing the operations defined in the *Stack* class.

Stack Applications

A stack can be used anywhere we need to reverse the order of a set of data items. We show two examples: changing a decimal number to its equivalent hexadecimal string and reversing characters in a string.

Converting a Decimal Number to Hexadecimal We can convert a decimal number to its equivalent hexadecimal number if we continuously divide the number by 16. The remain-

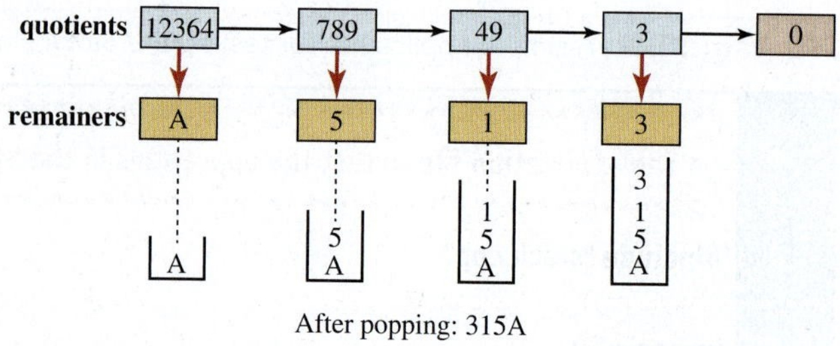

Figure 18.13 Converting a decimal number to a hexadecimal number

der is the value of the current hexadecimal digit, and the quotient is used to create the next digit. The process is repeated until the quotient is zero. However, the hexadecimal digits created are in the reverse order. We can push them into a stack and then pop them from the stack to put them in order, as shown in Figure 18.13.

Program 18.7 is a simple program for changing a decimal number to a hexadecimal number. To print the hexadecimal number, we must insert it in a string because the characters A to F are not digits in C++. We also use a string object named converter that holds the characters that can be found in a hexadecimal number. This string avoids a *switch* statement with 16 cases. We use the value created as the remainder as the index to the converter string.

Program 18.7 Converting from decimal to hexadecimal

```
/***************************************************************
 * The application program to change a decimal number to its  *
 * hexadecimal equivalent                                      *
 ***************************************************************/
#include "stack.cpp"

int main ( )
{
  // Instantiation of a Stack object
  Stack <char> stack;
  // Instantiation of two string objects and two integer variables
  string converter ("0123456789ABCDEF");
  string hexadecimal;
  int decimal;
  int index;
  // Input the decimal number
  do
  {
      cout << "Enter a positive integer: ";
      cin >> decimal;
  } while (decimal <= 0);
  cout << "The decimal number: " << decimal << endl;
```

(*continued*)

Program 18.7 Converting from decimal to hexadecimal (Continued)

```
    // Creation of hexadecimal characters and push them into stack
    while (decimal != 0)
    {
        stack.push (converter [decimal % 16]);
        decimal = decimal / 16;
    }
    // Pushing the characters from the stack into the hexadecimal string
    while (stack.size () > 0)
    {
        hexadecimal.push_back (stack.top());
        stack.pop ();
    }
    // Printing the hexadecimal number
    cout << "The hexadecimal number : " << hexadecimal;
    return 0;
}
```

```
Run:
Enter a positive integer: 124
The decimal number: 124
The hexadecimal number : 7C
```

```
Run:
Enter a positive integer: 1345
The decimal number: 1345
The hexadecimal number : 541
```

```
Run:
Enter a positive integer: 11
The decimal number: 11
The hexadecimal number : B
```

Reversing a String The nature of a stack, as a reverser, can help us in many applications. We used recursion to reverse the order of characters in a string. We can use a stack instead. We can get the characters in the input string, one by one, and push them in a character stack. Then we can remove the characters from the stack and create the output string, as shown in Program 18.8.

Program 18.8 Reversing a string using a stack

```
/***************************************************************
 * The application program to reverse a string using a stack   *
 * instead of recursion                                        *
 ***************************************************************/
#include "stack.cpp"

```

(continued)

Program 18.8 Reversing a string using a stack (Continued)

```
int main ( )
{
   // Instantiation of a stack object and two string objects
   Stack <char> stack;
   string origin;
   string reversed;
   // Input a string
   cout << "Enter a string to be reversed: ";
   getline (cin, origin);
   // Pushing the copy of characters in the origin string into the stack
   for (int i = 0; i < origin.size() ; i++)
   {
         stack.push (origin [i]);
   }
   // Popping the stack and adding characters to the reversed string
   while (stack.size () > 0)
   {
         reversed.push_back (stack.top());
         stack.pop ();
   }
   // Printing both string for comparison
   cout << "Original string: " << origin << endl;
   cout << "Reversed string: " << reversed;
   return 0;
}
```

```
Run:
Enter a string to be reversed: Hello my friends.
Original string: Hello my friends.
Reversed string: .sdneirf ym olleH
```

```
Run:
Enter a string to be reversed: rotor
Original string: rotor
Reversed string: rotor
```

18.3.2 Queues

A **queue** is a linear list in which data can only be inserted at one end, called *back,* and deleted from the other end, called *front.* These restrictions ensure that the data are output through the queue in the order in which they are input. In other words, a queue is a *first-in-first-out* (*FIFO*) structure.

A queue is the same as a line. A line of people waiting for the bus in a bus station is a *queue*; a list of calls put on hold to be answered by a telephone operator is a queue; and a list of jobs waiting to be processed by a computer is a queue.

Figure 18.14 shows two representations of a queue: one a queue of people and the other a queue of data items. Both people and data enter the queue at the back and progress through the queue until they arrive at the front. Once they are at the front of the queue, they can leave the queue.

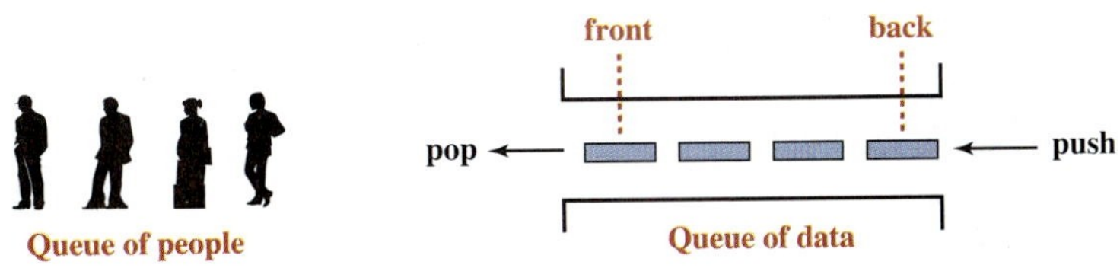

Figure 18.14 Queue

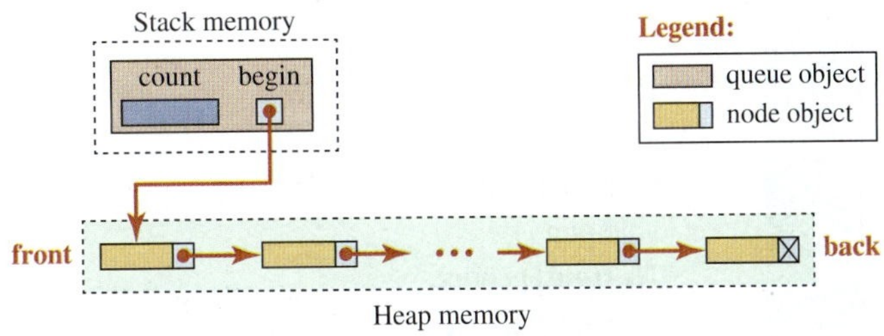

Figure 18.15 Queue implementation as a linked list

Although the literature sometimes refers to the *push* operation as *enqueue* and the *pop* operation as *dequeue,* we use the same terminology as used in the STL library. We also use *front* and *back* to define accessing the front element and the back element.

Implementation

A queue can be implemented either as an array or a linked list. Although the array implementation is easier, the size of the array must be fixed at compilation time. A linked-list implementation allows the size of the queue to grow and shrink dynamically. Figure 18.15 shows how we implement a queue as a linked list.

Figure 18.15 suggests that we can use the code we developed for the linked-list class to create a queue class. A queue class cannot be derived from a linked-list class, because a queue is not a linked list; it has less features. We either derive the queue class from the linked list privately (code reuse) or let a queue class compose a linked-list object. The first choice, as we mentioned in the case of a stack, may be troublesome when using a template class. We use the second choice, *composition.*

The Code

We create the interface file, the implementation file, and a simple application file for queue objects.

Interface File Program 18.9 shows the interface file. Note that we include the interface file of our *List* class.

Program 18.9 File queue.h

```
/***************************************************************
 * The interface file to define a Queue class using a List      *
 * object as the only data member                               *
 ***************************************************************/
```

(continued)

Program 18.9 File queue.h (Continued)

```
#ifndef QUEUE_H
#define QUEUE_H
#include "list.cpp"

template <class T>
class Queue
{
   private:
         List <T> list;
   public:
         void push (const T& data);
         void pop ();
         T& front() const;
         T& back() const;
         int size() const;
         void print() const;
};
#endif
```

As we discussed in the case of the *Stack* class, the *Queue* class uses one single data member, an instance of the *List* class. Again, there is no need to declare a constructor and a destructor. The *Queue* class uses the synthesized default ones.

Implementation File The implementation file for the *Queue* class is very simple; the definitions of member functions are given in terms of the definition of member functions for the *List* class as, shown in Program 18.10.

Program 18.10 File queue.cpp

```
/***************************************************************
 * The implementation for the Queue class in terms of operations  *
 * defined for the List class                                     *
 ***************************************************************/
#ifndef QUEUE_CPP
#define QUEUE_CPP
#include "queue.h"
#include "list.cpp"

// Definition of push operation
template <typename T>
void Queue <T> :: push (const T& value)
{
  list.insert (list.size (), value);
}
```

(continued)

Program 18.10 File queue.cpp (Continued)

```
// Definition of pop operation
template <typename T>
void Queue <T> :: pop ()
{
   list.erase (0);
}
// Definition of front operation
template <typename T>
T& Queue <T> :: front () const
{
   return list.get( 0);
}
// Definition of back operation
template <typename T>
T& Queue <T> :: back () const
{
   return list.get (list.size () – 1);
}
// Definition of size operation
template <typename T>
int Queue <T> :: size () const
{
   return list.size ();
}
// Definition of print operation
template <typename T>
void Queue <T> :: print () const
{
   list.print ();
}
#endif
```

Application File We use a very simple application to test the interface and implementation file, as shown in Program 18.11.

Program 18.11 Application file for testing the Queue class

```
/*****************************************************************
 * The application to test the Queue class                       *
 *****************************************************************/
#include "queue.cpp"

int main ( )
{
```

(continued)

Program 18.11 Application file for testing the Queue class (Continued)

```
	// Instantiation of a queue object
	Queue <string> queue;
	// Pushing four nodes into the queue
	queue.push ("Henry");
	queue.push ("William");
	queue.push ("Tara");
	queue.push ("Richard");
	// Checking the element at the front and the back of the queue
	cout << "Checking front and back elements";
	cout << "after four push operations:" << endl;
	cout << "Element at the front: " << queue.front () << endl;
	cout << "Element at the back: " << queue.back () << endl << endl;
	// Popping two elements from the queue
	queue.pop ();
	queue.pop ();
	// Checking the front and the back node after two pop operations
	cout << "Checking front and back elements";
	cout << "after two pop operations:" << endl;
	cout << "Element at the front: " << queue.front () << endl;
	cout << "Element at the back: " << queue.back () << endl;
	return 0;
}
```

```
Run:
Checking front and back elements after four push operations:
Element at the front: Henry
Element at the back: Richard

Checking front and back elements after two pop operations:
Element at the front: Tara
Element at the back: Richard
```

Queue Applications

Queues are one of the most common of all data-processing structures. They are found in virtually every operating system and network and in countless other areas. For example, queues are used in business online applications such as processing customer requests, jobs, and orders. In a computer system, a queue is necessary for job processing and for system services such as print spools.

Event Simulation The nature of a queue, as a first-in-first-out structure, makes it very helpful in applications in which entities are waiting to be served by servers. For example, in a bank the customers form a line (queue) to be served by one or more tellers. Program 18.12 shows a simulation using a queue. We simulate a bank with only one teller. The customers arrive and form a line (queue) to be served by the teller. The only two pieces of information we need for the simulation are the arrive time and service period. However, to avoid using the time for arrival, we assume that the time starts with the arrival of the first customer. We assume that the second customer arrives a random number of minutes after the previous customer. The service time is also a random number. In other words, each customer is defined with two randomly generated integers. The two random numbers are encapsulated in a *pair* object, which is defined in the <utility> header. The queue object in this case uses a *pair* object as the data part.

Program 18.12 Using a queue object to simulate a waiting line

```
/****************************************************************
 * A program to use a queue to simulate the queue of customers   *
 * in a bank and find the corresponding statistics               *
 ****************************************************************/
#include "queue.cpp"
#include <cstdlib>
#include <ctime>
#include <iomanip>
#include <utility>

// Definition of a randNum function
int randNum (int low, int high)
{
   int temp = rand();
   int num = temp % (high - low + 1) + low;
   return num;
}

int main ( )
{
   // Declaration of variables
   int size = 15;
   int arriveDelay;
   int serveTime;
   int arrive = 0;
   int start = 0;
   int leave = 0;
   int wait = 0;
   int totalServeTime = 0;
   int totalWait = 0;
   // Instantiation of a queue object called line
   Queue <pair <int, int > > line;
   // Simulation of customer arrivals and push the information into queue
   srand (time (0));
   for (int i = 0; i < size; i++)
   {
        pair < int, int> p (randNum(1, 6), randNum (5, 10));
        line.push (p);
   }
```

(continued)

Program 18.12 Using a queue object to simulate a waiting line (Continued)

```
    // Printing the header for statistical data
    cout << left << setw (10) << "Arrive" << setw (10) << "Start" ;
    cout << left << setw (10) << "Delay" << setw (10) << "Leave" ;
    cout << left << setw (10) << "Serve time" <<endl;
    // Calculation and printing statistics
    while (line.size () > 0)
    {
        arriveDelay = line.front().first;
        serveTime = line.front().second;
        arrive = arrive + arriveDelay;
        if (arrive >= leave)
        {
            start = arrive;
        }
        else
        {
            start = leave;
        }
        leave = start + line.front().second;
        wait = start - arrive;
        cout << left << setw (10) << arrive << setw (10) << start;
        cout << left << setw (10) << wait;
        cout << setw (10) << leave;
        cout << left << setw (12) << serveTime << endl;
        totalServeTime += serveTime;
        totalWait += wait;
        line.pop();
    }
    // Printing the summary
    double averageWait = static_cast <double> (totalWait) / size;
    cout << "--------------------------------------------------" << endl;
    cout << "Total serve time: " << totalServeTime << endl;
    cout << "Average Delay: " << averageWait << endl;
    return 0;
}
```

```
Run:
Arrive    Start     Delay     Leave     Serve time
5         5         0         12        7
6         12        6         22        10
8         22        14        32        10
10        32        22        39        7
13        39        26        48        9
16        48        32        54        6
20        54        34        63        9
```

(continued)

Program 18.12 Using a queue object to simulate a waiting line (Continued)

```
24      63      39      73      10
29      73      44      78      5
34      78      44      85      7
38      85      47      93      8
39      93      54      102     9
45      102     57      108     6
47      108     61      116     8
49      116     67      121     5
-------------------------------------------------------
Total serve time: 116
Average Delay: 36.4667
```

The statistics show that the total serve time is 116 minutes, which means that the teller has been busy for 116 minutes serving 15 customers. This gives a clue to the manager to determine how many tellers she needs. The statistics also show that the average delay time for each customer is almost 37 minutes, which is not acceptable. The manager must add tellers reduce customer wait times.

Categorizing Data It is often necessary to rearrange data without destroying their basic sequence. As a simple example, consider a list of numbers. We want to group the numbers while maintaining their original order in each group. This is an excellent multiple queue application. For example, assume a charity organization asks its advocates to donate between 0 and 49 dollars to a charity event. The donations come in order, but the organization must arrange them into five categories based on the dollar values: 0 to 9, 10 to 19, 20 to 29, 30 to 39, and 40 to 49. A program using multiple queues can help. Program 18.13 uses a random number generator that simulates the amount of the donation. It then pushes each donation into the corresponding queue based on the donation value. The program then prints the contents of each queue. The printout shows the order in which the donations are received in each category.

Program 18.13 Using queues to categorize data

```
/*****************************************************************
 * The program to simulate receiving donations and categorize     *
 * into five groups based on the value using queues               *
 *****************************************************************/
#include "queue.cpp"
#include <cstdlib>
#include <ctime>

int main ( )
{
   // Instantiation of queues and declaration of variables
   Queue <int> queue1, queue2, queue3, queue4, queue5;
   int num;
   int donation;
```

(continued)

Program 18.13 Using queues to categorize data (Continued)

```
    // Simulation of donations arrival and pushing into queues
    srand (time (0));
    for (int i = 0; i < 50; i++)
    {
        num = rand ();
        donation = num % (50 - 0 + 0) + 0;
        switch (donation / 10)
        {
            case 0: queue1.push (donation);
                    break;
            case 1: queue2.push (donation);
                    break;
            case 2: queue3.push (donation);
                    break;
            case 3: queue4.push (donation);
                    break;
            case 4: queue5.push (donation);
                    break;
        }
    }
    // Print the queue to see different categories
    cout << "Donations between 0 and 9: ";
    queue1.print ();
    cout << endl;
    cout << "Donations between 10 and 19: ";
    queue2.print ();
    cout << endl;
    cout << "Donations between 20 and 29: ";
    queue3.print ();
    cout << endl;
    cout << "Donations between 30 and 39: ";
    queue4.print ();
    cout << endl;
    cout << "Donations between 40 and 49: ";
    queue5.print ();
    cout << endl;
    return 0;
}
```

Run:

```
Donations between  0 and  9: 3 6 9 4 8 1 7 6 7 0 5 5 9
Donations between 10 and 19: 14 13 12 16 13
Donations between 20 and 29: 23 22 24 20 20 26 21 26 21 25 26 20
Donations between 30 and 39: 34 31 39 32 36 37
Donations between 40 and 49: 43 48 41 45 42 46 44 40 45 42 41 44 43 44
```

The output of the program shows that although the donations arrived randomly, we can organize them into five categories. We could also add some code to find the total and average of donation value in each category, but we leave that as an exercise.

18.4 BINARY SEARCH TREES

Linked lists, stacks, and queues are linear collections; a *tree* is a nonlinear one. In a general tree, each node can have two or more links to other nodes. Although general trees have many applications in computer science (such as directories), we encounter more **binary trees,** trees with a maximum of two subtrees. A special case of a binary tree is called a **binary search tree** in which the values in the nodes in the left subtree are less than the value in the root, and values in the right subtree are greater than the value in the root. Figure 18.16 shows a binary search tree.

18.4.1 Traversals

A binary search tree traversal requires that each node of the tree be processed once and only once in a predetermined sequence. We discuss three common traversals: *pre-order*, *in-order*, and *post-order.*

Pre-Order Traversal

In the **pre-order traversal,** the root node is processed first, followed by all the nodes in the left subtree traversed in pre-order, and then all the nodes in the right subtree traversed in pre-order. The pre-order traversal of the subtree in Figure 18.16 gives us the following sequence. Note that the root comes at the beginning.

80	62	45	72	84	-	86

The pre-order traversal is useful whenever we want to access the root in the tree or in the subtree first.

In-Order Traversal

In the **in-order traversal,** the processing of the root comes between the two subtrees. In other words, we need to traverse the whole left subtree first, then the root, then the right subtree. This rule should be followed in each subtree. The in-order traversal of the subtree in Figure 18.16 gives us the following sequence. The root of the whole tree comes in the middle. Note that in the in-order traversal of a binary search tree, the values are processed in ascending sequence.

45	62	72	80	-	84	86

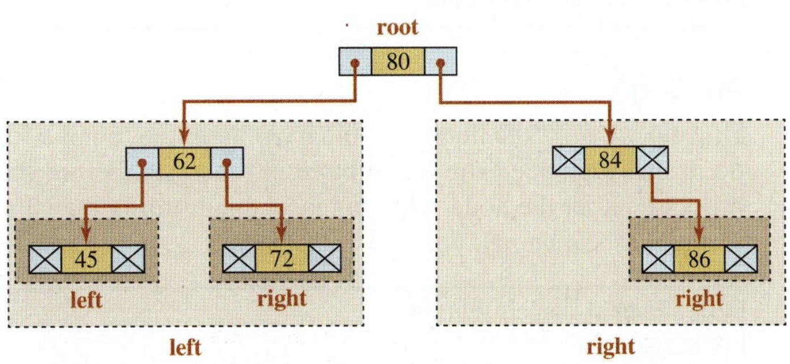

Figure 18.16 A binary search tree of integers

Post-Order Traversal

In the **post-order traversal,** the processing of the root comes after the processing of two subtrees. In other words, we need to traverse the left subtree first, then the right subtree, and finally the root. This rule should be followed in each subtree. The post-order traversal of the subtree in Figure 18.16 gives us the following sequence. Note that the root of the whole tree comes at the end.

45	72	62	-	86	84	80

18.4.2 Implementation

We discuss three traversals for a binary search tree. When a binary search tree is implemented correctly, the data values in the binary search tree are sorted, which means that we can search the tree more easily (hence the name binary search tree). The three traversals help us build a binary search tree, search a binary search tree, and destroy a binary search tree. However, for each activity, we must use the correct traversal.

Insertion

How do we insert nodes in a binary search tree? The answer is that we must find the position of the node to be inserted. The search for the position should start from the root. We must insert the root and then insert the left subtree or the right subtree. In each subtree, we do the same. This means we can write a recursive algorithm as shown below:

```
If the tree is empty, insert as the root.                          // Base case
Insert at the left subtree if value is less than root value.       // General case
Insert at the right subtree if value is greater than root value.   // General case
```

Destruction

How do we destroy a binary search tree? The answer is that we do it node by node. However, to delete a node, the left subtree and right subtree must be empty. This suggests that destroying a binary search tree requires post-order traversal because the last node that must be destroyed is the root. We must destroy the left subtree, then destroy the right subtree, and finally destroy the root. This means we can write a recursive algorithm as shown below:

```
Destroy the left subtree.        // General case
Destory the right subtree.       // General case
Delete data item in the root.    // Base case
```

Printing

How do we print the items in a binary search tree to get a sorted list? The answer is that we do it node by node. The left subtree is processed before the node, and the right subtree is processed after the node. This suggests that printing the value of all the nodes is a recursive process, as shown below:

```
Print items at the left subtree.    // General case
Print the root.                     // Base case
Print the items in right subtree.   // General case
```

The Code

Based on previous discussions, we create the interface file, the implementation file, and a simple application file for binary search tree objects.

Interface File Program 18.14 shows the interface for our binary tree.

Program 18.14 File binarysearchtree.h

```
/***************************************************************
 * The interface for a binary search tree that uses a recursive   *
 * member function to insert, erase, search, and traverse nodes   *
 ***************************************************************/
#ifndef BINARYSEARCHTREE_H
#define BINARYSEARCHTREE_H
#include <iostream>
#include <cassert>
using namespace std;

// Definition of Node struct
template <class T>
struct Node
{
   T data;
   Node <T>* left;
   Node <T>* right;
};
// Definition of BinarySearchTree class
template <class T>
class BinarySearchTree
{
   private:
         Node <T>* root;
         int count;
         Node <T>* makeNode (const T& value);
         void destroy (Node <T>* ptr); // Helper
         void insert (const T& value, Node <T>*& ptr); // Helper
         void inorder (Node <T>* ptr) const; // Helper
         void preorder (Node <T>* ptr) const; // Helper
         void postorder (Node <T>* ptr) const; // Helper
         bool search (const T& value, Node <T>* ptr) const; // Helper
   public:
         BinarySearchTree ();
         ~BinarySearchTree ();
         void insert (const T& value);
         void erase (const T& value);
         bool search (const T& value) const;
```

(continued)

Program 18.14 File binarysearchtree.h (Continued)

```
        void inorder () const;
        void preorder () const;
        void postorder () const;
        int size () const;
        bool empty () const;
};
#endif
```

Note that we have some public member functions and some private member functions. The public member functions are the nonrecursive functions called by the user (or the system in the case of the destructor). These functions are called with the minimum number of parameters. The private member functions are recursive helper functions called by the corresponding nonrecursive member function. For example, we have a nonrecursive member function that is called by the system when the tree object goes out of scope, but it calls the destroy member function to destroy the whole tree using post-order traversal. We also have an insert function that is called by the user, who gives only the value of the node data, but it calls a recursive helper function to insert the node at the appropriate position and maintain the properties of the binary search tree (sorted set of data items). We have also created three traversal functions that in turn call the recursive helper functions.

Implementation File Program 18.15 shows the implementation file for the interface file in Program 18.14.

Program 18.15 The implementation file for a binary search tree

```
/*****************************************************************
 * The implementation file to define the member function        *
 * declared in the interface file                               *
 *****************************************************************/
#ifndef BINARYSEARCHTREE_CPP
#define BINARYSEARCHTREE_CPP
#include "binarySearchTree.h"

// Constructor
template <class T>
BinarySearchTree <T> :: BinarySearchTree()
:root (0), count (0)
{
}
// Destructor
template <class T>
BinarySearchTree <T> :: ~BinarySearchTree ()
{
  destroy (root);
}
```

(continued)

Program 18.15 The implementation file for a binary search tree (Continued)

```
// Insert member function
template <class T>
void BinarySearchTree <T> :: insert (const T& value)
{
  insert (value, root);
  count++;
}
// Search member function
template <class T>
bool BinarySearchTree <T> :: search (const T& value) const
{
  return search (value, root);
}
// Preorder traversal function
template <class T>
void BinarySearchTree <T> :: preorder () const
{
  preorder (root);
}
// Inorder traversal function
template <class T>
void BinarySearchTree <T> :: inorder () const
{
  inorder (root);
}
// Postorder traversal function
template <class T>
void BinarySearchTree <T> :: postorder () const
{
  postorder (root);
}
//Size member function
template <class T>
int BinarySearchTree <T> :: size () const
{
  return count;
}
// Empty member function
template <class T>
bool BinarySearchTree <T> :: empty () const
{
  return (count == 0);
}
```

(continued)

Program 18.15 The implementation file for a binary search tree (Continued)

```
// Recursive helper member function called by the destructor
template <class T>
void BinarySearchTree <T> :: destroy (Node <T>* ptr)
{
  if (!ptr)
  {
      return;
  }
  destroy (ptr -> left);
  destroy (ptr -> right);
  delete ptr;
}
// Recursive helper member function called by insert member function
template <class T>
void BinarySearchTree <T> :: insert (const T& value, Node <T>*& ptr)
{
  if (!ptr)
  {
      ptr = makeNode (value);
      return;
  }
  else if (value < ptr -> data)
  {
      insert (value, ptr -> left);
  }
  else
  {
      insert (value, ptr -> right);
  }
}
// Recursive helper member function called by preorder function
template <typename T>
void BinarySearchTree <T> :: preorder (Node <T>* ptr) const
{
  if (!ptr)
  {
      return;
  }
  cout << ptr -> data << endl;
  preorder (ptr -> left);
  preorder (ptr -> right);
}
// Recursive helper member function called by the inorder function
template <class T>
void BinarySearchTree <T> :: inorder (Node <T>* ptr) const
```

(continued)

Program 18.15 The implementation file for a binary search tree (Continued)

```
{
    if (!ptr)
    {
        return;
    }
    inorder (ptr -> left);
    cout << ptr -> data << endl;
    inorder (ptr -> right);
}
// Recursive helper member function called by the postorder function
template <class T>
void BinarySearchTree <T> :: postorder (Node <T>* ptr) const
{
    if (!ptr)
    {
        return;
    }
    postorder (ptr -> right);
    postorder (ptr -> left);
    cout << ptr -> data << endl;
}
// Recursive helper member function called by the search function
template <typename T>
bool BinarySearchTree <T> :: search (const T& value, Node <T>* ptr) const
{
    if (!ptr)
    {
        return false;
    }
    else if (ptr -> data == value)
    {
        return true;
    }
    else if (value < ptr -> data)
    {
        return search (value, ptr -> left);
    }
    else
    {
        return search (value, ptr -> right);
    }
}
// Recursive helper member function called by the makeNode function
template <typename T>
Node <T>* BinarySearchTree <T> :: makeNode (const T& value)
```

(continued)

Program 18.15 The implementation file for a binary search tree (Continued)

```
{
    Node <T>* temp = new Node <T>;
    temp -> data = value;
    temp -> left = 0;
    temp -> right = 0;
    return temp;
}
#endif
```

Application File Program 18.16 shows how to use the implementation file to create a binary search tree and then print the data items in pre-order, in-order, and post-order sequence. Note that only the in-order gives us the sorted list of data value (from smallest to largest). The other two traversals give the structure of the tree (which element is the root, which elements are in the left subtree, and which elements are in the right subtree).

Program 18.16 The application file for testing the binary search tree

```
/*****************************************************************
 * The application file that tests the binary search tree class  *
 *****************************************************************/
#include "binarySearchTree.cpp"

int main ( )
{
    // Instantiation of a binary search tree object
    BinarySearchTree <string> bct;
    // Inserting six nodes in the tree
    bct.insert ("Michael");
    bct.insert ("Jane");
    bct.insert ("Sophie");
    bct.insert ("Thomas");
    bct.insert ("Rose");
    bct.insert ("Richard");
    // Printing values using preorder traversal
    cout << "Using preorder traversal" << endl;
    bct.preorder ();
    cout << endl << endl;
    // Printing values using inorder traversal
    cout << "Using inorder traversal" << endl;
    bct.inorder ();
    cout << endl << endl;
    // Printing values using postorder traversal
    cout << "Using postorder traversal" << endl;
    bct.postorder ();
    cout << endl << endl;
```

Program 18.16 The application file for testing the binary search tree (Continued)

```
    // Searching for a two values
    cout << "Searching: " << endl ;
    cout << "Is Sophie in the tree? " << boolalpha;
    cout << bct.search ("Sophie") << endl;
    cout << "Is Mary in the tree? " << boolalpha;
    cout << bct.search ("Mary") << endl;
    return 0;
}
```

```
Using preorder traversal
Michael
Jane
Sophie
Rose
Richard
Thomas

Using inorder traversal
Jane
Michael
Richard
Rose
Sophie
Thomas

Using postorder traversal
Thomas
Richard
Rose
Sophie
Jane
Michael

Searching:
Is Sophie in the tree? true
Is Mary in the tree? false
```

Key Terms

binary search tree
binary tree
doubly linked list
in-order traversal
post-order traversal
pre-order traversal
queue
singly linked list
stack

Summary

In computer science, objects are normally presented in collections: linear and non-linear. To implement a collection, we normally have two choices: using an array or using a linked list.

To implement a container as a singly linked list, we use two different object types: *list* and *node*. The list object is implemented in stack memory; the nodes are implemented in heap memory. Two common adaptations of a list are stack and queue. A *stack* is a linear list in which all additions and deletions are restricted to one end, called the top. A *queue* is a linear list in which data can only be inserted at one end, called the *back*, and deleted from the other end, called the *front*.

As an example of a non-linear collection, we introduced the binary search tree in which all elements in the left subtree have values smaller than the root and all elements in the right subtree have values larger than the root. To use a binary search tree, we need three traversals. The pre-order traversal is used to create a binary search tree. The in-order traversal is used to get the values of nodes in a sorted list, and the post-ordertraversal is used to erase the nodes in the tree when we destroy it.

Problems

PR-1. Assume we decide to use a doubly linked list as shown below (only three nodes are shown for simplicity). Give the step-by-step operations needed to add a node to an empty list.

PR-2. Repeat PR-1 for the case of inserting a node at the beginning of the list.

PR-3. Repeat PR-1 for the case of inserting a node at the end of the list.

PR-4. Repeat PR-1 for the case of adding a node at the middle (between the second and the third node).

PR-5. Using the doubly linked list in PR-1, show how we can erase the first node.

PR-6. Using the doubly linked list in PR-1, show how we can erase the last node.The following shows the operations and their effects in erasing the last node of a linked list.

Before

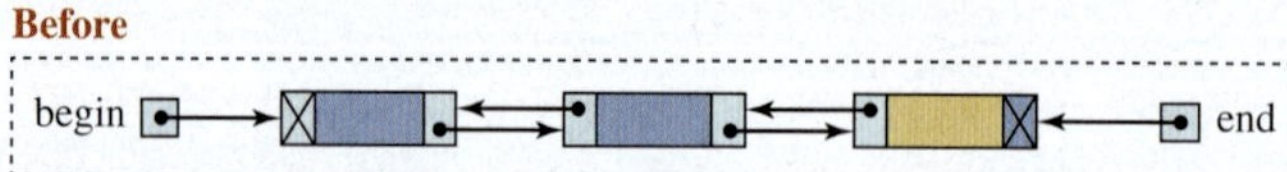

del = end

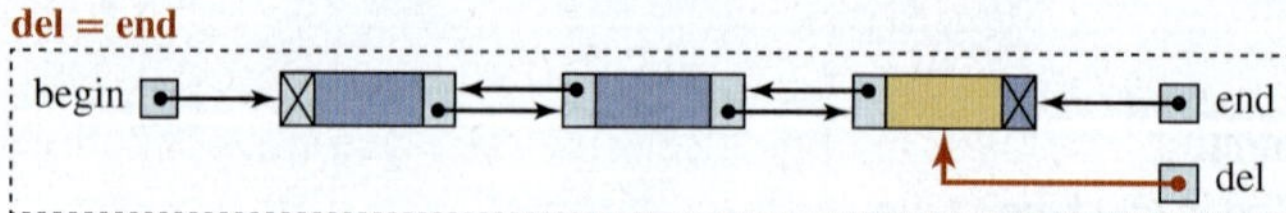

end = end -> prev

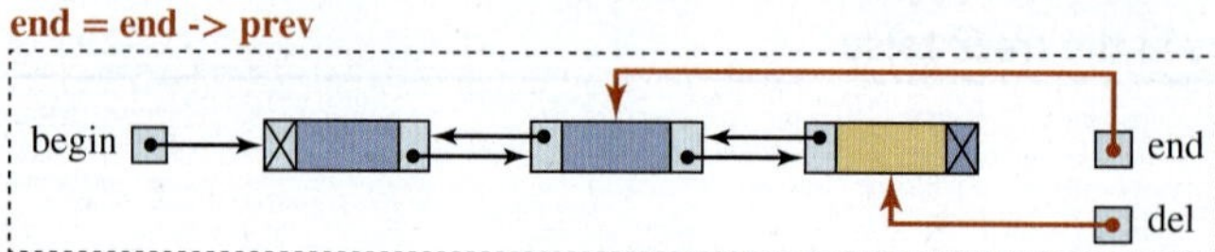

end -> next = 0

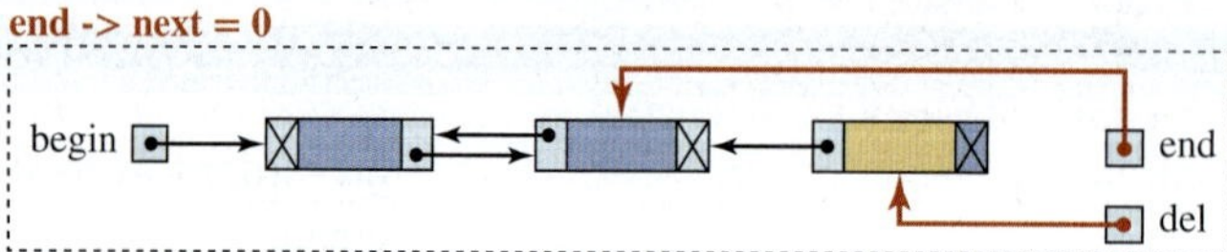

delete del

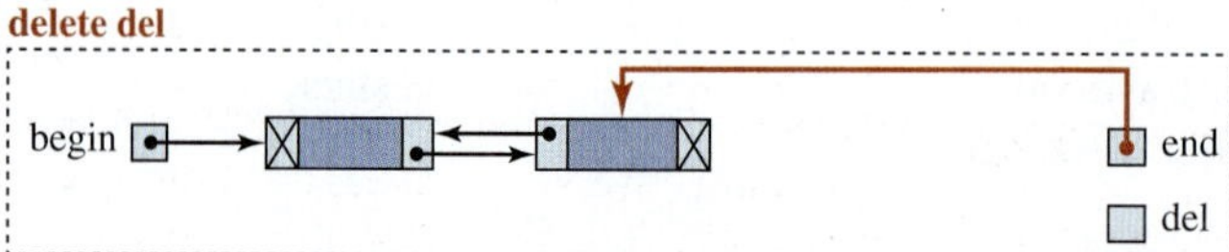

PR-7. Using the doubly linked list in PR-1, show how we can erase a middle node.

PR-8. Assume that we have a stack of five elements. We need to delete the third element from the top. Show the operations using another stack as a helper container.

PR-9. Assume that we have a queue of five elements. We need to delete the third element. Can we use another queue to hold the two elements at the front of the queue, delete the third element, and then push back the top elements?

PR-10. What do you think is the solution to deleting an element from the middle of the queueing and keeping the original order of the element?

PR-11. What is the output from the pre-order, in-order, and post-order traverals of the following binary search tree?

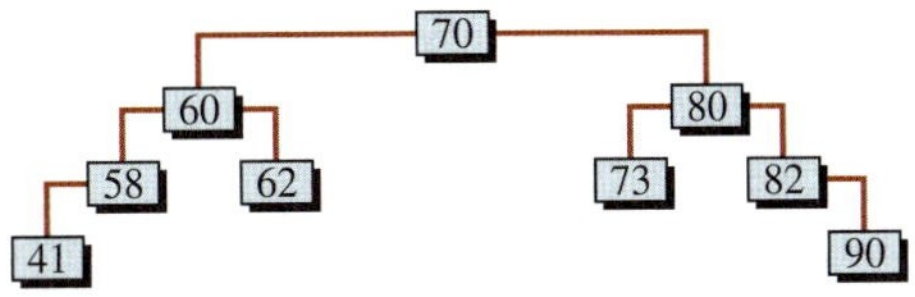

PR-12. Create a binary search tree from the following list.

```
32 45 47 23 24 41 39 15 26 47
```

Programs

PRG-1. Add a void tail recursive function and nonrecursive functions to the *List* class so that we can print the contents of the linked list in reverse order. The recursive function starts from the first node and moves to the end of the list. When it returns, it prints the data value of each node as shown below.

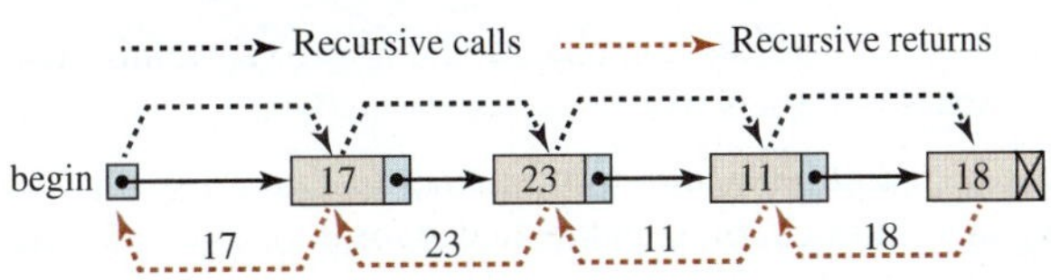

PRG-2. Assume we decide to change our singly linked list in Figure 18.4 to a doubly linked list as shown below. Rewrite and test the interface file, the implementation file, and the application files (Programs 18.1, 18.2, and 18.3) to use this new design. Also show how we can print the list in reverse order using this design.

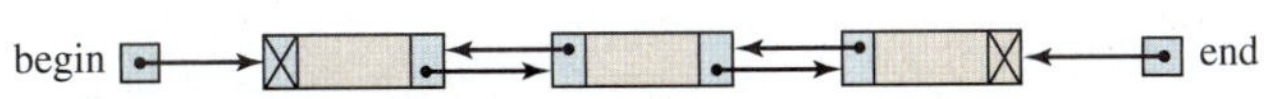

PRG-3. Modify Program 18.7 to let the program change any decimal number to its equivalent binary number.

PRG-4. Change the code in Program 18.7 to let the program change any decimal number to its equivalent octal number.

PRG-5. Rewrite the interface file, the implementation file, and the application file for the *Stack* class using an array created in the heap. One approach is to use a larger array and an index to serve as the top of the stack indicator.

PRG-6. Rewrite the interface file, the implementation file, and the application file for the *Queue* class using an array created in the heap. One approach is to use two indexes to serve as the front and rear of the queue.

In this chapter we give an overview of the Standard Template Library (STL) in C++. This library is large, and a thorough discussion of it would fill a book, but we devote a chapter to it so you will be familiar with its principal ideas.

Objectives

After you have read and studied this chapter, you should be able to:

- List the four components of the STL: containers, algorithms, iterators, and function objects.
- Discuss iterators and explain their different types.
- Discuss sequence containers (*vector*, *deque*, and *list*) that define collections of items organized as sequences.
- Discuss container adapters (*stack*, *queue*, and *priority_queue*) as special cases of sequence containers in which items can be accessed, inserted, or erased only from the front or the back of the container.
- Discuss associate containers (*set* and *map*) as sorted elements in which an element can be accessed using a key.
- Discuss functions and function objects and how to customize them for use in the algorithms that we discuss in this chapter.
- Discuss selected generic algorithms defined in the STL such as non-mutating algorithms, mutating algorithms, sorting and related algorithms, and numeric algorithms.

19.1 INTRODUCTION

The Standard Template Library (STL) is the result of years of research aimed at solving two important issues: reusability of software and separation of functionality.

19.1.1 Components

STL is comprised of four components, as shown in Figure 19.1.

Containers

Containers are the heart of the STL. The library defines four categories of containers, each for a different purpose: sequence containers, associate containers, container adapters, and pseudo-containers. Each container category has been defined for a group of applications. Each container in each category is used for a specific purpose. We discuss only the first three categories in this chapter. For the fourth category, pseudo-containers, we discuss only the *bitset* class (see Appendix R).

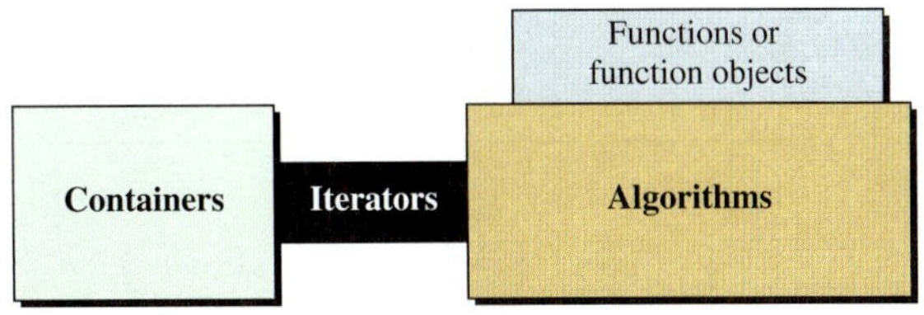

Four components of STL

Figure 19.1 STL components

Algorithms

Algorithms are operations that we apply to the container elements. They are divided into four categories: non-mutating algorithms, which do not change the container structure; mutating algorithms, which change the structure; **sorting algorithms,** which reorder elements in a container; and numeric algorithms, which apply mathematical operations to the elements.

Iterators

Research and experience have shown that the operations we perform on the elements of a container are independent from the type of the element and the type of the container. We have learned from childhood that if we want to count a collection of items, it does not matter if the items are pebbles, balls, or anything else. It also does not matter if the items are given to us in a bag, in a box, ordered, or unordered. We access the elements in the container one by one. An **iterator** allows us to access each element individually and apply the desired operation to it. This means that we do not need one algorithm that counts one type and another that counts another type. An algorithm can be applied to any container that provides the type of iterators that the container supports.

Functions and Function Objects

To apply algorithms to the container, STL uses *functions* or *function objects* in the algorithm definition. They allow the STL to define a generic algorithm and use functions or function objects to make the algorithm specific. In the first case, we need a function definition; in the second case, we need a class for which the *operator*() is defined. The user defines a function for the first case, but the class is normally defined in the STL library and the user can only call the constructor of the class.

19.1.2 Applications

The applications we present in this chapter use STL. Some of these applications have been defined in previous chapters without using STL. Some are new to this chapter.

19.2 ITERATORS

In previous chapters, we learned that we can declare a *pointer,* a system-defined type with a number of operations, that points to an element of a container, such as an array or a linked list. We can then use the operations defined for pointers to access the elements of the container one by one.

19.2.1 Introduction

An **iterator** is an abstraction of a pointer. It is a class type that has a pointer as a data member and predefined operations that can be applied to the pointer member. We can instantiate an object of an iterator and then apply the operations defined for it.

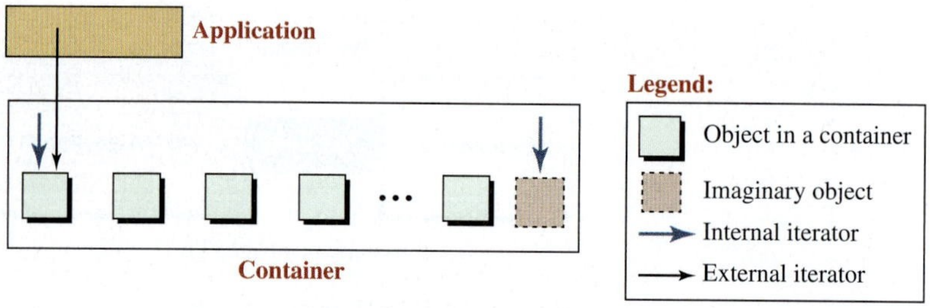

Figure 19.2 Internal and external iterators

One benefit of an iterator over a pointer is that we cannot limit the operations defined for a pointer, nor can we augment the operations defined for a pointer. But we can do both for an iterator. For example, we can define an iterator that can move only forward by including the ++ operator and excluding the −− operator. We can define an iterator that cannot jump from one object in a container to another by not defining the plus (+) or the minus (−) operator for the class. We can say that an iterator can only access an element or can only change an element, or can do both.

Another advantage of an iterator is that it can hide the internal structure of a container. Each container can define its own iterator type whose design is hidden from the user, but the user can create an iterator of that type and access the objects in the container.

The way iterators work with most containers is that the STL defines several internal iterators that are fixed and cannot move. They are used to control the external iterators instantiated by the applications. Figure 19.2 shows an example.

In the figure, the left internal iterator is pointing to the first object in the container. The external iterator is initialized to point where the left internal iterator is pointing. The application can move the external iterator through the container until it reaches the right internal iterator, which is pointing to a nonexistent object at the end. In this way, the external iterator can access all of the objects in the container without knowing anything about the structure of the container.

19.2.2 Five Types of Iterators

We can categorize iterators into five types: *input iterator*, *output iterator*, *forward iterator*, *bidirectional iterator*, and *random-access iterator*, as shown in Figure 19.3.

Table 19.1 shows five iterator types and their supported operations.

Input Iterator

An **input iterator** can use the dereference operator only to read from a container; it is not allowed to write to it. In other words, an input iterator treats the container as a *source* of data items to read.

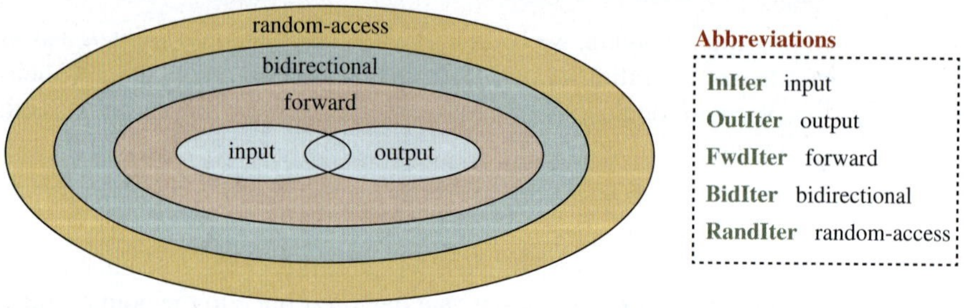

Figure 19.3 Hierarchy of iterator types

Table 19.1 Iterator types

Iterator	read	write	*	++	- -	== !=	<, <=, >, >=	+ -
input	✓		✓	✓		✓		
output		✓	✓	✓		✓		
forward	✓	✓	✓	✓		✓		
bidirectional	✓	✓	✓	✓	✓	✓		
random-access	✓	✓	✓	✓	✓	✓	✓	✓

Output Iterator

An **output iterator** can use the dereference operator to only write to a container; it is not allowed to read from it.

Forward Iterator

A **forward iterator** can read or write elements. Its functionality is the combination of the input and output iterators.

Bidirectional Iterator

A **bidirectional iterator** can move in both directions: backward and forward. The ++ and −− operators are defined for this iterator. In the following section we discuss the meaning of forward and backward movements in a container.

Random-Access Iterator

A **random-access iterator** has the capabilities of a bidirectional iterator, and in addition it supports the add (+) operator and the subtract operator (−). It also provides four relational operators (<, <=, >, and >=) that are not provided by the other iterators. These operators allow us to use the index operator [ ], which requires the +, −, and relational operators for forward or backward movement.

19.2.3 Moving Directions

A container normally defines two categories of iterators: regular (called *iterator*) and reverse (called *reverse_iterator*). The moving directions for these two types of iterators are shown in Figure 19.4.

In a regular iterator, the operators ++ and + mean moving toward the back; the operators −− and − mean moving toward the front. In a reverse iterator, the operators ++ and + mean moving toward the front; the operators −− and − mean moving toward the back. We can think of a reverse operator as similar to making a U-turn when driving.

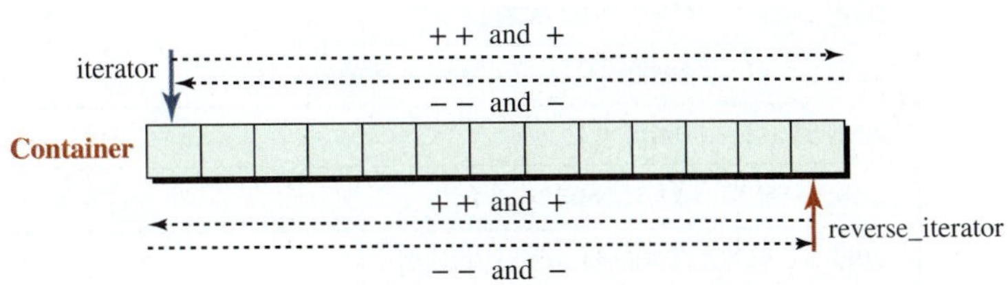

Figure 19.4 Moving directions of a regular and a reverse iterator

19.2.4 Constantness

A container can also define two types of iterators: *const iterator* and *const_iterator.*

Type: const iterator

The type *const iterator* defines an iterator type that is a constant object. In other words, it cannot be changed after it is created. We cannot move the *const iterator* to point to another element. It is like the name of an array that is a constant pointer.

Type: const_iterator

The type *const_iterator* defines an iterator type in which the dereferenced item is an *rvalue* (cannot be changed by the iterator). This is similar to when we declare an array whose elements are constants.

19.3 SEQUENCE CONTAINERS

A **sequence container** is a collection of objects in which the programmer controls the order of storing and retrieving elements. The STL provides three sequence containers: *vector*, *deque*, and *list*. The first two are normally implemented as dynamic arrays; the third is normally implemented as a doubly linked list.

19.3.1 Public Interface

Before discussing sequence containers, we provide a general public interface for them in Table 19.2. The abbreviation SC must be replaced with one of the three sequence containers (*vector*, *deque*, or *list*) when the corresponding column is ticked. Each of these containers is a template class in which T defines the type of the element in the container. The *typename* T can be any built-in or user-defined type. We have used *iter* for an iterator, *inIter* for an input iterator, and *pred* for a Boolean function returning *true* or *false*. The abbreviation V stands for *vector*, D for *deque*, and L for *list*.

Table 19.2 Interface of sequence containers classes

Constructors, assignment, and destructor	**V**	**D**	**L**
SC <T> :: SC()	✓	✓	✓
SC <T> :: SC(size_type *n*, const T& *value* = T())	✓	✓	✓
SC <T> :: SC(const_iter *first*, const_iter *last*)	✓	✓	✓
SC <T> :: SC(const SC <T>& *other*)	✓	✓	✓
SC <T>& SC <T> :: operator =(const SC <T> & *other*)	✓	✓	✓
SC <T> :: ~SC()	✓	✓	✓
Size and capacity			
size_type SC <T> :: size()	✓	✓	✓
size_type SC <T> :: max_size()	✓	✓	✓
void SC <T> :: resize(size_type *n*, T *value* = T())	✓	✓	✓
bool SC <T> :: empty()	✓	✓	✓
size_type SC <T> :: capacity()	✓		
void SC <T> :: reserve(size_type, *n*)	✓		
Accessing elements (constant and nonconstant versions)			

(continued)

Table 19.2 Interface of sequence containers classes (Continued)

T& SC <T> :: front()	✓	✓	✓
T& SC <T> :: back()	✓	✓	✓
T& SC <T> :: operator[ ]()(size_type *index*)	✓	✓	
T& SC <T> :: at(size_type *index*)	✓	✓	
Iterators (regular and constant_ iterator versions)			
iter SC <T> :: begin()	✓	✓	✓
iter SC <T> :: end()	✓	✓	✓
reverse_iter SC <T> :: rbegin()	✓	✓	✓
reverse_iter SC <T> :: rend()	✓	✓	✓
Insertion			
void SC <T> :: push_front(const T& *value*)		✓	✓
void SC <T> :: push_back(const T& *value*)	✓	✓	✓
iter SC <T> :: insert(iter *pos*, const T& *value*)	✓	✓	✓
void SC <T> :: insert(iter *pos*, size_type *n*, const T& *value*)	✓	✓	✓
void SC <T> :: insert(iter *pos*, InIter *first*, inIter *last*)	✓	✓	✓
Erasure			
void SC <T> :: pop_front()		✓	✓
void SC <T> :: pop_back()	✓	✓	✓
iter SC <T> :: erase(iter *pos*)	✓	✓	✓
iter SC <T> :: erase(iter *first*, iter *second*)	✓	✓	✓
void SC <T> :: clear()	✓	✓	✓
void SC <T> :: remove(const T& *value*)			✓
void SC <T> :: remove_if(pred *p*)			✓
void SC <T> :: unique(pred *p*)			✓
Splice, merge, and sort			
void SC <T>::splice(iter *pos*, SC<T> *other*)			✓
void SC <T>::splice(iter *pos*, SC<T> *other*, iter *other*)			✓
void SC <T>::splice(iter *pos*, SC<T> *other*, iter *i*, iter *j*)			✓
void SC <T>:: merge(SC<T> *other*)			✓
void SC <T> :: sort()			✓
Swapping			
void SC <T> :: swap(SC<T>& *other*)	✓	✓	✓
Global functions (*op* means <, <=, >, >=, == or !=)			
bool operator *op*(const SC<T> *left*, const SC<T> *right*)	✓	✓	✓
void swap(SC<T>& *left*, SC<T>& *right*)	✓	✓	✓

Note that each accessing member also has a constant version that creates an *rvalue*, but to make the interface shorter we did not include them. Also note that each iterator has a *const_iterator* version that we did not include for the same reason.

19.3.2 The vector Class

The **vector class,** defined in the <vector> header, implements a sequence container that provides fast random access to any element and fast insertion and deletion at the back. This means that if we need a sequence container with a lot of insertions and deletions at the front or the middle, a vector is not the best choice. A vector is a sequence of elements with an open end, as shown in Figure 19.5.

The vector class is implemented as an array allocated in heap memory but with additional features. Like an array, it has an indexing mechanism to access each element. Unlike an array, a vector resizes itself whenever more elements are needed.

Operations

The syntax of member functions for the vector class can be obtained from the general public interface (Table 19.2). In the next few sections, we discuss, some of these operations.

Constructors and Assignment Operator The vector class has one default constructor, two parameter constructors, one copy constructor, and one assignment operator. The following shows how we use these member functions.

```
vector <T> vec;                  // Constructs an empty vector
vector <T> vec(4 , value);       // Constructs a vector of 4 elements of given value
vector <T> vec[from,to);         // A vector created from another sequence
vector <T> vec(otherVec);        // Copy constructor
vector <T> vec = otherVec;       // Assignment operator
```

The first line shows how to create an empty vector. The second line shows how to create a vector of four elements, all of the same value. Note that if the second argument is missing, it uses the default value (for example, zero for an integer). The third line shows how to copy elements from another structure to make a vector. The arguments *from* and *to* are iterators that copy those elements. Note that the copied sequence is an open-ended sequence [from, to), which means the *from* is in the sequence, but the *to* is not. The next line is a copy constructor that creates a copy of *otherVec*. Finally, the last line is the assignment operator, which does the same job as the copy constructor but for which the *vec* object must be already instantiated.

Destructor The destructor is called automatically when a vector container goes out of scope. The destructor is designed to delete the whole array from the heap.

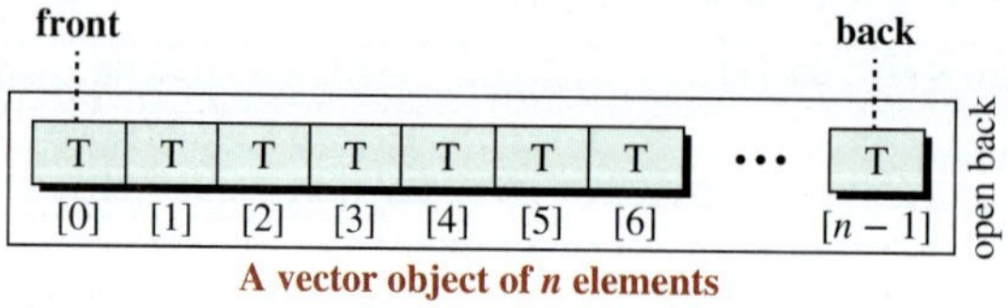

Figure 19.5 A vector as a sequence structure with indexes

Size and Capacity As the public interface (Table 19.2) shows, the vector class has six member functions related to the size and capacity of a vector. The following shows how we use them on an instance of the vector class (which we call *vec*).

```
vec.size();                // Returns the current size
vec.max_size();            // Returns the maximum size
vec.resize(n, value);      // Resizes the vector
vec.empty();               // Returns true if vector is empty
vec.capacity();            // Returns potential size
vec.reserve(n);            // Reserves more memory locations
```

The *size* function returns the number of elements currently in the vector. The *max_size* function defines the maximum number of elements the vector can have (a large number that is defined in the STL). The *empty* function returns `true` if the size is 0. The *resize*(*n*, *value*) function inserts elements to the back of the vector if $n > size$; it removes elements from the back of the vector if $n < size$. If the *value* is not given, a default value is used. The *capacity* function returns the number of allocated locations. In other words, *capacity* returns the potential size before the vector resizes itself. The function *reserve* ensures that the capacity is at least *n*. A vector normally estimates how many elements we must use and allocates memory from the heap based on that estimate. If, during the execution, more memory is needed, the function allocates a bigger storage chunk, copies all elements to that chunk, destroys the old object, and releases the memory used by the old chunk—a time-consuming activity.

Accessing Elements (for retrieve or change) As the public interface (Table 19.2) shows, the vector class provides the following member functions to access elements already in the vector.

```
vec.front();               // Access the first element
vec.back();                // Access the last element
vec [i];                   // Access the element at index i
vec.at(i);                 // Access the element at index i
```

Although, we can use *vec*[i] or *vec.at*(i) to access an element at index *i*, we recommend *vec.at*() because it controls the range and throws an exception when the index is out of range.

Iterators The vector class defines two regular iterators and two reverse iterators. We have shown only the regular ones in Table 19.2. In each category, we can have a constant and a nonconstant operator. Figure 19.6 shows these iterators.

Note that the iterators returned from *begin*(), *end*(), *rbegin*(), and *rend*() are fixed iterators and cannot move. They are used as a controlling wall for the domain of the user-defined iterators (*iter* and *riter*).

To use iterators in our program, we must first instantiate them. Since each container has its own iterators, we must create one or both of the iterators for that specific class as needed. We may need one or both of them depending on the application. We have called the two iterators *iter* and *riter* for convenience.

```
vector <T> :: iterator iter;               // A regular iterator
vector <T> :: reverse_ iterator riter;     // A reverse iterator
```

After instantiating the user iterators, we must set them. The iterator *iter* must start where the iterator returned from *begin*() is set; we must set the iterator *riter* to where the iterator returned from *rbegin*() is set, as shown below:

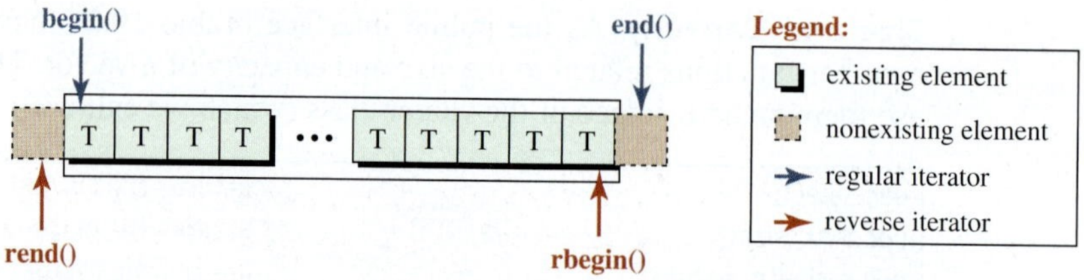

Notes:
The **begin()** function returns a regular iterator that points to the front element.
The **end()** function returns a regular iterator to a nonexisting element after the back element.
The **rbegin()** function returns a reverse iterator that points to the back element.
The **rend()** function returns a reverse iterator to a nonexisting element before the front element.
Both iterators are random-access iterators that can jump forward and backward.

Figure 19.6 Iterators and reverse iterators in a vector

```
iter = vec.begin();          // iter starts when the vec.begin() points to
riter = vec.rbegin();        // riter starts when the vec.rbegin() points to
```

We create a vector of size 10 and use regular and reverse iterators to access elements (Program 19.1).

Program 19.1 Testing iterators in a vector

```
/*****************************************************************
 * A simple program to test regular and reverse navigation      *
 *****************************************************************/
#include <vector>
#include <iostream>
#include <iomanip>
using namespace std;

int main()
{
    // Constructing a vector of 10 elements and two iterators
    vector <int> vec(10);
    vector <int> :: iterator iter;
    vector <int> :: reverse_iterator rIter;
    // Changing the value of elements
    for (int i = 0; i < 10; i++)
    {
        vec.at(i) = i * i;
    }
    // Printing the elements using the forward iterator
    cout << "Regular navigation: ";
    for (iter = vec.begin() ; iter != vec.end() ; ++iter)
    {
        cout << setw(4) << *iter;
    }
```

(*continued*)

Program 19.1 Testing iterators in a vector (Continued)

```
26      cout << endl;
27      // Printing the elements using reverse iterator
28      cout << "Reverse navigation: ";
29      for (rIter = vec.rbegin() ; rIter != vec.rend() ; ++rIter)
30      {
31          cout << setw(4) << *rIter;
32      }
33      cout << endl;
34      return 0;
35  }
```

```
Run:
Regular navigation:    0   1   4   9  16  25  36  49  64  81
Reverse navigation:   81  64  49  36  25  16   9   4   1   0
```

We are using ++ operators for both the regular iterator and the reverse iterator. In the first case, the iterator is moving from the front to the back of the vector; in the second case, it is moving from the back to the front of the vector. At line 22, the regular iterator starts at the element returned from *vec.begin*() and stops before the element returned from *vec.end*(). At line 29, the reverse iterator does the same but uses the iterators returned from *vec.rbegin*() and *vec.rend*(). Note that we are using ++ in both cases. Both iterators are moving forward.

To show that the iterators for a vector are in fact random-access iterators (they can jump in both directions), we create a vector with the following elements:

```
0   10   20   30   40   50   60   70   80   90
```

We first use a regular iterator to print 40 and come back and print the value of 20. We then use a reverse operator to print 50 and then come back and print 70. In other words, we randomly access the element in each direction (regular and reverse) using both operators + and – (see Program 19.2).

Program 19.2 Showing the random-access nature of iterators

```
/***************************************************************
 * A simple program to test random-access iterators in both    *
 * regular and reverse iterators                               *
 ***************************************************************/
#include <iostream>
#include <vector>
using namespace std;

int main()
{
// Instantiation of a vector and two iterators
    vector <int> vec;
```

(*continued*)

Program 19.2 Showing the random-access nature of iterators (Continued)

```
    vector <int> :: iterator iter1;
    vector <int> :: reverse_iterator iter2;
    // Filling the vector with 10 elements
    for (int i = 0; i < 10; i++)
    {
        vec.push_back(i * 10);
    }
    // Using the regular iterator to print 40 followed by 20
    cout << "Printing 40 followed by 20" << endl;
    iter1 = vec.begin();
    iter1 += 4;
    cout << *iter1 << " ";
    iter1 -= 2;
    cout << *iter1 << endl;
    // Using the reverse iterator to print 70 followed by 50
    cout << "Printing 50 followed by 70" << endl;
    iter2 = vec.rbegin();
    iter2 += 4;
    cout << *iter2 << " ";
    iter2 -= 2;
    cout << *iter2 << endl;
    return 0;
}
```

```
Run:
Printing 40 followed by 20
40  20
Printing 50 followed by 70
50  70
```

Figure 19.7 shows how the regular and reverse iterators can move backward and forward randomly.

Insertion The vector class defines several member functions that insert one or more items into the container. The insertion at the back is very efficient and does not require relocation of the items in the vector. Insertion in the middle and at the front require reallocation of items

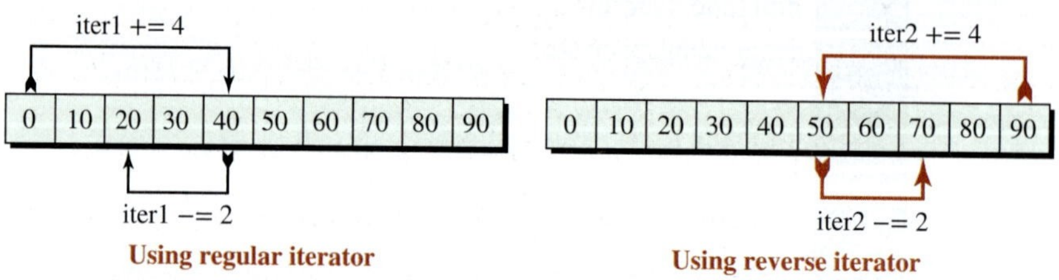

Figure 19.7 Movement of regular and reverse iterators in a vector

in memory. The following shows how we can use member functions to insert new elements into a vector. Note that the last example copies the elements from the first to the next-to-last element.

```
vec.push_back(value);              // Insert value at the back
vec.insert(pos, value)             // Insert value before pos
vec.insert(pos, n, value);         // insert n copies of value before pos
vec.insert(pos, first, last);      // Insert elements [first, last) before pos
```

The *pos* parameter is the position pointed to by the defined iterator. The *first* and *last* parameters are input iterators that define the range [first, last). They can be used to copy the elements in the host vector or another container.

Erasure The vector class defines several member functions for erasure of one or more items in the container. Erasure at the back is very efficient and does not require relocation of any items. An erasure from the middle or from the front requires reallocation of memory and should be avoided. The following shows the member functions we can use to erase elements from a vector.

```
vec.pop_back();                    // Erase the back (last) element
vec.erase(pos);                    // Erase the element before pos
vec.erase(first, second);          // Erase elements in the range [first, last)
vec.clear();                       // Erase all elements
```

Application

The vector class is designed to look like an array. It has the same functionality as an array, but with some advantages. First, the vector is a class with built-in type operations. Second, it is allocated in the heap and can be resized as needed. Third, it has a well-defined iterator mechanism that allows us to access, insert, and erase elements. In summary, we can use a vector anytime we need an array and benefit from its advantages.

In Chapter 8 we learned how to use a two-dimensional array. We can do the same with a vector. We can create a two-dimensional vector, which is a vector of vectors. A vector of vectors has the same advantages over a two-dimensional array that a vector has over a one-dimensional array. In Program 19.3 we create a two-dimensional vector that simulates the multiplication table that is taught in elementary schools. To understand the instantiation, we show, step by step, how we code the definition of the two-dimensional vector.

```
vector <type> table(rows, value);
vector <vector <int> > table(rows, value);
vector <vector <int> > table(rows, vector <int>(cols));
```

In the first line, we define a vector named *table* of *rows* elements, each initialized to *value*. In the second line, we see that the type of the table is a vector of integers. In the third line, we see the value of each row is a vector of type integer and we have *cols* number of them. Note that a space between the two symbols (> >) is needed to show that the combination is not the >> operator.

Program 19.3 A vector of vectors (table)

```
/***************************************************************
 * A program to simulate a table using a vector of vectors     *
 ***************************************************************/
#include <vector>
#include <iostream>
#include <iomanip>
using namespace std;

int main()
{
  // Creation of a vector of vectors
  int rows = 10;
  int cols = 10;
  vector < vector <int> > table(rows, vector <int>(cols));
  // Changing values from default
  for (int i = 0; i < rows ; i++)
  {
      for (int j = 0 ; j < cols; j++)
      {
            table [i][j] = (i + 1) * (j + 1);
      }
  }
  // Retrieving and printing values
  for (int i = 0; i < rows ; i++)
  {
      for (int j = 0 ; j < cols; j++)
      {
            cout << setw(4) << table [i][j] << " ";
      }
      cout << endl;
  }
  return 0;
}
```

Run:

```
1     2     3     4     5     6     7     8     9     10
2     4     6     8     10    12    14    16    18    20
3     6     9     12    15    18    21    24    27    30
4     8     12    16    20    24    28    32    36    40
5     10    15    20    25    30    35    40    45    50
6     12    18    24    30    36    42    48    54    60
7     14    21    28    35    42    49    56    63    70
8     16    24    32    40    48    56    64    72    80
9     18    27    36    45    54    63    72    81    90
10    20    30    40    50    60    70    80    90    100
```

In Chapter 8 we used a ragged array to create the coefficients of a polynomial $(x + y)^n$. We now solve the problem using a vector of vectors (Program 19.4).

Program 19.4 Using a ragged vector to create a Pascal triangle

```
/***************************************************************
 * A program to print Pascal coefficients                      *
 ***************************************************************/
#include <vector>
#include <iostream>
#include <iomanip>
using namespace std;

int main()
{
   // Declaration
   int power = 5;
   vector < vector <int> > pascal(power + 1, vector <int>());
   // Creation of ragged vector
   for (int i = 0; i <= power; i++)
   {
        for (int j = 0; j < i + 1; j++)
        {
              pascal[i].push_back(0);
        }
   }
   // Filling ragged table to create a Pascal triangle
   for (int i = 0; i <= power ; i++)
   {
        for (int j = 0 ; j < i + 1; j++)
        {
              if (j == 0 || i == j)
              {
                   pascal [i][j] = 1;
              }
              else
              {
                   pascal [i][j] = pascal [i-1] [j-1] + pascal [i-1][j];
              }
        }
   }
   // Printing the triangle
   for (int i = 0; i <= power ; i++)
   {
        cout << "Coefficients of (x + y)^" << i << " =====> ";
        for (int j = 0 ; j < i + 1; j++)
```

(*continued*)

Program 19.4 Using a ragged vector to create a Pascal triangle (Continued)

```
45          {
46                  cout << setw(4) << pascal [i][j] << " ";
47          }
48          cout << endl;
49      }
50      return 0;
51  }/
```

Run:

```
Coefficients of (x + y)^0 =====>    1
Coefficients of (x + y)^1 =====>    1    1
Coefficients of (x + y)^2 =====>    1    2    1
Coefficients of (x + y)^3 =====>    1    3    3    1
Coefficients of (x + y)^4 =====>    1    4    6    4    1
Coefficients of (x + y)^5 =====>    1    5   10   10    5    1
```

Note that in the constructor, we define the number of rows (power + 1), but the size of the columns is set to zero. The column in each row grows as we insert new elements using the *push_back*() operation. The values are set to 0 during insertion (line 19), but they change in the inner *for* loop (lines 25 to 35).

19.3.3 The deque Class

The **deque class,** defined in the <deque> header file, is a sequence container similar to a *vector* but with two open ends. The name deque (pronounced deck) is short for *double-ended queue*. This means that we can insert and erase at both ends of a deque. Figure 19.8 shows a deque of *n* elements.

The operations for inserting and erasing elements from both ends are fast. However, the extra capability to insert at the beginning makes a deque less efficient than a vector because doing so requires that the system allocate extra memory to extend the deque at either end. This means if we need a structure that does not need insertion and erasure in the front, it is more efficient to use a vector than a deque. Insertion and erasure in the middle of a deque have the same inefficiency as in the case of a vector.

Operations

The syntax of member functions for the *deque* class can be obtained from the general public interface (Table 19.2). Its functions are very similar to the ones for the vector class with some minor differences. We list only the differences.

Operations Added for deque The *deque* class uses the same set of operations as the vector but uses two additional operations.

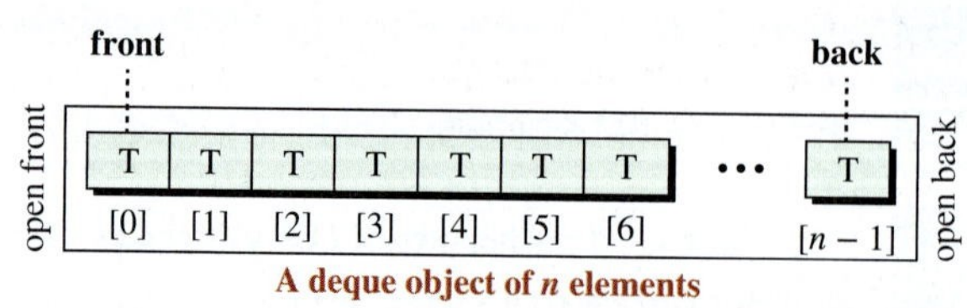

Figure 19.8 A deque as a sequence container

```
deq.push_front(value);          // Insert value at the front
deq.pop_front();                // Delete value at the front
```

Operations missing in deque As the public interface (Table 19.2) shows, the *capacity*() and *reserve*() member function are missing in the *deque* class. The reason is the implementation. Since a *deque* can grow or shrink from both ends, the standard normally implements the *deque* as a set of blocks in heap memory.

Application

The *deque* class was designed to be the foundation for the *queue adapter* class that we discuss later. However, it can be used in any application that needs insertion and deletion at both ends. One application that normally uses a *deque* is *rotation,* in which we have a list of data items we want to rotate *n* times. Clockwise rotation requires that we remove an element from the back and insert it at the front; counterclockwise rotation requires that we remove an element from the front and insert it at the back.

Program 19.5 shows how we can rotate a list of names to the right and then to the left to get the original list.

Program 19.5 Using deque to rotate a list to the left and right

```
/*********************************************************************
 * A program to demonstrate rotation                                 *
 *********************************************************************/
#include <deque>
#include <string>
#include <iostream>
#include <iomanip>
using namespace std;

// Global print function
void print(deque <string> deq)
{
   for (int i = 0; i < deq.size (); i++)
   {
       cout << deq.at(i) << " ";
   }
   cout << endl;
}

int main()
{
   // Create a deque of five string and print it
   deque <string> deq(7);
   string arr [5]= {"John", "Mary", "Rich", "Mark", "Tara"};
   for (int i = 0 ; i < 5; i++)
   {
```

(*continued*)

Program 19.5 Using deque to rotate a list to the left and right (Continued)

```
27          deq [i] = arr [i];
28      }
29      print(deq);
30      // Rotate the deque clockwise one element
31      deq.push_back(deq.front());
32      deq.pop_front();
33      print(deq);
34      // Rotate the deque counter-clockwise one element
35      deq.push_front(deq.back());
36      deq.pop_back();
37      print(deq);
38      return 0;
39  }
```

Run:

```
John    Mary    Rich    Mark    Tara
Mary    Rich    Mark    Tara    John
John    Mary    Rich    Mark    Tara
```

In lines 23 to 29, we create a deque of five strings. In lines 31 to 33, we copy the front element and push it at the back and then delete it. In lines 35 to 37, we copy the back element and push it at the front and then delete it.

19.3.4 The *list* Class

The **list class,** defined in the <list> header file, is a sequence container with fast insertion and deletion at any point. This means that we can insert or delete easily at any point in a *list*. On the other hand, a *list* does not support random access for retrieving or changing the value of an element using the index operator or the *at*() member function because the *list* is implemented as a doubly linked list, not an array in the heap. If we want to access the list randomly, we must use an iterator that moves to the desired element and then accesses it. Figure 19.9 shows a list made of five elements. The figure shows that each node has a data section and two pointers, one pointing to the previous node and the other pointing to the next node.

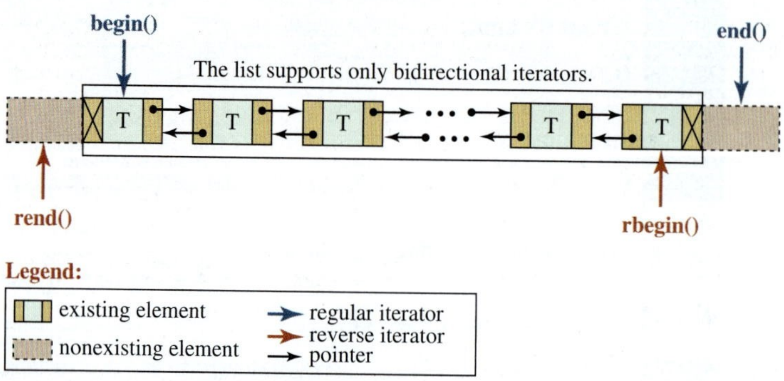

Figure 19.9 A list of elements

Operations

The syntax of member functions for the *list* class can be obtained from the general public interface (Table 19.2). These member functions are similar to the ones for the *vector* class and *deque* class with some differences. We discuss only the differences.

Iterators The *list* class supports only bidirectional iterators (not random-access iterators). This means that the list elements cannot be accessed using the index operator or the *at*() member function because it requires the operators + and – defined for random-access iterators.

Capacity and Reserve The *capacity*() and *reserve*() member functions do not exist in the *list* class because the system adds an element at the front, at the back, and in the middle using the pointers in the doubly linked list.

Accessing Elements The operator [ ] and the *at*() function are not supported for the *list* class because the *list* class does not support the random-access operator (only bidirectional). We must explicitly use an iterator to access elements.

Erasure The *list* class provides three new operations to erase an element or elements from the list as the public interface shows. The following shows how we call these operations.

```
remove(value);              // Erases all occurrences of value
remove_if(predicate);       // Erases all occurrences for which parameter is true
unique(predicate);          // Erases adjacent duplicates if parameter is true
```

Splice, Merge, and Sort The list class defines three other operations: *splice*(), *merge*(), and *sort*() as defined in the public interface.

```
splice(pos, first, last);   // Inserts elements [first, last) from another list before pos
merge(other);               // Merges two sorted lists to a new sorted list
sort();                     // Sorts the list
```

Figure 19.10 shows the idea behind splicing. The iterator *firstIter* defines the insertion position in the first list; the iterators *secondIter1* and *secondIter2* define the range to be moved in the second list.

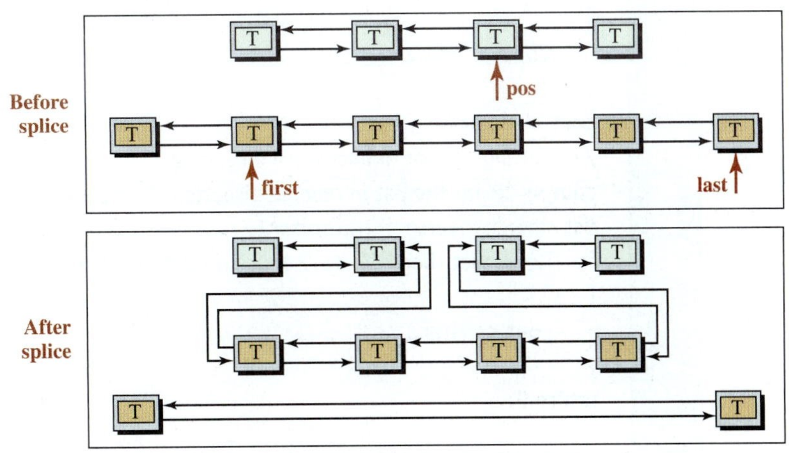

Figure 19.10 Splicing of two lists

Application

Since the *list* class can easily grow or shrink from both ends, it has many applications. We give some examples next.

As a simple example, we create a list of five integers input by the user. We then print the list in the forward and reverse directions. Program 19.6 shows the code.

Program 19.6 Printing list elements

```
/*****************************************************************
 * The program that creates a list of five integers and prints    *
 * in both forward and reverse direction                           *
 *****************************************************************/
#include <list>
#include <iostream>
using namespace std;

int main()
{
  // Instantiation of a list object and declaration of a variable
  list <int> lst;
  int value;
  // Inputting five integers and store them in the list
  for (int i = 0; i < 5; i++)
  {
       cout << "Enter an integer: ";
       cin >> value;
       lst.push_back(value);
  }
  // Printing the list in forward direction
  cout << "Print the list in forward direction. " << endl;
  list <int> :: iterator iter1;
  for(iter1 = lst.begin(); iter1 != lst.end(); iter1++)
  {
       cout << *iter1 << " ";
  }
  cout << endl;
  // Printing the list in backward direction
  cout << "Print the list in reverse direction. " << endl;
  list <int> :: reverse_iterator iter2;
  for (iter2 = lst.rbegin(); iter2 != lst.rend(); iter2++)
  {
       cout << *iter2 << " ";
  }
  return 0;
}
```

(continued)

Program 19.6 Printing list elements (Continued)

```
Run:
Enter an integer: 25
Enter an integer: 32
Enter an integer: 41
Enter an integer: 72
Enter an integer: 95
Print the list in forward direction.
25    32    41    72    95
Print the list in reverse direction.
95    72    41    32    25
```

We can rewrite Program 19.2 without using the + or – operators, which are not defined for bidirectional iterators. Program 19.7 shows a solution.

Program 19.7 Printing some elements in a list

```
/***************************************************************
 * Rewrite of Program 19-2 using list instead of vector        *
 ***************************************************************/
#include <iostream>
#include <list>
using namespace std;

int main()
{
  // Instantiation of the list container and defining two iterators
  list <int> lst;
  list <int> :: iterator iter1;
  list <int> :: reverse_iterator iter2;
  // Inserting 10 integers into the list
  for (int i = 0; i < 10; i++)
  {
      lst.push_back(i * 10);
  }
  // Moving two steps forward and two steps backward using iter1
  cout << "Printing 40 followed by 20" << endl;
  iter1 = lst.begin();
  iter1++;
  iter1++;
  iter1++;
  iter1++;
  cout << *iter1 << " ";
  iter1--;
```

(continued)

Program 19.7 Printing some elements in a list (Continued)

```
    iter1--;
    cout << *iter1 << endl;
    // Moving two steps forward and two steps backward using iter2
    cout << "Printing 50 followed by 70" << endl;
    iter2 = lst.rbegin();
    iter2++;
    iter2++;
    iter2++;
    iter2++;
    cout << *iter2 << " ";
    iter2--;
    iter2--;
    cout << *iter2 << endl;
    return 0;
}
```

```
Run:
Printing 40 followed by 20
40    20
Printing 50 followed by 70
50    70
```

We create a big integer class that handles any integer with any arbitrary number of digits. We provide only the addition operation of two big integers. Program 19.8 shows the interface for a simple big integer class with only the addition (+) operation. We use a list in which each element holds a digit. Another solution is to allow each element to hold three or six digits, but the coding is more complicated.

Program 19.8 The file bigInteger.h

```
/***************************************************************
 * The interface for the big integer class                     *
 ***************************************************************/
#include <string>
#include <list>
#include <iostream>
#ifndef BIGINTEGER_H
#define BIGINTEGER_H
using namespace std;

class BigInteger
{
  private:
      list <int> lst;
  public:
```

(*continued*)

Program 19.8 The file bigInteger.h (Continued)

```
        BigInteger();
        BigInteger(string str);
        ~BigInteger();
        string toString();
        friend BigInteger operator+(BigInteger first, BigInteger second);
};
#endif
```

Program 19.9 shows the implementation file for the big integer class. We have coded two constructors, one destructor, one addition operator, and one member function called *toString*(). It is customary in computer programming to define a *toString* function that creates a string object out of a value so that the object can be exported to other programs.

Program 19.9 The file bigInteger.cpp

```
/*****************************************************************
 * The implementation file for the BigInteger class              *
 *****************************************************************/
#include <iostream>
#include <string>
#include <iomanip>
#include "bigInteger.h"
using namespace std;

// Default constructor
BigInteger :: BigInteger()
:lst (list<int>())
{
}
// Parameter constructor
BigInteger :: BigInteger(string str)
:lst(list <int>())
{
   for (int i = 0; i < str.length(); i++)
   {
       int num = str[i] - 48;
       lst.push_back(num);
   }
}
// Destructor
BigInteger :: ~BigInteger()
{
}
// Changing a list to a string for printing
```

(*continued*)

Program 19.9 The file bigInteger.cpp

```
string BigInteger :: toString()
{
   string strg;
   list <int> :: iterator iter;
   iter = lst.begin();
   while (iter != lst.end())
   {
       strg.append(1, *iter + 48);
       iter++;
   }
   return strg;
}
// Friend operator+
BigInteger operator+(BigInteger first, BigInteger second)
{
   list <int> :: reverse_iterator iter1;
   list <int> :: reverse_iterator iter2;
   BigInteger result;
   int num1, num2, sum;
   int carry = 0;
   iter1 = first.lst.rbegin();
   iter2 = second.lst.rbegin();
   while ( (iter1 != first.lst.rend()) && (iter2 != second.lst.rend()))
   {
       num1 = *iter1;
       num2 = *iter2;
       sum = (num1 + num2 + carry) % 10;
       carry = (num1 + num2 + carry) / 10;
       result.lst.push_front(sum);
       iter1++;
       iter2++;
   }
   while ( (iter1 != first.lst.rend()))
   {
       num1 = *iter1;
       sum = (num1 + carry) % 10;
       carry = (num1 + carry) / 10;
       result.lst.push_front (sum);
       iter1++;
   }
   while ( (iter2 != second.lst.rend()))
   {
       num2 = *iter2;
       sum = (num2 + carry) % 10;
```

(continued)

Program 19.9 The file bigInteger.cpp (Continued)

```
            carry = (num2 + carry) / 10;
            result.lst.push_front(sum);
            iter2++;
    }
    if (carry == 1)
    {
            result.lst.push_front(carry);
    }
    return result;
}
```

In Program 19.9 the default constructor creates an empty list. The parameter constructor takes a string representing a big integer, such as "4572349876509", extracts the digits, one by one as ASCII characters, subtracts 48 from the integer value of the ASCII character to create a digit, and then pushes it to the back of the list. Note that the character is copied from the front of the string, but it is pushed to the back of the list. The next digit pushes the digit at the back of the list toward the front. When the big integer object is instantiated, we have a list of integers in which each element holds one digit.

The next member function is the *toString*() function, which does the reverse. It copies digits one by one from the list and appends them to a string.

The heart of the implementation is the *friend operator*+() function, which takes two big integer objects, adds the digits from the right, and creates a sum and a carry. We need to use three *while* loops. If the two lists are of the same size, the first loop does the job. If either of the lists is exhausted, one of the other two loops continues. Note that if both loops are exhausted, we may still have a carry from the last two digits added; the *if* statement at the end takes care of this situation. Program 19.10 shows a sample application that uses our *BigInteger* class.

Program 19.10 The application file (app.cpp)

```
/*******************************************************************
 * Application file to test the BigInteger class                   *
 *******************************************************************/
#include <iostream>
#include <iomanip>
#include "bigInteger.h"
using namespace std;

int main()
{
    // Inputting two strings
    string strg1, strg2;
    cout << "Enter the first big integer: ";
    cin >> strg1;
    cout << "Enter the second big integer: ";
    cin >> strg2;
    // Creation of two objects of type BigInteger
```

(*continued*)

Program 19.10 The application file (app.cpp) (Continued)

```
    BigInteger first (strg1);
    BigInteger second (strg2);
    // Adding two big integers and storing the result in the third object
    BigInteger result = first + second;
    // Changing big integers to strings
    strg1 = first.toString();
    strg2 = second.toString();
    string strg3 = result.toString();
    string dashes(strg3.length(), '-');
    // Printing the result
    cout << "First big integer " << setw(strg3.length());
    cout << right << strg1 << " + " << endl;
    cout << "Second big integer" << setw(strg3.length());
    cout << right << strg2 << endl;
    cout << "                  " << dashes << endl;
    cout << "Result            " << setw(strg3.length());
    cout << right << strg3 << endl;
    return 0;
}
```

```
Run:
Enter the first big integer:346786543098762378
Enter the second big integer:78654329876

First big integer     346786543098762378 +
Second big integer           78654329876
                      ------------------
Result                346786621753092254
```

```
Run:
Enter the first big integer: 3478654212345690
Enter the second big integer:7654329876534567

First big integer       3478654212345690 +
Second big integer      7654329876534567
                       -----------------
Result                 11132984088880257
```

```
Run:
Enter the first big integer: 356709876567
Enter the second big integer:19283848484848987654356

First big integer                356709876567 +
Second big integer      19283848484848987654356
                        -----------------------
Result                  19283848485205697530923
```

In the first run, the first integer is longer; in the second run, the two integers are of equal length and create an extra carry; in the third run, the first integer is shorter.

19.4 CONTAINER ADAPTERS

The Standard Template Library also defines three **container adapters** that have a smaller interface for easier use. The container adapters defined in the library are *stack*, *queue*, and *priority_queue*. We cannot apply the algorithms defined in the library to container adapters because they lack iterators; they do not provide the member functions, such as *begin* and *end*, to create iterators.

> **Container adapters cannot be used with algorithms because they do not provide support for iterators.**

19.4.1 Public Interface

Table 19.3 provides a general public interface for container adapters. The abbreviation **Ad** can be replaced with one of the three adapters (*stack*, *queue*, or *priority_queue*) when the corresponding column is ticked. Each of these adapters is a template class in which **T** defines the type of the element in the container. The abbreviations are **S** (stack), **Q** (queue), and **P** (priority queue).

Note that the interface for *stack* and *priority_queue* is similar although their purpose and applications are different. We can only use the *top*() member function to access an element in a *stack* or *priority_queue*. On the other hand, we can use the *front*() and *back*() member functions to access the front or the back element in a *queue*.

19.4.2 The stack Class

The ***stack* class,** which is defined in the <stack> header file, is a container adapter class that is designed for three simple operations: *push*, *pop*, and *top*. The *stack* class is designed for insertion into and erasure from one end (the top). It is also referred to as a *last-in-first-out* (LIFO) structure because the last item pushed into the stack is the first item popped from the stack.

Table 19.3 Public interface for the container adapter classes

Constructor	S	Q	P
Ad <T> :: Ad ()	✓	✓	✓
Checking size and emptiness			
size_type Ad<T> :: size() const	✓	✓	✓
bool Ad <T> :: empty() const	✓	✓	✓
Accessing elements			
T& Ad <T> :: front()		✓	
T& Ad <T> :: back()		✓	
T& Ad <T> :: top()	✓		✓
Insertion			
void Ad <T> :: push(const T& *elem*)	✓	✓	✓
Erasure			
void Ad <T> :: pop()	✓	✓	✓

Operations

The stack interface creates an empty constructor. We can check the size and emptiness of a stack. The only member function that we can use to access the elements in the stack is the *top*() member function. The *push*() and *pop*() operations are used to insert into and erase an element from the stack, respectively.

Application

The last-in-first-out nature of a stack makes it ideal for applications in which the first object we need to use in a collection of objects is the last one that we created.

In Chapter 10 we showed how to convert a decimal number to its equivalent hexadecimal number using a user-defined stack class. We repeat that example using the stack class defined in STL as shown in Program 19.11. Although the code is very similar to the one in

Program 19.11 Coverting a decimal to hexadecimal

```
/***************************************************************
 * Using a stack to change a decimal number to hexadecimal     *
 ***************************************************************/
#include <stack>
#include <iostream>
using namespace std;

int main()
{
   // Instantiation of a stack
   stack <char> stk;
   // Creation of two strings and a declaration of a variable
   string converter("0123456789ABCDEF");
   string hexadecimal;
   int decimal;
   // Inputting a decimal number
   do
   {
       cout << "Enter a positive integer: ";
       cin >> decimal;
   } while (decimal <= 0);
   // Creation of hexadecimal characters and push them into stack
   while (decimal != 0)
   {
       stk.push(converter [decimal % 16]);
       decimal = decimal / 16;
   }
   // Popping characters from stack and pushing into hex string
   while (!stk.empty())
   {
       hexadecimal.push_back(stk.top(());
       stk.pop();
   }
   cout << "The hexadecimal number : " << hexadecimal;
   return 0;
}
```

(*continued*)

Program 19.11 Coverting a decimal to hexadecimal (Continued)

```
Run:
Enter a positive integer: 182
The hexadecimal number : B6
```

```
Run:
Enter a positive integer: 1234
The hexadecimal number : 4D2
```

```
Run:
Enter a positive integer: 23
The hexadecimal number : 17
```

Chapter 10, but we do not have to define a linked list and a *stack* class. We use the available *stack* class in the STL library.

Another example is found in compiler design. The compiler must verify that the parentheses used in an expression are properly paired; every opening parenthesis must be paired with a closing parenthesis. The following shows examples of paired and unpaired parentheses.

Paired parentheses	Unpaired parentheses
(2 + 5) * (3 − 4) 4 + 5 * (6 + 7)	10 − (5 * (6 + 7) 8 − (5 * 6 + 7) + 4)

Note that we do not mean that the number of opening and closing parentheses should be the same; we mean that each open parentheses must be paired with a closing parenthesis. For example, in the expression

$$(3 + 4 (7 + 4))) \; 7 \; (8$$

the number of opening and closing parentheses are the same, but they are not paired. Program 19.12 uses a stack to check if the parentheses are paired in an expression.

Program 19.12 Checking pairing of parentheses

```
/*****************************************************************
 * A program to check if parentheses are paired in an expression *
 *****************************************************************/
#include <stack>
#include <string>
#include <iostream>
using namespace std;

int main()
{
   // Declaration of a stack, a string, and a Boolean object
   stack <char> stk;
   string expr;
   bool paired = true;
   // Inputting an expression and pushing it into or popping the stack
   cout << "Enter an expression: " ;
```

(continued)

Program 19.12 Checking pairing of parentheses (Continued)

```
    getline(cin, expr);
    int i = 0;
    while (i < expr.size() && paired)
    {
        char next = expr[i];
        if (next == '(')
        {
                stk.push(next);
        }
        else if (next == ')')
        {
                if (stk.empty())
                {
                    paired = false; // If stack is empty here, no pairing
                }
                else
                {
                    stk.pop();
                }
        }
        i++;
    }
    // If stack is not empty at the end, parentheses are not paired
    if (!stk.empty())
    {
        paired = false;
    }
    // Print the result
    if (paired)
    {
        cout << "Parentheses are paired!" << endl;
    }
    else
    {
        cout << "Parentheses are not paired!" << endl;
    }
    return 0;
}
```

```
Run:
Enter an expression:3 + (4 + 7 + 6)
Parentheses are paired!
```

```
Run:
Enter an expression:2 + (4 + (6 + 7)
Parentheses are not paired!
```

```
Run:
Enter an expression: 6 + 7 + (10 * 2 - 4) + 8)
Parentheses are not paired!
```

19.4.3 The queue Class

The **queue class,** which is defined in the <queue> header file, is a container adapter class that is designed for three simple operations: insertion at one end, erasure from the other end, and accessing at both ends. It is also referred to as a *first-in-first-out* (FIFO) structure because the first item pushed into the queue is the first item to be popped from the queue.

Operations

The queue interface allows us to create an empty queue. We can check the size and emptiness of a queue. The only two member functions that we can use to access the elements in the queue are the *front*() and *back*() member functions, each in two versions. The *push*() and *pop*() operations are used to insert an element into and erase an element from the queue, respectively.

Application

The first-in-first-out nature of a queue makes it the best application for entities waiting to be served by servers. For example, in a bank the customers form a line (queue), where they wait to be served by one or more tellers. In a post office, the customers wait in a line to be served by one or more employees. In a typical queue, the customers arrive randomly and need a random amount of time (number of minutes, for example) to be served. We studied an application of this nature earlier in the text.

In Chapter 18 we created a program to categorize charity donations to different groups using a user-defined queue class. We repeat the problem using the STL *queue* class. Although the application code is almost the same, we do not have to create a list and a queue class to do so. We use the library-defined *queue* class instead (Program 19.13).

Program 19.13 Grouping charity donations

```
/***************************************************************
  * Using a queue to categorize a list of donations              *
  ***************************************************************/
#include <queue>
#include <cstdlib>
#include <ctime>
#include <iostream>
using namespace std;

// Declaration of print function
void print(queue <int> queue);

int main()
{
   // Instantiation of five queue objects and two variables
   queue <int> queue1, queue2, queue3, queue4, queue5;
   int num;
   int donation;
   // Random creation of donation values and push them in queues
   srand(time(0));
```

(continued)

Program 19.13 Grouping charity donations (Continued)

```
    for (int i = 0; i < 50; i++)
    {
        num = rand();
        donation = num % (50 - 0 + 0) + 0;
        switch (donation / 10)
        {
                case 0: queue1.push(donation);
                        break;
                case 1: queue2.push(donation);
                        break;
                case 2: queue3.push(donation);
                        break;
                case 3: queue4.push(donation);
                        break;
                case 4: queue5.push(donation);
                        break;
        }
    }
    // Printing the donations in each group
    cout << "Donations between 00 and 09: ";
    print(queue1);
    cout << "Donations between 10 and 19: ";
    print(queue2);
    cout << "Donations between 20 and 29: ";
    print(queue3);
    cout << "Donations between 30 and 39: ";
    print(queue4);
    cout << "Donations between 40 and 49: ";
    print(queue5);
    return 0;
}
// Definition of the print function
void print(queue <int> queue)
{
    while (!queue.empty())
    {
        cout << queue.front() << " ";
        queue.pop();
    }
    cout << endl;
}
```

Run:

```
Donations between 00 and 09:  3  1  3  7  9  1  8  8  9  7  4  3
Donations between 10 and 19:  18  14  13  15  16  15
Donations between 20 and 29:  23  26  28  29  23  21  26  21  22  27  28  23
Donations between 30 and 39:  32  31  39  39  39  34  30  38  30  36  32
Donations between 40 and 49:  41  49  49  43  47  43  45  46  41
```

19.4.4 The priority_queue Class

The ***priority_queue* class** defined in the <queue> header file is a container adapter in which each element has a priority level. The elements can be inserted into the *priority_queue* in any order; the elements are retrieved based on their priority. In other words, the front element is the element with the largest value in the container.

Operations

The interface of a *priority_queue* is given in Table 19.2. Like a *queue*, we push at the *back* and pop in the *front*, but the access is limited only to the *front*, which is called *top*(), like a stack; we cannot access elements at the back.

An implementation difference between a *queue* and a *priority_queue* is that the *priority_queue* does not support relational operators (see Table 19.3). In other words, two priority queues cannot be compared.

Application

The *priority_queue* is the only structure available when we need to access the elements in the order they enter the container while at the same time giving priority to those that need faster access. For example, in a restaurant, people with reservations have seating priority.

Although we can use a *pair* class, a *tuple* class, or a user-created class to define the type of elements in a *priority queue*, all approaches require that we define the comparison for the data type or use a *function object* to do so. We leave this until we learn about *function objects*. Program 19.14 shows a simple example of a *priority queue* application of type integer that reorders the elements according to their integer values.

The result shows that the elements with a higher priority (value) are printed before the elements with a lower priority (value).

Program 19.14 Using a priority queue

```
/***************************************************************
 * A program to test the priority_queue class                  *
 ***************************************************************/
#include <queue>
#include <iostream>
using namespace std;

int main()
{
  // Create a priority_queue object
  priority_queue <int> line;
  // Push some elements
  line.push(4);
  line.push(7);
  line.push(2);
  line.push(6);
  line.push(7);
  line.push(8);
  line.push(2);
```

(continued)

Program 19.14 Using a priority queue (Continued)

```
    // Print the elements according to their priorities
    while (!line.empty ())
    {
        cout << line.top() << " ";
        line.pop();
    }
    return 0;
}
```

Run:

```
8  7  7  6  4  2  2
```

19.5 ASSOCIATIVE CONTAINERS

Elements in an **associative container** are stored and retrieved by a *key*. To access an element in an associate container, we use the *key* of the element. Associative containers are normally implemented as a binary search tree. Associate containers discussed in this chapter are divided into two classes (*set* and *map*). The standard has recently added *multiset* and *multimap* with duplicate values and duplicate keys, but we do not discuss them in this book.

- A **set** is an associative container in which the *key* and *value* are the same data item.
- A **map** is an associative container in which the *key* and the *value* are separate data items.

19.5.1 Public Interface

Before discussing associative containers, we provide a general public interface for them in Table 19.4. The abbreviation **AS** must be replaced with one of the two associative containers (*set* or *map*) when the corresponding column (S or M) is ticked. S means *set* and M means *map*. Each of these containers is a template class in which **K** defines the type of key for both *set* and *map* and **T** defines the type of the value for *map* only. The abbreviation <...> means <**K**> for the set and <**K**, **T**> for the map.

Table 19.4 The public interface for the set and map classes

Constructors, assignment, and destructor	**S**	**M**
AS <...> :: AS()	✓	✓
AS <...> :: AS(const_iterator *first*, const_iterator *last*)	✓	✓
AS <...> :: AS(const AS <...>& *s*)	✓	✓
AS <...>& AS <...> :: operator =(const AS <...> & *right*)	✓	✓
AS <...> :: ~AS()	✓	✓
Controlling size		
size_type AS <...> :: size()	✓	✓
size_type AS <...> :: max_size()	✓	✓
bool AS <...> :: empty()	✓	✓

(continued)

Table 19.4 The public interface for the set and map classes (Continued)

Iterators		
iterator AS <...> :: begin()	✓	✓
iterator AS <...> :: end()	✓	✓
reverse_iterator AS <...> :: rbegin()	✓	✓
reverse_iterator AS <...> :: rend()	✓	✓
Accessing		
T& AS <...> :: operator [ ](const K& *k*) const		✓
Searching		
size_type AS <...> :: count(const K& *k*) const	✓	✓
iterator AS <...> :: find(const K& *k*) const	✓	✓
iterator AS <...> :: lower_bound(const K& *k*) const	✓	✓
iterator AS <...> :: upper_bound(const K& *k*) const	✓	✓
pair <iterator, iterator> AS <...> :: equal_range(const K& *k*) const	✓	✓
Insertion		
pair <iterator, bool> AS <...> :: insert(const K& *k*)	✓	
pair <iterator, bool> AS <...> :: insert(const pair < const K, T > & p)		✓
iterator AS <...> :: insert(iterator *hintpos*, const K& *element*)	✓	✓
void AS <...> :: insert(InputIterator *first*, InputIterator *last*)	✓	✓
Erasure		
size_type AS <...> :: erase(const K& k)	✓	✓
void AS <...> :: erase(iterator *pos*)	✓	✓
void AS <...> :: erase(iterator *first*, iterator *last*)	✓	✓
void AS <...> :: clear()	✓	✓
Swapping		
void AS <...> :: swap(AS <...>& v)	✓	✓
Global functions		
bool operator oper(const AS <...> *left*, const AS <...> *right*)	✓	✓
void swap(AS <...>& c1, AS <...>& c2)	✓	✓

To discuss the classes *set* and *map*, we introduce a library *struct* named *pair* defined in the <utility> header. A *pair* defines a template *struct* with two template data members possibly of different types. The elements are called *first* and *second*, respectively, as shown below:

```
template <typename T1, typename T2>
struct pair
{
   T1 first;
   T2 second;
};
```

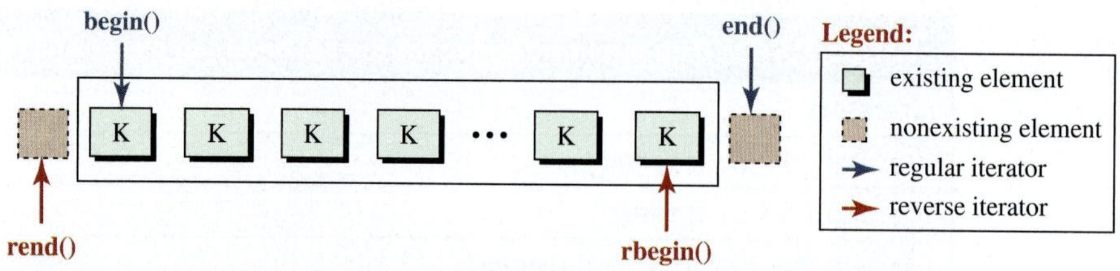

Notes:
The keys are unique in a set.
The objects are in a nonlinear relationship with each other.
The *set* class uses bidirectional iterators.

Figure 19.11 A set

19.5.2 Set

The *set* class is defined in the <set> header file. In a *set*, each element in the container stores one template value, which is referred to as the *key*. The elements are sorted in ascending order, and duplicates are not allowed. Figure 19.11 shows an example of a *set*.

Although the objects in Figure 19.11 appear to be one after another, they are not linearly connected. There is a nonlinear relationship among them. Although the library does not reveal the implementation, they are most likely implemented as a binary search tree.

Operations

We briefly discuss the operations that we can use with a set.

Constructors, Destructor, and Assignment We can create a new set using a default constructor (empty set). We can also create a new set using a parameter constructor by copying the elements of another set in which the range is indicated by [first, last). We can also create a set by using a copy constructor or an assignment operator. The following shows how to create a set of integers.

```
set <type> set1                 // Create an empty set
set <type>(pos1, pos2) set2     // Create a set copying elements of another set
set <type>(set2) set3           // Create a set copying all elements of another set
set4 = set3                     // Create a set copying all elements of another set
```

Controlling Size There are three member functions that we can use to check size, maximum size, and emptiness. They are the same as discussed for sequence containers.

Iterators The *set* class uses bidirectional (not random-access) iterators because it is normally implemented as a nonlinear linked list. It provides the same eight internal iterators as the sequence containers, in which four are constant and four nonconstant. Both constant and nonconstant iterators have the same syntax.

```
set1.begin()       // Returns a regular iterator to the first element
set1.end()         // Returns a regular iterator to the element after the last
set1.rbegin()      // Returns a reverse iterator to the last element
set1.rend()        // Returns a reverse iterator to the element before the first
```

Searching Since the elements in a set are sorted, searching is possible and efficient. There are five members for searching, as shown below:

```
set1.count(k)            // Returns number of elements equal to k
set1.find(k)             // Returns an iterator pointing to the first k found
set1.lower_bound(k)      // Returns the first position where k can be inserted
set1.upper_bound(k)      // Returns the last position where k can be inserted
set1.equal_range(k)      // Combination of lower and upper bound
```

Note that the *count*(k) for a set returns either 0 or 1. The *find*() member tries to find the value in the set and returns the iterator to the value if it is found. If the value is not found in the set, it returns the *end*(). The *lower_bound*() returns the first position where the value can be inserted; the *upper_bound*() returns the last position where the value can be inserted. The *equal_range*() returns a pair object showing the combination of *lower_bound* and *upper_bound*. Note that the set has no operations to access the elements in the set using an index operator or *at*() function. We must use the key to do so.

Insertion There are no push members to insert an element in a set. Insertion must be done using the key or through iterators.

```
set1.insert(k)           // Insert k and returns a pair <pos, bool>
set1.insert(hint, k)     // Returns an iterator to the element after the hint
set1.insert(pos1, pos2)  // Returns a pair where k can be found
```

The first member function inserts the key *k* and returns an iterator showing the position and a Boolean value (success or failure). The second member function also inserts *k*, but the user can give a hint (iterator) to the position to reduce the search. The third member function copies an open range [pos1, pos2) from another set and inserts it at the appropriate place.

Erasure There are no pop members for deleting an element from a set. Deletion must be done through the value or iterator.

```
set1.erase(k)            // Erases k and returns a pair <pos, bool>
set1.erase(pos)          // Erases an element pointed to by pos
set1.erase(first, last)  // Erases elements in the range [first, last)
set1.clear()             // Returns an iterator to the element after the last
```

The first member deletes the element with the key *k* and returns the number of elements, which can be 0 or 1 for a set. The second erases the item at *pos*. The third one erases a range. The last one erases all elements.

Other Operations Just like the sequence containers, the *swap*() operation is defined for sets. Also, we can compare two sets with relational operators.

Applications

We show two simple applications of sets in this section. In the first example we use a program to show how we can create a set of integers, print in the ascending and descending order, and print an integer before a given integer and an integer after a given integer (Program 19.15). In the second example we create a student set and overload the less-than

Program 19.15 Handling a set of integers

```
/*****************************************************************
 * Using a set to create a sorted container of integers          *
 *****************************************************************/
#include <set>
#include <iostream>
#include <iomanip>
using namespace std;

int main()
{
   // Create an empty set of integers
   set <int> st;
   // Insert some keys in the set (with duplicates)
   st.insert(47);
   st.insert(18);
   st.insert(12);
   st.insert(24);
   st.insert(52);
   st.insert(20);
   st.insert(24);
   st.insert(92);
   st.insert(53);
   st.insert(77);
   st.insert(98);
   st.insert(87);
   // Print the set elements from smallest to largest
   cout << "Printing set elements from smallest to largest." << endl;
   set <int> :: iterator iter;
   for (iter = st.begin(); iter != st.end(); iter++)
   {
        cout << setw(4) << *iter;
   }
   cout << endl << endl;
   // Print the set elements from largest to smallest
   cout << "Printing set elements from largest to smallest." << endl;;
   set <int> :: reverse_iterator riter;
   for (riter = st.rbegin(); riter != st.rend(); riter++)
   {
        cout << setw(4) << *riter;
   }
   cout << endl << endl;
   // Print the element after 52
   set <int> :: iterator iter1 = st.find(52);
   iter1++;
   cout << "Element after 52: " << *iter1 << endl;
   // Print the element before 20
   set <int> :: iterator iter2 = st.find (20);
```

(continued)

Program 19.15 Handling a set of integers (Continued)

```
    iter2--;
    cout << "Element before 20: " << *iter2 << endl;
    return 0;
}
```

```
Run:
Printing set elements from smallest to largest.
  12  18  20  24  47  52  53  77  87  92  98

Printing set elements from largest to smallest.
  98  92  87  77  53  52  47  24  20  18  12

Element after 52:  53
Element before 20:  18
```

operator for the *Student* class so we can list students according to their student identification (Program 19.16, Program 19.17, and Program 19.18).

Program 19.16 shows the interface file for the *Student* set.

Program 19.16 The interface file (student.h)

```
/***************************************************************
 * The interface file for the Student class                    *
 ***************************************************************/
#ifndef STUDENT_H
#define STUDENT_H
#include <string>
#include <set>
#include <iostream>
#include <iomanip>
using namespace std;

class Student
{
  private:
       int identity ;
       string name;
       double gpa;
  public:
       Student(int identity, string name, double gpa);
       ~Student();
       void print() const;
       bool friend operator< (const Student& left, const Student& right);
};
#endif
```

Program 19.17 The implementation file (student.cpp)

```
/***************************************************************
 * The implementation file for the Student class              *
 ***************************************************************/
#include "student.h"

// Constructor
Student :: Student(int id, string nm, double gp)
: identity (id), name (nm), gpa (gp)
{
}
// Destructor
Student :: ~Student()
{
}
// Print member function
void Student :: print() const
{
    cout << setw(3) << right << identity << " " ;
    cout << setw(12) << left << name << " " ;
    cout << setw(6) << right << showpoint << setprecision(3) ;
    cout << gpa << " " << endl;
}
// Friend less-than operator
bool operator<(const Student& left, const Student& right)
{
    return (left.identity < right.identity) ;
}
```

Program 19.17 shows the implementation file for *Student* class.

The application file instantiates *Student* objects and inserts them in the set to be sorted based on their identity. It then prints the information in each object (Program 19.18).

Program 19.18 The application file (app.cpp)

```
/***************************************************************
 * The application file for the Student class                 *
 ***************************************************************/
#include "student.h"

int main()
{
    // Creating six instance of the Student class
    Student student1(120, "George", 3.78);
    Student student2(185, "Mary", 3.95);
    Student student3(110, "Richard", 4.00);
    Student student4(245, "Alen", 3.70);
    Student student5(172, "John", 3.00);
    Student student6(195, "Lucie", 3.80);
```

(continued)

Program 19.18 The application file (app.cpp) (Continued)

```
    // Insert the above six objects into the set
    set <Student> stdSet ;
    stdSet.insert(student1);
    stdSet.insert(student2);
    stdSet.insert(student3);
    stdSet.insert(student4);
    stdSet.insert(student5);
    stdSet.insert(student6);
    // Printing the contents of student objects
    set <Student> :: iterator iter;
    for (iter = stdSet.begin(); iter != stdSet.end(); iter++)
    {
        iter -> print();
    }
    return 0;
}
```

```
Run:
110     Richard     4.00
120     George      3.78
172     John        3.00
185     Mary        3.95
195     Lucie       3.80
245     Alen        3.70
```

19.5.3 Map

A *map*, which is also called a *table*, a *dictionary*, or an *associate array*, is defined in the <map> header file. It is a container that stores a template *pair* of *key* and *value*. The elements are sorted in ascending order based on the key. In a *map*, the keys are unique. Figure 19.12 shows an example of a map.

Operations

The operations defined for the *map* class are very similar to the ones for the *set* class. The main difference is the ability to access the elements in the *map* using the *operator* [ ]. This

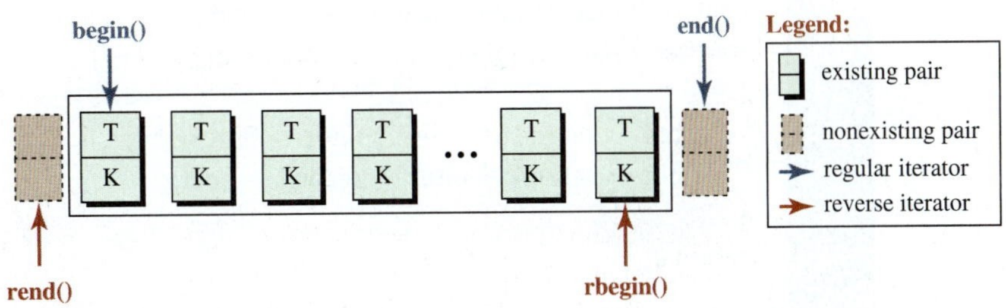

Notes:
The keys are unique in a map.
The objects are in nonlinear relationship to each other.
The *map* class uses bidirectional iterators.

Figure 19.12 A map

operator makes a *map* object look like an array in which the index is a key value instead of an integer. In other words, if we know the value of the key in an element, we can access the element using the expression *map* [key]. However, the operator [ ] does not act like the one used for an array or a *vector* or a *deque*. It is just a notation to create a *pair* consisting of key-value. A *map* uses only bidirectional iterators and cannot jump from one *pair* to another using the + or – operator.

Applications

We discuss two applications that use a map. In the first, we create a *map* of student scores in which each element is a pair of student name and student score on a test. We then find the minium and maximum score (Program 19.19). In the second, we create a program that finds

Program 19.19 A student table (name and score)

```
/*****************************************************************
  * A program to create five pairs of student and score in a map      *
  *****************************************************************/
#include <map>
#include <iostream>
#include <iomanip>
#include <utility>
using namespace std;

int main()
{
// Creation of a map and the corresponding iterator
  map <string, int > scores;
  map <string, int > :: iterator iter;
// Inputting student name and score in the map
  scores ["John"] = 52;
  scores ["George"] = 71;
  scores ["Mary"] = 88;
  scores ["Lucie"] = 98;
  scores ["Robert"] = 77;
// Printing the names and score sorted on names
  cout << "Students names and scores" << endl;
  for (iter = scores.begin (); iter != scores.end(); iter++)
  {
      cout << setw(10) << left << iter -> first << " ";
      cout << setw(4) << iter -> second << endl;
  }
  return 0;
}
```

Run:

```
Students names and scores
```

(continued)

Program 19.19 A student table (name and score) (Continued)

```
George      71
John        52
Lucie       98
Mary        88
Robert      77
```

the frequency of words in a string. We use a *map* object named *freq* in which the key is the word encountered in the text and the value is the frequency of words. Note that we have used the ctrl + Z character to signal the end of the input file (Program 19.20).

Program 19.20 Frequency of words in text

```
/*****************************************************************
 * A program to count the number of words in a text              *
 *****************************************************************/
#include <map>
#include <string>
#include <iomanip>
#include <iostream>
using namespace std;

int main()
{
    // Declaration of map, iterator, and a string
    map <string, int > freq;
    map <string, int > :: iterator iter;
    string word;
    // Reading and storing words in the map
    cout << "Enter a sentence to be parsed: " << endl;
    while (cin >> word)
    {
        ++freq [word];
    }
    // Printing the words and their frequency
    for (iter = freq.begin(); iter != freq.end(); iter++)
    {
        cout << left << setw(10) << iter -> first << iter -> second << endl;
    }
    return 0;
}
```

```
Run:
Enter a sentence to be parsed:
we are in the world of this and that and this and that
^Z
```

(continued)

Program 19.20 Frequency of words in text (Continued)

```
and          3
are          1
in           1
of           1
that         2
the          1
this         2
we           1
world        1
```

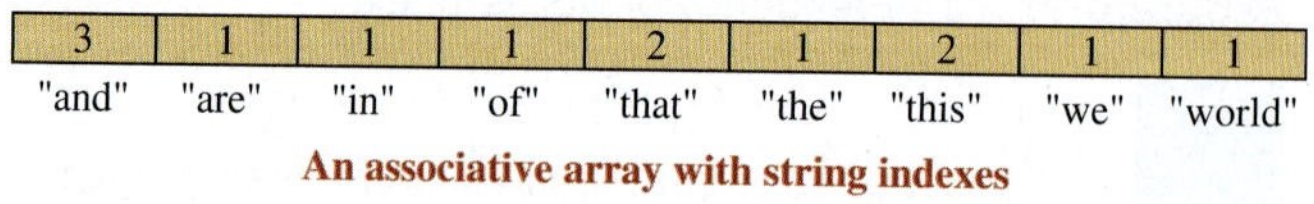

Figure 19.13 A map serving as an associative array

Note that we type all words in lowercase to make easier to see that the keys are sorted. The words and frequency form an associative array, an array whose index does not have be integers (Figure 19.13).

19.6 USING FUNCTIONS

We can use library algorithms or define our own algorithms. In each case, an algorithm applies an operation to a number of elements in the container. The question is how this operation can be defined as a parameter in the algorithm. It can be done in two ways: a pointer to function or a function object (*functor*). We discuss each approach next.

19.6.1 Pointer to Function

We know that the definition of a function is stored in memory. Every entity that is stored in memory has an address. In fact, the name of a function is a pointer to the first byte of memory where the function is stored, just as the name of an array is a pointer to the first element of an array. Figure 19.14 shows how the name of an array and the name of a function are pointers. The figure also shows how a pointer to an array and a pointer to a function are declared.

We write an example of a pointer to function (Program 19.21). We want to use a function, *fun*, that uses another function, *print*, as an argument. We define both functions. In *main*, we call *fun* two times, which calls the *print* function in each call. Note that the definition of *fun* does not define which function is to be called as the second parameter. The calling statement passes a pointer to the *print* function (*print* is a pointer to the beginning of the print function).

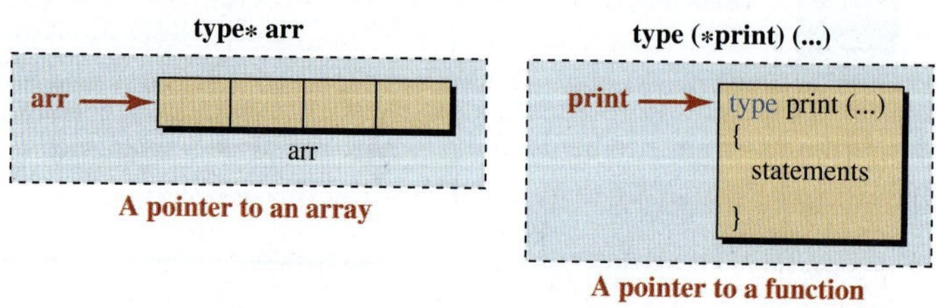

Figure 19.14 Pointer to an array and pointer to a function

Program 19.21 Using pointer to functions

```
/*****************************************************************
 * Using functions that call another function                    *
 *****************************************************************/
#include <iostream>
using namespace std;

// Definition of print function
void print (int value)
{
  cout << value << endl;
}
// Definition of fun function
void fun (int x, void(*f)(int))
{
  f(x);
}

int main()
{
  fun(24, print); // Calling function fun
  fun(88, print); // Calling function fun
  return 0;
}
```

```
Run:
24
88
```

In Program 19.21 the declaration of a pointer to function, *void*(*f)(*int*), may look unusual, but the good news is that most algorithms in STL have already defined functions that use a pointer to functions (such as *print*). We do not have to declare them. In other words, if an STL algorithm uses a pointer to function, we need to give only the name of the function in the call.

We use the STL generic algorithm, *for_each*, that applies a function to a range of items in a container. The algorithm applies the function defined as the third parameter to the range [first, last) as shown in Program 19.22. The algorithm defines that the third algorithm must

Program 19.22 Using for_each with a user-defined function

```
/*****************************************************************
 * Applying a function to all elements in a range using the      *
 * algorithm for_each in the library                             *
 *****************************************************************/
#include <vector>
#include <algorithm>
```

(continued)

Program 19.22 Using for_each with a user-defined function (Continued)

```
#include <iostream>
using namespace std;

// Definition of the print function
void print(int value)
{
  cout << value << " ";
}

int main()
{
// Instantiation of a vector object and storing three values
  vector <int> vec;
  vec.push_back(24);
  vec.push_back(42);
  vec.push_back(73);
// Using a print function to print the value of each element
  for_each(vec.begin(), vec.end(), print);
  return 0;
}
```

Run:

```
24 42 73
```

be a pointer to a function. We pass the name *print* and then we define a function named *print* with one argument. The *print* function takes the value of its argument from the iterator (*iterator).

19.6.2 Function Objects (Functors)

In Chapter 13 we learned that we can overload the *function operator*, a pair of parentheses, to create a *function object* (sometimes called a *functor*). Figure 19.15 shows how we write a regular function and a function object.

Program 19.23 shows how we can call a *functor* from another function (*main*). We create a class named *Print*, overload the *operator*(), create an object of the class, and call the operator. Note that calling the overloaded operator is simply calling the object instantiated from the class and inserting the arguments inside the parentheses. In fact, we are calling *print.operator*()(45) in line 16.

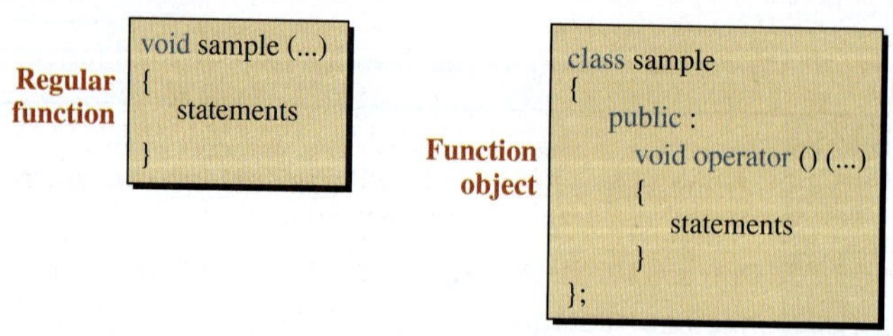

Figure 19.15 A regular function versus a function object

Program 19.23 Using a functor

```
/***************************************************************
 * Calling a function object to print the same value           *
 ***************************************************************/
#include <iostream>
using namespace std;

class Print
{
  public:
  void operator()(int value) {cout << value;}
};

int main()
{
  Print print; // Instantiation of an object of type Print
  print(45); // calling operator()
  return 0;
}
```

Run:

```
45
```

We can see that the definition of a function object is longer than a regular function, but a function object has advantages that justify its longer definition:

- As an object, a function object can be used wherever an object can be used. In particular, it can be passed to a function as an argument, and it can be returned from a function.
- A function object can have a state, which means that it can hold information from one call to another.
- We can define a class to be used as a function object and then inherit from it to create other function objects.

Function Objects in STL Algorithms

To facilitate the use of algorithms, the STL library defines many function objects. They can be divided into unary (taking one argument) and binary (taking two arguments). These function objects are defined in the <functional> header file and can be used in our programs. Table 19.5 lists some of these functions.

Table 19.5 Function objects in STL

Function object	Type	Arity	Operator
negate <T>	arithmetic	unary	−
plus <T>	arithmetic	binary	+

(continued)

Table 19.5 Function objects in STL (Continued)

minus <T>	arithmetic	binary	–
multiplies <T>	arithmetic	binary	*
divides <T>	arithmetic	binary	/
modulus <T>	arithmetic	binary	%
equal_to <T>	relational	binary	==
not_equal_to <T>	relational	binary	!=
greater <T>	relational	binary	>
greater_equal <T>	relational	binary	>=
less <T>	relational	binary	<
less_equal<T>	relational	binary	<=
logical_not <T>	logical	unary	!
logical_and <T>	logical	binary	&&
logical_or <T>	logical	binary	||

Each function simulates one of the built-in operators. However, the naming is different from what we have seen for built-in operators. For example, *negate* means the minus operator (unary) and *minus* means the subtraction operator (binary).

We discuss algorithms in the next section. For the moment, we show how we use the transform algorithm to negate all elements in a vector, as shown in Program 19.24. Note that we do not see any object of type *negate* in the call to the transform algorithm. The reason is that the *transform* function directly calls the default constructor of the *negate* class (with a pair of parentheses). The algorithm then calls the *operator*() in the background and passes the value returned from the dereferencing iterator to that operator. However, this happens in the background and is hidden from the user.

Program 19.24 Using a unary functor

```
/****************************************************************
 * A program to use a pointer to function and a functor          *
 ****************************************************************/
#include <vector>
#include <algorithm>
#include <iostream>
#include <functional>
using namespace std;

// User-defined print function
void print(int value)
{
```

(continued)

Program 19.24 Using a unary functor (Continued)

```
    cout << value << " ";
}

int main()
{
    // Creation of a vector with four nodes
    vector <int> vec;
    vec.push_back(24);
    vec.push_back(42);
    vec.push_back(73);
    vec.push_back(92);
    // Printing the node using a pointer to user-defined function
    for_each(vec.begin(), vec.end(), print);
    cout << endl;
    // Negating the values of all nodes and print them again
    transform(vec.begin(), vec.end(), vec.begin(), negate <int>()());
    for_each(vec.begin(), vec.end(), print);
    return 0;
}
```

```
Run:
24 42 73 92
-24 -42 -73 -92
```

19.7 ALGORITHMS

Another piece of the STL is a set of generic algorithms. Instead of defining these operations inside each container type, the C++ language defines template global functions that can be applied to any container type that supports the iterators required by the algorithm. For our purpose, we divide generic algorithms into four groups based on their functionality: *non_mutating*, *mutating*, *sorting*, and *numeric*.

Before discussing some of the algorithms in this group, we must mention a point that is sometimes misunderstood: The algorithms are template global functions, but the template type does not define the type of the elements in the container; it defines the type of the iterator the algorithm itself uses. In other words, if a container does not support the type of iterator (or a higher one in the hierarchy of iterators) defined in the algorithm, that algorithm cannot be applied to that container. A good example is the sorting algorithm, which we discuss later in this section. This algorithm requires a random-access iterator, but the list <T> container does not provide this type of iterator, which means the generic sorting algorithm cannot be applied to the list <T> class. This is why sorting is defined in the list <T> class as a member function. Another example is that we cannot apply generic algorithms to container adapters, because they do not support iterators.

Space does not allow discussion of all the algorithms defined in the STL. We discuss only some of them in this section and give a brief description of each with the type of iterator it needs. Our purpose is to familiarize you with the use of containers.

Table 19.6 Non-mutating algorithms
difference_type count(InIter *first*, InIter *last*, const T& *value*);
difference_type count_if(InIter *first*, InIter *last*, Predicate *pred*);
InIter find(InIter *first*, InIter *last*, const T& *value*);
Function for_each(InIter *first*, outIter *last*, Function *func*);

19.7.1 Non-Mutating Algorithms

Non-mutating algorithms, which are defined in the <algorithm> header file, do not change the order of the elements in the container that they are applied to. They can be modifying or non-modifying. The non-modifying algorithms do not change the value of elements in the container; the modifying algorithms can change the values if the operation is designed for that purpose. Table 19.6 shows some of the most commonly used algorithms in this category. Note that we use *InIter* as an abbreviation for Input Iterator. A predicate is a function that returns a Boolean value. In this category, the only algorithm that can be modifying or non-modifying is the last one. If the function uses a reference to its argument and returns a reference, it can be modifying.

The first function counts the number of elements equal to *value*. The second function counts the element if they meet the criteria in *pred*. The third function finds the position of an element with a given value. The fourth function applies the parameter *func* to the member elements in the range [*first*, *last*).

We apply some of these algorithms on a vector object of integers, as shown in Program 19.25. We use *for-each*, *count*, and *count_if* algorithms. The *for_each* applies a function to all elements. The function *count* counts some specific values, and *count_if* applies a Boolean function to each element.

Program 19.25 Testing non-mutating algorithms

```
/***************************************************************
  * A program to use some non-mutating algorithms              *
  ***************************************************************/
#include <vector>
#include <algorithm>
#include <iostream>
using namespace std;

// Definition of isEven
bool isEven(int value)
{
  return (value % 2 == 0);
}
// Definition of timesTwo
void timesTwo(int& value)
{
  value = value * 2;
}
```

(continued)

Program 19.25 Testing non-mutating algorithms (Continued)

```
// Definition of print
void print(int value)
{
  cout << value << " ";
}

int main()
{
  // Instantiation of a vector of integers
  vector <int> vec ;
  // Pushing ten values into the vector
  vec.push_back(17);
  vec.push_back(10);
  vec.push_back(13);
  vec.push_back(13);
  vec.push_back(18);
  vec.push_back(15);
  vec.push_back(17);
  vec.push_back(13);
  vec.push_back(13);
  vec.push_back(18);
  // Printing original values
  cout << "Original values in vector" << endl;
  for_each(vec.begin(), vec.end(), print);
  cout << endl << endl;
  // Counting number of 10's
  cout << "Count of 10's: ";
  cout << count(vec.begin(), vec.end(), 10);
  cout << endl << endl;
  // Counting the even values
  cout << "Count of even values: ";
  cout << count_if( vec.begin(), vec.end(), isEven );
  cout << endl << endl;
  // Doubling each value and printing vector
  cout << "Values after multiplying by 2" << endl;
  for_each(vec.begin(), vec.end(), timesTwo);
  for_each(vec.begin(), vec.end(), print);
  return 0;
}
```

Run:

```
Original values in vector
17  10  13  13  18  15  17  13  13  18
```

(*continued*)

Program 19.25 Testing non-mutating algorithms (Continued)

```
Count of 10's:  1

Count of even values:  3

Values after multiplying by 2
34  20  26  26  36  30  34  26  26  36
```

Table 19.7 Some mutating algorithms
void generate(BdIter *first*, BdIter *last*, *gen*);
void reverse(BdIter *first*, BdIter *last*);
void rotate(FwIter *first*, FwIter *middle*, FwIter *last*);
void random_shuffle(BdIter *first*, BdIter *last*);
outIter transform(inIter *first*, inIter *second*, outIter start, oper);

19.7.2 Mutating Algorithms

The **mutating algorithms,** which are defined in the <algorithm> header file, change the structure of the container they are applied to. The list of these algorithms is long, but we show three of them in Table 19.7 (*BdIter* means bidirectional iterator and *FwIter* means forward iterator).

The first function in Table 19.7 creates a sequence with the result of running the *gen* function. The second function reverses the order of elements in the container. The third function rotates the elements to the left so that the middle element becomes the first element and the element before the middle element becomes the last. The *random_shuffle* function changes the order in the container to a random order. The *transform* function changes the values from the member pointed to by *first* to *second* (using the *oper* function) and puts the result starting from the element pointed to by *start*. It returns a pointer to the last modified element.

We use the three mutating algorithms in Program 19.26. We create a vector of integers, we then reverse the elements in the vector, we then rotate the elements, and finally we create a random shufflle of the vector.

Program 19.26 Testing mutating functions

```
/***************************************************************
 * A program to use some mutating algorithms                   *
 ***************************************************************/
#include <vector>
#include <algorithm>
#include <iostream>
#include <iomanip>
using namespace std;

```

(*continued*)

Program 19.26 Testing mutating functions (Continued)

```
// Definition of print function
void print(int value)
{
  cout << value << " ";
}

int main()
{
  // Instantiation of a vector object
  vector <int> vec ;
  // Adding six values
  vec.push_back(11);
  vec.push_back(14);
  vec.push_back(17);
  vec.push_back(23);
  vec.push_back(35);
  vec.push_back(52);
  // Printing original values
  cout << "Original vector" << endl;
  for_each(vec.begin(), vec.end(), print);
  cout << endl << endl;
  // Reversing the values and print the vector
  cout << "Vector after reversing the order" << endl;
  reverse(vec.begin(), vec.end());
  for_each(vec.begin(), vec.end(), print);
  cout << endl << endl;
  // Rotate the values and print the vector
  cout << "Vector after rotating the order" << endl;
  rotate(vec.begin(), vec.begin() + 2, vec.end());
  for_each(vec.begin(), vec.end(), print);
  cout << endl << endl;
  // Random shuffle the value print the vector
  cout << "Vector after random shuffle" << endl;
  random_shuffle(vec.begin(), vec.end());
  for_each(vec.begin(), vec.end(), print);
  cout << endl << endl;
  return 0;
}
```

Run:

```
Original vector
11  14  17  23  35  52
```

(continued)

Program 19.26 Testing mutating functions (Continued)

```
Vector after reversing the order
52  35  23  17  14  11

Vector after rotating the order
23  17  14  11  52  35

Vector after random shuffle
23  14  35  52  17  11
```

Table 19.8 Sorting and related algorithms
void sort(RndIter *first*, RndIter *last*);
bool binary_search(FwIter *first*, FwIter *last*, const T& *value*);
FwIter min_element(FwIter *first*, FwIter *last*);
FwIter max_element(FwIter *first*, FwIter *last*);
OutIter set_difference(InIter *first1*, InIter *last1*, InIter *first2*, InIter *last2*, OutIter *result*);
OutIter set_intersection(InIter *first1*, InIter *last2*, InIter *first2*, InIter *last2*, OutIter *result*);
OutIter set_union(InIter *first1*, InIter *last1*, InIter *first2*, InIter *last2*, OutIter *result*);
OutIter set_symmetric_difference(InIter *first1*, InIter *last1*, InIter *first2*, InIter *last2*, OutIter *result*);

19.7.3 Sorting and Related Algorithms

The <algorithm> header file also defines several algorithms that either sort the sequence or apply operations that are related to sorting. We list eight of these algorithms in Table 19.8 and give some examples.

The first algorithm in Table 19.8 sorts a sequence, but we must be sure that the sequence supports random-access iterators. The second uses the binary search algorithm to find an element in a sequence. The third finds the first minium element, and the fourth finds the first maximum element. The last four algorithms apply set operations on sorted sequences. In other words, they take a sorted sequence as a set and apply the *set_difference*, *set_intersection*, *set_union,* and *set_symmeteric_difference* to these sorted sequences. Since a set container is already a sorted sequence, we can apply these operations to the set associate.

In Program 19.27 we create a vector of integers and then sort them first in ascending order and then in descending order. The sort algorithm is controlled by one of two function objects: *less* <T> and *greater* <T>. To sort in ascending order, we use the default function *less* <T>. To sort in descending order, we change the behavior of the sorting algorithm by using the *greater* <T> function object as the third algorithm in the parameter list.

Program 19.27 Using sorting algorithms

```
/***************************************************************
 * A program that sorts a vector using sort algorithm          *
 ***************************************************************/
#include <vector>
#include <algorithm>
#include <iostream>
using namespace std;

// Definition of print function
void print(int value)
{
  cout << value << " ";
}

int main()
{
  // Instantiation of a vector object
  vector <int> vec ;
  // Pushing six elements into the vector and print them
  vec.push_back(17);
  vec.push_back(10);
  vec.push_back(13);
  vec.push_back(18);
  vec.push_back(15);
  vec.push_back(11);
  cout << "Original vector" << endl;
  for_each(vec.begin(), vec.end(), print);
  cout << endl << endl;
  // Sorting the vector in ascending order and print it
  cout << "Vector after sorting in ascending order" << endl;
  sort(vec.begin(), vec.end());
  for_each(vec.begin(), vec.end(), print);
  cout << endl << endl;
  // Sorting the vector in descending order and print it
  cout << "Vector after sorting in descending order" << endl;
  sort(vec.begin(), vec.end(), greater <int>());
  for_each(vec.begin(), vec.end(), print);
  cout << endl << endl;
  return 0;
}
```

```
Run:
Original vector
17 10 13 18 15 11
```

(continued)

Program 19.27 Using sorting algorithms (Continued)

```
Vector after sorting in ascending order
10  11  13  15  17  18

Vector after sorting in descending order
18  17  15  13  11  10
```

We now test the *binary_search*() algorithm. The sequence must be sorted for this algorithm to work correctly. Program 19.28 shows a simple example in which we create a vector of integer values, we sort it, and then we search the vector for two values: one in the vector and the other not in the vector.

Program 19.28 Using a binary search algorithm

```
/*****************************************************************
 * A program that uses binary search on a vector                 *
 *****************************************************************/
#include <vector>
#include <algorithm>
#include <iostream>
using namespace std;

int main()
{
   // Instantiation of a vector object
   vector <int> vec ;
   // Adding six elements to the vector
   vec.push_back(17);
   vec.push_back(10);
   vec.push_back(13);
   vec.push_back(18);
   vec.push_back(15);
   vec.push_back(11);
   // Sorting the vector
   sort(vec.begin(), vec.end());
   // Searching vector for two values
   cout << "Found 10 in vector? " << boolalpha;
   cout << binary_search(vec.begin(), vec.end(), 10) << endl;
   cout << "Found 19 in vector? " << boolalpha;
   cout << binary_search(vec.begin(), vec.end(), 19) << endl;
   return 0;
}
```

```
Run:
Found 10 in vector? true
Found 19 in vector? false
```

Figure 19.16 Graphical representation of set union

Figure 19.16 shows union operations applied to *first* and *second* sets. The result is the shaded area. The *union* is a set that includes all elements in *first* and *second*.

Program 19.29 shows how we can apply the union operation on the two sets (*first* and *second*).

Program 19.29 Finding the union of two sets

```
/*****************************************************************
 * A program that finds the union of two sets                    *
 *****************************************************************/
#include <set>
#include <vector>
#include <iostream>
#include <algorithm>
using namespace std;

// Print function
void print(int value)
{
  cout << value << " ";
}

int main()
{
  // Creation of the first set
  set <int> first ;
  first.insert(10);
  first.insert(19);
  first.insert(14);
  first.insert(17);
  first.insert(13);
  cout << "Elements of first set" << endl;
  for_each(first.begin(), first.end(), print);
  cout << endl << endl;
  // Creation of the second set
  set <int> second;
  second.insert(16);
  second.insert(14);
```

(continued)

Program 19.29 Finding the union of two sets (Continued)

```
    second.insert(13);
    second.insert(11);
    second.insert(20);
    cout << "Elements of second set" << endl;
    for_each(second.begin(), second.end(), print);
    cout << endl << endl;
    // Finding the union of two sets and storing in a vector
    vector <int> temp(10);
    vector <int> :: iterator iter;
    vector <int> :: iterator endIter;
    endIter = set_union(first.begin(), first.end(), second.begin(),
                                        second.end((), temp.begin());
    // Copying elements from the vector to the result set
    set <int> result;
    for (iter = temp.begin(); iter != endIter; iter++)
    {
        result.insert(*iter);
    }
    cout << "Elements of result set" << endl;
    for_each(result.begin(), result.end(), print);
    cout << endl << endl;
    return 0;
}
```

```
Run:
Elements of first set
10 13 14 17 19

Elements of second set
11 13 14 16 20

Elements of result set
10 11 13 14 16 17 19 20
```

In Program 19.29 the size of the target sequence must be large enough to accommodate the result. This is not possible with a set because any set when created is empty. To solve the problem, we have created a vector to temporarily hold the result of an operation and then copied the part of the vector that holds the result to the resulting set. Figure 19.17 shows the process we have used.

19.7.4 Numeric Algorithms

There are a few **numeric algorithm,** defined in the <numeric> header file, that perform simple arithmetic operations on the elements of a container or containers. Note that these algorithms do not have to be applied on arithmetic types (such as *int* or *double*); as long as the corresponding operation is defined for a type, these algorithms can be applied to them. Table 19.9 shows one commonly used numeric algorithm.

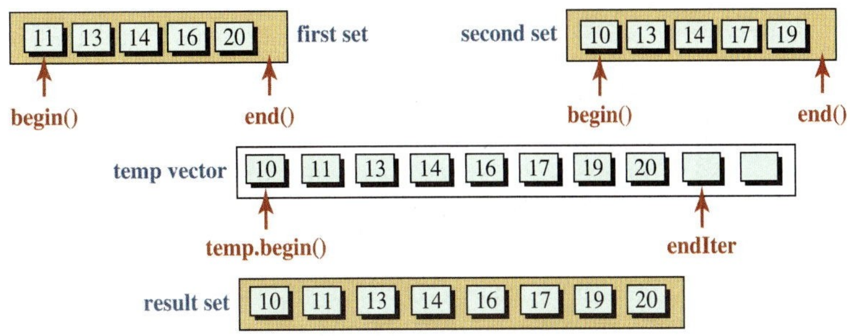

Figure 19.17 Using the set_intersection operation

Table 19.9 The accumulate algorithm
`T accumulate(InIter first, InIter last, T init);`

The *accumulate* algorithm finds the sum of the value in a range [first, last) and adds the result to the *init* value.

Program 19.30 uses the *accumulate* algorithm.

Program 19.30 Testing the accumulate algorithm

```
/***************************************************************
 * A program to test the numeric algorithm accumulate          *
 ***************************************************************/
#include <vector>
#include <numeric>
#include <iostream>
using namespace std;

// A print function
void print(int value)
{
   cout << value << " ";
}

int main()
{
   // Instantiate and print a vector
   vector <int> vec ;
   vec.push_back(17);
   vec.push_back(10);
   vec.push_back(13);
   vec.push_back(13);
   vec.push_back(18);
```

(continued)

Program 19.30 Testing the accumulate algorithm (Continued)

```
    vec.push_back(15);
    vec.push_back(17);
    for_each(vec.begin(), vec.end(), print);
    cout << endl;
    // Calculate the sum and print it
    int sum = accumulate(vec.begin(), vec.end(), 0);
    cout << "Sum of elements: " << sum;
    return 0;
}
```

```
Run:
17  10  13  13  18  15  17
Sum of elements: 103
```

Key Terms

algorithm
associative container
bidirectional iterator
container
container adapter
deque class
forward iterator
input iterator
iterator
list class
map
mutating algorithm
non-mutating algorithm
numeric algorithm
output iterator
priority_queue class
queue class
random-access iterator
sequence container
set
sorting algorithm
stack class
vector class

Summary

The Standard Template Library (STL) is the result of years of research to solve two important issues: reusability of software and creation of components each with a distinct functionality. STL is made of four components: iterators, containers, functions, and algorithms.

Iterators are tools that allow us to access objects in a container. They are based on the pointer concept that allows us to reference objects using their addresses.

A sequence container preserves the original order of items added to the container. It consists of three classes: *vector*, *deque,* and *list*. Container adapters include *stack*, *queue*, and *priority-queue* classes. Associative containers hold elements stored and retrieved by a key. We discussed two classes of associative containers: *set* and *map*.

STL uses either a pointer to function to a function object in algorithms. If an algorithm uses a pointer to function, the user needs to provide the function definition. If an algorithm uses a function object, it is normally defined in the collection.

Algorithms consist of template global functions that can be applied to any container type that supports the iterators required by the algorithm. We have divided algorithms into four groups: non-mutating, mutating, sorting, and numeric.

Problems

PR-1. Write the definition of a generic function that prints the value of all elements in a *vector* of any type.

PR-2. Write the definition of a generic function that prints the value of all elements in a *list* of any type.

PR-3. Write the code to create a vector of 0, 1, 2, 3, 4, 5, 6, 7, 8, 9 values using the *at*() member function.

PR-4. Write the code to create a list of 0, 1, 2, 3, 4, 5, 6, 7, 8, 9 values.

PR-5. Write the statements to swap the values at index 2 and index 3 in a vector of type integer named *vec*.

PR-6. Write the statements to swap the values of second and third elements in a list of type integer named *lst*.

PR-7. The *push_front* operation is not defined for a vector. Write code to insert a value at the front of a vector of type integer.

PR-8. The *pop_front* operation is not defined for a vector. Write code to remove the first element from a vector of type integer.

PR-9. The remove function is not defined for a vector. Write code to simulate the remove function for a vector.

PR-10. Assume we insert the following integer values into an empty priority queue: 14, 24, 76, 18, 20, and 54. We then pop two integers. What is the next integer to be popped?

PR-11. Assume we insert the following values into a set: 20, 17, 20, 14, 15, 19, 17, and 10. What would be printed from the *size*() member function after all insertions?

PR-12. Assume we insert the following pairs into a map: (20, 10), (14, 40), and (17, 3). What is the order of these items in the map?

PR-13. Assume we have the following items in a set named *st*: 20, 14, 18, 22, 76. Write the code to print 18 and 22.

PR-14. Assume we have inserted the pairs (15, 10), (16, 10), (6, 16), and (12, 8) into a *map* named *mp*. What would be printed from the following code?

```
cout << mp [6] << endl;
cout << mp [16] << endl;
cout << mp [10] << endl;
```

PR-15. Write the code to create a map and use the *insert* member function to insert the following pairs in it: (3, 10), (5, 12), and (7, 8).

Programs

PRG-1. Since the pointers in an array are compatible with random-access iterators, we can use some algorithms defined in the STL with arrays. Write a program that initializes an array of five elements, defines a print function, and uses the *for_each* algorithm to print the values in the array.

PRG-2. The *max* and *min* functions defined in <algorithm> can be used to compare any two objects for which the less-than (<) and greater-than (>) operators are defined. Use these functions in a small program to compare two integers, two doubles, and two strings. These two templated functions are defined as shown below:

```
const T& max (const T& first, const T& second)
const T& min (const T& first, const T& second)
```

PRG-3. Write a program that creates a *vector* of a few names. Then print the names, sort the names, and print the sorted names.

PRG-4. Since a list does not support random-access iterators, we cannot apply the generic sort algorithm to a list. The STL library, however, provides a customized sort operation for a list. Write a program that creates a list of integers, and then sort the list.

PRG-5. Since array pointers have random access capability, we can use the generic sort algorithm with an array. Create an array of 10 characters and then sort and print it.

PRG-6. Write a program to create a vector of 10 elements, and then create another vector. Copy only elements at locations 2 to 6 to the new vector. Print the elements of both vectors.

PRG-7. Create a *vector* of 10 random values, and then use the *for_each* and the *accumulate* algorithms to print the values and the sum of them.

PRG-8. Another approach to store random values in a vector is to use the *generate* algorithm to assign the return of a function to each member of a container. Write a program to store 10 random values between 100 and 200 in a vector using a function named *randGen.*

PRG-9. Use the *min_element* and *max_element* algorithms to find the minimum and maximum elements in a vector.

PRG-10. One approach to sort an array is to make a *set* of the array and then copy the set back to the array. Write a program to do so.

PRG-11. Program 19.29 finds the *union* of two sets. Design a program that finds the *intersection* of two sets. The *intersection* of two sets is a set that includes only common elements in the set as shown below:

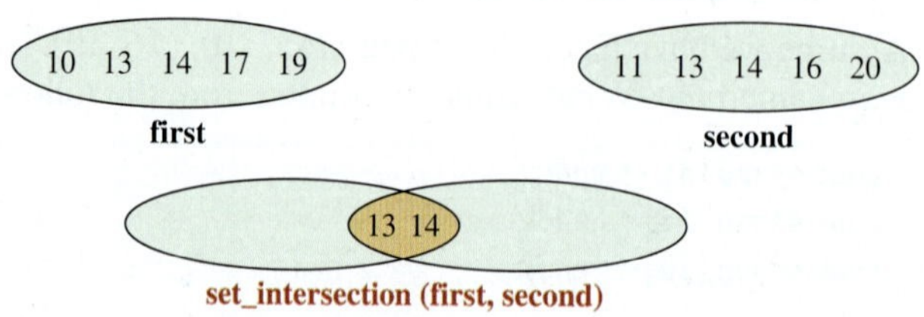

PRG-12. Program 19.29 finds the *union* of two sets. Design a program that finds the *difference* of two sets. We can have two *set differences*: first-second and second-first. The set first-second contains all elements that are in the first but not in the second. The set second-first contains all elements that are in the second but not in the first, as shown below:

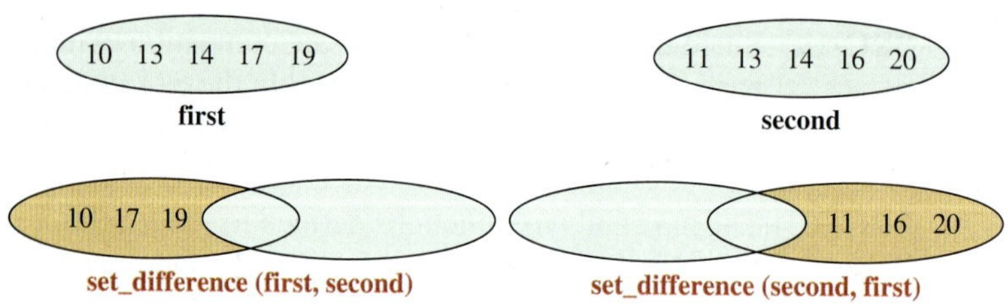

PRG-13. Program 19.29 finds the *union* of two sets. Design a program that finds the *symmetric difference* of two sets. The *symmeteric difference* of two sets contains elements that are in the first or the second, but not in both.

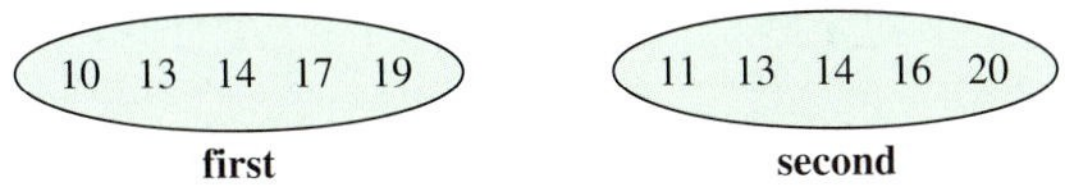

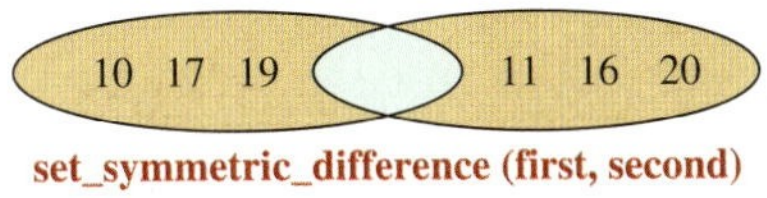

PRG-14. We can use the *generate* algorithm with a function object to create a list of items in which each item depends on the previous one. For example, we can create a list of even integers using a functor named *Even*. The functor returns the previous value plus 2. Write a class *Even*, overload the function operator, and then use the *generate* algorithm to create a list of the first 10 even values.

PRG-15. One of the functions that is a good candidate for a function object is the Fibonacci sequence. We know that $fib(n) = fib(n - 1) + fib(n - 2)$. In other words, we must keep the values of two previous terms to calculate the new term. Write a program to design a class *Fib*, and overload the function operator for the class. Then use the function object to store 11 Fibonacci numbers in a vector: $fib(0)$ to $fib(10)$.

A

D

E

F

M

Q

R

S

T

U

V

W